SLAVE TRADERS BY INVITATION

FINN FUGLESTAD

Slave Traders by Invitation

*West Africa's Slave Coast
in the Precolonial Era*

HURST & COMPANY, LONDON

First published in the United Kingdom in 2018 by
C. Hurst & Co. (Publishers) Ltd.,
41 Great Russell Street, London, WC1B 3PL

© Finn Fuglestad, 2018

All rights reserved.

Printed in India

The right of Finn Fuglestad to be identified as the author of this publication is asserted by him in accordance with the Copyright, Designs and Patents Act, 1988.

A Cataloguing-in-Publication data record for this book is available from the British Library.

ISBN: 9781849049061

www.hurstpublishers.com

The book benefitted from a grant from the Department of History, University of Oslo (Norway).

Dedicated to the memory of Stephen Ellis (1953–2015)

Y para Elisa Pérez-González de la Barreda

CONTENTS

Acknowledgements ix
List of Illustrations xi
List of Abbreviations xiii
Maps xv

Introduction 1

PART A
STRUCTURES AND TRENDS

1. The Slave Coast: A General Presentation 21
2. Historiography, Sources and Epistemology 37
3. Societal, Religious and Political Structures: A Model 57
4. Some Concrete, Practical Implications 69
5. A Few Comments on Certain Economic Matters 81
6. The Database and the Slave Trade from the Slave Coast 91

PART B
CHRONOLOGICAL OVERVIEW: EARLY DAYS TO THE 1720s

1. Focus on the European Side 113
2. The African Side: Early/Legendary Past 129
3. Allada, Its Vassals and Neighbours, and the Europeans 139
4. Dahomey and Its Neighbours: Early Beginnings and After 159
5. Convulsions Further West 171
6. The 1680s-1720s: An Overview 179

PART C
CHRONOLOGICAL OVERVIEW: THE 1720s –1850/51

1.	The Dramatic and Decisive 1720s	199
2.	Aftermath and General Considerations	215
3.	Near Disaster: The First Years of the Tegbesu Era	225
4.	More about the Tegbesu Era	237
5.	Continuation	249
6.	The Long Goodbye	265

Epilogue   289

Notes   295
Bibliography   393
Index   435

ACKNOWLEDGEMENTS

The author of the present manuscript written in English is a Norwegian whose first foreign language is French, and who took up residence in Spain many years ago. The implication is that if the manuscript has become at all readable, it is thanks to the toiling of my good friend Ms Juliet Wrightson who has done a tremendous job in correcting my English. My debt and gratitude to her are beyond words. Juliet agreed to take over after her sister, the late Penelope Wrightson, who had offered to help me out with my English, was struck down by a terminal disease.

Another friend of mine who has left us is Selena Axelrod Winsnes, with whom I have had many inspiring conversations, and who provided me with many hints and suggestions with regard to the Danish sources especially.

After completing the first version of the present manuscript, I most fortunately succeeded in persuading fellow-Africanists Adam Jones and Edna G. Bay into reading parts of it: the former read the Introduction, the latter the Introduction and Part A. Those two sections contain the ideas and viewpoints developed in the rest of the manuscript. Ms Bay in particular has saved me from some embarrassing misinterpretations, plus a number of errors. Her endeavour is all the more admirable since she and I continue to part company on certain fundamental matters, as will become clear later on.

I have also had the honour and pleasure to discuss some of the ideas expressed in the following with the legendary Professor John Donnelly Fage (1921–2002). I still hear his voice.

I would like finally to express my gratitude to all those archivists and librarians in many countries and on three continents who assisted me during my research, which I initiated, if my memory does not fail me, nearly forty years ago.

ACKNOWLEDGEMENTS

If these acknowledgements are unusually short, it is because the present manuscript belongs, for many reasons, to the "in-spite-of" category, rather than the "thanks-to" one.

As for the rest, the usual disclaimers pertain.

LIST OF ILLUSTRATIONS

Figure 1: European lodges in the inland town of Savi, then the capital of Hueda and hub of the local slave trade (17th century). From the Des Marchais archive, British Library

Figure 2: Map of the Slave Coast before 1724. From the Des Marchais archive, British Library

Figure 3: Restored main building of Ouidah's Portuguese "fort" (2010). Photograph by Finn Fuglestad

Figure 4: View of the River Weme at Porto Novo (1980s). Photograph by Finn Fuglestad

LIST OF ABBREVIATIONS

AAP/EB or Anais	*Anais/Annaes do Archivo Público/do Arquivo do Estado da Bahia* (Salvador da Bahia, Brazil)[1]
AAR	*African Archaeological Review*
AD	Archives Départementales
ADM	Admiralty
AEH	*African Economic History*
AHR	*American Historical Review*
AHU	Arquivo Histórico Ultramarino, Lisbon
AM	Archives Municipales
AN	Archives Nationales, Paris
APEB	Arquivo (Público) do Estado da Bahia
BCEHSAOF	*Bulletin du Comité d'Études Historiques et Scientifiques de l'Afrique Occidentale Française* (predecessor of *BIFAN*)
BIFAN	*Bulletin de l'Institut Français/Fondamental d'Afrique Noire*
BNE	Biblioteca Nacional de España
BT	Board of Trade (UK)
CAOM-DFC	Centre des Archives d'Outre-Mer, Aix-en-Provence Dépôt des Fortifications des Colonies, Côtes d'Afrique
CÉA	*Cahiers d'Études Africaines*
CO	Colonial Office records
CUP	Cambridge University Press
ÉD	*Études Dahoméennes*

ABBREVIATIONS

EHR	*Economic History Review*
HA	*History in Africa. A Journal of Method*
HAHR	*Hispanic American Historical Review*
IAI	International African Institute
IFAN	Institut Français/Fondamental d'Afrique Noire
IJAHS	*International Journal of African Historical Studies*
JAH	*Journal of African History*
JHSN	*Journal of the Historical Society of Nigeria*
NA	The National Archives (formerly Public Record Office), Kew
NS	Nouvelle série/New series
OR	Ordens régias/regiaes[2]
O.s.	Old style (to 1751)[3]
PRO	Public Record Office, Chancery Lane (later renamed The National Archives and transferred to Kew)
RAC	Royal African Company
SA	*Slavery and Abolition*
SFHOM	Société Française d'Histoire d'Outre-Mer
T (as for instance T70)	Treasury records in NA
THSG	*Transactions of the Historical Society of the Gold Coast and Togoland/of Ghana*
UP	University Press
WIC	Generaele/Geoctroyeerde West-Indische Compagnie

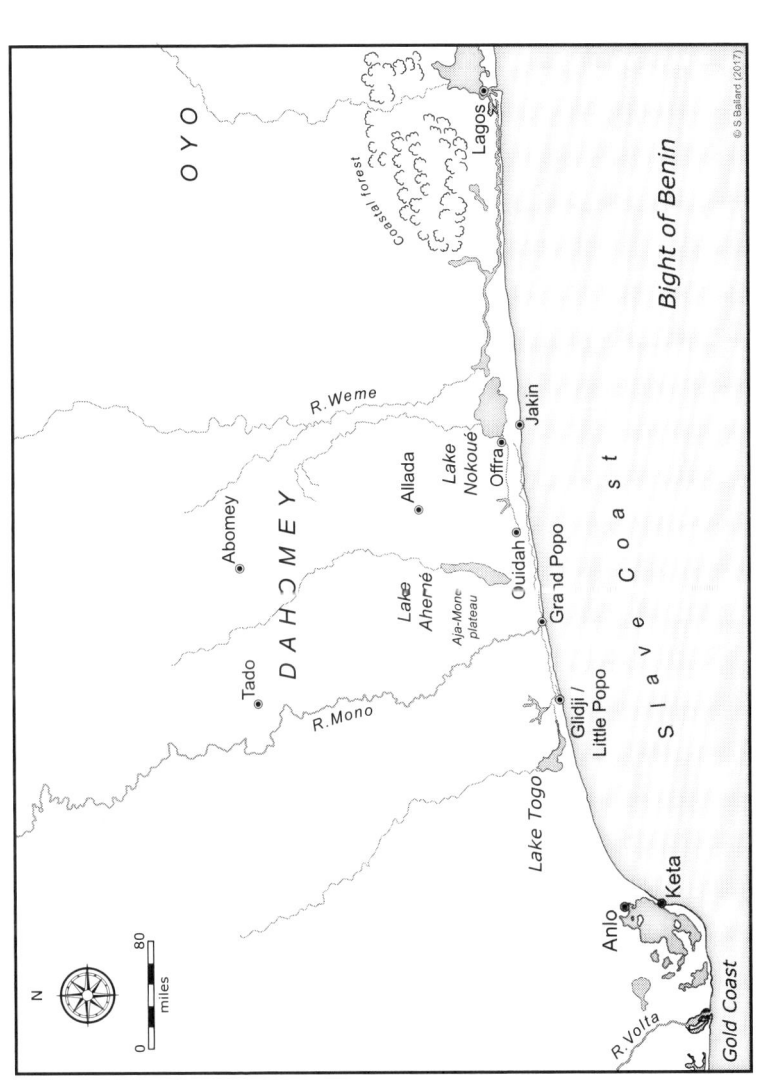

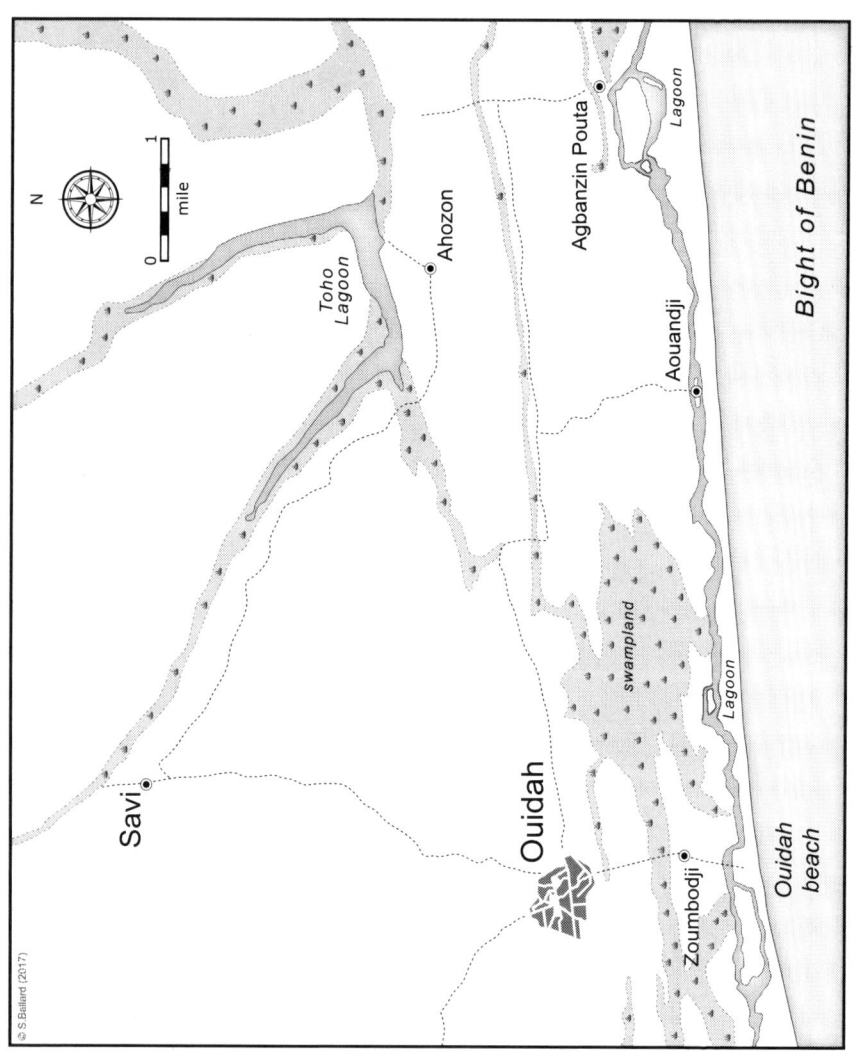

INTRODUCTION

Common sense may tell us that trade on a significant scale cannot flourish for long on a heavily surf-ridden beach without any permanent human settlement. But if so, common sense turns out to be a poor guide to the past of that part of the coast of Guinea that we call the Slave Coast. In fact, the Slave Coast, whose shore line corresponds to the description above, was the site of a considerable trade for more than 240 years, between around 1616 and 1850/51, before it petered out during the next 12–13 years. This was a very special trade, a trade in human beings, a slave trade.[1]

Indeed, the 320 km long beach between the River Volta and Lagos known as the Slave Coast, and especially the central part around the towns of Ouidah and Offra, ranks as one of the major epicentres of the Atlantic slave trade, and as the leading West African centre. The Slave Coast "exported", according to the best available estimates (but veering probably on the low side), some two million slaves: that is, about sixteen per cent of the (probably) twelve and a half million human beings (or more) sent from Africa to America in the era of the Trans-Atlantic slave trade. It means that on average some 20 slaves were embarked from the Slave Coast each and every day for more than two centuries. Of those two million, probably more than half transited at one single spot, the beach south of Ouidah[2] – an open roadstead with no port facilities whatsoever. Note that the figures above refer to the slaves who were *alive* by the time the ships set sail, and who had survived the notorious loading and waiting time, of which more later.

The paradox then is that this large-scale trade in human beings took place in a particularly inhospitable, even dangerous environment. To quote an employee of the company in charge of the upkeep of the English forts,

Justly Watson, who went ashore on the beach south of Ouidah on 20 December 1755:

> The landing is the worst I ever saw, and I believe one of the worst in the whole world (yet we arrived in the best season). I was informed, sometimes ships have been four or five weeks before anybody could get ashore, or any boat go off to them. There is a bar before the shore, in which the sea breaks prodigiously, & the canoes frequently overset in what is called good weather. After one gets ashore there are several rivers to pass over, which makes it very tiresome & dangerous[3]

to reach the town of Ouidah, Watson's destination, some four kilometres *inland*.

Watson was certainly not exaggerating, quite the contrary. In fact, he noticed only one bar, whereas there were actually two moving underwater sandbars which ran parallel to the coast, implying that the surf broke three times during most seasons, the third time over the shoreline itself.[4] It has been described by other visitors as a wall of water, with waves reaching truly impressive heights, altogether not bereft of majesty.[5] It has also been described as a dangerous belt of death owing to the frequent capsizing of canoes and the presence of man-eating and reputedly enormous and "gluttonous" sharks, sharks that there is every reason to believe were well fed in the era of the slave trade.[6] It is claimed that during certain periods human lives, and not exclusively slave lives, were lost nearly every day.[7] As for the average loss of goods (other than slaves, who were regarded as goods), it has been estimated at five per cent of the cargo by Patrick Manning.[8]

We can deduce from the existence of the exceptionally heavy surf and the sandbars that the European ocean-going ships could not go anywhere near the coast in what were also shallow waters. In fact, they always had to stand 2–3 km off the coast[9] in what was called the "roads", for example, the Ouidah road.

The references and quotations listed above have been chosen at random from many available sources. The forbidding conditions under which the slave trade was conducted on the Slave Coast loom in fact large in our sources.[10] Obviously, those conditions functioned as an effective barrier against intruders coming from the sea, which was where the Europeans came from in our period. But there was an additional barrier inland south of Ouidah behind the kilometre-deep beach – a natural moat in the shape of a lagoon. Its width varied according to the season, but was never less than two to three hundred metres at Ouidah. The lagoon ran parallel to the coast for several hundred kilometres. It was mostly shallow, generally less than one metre, but in several places reached a depth of three to four metres, and hence was not always possible to ford.[11] Behind the lagoon there were wetlands, swampy grounds and streams (Watson's "rivers") whose extension obviously also varied according to the seasons. As for the town of Ouidah and the region of permanent human settlement, that is, the area of permanently dry and therefore cultivable land, that, as can be deduced from the above, was some three kilometres north of the lagoon.[12]

So there was a total of a distance of seven to eight kilometres between the ships and Ouidah. One question is how it was possible to drive unwilling and underfed slaves from Ouidah town, the centre of the slave trade, to the beach via the lagoon, where no bridge existed, and then out to the waiting ships. Another is how it was possible to carry goods in the opposite direction, and the Europeans in both – Europeans who usually travelled in hammocks once on shore,[13] in this country where no wheeled carriage existed and where horses were few, small and condemned to an early death due to trypanosomiasis borne by the tsetse fly[14] (horses were reserved in theory for the king and the Europeans).[15] As for the canoe crossings between the ships and the beach, it goes without saying that one was almost guaranteed to reach one's destination soaking wet. Thus many Europeans confronted the surf wearing only the minimum.[16] But then, if we are to believe a local proverb, even the water is dry in Guinea.[17]

Actually, what we have described above is the situation that came to prevail after about 1727 and the famous but long drawn-out Dahomean conquest of the coast (in fact the beginning of a long, chaotic period, as we shall see). However, before 1727 the slaves were gathered together not at Ouidah, but at Savi, some nine kilometres further north (about 16–17 km from the ships), and driven from thence down to the shore and the ships. Savi was the palatial capital of the pre-1727 and rather Lilliputian polity ("kingdom") of Hueda.[18] As for the question of how the slaves arrived at Savi, later at Ouidah, in the first place, it is formally outside the scope of this book, but will nevertheless be touched upon later.

We do not really need any sources to convey to us the near-absurdity of it all. Anyone who has set foot on the small melancholy backwater town of Ouidah[19] before the (modest) transformations of the 1990s (about which more in the Epilogue), and who made at that time the short but difficult journey – still no road then, although there was a bridge – down to the absolutely desolate and empty but imposing beach, would have had considerable difficulty in imagining that he found himself right in the middle of the old epicentre of the slave trade in West Africa. That is especially true if he had been to the Gold Coast and contemplated the many imposing European forts that grace its seashore, forts that were *not* constructed originally for the purpose of the slave trade. On the Slave Coast he would have encountered only what is presented as one of the original three, the not very impressive Portuguese fort as it now stands (the present layout dating from 1865, that is, long after the end of the slave trade).[20] He would have wondered anyway what that fort was doing some four kilometres inland. The point is that what some call "visible memory" is near-absent from the Slave Coast. Given all this, our visitor must be forgiven for expressing incredulity when told that Ouidah was often, and frequently still is, referred to as a port in the literature.[21]

But apart from the "how-was-it-possible" question, here we must draw a number of preliminary conclusions. The first is that although the local conditions functioned as an efficient barrier against foreign intruders, they also functioned as a barrier in the opposite direction. We have explained then why the local people turned their back on the ocean, why they never developed a maritime tradition. They did not have to, since the lagoon and the extensive wetlands were overflowing with not only fish and other aquatic animals, but also all sorts of wildlife, even big game.[22] The lagoon is in fact part of a vast inland aquatic ecosystem. The paradox here is that the locals' lack of navigational skills contributed to guarantee, in a sense, the success of the slave trade.

The next and really crucial point is that for a slave trade, or for that matter any sort of trade over time on a substantial scale to develop between the Africans and the Europeans in this very special environment, one basic requisite had to be met: a strong determination on the part of the former to overcome the natural barrier that protected them against the latter, that is, a strong determination to enter into contact with the Europeans, and to maintain that contact. The locals also needed to guarantee the safety of the European slave traders to a certain extent. The conclusion is that the Europeans could not and would not have got anywhere without the very active collaboration of the locals (not that they ever tried), without having been invited ashore, so to speak.[23] Indeed, the Europeans were and remained totally dependent on the local inhabitants: that is, the few Europeans *stationed* on the Slave Coast, no more than a hundred most of the time and frequently far less. The hostility that Joseph Inikori believes characterized the inhabitants of the coast towards the Europeans[24] is nowhere evident on the Slave Coast.

INTRODUCTION

The Europeans erected all told, and long after the beginning of the slave trade, three forts grouped together within a short distance of each other in Ouidah town,[25] that is, we repeat, about four kilometres inland (from the English William's fort one could at least glimpse the sea, because of the down-sloping configuration of the land).[26] This is to be contrasted with the situation on the Gold Coast where there were some 26–27 forts, all built with solid material (not the case in Ouidah), and all situated on the seashore or close to it.[27] The Europeans began constructing those forts some two centuries before the first emerged from the ground at Ouidah. The implication is that the Slave Coast forts, as opposed to those on the Gold Coast, were out of artillery range of the European ships. The implication is also that they could not command the landing places for their own supplies, which in turn meant that they could be starved to surrender any time if the local population so decided. In fact, the Slave Coast forts, constructed of dried earth[28] – it was said that not a single pebble could be found on the Slave Coast – and with thatched roofs, were simply indefensible, as the Europeans knew full well (the forts also caught fire easily and were constantly in need of repair). This was true even though they may have looked imposing enough in the local context: two-storey quadrangular buildings of considerable size (100 by 80 metres) surrounded by dry moats, across which were moveable bridges of boards in the manner of their medieval predecessors in Europe, and provided with a number of cannon.[29] But if they were not defendable, the cannon notwithstanding, what then exactly was their purpose? We suggest that they may have served as embassies of sort, plus information centres – and finally as social clubs for the captains and officers of the ships in the roads.[30] Or, if one prefers, forts served the function of facilitating contacts and organizing services for visiting traders and to some extent also as warehouses, or barracoons for slaves.[31]

But the forts may also have been considered valuable markers for the various companies' ongoing trade at particular places on the African coast. That is, they may have been built to defend and to maintain the interests of those who constructed them against European competitors.[32] That being said, the forts turned out to perform, unexpectedly, a crucial, even strategic, role in many circumstances from especially 1727 onwards, as a result of wars between Africans, serving for instance as refuges. Ouidah became, as we shall see, the object of a long drawn out local internecine war with the Europeans caught in the middle not always knowing which party to support.

We add however that there could also be at any time a number of factories or lodges (the difference between the two, if any, is not clear – the French word is *comptoirs*); these were much less imposing edifices, unfortified, and in many cases simply temporary installations. For instance, the Dutch never had forts on the Slave Coast, but they were very much present nevertheless until the 1750s, thanks in part to their factories[33] (the same also applies, but to a far lesser extent, to the Danes and the Germans of Brandenburg-Prussia).

In any case, many Europeans began early to question the usefulness of forts or even of factories, that is, of permanent land bases.[34] The point is that land bases were not a necessary requisite for trade. Many Europeans did without, especially the private traders, those we call interlopers in the period of the monopolistic companies.

To return to the main track, the active collaboration of the locals was not enough. Somehow some people would have to be able to go through the surf both ways. And since the European light boats were totally inadequate for the purpose, and the locals had, as noted, no maritime tradition, the question was where to find such people. They were recruited from two of the three known maritime communities along the coast of Guinea: the Ga and especially the Fante of the neighbouring and very different Gold Coast west of the river Volta (the third such community were the Kru of Liberia).[35] But although the coastal Fante people did have a tradition of venturing into the open sea, it must have taken the first generations of them quite some time, and a considerable number of casualties, to master the surf, the likes of which they cannot have been familiar with from home. What is certain is that they had to be, and became in fact, accomplished athletes, and especially excellent swimmers and divers.[36]

That, then, is the short answer. However, it begs a number of unanswerable questions. The central one is simply why the Fante canoemen volunteered at all. But more generally, those canoemen, the famous *remaderos* or *remidors* of the sources,[37] present us with a problem of some magnitude: we know next to nothing about them. We are well informed about the ethnic group we call Fante, but not about the Fante (also called Mina) canoemen. The latter have been severely neglected by historians, formally for the same reason that there remain so many other blanks in the past of the Slave Coast: the dearth of sources. But even so, the very fact that historians (the present author included) have not even given it a try calls for attention. As it is, we can only state the obvious, that the Fante and their occasionally enormous flat-bottomed dugout canoes, manned by from seven up to over 30 paddlers,[38] were absolutely indispensable. In fact, the Europeans had no alternative but to entrust them with all that they needed,[39] and indeed with their very lives,[40] which incidentally not a few of the Europeans lost in the venture.[41] The bitter complaints that the Europeans occasionally lodged in their reports in the early days[42] against the canoemen obviously served no practical purpose.

The only certain information that the present author has been able to glean about the Fante canoemen is, first, that they were very religious[43] – as everyone was, but obviously it was very understandable in their case since they put their lives on the line on each and every trip; second, that the best and most expensive were from the region of Shama;[44] and third, that some of them (probably a minority) were formally slaves,[45] a fact which does not make much sense, although we presume they would have been very privileged slaves. Fourth, and finally, since many Fante canoemen settled down on the Slave Coast, it seems legitimate to speak of a sort of Fante colonization of the coast east of the Volta.[46]

Were the Fante canoemen ever conscious of their power and what they were actually doing? To give an idea of that power, here is a quotation from the famous slave trader Thomas Phillips, who wrote in the 1690s:

> the canoes frequently over-setting, but the canoe-men are such excellent divers & swimmers, that they preserve the lives of those they have any kindness for, but such as they have any displeasure to…(so) very prudent for all commanders to be kind & obliging to them, their lives lying in their hands, which they can make them lose at pleasure, & impute all to accident, and they could not help it.[47]

Another European, the Portuguese Father Vicente Ferreira Pires, claimed a century later that the canoemen were occasionally paid by Europeans to get rid of fellow Europeans.[48]

If more proof were needed of the Europeans' total dependence on the local population and on the Fante canoemen, we can turn to the period of the so-called illegal slave trade after 1807/8, that is, after Europeans, principally the British, abolished and then tried to stop the slave trade. And here the point is that the Commodore of no less a force than the anti-slave-trade squadron of the Royal Navy, amounting to one-tenth of British warships on active service, found it impossible to bring the main slave-trading mart, Ouidah and its beach, under his control.[49] Britannia never ruled the waves off Ouidah. The reason was that the local population was opposed to abolition, and the Fante canoemen were uncooperative.

Since the picture drawn above refers primarily to the region of Ouidah, we need to add a few qualifications. The first is that, in order to avoid any misunderstanding, the slave trade did not get under way first at Ouidah, but some 30 kilometres further east, at Offra in the kingdom of Allada. However, Ouidah (in the kingdom of Hueda) took over very quickly as the leading emporium.⁵⁰ Furthermore, if we are correct in believing, as most do, that Offra, which has disappeared as such, corresponds to modern Godomey, then it was situated slightly further away from the sea than Ouidah, and with equally forbidding landing conditions. There were other centres on the Slave Coast which were situated closer to the coastline, and several, such as Little Popo-Aneho and Keta (or Kitto), even on the shore itself. But they were always statistically insignificant compared with Offra, and later Ouidah, as far as the slave trade is concerned.

Our second qualification is that the surf was not uniformly as strong as implied above all the year round or even on the whole of the Slave Coast. The best period seems to have been between January and March, that is, towards the end of the dry season⁵¹ (our source Watson was wrong, he arrived not in the best season, but slightly too early). But the surf could be formidable even in calm weather (see below).

There is in any case no doubt that the worst surf-ridden part of the Slave Coast was precisely and surprisingly that of Offra-Ouidah,⁵² that is, the Central Slave Coast, where it really happened.

Our next qualification is that the figures above refer, strictly speaking, to the export of slaves from the Bight of Benin, of which in geographical terms the Slave Coast constitutes only the small western part. But there is reason to believe, as we shall see, that during the period we are interested in the export of slaves from the rest of the Bight of Benin, that is, east of the Slave Coast, was close to negligible.

Let us add finally that the beach was certainly not empty all along the coast, as the previously mentioned examples of Little Popo-Aneho and Keta indicate. In the more general case of Anlo in the west, the beach was at places much larger in depth than at Ouidah (but in others actually smaller), and in fact inhabited far in the past.⁵³ But again, the slave trade from Anlo, and from the Western Slave Coast generally, was on a modest scale compared with what went on further east.

* * *

It is important to bear in mind what we have hinted at already, namely that the Slave Coast was (and is) unique compared with the other coasts of Guinea, and in particular with that of the neighbouring Gold Coast (now Ghana). About the Gold Coast we need to know first that, as its name indicates, it was

INTRODUCTION

gold that attracted the Europeans, not slaves. However, the Gold Coast did eventually become what has been described as a second Slave Coast – from the early 1700s, as we shall see. We also need to know that the Gold Coast was always the epicentre of European activities on the coast of West Africa during the precolonial era – as the many forts still standing along the coast bear witness. The Europeans in question were first the Portuguese, who arrived in 1471,[54] and later especially the Dutch and the English, but also the French, plus the Danes and the Germans from Brandenburg-Prussia,[55] and finally the Swedes for a short period.[56] The oldest section of the presidential palace of the present-day Republic of Ghana in Accra is actually a former Danish fort (Christiansborg) that dates to 1661. Christiansborg, in its time reputedly one of the most impressive forts on the coast, together with the Dutch (originally Portuguese) Elmina and the English Cape Coast Castle, was for long the only Danish establishment on the whole of the coast.[57] It was also the easternmost of all the Gold Coast forts. Hence, if the Danes wanted to expand – which they did, especially towards the end of the eighteenth century – they could do so only eastwards, aided by the fact that between Christiansborg and Ouidah, a stretch of some 280 km, there was for most of the period no fort and little European activity. In brief, the Danes always took a keen interest and dabbled increasingly in the affairs of the Western or Little Slave Coast, as they called it.[58] In the process they converted themselves into privileged observers of the Slave Coast scene, for which reason they will appear frequently in this work.[59] Actually, the Danes erected the only known fort on the Western Slave Coast; but that happened rather late in the day, in 1784, and the Danish fort was and remained of very marginal importance.

The three nations that erected forts where it really mattered, on the Central Slave Coast, were the English, the French and the Portuguese, in chronological order. Among them, only the English had permanent establishments on the Gold Coast throughout our period. The French tried hard for a long time to establish a permanent base on the latter coast, but never really succeeded.[60] Neither did the Portuguese. In their case it was a question of trying to *return* to a coast from which they had been ousted by the Dutch in the 1640s, a fact that did not stop Portuguese vessels from trafficking on the Gold Coast.[61]

The reasons for the Gold Coast's central position are many, one having to do with the fact that all the indispensable canoemen came from there; but the other reasons are purely physical. Its coastline was characterized by inlets, bays, rocky promontories and pronounced headlands where it was easy to construct, and which gave shelter from prevailing winds and currents and allowed for relatively safe anchorage.[62] There was then no beach of the Slave Coast type, and no lagoon. That said, conditions on the Gold Coast were far from optimal.[63] There were in particular no genuinely natural harbours (except possibly at the Shama river).[64] And the surf could be occasionally a problem on the Gold Coast too.[65] Nevertheless, the Dane Erick Tilleman was certainly correct when he noted in 1697 that "the land of the Slave Coast is different in every way" to the Gold Coast.[66]

What then about the coast to the east and the south-east between Lagos and the Niger Delta where the Europeans never erected forts, and whose centre was the old kingdom of Benin? (Not to be confused with the present-day Republic of the same name much further west.) Here the conditions were different again, owing to the swamp vegetation and the problem of navigating the many rivers characteristic of the region. But the central point for our purpose is that the slave trade was statistically close to insignificant in that part of West Africa.[67] The Slave Coast, and especially the central part, was the main exporter of slaves in West Africa west of the Niger Delta, followed by the Gold Coast, and – far behind – Senegambia with the famous islet of Gorée.

* * *

One obvious conclusion that can be drawn from the above is that along the Slave Coast Africans played a very active role in the emergence of what we call the South Atlantic system. Hence the sad but inevitable contention summed up in the title of this work: slave traders by invitation.

But is this contention based exclusively on the physical conditions under which the slave trade was conducted, or do we know of any genuine invitation that was actually extended, formally or otherwise, to the Europeans? The European sources are not very eloquent. We know, though, that the Portuguese had a good idea of the configuration of the Slave Coast by the middle of the sixteenth century.[68] Nevertheless, for a long time they simply sailed past it on their way to Lagos with its very dangerous bar, or regions further to the south-east:[69] perhaps while waiting for an invitation.

According to the local traditions from Ouidah (those of Offra have disappeared along with the town itself), the first locals who spotted the Portuguese and managed to persuade and/or lure them to venture ashore were later elevated to the dignity of divinities (they are so worshipped to the present). And they were so elevated because they were considered as benefactors to society.[70] The trouble was, however, that the locals had nothing to offer but slaves, and the Portuguese at that early stage were not particularly interested (it was gold, not slaves, that originally attracted the Europeans to the coast of Guinea).

According to one version, Kpatè, the one who spotted the Portuguese became the divinity of shipwrecks – that is, the divinity to which one offered sacrifices to make ships run aground. Indeed, according to the custom on the coast the locals had the right to loot any ship wrecked on the beach[71] (a custom not unknown elsewhere, including parts of Western Europe). That happened with some frequency in the following centuries. It is tempting to argue that the Kpatè story testifies to the difficulties of establishing contact, and more generally to the dangers the Europeans were confronted with in these waters.

Whatever the case, we suppose that there was a considerable time lag between the first contact and the time when regular trade relations developed, an extensive period of trials and failings. The Slave Coast was in fact the last region of coastal West Africa to establish regular relations with the Europeans.

It is at this juncture that we must lament the disappearance of the oral traditions of the Offra region, since we suspect that they may have had a somewhat different story to tell. We know for certain that the polity of Allada, which included Offra, exported in the early days considerable quantities of cloth, and cotton cloth at that, to the Gold Coast, as well as other "normal" merchandise.[72] This trade went on until at least the 1680s and co-existed for some time with the slave trade.[73] Why and how that non-slave trade disappeared, and why Offra-Allada was superseded rapidly by the neighbouring region of Ouidah, are questions which still await answers.

The next point is that the invitation (we consider it as such) to trade in slaves, once extended, was never withdrawn. Indeed, in the end it was, as we shall see, the slave trade that abandoned the Slave Coast, not the other way around.[74] It is significant in this respect that when the region was rocked by warfare, the slave trade does not seem ever to have been an issue, all sides vying for the control of that trade – for the very simple reason that it constituted a major source of material enrichment, and all sides tried to enlist the Europeans as allies, while attempting at the same time, and with success, to keep those same Europeans in their place. Regarding warfare, there was a contradiction inherent in the slave trade, which was certainly not like any other trade. It is true that like all trade, it needed peaceful conditions (and predictability) to thrive. But, to state the obvious, it needed also exactly the opposite, namely violence, since violence in whatever form was clearly an important way of procuring slaves. The question was, however, *where* that violence took place. It had to take place away from those centres where the trade as such was conducted.

As for the Europeans, although possibly lukewarm initially, they quickly proved themselves to be over-eager to respond to the invitation. The so-called sugar revolution in the Caribbean around the 1670s (see later) had created an insatiable demand for slaves. But why slaves from *Africa*? The short answer is, because that was where slaves could be had (apart from obvious climatic and microparasitic-epidemiological reasons). But how so? J.D. Fage suggested some time ago that "the possession of men and women was both the source and symbol of wealth and power, particularly perhaps because they seem to have been a scarce resource in relation to...land".[75] In other words, wealth and power were rooted not in ownership of land (a non-existent notion anyway), but in control of people – the wealth-in-people paradigm. Hence Fage posits the emergence of an important group of dependents, and the temptation to use those dependents as money with which to purchase the commodities the Europeans had to offer.[76] Convincing or not, Fage's theory remains to date the only one on offer. But if the selling of dependents was how it all began, it does not explain the continuation, that is, how and why it developed into a large-scale enterprise and why it lasted for so long. Clearly dependents constituted only a small fraction of the totality of slaves sold. The question is where the others came from, how they were "produced", so to speak. And as we shall see, the answer is far from evident.

An important point in this context is that from the European side it was in a sense "safe" to fetch slaves in Africa, and especially so on the Slave Coast. For as Seymour Drescher has underlined,[77] the slaves had no sailing skills, so that in case of a successful revolt they could not steer a ship back to Africa, where there was no safe haven waiting for them anyway, since most of the people living along the coast were involved in the slave trade one way or the other. In addition, there was no risk that anyone would come after the slave ships in order to liberate the slaves, or for that matter to mount a rescue expedition to the Americas. In brief, the slaves, once the Middle Passage had begun, had nowhere to go and no-one to turn to. They were absolutely alone in the world.

* * *

As we have seen, the slave trade on the Central Slave Coast was conducted under extremely adverse physical conditions. The wider theme is what happened to the slaves from the moment they came into the purview of the Europeans up to the moment the slave ships, after having set sail, lost sight of

INTRODUCTION

the coast. We call it the loading and waiting time and we consider it to be a neglected theme in the history of the slave trade. The contention here is first, that it was a very long-lasting stage; and second, that it was a stage during which a frightful number of human lives was lost, not only because of the physical conditions, but also because of what some sources refer to as the local "ill usages" and "ill conducts",[78] which were certainly deadly, whatever they may have consisted of exactly – our sources do not really tell.

The casualties during the waiting and loading time on the Slave Coast far exceeded, we suspect, those on the better-known Middle Passage – the Atlantic crossing.[79] The loss of life during that crossing was due in large part precisely to the conditions endured by the slaves during the waiting and loading time. Indeed, the squandering of human life on the Slave Coast must have been on a scale not seen anywhere else on the coast, or perhaps even anywhere else in the context of the history of slavery and the slave trade. That, at least, is the contention. To prove it, we would have had to conduct a vast comparative study, complete with reliable figures, and this we cannot do. We cannot even quantify what happened on the Slave Coast (can archaeology help?). Yet the evidence, circumstantial and as presumptive as it may be, does point unequivocally in the direction suggested.

* * *

All this brings us to the epistemological and especially philosophical-ethical problems at hand, problems we can no longer avoid. They are like the proverbial hobgoblins of Nordic folklore, impossible to ignore and impossible to get rid of. The epistemological problem (which will be investigated in depth later) is multi-dimensional, one dimension having to do with the problem of imbalance in the sources, those sources being certainly voluminous but nevertheless vastly inadequate in many ways and, in particular, terribly one-sided. Hence the tentative and incomplete nature of the history we present to the reader. Another dimension is whether the past of Africa can be fully understood in terms of our Western conceptual categories, unsatisfactory but so far the only ones we have at our disposal.[80]

As for the philosophical-ethical problem, the sources, for all their shortcomings, are more than adequate in one particular aspect. They provide us with an idea of the practical day-to-day functioning, the routine as it were, of the slave trade. The inescapable impression we are left with is that we are confronted with an authentic horror story in which the superlatives become quickly exhausted. Hence the problem for the historian who looks into precisely the day-to-day functioning, as opposed to the more abstract quantitative dimension, is how to maintain the required clinical detachment from the subject, what is known as academic restraint.

The point is that there is something very special about the slave trade. For it went on day in, day out, year after year, decade after decade, and indeed century after century, in a routinely, not to say monotonous-bureaucratic and starkly callous fashion, and on an unrivalled scale, and even in the teeth of formidable natural barriers, as in the case of the Central Slave Coast.[81]

In fact, the routine aspect, the very long time span and the enormous distances involved, and the gigantic infrastructural apparatus and logistical organization necessary, tempt one to ask if there is really anything comparable in the history of mankind. If we add the genocide-like fate which awaited the majority of the slaves, those who ended up in the Caribbean and Brazil,[82] it seems entirely possible to suppose, that no, there may not have been anything like it in the past. (Note that we are talking here exclusively about the Atlantic slave trade. Had we added the little-studied but obviously statistically significant Trans-Saharan slave trade,[83] we would have ended up with an even bleaker picture.)

It is this unremitting, large-scale, mass-production aspect, this big-business, capitalist, modern, or industrial dimension, which is particularly striking, and which in our opinion sets the Atlantic slave trade apart from whatever may have occurred earlier, later, or elsewhere.

While we are at it, and in relation to the possibly un-academic "how-could-they" question, and at the risk of falling into several traps, including that of anachronism, we may as well go on to wonder what would have happened if the Pope, the Archbishop of Canterbury and/or some leading Lutheran and Calvinist theologians (plus, say, an influential rabbi) had promised the slavers eternal doom and damnation. They never did, quite the contrary, as is well known.[84] Can we take refuge in the argument that the Atlantic slave trade happened a long time ago, that the world and what the Germans call our *Weltanschauung*, have changed radically since then – if they have so changed?

It is true that many Europeans considered the slave trade and slavery to be a problem, moral or otherwise, that its supporters were often on the defensive,[85] and that something akin to bad conscience among the direct participants surfaces occasionally in our sources. One of those participants, the Frenchman Antoine Pruneau de Pommegeorge, even went as far as to pray for the Almighty's forgiveness for what he had taken part in. He went on to label the slave trade as a profanation of the Christian religion.[86] But Pruneau, who was stationed in Ouidah in the 1750s and 1760s – ending his local career as director-governor of the French fort, and as such directly responsible for the slave trade – had no success in convincing his superiors.

It is equally true that the Europeans, and especially the British, did in the end conclude that the slave trade (and later slavery) was incompatible with their own basic values and norms (in 1807 in the British case).[87] But not with those of capitalism. To paraphrase a sarcastic historian, one gets at times the impression that the slave trade and slavery were and are perceived as some sort of regrettable but "inevitable" collateral damage of capitalism's triumphant – and applauded – progress.[88] However, the British "were a long time finding it out to be wrong", as noted ironically by none other than possibly the leading African slave-trader of the day, King Gezo of Dahomey on the Slave Coast.[89] The other Europeans were even slower in finding it out.[90]

On the African side, one cannot but wonder what would have happened if the local rulers had followed the example of a certain seventeenth-century Hindu warlord on the Coromandel coast of India who refused to supply the Dutch with slaves, in spite of the latter's insistence. His argument was that to do so would have been a great sin in the eyes of the gods. As a result, the slave trade from that coast never took off, and in fact petered out quickly, much to the disappointment of the Dutch.[91] Actually, we do know of at least one African ruler who did something of the sort, as we shall see – the king of Benin in present-day southwestern Nigeria; he decreed a ban on the sale of male (although not female) slaves, a ban that lasted for more than two centuries. But his was and remained an exceptional case.

On the African side, furthermore, or rather that part of the African side that we know about, there is no hint of anything even remotely resembling remorse or moral scruples, not to mention an abolitionist movement, and certainly not in Ouidah. Consider Robin Law's assertion, based on his extensive fieldwork in the area, that there was "until very recently [this was written in 2004], a local consensus that the slave trade was a good thing for Ouidah". He added that he did not detect any feeling of shame anywhere.[92] Law, who is not taken to verbal excesses, notes also that references to the slave trade in the remembered praise names of prominent traders are sometimes "by the standards of modern susceptibilities, alarmingly callous".[93] In fact, and as we intend to demonstrate later, the treatment of the slaves destined for America, before they ended up in the custody of the Europeans, demonstrates that their fate was of no concern to the local population. If one asks why, the answer may perhaps be something to the effect that a slave was an "other", someone without kin relations in this kinship-type society, and as such no longer considered to be a genuine human being, in the sense of not belonging to any human community.

It could be, nevertheless, that the slave trade represented a problem for the Africans involved too, including a spiritual one. We can deduce from works concerning the slave trade in other regions that capturing and selling slaves may have been considered in a sense a polluting exercise, placing the traders (but only the traders?) in spiritual danger. Hence the need for some sort of ritual-spiritual purification, assistance and/or protection, even some kind of religious redemption.[94] But the problem is that there is nothing whatsoever in our sources from the Slave Coast on the subject. We can therefore do no more than repeat Robin Law's speculative suggestion that the slave trade may have been understood in the idiom of witchcraft,[95] and that there may have existed some attempt to establish some sort of "psycho-religious control" of the operation of the slave trade,[96] whatever all that really means.

Incidentally, the frequent references to the works of Robin Law above are not fortuitous. Law's corpus constitutes an important part of the existing historiography on the past of the Slave Coast, and will therefore be with us throughout. However, the present author begs to dissent from *some* of Law's conclusions, one of the reasons why the present book has been written.

In the more global context, it remains true what the Cameroonian sociologist Axelle Kabou – as far as we know only she – has underlined on the African side, namely that the Africans hold the regrettable record of being the only people in the world to have sold their own kin (although perhaps they were not considered as such) into slavery on a vast scale.[97] However, we hasten to add (recalling the case of the kingdom of Benin), certainly not all Africans, and certainly not all the time.

But nothing of this really answers the "how-could-they" question, and certainly not on the European side. It is a question we have in the final analysis to leave unanswered, unless we argue that all, or at least most, European participants were really confident about the "subhuman identity" of the Africans or believed seriously that the Africans "filled up the space between mankind and the ape".[98] In brief, the Europeans simply could and did, they "slaved", to use a verb (accompanied by an adjective, "halve [half] slaved")[99] which has disappeared from current English, while usually claiming at the same time to be good Christians. Allow us to quote in this context two typical contemporary justifications, for whatever they may be worth. The first is the standard Pontoppidanian one (see above) that, as a Portuguese official (but not a clergyman this time) put it, the Africans were freed through slavery, that is, given the opportunity to "see the light".[100] Note in this respect that the prudish Portuguese did not officially take part in the slave trade at all, they did not "slave". What they did was to *resgatar* slaves, a verb which can be translated as to buy back, to redeem, to ransom, to set free.[101]

The second justification is, as pointed out by no less a figure than King Louis XIV of France in 1696 (or by someone expressing himself in the king's name), that the Negroes (the word "slaves" was avoided) were essential for the cultivation of useful crops in America (no moral objections raised).[102] Or as expressed somewhat more straightforwardly by an anonymous French official in possibly 1775: "May humanity pardon us, but the case is that the negroes [he too avoided the word "slaves"] are as indispensable to the cultivation of the land in our colonies as the oxen and the horses are to the same in Europe".[103] All this is echoed by another Portuguese official who as late as 1811 referred to "this sad but necessary trade".[104]

* * *

We have allowed the questions and thoughts formulated above to surface in this Introduction, in the hope that they will not colour, or at least not colour unduly, the rest of this work, whether one believes they should do so or not. We need, however, to make a few comments on the problem of objectivity. We have been told repeatedly that objectivity is but a dream, be it a noble one.[105] But that is true in our opinion only in the absolute, fundamentalist sense of the term. In the historian's real world, a skewed, biased, or partisan account is, apart from being generally boring, easily detected; we all know what the reverse of objectivity and impartiality is. The question is in fact whether we pursue the goal of objectivity or not, while knowing full well that it is unobtainable. If we do, as we must, and do so displaying what is called intellectual honesty, we respect (however sermon-like this may sound) the ethical and moral obligations of our craft, which is, we believe, what we as historians must demand of ourselves, and what the rest of the world is entitled to expect from us.

Intellectual honesty compels us, among other things, to abide – if necessary – by conclusions we find repugnant, such as the one which appears in the title of the present work. It also compels us to distinguish between what we know for certain, what we *think* we know, and what we do not know, or know loosely, but allow ourselves to speculate about. The point is important, and especially so in the context of the Slave Coast with regard to the epistemological problem at hand, and leads us to make a programmatic declaration about the type of history we believe we always try to write, trying again in this work. We favour a problematizing approach, that is, one in which we focus on the problems the past presents us with, which are always legion, given that very little about the past is absolutely certain, even at times at the purely chronological-factual level (leaving aside the problem of what an absolutely certain and irrefutable fact really *is*). The task of the historian in this context is not necessarily to resolve those problems, but to discuss and above all to define them. It makes for a kind of history-writing which implies necessarily more questions than answers, and is therefore not universally favoured. We think, however, that probabilizing history, as we call it, contributes powerfully to our insight and understanding, which is in the final analysis what history is, or ought to be all about. Or so the present author argues.

* * *

It is time to redress the balance somewhat. Although the local environmental conditions and the slave trade must necessarily loom large in the history of the Slave Coast – they represent a sort of backdrop to the rest – and although it seemed natural to focus on them in this Introduction, they do not constitute the whole story. In fact, our ambition is to present something approaching a global overview of the history of the Slave Coast in the relevant period. Due attention will then have to be paid to a variety of other, necessarily related themes, among them especially the nature of the polities which existed or emerged on the Slave Coast, in a comparative context. We frequently use the neutral term "polity" instead of "kingdom", and especially of "state", whether archaic, primary or secondary. We are in fact not certain that the existing definitions of those terms are applicable to the African political entities of olden times;[106] if, that is, they were really *political* entities...).

PART A

STRUCTURES AND TRENDS

1

THE SLAVE COAST

A GENERAL PRESENTATION

A general presentation of the Slave Coast is long overdue. So to begin at the beginning, the term Slave Coast refers to a maritime *region*; that is, we repeat, the long stretch of the Lower Guinea coast[1] in West Africa, roughly 320 km in length, between the river Volta in present-day eastern Ghana and the Lagos channel (the outlet of the vast Lagos lagoon) in western Nigeria, as well as that coast's hinterland (except in the small easternmost Apapa-Badagry-Lagos part where one does not normally include the Yoruba hinterland). How far inland is a matter of choice. We settle for about 150 kilometres, and we do so for sound linguistic reasons. However, we have noted that Robin Law opts for another 70 kilometres further north.[2] The problem is that about 120 km inland we enter progressively into a sort of heterogeneous frontier zone, characterized by a mixture of peoples, ethnic groups and languages. And the question is where exactly that zone begins, how extensive it is northwards, and how much of it can or should be defined as pertaining to the region we call the Slave Coast. 150 kilometres inland (our choice) gives us an area slightly larger than Belgium, that is, a very small proportion indeed of the enormous African continent, but a globally significant one for many centuries.

In modern terms the Slave Coast corresponds approximately to the southern ten per cent or less of the Republics of Togo and Benin, together with small parts of southeastern Ghana and southwestern Nigeria: more precisely, nowadays, the southern half of the Volta region in the former case, and Lagos

State in the latter. The Slave Coast is divided then between no less than four modern states, two officially Anglophone and two Francophone. It constitutes nevertheless a clearly delineated region, and not only for historical and linguistic reasons, but also for geographical-vegetational ones. Most of the Slave Coast coincides with a significant ecological feature, the so-called Benin Gap, where what is called the forest-savanna mosaic zone, comprising vast stretches of open grassland, breaks through the belt of tropical rainforest and reaches all the way down to the coast.[3] The reason has to do with the local microclimate:[4] this region receives much less rain than its eastern or western neighbours, a fact usually attributed to the roughly south-north-running Akwapim-Togo-Atakora hills and mountains along the Ghana-Togo border in the west,[5] and hence rainfall increases from west to east. Hence also, whereas the Benin Gap extends panhandle-like on the coast westward beyond Accra in Ghana,[6] the easternmost tip of the Slave Coast is covered by rainforest and is thus situated outside of the Benin Gap. (The name "Benin" refers then not only to a precolonial polity in southern Nigeria, and to a modern Francophone republic much further west, but also to a vegetational-environmental zone, as well as to a part of the Gulf of Guinea, etc.)

The Central Slave Coast centred on the towns of Ouidah and Offra (or Offra/Jakin) is no more than 100 kilometres in length, between Lakes Ahémé and Nohoué. But it was from this Central Slave Coast (the genuine Slave Coast, one may call it) that the great majority of the slaves was exported. The rest, the Western and Eastern Slave Coasts respectively (some 220 kilometres altogether), may be called peripheral, in the sense that it played only a marginal role in the slave trade to the 1770s. However, from that decade onwards the slave trade soared on the *Eastern* Slave Coast, owing in part to the considerable influx of people from the Central Slave Coast after 1724/27 (about which more later).

West of Lake Ahémé (and east of the river Mono, north of Grand Popo), we come to a curious small and sparsely populated sort of no-man's land, the Aja-Mono (or Adja-Mono) plateau. There, more or less "archaic" structures survived to the nineteenth century if not longer, that is, the structures associated with what we call acephalous ("headless") societies.[7]

As for the region west of the Mono, the Western Slave Coast – the Little Slave Coast of the Danes – it corresponds *grosso modo* to Eweland, plus regions occupied by the Hula, the Bê of Lake Togo being the westernmost Hula as far as we know.

Obviously the term Slave Coast, which was coined by European slave traders in the seventeenth century,[8] is highly pejorative. Yet it has stuck, and has survived so far both the era of decolonization and that of political correctness. Indeed, the term is still widely used, as atlases, encyclopedias *and* many scholarly works testify. Why the name? Because the Slave Coast came to export *only* slaves once the cloth trade from Allada disappeared – as opposed to the Grain, Pepper, Ivory, and especially Gold Coasts, where, as their names indicate, other goods were, had been or remained of importance.

Since the Slave Coast can be defined as an historical region, it makes sense to study its past more or less separately from the rest of West Africa, even from the neighbouring Gold Coast, with which interrelations were intense, although certainly not in isolation from those other areas. For instance, we will encounter frequently in the following pages such polities as Oyo and Akwamu, the former a mighty and enormous Yoruba polity in the north-east,[9] the local superpower as it were; and the latter originally a realm in the inland of the Gold Coast.[10] Then there were, as we have seen, the Fante canoemen, together with the Ga of the region of Accra, and finally the Europeans, who, although they often distinguished between the Upper or Windward and the Lower or Leeward coasts (the Gold Coast and the Slave Coast respectively), also tended at times to consider the two as one region, and certainly to trade on both.

If one argues that it would have made more sense to choose as one's frame of study the whole of the Lower Guinea coast, one certainly has a point. But although that would have been too big a cake to swallow for the present author, in fact comparisons with the neighbouring regions are unavoidable, so that the present work does at times resemble something approaching the history of that broader region. It may also be that what follows has been inflated, somewhat unintentionally, with a certain global dimension ("the pen took charge").

As for the linguistic and ethnic distribution, the salient feature is that most people of the Slave Coast apparently speak what is basically the same language. The exception is, and especially was, a small section situated east of the Weme river and part of the wider Yorubaland. Ketu, a neighbour of Oyo, is the best-known and largest Yoruba polity inside the Slave Coast.[11]

Those who argue that with that exception there is only one language are a number of linguists, including the Beninese Hounkpatin Capo,[12] whom we choose to follow. Should one argue the opposite, namely that there are several languages (about twenty), one would have to add, our linguists say, that those languages are very closely related indeed. It all hinges on one's definition of what constitutes a language, what constitutes a dialect, and at which stage a dialect becomes a separate language (or vice versa). The problem of considering that there is only one language is that no agreement has been reached on any measure of standardization, not to mention a *name* for that language. However, *Gbe*, meaning "tongue" or "language" in all the relevant dialects (hence for instance Fongbe and Ewegbe, the Fon and Ewe tongues), has been proposed, and has been adopted by many scholars, Hounkpatin Capo included. Other names proposed are Xwegbe and Egaf, the latter short for Ewe-Gen-Aja-Fon.[13]

What is beyond doubt is that Gbe differs sharply from the other languages spoken in the wider region, whether Yoruba in the east (and in the north, as we shall see), Ga-Adangbe in the west between the Volta and the Densu river west of Accra,[14] or Twi of the Akan and the Fante even further west.

But the apparent linguistic unity has not fostered any other kind of unity, and certainly not an ethnic one. Indeed, the people of the Slave Coast belong, and belonged traditionally, to a bewildering number of more or less fluid ethnic groups. Hence we have to confront and tolerate quite a few ethnonyms – that is, names of ethnic groups. In brief, the literature presents us with (roughly from east to west, to the west of Yorubaland) the Gun or Egun, the Tofinu, the Hula, the Wemenu or Oueneou, the Hueda, the Mahi, the Guedevi, the Fon, the Aïzo, the Aja, the Ewe, also written Eve or Vhe (the two occasionally put together as Aja-Ewe); the Guin (also called Ge or Gen), the Mina, the Anlo, the Watchi or Ouatchi, the Krepi, and a few more. Some may be considered to be subgroups of others (the three last mentioned are for instance often also catalogued as Ewe, and Krepi is frequently used in the sources as synonymous with Ewe).[15] One (Aïzo) does not really refer to a specific ethnic group as such, but denotes in general terms indigenous peoples or firstcomers. Other groups have disappeared more or less, especially the Guedevi. And some ethnonyms are of relatively recent date, Gun/Egun and Tofinu in particular. We must remember in this context that ethnic identity is bound to and by historical development, and that ethnic affiliation can be fairly unstable and fluctuating. That being said, we may define ethnicity (loosely) as perceived common ancestry, plus common customs and common language, together with in many cases boundary maintenance towards other groups.

Some minorities there are, in the north, in the region shading into the above-mentioned frontier zone. And here it is noteworthy that we find Yoruba-speakers in the north too. In fact, they inhabit a sort of southwest-bending panhandle all the way to, and including, Atakpamé far to the west in the Plateau region of present-day Central Togo.[16] Thus they constitute partly a buffer zone between the land of the Gur-speaking peoples to the north and our Gbe in the south. What is noteworthy about the panhandle-Yoruba – Peel's Western Yoruba Groups[17] – is that, apart from two small polities,[18] they display what is qualified as marked archaic traits: they have no kings (contrary to those of the vast Yoruba heartland). They too are, in short, classified as acephalous.[19] Are we dealing with the advance guard of a migration which petered out, as Robert Smith has suggested?[20]

As for the present-day Mahi in the hilly region of central Benin (and clearly in the frontier zone), they do not constitute a linguistic minority properly speaking, they are in fact Gbe-speakers. But theirs is a relatively new ethnic group, a mixture of Yoruba and Fon, the latter being refugees from the south in the eighteenth century especially.[21] Since they were the northern neighbours of Dahomey, the main polity on the Slave Coast after 1727, and became possibly the principal victims of the slave-raids of that polity, the Mahi will appear frequently in the following.

We find genuine linguistic minorities in the Plateau region of Central Togo and especially its continuation into modern Ghana, north of Ho, that is from the shores of the modern Volta Lake and eastwards, yet another typical hilly refugee zone.[22] Those (small) minorities "speak languages which are unique to themselves".[23] We are referring to the more or less mysterious people who speak the so-called Ghana-Togo Mountain Languages (GTML-Togo *Restsprachen* in the German literature). They were and are clearly acephalous.[24] We mention these people because they pop up now and then in the traditions of the neighbouring Ewe. As for making head and tail of their past, it seems like even the specialists have given up the attempt, noting that their oral traditions, and the available linguistic evidence, sprawl out in all directions. Hence our leading authority, Paul Nugent, has described them as the first postmodernists.[25] But at least one linguist believes that their languages may be related to Guan[26] (the language of one group is actually classified as Guan[27]). And people who speak Guan constitute also an enigma of sorts – they are scattered in small and not so small groups nearly all over Ghana,[28] as well as possibly also in Central Togo.

After this brief overview of the linguistic situation, it remains for us to lament the rather strange fact that research in historical linguistics has, as far as we know, not yet been undertaken in the case of the Slave Coast. It is indeed one of the few fields one can think of which has the potential of broadening and deepening our understanding of its past. One wonders in particular what a systematic study of the etymological origins of place names might result in.[29]

The local political situation, past and present, implies that there was, and is, no authority capable of imposing a common language, or even of standardizing any of the component dialects (if dialects is the correct term). Hence there is no agreed-upon orthography. If we add that the Europeans wrote down the words and names as they saw fit or thought they heard them, the result is an onomastic nightmare for the modern researcher.

Take for instance Ouidah, admittedly an extreme case. Ouidah, so spelt, is how the name appears on modern road maps and on the local roadsigns, and is also the orthography adopted by Robin Law in his work on its history already cited. Hence it is also adopted, in the present work, though reluctantly – somehow it does not sound right. But in the sources the town is more often referred to as Whydah (our favourite), or alternatively as Widah, Whidawe, Wheda, Guydah or Vida (all mainly English and Danish styles), Juda or Judas (French style), Ayuda or Ajuda (Portuguese style), and finally Xweda and Fida. But the problem is that the town was (and perhaps is) also called Glehue, Gléhoué, Gregory, Gregoy, Grighwe, Grighue and Agriffie etc. (I.A. Akinjogbin adds to the confusion by using what he presents as the Yoruba name for the place, Igelefe).[30] This second class of names has obviously another origin than the first. So what is the explanation? Ouidah/Whydah etc. is derived from Hueda, also written Xueda, Weda or Pédah, which is the name of the local ethnic group (not necessarily that of the original inhabitants of the place, who may have been Hula).[31] But it was also, we have learned, the name of a pre-1727 polity, of which Ouidah was part, with its capital at Savi some nine kilometres further north (also written Sahè, Saxè, Xavier, Sabba etc.). The original name of the *village* of Ouidah was in fact Glehue etc. Why and how the original name was replaced by one derived from that of a local ethnic group and the corresponding polity, we do not know. Hence Agriffie in Whidawe – that is, Glehue in Hueda – in the earliest extant document written from Ouidah in 1681 may be the correct way of putting it, according to Robin Law.[32] An additional problem is that the *polity* of Hueda disappeared in 1727, but certainly not the *town* of Ouidah-Glehue. However, the real problem is that when reference is made in the sources before 1727 to Ouidah or Whydah, we are not always certain whether it refers to the Hueda polity or to the town (village?) of Ouidah. To avoid confusion, we have tried to use the double name Ouidah-Glehue for the town and that of Hueda for the polity.

To take another possibly confusing example from some kilometres further east, there is Jakin (the twin town of Offra), also written Djèkin,[33] Diaquin, Djaquin and Jacquin; this is incidentally a Hula polity – Hula being also written Houla, Kpla, Xula, Xwla, Huda or Pla – at some points neighbouring the

Weme, also written Ouémé (note that Weme is the name of a river, an ethnic group *and* a polity; the original name of the river seems to have been Wo).

* * *

Let us pause for a while and have a closer look at the Hula, because they provide us with a sort of introductory glimpse into the logic of the societies of the Slave Coast even in remote times. The Hula are, or were, the famous water people, so called, those who worshipped Hu, the *vodun* or deity of the sea,[34] the meanest of the deities[35] since the sea was never really calm (*hu* means actually the sea – hence, we suspect, the names Hula and Hueda). To-day only a few scattered groups who call themselves Hula remain. But they constituted, one is inclined to suppose, the indigenous people of the south of possibly the whole of the Slave Coast[36] – Eweland included, or at least that part of the indigenous population whose domain was the lagoon and the marshlands, devoting themselves principally to fishing and salt-making.[37] It is in this context significant that they, like the Hueda, claim to have emerged from a hole in the earth[38] (incidentally not from the sea), usually a sure sign of indigenous status.

The point here is that although the name Hula may refer to the original inhabitants of the coast itself, possibly the people who greeted or invited the Portuguese on shore, it refers also to a specific way of life, one connected with water. Hence, people who were distinct from economic and religious points of view (the two being very much interconnected) also tended to constitute a distinct ethnic group. And when that specific way of life began to be eroded, the same happened to the corresponding ethnic group, its members shifting simply their ethnic affiliation. Note in addition that when the Hula of the Ouidah-Glehue region came under the sway of the Hueda, this was reflected in the religious domain too, in the sense that Hu was relegated to the position of younger brother of Dangbe the python,[39] the tutelary deity of the Hueda. In what we may call the official Huedan pantheon, Hu remained very much in evidence at Ouidah-Glehue.[40]

Finally, let us present a very curious Hula personage who lived at Agbanakin (or Agbananken) on an island in the lagoon; Agbanakin, together with the surrounding hamlets on both sides of the lagoon, is called Grand Popo or Hulagan (which is a direct translation of Great Hula). Grand Popo-Hulagan could be the (mythical) ancestral home of the Hula.[41] Agbanakin, whose title was *hulaholu* according to Félix Iroko[42] (who unfortunately does not explain what it means) called himself the "Master of the Lagoon", according to the eighteenth-century German-Dane Paul Erdmann Isert.[43] The *hulaholu* has been variously presented as a chief, a priest, and even a sacred king.[44] As such he exercised some sort of undefined power, perhaps primarily a ritual one, over a vast area.

* * *

We repeat that although most people of the Slave Coast speak basically the same language, this linguistic unity is not mirrored in the ethnic field. Nor for that matter in the political one. That is, we cannot exclude the possibility that the above-mentioned *hulaholu* of Hulagan, and (afterwards?) the rulers of Tado in the interior, once held some kind of sway over a considerable portion of the Slave Coast. It is also fairly certain that those of Allada did so some time later.[45] Tado is situated ca. 100 km inland, in present-day Togo, but close to the modern Benin Republic border; the town of Allada, also called Ardres, Arida etc., is situated some 38 km inland in what is now central Benin; Offra and Jakin were for long dependencies of Allada. If the rulers of Tado did rule such a wide area, they sank early into oblivion, and those at Allada lost their prominent position after a short while. And the later dominant polity, that of Dahomey, controlled probably less than half of the Slave Coast.[46]

In fact, should one choose to consider the Slave Coast as one entity, as we do, we would have to add that it was an entity rocked by a more or less permanent civil war during the whole era of the slave trade, the rise and expansion of Dahomey in the first half of the eighteenth century being the most notorious episode in this context. The temptation is to argue that this permanent civil war may explain, in part at least, the slave trade.

One may wonder if there existed any kind of feeling of unity even at the level of the various ethnic groups. The Ewe or Vhe, who occupy roughly the western half of the whole Slave Coast (the Hula excepted), and who are often presented as a bloc, do apparently display such a feeling – there is even reference today to Ewe nationalism. But there are scholars who argue that this pan-Ewe identity, as we may call it, was fashioned, if not fabricated, by the German missionaries who were active in the region from 1847.[47] Indeed, according to the anthropologist Paul Nugent, the very term Ewe, as a unifying designation, was probably not in common currency before the 1920s.[48] Hence the contention that "The very term 'Ewe' has its origins in missionary ethnography".[49]

A closer look reveals that the term Ewe dissolves itself into a number of more or less separate, although closely related, groups. There is for instance the case of the coastal Anlo in the south-west who adopted what is called Ewe-ness, whatever that may mean exactly, only recently.[50] They were traditionally opposed to, and kept aloof from, those of Ewedome (inland Eweland[51]), that is, principally the Krepi or Peki in the west around Ho, and the Watchi on the plateau that bears their name in the east.[52] In fact, most slaves in Anlo came from Ewedome and thus spoke conveniently the same language as their masters ("Domestic slavery was widely practised in precolonial Anlo").[53]

It is probable that the various groups which made up the population of the Slave Coast in the period under scrutiny, and still do in large part, have occupied their present habitat since time immemorial.[54] This in spite of all the migration stories we encounter in the traditions. Those stories, if they really correspond to actual events, probably refer to migrations over short distances, involving only a limited number of people. However, we do know of several apparently fairly large-scale exoduses in our period, including many waves of Ga-Adangbe from the Accra region of the eastern Gold Coast, who fled east of the Volta after their homeland was conquered by Akwamu in about 1680. Some of them established the polity of Glidji or Genyi about 55 km west of Ouidah-Glehue, and formally including Little Popo-Aneho. But regardless of how numerous or few the fleeing Ga were, the fact remains that they were linguistically assimilated by the local Gbe-speakers.[55]

The expansionist wars of Dahomey also provoked migrations (as we shall see), mainly southwards and eastwards towards the sparsely populated Yoruba-speaking Eastern Slave Coast. The Yoruba were either pushed back or assimilated by the Gbe. The phenomenon affected especially the ethno-linguistical composition in the flood-plain of the Weme river and eastwards.

* * *

As noted, the people of the Slave Coast live in a region which corresponds roughly to what is called the Benin or Dahomey Gap, and which is part of the forest-savanna mosaic zone. Has the area covered by forest decreased in the last two to three hundred years? With modern ecological consciousness, it is tempting to believe so.[56] But the specialists tell us, first, that the forest-savanna mosaic type of vegetation and not forest was the original one, and second, that the change could actually be in the contrary direction, that the forest is *advancing*.[57] However, what does seem certain is that the fauna has declined sharply. One is particularly struck, when combing the sources, by the frequent reference to elephants, an animal of the savanna; and in fact to a somewhat lively trade in ivory, especially on the Western Slave Coast. There was even from old times a sort of corps of elephant huntresses in Fon country known as *gbeto*, possibly the predecessors of the later famous Amazons.[58] To the best of our knowledge, there are few if any elephants, or any kind of big game, left on the Slave Coast today.[59] But of course, the reason may have more to do with demographic expansion than with ecological deterioration.

It is tempting to argue that the Benin Gap phenomenon also explains in part the predominance of the Slave Coast in the slave trade. One may in fact surmise that the forest-savanna mosaic, and the low-lying undulating plain which makes up most of the region, implying the absence of serious physical obstacles to human movement, facilitated the circulation of slave caravans, although obviously also of armies and of robber bands and others. However, we imagine that the many rivers, floodplains, lakes, wetlands and muddy depressions, not to mention the lagoons and other features, forced people on the move to adopt at times complicated zigzag-like itineraries.

We need more detail about the local climate. We note, first, that the era of the slave trade corresponds roughly to a relatively dry phase (c.1300–c.1850) in the climatic history of West Africa.[60] We note, second, that although the climate is tropical, it is characterized by four seasons, two dry and two rainy ones. The main rainy season begins normally in mid-March and lasts until mid-July. It is also called the *travat* season in the European sources, because of the frequent thunderstorms which often wreak a great deal of havoc from May onwards, owing in part to the nature of the soil (*travat* is possibly derived from the Portuguese *trovoada*, and not *travado* as some authors would have it). The little dry season lasts from mid-July to mid-September, and is followed by the little rainy season from mid-September to mid-November.[61]

The main dry season (mid-November to mid-March) is accompanied between December and February by the famous Harmattan, a relatively cold and dry wind from the north-east or east, which often provokes the forming of fog.[62] It was called the "Doctor" by the Europeans because of its beneficial effects on their health.[63]

For our purpose, it is important to note that the Harmattan alters the direction of the maritime currents close to the coast: they flow for a short while from east to west, instead of the reverse as in the rest of the year. Harmattan-time was then the only time of the year when it was possible for the canoemen to make the return trip to the Gold Coast, thanks to their use of sails.[64] What also facilitated the maritime-coastal communications during the dry season was the reduction in the outflow of the Volta, a river which could not be passed at sea by canoe for the rest of the year, and thus functioned as a barrier of sorts.[65]

The main dry season, including Harmattan-time, was the time of the year when the sea was *relatively* calm, and the surf much less formidable. But it was still there, owing to the continual presence of the underwater sandbars. Those sandbars are usually presented as the main cause of the famous surf. But the matter is somewhat more complicated, and is actually related to meteorological conditions far away in the south Atlantic. Hence the calming of the surf during the dry season is primarily ascribed to the fact that that season corresponds to summer time, and hence stable weather, in the Southern Hemisphere.[66]

The main dry season was obviously the "best" period for the slave traders. But was the slave trade really a seasonal business? One is tempted to believe so, considering what we know about the local climate. However, the strange point is that I have been unable to dig up any convincing evidence to that effect. One of the problems is that the slave trade as a seasonal activity would have required a strict timing, something which was possibly outside the reach of the slave-traders, among other reasons because they could not know beforehand how many months they had to stay on the coast in order to complete their cargoes.[67] Besides, the supply of slaves did not in any way respect the seasonal changes.[68]

The beach is in general between 500 and 1,000 metres deep, says Nicoué Gayibor[69] – that is, as noted, less than a kilometre south of Ouidah-Glehue, but a mere 30 metres in some parts of Anlo. At Anlo one is struck by the inescapable and in a sense oppressive presence of the ocean, and behind the beach of the huge inland lake-like lagoon.[70] Indeed, behind the beach, there is the famous lagoon whose size has varied enormously, but which has always been by far at its largest at Anlo, and which may have extended (the seasons and the climatic cycles permitting) from Anlo in the west to far east of Lagos. Or it may also always have been broken at two sites, as in recent times, one site being situated east of Jakin, where the lagoon loses itself in the earth.[71] The lagoons (the plural is in fact required) broaden at times into veritable lakes, and not only at Anlo-Keta. Mention must be made, especially, of Lake Togo or Haho in the middle, of Lake Ahémé – the residual estuary of the Couffo river[72] – and especially of Lake Nokoué in the east. Lake Nokoué in turn is connected with the river Weme west of Porto-Novo, which flows into what is called the Lagos lagoon, a very large such lagoon complete with many islands, one on which the town of Lagos emerged.[73] This extensive inland waterway system was part of a vast amphibian landscape, a sort of strange intermixture of water and land; an aquatic ecosystem complete with rivers, floodplains, swamps, marshlands, and so on – and, we repeat, a perpetually changing one, waxing and waning according to the seasons and the climatic cycles. But note that it is a landscape which is, since the onset of colonial rule, slowly disappearing owing to drainage, construction of artificial harbours, and so on.

As indicated, the lagoons had two permanent openings. But only one was navigable, the Lagos channel in the east – navigable, although barely so, and deemed in fact unapproachable by many Europeans in the relevant centuries.[74] The other opening was and is at Little Popo in the west.[75] As for temporary openings, especially at high water, there may have been quite a few, beginning with the famous and presently impressive Boca del Rio ("mouth of the river") east of Grand Popo, which is reported to have moved eastwards over the centuries. It is usually presented as a permanent opening, but was in fact closed during certain periods of the colonial era, and therefore possibly also earlier. Other earlier known openings were at Great Popo proper and at present-day Cotonou.[76] These openings, plus near-regular flooding at high tide, explain why salty water frequently penetrated the lagoon, creating propitious conditions for a teeming aquatic life.

This watery region, a luxuriant natural setting, must have been an important source of food for the local population.[77] As for the principal lagoon itself, it seems also to have been an important medium of lateral communication,[78] although a rather slow one, because of its shallowness which made it necessary to "pole" or punt the canoes, as opposed to paddling them[79] (the exception here is the Lagos lagoon). A trip on the lagoon from Ouidah-Glehue to Grand Popo, a distance of less than 25 kilometres, is reported to have lasted some eight hours.[80]

* * *

Inland, on the central-eastern Slave Coast, the land rises slowly to the Abomey plateau situated no more than some 260 metres above sea level (and some 97 km from the coast in the case of the town of Abomey). On the western Slave Coast the rise is much more marked. First, there is the Watchi plateau, and then the Akwapim-Togo ranges, a narrow belt of ridges and hills which extends in a northeast direction from near Accra on the eastern Gold Coast. They become the Atakora mountain range in Togo and culminate at nearly a thousand metres above sea level in the above-mentioned Plateau region.

One more feature of the landscape needs to be mentioned, namely the extensive low-lying area of marshy and heavily wooded country called Lama, meaning "mud" in Portuguese (also called the Agrimey swamp), and teeming with wildlife in our period – separating the Abomey and Allada plateaux. North-south it is situated roughly halfway between Abomey and the coast, and east-west between the rivers Koufo and Weme. This "no-man's-land" was reputed to be close to impassable in the rainy season, and served therefore as a barrier of sorts between the coastal regions and the interior of the Central Slave Coast.[81]

* * *

The vast majority of the people of the Slave Coast living north of the lagoons and outside of the wetlands were and still are agriculturalists tilling the soil. That soil is usually referred to as *terre de barre*;[82] a lateritic-reddish-leached, iron-bearing and clay-rich soil, it is considered to be relatively fertile, in fact exceptionally rich according to some observers, who argued that the land could produce absolutely everything one needed and wanted.[83] But the system of cultivation was of the reputedly primitive itinerant slash-and-burn type, although of a kind, we learn, which did not entail any negative ecological consequences.[84] It permitted three harvests a year[85] (four according to James Houstoun who wrote in the early eighteenth century).[86] Originally, the local peasants may have cultivated especially yams, possibly also millet and sorghum. But with the beginning of the first globalization – that is, the arrival of the Europeans – the local agriculture underwent some sort of revolution due to "the introduction of a complete foodcrop complex from the Americas".[87] Among those foodcrops were cassava and above all the miraculous maize, making possible as many as four harvests a year. The Watchi Ewe in particular acquired the reputation of being exceptional cultivators of maize.[88] In addition the coconut palm and rice arrived from Asia.

But if Jouke Wigboldus is correct in arguing that the Guinea coast "was the habitat of no other domestic animal than the dog before the 1470s",[89] we will have to postulate a much broader agricultural revolution, since we have to include the introduction of a vast number of smaller domestic animals: pigs, sheep, goats and poultry in particular (the climate did not favour horse and cattle breeding). Note the possibly central role of the Portuguese islands of São Tomé and Príncipe in the introduction and dissemination of new crops and new animals, together with the gardens the Europeans set up in or outside their forts.[90] Note also that European iron bars enabled African smiths to turn out considerably more and better farm tools, as well as improved fishhooks, which boosted catches.[91]

In view of all this, and the abundant wildlife, it comes as a surprise to learn that famine was not an altogether unknown phenomenon on the Slave Coast, that is, if we are to believe especially Willem Bosman, who wrote in the early eighteenth century, and Alexis Adande, a modern scholar.[92] But the question here is whether the people of the Slave Coast were able to feed themselves *and* the slaves destined for America, the latter including during the Atlantic crossing. The question is then more generally where the necessary food for the functioning of the Atlantic slave trade came from. In this connexion we may note that the French slave ships in particular had often to make stops on the Gold Coast in order to take in water, wood and victuals, which seem to have been in short supply on the Slave Coast, and to hire the indispensable canoemen.[93] We must also note that most slave ships, after leaving the Slave Coast, did not sail directly for the New World but made, as we shall see, a rather long stopover on one of the Portuguese islands, for reasons of provisioning, among others. But even so, it is tempting to believe that what we may call the maize revolution contributed to the "success" of the slave trade.

* * *

We have so far avoided the subject of demography. The reason why is unfortunately all too evident: we have no idea how many people lived on the Slave Coast in our period, and how the local demographic regime evolved. We can note, as we shall see, that the Europeans came away with the impression that the first polities they entered into contact with, Allada and Hueda, were very densely populated. We can also note that today the southern parts of the modern Republics of Togo and Benin, corresponding to the major part of the Slave Coast, are by far the most densely populated regions of those two states. But that is about all.

* * *

If one wonders how the Europeans stationed on the coast, basically in the Ouidah-Glehue and Offra region, perceived the environment they lived in, the surprising answer is that they found it literally enchanting. It is true that many complained about the local facilities and various nuisances such as the insects, including very dangerous ants.[94] But others seem to have had the time of their lives in Ouidah-Glehue.[95] And virtually all were full of praise for the country which, according to the most enthusiastic Britons, compared favourably, it almost seems, even with "England's green and pleasant land".[96] Possibly the most rapturous description is by James Houstoun from 1725: "an open, pleasant, plentiful fine champaign country, as any this globe can produce. Nature has made this country vie, if not exceed, for pleasure and plenty...any in Europe" [It was, in fact, a country which offered] "everything for the support of human life, nay, even to feed luxury"[97]. Note also that Houstoun was among those who thought the country "prodigiously populous".[98]

What can we say more generally about the (few) European employees on the coast, those who did the dirty work in sum?

They were all men, bachelors mostly, or at least not with their wives in Africa, and very young, arriving often as teenagers and attaining positions of responsibility in their twenties, if not earlier.

But although the Europeans were enchanted with the country, we learn from the literature that they were prone to homesickness, alcoholism, depression, paranoia etc.; that some were converted into jittery melancholics, and some went berserk; that some (most?) led dissolute, intemperate, not to say extravagant ways of life, often at the expense of whichever company employed them; and that most saw to it that their wages "were supplemented by proceeds of fraud and deception".[99] Can we conclude by arguing that what Johannes Postma has to say of the Dutch – the "dregs of the nation"[100] – is valid for all? The description strikes us as unjustifiably unkind. The problem is that the Europeans on the coast constitute an all too easy target, they are the obvious scapegoats. If one wants to go looking for those really responsible on the European side, one has to look elsewhere, in the boardrooms of the various companies and in the chancellery offices of many European states; people to whom those left to face the reality on the spot in Africa were of little concern.[101]

The latter had at least two excuses, they were involved in a trade which must have wrought havoc with their sensibilities; and they expected their lives to be short, owing principally to the famous coast fever, "the country illness".[102] Indeed, the Europeans died literally like flies on the Guinea coast, the notorious "white man's grave". One historian has characterized going to that coast as a "Russian roulette in which more chambers were loaded than empty".[103] For example, at Ouidah-Glehue and Offra, the English presence was nearly interrupted various times between 1680 and 1687, because most employees died.[104] And Johannes Postma has found that of the personnel the Dutch West Indies Company sent out, some sixty per cent died during the first eight months.[105] Was it always possible to fill the vacancies?

That being said, among those who survived the first year or so, some went on to spend decades on the coast, and to exercise considerable influence on the course of events. We shall meet some of them later. We add that the local Europeans, and not only those who served as directors or governors,[106] have left us the main bulk of our sources; sources which are often eminently readable – dregs do not usually write thus. In fact, some of them even published books. And some went on to make quite respectable careers – Archibald Dalzel (about whom more later) and Pruneau de Pommegeorge, to cite but the best known.

Less well known, but possibly more spectacular is the case of William Devaynes. He took over as director of William's Fort Ouidah at the tender age of 17 because he was an officer on a naval ship which chanced to be there at a time (1747) of acute staff shortage.[107] He was appointed to that position three times, spending some twelve years altogether in Ouidah-Glehue between 1747 and 1763. After that he ended up sitting in the House of Commons as an MP during thirteen years (1774–80, 1784–86 and 1796–1801). He also became one of the directors in London of the famous East India Company.

Among the naval officers who spent time on the coast, we will encounter *inter alia* the Dutch national hero Michiel de Ruyter (1607–76) and the Frenchman Jean-Baptiste Ducasse (1646–1715), who held many prominent positions, including that of Governor of Saint Domingue (1697–1700).

It is true that we find at the other end of the scale the case of Charles Whitaker, also Director of the fort in Ouidah-Glehue (in 1733–4), who simply ran away[108] (in his defence, 1734 was a very dangerous time in Ouidah-Glehue). A third category is represented by the famous Lionel Abson, another director in Ouidah-Glehue but much later (1770–1803), who "went native", as we shall see.

The only genuine mutiny among the Europeans in the Lower Guinea that the present author is aware of took place outside the Slave Coast, in Accra on the Gold Coast, and in the Danish fort of Christiansborg, in October 1744.[109]

We add that some Europeans were, as we shall also see, confronted unexpectedly with very perilous situations in which they displayed considerable courage. Some paid for it with long periods of captivity in wretched conditions, others with their very lives.

* * *

For those familar with the stranger-king phenomenon well-known from other parts of the world,[110] and with the frequently encountered contention that the Europeans were considered to be spirits of deceased Africans and/or returning ancestors and/or deities,[111] the Slave Coast must be considered to a be disappointing case, since nothing of the sort appears in the sources. We have, it is true, one Englishman in the seventeenth century called Petley Wybourne and a Dutch-German by the name of Hendrik Hertogh in the next century, who acquired very special positions, as we shall see. But those positions fell probably rather short of the categories just listed. Even so, it carried prestige for a local African king or chief to have a fort or a factory in his domain and/ or Europeans in his entourage.

2

HISTORIOGRAPHY, SOURCES AND EPISTEMOLOGY

The quantitative-statistical dimension of the slave trade, the "numbers game", has made great strides since the pioneering work of Philip Curtin from 1969.[1] It has culminated so far in the Trans-Atlantic Slave Trade Database, the result of an admirable disinterested collective endeavour, easily available on the Internet.[2] Its aim is to provide regularly updated estimates for the number of slaves exported from Africa to America – *estimates* we repeat, not absolute figures, a fact we must not lose sight of. That being said, the figures of the Database are not without their problems for our purpose. We shall return to the matter in some detail in the next chapter.

We are also fairly well informed about many related topics – slave and crew mortality on the Middle Passage, prices and profits, conditions aboard, sex ratios, and so on. That is, everything related to the European side of the story.

But outside of the Database, figures which speak for themselves are close to non-existent. Actually, once one goes "upstream" as it were, that is, once one goes ashore on the Slave Coast, genuine hard facts of whatever kind, including precise dates, become difficult to encounter. Hence we are left often with what one is tempted to describe as soft facts – hearsay, impressionistic, anecdotal and/or subjective evidence etc. – and forced to content ourselves with suppositions, extrapolations, probabilities, educated guesses and so on.[3] This may sound somewhat surprising in the light of a book such as Patrick Manning's which presents us with economic statistics going back to the 1640s, no less;[4] considering also more generally the apparently abundant sources and the impressive historiography on the Slave Coast – a historiography dominated by Robin Law. But, to put it briefly, the part of Manning's book dealing with the economy is empirically unsound and cannot be accepted, as Jouke Wigboldus, among others, has demonstrated.⁵ And the historiography in general may be said to be often based on a quicksand-like empirical foundation, as it seems to us that Law himself has emphasized time and again. Finally, abundant sources do not necessarily tally with reliable or informative ones, or for that matter with original, as opposed to repetitive or derivative ones.

In fact, certain parts of the historiography, and particularly the book by Manning with his extravagant theory of early economic growth cut short by the slave trade, may be said to illustrate a syndrome not unknown among historians, and certainly evident among Africanists: the temptation to elucidate from the sources more information than what they can actually yield, or, one might say, the urge to fill in the blanks (to avoid misunderstanding, we are not arguing that Manning is necessarily wrong, only that his work is guesswork in statistical disguise).

We have, then, a severe epistemological problem at our hand (epistemology being usually defined as the theory of knowledge – how we can know what we believe we know).

* * *

"...from Whydah [Ouidah-Glehue] beach to Abomey [the capital of Dahomey], which is perhaps the most beaten track, by Europeans, of any in Africa..." Thus the anonymous writer of the Preface to Archibald Dalzel's history of Dahomey.⁶ Dalzel's book was the first full-fledged history of that polity, and it appeared as early as 1793. But as can be deduced from the quotation, at that time Dahomey was already well known in Europe, although in a rather unfavourable light.

Dalzel's book was the first genuine history of any part of the Slave Coast, which is why we need to devote some space to it. There are three elementary and obvious points about Dalzel's book that we need to stress. First, it was written by a European, symbolizing the fact that most of what we know about the past of the Slave Coast we owe to foreigners, that is, Europeans: a problem, whichever way one puts it. The second point is that Dalzel was mostly not a private trader (although he was also that at times) but an official, first of the slave-trading Royal African Company of England, and after 1751 of the Company of Merchants trading in Africa (often called the African Company, a similarity of names which has generated some confusion). The latter was a regulating company exclusively in charge of the upkeep of the forts, and hence dependent on grants from Parliament. And here the essential point is that most of the sources emanate precisely from the officials on the coast, not from, for instance, the so-called interlopers, as the private traders were known in the days of monopolistic trade. The implication is that even within the European sources there is a heavy bias, in favour of officialdom.

A third point: Dalzel chose to write a history not of the Slave Coast, but of the polity of Dahomey, a relative latecomer. In fact, Dalzel set the tone. For as Patrick Manning has expressed it, the study of the past of the Slave Coast has tended to be organized around the history of Dahomey.[7]

It is not difficult to understand why: the case of Dahomey is a fascinating, not to say sensationalist one, with, as presented by Dalzel, its endless stream of wars, executions and human sacrifices, not to mention the despotic character of its absolutist rulers – and with Europeans as witnesses to nearly all of it. We are in fact well informed about Dahomey and the Central Slave Coast, whereas we know next to nothing about many other parts of that region. What has been said about the Watchi-Ewe, that "they appear spuriously in the midst of information about other groups, without (ever) taking centre-stage",[8] is true in an embarrassing number of cases. The result has been an imbalanced historiography, one that reflects the nature of the sources. The ambition of the present author is to *try* to redress that imbalance – to the limited extent that it is possible. But we too must take as our point of departure the case of Dahomey, especially the controversy occasioned by the image presented by Dalzel; or, if one prefers, the image presented by those who have interpreted Dalzel.

Dahomey was conquered by the French in 1892–94, that is, nearly a century after the appearance of Dalzel's book. The unanswerable question is whether the nineteenth-century authorities in Dahomey knew about the contents of Dalzel's book, and if so, whether, to what extent, and how, the oral traditions of Dahomey were coloured by its content. It is highly unlikely, we have been told. But the point has the merit of alerting us to the eternal problem of feedback from the written sources.

Second, there is no doubt that Dalzel (Dalziel before he changed his name), a naval surgeon by training, knew his subject intimately from his many years on the Guinea coast, including three (1767–70) as director of the British fort at Ouidah-Glehue (while leaving at the age of 29–30, he nearly perished in the famous surf).[9] In addition, a large section of the book (pp. 156–230) is based on communications from Lionel Abson, who arrived with Dalzel in

1767 aged 17, succeeded him as director, and remained in that position for the next 33 years – an absolute record on the coast – until his death in 1803, actually functioning in the end more as an African chief than as a European employee.[10] The section based on the testimony of Abson may then be qualified as a primary source.

As for Dalzel himself, after having tried his luck directly in the slave trade for quite some time,[11] he re-emerged in 1792 as no less than the governor of Cape Coast Castle, that is, as the head of all the British establishments on the Guinea coast, a position he held for some eight years altogether (1792–98 and 1800–2).[12] Before and after that he was a somewhat active participant in the public debate in Britain over the slave trade, generally defending it, although with an eye to the nuances.[13] What is not in doubt is that Dalzel, who has left traces in many archives,[14] was a person of some standing whose testimony must be taken seriously.

Did Dalzel write his book to justify and/or to legitimize the slave trade? It has been argued that Dalzel's aim was to demonstrate that the Africans were naturally warlike, thus refuting those who contended that it was precisely the slave trade which had triggered off wars in Africa.[15] But if that was Dalzel's intention, it is nowhere made explicit in a book which is purely descriptive, and which could in our opinion as easily be interpreted as a blaze *against* the slave trade. We note in this context that Dalzel was not the only former Director at Ouidah-Glehue who wrote books. We have also the one by the Frenchman Pruneau de Pommegeorge who was stationed there for a long time and whose book was published four years before Dalzel's.[16] It contains a large section on Dahomey – basically a witness account – and in that section Pruneau confirms, it seems to us, Dalzel's image of Dahomey; in spite of the fact that Pruneau's intention was clearly not to justify the slave trade, but, as argued earlier, exactly the opposite.

Whatever the case, Dalzel's book set the tone in a sense. And it is no coincidence that in the next general history of Dahomey to appear, some 174 years later, the Nigerian historian Isaac A. Akinjogbin, reacting against the perception of Dahomey as the classic slave-trading polity characterized by a rule of terror, tried to refute Dalzel, or rather the standard interpretation of Dalzel.[17] He thereby triggered off a major controversy which we must investigate in some detail, since it is related intimately to one of the main contentions we intend to make in the present work. Before going on, we must note that it may perhaps not be correct to put the blame for Dahomey's negative reputation exclusively on Dalzel. What must also have contributed was that Dahomey, like other polities on the Slave Coast, including notably Lagos, insisted on carrying on with the slave trade in the nineteenth century long after it had come to an end elsewhere in West Africa. During that period, the period of the so-called "illegal" slave trade, many Europeans visited or had dealings with Dahomey. Most wrote about what they saw or experienced, depicting Dahomey in a rather unfavourable light.

As for Akinjogbin, he argued famously that Dahomey was an innovative polity, a new and revolutionary one at that, in the sense that it did not conform to what Akinjogbin called the Ebi social theory, which according to him was the norm in West Africa at that time[18] (*ebi* means lineage or kindred among the Yoruba, it is synonymous with *idile*[19]). The Ebi social theory implies, according to Akinjogbin, that most polities were of a federal structure, and as such made up of autonomous entities, with kinship ties, mostly fictive, having been established between those in command: families writ large, if one prefers. This is certainly logical, considering the fact that we are in a region and an epoch where the social structure was a kin-based one. However, Dahomey was different, according to Akinjogbin, in the sense that the Dahomean rulers rejected the Ebi social theory and tried consciously to destroy the old order. All this impelled Dahomey to conquer the coast in order to put an end to the slave trade. But unfortunately, King Agaja, the real founder of Dahomey who died in 1740, was forced by the Europeans to reactivate that trade, much against his will.[20] Akinjogbin evokes in this context "the desecrating hands of the European factors"....[21] And of course, once Dahomey and other polities were drawn into the slave trade, that trade "entangled African societies in destructive relationships of dependency".[22]

In order to see clearly, it may be worthwhile to split the controversy in two. There is on the one hand the nature of the Dahomey polity and Akinjogbin's Ebi social theory, and in this case we believe that Akinjogbin was in a sense on the right track, although he overdid it. On the other hand, there is the topic of Agaja and the slave trade. And in this context Akinjogbin's case rests, as far as we can see, first on the fact that all the European permanent trading establishments at Savi were burned down in 1727 and the Europeans encountered there made prisoners, and second on a letter that king Agaja is supposed to have written in 1726 (that is, before the beginning of the conquest of Hueda) in which he advocated the establishment of plantations on the Slave Coast. (The letter was incidentally read aloud in the House of Commons in 1789 by an MP opposed to the proposed abolition of the slave trade.)[23]

As for what happened at Savi, Akinjogbin is certainly correct. But the Europeans were released quickly, the forts at Ouidah-Glehue, as opposed to the trading establishments at Savi, were *not* destroyed, and Agaja went out of his way, as we shall see, to reassure the Europeans of his desire to carry on as usual. What Agaja was bent on erasing was, it seems to us, an intermediary and a rival, namely the Huedan polity, not the European presence, nor the slave trade. Had he really wanted to put an end to that presence and that trade, the events of 1727 presented him with a golden opportunity to do so – and anyway he did not need such an opportunity, he had it in his power to do so at any time. As for the letter, assuming that it is genuine (as Robin Law does, I am less certain), it indicates simply that Agaja wanted plantations *and* slave trade. Nevertheless, the idea that he was opposed to the slave trade, an idea first formulated by John Atkins as early as 1735[24] and repeated by Akinjogbin, turned out to be a success. It has in fact been seized upon, one could say eagerly, by the historians of the so-called Radical school –Walter Rodney and Basil Davidson among others.[25] But the very idea that an external agent could force a ruler on the Slave Coast to engage in the slave trade against his will strikes us as being frankly absurd considering the local conditions.

As for Akinjogbin's reconstruction of the history of Allada and the early years of Dahomey,[26] the problem is that it is in a sense too detailed. Like Manning, he knows "too much". However, the Ebi social theory, and the contention that Dahomey was different, is something else. In this case, the most critical voice has been Robin Law who denied originally any validity to the Ebi social theory.[27] He argued that that theory simply did not exist, implying, we suppose, that it did not exist as a sort of ideology which some people proposed consciously at some stage. But the way we read Akinjogbin, his Ebi social theory is simply a model which purports to convey to us how the polities of Yorubaland, and in fact of most of West Africa, were constructed and functioned. If so, Akinjogbin's point is that Dahomey did not conform to what we may call the traditional pattern of polities in that part of the world. This is in sum Akinjogbin's rupture theory. Law's central argument is, on the other hand, that the differences between Dahomey and the other polities of the region, although substantial, were in the final analysis of degree, not of kind. Indeed, according to Law "The evidence suggests…that the type of government which Dahomey evolved was essentially an adaptation of what was already known".[28] Edna Bay, another distinguished historian of Dahomey, agrees.[29] The principal difference between Dahomey and the rest, according to Law, is the fact that Dahomey was a much more militaristic entity, employing means of destruction hitherto unknown in the region – firearms, and more generally a military organization clearly geared to the gathering of slaves.[30] Dahomey was, in sum, a predatory polity. Hence, "If the rise of Dahomey was a revolution, it was a revolution of destruction".[31] Nevertheless, "by the 1770s, the Dahomians clearly had…won the consent of many of the conquered to the legitimacy of their rule". In fact, under King Tegbesu (1740– 74), Agaja's successor, whatever problems may have existed at whatever level of legitimacy had been resolved.[32]

This is what we may call the continuation theory, which in Law's presentation looks in our view rather like its opposite, the rupture theory. The present author finds it in any case difficult to reconcile the continuation theory with the predatory, militaristic nature of Dahomey. As for the historian who has presented most forcefully Akinjogbin's original rupture theory, J. Cameron Monroe, he argues that we are confronted with "a revolutionary militaristic, and increasingly bureaucratic, ideology that differed dramatically from the ritually based principles of political order established [earlier]".[33] But if that was the ideology the Dahomean rulers tried to impose (it may actually have been so), the question is whether they were successful in doing so. And the present author's opinion is that they were not.

Our position is, first, that we find Law's portrayal of the reign of Tegbesu, an absolutely crucial period in this context, difficult to reconcile with the empirical basis; second, that we disagree with the continuation theory; but third, that the rupture theory needs to be seriously modified.

The heart of the matter is this: Dahomey was founded by outsiders, that much all are agreed upon – whether bandits, outlaws[34] or members of the royal sib of Allada, as Akinjogbin and many oral traditions would have it.[35] But as outsiders they had to abide by a certain number of rules if they were to be accepted, in particular that of respecting the indigenous "earth-priests" and their ritual control of the land. Here we have entered into a subject which is fundamental in our sense, but which has not received the attention it merits. The central point is that the early rulers of Dahomey, by not respecting the indigenous "earth-priests" (about whom much more later), and in fact killing them (or claiming to have done so), *and* by usurping their position, committed an unheard-of and unforgivable sacrilege according to the prevailing beliefs and/or customs of the time in that part of the world (and according to the model which will be presented shortly).[36] Those who founded Dahomey violated just about every rule in the book, as they admitted in their oral traditions. If they expected to get away with it, they were mistaken, which is why they found themselves saddled with a severe problem of legitimacy. In fact, our newcomers were left with little choice but to establish a polity based on force and terror, that is a bloodstained militaristic one (here one can say that we rejoin Law again). However, we are not certain it was a consequence of deliberate innovations or a new ideology. The alternative is that we are dealing with some kind of continuous *fuite en avant*.

Once in power, the newcomers who founded Dahomey tried naturally to explore avenues to legitimate their position, a legitimation which would necessarily have to be of a religious character. Hence very extensive attempts at manipulation and engineering in the religious domain, as we shall see. But in this they never really succeeded (here we part company with Law once more), they were never able to get around their "original sin". For as Jacques Lombard pointed out, religion always escaped the complete control of the Dahomean kings[37] – a very uncomfortable, not to say impossible situation for any monarch to be in at that time and in that part of the world. In addition those kings were not very successful in what was supposed to be their very raison d'être, in which success might perhaps have made up for everything else: expansion, that is to say war, which meant in turn spoils, especially in the shape of slaves. Worse, Dahomey was forced early on to become a tribute-paying vassal of Oyo, and remained so until the decline of that once mighty polity, not a very glorious position for a self-declared warrior polity.

To sum up: the results of Dahomey's very marked militaristic-aggressive policy were in the end not very impressive, even measured by their own yardstick.[38] In fact Dahomey, although certainly the leading power on the Slave Coast after 1727, was in the final analysis a small and, we may add, second-rate polity, completely dwarfed in the larger region by such entities as Oyo and Asante, possibly also by old Benin at its height. Sir Richard Burton, who visited Dahomey at the moment of its greatest extension in the 1860s, perhaps summed it up adequately when he qualified Dahomey as "a *small black Sparta* [our italics]...hedged in by hostile accolents", that is, neighbours.[39] With those neighbours, Dahomey had exclusively relations of war.[40]

As for the slave trade, there is every reason to believe that the Dahomeans did what they could to encourage it, which was not very much. Like "barbarians", as they were from the point of view of the people of Allada and Hueda, the two principal polities they conquered, the Dahomeans, lacking in commercial acumen and trans-cultural experience, did it all wrong, driving away the Europeans little by little, one of the consequences being that they were faced with increasingly stiff competition from new centres on the eastern

HISTORIOGRAPHY, SOURCES AND EPISTEMOLOGY

Slave Coast, a competition Dahomey sought to eliminate simply by physically destroying those centres. In fact, the Dahomean rulers provoked a sharp decline in the slave trade from the central Slave Coast: that is, exactly the opposite of what we suspect they had aimed at.

In order to avoid any possible misunderstanding, we consider that the praise Robin Law has received recently in the shape of a voluminous *Festschrift* is certainly merited.[41] Law's contribution to the exploration of the past of West Africa is indeed nothing less than colossal (in some periods he published articles and books faster that the rest of us could read them). The aspect of Law's endeavour which we find particularly admirable, because totally disinterested, is his editing and publishing of a number of collections of archival sources, which has made life much easier for the rest of us. It is an activity which is not considered too glamorous in certain more prestige-focused quarters.

All this serves to explain why the present book relies on the works of Law to an embarrassing, some would say, unbecoming degree. But then, as Law himself has written, appropriately modestly, and elegantly: "I have no desire to have the last word, only that the debate should continue".[42] As indeed it should, since the evidence at hand is often capable of more than one interpretation, and some of Law's theories and conclusions need to be questioned. Among these are especially those pertaining to the origin and nature of the Dahomean polity. That being said, Law's "I have no desire" statement expresses my view also.

* * *

Now for the sources. Respecting the conventional division between written and oral sources, and as far as the written sources are concerned between archival and printed sources, we must begin by noting that the huge corpus of archival sources is exclusively European, and preserved exclusively in European and American archives, one of the negative consequences being that one does not have to take the trouble to travel to Africa to write about the past of the Slave Coast (but as we hope to have demonstrated in the Introduction, a geographical reconnaissance is absolutely indispensable for the comprehension of that past). Even when we are told that the contents of a particular manuscript were dictated by a certain local king, we cannot be certain that the words are those of the relevant king (the classic case is the letter from Agaja mentioned above). After all, whoever wrote down the dictates of the king in question was a European, and the king had no means of controlling what the European penned.

The European archival sources that have been preserved emanate in the main from the trading companies on the coast. As such they are concerned principally with company affairs. But although they are often far less informative than one would have liked – they contain a lot of hearsay – they are nevertheless indispensable. Robin Law has an excellent point when he argues that the main problem with those sources is that there is not more of them.[43] Since Law wrote those lines, the task of the historian has been immensely facilitated thanks to the publication of a good many archival sources, often duly edited and translated, in many cases by Law himself. What is still missing, however, are the sources emanating from the so-called interlopers, many increasingly organized in private firms, which were responsible for an ever larger share of the slave trade.[44]

Next there is the rather impressive bulk of printed reports, and above all travel accounts, personal recollections and so on by Europeans, mostly employees of the trading companies, who thought they knew well the Guinea coast and the slave trade, and who felt the need to share their experience with European readers. Some did so with remarkable success, especially the Dutchman Willem Bosman, whose reminiscences from his 14 years' stay on the coast, ending up as the Dutch second-in-command at Elmina before being swept out in 1701 at the age of 29,[45] became an international best-seller – and an all-time classic. Many others also enjoyed a wide international readership, including those of two other Dutchmen, Pieter de Marees and Olfert Dapper (the latter actually never set foot on Africa),[46] and the German-Dane Paul Isert.[47] Not to mention Dalzel and a host of other Britons.

Whether or to which extent books like these should be classified as primary or secondary sources is a complex matter we need not go into.[48] But we note that they include more or less everything, from the seventeenth-century Spaniard Alonso de Sandoval who, like Dapper, never went to Africa but, also like Dapper, had privileged access to information unavailable to the modern scholar;[49] to the eighteenth-century French-English Huguenot slave-trader Jean/John Barbot, who spent no more than 30 days ashore in Africa;[50] to long-term residents like Bosman, Dalzel and Pruneau de Pommegeorge etc. What is certain is that this corpus still constitutes a very important bulk of our sources for the past of the Slave Coast (and of the Guinea coast generally), and an easily accessible one. But of course the perennial question is how trustworthy they are (note Edna Bay's warning that "pre-colonial travelers have seldom been read critically").[51] They borrowed freely from each other, they plagiarized, in sum they often committed a sort of literary robbery, as one expert in these matters, a certain John Green, put it in 1745–46.[52]

The next wave of Europeans to write on the Slave Coast were the missionaries and above all the first official envoys (including after a while colonial administrators), who began to arrive in the nineteenth century. In both groups there were many who tried their hands as amateur historians and especially as amateur anthropologists. In so doing, they undertook in a sense a rescue operation, confining to paper many customs, cultural traits, and above all oral traditions which would otherwise certainly have been lost. The famous case is that of Auguste Le Hérissé, to which we will return shortly. The temptation for the modern scholar is to rely heavily on this sort of evidence, since it is at times the only one available.

The next to arrive on the scene were the professional anthropologists, whose works are certainly indispensable to the historians.[53] But as we all know, the anthropological literature presents the historian with a number of problems. The first is the tendency to convey to us a somewhat timeless view of whatever society they study. And the second is how far back in time we can risk extrapolating from the findings of early twentieth century and later anthropologists, especially considering the break the colonial conquest represents. Robin Law in particular warns against "the persisting influence of an assumption of effective social stasis in the pre-colonial period, implicit in the still common use of extrapolation from twentieth-century ethnography to provide an imputed cultural background for pre-colonial history".[54] This warning is easy to agree with but difficult to abide by, and incidentally works in both directions – it is at times tempting to assume that conditions in, say, the seventeenth and eighteenth centuries turned out to be permanent.

The third problem is simply how trustworthy or reliable and representative the anthropological studies are: what about their sources? How long did a particular anthropologist stay on the coast, what was his or her relationship with the local colonial administration (often a very touchy point), and above all, how many informants did he or she consult and where did those informants come from? What kind of version did those informants propagate? The answers to those questions are not always reassuring.[55]

Then finally arrived (in the 1960s) the historians, with Akinjogbin and the French-Brazilian Pierre Verger as the undisputed pioneers, although the latter was never trained as such, and did not claim to be one. Nevertheless, Verger is the only scholar so far to have genuinely explored the voluminous Portuguese-language sources mostly in Salvador da Bahia in Brazil.[56] He did such a thorough job that his successors have, somewhat surprisingly, not deemed it necessary to consult even the easily accessible sources in the

Arquivo Histórico Ultramarino in Lisbon, including the many duplicates of those in Salvador.[57]

And the archaeologists? They have appeared at long last – Danes and Americans in particular. The latter have concentrated on the ruined town of Savi and on the pre-1727 polity of Hueda,[58] the former on the Abomey plateau further north, the old heartland of Dahomey.[59] The Danes in particular have added substantially to our understanding of the past of the Slave Coast, as we shall see. It is however surprising that the archaeologists have so far paid little attention to places like Tado and Notsé (Nuatja) which loom so large in the oral traditions.

The archival sources present the researcher with a number of daunting practical problems, the principal one being the fact that they come in no less than nine European languages, including Latin. The scholars who master nine languages are few and far between, and the present author is not among them. The second problem is that they are spread over a great many archives, in nine countries altogether, and on two continents (one apparently important manuscript even turned up recently at Yale University in the USA).[60]

The third problem is that a fair amount of the archival sources are simply illegible one way or the other. This may be either because they have been severely damaged, or because they are written in a script unfamiliar to the historian – the so-called 'Gothic' script of the Danish sources in particular[61] – or because they are written in a European language which has undergone such profound transformation since the time they were penned that a fair knowledge of the modern language does not help much; this is the case with the Dutch sources.[62] These problems taken together are simply insoluble, the implication being that we all have to take short cuts. It must be said, though, that the recent publication of a fair amount of precisely the Dutch and Danish sources translated into English has alleviated the situation considerably.[63]

We repeat that absolutely all the written sources emanate from Europeans. This we allow ourselves to consider a problem. The point here is that with the exception of a few locals who had worked closely with the Europeans, the peoples of the Slave Coast were totally and, we may add, staunchly illiterate in the precolonial era – in spite of king Agaja's apparent fascination with literacy ("he much loving to look in a book, and commonly carries a Latin Mass-book in his pocket").[64] Indeed, the locals seem to have actively combated literacy,[65] as did certainly the Akan of Asante on the Gold Coast,[66] and possibly others. What should we make of it? Let us note that the people of the Slave Coast had active intercourse with the Europeans for some 2–300 years before the beginning of the colonial period (which incidentally lasted for "only" 70–80 years), and those of the Gold Coast for even longer, some 400 years. The result was that the locals did adopt new crops, new domestic animals, and European firearms, as well as umbrellas (an important symbol of status)[67] and a few more items, but little else; certainly not literacy, nor for that matter the many tools and "arts" the Europeans made use of or practiced in their gardens in the forts[68] (not to mention ocean-going ships). We add one minor detail which may or may not be significant, but which certainly surprised many Europeans: the locals never tried to tame and use elephants.[69] Clearly the locals were not genuinely receptive to European technology, ideas, values and religion.

It is also noteworthy that we do not know of attempts to make practical use of technical assistance from foreigners, as administrators, mercenaries and/or military advisers, as happened occasionally elsewhere[70] (there is one exception, that of Francisco Nunes, a Portuguese adventurer, who served briefly as secretary and private councillor to Agaja in the 1730s).[71] And as far as we know, no-one from Hueda or Dahomey or any other polity on the Slave Coast was ever sent to be educated in Europe;[72] there are however indications that one or two future Alladan kings spent time in their youth in São Tomé, as we shall see. Nor is there any sign of cultural transformation, or of what Kenneth Kelly calls cultural creolization.[73] In sum, the European presence did not foster any cultural conversation. Is this as it should be, or have we got a problem here? It is a question of words and what sense, ideological or otherwise, one infuses them with. If we say that the locals were in general change-averse, it may sound somewhat unattractive. But if Dahomey was different in whatever sense, then at least the rulers of that polity should in pure logic be receptive to new ways in many fields. There is no reason to believe that they were. Was the continuing ancestor cult a powerful impediment in this context?[74]

Incidentally, what about the other way around – were the Europeans on the spot, many of them very young, even teenagers, as we have seen, influenced by the African environment? If so, how, and to what extent? Were there others besides Lionel Abson who "went native"? And were there people who nourished projects like the one portrayed in Rudyard Kipling's *The Man Who Would be King*?[75]

* * *

We now come to an apparently complicated topic, the oral sources and the oral traditions. Oral sources are what anthropologists consult, plus some historians, interviewing (preferably older) people, who then acquire the status of oral informants, about their more or less personal reminiscences, including what earlier generations have transmitted to them. It is called fieldwork and may not be relevant for a work such as this which is concerned with a period too remote in time. Oral traditions on the other hand are more fixed myths, legends and tales. Some of them circulated only among a certain stratum of the population or were confined to a small select group.

The problem is that what goes under the name of oral traditions constitutes a rather heterogeneous mix (those of the Slave Coast are incidentally considered to be much poorer than those of the neighbouring Gold Coast).[76] We do not have, for instance, a multi-volume and easily accessible collection called "The oral traditions of the Slave Coast".[77] Nor do we have a sort of official version of the oral traditions written down for all posterity, as is the case with Samuel Johnson's *History of the Yoruba*.[78] Instead, what are presented as oral traditions come in bits and pieces. Above all, and as Patrick Manning has pointed out, none of these traditions were collected scientifically: "That is, you cannot distinguish the tradition itself from modifications given to it by the researcher, nor can one separate the tradition from material and ideas gathered by the researcher from [already] published materials".[79]

In addition, those who first penned down the oral traditions were amateurs: they were missionaries or colonial administrators. In the case of the latter theirs was not always, we imagine, a disinterested task, since they were often looking for traditions which might confirm or bolster whichever "indigenous" policy they were pursuing. One suspects that the locals knew it and shaped their tales accordingly.

We can say more generally that oral traditions are no longer the panacea they once were considered to be.[80] Apart from being close to useless at the level of chronology, the problem with the oral traditions is that they are mostly about kings and rulers. As such they reflect nearly always the perspective and perceptions of the ruling strata, and have therefore little to do with "history from below", one of the present fashionable trends.

The dilemma the modern historian is faced with is in any case, and once more, one of credibility: whether to believe or not an author who claims that what he/she presents us with are oral traditions collected and written down by that author. If the relevant information is corroborated (more or less) by written sources, fine. But if not, the historian has a problem.

In this context we need to know that, as Edna Bay has noted, "Dahomian history claims perhaps the most blatant manipulation of oral memory ever documented",[81] the elimination of the reign of a king (Adandozan) who we are certain reigned for a long time, from 1797 to possibly 1818. But there are of course other manipulations, since the Dahomean authorities "sought to suppress discrepant versions circulating outside official circles".[82] Most traditions are, in brief, the official and authorized versions of the past.

Let us take the case of the famous account by August Le Hérissé published in 1911, and the corner-stone of almost everything which has been written on precolonial Dahomey since then.[83] This is in a sense as it should be, since Le Hérissé's book contains a lot of general and interesting information, including the myths of the origin of the royal lineage or clan, which were published for the first time (the true history of the royal family is said to have been esoteric knowledge[84] – in fact all clans kept their traditions secret one way or the other).[85] But who was Le Hérissé? A French colonial administrator, none other than the *Commandant de cercle* (equivalent to District Officer) of Abomey, and as such a man who wielded considerable power at the local level. In addition, he was married to a daughter of Béhanzin, the last king of independent Dahomey (1889–93).[86] In addition, Le Hérissé got most of his information from one of his brothers-in-law, that is, from a son of the same Béhanzin called Agbidinukun, who was *chef de canton*, and as such integrated into the colonial administration.[87] No wonder that Le Hérissé's book – or is it Agbidinukun's? – was the first pro-Dahomey study of the kingdom. No wonder, either, that it omits Dahomey's many defeats in war.

Faced with all this, the modern historian finds himself in a somewhat awkward position. He knows that he ought to consider Le Hérissé's book with scepticism since it may be labelled as "official history", that is, propaganda. But he also knows that he cannot do without it.

Another example: Edna Bay's authoritative and informative work on the institution of *kpojito*,[88] which she defines as that of the Queen Mother of Dahomey, that is, the most important women's office in Dahomey. But the problem here is the section on the origins of that institution and its nature in the early days, a section based exclusively on oral traditions. Ms Bay interprets those traditions as indicating that the *kpojito* represented in some sense the local indigenous population, the implication being that the conquerors established some sort of *modus vivendi* with the indigenous people.[89] But first, it takes, as we shall see, more than just one office to establish the above-mentioned *modus vivendi* (which is incidentally never associated with the figure of the Queen Mother in the cases that we know of); and second, Ms Bay's interpretation of the origins of the institution is after all based on oral sources collected some two hundred and fifty years after its supposed founding. If we add that, as Ms Bay herself notes, "enormous problems of documentation surround the kpojito", and that "Written sources and [even] oral accounts are oddly vague about [her]",[90] one feels that some caution is called for.

All that being said, we can be allowed nevertheless to present a short defence of oral traditions. We need to understand what they really are: not sources in the generally accepted sense of the term, but in the main propaganda designed to legitimate and if possible to enhance the position of whoever holds power. As such they inform us about the bases of legitimacy, and thus also about the mindsets and cosmologies of the relevant population. In other words, we need to focus on the *themes* the oral traditions evolve around, not on whatever more or less reliable information they may contain. And we must certainly forget trying to elicit any reliable chronological framework from those traditions.

Furthermore, since oral traditions are mostly propaganda, they aim deliberately at manipulating what we may call the "truth". But the interesting questions become how they do that, in what sense and for what purpose, and how far they succeed (one of the theories of the present work is that the kings of Dahomey were not particularly successful in this respect). And when the oral sources become clouded, as often happens, did someone intend them to be so, and if so, why?

We can conclude by arguing that the oral traditions of the Slave Coast provide us, in the final analysis, with an invaluable glimpse into the functioning and world outlook of the societies of old.

One interesting subsection of oral traditions can be said to be the many festivals celebrated in most polities. During those festivals, the founding moment of the polity is reenacted (or rather, the past and the present fuse), and the ideal order which the founding moment represents is considered to have been restored. There is in addition a strong element of fertility cult present.[91] We shall return to the subject.

* * *

Here then is the epistemological problem, which has many facets. The most obvious one is the tremendous culture gap between the "producers" of the sources (the Europeans) and most of the "observed" (the Africans). The "producers" occasionally admitted their perplexity, not to say their ignorance, regarding the surrounding African societies. The problem is made even more poignant by the obvious fact that the modern historian, even an African one, has much more in common with the "producers" than with the "observed", and that the "observed" belong to a world which has since disappeared. In short, if we argue that we need to understand the people and the societies of the Slave Coast in the light of their own logic in order to reconstruct their past, the question is whether it can be done. This without denying the existence of what goes under the name of transculturation.

But the epistemological problem goes deeper. It has to do, first, with what the present author has called earlier the Trevor-Roper trap; that is, the need, apparently never satiated, to demonstrate that Professor Hugh Trevor-Roper was wrong when he argued that Africa has no history.[92] That is, many Africanists committed (in our view) the fatal blunder of accepting Trevor-Roper's logic, his dichotomy between "barbarians" and "civilized" peoples. Hence the rush away from the "barbarian" label. In brief, the Africanists, instead of rejecting Trevor-Roper's very logic, set out to "prove" that the history of Africa is "as rich and as interesting" (whatever that may mean) as that of Europe. This involved erasing what we see as the most fascinating part of it all, the cultural differences – if one prefers, the truly "other". The result has been what we have called "Europeanized" African history: the Africans reason, think, behave, act, smell etc. the same way as the Europeans do – or vice versa if one prefers. And kings and kingdoms, for instance, are construed as similar to the European institutions that go under the same names – what Paul Nugent calls an optical illusion.[93]

We can illustrate the Trevor-Roper trap by taking as examples the excesses (we consider them so)[94] of Akinjogbin and his followers. Indeed, Akinjogbin, in addition to the arguments and theories referred to above, went on to argue that Dahomey was founded by a group of patriotic Aja, who then set about constructing a European-like nation state. Hence, Dahomey came to be organized on principles which "ran very close indeed to the modern European idea of a national state".[95] As for the rulers, they were comparable to the eighteenth-century European benevolent despots.[96] Note that in this Akinjogbin was in a sense merely following Robert Norris who wrote in the eighteenth century, and had already portrayed Agaja as a nation builder.[97]

Maurice Glélé abounds in the same sense, celebrating Dahomey's achievement in fusing communities of disparate origins into a single national identity: the end result was obviously a "nation state".[98] As for John Yoder, the most extreme, he is on record for having argued that the Dahomean king was a constitutional rather than an absolute monarch, and that the Dahomean regime was, in the nineteenth century, actually a constitutional monarchy endowed with something resembling a Parliament.[99] We add that J. Cameron Monroe obligingly provides Dahomey with, not necessarily a fully developed centralized state bureaucracy, but certainly one in the making – this in a non-literate society. Incidentally, Monroe goes on to argue that Dahomey achieved order in this period of dramatic instability (the eighteenth and nineteenth centuries).[100] The present author believes the reverse, that Dahomey destabilized the region.

Even Robin Law has allowed himself to be somewhat contaminated, moving into perilous territory when he argues that there is no question that in the long run many of the conquered peoples came to adopt the Dahomean language and culture and to identify themselves as Dahomeans.[101]

This then is the Trevor-Roper trap in all its splendour, the urge always to compare with the European model, a model which is implicitly conceived as the ideal one. And the aim? Always the same, to demonstrate that the Africans were in no way inferior to the Europeans; as if the task of the historians were to establish a ranking-list of societies, cultures, peoples or whatever. If it were, the immediate question becomes, according to which criteria, and chosen by whom? Those criteria must necessarily be neutral from a cultural-civilizational point of view. And that is where the trouble begins. For since history is a science, it must necessarily, or ideally, lay claim to universality. It follows that its conceptual framework must be adequate for the study of *all* the civilizations and/or cultures of the past. Or put differently, we must be able to separate the lenses through which we study the past from the past itself, that is, from our object. But this, as we all know, is not what happens.[102]

The heart of the matter is the incestuous relationship between history and what is traditionally called Western Civilization – history as we know it originated within that civilization, and may be said to constitute one of its defining parts (history as "the quintessential Western discourse").[103] More concretely, our conceptual framework, which is by definition a cultural-civilizational product, originated from within Western Civilization, from within the past of that civilization. Hence we cannot separate history from its own object, or rather, from *one* of its objects of study. History is in fact the product of its own object of study, the only academic discipline or science of which this can be said; the only discipline or science which can study itself. In conclusion, what we "see" through is also part and parcel of what we see. Our conceptual framework is therefore "Eurocentric", and leads to the aberrations listed above. The question is whether it is condemned to remain so. (Actually, that framework is not only "Eurocentric" but also "presentist", in the sense that, if we have understood correctly, even the students of Europe in the Middle Ages, not to mention earlier periods, feel at times uneasy within that framework.)[104]

Or put differently, the broadening of history's vision to encompass the non-Western world, something which happened not that long ago (a surprising fact in its own right), has not yet been accompanied by a corresponding effort to accommodate our conceptual framework to that new reality. The logical next step would be to propose a new or modified framework. But that is easier said than done, if it can be done, for a variety of reasons which it would take too long to enumerate here. It is possible to argue, though, that the process has been set in motion; we would like to think that the present work is part of that process.

There is, anyway, all the difference in the world between on the one hand adopting the existing Western-centric conceptual framework lock, stock and barrel, and on the other being aware of the problem, conscious of the inadequacies of our framework, and to propose, if only in certain limited circumstances, possible alternatives.

In other words, if we argue that any given society deserves to be studied on its own terms, not by the yardstick of another, we are confronted with a very difficult task, especially in the African case. The easy way out is in fact the Trevor-Roper stance, to establish a hierarchy of societies, and to label everything one does not understand as "barbarian" in order to eliminate it from the historical discourse. But again, an awareness of the difficulties certainly helps.

* * *

Implicit in the above is the contention that the subject under scrutiny, the past of the Slave Coast, presents a challenge to the very nature of the science or academic field we call history – at a time, incidentally, when our confidence in history as a way of knowing is crumbling, according to certain authors.[105] The point is that the Africans who lived on the Slave Coast in the period under scrutiny certainly did not think of making life easy for the future historians; they did not in any way try to make certain that their experience would be remembered by future generations.[106] Is it legitimate to wonder why?

* * *

In the end we are forced, as usual, to pick our way as we can through the evidence as it stands, that is, we must reconstruct what we can.[107] But as Igor

Kopytoff has pointed out, granted the paucity of written records, and in order to reconstruct from the few pieces that we know, we must have what Kopytoff calls a structured understanding of what we do not and may never know[108] – the known unknowns, in sum. Put differently, we need to develop a model, a task we now turn to.

3

SOCIETAL, RELIGIOUS AND POLITICAL STRUCTURES

A MODEL

What follows may be considered arduous reading by many. We will have to present the reader with a number of words, expressions and concepts which are not frequent in the historical literature, but which are highly central to our purpose. Among them are ritual control of the land, contrapuntal paramountcy, "earth-priests" and "owners of the land" ritually speaking – all of which will be explained in due course (the quotation marks are used because we are not talking about priests or owners in the commonly accepted sense of the terms). Somewhat more familiar may be expressions such as sacred society, sacred kingship, stranger-kings, ritual regicide, kinship-type societies, fertility cults, non-linear concepts of time, and so on.

* * *

"With respect to Dahoman religion, it will hardly be expected that we should be able to say much".[1] So wrote Archibald Dalzel in 1793. Understanable in light of what Dalzel admitted in a hearing some years earlier, namely that he had never been able to understand the religion of the "natives".[2] The frank Dalzel was certainly not alone, and some Europeans, despairing of understanding, opted for the easy way out, by arguing simply that the Africans *had* no religion[3] – early soulmates of Professor Trevor-Roper in a sense. There were however Europeans on the Slave Coast who concluded that the Africans did in fact believe even in an Almighty God, the Creator of all, and who governs everything in the world.[4] Were they correct in concluding so?

However, the real point is that Dalzel made it easy on himself by simply ignoring what is certainly an excruciatingly complicated subject, but which according to the present author constitutes the most fundamental aspect of the past of the Slave Coast, and in fact more generally (to make an apparently extravagant claim) of a very large part indeed of the past of humanity: the religious aspect. Dalzel is in good company, however, in the sense that religion is not fashionable among modern historians – ever since the Enlightenment it has in fact been difficult to know what to do with "religion". This is especially the case among the Marxist-leaning historians, a category to which Robin Law has proclaimed he belongs.[5]

The modern historians have an excellent excuse since we all live in a secularized world where for many people religion no longer takes centre stage. But once we move sufficiently backwards in time, and especially once we move to what may be called the overseas world (for want of a better expression), the historian is confronted with a very different reality in our opinion. For then we encounter in many instances what the present author believes can be labelled *sacred societies*. The expression is meant to refer to societies where religion was all-pervading and all-permeating; that is, societies in which everything had to be legitimized and explained via religious beliefs and where no human pursuit could be accomplished without it being secured successfully first in the spiritual realm.[6] Or to quote from some works concerned with our region: "All life, public and private, is pervaded by the worship of the *trowo*",[7] that is, the deities, among the Ewe; for the Mahi, "Religion encompassed their entire existence".[8] For the Yoruba "religion was the binding force which held society together, and the relevant people saw the whole world as a sign of supernatural reality, implying that everything is both what it is itself and also a sign of something else, a higher and deeper truth".[9] And in the case of the Fon, "what we see is only the surface of a more profound reality, invincible, the real reality, which upholds [*soutient par la force*] the visible world".[10]

It is significant that religion took centre stage even in the military field: spies were sent out to destroy the power of protective gods and other supernatural forces,[11] and defeat in war was attributed to the loss of war charms. Cruickshank noted the idea seemed to be that in wars, "the protecting deities of one nation are contending against those of the other".[12] Or as it has also been expressed: warfare was primarily about neutralizing, capturing or even destroying the enemy's deities.[13]

And in the economic field? We learn that the establishment of a market supposed magico-religious ceremonies, including a human sacrifice – markets had to be consecrated. In fact, the market-places were considered to be holy ground, and as such the regular scene of religious rituals.[14] As for the ironworks, they were ritual shrines or sanctuaries.[15] More generally, each and every occupation and/or economic activity had its own deities, the canoemen very much included.[16] We learn also that for each and every undertaking there was a corresponding ritual, often one of divination.[17]

With regard to the headmen or rulers, they all had, as we shall see, religious rituals to perform, rituals which constituted in a sense their veritable raison d'être.

There is in short no doubt about the centrality of what we may call religious beliefs in the lives of the people of the Slave Coast; people displaying incidentally a devotion to their gods provoked the envy of at least one European Christian priest.[18]

In all this there was nothing unique or special about the societies of the Slave Coast. They were similar to most societies of Atlantic West Africa, and in fact, to make another extreme claim, to a great many societies all over the world for thousands of years. To make this claim seem somewhat less extravagant, when we are talking about similarities we mean a certain number of archetypes, plus above all what we may call the underlying logic. The end result at the concrete or superstructural level could of course be, and was, very dissimilar according to the cases and according to the epochs. It is for instance obvious that there was an enormous difference between on the one hand the great polities ("kingdoms") and on the other the so-called acephalous ("stateless") societies. But the contention here is that the differences were not of kind but of degree, both cases displaying (once more) the same archetypes and the same underlying logic. What then was this logic?

This is where the real difficulties begin. It is indeed very well to argue that religion was all-important and needs to occupy a, or *the* central position in the historical analysis in many cases. It is also very well to lament the apparent fact that the religious dimension was left out to a considerable extent when African history began to emerge.[19] But if so, we will have to explain what kind or sort of religion we are dealing with – what exactly was it that the people of the Slave Coast believed in and how were those beliefs structured? We need to understand it in other words, and we will have to find out how we can genuinely integrate religion in the historical discourse, especially at the analytical level. The task is a daunting and probably impossible one. But that is no excuse for not trying to elucidate at least some central or pertinent points.

Part of the problem is the word religion itself, because it carries connotations which are peculiar to the so-called revealed religions, like Christianity and Islam. For instance, and as Winston King has underlined, "a distinction between a transcendent deity and all else" does not make sense outside of the revealed religions.[20] The religions classified as non-revealed (for want of a better expression), such as those of the Slave Coast, were quite something else, of a different nature so to speak. Exactly *what* nature is hard to define. But what we can say in any case is that our non-revealed religions were certainly not fixed or static; there were no theologians or genuine priests, no church, and no holy script. As for pantheons, opinions vary. But if there were, one or several, or pantheons within pantheons etc., they must have been extremely unstable and varying almost from one locality to another.

What was there then?[21] Let us say tentatively a belief in a powerful and invisible spirit world that is inextricably linked to the visible human one. Or if one prefers, a bundle of basic creeds, always roughly the same, and all connected in turn with the belief in an immaterial supranatural world which in the final analysis commands everything, is the source of everything, and which it is essential to communicate with one way or the other, and perhaps above all to get as close to as possible.[22]

Another part of the problem is that it does perhaps not make much sense in the context of the Slave Coast or elsewhere to study more or less in isolation something called religion. For as Louis Brenner has pointed out, "most African languages did not include a word which could be convincingly and unequivocally translated as 'religion'".[23] He could have added that the same goes probably for many other languages around the world, including those of India.[24]

The point here is that the very existence of the word religion implies the existence of a corresponding more or less separate or autonomous religious *sphere* (alongside political, economic etc. spheres). But in a society where everything is religion, no such autonomous religious sphere exists and no corresponding word either. That is, we cannot separate the religious from the rest, the intertwining is absolute.[25] It does not imply, as some seem to believe, that material considerations or motives of a non-religious character are absent, or that manipulations do not happen, far from it. But the point is how they are clad, how they are presented, how they are *legitimized*, in sum.

* * *

SOCIETAL, RELIGIOUS AND POLITICAL STRUCTURES

Let us start all over again by asking what the societies of the Slave Coast of yesteryear were like, and how they were structured. Furthermore, what did the people of those societies believe in, what do we know about their cosmology, their *Weltanschauung*, and more generally their religion? In brief, what kind of universe are we entering into? What follows then is supposed to be about the local cognitive universe, which implies testing the boundaries of the comprehensible, and delving into matters theoretically "unknowable".

Our first point is that we are dealing in West Africa of old (and elsewhere) with what we may call kinship-type societies: societies made up, not of individuals as such, but of what is called alternatively kindreds, sibs or descent groups – collectivistic in a sense. "I am because *we* are": hence the notion of collective responsibility and solidarity, leading in extreme cases to what we may call virulent egalitarianism. For instance, in Eweland (and elsewhere) "The notion of collective responsibility hangs like the threatening sword of Damocles upon the group and compels individual members to have a say in the lifestyles of others",[26] one of the implications being that the very notion of a private sphere is virtually unknown ("threatening sword of Damocles" from an individualistic European point of view, that is). A king, in those societies where the institution of kingship existed, is often, apparently, the only clearly discernible individual around. The king is, incidentally, always the head of a kindred, generally the largest one. One of the implications of all this is that each and every title or position, including that of the king, in whatever kind of hierarchy that may have existed, was in a sense the property, as it were, of a kindred. This is of course the exact opposite of the bureaucratic model which holds that only the individual counts, and where no position is hereditary – at least not in principle.

A kinship-type society is based on roles, that is to say that an individual assumes or, put another way, is hedged in by pre-determined rules which define how he or she is supposed to behave and act at each and every stage of his/her life. One is in a sense caught in a web, defined once and for all by the ancestors. For those who fail to comply, expulsion is the supreme sanction. And expulsion means the loss of place and rights in the ancestral cult, and especially the loss of protection by the ancestors, a very serious matter; *and* the loss of the possibility of reincarnation, a not infrequent belief, attested among the Ewe, and also widespread among the Fon (that is, a special type of reincarnation in the latter case, since only the portion called *joto* of an ancestral spirit is reborn in a child).[27] Death is in any case seen as a mutation, not an end – the dead converted into ancestors and spiritual forces continue to influence the lives of their descendants.²⁸ In fact, the intercourse between the living and the ancestors is intense, and the spiritual linkage with the ancestors must not be broken.

From all this it can be deduced that a kindred is made up of the living and the dead, and of the not yet born, that is to say, future reincarnated ancestors in some sense.

In most parts of the Slave Coast there were two types of kindreds: the clan and the (smaller) lineage. Clans are usually dispersed and of secondary importance, the lineages or lineage segments the opposite. Each clan and each lineage has a founding ancestor or *vodun*, in the Fon case respectively *akovodun* and *henuvodun*, but also called *tohwiyo*, who protect the kindred and to whom offerings are due.²⁹ But each household within a lineage has its own (lesser) ancestors, and therefore also its own spirits. One is in fact struck by the private character of much of the religious worship.³⁰

It is logical to assume furthermore that a society based on ancestor worship will necessarily be a conservative one in the sense that the original community created precisely by the ancestors constitutes the ideal, that is, a community of the past.

As for those without kin, they were necessarily slaves, and as such no longer human beings in a sense. They could therefore be disposed of at will, for instance exported to the New World.

* * *

Armed with these notions, we can take as our point of departure at the concrete-practical level the societies of Yorubaland of old. That choice may not seem logical at first glance, considering that most of Yorubaland is situated outside of the Slave Coast. But since we hold that what we have called the underlying logic, plus in fact the social fabric generally, were roughly the same all over West Africa (at the very least), the well-documented case of Yorubaland can help us to make sense of those, such as that of the Slave Coast, which are somewhat less so.

The specialists tell us that the Yoruba lived in what they call towns. But note that the word for "town" is the same as that for "community" – *ilu*, synonymous with *ebi*.³¹ And all the towns/communities were composed of lineages. Also, those towns/communities were ruled by hereditary and *sacred* "kings", the famous *oba*s – each and every one possessing "a power like that of the Gods",³² and each and every one being regarded by his people as a deity with whose well-being their own condition was bound up. As such the *oba* had to be free of physical blemish. As such, also, he was by definition the titular head of all religious cults; he was in fact the supreme religious authority of his realm, be it the *oni* of Ife or the *alafin* of Oyo, to name but the two best known *obas*.[33]

On succession it is argued that the new *oba* had to eat the heart of his predecessor, possibly not literally, and was in any case considered to have been born anew after having gone through very elaborate enthronement rituals.[34] A sacred king, then, which is not the same as a divine king – the latter being the living incarnation of a god as in Pharaonic Egypt of old;[35] but both sorts of king are invested with a "force" of divine provenance, the famous *mana*, to use what has become a generic term (it is actually a Polynesian word), which allows him to command nature in a sense.[36] This means he must keep himself in a state of physical perfection, as an outward sign of his inner moral perfection. We dare to compare *mana* with electricity for illustrative reasons, noting that it was dangerous simply to get near a sacred king (*acè*, *ase* or *aché* may be the local variants of *mana* among certain ethnic groups of the Slave Coast outside of Yorubaland).[37] But if the deities withdraw their favour, as it were, if the king's *mana* is as a consequence dwindling, he is in trouble. Pursuing the analogy with electricity, one could say that the king needs to recharge his batteries. Or in some polities (and in extreme cases?), as in Oyo, the king could be sacrificed, ritually or concretely so – in the case of Oyo "asked" to commit suicide.[38] This, then, is the custom of ritual regicide or king-slaying of Frazerian fame.[39] In other polities he was destooled, that is, desacralized.[40] Note that there are scholars who argue that human sacrifices are an integral part of the concept of sacred kingship: "a means of enhancing [the king's] divine attributes".[41]

But if the king wields tremendous power, it is mostly in theory; the reality is somewhat different. In fact, Montserrat Palau-Martí has a point when she argues that the king is above all a symbol.[42] For as Lucien Scubla has put it regarding sacred kingship generally, "The king is a sacred figure, but for this very reason he is 'bound' by the ritual. Under house arrest and a recluse in his palace, he (has to submit to a great many) restrictions"[43] – a plethora of taboos and inhibitions. So this is "a monarchy trapped by its own ideology of power", according to Nii Quarcoopome.[44]

In fact, the king is always surrounded by a sort of state council which severely circumscribes his power; a state council composed moreover of hereditary dignitaries whom he cannot remove or displace – each seat in the council being the "property", as it were, of a particular lineage.[45] It is this council, for instance the famous *oyo mesi* in Oyo, which has the power to decide whether it is time for the king to depart from this world – that is, if the king has lost his *mana* for whatever reason (defeat in war, failing harvests, even impotence).[46]

We must have a look at the founding myths and legends of Yorubaland. And here we note that all the *oba*s trace their descent from the famous culture-hero Oduduwa; the one sent, the myths have it, from heaven to create the world, who founded Ife, the traditional site of creation and cradle of the Yoruba.[47] From there, according to the orthodox version, the kinsmen of Oduduwa spread out in all directions, establishing themselves everywhere as *oba*s (that is, all *oba*s are required to claim descent from Oduduwa and Ife, whether that filiation is historically correct or not). What then about the members of the various state councils? It is tempting to argue that they represented the lineages of the pre-Oduduwa or autochtonous population – the "owners of the land"[48] – in which case Oduduwa and others could have been in some sense foreign conquerors. The acephalous panhandle-Yoruba north of the Slave Coast are perhaps what is left of pre-Oduduwa Yorubaland.

The "owners of the land": this is where the really complicated (and long) part begins. And this is where we have moved to the acephalous societies of old. Let us take as our point of departure the fact that the earth was sacred in Africa of old (and elsewhere), it was and remained in fact a deity, let us say Mother Earth the nourisher (that is, a *vodun* in the language of the people of the Central Slave Coast).[49] We are dealing with possibly the world's oldest or original deity among societies made up of farmers. Since it was a deity, no-one could "own" the earth or the soil in the modern sense of the term, one could only claim usufructuary rights, rights normally vested in the lineages, and especially in the most ancient local lineage or considered as such. The way we have understood it (and we present it in a somewhat plain language dress for reasons of clarity),[50] the head of this lineage was considered according to the relevant legends to be the descendant of the first settler (or settlers), the one who originally "married" the earth (Mother Earth), who inseminated Her, so to speak, by sowing, and who was thus granted the permission to till the earth. The task of his descendants was to see to it that the original pact (matrimony) with Mother Earth was upheld, that is, that the earth and the first settler(s) converted into ancestors were revered and provided with adequate offerings. Otherwise the harvest would be in danger, or there could be other perils. This is, it seems to us, the essence of what is referred to usually as fertility cults.

But to return to the lineage of the founding ancestor(s), it exercised in sum what has been called "ritual control" over the earth, a very central but somewhat vague term which is not easy to grasp. In any case, the head of this lineage is the famous "earth-priest", so called in the literature (*aïnon* among the Adja-Fon, *balè* among the Yoruba – as noted earlier the word *aïzo*, written earlier Aïzo, always indicates indigenous or local people on the Slave Coast).[51] As such, the "earth-priest" is the intermediary between the humans and the world of the deities and the ancestors. He and his companions and/or the members of his lineage are then the so-called "owners of the land" by virtue of their status as those who came first – the famous firstcomer principle which looms so large in the past of Africa[52] (we use the term "owners of the land" always between inverted commas because they were in no way owners in the modern sense of the word). We have here, in our opinion, a universal institution.[53]

The "earth-priest" is, in a sense, the head of the council of elders or lineage heads of the society (remember, we are in an acephalous society). If one wonders what happens to those who are not farmers but rather fishermen, the answer is that we also know of "water-priests" (possibly the case of the *hulaholu* of Hulagan/Grand Popo mentioned earlier). In addition we have "iron-priests" among the blacksmiths. "Bush-priests" too figure in the literature and refer probably to hunters.[54]

The next and most important point is that the ritual control of the land (or the water or the iron, etc.) is formally inalienable – for reasons we are at a loss to explain.

The "earth-priest" is, then, the first among equals in an acephalous society, the visible head, as it were, of that society. But not all acephalous societies may have been blessed with "earth-priests"; we can in fact imagine cases where all the lineage-heads of the "owners of the land" collectively exercise the functions of "earth-priest".[55]

What happens when an acephalous society is transformed into something else – let us say a genuine polity, or "realm" if one prefers, a transformation usually related to the "wealth-in-people" paradigm? Concretely, where does the king come from? The "earth-priest" is obviously a likely candidate. But so is also the "iron-priest" in societies where there is a local lineage of blacksmiths, which is usually the case (the blacksmiths always constitute a separate kindred,[56] and blacksmiths are renowned for their magical acumen). An "earth-priest"-turned-king (to take that example) ceases to be a *primus inter pares*. But if he acquires more power, the logic of the sacred societies holds that he also acquires more responsibilities. He becomes in short a sacred king, and as such the head of what we may call a "kingdom" (the persistent contention that a kinship-type society is incompatible with "states" or "kingdoms" is one which should be put to rest).

But the problem is that we know of many cases where the king and those of his lineage either claim a foreign origin or are considered to have come from somewhere else. This is the case of Yorubaland generally, as we have seen, including Oyo (whose ruling kindred may have come from the land of the Bariba, and not from Ife, as the traditions claim, indeed *have* to claim).[57] We are entering the field of the stranger-king, yet another universal archetype.[58] Here we are dealing with what we choose to call *contrapuntal paramountcy*, a term originally coined by the anthropologist Jack Goody.[59] What does it mean? We must take as our point of departure the inalienable ritual control over the earth exercised by the "owners of the land". It is inalienable, and cannot then be abolished by the incomers. Put differently, the right of conquest as such does not exist, it is unfathomable. Hence an invading group of people needs to placate the spirits of the indigenous inhabitants of the land they have conquered. What this means in practice is that the newcomers have to establish, as noted already in the preceding chapter, some sort of *modus vivendi* with the "owners of the land"; a *modus vivendi* often sealed by a marriage arrangement, the incoming king "marrying" in some sense a daughter of the "earth-priest", a daughter who, still in some sense, symbolizes Mother Earth. The result is precisely a contrapuntal paramountcy, often presented as a sort of power-sharing arrangement, in which the (incoming) king is surrounded by a council composed of the lineage-heads of the firstcomers, the former "earth-priest" being perhaps the head of that council. It is then this council which decides in the relevant cases whether the king is still worthy of the favour of the deities, and hence of the humans, or not.[60] But note that the king is frequently portrayed as the political-military head, and the council-members as the religious leaders – and this cannot be the case. In fact, the king is, by virtue of being a sacred king, always, and by definition, the religious head of the polity, his sacredness having in a sense been delegated to him by the "owners of the land" in the case of a contrapuntal-paramountcy arrangement.[61] Besides, the king has important religious functions to perform in his own right, as the supreme priest of the cult of the ancestors of the royal lineage, a lineage which is as a rule by far the most numerous. As a rule, because we know of cases where the new ruler is expelled from his lineage and forced to establish, so to speak, his own (fictitious) kindred.[62]

That being said, we think it can be argued that contrapuntal paramountcy implies a sort of inbuilt tension in the relevant polities, Oyo being in this case a paradigmatic example.[63]

One may imagine that the set-up outlined above could have been perceived as a sort of straightjacket from the point of view of certain kings. An important but complicating point is that contrapuntal paramountcy, another universal phenomenon in our view, is not necessarily linked to the stranger-king phenomenon and may not necessarily result from conquest as such. It may be, for instance, that the local society finds it expedient for one reason or another to appeal to a warrior-band for protection against external enemies (or for that matter to appeal to a lineage of iron-smiths for the necessary weapons). Furthermore, since an acephalous society is as a general rule marked by a strong egalitarian ideology, and opposed to any "state"-like setup, it makes sense, one could argue, to recruit the king, in case one turns out to be needed, from outside the local society.[64] Indeed, a sacred king is reputed always to be over and above but also *outside* of the society, or at least outside of the ranks of the farmers, always the vast majority of the local population. Hence the cases of iron-priests becoming sacred kings, as in the old kingdom of Kongo in our opinion (as we shall see). Also in Oyo? The possibility cannot be excluded.[65]

The next question is what happens if a polity, whether characterized by a contrapuntal paramountcy or not, tries or begins to expand. Generally, larger entities came into being when, as in the Yoruba case, one "town" forced the neighbouring ones into subjection (or persuaded them to submit), but without annexing or annihilating them – they lost their independence, but little else (the ruling community becoming, let us say, the metropolitan area of the new enlarged polity, like Oyo Ile in Oyo). But if so, the principle of the inalienable ritual control of the "owners of the land" remains, implying that the "right of conquest" does not exist in this case either. What it means is that if one conquers a neighbouring polity, one has to content oneself with what could be called indirect rule, that is, with exacting some sort of tribute and possibly imposing a governor in charge of supervising the locals, but otherwise leaving intact the local institutional set-up and the local rulers,[66] since the position of those rulers has been sanctioned by supernatural powers. It is in fact customary to retain the vanquished ruler as vassal lord, and/or to install a close relative in his place. If the submitting polity is of the acephalous sort, one can imagine that the king of the conquering polity sends out, say, a younger son as governor, and that this younger son becomes the king of that entity (in which case one can further imagine that a contrapuntal paramountcy emerges). The new king and his successors will then all be considered as the sons of the overall-king – in perpetuity.

But again we do not need to stipulate conquest. One may imagine for instance that a local society (whether acephalous or not) finds it expedient in some sense to relate itself to a powerful and prestigious centre which has arisen somewhere close by, perhaps because the king of that centre is renowned for his privileged access to supernatural powers, or/and for his exceptional *mana* etc. In which case one could perhaps talk of ritual overlordship. Or it could be that the above-mentioned local society simply acknowledges the overlordship of that centre, or even invites some junior prince from thence to establish himself as vassal-lord. Whatever the case, the kinship ideology (if so it can be called) often permeated the relationship between the centre and its vassals (Akinjogbin's Ebi social theory, it can be suggested).

Now, having outlined the rules of the game, there were of course ways of trying to get around them, of manipulating them. One way of doing so would be to argue in the case of incomers that there *were* no local "owners of the land", that the land was simply empty when they arrived. Or alternatively that the "owners of the land" were so few that they were quickly assimilated and hence could be forgotten.[67] Or it might be possible to manipulate the genealogies to such an extent that the head of the incomers appears in some sense to be the direct descendant of the founding ancestor(s) in lieu of the "earth-priest". But to manipulate implies acknowledging, in a sense, the rules of the game. What is *not* acceptable is to blatantly disregard those rules, which is precisely what the founders of Dahomey did. Besides, of course, it was one thing to try to manipulate, quite another to succeed.

There existed actually at least one way of undoing altogether the rules of the game listed above: to convert to a revealed religion. Those on offer in Africa were Christianity and Islam. Neither holds the earth to be sacred, and both are formally incompatible with a kinship-type society and with ancestor worship, and also with sacred kingship. Christianity or Islam implies, in other words, doing away with "earth-priests", the "owners of the land", contrapuntal paramountcy, ritual regicide, sacred kingship and so on. It can also imply replacing lineage-appointed senior chiefs with royal appointees.

But again, it was one thing to *try* to impose a revealed religion – and as we shall see, surprisingly many rulers on the Slave Coast seem to have toyed with the idea – and quite another to succeed.

4

SOME CONCRETE, PRACTICAL IMPLICATIONS

We need a description of what we may call the religious world of the people of the Slave Coast. The idea is not to present a comprehensive overview but to extract what we need for our understanding.

There were two worlds: Kutome, the invisible one, and Gbetome, the land of people, the two constituting a coherent whole.[1] The invisible world was inhabited by the deities, often deified ancestors, *vodun* among the Fon and related groups, *trowo* (sing. *tro*) among the Ewe and *orisha*s among the Yoruba.[2] And according to Roberto Pazzi, happiness consisted for a human being in maintaining oneself in perfect equilibrium with the invisible world.[3] Communications or links between the two worlds were through prayers, sacrifices, rituals, oracles, divination, and later also possession dances.[4] Each world could affect the other. And neglected and/or angered deities could injure and even kill.[5] But humans could also try to appropriate the deities, manipulate them, as it were, for their own purpose.[6]

The *vodun* could then be good or bad, benevolent or nasty, even lethal in the case especially of Legba, the "trickster", or devil, to whom everyone everywhere presented offerings (unless Legba the devil is the product of missionary conception).[7] That is, some provided protection, others one needed to protect oneself against; some were dormant, waiting to be "captured"; and some dwindled into oblivion for lack of attention on the part of the humans, although they could "resurrect" at a later stage.[8] Or as it has been expressed, humans and deities mirrored one another in West African philosophies.[9]

Naturally, there are scholars who argue that it is more complicated than that. Suzanne Preston Blier has for instance defined the *vodun* as "mysterious forces or powers that govern the world and the lives of those who reside within it"[10] – the word "power" (or force) again. And Roger Brand argues that the word *vodun* is untranslatable. According to him, *vodun* calls to mind or relates to an idea of mystery and designs what partakes of the divine; it relates to all manifestations of a force we cannot define. Or else *vodun* means power and to tap into that power source means access to authority.[11] All this is noted. But before going on, a parenthesis for those who wonder about the link between the *vodun* of the Slave Coast and the *vodou* or *voodoo* cults of Haitian fame, but also known from places such as New Orleans: there is no question that the latter derive from the former, but the specialists tell us that it is an error to postulate a simple transfer of religious beliefs from the Slave Coast to America. Haitian *vodou*, which we associate primarily with magic, has in fact been deeply transformed, we are also told, by the experience of the local slave population.[12] That being said, the existence of voodoo cults in Haiti, and similar cults elsewhere in America, and their survival to the present day, indicate that many slaves imported to America from the Slave Coast must have come from that coast itself, as opposed to other places further afield.[13]

Now, there were different types of *vodun* (or *trowo*). There were the tutelary deities, there were the deified ancestors, there were the *vodun* who personalized the various forces of nature. Some of those deities became "national", in the sense that they received a name and were worshipped by many different groups. A pantheon in the making? We repeat that opinions vary.

But if a pantheon there was (from what time?), the most obvious candidate for the top position is Mawu-Liisa, a dual or twin *vodun*, often presented as the all-powerful supreme being or beings, the master(s) of the universe[14] – but with Mawu often as the leading of the two (called Nyigble among the Ewe according to certain authors, and both male and female,[15] except in Anlo where the name is Awu, obviously a variant of Mawu[16]). As the supreme deity, Mawu-Liisa (he and she) created the world, but then retired, so to speak. A classic *deus otiosus* in other words, and as such not the object of any cult.[17] In some versions, the other *vodun*s are presented as the "children" of Mawu-Liisa,[18] including the famous Sakpata sent to rule the earth.[19] If so, Mawu-Liisa had an enormous amount of children, since the *vodun*s were literally without number.[20] But we cannot rule out the possibility of "contagion" from Christianity, since Mawu is the name adopted locally for the Christian God.[21] There are of course many complicating details, one being the belief that Aido-

Hwedo, the primordial serpent, was not the child of Mawu and even existed before Mawu-Liisa.[22]

Apart from Mawu-Liisa, among the best-known *vodun* who have names we have already encountered Sakpata, Legba and Hu; the latter being, as already noted, the meanest of the deities.[23] We may mention in addition, *inter alia*, Hevioso – a thunder-god, but also linked to water[24] – and Gu, the deity of the blacksmiths (Ogun among the Yoruba).[25] But their shape was often very imprecise, they floated over one another and may have been in actual fact manifestations, or personifications or something of the sort, of others, including Mawu-Liisa; or they may have constituted, say, "a separate conception" of the Supreme Being,[26] whatever that may mean exactly; or there may have been many *vodun*s in one. Also, the deities interacted with one another in the spirit world.

But the deity which is of supreme interest for our purpose is Sakpata. In order to understand the role and position of Sakpata, we will have to both recapitulate and anticipate: Dahomey was founded, we have learned, by a group of outsiders who did not respect the rules of the game as defined above. That is, instead of seeking a *modus vivendi* with the indigenous population, that is, the "earth-priests", they killed them and usurped their position. Hence no contrapuntal paramountcy emerged. What is more, the conquered polities were simply annexed, incorporated into Dahomey, and erased from the map. It is in this context highly significant that the Dahomeans always tried, as we shall see, to wipe out completely the ruling lineages of the polities they conquered.

But nothing of this went unchallenged. And this is where Gu and especially Sakpata come into the picture. Sakpata was or became a many-faceted *vodun* or even perhaps a series of *vodun*s, which seems originally to have been the deity (or deities) of the smallpox, but were also linked to thunder and lightning – and hence possibly the "rival" of Hevioso earlier. But above all, Sakpata, whenever that *vodun* emerged, replaced and/or took up in him the cult of the earth, the earth deities and fertility. Sakpata became in sum the "fetish" of the earth, the *aïkoungbanvôdun*.[27] Sakpata's ritual names were in fact *ayihosu* or king of the earth and *aïnon*,[28] the latter being precisely the "title" of the old "earth-priests" as indicated above (*aï* or *ayi* alone means earth and the earth deity,[29] *anyigba* among the Ewe). In brief, Sakpata became the symbol, the rallying cry, the banner and so on, of those who had not accepted, and in our view never accepted, what it is tempting to qualify as "foreign illegitimate rule". Indeed, Sakpata (together with Gu of the black-smiths) provided the basis for a solid and durable opposition to the monarchy,[30] one which wielded a redoubtable arm, that of smallpox, a major scourge on the

Slave Coast then, earlier and later, including among the slaves exported to the Americas.[31] In fact, Sakpata manifested his wrath on many occasions; several Dahomean kings died of the disease, and important military campaigns failed because it wrought havoc in the ranks of the army.[32]

In brief, the rulers of Dahomey never managed to eliminate or even to get around the opposition symbolized by Sakpata. Not for want of trying – they had in a sense no choice but to try, since in Africa of old the golden rule was that political and religious power were always inextricably linked.

Our point of view is that the rulers of Dahomey were always short on legitimacy, and that was why they had to resort to what we would call terror. Indeed, they tried to institute a regime of a markedly totalitarian bent; a regime in which the subjects were all simply slaves of the king. They tried but never really succeeded. We disagree, in sum, with those historians who argue that the religious prestige of the king of Dahomey was enormous.[33]

* * *

We consider it necessary to try to place the Dahomean case in a wider comparative context. In brief, was Dahomey the sole exception that confirms the rule in the larger region, if not Africa-wide, or are there other exceptions as well?

We begin with the ancient polity of Kongo far to the southeast. The way we interpret the relevant literature[34] is that Kongo, before the arrival of the Portuguese towards the end of the fifteenth century, was certainly characterized by contrapuntal paramountcy. But with the Portuguese came the "temptation" represented by Christianity. In brief, the sacred kings of Kongo, especially the one known as Afonso I (1509–42),[35] tried to impose the new creed on the local population. But in this they failed, in our opinion. For although Christianity did acquire a certain foothold, the Kongolese kings triggered off a sort of permanent civil war which fuelled the slave trade, converting the Congo-Angola region (the West-Central region of the Database) into the leading purveyor of slaves for America (Kongo is the name of a polity, Congo that of a region).

The little-known, small and nearly inaccessible Warri kingdom of Itsekiri in the Niger delta is perhaps another case in point. It was founded by a royal prince from Benin, one of whose successors converted to Christianity late in the sixteenth century, followed by his subjects, who were described as enthusiastic converts. In fact, the royal dynasty remained Christian throughout the seventeenth and eighteenth centuries, even though missionary

SOME CONCRETE, PRACTICAL IMPLICATIONS

visits were very few and infrequent – but apparently not longer.[36] What happened? We do not know.

In the case of the northern neighbour of Itsekiri-Warri, the much more imposing kingdom of Benin, we believe that a strong case can be made for arguing that the establishment of a typically sacred kingship, by people connected in some way with Ife, was accompanied by the emergence of contrapuntal paramountcy. But at some later stage the local king tried to put an end to that system, apparently without the aid of Christianity, although it is said that the king in question showed himself willing to receive missionaries from São Tomé. However, in Benin too the consequences were negative, namely a long civil war (we are possibly in the 1680s and 1690s), with the result that Benin lost its position as the dominant polity of the wider region.[37]

North of Benin we come to the vast Yorubaland where, we repeat, everything is clear cut (to the present author, that is): most Yoruba polities were apparently established by outsiders and virtually all were characterized by a contrapuntal paramountcy, Oyo very much included. And in Yorubaland as elsewhere, kingship is in a sense incompatible with the ideals implied in a kinship-type society, yet is at the same time indispensable for avoiding discords among the descent groups.[38]

There are, however, some polities which show certain "anomalies", primarily the "new" polity of Lagos (on the Slave Coast this time) which emerged from late in the seventeenth century onwards when the office of viceroy of Benin became hereditary and was turned into an autonomous monarchy, and the viceroy converted into an Oba. There existed a group, the *idéjo*, who represented, and were considered to be, the original "owners of the land". But the relationship between the Oba and the *idéjo* does not seem to have amounted to a full-fledged contrapuntal paramountcy. In fact, the leaders of the *idéjo*, the *olófin*, after leading the resistance against the incoming Edo from Benin, disappeared out of sight. But the relationship between the royal dynasty and the *idéjo* chieftaincy families continued (significantly?) to be an uneasy one.[39]

As for the small Yoruba polities just north of the Slave Coast, in the case of Dassa-Zoumé all we know is that the indigenous people, the *máhàhún*, were recognized as the rightful owners of the land and as such had the custody of rituals connected with the land.[40]

With regard to Ketu, a polity founded by immigrants from Ife, the ritual murder of several kings and the position and role of the "owners of the land" loom large. Some, possibly many, of the indigenous lineages were at least represented in the state council.[41]

North and west of the Yoruba, among the Gur-speaking Bariba of Borgu whose ruling elite speaks a Manding language, there seems to be little doubt that we encounter a typical contrapuntal paramountcy set-up.[42]

Let us now move to the Akan of the Gold Coast and especially to the imposing kingdom of Asante which emerged around 1701 at the expense of Denkyira (and in the tropical rain forest, an environment not considered appropriate for "state formation").[43] Asante was certainly not characterized by a contrapuntal paramountcy, and there was no reason for it to be so characterized, for the simple reason that there is nowhere any trace of non-Akan people or of migration, whether in the oral traditions or in the European sources (no Guan people having been encountered).[44] Indeed, the Akan and their rulers claim that they emerged from a number of holes or caves in the ground (at Adansi), or alternatively descended from the sky,[45] types of legend generally considered, as noted, to be a sure sign of indigenous status. There are then no "owners of the land" distinct from the rest of the population. In fact, the *amanhene* (sing. *omanhene*), the heads of the original and component Asante polities (*aman*, sing. *oman*) held significantly also the title of *asase wura* which can be translated as "earth-priest" (derived from *asase yaa*, the female deity or spirit of the earth).[46] It should be noted that inside Asante each territory and each village was a self-governing community[47] – fitting almost perfectly Akinjogbin's Ebi social theory. Note also that when Asante expanded, subjugating a great number of polities, the internal autonomy of those polities was respected,[48] that is, the Asante conquerors abided by the rules of the game (although resident commissioners were appointed from the 1760s).[49] That this led at times to rather confusing situations in which polities which were vassals of the Asantehene, the supreme ruler in Kumasi (originally the omanhene of the oman of Kumasi), waged war against each other and occasionally even against the Asantehene, is another matter.[50]

Moving north of the Akan (and even further away from the Slave Coast), we come to the quintessential "contrapuntal paramountcy" region, if so it can be expressed, that of Gonja and its neighbours, a region conquered by Asante (note, however, that many local societies were and remained acephalous).[51] Contrapuntal paramountcy is also very much in evidence among the Mossi even further north, in present-day northern Ghana and especially in neighbouring Burkina Faso.[52]

Moving south again, to the central coastal region of the Gold Coast, the land of the southern Akan, or Fante, we note that the Fante have a tradition of migration from the north. There are in fact ample traces of a pre-Fante population in the shape of the Kpesi and/or Etsi (Guan people?) who were considered to be the local original "owners of the land". But since no genuine monarchy emerged – the Fante remained acephalous, or were constituted in what Rebecca Shumway calls mini-states which eventually formed a sort of confederation[53] – there was in a sense no need for a contrapuntal paramountcy.

There were also Kpesi (and/or Kple) among the Ga further east – they too were considered to be the "owners of the land". Note the position of the *sitse*, the senior *wulomo* or priest, and obviously a Kpesi. In fact, land was considered to be "owned" by the gods of the Kpesi.[54]

But then there is Akwamu, a polity which rose to prominence after it conquered the Ga kingdom of Accra in ca. 1680. And in fact Akwamu is of considerable interest for our purpose. Akwamu may be another polity which did not respect the rules of the game, at least not after 1689, which is the date Ivor Wilks gives for a sort of coup d'état organized by the military leaders and resulting in the loss of power by the traditional chiefs.[55] What is more, the rulers of Akwamu after 1689 certainly did not behave like, and cannot possibly be described as, sacred kings.

Given all this, our conclusion is that we are dealing with, not one but *two* exceptions that confirm the rule: Dahomey and Akwamu. But Akwamu, which also became heavily involved in the slave trade, displayed much less staying-power than Dahomey, since the polity was destroyed in 1730 – although a sort of rump-Akwamu survived east of the Volta river after that date, where it subjugated Ewe communities, and made its presence felt now and then on the rest of the Slave Coast.

* * *

We return to the Slave Coast properly speaking. And here we repeat what is implicit in the above, that Dahomey was unique, implying that all the other polities, including those which Dahomey conquered, conformed roughly to the "traditional" model elaborated above. We will have occasion to test those claims when we turn to the chronological overview.

However, for the time being we deem it necessary to have a closer look at the Ewe (or Vhe) block of the Western or Little Slave Coast between the rivers Volta and Mono. The Ewe do not fit into the dichotomy with which we have operated so far, that between acephalous societies on the one hand and societies which developed kingly institutions on the other, whether within the framework of the contrapuntal-paramountcy variant or not. Eweland presents us with a sort of third in-between case, that of "chieftainship" societies – for want of a better expression.

Our point of departure is that according to many local traditions, all the Ewe originated from one place, namely the town of Notsé (so named on modern road maps – Nuatja earlier), which still exists to-day, a small backwater town (possibly 22,000 inhabitants) situated some 95 km from the coast in present-day central Togo. The traditions speak of a wholesale exodus from Notsé in order to escape the tyrannical rule of the king of that locality. The view is that the Notsé experience cured the Ewe forever of anything to do with kingship.[56]

Is it really the case that all the Ewe came from Notsé (Nuatja) and that they spread out over and settled a region previously empty of people, or at least so thinly populated that the original inhabitants were quickly and easily assimilated? Many modern historians and anthropologists have their doubts.[57] They argue in substance that the story was fabricated by, once more, the German missionaries, who felt it necessary to try to convert the Ewe into a genuine nation, a *Volk*. They point in particular to the apparent fact that there were several traditions, later suppressed, which refer to other origins than Notsé. Also, many Ewe traditions admit earlier settlers, a point we shall return to, whoever those earlier settlers may have been[58] – we do not know, although the Hula come to mind.

It is, above all, a fact that many of the small polities (*dukowo*, singular *duko*) – no less than 120, approximately – of which Eweland was traditionally made up[59] were characterized by an institutional set-up reminiscent of, if not identical to, contrapuntal paramountcy. Hence the by now familiar distinction between the original "owners of the land" and the latecomers, and the title of *duto* (or *anyigtao*, also written *anyigbafio/fia*), which may be translated as "earth-priest".[60] What is clear also is that the "political" chief, the *dufia*, is not of the stock of the "owners of the land" (nor is he, for that matter, a genuine sacred king). Incidentally, the office alternated often between two or more lineages, a device designed obviously to avoid any excessive accumulation of power. There was also a state council, the *fiaha* made up among others of the "great priests", a council which could destool the *dufia*.[61]

A case somewhat apart, even in Eweland, is that of coastal Anlo, by far the largest of the Ewe polities (followed incidentally by that of Peki in the interior).[62] Anlo is variously presented as one *duko* or as a confederation of *dukowo* (no less that 36 according to Gayibor),[63] that is, *dukowo* which had decided to cooperate for defensive purposes[64] (the *-wo* ending indicates the plural). The ruler, the *awoamefia* in Anloga (compare with the title of *mawoafia* in Notsé, and with Awu, the local name for Mawu, alongside with Nyigble), is presented as a rain-maker, who had to be free from any physical blemish and lived in seclusion indoors. In fact, only a few elders of the nation had access to him.[65] In sum, the *awoamefia*, who could be destooled if necessary,[66] strikes one as more akin to a sacred king than a "mere" chief.

But we need to add that the position of the *awoamefia* alternated between two (or possibly more) clans, primarily the Bate and the Adzovia.[67] In addition he was surrounded by a state council of kingmakers, made up of other clans (especially Lafe and Almade), precisely those clans which provided the hereditary religious specialists in each settlement, and as such were recognized as the ritual "owners of the land". A near-perfect contrapuntal paramountcy in sum, had it not been for one jarring detail: *all* the clans mentioned above, and in fact all the people of Anlo, claim descent from Notsé.[68] The easy way out would be to argue that it cannot be the case and that the specialists have got it wrong somehow. Or that the events of the seventeenth century and later, to which we shall return shortly, altered the situation. But if the original population has disappeared officially, it so happens that the last to disappear were deified, because it was recognized that the indigenous inhabitants had spiritual authority over the land.[69] Among those last indigenes-turned-deities we find especially Mama Bate, possibly the leading local divinity alongside with Nyigble.[70] But here comes another jarring detail: Mama Bate has given her name to, and is associated with the Bate clan, which as we have seen is one of the clans which provides the *awoamefia*. The other one, that of the Adzovia, is incidentally associated with strong supernatural forces having to do with blacksmithing,[71] possibly a significant detail.

But if all the details do not fit together, assuming that the anthropologists can be trusted – or that some people have somewhere along the line indulged in extensive manipulation for reasons unknown – the conclusion is clear: this case (that of Anlo plus that of Eweland more generally) belongs to the "traditional" variant, not the Dahomey/Akwamu one.

So what about the Notsé story in all this? It is difficult to tell, one of the reasons being that we have, as far as the present author knows, no genuine in-depth study of Notsé itself, whether historical or anthropological.[72] We limit ourselves to pointing out that numerous Ewe polities still acknowledge the ritual primacy of the ruler of Notsé, according to Robin Law,[73] a ruler who also wore the title of *anyigbafio*, and that there used to be an exchange of gifts with the chief of Notsie on the accession of each new *awoamefia*.[74]

* * *

We have to return to a theme mentioned fleetingly earlier, that of the so-called festivals celebrated in most polities, such as for instance the famous annual Odwira festival in Asante,[75] and the many similar festivals known from Yorubaland.[76] They represent the moment when the past, rehearsed in the present, was projected into the future, according to Tom McCaskie.[77] That is, the distance between the past and the present is abolished, what happened in the past, often the founding of the polity, is actually happening again. All this has to do with an important concept, namely that of time, a concept the Africanists have been reluctant to explore, and one that our sources are certainly not very eloquent about. However, it does seem possible to argue that most Africans of old had very different understandings and representations of space and especially of time compared with those prevalent in the modern Western world.

Now, the way we have understood it,[78] the past presents us with basically three different concepts of time. The first and most obvious is the familiar linear one which has it that whatever happened in the past will never happen again. It is associated with the emergence of the revealed religions which all introduced a year zero (or year one, if one prefers): the birth of the Christ, the flight of the Prophet from Mecca to Medina, and so on. The opposite, the circular time concept, naturally implies the contrary. We doubt, however, that many societies of the past were characterized by such a time concept. Which leads us to the third and in-between category, a linear concept encapsulated in a circular one:[79] that is, one counts days, weeks, months, years etc. in a linear fashion, but at the end of a certain cycle (possibly after a long process of deterioration), the past will eventually return some way or other and one starts afresh. And/or the past returns and/or is reenacted at regular intervals, in ceremonies and rituals, including the festivals mentioned. In societies like this the past of the historian is in a sense irrelevant. Or if it exists, only those moments of the past which are of transcendental importance for a society, again basically the founding moments, are remembered.[80]

It is difficult to back this general overview up with hard evidence in the concrete case of the Slave Coast. It is true that the only scholar who has investigated the matter in some depth, the anthropologist Claude Savary, argues that the concept of time of the Fon and neighbouring groups was clearly of the non-linear type.[81] But in the sources there are only references to "the utter insignificance of the value of time with" the locals[82] or the "very vague notions of time" they displayed.[83] As for Robin Law, he argues that the Dahomeans possessed a sense of linear chronology at least superficially analogous to that of modern historical thought,[84] a suitably ambiguous statement. But he also notes that what he calls historical knowledge was treated as having inherent power, analogous to certain ritual objects,[85] thus echoing Jacques Lombard's point that history was a royal monopoly.[86] We are dealing here with a concept of the past and hence also of time which does not square well with the linear scheme.

Our conclusion is that a linear concept of time is not much in evidence among the people of the Slave Coast of old. The implications should be obvious.

5

A FEW COMMENTS ON CERTAIN ECONOMIC MATTERS

It is time to change the subject and to turn to economic matters. The first purpose of this short chapter is to have a cursory look at the existing models and theories regarding the economy of the Slave Coast (mainly Dahomey) and the slave trade. The second is to propose some alternative points of view.

The pioneer in this context was Karl Polanyi, who had an enviable reputation before he plunged into the past of Dahomey in the 1960s.[1] Polanyi argued that Dahomey was characterized by an archaic economy, a relatively new concept which he did not define properly, and that the slave trade forced itself upon that inland country. The reaction of the rulers, rulers incidentally accepted as of divine origin, was to isolate the slave trade from the rest of the economy and society through a tight royal monopoly, and especially through establishing a sort of administered port, that of Ouidah-Glehue, cut off from the rest of the economy. In brief, the purpose was to control and to minimize the economic influence of the European trade, in order to protect indigenous social institutions and values from the corrosive impact of market forces. Polanyi noted in this context the irrelevance of the profit motive, and talked about gainless barter (implying thus that the slave trade *was* a barter).[2] Note that in Polanyi's scheme of things Dahomey and the Dahomean monarchy predated the slave trade.

As one can see, Polanyi's affirmations are not easily reconciled with what has been argued so far in this book. They are in fact "empirically unsustainable", as Robin Law has pointed out.[3] Polanyi committed the deadly sin of indulging in some quite extravagant extrapolations, based on inadequate research – he does not seem to have visited any archive, or collected oral traditions. That said, we need to add that many of Polanyi's articles on the slave trade and the Slave Coast do provide food for thought.

Other scholars believe that the classic Marxist concept of mode of production is applicable. Georg Elwert in particular argues that "*Sklavenraub*" – that is, robbery of slaves – must be considered as a separate mode of production, and that it was characteristic of Dahomey.[4] As for Roberta Kilkenny, she opts, quite simply, for the slave mode of production, defined by her as the domination of the production process by slave labour, with effective possession of slave labour by a separate class of slave owners.[5]

There is also the family mode of production, as befitting a kinship-type society. There is finally the interesting twist proposed by Jack Goody who wonders if it may not be more relevant to talk of the means of *destruction* rather than production.[6]

Goody apart, what can we say? That it all sounds appealing, but that it is not very informative, and does not get us very far.

Among those who have tried to be somewhat more specific, David Eltis and Lawrence C. Jennings have argued that the Atlantic slave trade was not on a sufficient in scale to have had a major impact on West African economic and political development, except for the case of some (unspecified) coastal regions. Their stance has been interpreted as implying that trade with the Atlantic world made no difference to the history of Western Africa between 1600 and 1860.[7] As for the (still unspecified) coastal regions themselves, J.E. Inikori (incidentally a critic of Eltis and Jennings) believes that "The coastal economies became typical parasitic enclave economies, with little productive but largely disruptive links to the economies in the hinterland".[8] Inikori also argues that the reduction of currency imports in the Bight of Benin is a clear sign that the internal trade, whether regional or interregional, and the development of the market economy were all in decline at the beginning of the nineteenth century.[9]

Are these scholars correct? Frankly, we have no idea. But we wonder how they can know what they claim to know.

Robin Law represents a reaction to all this. Indeed, he tried in a number of articles, following in the footsteps of Marion Johnson, to lay a solid empirical foundation for the economic history of the region, a genuinely quantitative economic history at that.[10] But to take a short cut, at the risk of not valuing justly that part of Law's scholarship (or of unveiling the present author's limited understanding of matters economic), it seems to us that beyond a certain general level, the results were not up to expectations, which prompted Law to abandon his scheme. The same occurred in a sense with Patrick Manning's attempt already alluded to, of writing a general and quantitatively oriented economic history of Dahomey from 1640, complete with statistics.

The very limited amount of hard statistical evidence and other economic facts that one can squeeze out of the sources is capable of defeating even the most tenacious of scholars.

* * *

We believe it necessary to start with two elementary points: the first is that the great majority of the people of the Slave Coast were farmers, with fishing and hunting as subsidiary activities. But one visitor emphasized that the people of Ouidah-Glehue/Dahomey manufactured "cotton cloths of a most excellent quality & possessing great durability". He went on to argue that they wove grass cloths, for common use, which in his opinion were "always beautifully variegated".[11] A handicraft industry in the making? Could something have come of it?

The second, but often somewhat strangely overlooked point is that if the societies of the Slave Coast were structurally very different from those of, for instance, the Western world, the same must also be the case of the economy. Indeed, if the Western world was during the period under scrutiny on the road to global hegemony thanks to the emergence of a capitalist growth economy blazing the way for an industrial revolution, the situation in Africa must have been very different. One could say in effect that its economy was the exact opposite of a capitalist growth economy. But what is that opposite?

At this stage we encounter yet another epistemological problem, the one the science of economy or economics presents us with. That science originated in an emerging capitalist world, a world that its central paradigms and assumptions reflect (yet another incestuous relationship, in sum). Indeed, economics are based on the rational actor model, or rational choice theory – that is, humans will rationally pursue profit,[12] and profit in the capitalist sense of the term. To this we must add the law of supply and demand. The trouble, however, is that theory and that law suppose an individualistic society, not a sacred kinship-type society in which the ideal of solidarity among the members of one's kindred is paramount. Hence the economic behaviour of the people of the Slave Coast cannot be adequately explained by concepts drawn from market economics. Nor, for that matter, can it be explained by Marxist concepts which constitute the antithesis of market economics, but function nevertheless within the same framework or logic.

The opposite of a capitalist growth economy may be said to be a moral and/or an ostentatory one, concepts which do not figure in the pages of Adam Smith's *Wealth of Nations*. We have to do with suitably vague concepts – they are meant to be so. However, the essence of the moral economy is first, that it is focused on the collective (the kindred), not the individual, and second, that what tradition (that is, the ancestors) prescribes is of prime importance. But if so, what were the consequences at the concrete, practical level? For instance, what happened to whatever the Africans earned from the slave trade? As far as we know, those earnings meant the possibility of lavishing more offerings to the supernatural world,[13] and accumulating wives, slaves and dependents, that is, retainers of all sorts, the traditional power-basis in Africa (the "wealth-in-people" paradigm again). They meant, finally, the possibility of cementing the important patron-client relations. In this context the big man, or rather the powerful kindred, is not the one that accumulates, but the one that publicly displays wealth, in part by spending lavishly (the ostentatory dimension), and distributes, or is at least perceived to do so – but at the end of the day somehow manages to end up with a huge profit (in Western terms). In the case of the polities of the Slave Coast what helped enormously in this respect were all the taxes, duties, excises, tolls, rents and gifts paid to the various monarchs, including very many paid by the Europeans.

Distribution was of what, exactly? Goods obviously, especially goods from far away, that is goods which carried prestige for one reason or another (not necessarily because of their value in the market), plus wives and retainers etc., but also, and perhaps above all, goods which might generate the indispensable blessings of the ancestors and of the supranatural sphere.[14] In this world, concepts such as entrepreneurship and investment (in productive undertakings, that is) are unknown. Therefore, and at the limit, whatever amounts one injects of, let us say, money and wealth in such societies has a tendency to disappear into thin air (from a "rational" point of view, that is). As for wealthy traders, to the extent that they exist, they are suspect by definition; first, because their wealth can only have been acquired through reprehensible means such as witchcraft (the idea that there is a link between hard work and wealth is not much in evidence); and second, because they pose a threat to those in command. Wealth has to follow one's formal position in society, by definition, not the other way around. The emergence of a more or less autonomous commercial-mercantile sector is therefore resisted. In Western Europe capitalism, in our view, broke through the moment those in power, the Catholic Church included, were no longer able to contain that sector, which attained some sort of autonomy. Or put differently, the economic sphere ceased to submit to the political and/or religious sphere, it liberated itself to some extent from those spheres (this happened first in the city-states of Northern Italy in the high Middle Ages).[15] Nothing of the sort occurred on the Slave Coast, where, as we have tried to demonstrate, the economic sphere was never divorced from the religious one.

In sum, to try to force the economy of West Africa of old into the concepts invented by Western economists will not work.

But to return to Robin Law – he may well be correct in stressing the highly commercialized and market-responsive character of the domestic economy of Dahomey, and in arguing that wealth derived from European trade had a multiplier effect.[16] That trade functioned as an enormous stimulus to the domestic economy, although it accentuated considerably what from a Western point of view were social inequalities.[17]

So there existed a commercial, market-based sector of some importance if we are to believe Law, and we do; a by-product of the European trade, and as such, by definition, monetized. But to embark on a very long detour, the money in question was principally the famous cowries. The cowries we are well informed about, they have aroused the curiosity of a number of researchers. Cowries are simply shells, but not any shells, in fact light, very solid and durable shells imported exclusively from the small Maldives islands in the Indian Ocean. They are the shell money of the slave trade, to quote the title of a well-known book.[18] Only the English and the Dutch had access to those islands and those shells, implying that the French, the Danes, the Portuguese and the others had to buy them from their Anglo-Dutch rivals.[19] But the cost of acquiring cowries was staggeringly high for all, it has been argued.[20] Now, it is quite clear that all slave ships had to carry a large amount of cowries. How large is however open to debate,[21] as is also, more generally, the role and function of that very special currency. The first point is that cowries are a very bulky currency, and hence limited to relatively small-scale transactions; it was the currency of the poor, says Polanyi.[22] And the second point is that the local authorities, whoever they may have been, could in no way control its supply. Nor, naturally, were the cowries convertible. In fact, they were often part of a multiple currency system, serving as small change alongside, for instance, gold – and slaves.[23] Note finally that cowries were at times more than just money, since they were also used in magico-religious ceremonies.[24]

Slaves as currency? On the Slave Coast the value of goods was indeed expressed in terms of the quantity of goods equivalent to one slave.[25] We presume that this is what is called in the sources a *pieza de Indias*, that is, a healthy adult male (*pieza* is Portuguese for "thing "or "piece").[26] Hence, for instance, one and a half female slaves, or, say, three child slaves could correspond at certain moments to one *pieza de Indias*. With regard to European goods, a basket of such-and-such a quantity of articles corresponded then to the price of a *pieza de Indias*. The question which immediately comes to mind is who decided upon the content of that basket, and how that decision was taken; and on those concrete questions the sources and our experts are remarkably silent. Is there something the rest of us have not understood?

Then, from probably the 1760s/70s the so-called ounce system spread to Ouidah from the Gold Coast where it originated.[27] So the question was which assortment of trade goods could be exchanged for one ounce of gold. Hence two units of account emerged, or put another way, two currencies existed at the same time.[28] But in the case of the ounce system, the problem is the same, namely who decided what was the equivalent in trade goods of the famous ounce, and how.

The broader questions are, first, what the Africans got for their slaves and second, who "won" or who "lost" – who got the "best" deal? A.G. Hopkins has argued in respect to the first question that the European ships came to resemble "floating supermarkets",[29] offering a very broad range of commodities. However, practical cloth, especially Indian fabrics, and metal goods clearly dominated. If we add cowries, alcohol, Brazilian tobacco plus pipes, and increasingly firearms and powder – consumer articles all – we have said what needs to be said[30] (pipes, clay pipes included, were also produced locally).[31] The trouble, from the European point of view, was that African tastes, and therefore also African demand, fluctuated widely with time and place, making it very difficult to compose an adequate cargo.[32]

The second question, the who-lost-and-who-won question, is basically unanswerable, since it all depends on what we compare with and in which context we contemplate it all, considering once more the fact that Africans and Europeans functioned in different economic worlds. Here is a case of cross-cultural trade in which it is futile to try to establish anything resembling a balance-sheet.[33] The same object may have different meanings and be valued differently depending on the different sides of the cultural divide -- Nicolas

Thomas' "Entangled Objects".[34] Hence, a bundle of goods which was expensive in Europe may have fetched fewer slaves in Africa than a less expensive one, or vice versa,[35] which could lead to a very complex bargaining situation. And, as hinted above, some items may have been regarded by the Africans as attributes of status and as such reserved for elite consumption.[36] But again, who fixed the price and how? However, Polanyi points out that no troubles arising from what he calls the "rates of trade" are on record.[37] In other words, it was perfectly possible for both sides to consider themselves the "winners". In fact, if the slave trade lasted for some 400 years, it is evident that both sides, or at least those in power on both sides, considered the trade to be to their advantage.

What is clear, in any case, is that the competition on the European side was intense. It leads us to believe that the prices were always close to the ceiling of what the Europeans thought they could afford to pay, and that no real "goods-dumping" occurred.

But to return to Robin Law's comments quoted above: as we see it, the point is not how many or few goods found their way to the market-place or how transactions were made and/or organized, and/or to what degree money entered into the picture. Rather, the point is what the earnings were fuelled into, the finality of it all. And in this respect we must remember that certain "modern" economic practices such as increased commercialization and monetarization, although they may in the end contribute to destroy structures which are more or less "traditional" – that is, anti-capitalist – may also have exactly the opposite effect, that of bolstering the "traditional" (or "neo-traditional") structures: if, that is, the doses are manageable, which they do seem to have been in West Africa.

Let us now move upstream, as it were, to the production of slaves. And here we begin by noting that slave-raiding (the production of slaves) has been defined at the macroeconomic level by E.W. Evans and David Richardson as a hunter-gatherer and rent-seeking activity which was the exclusive domain of "states".[38] Hence, "earnings from the slave trafficking largely accrued to the social and political elites...for whom rent seeking became an important activity".[39] But the present author fails to understand why slave-raiding, defined as a hunter-gatherer activity, has to be the exclusive domain of "states". He notes, furthermore, that the sources are full of transactions in which only one or two slaves were sold, and sold by individuals.[40]

But more generally, what is the link between warfare and the slave trade? For instance, is it true, as Robin Law has argued, that war was a major source of material enrichment?[41] It does sound logical. It is in fact tempting to agree with Law that warfare was probably "an especially important activity in precolonial West Africa...an industry in its own right". Indeed, "The importance of slaves, both in the internal economies and as a commodity for export, contributed to the institutionalization of warfare: for the procuring of slaves depended upon organized violence. War, therefore, was an economic activity."[42] To which one feels like adding that it always is, anyway.

But if we are correct in believing that Dahomey, the most militaristic and belligerent of the Slave Coast polities, was not particularly successful in the economic field, including the slave trade, then we can go on to argue that warfare proved in the end detrimental to trade. It is of course true that "the procuring of slaves depended upon organized violence", though probably far from exclusively so. But the problem is *where* that violence occurred and in which forms; for instance, how "decentralized", how "spread out" it was, how large the "catchment area" was. And in this respect we are left with the impression that Dahomey committed two major sins, first that of neglecting the middleman trade (as Robin Law emphasizes), and second that of concentrating its raiding activities on a much too small area, rarely venturing further afield than its own backyard. Obviously, frequently raided communities will react very differently to infrequently raided ones.

Law's line of argument, plausible as it may be, consists of deductions based more on common sense than on hard facts. But as we know by now, common sense does not always function well in the case of the Slave Coast.

* * *

Finally, a central question in global (and macro-economic) history: was there a link between the slave trade and what is usually referred to as the rise of the Western world? But since most historians are now agreed, it seems to us, that there *was* such a link, the question has become what exactly that link was. To cut the discussion short, we believe that the slave trade had a beneficial *indirect* effect on the economy of the West. There is, however, also a direct one: African slaves comprised the vast majority of the immigrants to the Americas before 1800.[43] What would have become of the New World without them?

Already many pamphleteers of the epoch were aware of the positive consequences of the slave trade: not necessarily that trade in isolation, but the vast economic circuit that it became part of, what we call the South Atlantic system: the slave trade, slaves, plantations, the Triangular Trade and so on.

We single out for attention two pamphlets, one English from 1680,[44] the other French from 1777,[45] because they are, in spite of their different origins and the time-lag between them, remarkably similar in content. What they say is that the slave trade implied expanding economic activity, it set wheels in motion, it stimulated, in particular, shipping and naval construction, and above all the labour market – one has only to think of all the seamen needed, they came from all over Europe. All told, the slave trade had a tremendously stimulating multiplier effect, that is, a synergetical one – never mind the cost in human lives. The English pamphleteer noted in addition that the slave trade had a quite direct effect on the economy in the sense that it challenged the English to come up with substitutes for all the manufactures they had previously had to import from the Netherlands, especially in order to participate in that trade (and in other fields of foreign trade). It was a challenge the English rose to,[46] it is part of the well-known story of how the English managed little by little to compete with the Dutch and finally to surpass them. But it was a challenge (now an increasingly Dutch-English one) which the French and above all the Portuguese were never really able to meet, as we shall see.

The slave trade, in part because of its hazardous nature and the long delays it involved, also constituted a challenge to, and hence a boost to another important sector of the economy, namely the service sector, banking and insurance in particular.[47]

By "expanding economic activity" we mean the fact that the slave trade contributed to enlarge the market-oriented, monetized sector of the economy, the capitalist sector if one prefers; that is, the most dynamic sector, the very locomotive which pushed the Western world towards "modernity". The level of profits becomes in this context of rather secondary importance.

In conclusion, as Roland Findlay and Kevin O'Rourke have put it: "the inhuman institution of slavery [hence also of the slave trade]...was an important factor underlying the transition to modern economic growth in Europe".[48] Exactly how important is obviously impossible to ascertain.

* * *

Why could not the slave trade, as inhumane as it was, have had the same, let us say, positive economic effect on Africa as it did on Western Europe? Why did not the slave trade generate some sort of long-term economic expansion? If what we suspect is correct – that the inhabitants of the "kingdom" of Hueda before 1727 had one of the world's highest standards of living at that time (see Part B) – why could not *something* have come out of it? Basically, we believe, because the economic structures were radically different in the two cases.

What was lacking most conspicuously in the Hueda case was an emerging capitalist sector capable of revolutionizing the economy; hence no synergetical effect emerged, or alternatively, it did emerge (witness the contention of Robin Law above) but was prevented from expanding to any significant level. The point can incidentally be illustrated by a comparison between Portugal and England. Portugal, in spite of being the leading European slave trading nation, did not really take off, whereas England, the number two, certainly did. They differed structurally, the Portuguese economy being much less capitalist (or proto-capitalist) than the English (or the Dutch). So they had limited ability to genuinely channel whatever profits they made into productive undertakings, or to integrate it all into a greater economic circuit – the multiplier effect being much more pronounced in the English case than in the Portuguese one.

The ultimate question is of course how an emerging capitalist sector surfaces in the first place. How is it that what we may call certain capitalist tendencies, habits or practices (which we imagine were present nearly everywhere) take off, or are allowed to take off and to expand, in some societies, but not in others? If one argues that it is a question of world-outlook and of mentality, the next question becomes what came first, what triggered off what – unless there was a joint, more or less synergetic emergence. The basic problem here, as elsewhere, is the origin of everything.

6

THE DATABASE AND THE SLAVE TRADE FROM THE SLAVE COAST

Since this is a work about the Slave Coast in the era of the trans-Atlantic slave trade, it is time to have a closer look at that trade. An indispensable point of departure is the earlier mentioned Database.[1]

But as noted, there are problems with the Database for our purpose. The principal problem is that it has adopted what we consider to be a regrettable convention in quantitative studies regarding the definition of areas of embarkation.[2] The Slave Coast, contrary to the Gold Coast, incomprehensibly does *not* figure among those areas. Instead it is subsumed under what is called the Bight of Benin, which is usually defined as the coastline about 640 km long, from the mouth of the Volta river all the way to the Niger Delta. Superficially this makes the Database useless for our purpose, since we cannot deduce from it how many slaves came from the western half of that coastline (the Slave Coast) and how many from the rest. Unless, that is, we can demonstrate that the latter half exported few if any slaves, at least in the period under scrutiny; and it so happens that we can do so.

The eastern part of the Bight of Benin region, where the Europeans never built forts, corresponds to the "kingdoms" of the Itsekiri of Warri and of Benin, both mentioned previously, and the territories of the acephalous Ijaw (Ijo). Benin certainly exported slaves, it took an active part in the early *Atlantic* slave trade (a wider category than that of the *Trans*-Atlantic slave trade). In fact, Benin had already entered into contact with the Portuguese by 1485,[3] that is, roughly some 140 years before the Slave Coast. But first, the local geographical conditions were, if possible, even more forbidding than on the Slave Coast, implying that the slave trade was and remained on a very modest scale.[4] And second, we repeat that the local rulers actually *banned* the trade in male slaves as early as the beginning of the sixteenth century (before the Trans-Atlantic slave trade really got under way); those were precisely the slaves the Europeans were most interested in, and very few females seem to have been sold.[5] Even after the ban was lifted, more than two hundred years later, in the 1720s, the slave trade remained close to negligible up to the 1780s.[6] In fact, A.F.C. Ryder, our leading authority, has stressed "Benin's general indifference to the demands and opportunities of the European slave trade",[7] the implication being that "Benin either could not or would not become a slave-trading state on the grand scale".[8] Instead, a limited trade was carried out in other commodities – cloth especially, but also ivory and gum and the marble-like beads called *akori*.[9]

Incidentally, the few slaves taken from Benin had a bad reputation. They were much more prone than those from other parts to lie down and simply die – 308 slaves out of 436 among one particular ship-load that we know of.[10]

All in all, it has been argued that about 6.5 per cent of the slaves embarked in the Bight of Benin came actually from the "Kingdom" of Benin,[11] and most before the sixteenth century; this suggests that 93.5 per cent came from the Slave Coast, possibly more in the period in which we are primarily interested in the present work. If these percentages come anywhere near the truth, then we can conclude that the Database's figures for the Bight of Benin reflect roughly those of the Slave Coast, at least up to the 1780s.

But there is a second problem with the Database: the distinction between the Gold Coast and the Gulf of Benin, that is, between the Gold and Slave Coasts, a distinction which did not stop the slave traders from trafficking indiscriminately on both. For instance, many ships bound for the Slave Coast stopped at Shama to take in wood and water, and to hire the necessary canoemen.[12] And of course most Dutch, English and Danish ships called at Elmina, Cape Coast Castle and Christiansborg respectively before proceeding further eastwards; the Portuguese were obliged in theory to call at Elmina and many did, as we shall see. This implies that many ships began purchasing slaves on the Gold Coast and continued to do so on the Slave Coast,[13] but not vice versa outside of the (short) Harmattan season. The question then is under which point of embarkation they are listed, and the more general problem is that the Database lists only one point for each ship, whereas many ships actually called at several places. But given the reputation of the Slave Coast as a reservoir of slaves – "the chiefest place for slaves in all these parts"[14] – it is more likely that many more slaves listed as having come from the Gold Coast actually originated further east than the other way round. For instance, we are told that the vast majority of the approximately 30,000 slaves exported by the Danes from the Gold Coast after 1792 did *not* come from that coast, but from its eastern neighbouring territory.[15] Part of the explanation has to do with what is called the coastal trade, the fleet of smaller vessels belonging to the trading companies (yachts, snows, barques, brigantines etc.) which roamed the coast, especially during Harmattan time when, as already noted, it was possible to sail from east to west, and which could transport up to 200 slaves. The slaves purchased in this way, mostly on the Slave Coast we suppose, were "stored" in the forts of the Gold Coast pending the arrival of ocean-going ships.[16]

We may add (although it is a minor point statistically speaking) that the Slave Coast was an important source of slaves for the Gold Coast labour market,[17] including the slaves the Europeans needed for their forts. One could argue that the opposite was equally the case, that most fort slaves on the Slave Coast came from the Gold Coast, from some distance away, and hence were less likely to run away.[18] But the number of slaves needed on the Gold Coast was obviously much superior to the needs of its eastern neighbouring territory. Incidentally, fort slaves must have made up a very special category of slaves who had to be very leniently treated and could certainly not be sold overseas. For as one English official noted very logically, if he sold any of them the rest would run away, something they could do very easily.[19] Our general conclusion is that probably a considerable number of slaves listed in the Database as having come from the Gold Coast actually came from the neighbouring Slave Coast.

Now for some definitions. The all-embracing term "Atlantic slave trade" refers to the export of slaves from any point of the African coast to any place in the Atlantic world. Hence it includes also the export of slaves from one African region to another, for instance the well-documented export of slaves from the Benin polity to the Gold Coast and São Tomé in the early days of the European presence – that is, the carrying trade within Africa.[20] The Atlantic slave trade lasted for some 400 years altogether, from the end of the fifteenth to the end of the nineteenth century.[21] As for the most important subsection, the one we call the "Trans-Atlantic slave trade" – the export of slaves to the Americas, it is reputed to have begun in 1501 and to have come to an end in 1866–7 (the extreme dates in the Database). But the first direct shipment of slaves from Africa to the Americas took place in 1525.[22] This trade therefore lasted thus 340 years or more. The Slave Coast was a latecomer in this context, since the first shipment of slaves from that coast to the New World may have taken place in 1616;[23] the last such shipment occurred in 1863. But within those 247 years, we will focus especially on the period between the 1670s, when the slave trade from our region really took off, and 1850–51, which marked the beginning of the end of that trade. We are left then with roughly 180 years, the period when the Trans-Atlantic slave trade must rank as a major organized enterprise on the Slave Coast. What went on before the 1670s may be qualified as "statistically insignificant". And what went on after 1850/51, up to 1863, when the last trans-Atlantic slavers ran the international blockade, may be qualified as residual, the last spasms of the slave trade as it were. Those spasms resulted in nearly 33,000 more slaves being embarked for the Americas, that is some 2,500 per year, but those numbers are insignificant compared with those of the period when the slave trade from the Slave Coast was at its height, the 1710s and the 1720s.

We also need to know that of the estimated 12.5 million slaves embarked from Africa for the New World during the era of the Trans-Atlantic slave trade, the majority came from the enormous region of West-Central Africa, that is, roughly the present-day Congo and Angola and neighbouring regions. But the next-largest number was taken from the Bight of Benin/Slave Coast and Gold Coast. As noted, possibly more than two million slaves came from the Bight of Benin, and over one million from the Gold Coast, making more than a quarter of the total. Of the two million, perhaps some 60 per cent ended up in Brazil,[24] and especially in the region of Salvador da Bahia, the famous South Atlantic port city and major slave mart where Europe met Africa in the Americas, and where the visitor in our own time may be forgiven for feeling at times that he has returned to Africa.

* * *

Slave trade figures according to the Database:

	Bight of Benin-Slave Coast/	Gold Coast/	Total Africa/
1601/16–25 (a)	2,921	68	352,843
1626–50	6,080	2,429	315,050
1651–75	52,768	30,860	488,064
1676–1700	207,436	75,377	719,674
1701–25	378,101	229,239	1,088,909
1726–50	356,760	231,418	1,471,725

THE DATABASE AND THE SLAVE TRADE FROM THE SLAVE COAST

	Bight of Benin-Slave Coast/	Gold Coast/	Total Africa/
1751–75	288,587	268,228	1,925,324
1776–1800	261,137	285,643	2,008,670
1801–25	201,054	80,895	1,876,992 (b)
1826–50	209,742	5,219	1,770,979 (c)
1851–63/7	33,867	0	225,609

(a) *from probably 1616 in the case of the Slave Coast*
(b) *of whom 1,160,601 went to Brazil*
(c) *of whom 1,299,969 went to Brazil*

Here are some slave trade figures divided into five-year periods for the Bight of Benin/Slave Coast, with the share of Lagos for certain periods (according to Mann [2007], 38) compared with the totals for Africa:

	Bight of Benin: Slave Coast	Lagos	Totals Africa:
1676–80	19,134		119,552
1681–5	40,705		145,546
1686–90	39,185		115,018
1691–5	47,931		128,356
1696–1700	60,480		211,201
1701–5	73,009		211,590
1706–10	63,934		182,651
1711–5	72,000		210,977
1716–20	77,463		242,431
1721–5	91,694		241,259
1726–30	102,736 (a)		307,133
1731–5	80,999		282,593
1736–40	64,806		315,410
1741–5	54,188		287,564
1746–50	54,032		279,025
1751–5	73,467		361,496
1756–60	49,099		281,462
1761–5	53,654		367,023
1766–70	56,729		451,937
1771–5	55,638		463,396
1776–80	54,248		292,271
1781–5	48,133	3,870	362,658

	Bight of Benin: Slave Coast	Lagos	Totals Africa:
1786–90	65,509	14,077	505,335
1791–5	47,594	4,186	459,366
1796–1800	45,603	3,282	389,040
1801–5	45,268	21,412	453,906
1806–10	50,160	28,418	369,648
1811–15	47,454	20,584	282,726
1816–20	26,369	22,683	403,117
1821–5	31,533	17,727	367,595
1826–30	27,717	(b)	488,153
1831–5	38,445	16,336	216,683
1836–40	34,636	27,582	469,601
1841–5	52,339	35,038	226,918
1846–50	56,604	37715	369,624
1851–5	7,784	5,410	66,361
1856–60	14,744	0	105,057
1861–3/5	11,339		53,315
1866	0		877

a) that is, on average, nearly 70 slaves exported every day of the year for five years.

b) Mann's figures for 1826–30 – 31 776 – have been left out, since they are higher than the total for the Slave Coast. Either Mann's figures or those of the Database are incorrect.

The data are explicit enough for our purpose. They demonstrate first, that the early and relatively massive European presence on the Gold Coast had nothing to do with the slave trade, but that the situation changed radically from about 1700 or slightly earlier.[25] They demonstrate second, that the real take-off of the slave trade from the Slave Coast occurred in the 1670s and 1680s, coinciding perfectly, as noted, with the sugar revolution in the Caribbean – whereas the take-off on the Gold Coast is probably linked to the wars of "state-formation" which culminated with the rise of Asante from 1701. Third, the heyday on the Slave Coast was from 1696 to 1730, during which period no less than a third of the slaves embarked in Africa came from that small stretch of coast, which took over from West-Central Africa as the leading supplier. If we add the figures from the Gold Coast, which may, as already noted, include slaves from the Slave Coast, the two regions together counted for more than half of all slaves exported from Africa between 1701 and 1725, clearly the "golden age"; that is, before the Dahomean conquest of the coast. Thereafter, however, decline set in, a very marked such decline from

1736, both absolute and relative. Actually, the decline from the *Central* Slave Coast, that is from the region controlled by Dahomey, was probably particularly pronounced, since it was from the 1770s that the slave trade centred on the *Eastern* Slave Coast, especially Lagos, began to expand, basically from nil.

The decline coincides perfectly with the beginning of Dahomey's dominance on the Central Slave Coast. We may conclude, therefore, that Dahomey's "success" as a slave trading polity was very limited. What is the explanation? One could of course argue that the region was running out of the necessary "raw material", that is, slaves. Certainly that is plausible – the Europeans wondered often how it was possible for such a small region to "produce" so many slaves, they feared "exhaustion".[26] An alternative theory is that the people of the "catchment area" had learned how to resist efficiently, which is also plausible. But the third possibility, that the rulers of Dahomey consciously limited the slave trade, can be safely disregarded; the sources make it very clear, as we shall see, that the sharp decline of the slave trade constituted a major preoccupation for the Dahomean elite. In fact, it looks very much as if the Dahomeans conquered the coast in order to confiscate for themselves all the gains from the slave trade; but that the end result proved rather disappointing. What went "wrong"? The principal problem, we believe, was the Dahomeans' lack of commercial and other acumen – that is, the apparent fact that they relied exclusively on their (overrated) military might, and hence on raiding, and raiding, we repeat, only their own backyard. Hence they neglected the important role of middlemen which Dahomey's predecessors had performed more or less satisfactorily. This provoked, we imagine, the ire of perhaps the leading inland supplier of slaves, namely Oyo, which redirected its slave caravans to the Eastern Slave Coast. One may presume, more generally, that the Dahomean conquests disrupted a sophisticated trading network.

One can also imagine that the very existence of Dahomey as a "new" type of polity proved both offensive and threatening, even to Oyo, though Dahomey remained for long formally a vassal of Oyo. Perhaps that allegiance explains in turn why Dahomey preferred to rely more on its own raiding than on the slave caravans from Oyo.

We note finally that the high figures for 1701–25 indicate that the slave trade was never seriously affected by warfare among the European powers. Indeed, the period was marked by the War of the Spanish Succession (1702–13/14), a nearly worldwide conflagration which involved most of the slave-trading nations. Actually, the war turned out to be a real bonanza for the slave trade from the Slave Coast, for reasons which will be explained later.

The overall figures for Africa indicate also more generally that the many wars fought between the Europeans later in the eighteenth century never disrupted the slave trade – though it is tempting to ascribe the decline from 1800 to the French Revolutionary and Napoleonic wars. But the alternative theory is that the decline is connected to the beginning of the campaign to abolish the slave trade.

The big surprise of the Database – at least to the present author – is that Portugal, with its dependency Brazil (independent from 1822), and not Britain, emerges as the leading slave trade nation, responsible for no less than 5.8 million slaves embarked, compared with 3.2 million for Britain. Together the two accounted then for 9 million out of the 12.5 million Africans embarked in Africa. Then followed France, Spain (absent 1701–50), the Netherlands, the future USA – from late in the day – and finally Denmark-Norway and Brandenburg-Prussia, lumped together in the Database.

But if we consider only the Bight of Benin, the ranking list is slightly different, the Portuguese being very much ahead this time, actually responsible for more than half of the total figure, entering the trade on a large scale during the second half of the 1670s. Then follow the French (from 1704), the British (from early in the seventeenth century), the Spanish (but only from 1800), and the Dutch (well in the lead until 1675, second from 1676 to 1701, and disappearing completely in the 1750s). Then finally, far behind, came Denmark-Norway, the USA being statistically insignificant.[27] (Note that Brandenburg-Prussia does not figure at all: a minor omission.)

However, it does not necessarily make too much sense to distinguish between the various European nations. Some nations contracted out part of the trade to others, and the flags many ships flew did not necessarily correspond to the nationality of most crew-members, coming as they did usually from many parts, or even to that of the owner(s) – especially during the era of the "illegal" slave trade. On the ground in Africa the personnel of the European establishments were often a cosmopolitan lot.[28]

* * *

There are historians who argue that the estimates of the Database err on the low side. J.E. Inikori especially believes that more than 15 million slaves were exported from Africa, as opposed to the 12.5 million of the Database.[29] Whether he is correct or not, or how he arrives at his figure, does not need to concern us here. But part of his argument is of interest for our purpose. What Inikori does is to list all the pitfalls concealed in the data, especially when using slave import data in America. Indeed, Inikori underlines the obvious, that "the institutional framework under which the trade was conducted encouraged fraudulent concealment."[30] He refers here to the many private freelance merchants known as interlopers in the era of formally monopolistic company trade. Those interlopers were legally smugglers, and as such avoided any sort of officialdom whenever they could. But even company trade had its share of smuggling in the shape of the many slaves not declared aboard the company ships.[31] We must note here that in the period which occupies us in this context smuggling was widespread, economically significant, and understood by participants not as a criminal activity but as a necessary adaptation to metropolitan commercial restrictions.

Inikori also wonders about all the slaving ships which were wiped out by captures and other losses.[32] Have they found their way into the figures of the Database?

Incidentally, Inikori might have added, for whatever it may be worth, that many contemporary and obviously impressionistic estimates, commonly partial, are usually higher than those of the Database. Whatever the case, personally we would not be surprised if in some years' time it turns out that even Inikori erred on the low side.

However, what is important for our purpose is not necessarily the overall figures, but how the slave trade varied over time and what the position of the Slave Coast was in the overall comparative context. And in these respects the Database presents us, as we have seen, with some essential clues. But once again, we consider that the really meaningful figures may not be the numbers of slaves still alive by the time the slave ships set sail, but the numbers of slaves destined for export. And those figures we do not, and may never, have.

* * *

The Database is concerned exclusively with the numbers game, or rather with one aspect of that game, namely the slaves exported from Africa (that means, as noted, the slaves alive after the end of the waiting and loading time). In brief, the Database pretends only to tell part of the story. Here we must turn to the other parts, and the other questions that that story generate, though they may be partly or totally unanswerable.

If we begin by asking where the slaves came from in the first instance, we already bump into a partly unanswerable question, one of the reasons being that the interior remained a *terra incognita* to the Europeans. They were permitted to travel no further north than the respective capitals of Hueda, Allada and Dahomey – in the latter case the towns of Abomey and Kana, situated less than 100 km from the coast (Kana, often written Cana, is located 11 km south-east of Abomey). And they made it under heavy escort.[33] The first who tried to venture further inland, the Briton Thomas Dickson as late as 1825–26, was killed two days' journey north of the Dahomean "frontier".[34]

Now, did the slaves come from the Slave Coast itself or from further afield, or both? Put differently, was the Slave Coast a slave-producing region or a slave-importing one, or was it both? Was there a so-called slaving frontier which moved gradually deeper into the African continent, as some specialists believe?[35] Patrick Manning has argued that 90 per cent of the slaves were obtained locally, implying a general and terrible depopulation.[36] Robin Law doubts the first part of Manning's theory, but seems to agree with the second, the depopulation bit, arguing that the repopulation by elephants after their near-extinction in the 1690s constitutes proof.[37] That many slaves *were* "produced" locally is something Law himself has demonstrated, by digging up a number of examples of survivals in the Americas of ethnic terms, and words and expressions, which obviously originated on the Slave Coast.[38] Then there is, as we shall see, evidence to the effect that even the pre-Dahomean polities, Hueda in particular, indulged in considerable local raiding. Nevertheless, there is no question that Manning, and also Law, overstated the point. We note first, for whatever it may be worth, that the south of the present-day Republics of Benin and Togo – that is, the old Slave Coast – is today by far the most densely populated region of the two countries. We note also that in a polygynous society the effects of the loss of a fair percentage of the *male* population may not necessarily affect radically the rate of natural increase. But more to the point, Manning and Law seem to have overlooked the existence of the mighty inland Yoruba polity of Oyo, which always looms large in the background in the history of the Slave Coast; and Oyo owed its rise to prominence precisely to the slave trade. So argues in fact Robin Law himself, presenting Oyo as a polity which, already from the 1640s, exported slaves to the south, through the Slave Coast, in order to finance the continual purchase of horses from the north.[39] Horses did not do well as far south as Oyo, because of the tsetse fly, and so Oyo had to replenish regularly the supply of horses it needed for its cavalry, which was the basis of its might.[40] Hence the necessity for Oyo to send slaves southwards for sale. Obviously, many of those slaves came from regions far in the north, deep inside the Sahel-Sudan belt. This also explains why Oyo took, as we shall see, a keen interest in the affairs of the Slave Coast, often intervening militarily so far as the environment permitted (the Slave Coast being of course situated even further south, and thus even more dangerous for horses).

The contention that many slaves came from far away, via Oyo and Borgu among other places,[41] tallies with a number of contemporary testimonies.[42] But the problem is how many – what percentage are we talking about? Perhaps it is in part, as already hinted at, a question of chronology. It may be in fact that many slaves came from far afield in the early days, the Huedan raiding notwithstanding, but that the situation changed with the destructive wars provoked by the rise of Dahomey in the 1720s. Dahomey seems indeed to have raided extensively its own or neighbouring communities, such as the Mahi. However, we cannot assign percentages, we have no idea of how many slaves came from remote parts and how many from the Slave Coast itself.[43] What we can say is the obvious, that those who came from far away must have had behind them many weeks, not to say months, of strenuous walking before they reached the slave marts in the south, passing possibly from hand to hand.

But if many slaves were after all "produced" locally, were wars waged in order to capture slaves, or were the slaves a by-product of wars made for other reasons, or both? Apart from war, did some groups organize slave-raiding expeditions? If so, who were the victims – people living in acephalous societies, or local rebellious villages, or both? Were regions that are characterized to-day by very low population densities victims of slave-raiding (as Kenneth Kelly believes, following Patrick Manning)?[44] (Unlikely, in our opinion.) If so, did warfare and banditry create pervasive violence throughout the region? Did some or many elders sell members of their own family, as the Spanish Capuchin missionary Naxara claimed that he witnessed in Allada already in 1660?[45] Actually, during famine times which did occur strangely enough, close kin *were* sold.[46] We also know that some of the kings were prone to sell some of their own subjects, including or even especially "wives", from time to time.[47] In fact, adulterous royal wives and their seducers (or victims), and even at times the latters' extended families, faced the worst.[48]

We know furthermore that those who lost out in power struggles were certainly sold.[49] We know finally, or at least seem to know, that the judicial system, including possibly witchcraft trials, produced slaves for export.[50] On the system of pawning (debt bondage) there is less certainty.[51]

What we have in sum are some clues here and there, but nothing in the way of any easily recognizable pattern.

Whatever the origin of the slaves, one imagines that there existed several markets in the region and elsewhere; Robin Law believes so, and with good reason.[52] But the principal one before 1727, as noted, was clearly at Savi, some 14 km from the seashore. And it so happens that we are relatively well informed about what went on in Savi. It was to Savi that the Europeans went to buy slaves, and all the Europeans had lodges there from a very early date, long before the forts were constructed at Ouidah-Glehue, and lodges situated within the precinct of the vast royal compound.[53]

The slaves were placed, or "stored", in an infamous place called a trunk – another word which has disappeared in the sense implied here – also called the shackle (or slave hole), a word which has also disappeared. And not surprisingly, conditions in the trunk were beyond imagination, as they were later in the "warehouses" in the compound of the ruler of Jakin.[54] An experienced slave trader such as Thomas Phillips, presumably not the most tender of human beings, often fainted when he bought slaves in the Savi trunk, because of the smell (this in the 1690s).[55] Those who guarded the slaves were officials of the king of Hueda, commanded by a "captain" of the trunk.

After having been examined by a European surgeon, including their "privities", and after the sellers had "liquor'd them well and sleek with palm oil", and they had been branded with a hot iron,[56] the slaves were driven to the coast, under the care of another "captain", also an official of the king of Hueda. This was, we repeat, a 14 km strenuous and perilous walk which involved among other things "three fords to pass where the water is up to the neck", and a lot of other difficulties.[57] The Brandenburger Johann Peter Oettinger, who accompanied a party of slaves southwards in 1692–93 (as the Europeans often did), and who obviously had problems with his conscience, could barely stand the "heart-rending cries" of the women especially that filled the air, "which often cut me to the quick", although there were efforts to drown them with the sound of drums or other noisy instruments managed by the guards.[58] At the end of it all, the slaves were confronted with the ocean and the surf, presumably for the first time in their lives, obviously another traumatic experience. On the beach the Europeans established tents, or occasionally open-air trunks, for the final inspection and branding of the slaves, if this had not been done before.[59] On the beach also, another "captain" of the king of Hueda was in charge of the security of the place.[60] The locals entrusted with guarding the slaves must have done a splendid job from the point of view of the Europeans, since we do not know of any slave revolts on land.

After 1727 and the disappearance of Savi the organisation changed radically. It is true that we know of other trunks elsewhere and later, notably at Jakin (as noted) and at Ekpe in the east.[61] But in Ouidah-Glehue there was no central trunk, only private prisons in most houses. According to Paul Isert, a broker criss-crossed the town every morning, going from one trader to another and asking if slaves had arrived (if yes, a factor would come around later to buy them). The purchased slaves were then branded with the factor's mark, and finally delivered to the fort or the factory which accumulated slaves at times.[62] Since prices were set in advance by the local authorities (but according to which criteria?), there was no auction, no slave market, the slaves being delivered as they became available.[63]

What happened to the not "merchantable" (unsaleable) slaves, those that the Europeans rejected? Pruneau de Pommegeorge argues that children/babies under the age of three or four were routinely "thrown to the wolves" (meaning wild beasts), as he expresses it, and those too old, equally routinely, had their throats cut[64] (this in the 1750s and 1760s). But since Pruneau became a staunch opponent of the slave trade, one may suspect him of exaggerating. However, James Houstoun (in the pre-Dahomean era) noted that "when we throw out our dead slaves on the fields" (no mention of how they died), they were immediately carried off and devoured by the local beasts (Houstoun thought tigers).[65] And Robert Norris stated laconically in 1788 that "Prisoners taken in war and not sold are put to death".[66] As for Robin Law, he presents evidence to the effect that the Dahomeans in their campaigns, at least the one against Hueda in 1727–28, adopted the practice of killing the wounded, the too old or the too young, something which was normally done on the battlefield.[67] Then there were the slaves the Dutch confiscated from those Luso-Brazilian ships which had not complied with the obligations the former imposed on the latter; many of those slaves were "of such poor quality" that the captains of the WIC's slave ships refused to take them; they were simply left to die.[68] We note finally in this context that at Lagos in the 1820s the sickly, old and infirm were drowned, according to Richard Lander the explorer.[69]

Again we have no idea of the percentages of the slaves killed as compared with those who succumbed to the conditions they were confronted with, including the new diseases the slaves from the interior encountered, against which they had no immunity.[70] Nor have we comparative figures for those selected for the American ordeal and those who were retained by the local authorities. The latter found their way to the huge royal estates that proliferated in Dahomey especially, or became household slaves (the enormous royal household included), or were redistributed as gifts, forced to become prostitutes, recruited as soldiers, or destined to become sacrificial victims.⁷¹

But we must return to the slaves destined for the Americas. And for those who survived the surf – again we have no idea how many perished, either because the canoes capsized or because the slaves took advantage of the situation, so to speak, and committed suicide by jumping overboard⁷² – and who arrived aboard the ships, the real waiting time began, especially for the first to arrive. Here we repeat that the slaves came in small batches, especially in the epoch of Dahomey: one day one could buy ten slaves, the next day two, and so on.⁷³ The first slaves to arrive obviously faced the longest waiting time. The point here is that, according to Bosman, it was cheaper to guard slaves on board ship than on land.⁷⁴ However, on the Gold Coast the waiting time was in the forts which were theoretically "equipped" for that purpose. But even so, slaves had at times to sleep out in the open air, even in the rainy season, with the consequences one can imagine.⁷⁵

To all this we must add that not infrequently, in certain periods, slaves were transferred from one ship to another while still in the road: the Portuguese in particular bought slaves from other Europeans instead of buying directly from the Africans.⁷⁶ We must also remember that many slave ships had to call at various places to complete their slave cargoes, with a corresponding lengthening of the time the slaves had to stay on board.

How long, then, did the waiting-time aboard the ships last for the firstcomers? It must have varied enormously, but let us say from one to eight months – although it could last more than a year, with three months being more or less the average. That is in any case far longer than the Middle Passage which lasted normally between 50 to 80 days.

Summing up, we arrive at the surprising conclusion that the most unfortunate had spent between one and two years on board ship before arriving in the New World.⁷⁷ That is in theory, since we doubt that many could survive such a long ordeal.

We know that, logically enough, the bigger the vessels, say, more than 200 tons, the longer the waiting time.⁷⁸ We also know, or rather seem to know, that the loading and waiting time increased from the 1750s onward, Africa-wide, and that it was especially high between 1751 and 1775, for reasons which remain obscure.⁷⁹ We know finally that the Europeans were very much aware of the problem. For as Archibald Dalzel argued in a hearing, "The mortality arises very much from being detained on the coast, and often from the conditions the slaves are in, when they come on board, from the scarcity of provisions in the Country".[80] Above all, the longer slaves laid in "the oven-like hold off the Guinea Coast", the fewer would be delivered in the Americas.[81] Those conditions determined, we imagine, the death rates on the Middle Passage.

In many of these matters the Portuguese of Brazil had some advantages compared to the others. First, their ships were generally smaller; and second, they had to make far shorter trips. In fact, theirs was a sort of shuttle traffic between (mainly) Salvador da Bahia and the Slave Coast. But even so, the authorities complained that too many slaves died because of lack of space aboard the ships.[82] The waiting time could also be deadly for the Europeans; there were at times simply not enough crew left to man a ship, or nobody fit to take command.[83]

If one asks what caused the slaves to die aboard the ships while still at anchor, or in the forts of the Gold Coast, the answer is disease, undernourishment – that is, hunger[84] – despair, or simply sitting or lying there.[85] Or they starved themselves to death, believing that they would be eaten otherwise (by the Europeans) and that if they died before that happened, they would return to their own country in some way or other;[86] as has been pointed out: "the horror of being eaten was not merely the fear of physical death but the additional dread that the soul of the victim would be consumed by the eater, extinguishing the survival of the individual in another world".[87] All this happened in a very noisy atmosphere if we are to believe Nigel Tattersfield, who talks about "the incessant chanting of woe and despair which rose and fell, but was never hushed, issuing from the slave-hold".[88]

It could also happen that the slaves (and crew members) were killed because the ship they were aboard was blown up or otherwise wrecked, perhaps because of slave revolts or pirates. Pirate attacks were not frequent but certainly occurred, for instance in 1683 and 1686,[89] and especially between 1718 and 1723. In January 1722 pirates led by the notorious Bartholomew Roberts blew up a slave ship in the Ouidah-Glehue road (the captain having refused to pay the ransom demanded), leaving us a heartbreaking description of slaves clapped in irons trying to save their lives in these shark-infested waters – "a Cruelty unparallel'd".[90] Or the slaves were caught in the crossfire between European battleships, whether this happened directly off the coast or further away.[91]

As for the revolts, it has been argued that more than half occurred before the vessels were filled to capacity and began the outward journey. When revolts did break out, the violence was horrific, the success rate minuscule, and the punishment meted out bestial.[92] We leave out the details. In fact, the period from when the departure approached and to when a ship began to distance itself from the shore was generally a particularly tense one, since the slaves seem to have known that once on the open sea they were irremediably lost.[93] Tattersfield adds the morbid detail that packs of sharks dogged the progress of every departing slave ship and fed upon the discarded bodies. Sometimes a dead slave was dragged behind the vessel as bait.[94]

As for Thomas Phillips, he has left us with some interesting details about the precautions taken by the slavers:

> When our slaves are aboard we shackle the men two and two, while we lie in port, & in sight of their own country... When we come to sea we let them all out of irons...we have some 30 or 40 gold coast negroes, which we buy...to make guardians & overseers of the Whydah [Ouidah] negroes, and sleep among them (as spies) when we constitute a guardian, we give him a cat of nine tails as a badge of his office, which he is not a little proud of, & will exercise with great authority.[95]

What Phillips does not say is what happened to those Gold Coast negroes; did they go with the ship all the way to the Americas or not? And if they did, what happened to them there? Incidentally, other slaves who also assisted in the task of surveillance were those females who had been chosen to serve as sex-slaves.[96]

* * *

It was easy to sail from Europe to West Africa thanks to the prevailing currents and winds (especially the Guinea current) but close to impossible to sail in the opposite direction. Hence most ships, once they had completed their cargo, had to drop down to the Equator, and hence to the islands of São Tomé and Príncipe, before heading westwards to the Americas, catching the south east trade winds to Brazil or the north west ones to the Caribbean.[97] It came in handy in this context that those two tiny but very fertile Portuguese islands could offer, abundantly, what the Slave Coast could not, or at least not in sufficient quantity considering the problem of transport across the surf: wood, water and victuals of all sorts (drinking water was actually a permanent problem at Ouidah-Glehue).[98] In addition, the islands, and especially Príncipe, possessed superb natural harbours.[99] In fact, the two islands (to which one may add the small Annobón, even more fertile according to Bosman),[100] constituted a necessary complement to the Slave Coast – the Key to the Guinea trade as one British official put it,[101] or the supply base of the slave trade. It was in a sense the existence of those islands which made possible the slave trade on the Slave Coast. What is certain is that the Europeans, after the fatiguing loading and waiting time on the Slave Coast, considered the islands to be some sort of paradise,[102] a paradise they thought it indispensable to reach as soon as possible, which they usually did after two to three weeks' sailing.[103] On the islands they stayed usually some three weeks, if we are to believe Stephen Behrendt *et al*.[104] And the slaves? We have no evidence of slave revolts aboard the ships while in the islands or of massive escapes, however that silence may be interpreted. What we do have evidence of are events not directly relevant, that is, of a Danish slave ship which blew up with more than 800 slaves on board in 1705,[105] and ships unfortunate enough to be caught up in the notorious doldrums around the Equator.[106] Once more it does not take much imagination to guess what happened to the slaves.

That the Portuguese authorities were apparently unable to take advantage of the strategic position of the islands and to turn them into a thriving emporium constitutes in our view a historical problem. Even some Portuguese had difficulties in understanding why the authorities neglected the islands,[107] why they functioned *de facto* as a sort of penal colony.[108]

After a three weeks stay on average, the slave ships finally embarked upon the genuine Middle Passage, which, although it too certainly claimed its share of human lives (which was very much, we repeat, a consequence of the debilitating waiting and loading time), strikes us as the least difficult stretch of the ordeal of the slaves[109] – that is, if no more revolts occurred and if, in war-time, no enemy ships appeared on the horizon.[110]

This is where we leave the slave ships.

* * *

Those Europeans who were under the impression that more slaves were lost at Ouidah-Glehue than elsewhere on the coast of Guinea[111] probably had a point. But what we would like to know is how many of, say, a thousand slaves who entered the trunk at Savi in the pre-1727 era (to take but that example) actually set foot in the New World after the incredible odyssey they had to go through? Or perhaps, how many were still alive after the crucial first months in the Americas, the period of adaptation to the climate? (According to one source, fully one-fourth of the slaves died after the first few weeks in the Americas).[112] Or if one prefers, how many survived to reach their final destination,[113] which in the Brazilian case could mean a long and strenuous overland journey to the mining regions of the interior.[114] Once again, we have no idea, and it is in our opinion futile even to try to make a so-called educated guess – apart from the obvious point that quite a few *must* have survived, otherwise the whole enterprise would simply have ground to a halt. What we are dealing with in any case is, we repeat, a possibly unparalleled squandering of human life. What we are also dealing with is a tremendous challenge awaiting the scholars devoted to quantitative history.

* * *

We need to backtrack, and to have a short look at the (rudimentary) organization of the slave trade on land. If we follow a ship's captain who arrived on, for example, the beach south of Ouidah-Glehue, the first thing he had to do was to ask the local authorities for permission to trade. To obtain that permission, he had to pay taxes, also called customs, plus more or less compulsory gifts, the famous *dashees* (from the Portuguese *dação* in the singular) – always excessive according to the Europeans, and obviously an important source of revenue for the locals.[115] If the captain had access to a fort or a factory, he and his officers could rely on the cooperation of its personnel, and even lodge there, while the members of the crew spread all over the place. And since more than ten ships could be at anchor simultaneously in the Ouidah-Glehue road, it meant a lot of Europeans and hence a lot of activity and fraternization (we presume, since our sources are close to silent about what we may call the daily life in the slave-trading centres). Note that the market in Ouidah-Glehue at least was provided with a fair assortment of imported European goods for sale in this partially monetized economy.[116]

After that it was time to discuss prices and to contract for the host of workers of all categories needed, "*les serviteurs de la traite*", as Dieudonné Rinchon has called them,[117] especially porters,[118] in this region without wheeled transport, and of course canoemen, if the captain did not already have those he needed on board. Indeed, the total African workforce servicing the slave trade must have been quite considerable. A fair portion of that workforce was recruited from among the inhabitants of the hamlets or quarters which had sprung up around the European forts and who usually had kinsmen among the slaves inside the forts:[119] slaves who outnumbered the Europeans by perhaps 20 to one, if not more. But as noted, these were very special slaves – some of them were even paid and worked regular hours, from 7 to 11 in the morning, and from 13 to 17 in the afternoon in the case of about 200 slaves in the French fort in Ouidah-Glehue in the 1760s/70s.[120]

The glimpses we have of the relationship between the Europeans on the one hand, and on the other the fort slaves, plus the inhabitants of the adjacent quarters, leave the impression of ambiguity and fear, and of stealing being a serious problem.[121] That said, the fort-slaves and their kinsmen outside identified at times with the Europeans, even to the point of taking up arms in their defence, as we shall see.

After all this it was time to decide upon the prices and to start buying slaves. The first seller was nearly always the king, and custom had it that the Europeans had to buy all the slaves the king offered, and at the price decided by him. Who sold the rest of the slaves – that is, did there exist a more or less autonomous commercial sector? As indicated earlier, after 1727 many individuals or families had slaves to sell, and sold them directly to the Europeans. But does that make for a private commercial sector? If it does, the chances are that that sector was severely controlled and restricted by the Crown, at least in the era of Dahomey.

It is in any case clear that the local African authorities on the Slave Coast had "a much greater command of the trade than any other on the coast".[122]

PART B

CHRONOLOGICAL OVERVIEW
EARLY DAYS TO THE 1720s

1

FOCUS ON THE EUROPEAN SIDE

As noted, in the beginning were the Portuguese – the first Europeans who, coming from the sea, went on land on the coast of the future Gold Coast, in 1471. They were responsible for integrating Lower Guinea into the wider world. A globalizing perspective cannot do without them. Furthermore, since the past of the Slave Coast is not fully comprehensible without a certain understanding of not only the role of the Europeans but also the relationship between them, we need an overview of who came when, where and why in the early days – which is what this section is about.

It was, as also noted, the gold of the Gold Coast that attracted the Europeans to Lower Guinea, which meant that the future Slave Coast continued to be, for some time, of peripheral interest.

The Portuguese were granted exclusive rights to Guinea by the Treaty of Tordesillas with Spain, for which reason the kings of Portugal attributed to themselves the title of *Senhor de Guiné* (Lord of Guinea), a title the Portuguese crown was anxious to give substance to, though it never succeeded.[1] The problem for the Portuguese was that they had little of interest to offer to the Africans, owing principally to the comparatively poor, underdeveloped state of the Portuguese handicraft industry – a chronic preoccupation for the rulers in Lisbon.[2] One way to remedy this state of affairs was for the Portuguese to develop inter-regional African trade with themselves as middlemen, for instance by buying slaves in the Benin polity and selling them on the Gold Coast.

The Portuguese came to call the coast *A Costa da Mina*, after their headquarters, the famous *Castelo* (castle) de São Jorge da Mina, usually known as Elmina, built in 1482, one of Portugal's string of fifty or so trading forts in Africa and Asia.³ Its position was ideal – with its protected bay it constituted by far the best site on the whole of the coast.⁴ In addition, it was situated in the midst of the region with the most maritime activity, thanks to the Fante canoemen.⁵

For the Portuguese the *Costa da Mina* (Mina coast) included the future Slave Coast to the east,⁶ a region with which, we repeat, it took a long time to establish relations. But in 1620 Garcia Mendes Castello Branco noted that two Portuguese ships sailed from the "kingdom" of Allada (that is, the beach south of the trading centres of Offra/Jakin) every year laden with slaves, plus ivory, cotton cloths, food⁷ and those gemstones called *akori* or simply beads.⁸ But every year since when? That is what we do not know.

Robin Law speculates that the scale of the early trade during the period of Portuguese monopoly (which lasted until 1635 according to him) and the Portuguese involvement more generally may have been underestimated, and that the significance of the Dutch entry in the 1630s–40s has been correspondingly exaggerated. Law argues in fact that the Portuguese exported until the 1620s about a thousand slaves a year from the Slave Coast,⁹ a figure which is certainly not incompatible with those of the Database.

Whatever the case, the Portuguese were the only Europeans on the Lower Guinea Coast for something like a hundred and twenty years, or at least the only Europeans who had genuine permanent establishments.

The next Europeans to arrive in number on the Guinea coast were the Dutch, from the 1590s,¹⁰ a decade which saw the beginning of the Dutch Golden Age.

The aim of the Dutch was not to compete with the Portuguese, but simply to expel them and to take over their monopolistic position,¹¹ something which they had succeeded in doing by 1642 (the conquest of Elmina took place in 1637). By then the Portuguese had lost all their establishments on the mainland. One reason for the Dutch interest must be sought in the fact that they had succeeded in conquering the north-eastern part (but only that part) of Brazil in 1630, where they began to establish sugar plantations based on African servile labour.¹²

The Dutch had an excellent excuse for attacking the Portuguese possessions in West Africa and elsewhere. It was in the midst of the eighty-year war of liberation (1568/1572–1648) that the Dutch waged against their formal suzerains, the Habsburg kings of Spain.¹³ And since the latter became also the kings of Portugal from 1580, the enemies of Spain became the enemies of

Portugal as well. But even after Portugal (somewhat miraculously) recovered its independence in 1640, the Dutch were not in a hurry to end the war. The Dutch had not completed their conquest of the Portuguese possessions in the Atlantic coast. But Luanda in Angola, the principal supplier of slaves, and the island of São Tomé both fell in 1641, although the Dutch hold over the latter was incomplete.[14] After that the Dutch finally agreed to an armistice in 1642. However, the hard-pressed Portuguese, also at war with Spain (which tried unsuccessfully to impede the Portuguese secession until 1668), managed somehow to fight back and to recover all of São Tomé in 1644, north-east Brazil between 1645 and 1654 and Luanda in 1648 – armistice or no armistice. But what was irremediably lost were the establishments on the Guinea coast.[15]

All this was reflected in the final peace treaty between Portugal and the Dutch Republic (formally called the United Provinces) in 1662. That treaty, as well as the armistice twenty years earlier, was interpreted by the Dutch as implying that the Portuguese had been officially banned from the Guinea coast.[16] The Dutch then clung firmly to the theory that they had by right of conquest taken over the Portuguese monopoly of the Guinea trade. For although the Dutch needed, and claimed, freedom of trade and free seas, *mare liberum*, in Europe, they always tried to enforce closed seas, *mare clausum*, overseas.[17]

It is important to remember in this context that we are entering into the era of mercantilism. This meant that the political authorities took a keen interest in matters economic, in fact tried to submit the economy to their aims (although often in alliance with whatever bourgeoisie existed). The result was that commerce and warfare became inseparable,[18] meaning that everyone strove to acquire a monopolistic position, and to eliminate if possible any competition. Hence what is called armed long-distance trading, one incidental consequence being a high level of smuggling.[19] In fact, if a European nation built a fort or a trading station in whatever part of the world, that nation felt entitled to deny access there to the other European nations, if necessarily by force, on the condition that the local habitants were either too weak or too little interested to hinder it. Hence, forts and settlements were considered to be marks of sovereignty and possession.[20] Or to put it differently, "Settlements [were] deemed valuable…as conferring an exclusive right of trade upon the Power possessing them".[21]

But on the Guinea coast the Dutch were unable to curb the interest of other nations, and notably of the English, who appeared already in 1631–2, in the shape of the newly established Guinea Company.²² They turned out to be redoubtable adversaries, in Guinea as elsewhere. The English were followed by the Swedes, the Danes, the Brandenburgers and the French.

As for the relations between the Dutch and the English, it took no less than a major war, the Second Anglo-Dutch Naval War (*de facto* 1664–67), which ended in a sort of draw,²³ to persuade both to agree upon some kind of peaceful coexistence, that is, to give up their claims to monopolistic rights over the whole region, though not over their respective spheres of interest within that region.

The exception to the rule is the Slave Coast where no European nation or trading company was ever able to establish monopolistic rights, even over small areas – although this was not for not trying. Indeed, the Slave Coast became from the very outset, and remained, a zone of what we may call free trade.

What happened locally on the Guinea coast was a consequence, and part, of a significant turning point in world history, the decay of the old-fashioned Iberian empires which lost their preeminence to the new emerging and more dynamic – because capitalist-oriented – states of north-west Europe: Britain, and especially the Dutch Republic. The latter was fast becoming characterized by what has been called "The First Modern Economy", to quote a famous and illustrative book title.²⁴

* * *

Dutch trading in Guinea came to be united under the formally private West Indies Company or WIC (Generaele or Geoctroyeerde West-Indische Compagnie 1621–1791, with monopoly rights 1630–1734/35). The WIC, which is possibly best known for founding and governing New Amsterdam, the future New York, between 1623 and 1664, was in a sense the sister company of the better-known United East India Company or VOC (Verenigde Oostindische Compagnie, 1602–1798).²⁵ Both belonged to the first generation of a new type of politico-economic entity, the so-called chartered companies, which were state-protected, each being *de facto* the long arm of its respective government, always a major share-holder. They were in fact the world's first joint-stock companies and multinational corporations. Actually, each represented "a unique combination of commercial and political power of a kind never seen before".²⁶ And each was "virtually a state within the state".²⁷ However, the WIC, contrary to the VOC, turned out to be "a losing proposition for almost every year of its existence".²⁸ And the WIC, although a commercial enterprise, was, according to Wim Klooster, in practice more of a war machine,[29] battling against the Habsburgs but also delivering, in fact smuggling, slaves into Spanish America. Indeed, after 1645 and their loss of north-east Brazil, the Dutch succeeded in capturing – formally as sub-contractors – the traditional Portuguese markets in Spanish America.[30]

The English followed quickly in the footsteps of the Dutch, and they too established chartered companies of the VOC-WIC type. But whereas the WIC was the only Dutch company on the coast from beginning to end, on the English side there was a succession of such companies.

* * *

According to A.F.C. Ryder, "Portuguese trade and influence in West Africa had suffered total eclipse" after 1642.[31] But that may perhaps be too harsh an assessment. After all, the Portuguese managed to hold on to their islands in the Gulf of Guinea – islands whose central role in the slave trade from the Slave Coast has already been emphasized – and São Tomé served as a basis for missionary forays on the coast of Guinea.[32] Later it also served, as we shall see, as the basis for what may be described as politico-military incursions on the coast organized by the local Portuguese, which it is tempting to call a sort of São Toméan "sub-imperialism".

Furthermore, what we may call the Portuguese cultural influence proved enduring. What was dubbed "Coastal Portuguese", Portuguese Creole, continued to be the coastal *lingua franca*, most notably the trade language; all the Europeans had to learn it.[33] Then there were all the Portuguese words which had crept into the local languages, the best known being perhaps "palaver", from *palavra* (word) or *palavrear* (to chat, to discuss). "Palaver" became in a sense the term for an informal institution designed to settle quarrels and disputes.[34]

We can add all the Portuguese place-names, many of which have endured to the present: Lagos, Porto Novo, Boca del Rio, Volta, to name but a few.

Although Portugal itself had been driven out, Portuguese ships from Brazil began increasingly to ply the waters of Guinea in the second half of the seventeenth century. The Luso-Brazilians (the Portuguese of Brazil),[35] and particularly those of Bahia in the north-east, found a very special niche in the trade of what to them remained the *Costa da Mina*, a niche based on a somewhat surprising product, namely tobacco. This was however not any tobacco, but a tobacco reputed to be of inferior quality, the so-called third-rate (*refugado*) tobacco called *soca* and sweetened with molasses, a sort of honey-like syrup made from sugarcane.[36]

This third-rate tobacco came nearly exclusively from Cachoeira in inland Bahia, for centuries the centre of the most important tobacco-growing region in Brazil,[37] but to-day, like Ouidah, another backwater-town where little testifies to past glory. This tobacco, smoked in pipes,[38] became something of an instant hit, developing in fact into some sort of craze among the people (or at least the upper social strata) of the Slave Coast,[39] and, increasingly also, of those of the Gold Coast.[40] The third-rate Brazilian tobacco remained very much in demand throughout our period. It is one of those occurrences in the past which defeats the analytical acumen of the historians. The profits from the slave trade went up in smoke, literally. There is another irony hidden here – the tobacco plant grows well on the Slave Coast.[41] However, as mentioned, the locals did not want just any tobacco, and certainly not a tobacco of superior quality, but exclusively the Brazilian third-grade variant; a type of tobacco the other Europeans tried time and again to imitate, never succeeding – the imitations were, we are told, easily detected and rejected by the Africans.[42] From the point of view of the Luso-Brazilians, tobacco solved their major problem, the fact that they had few products of interest to offer. Hence the small but rapid Portuguese ships known as *sumacas*[43] became a familiar sight on the Slave Coast.

How did the Portuguese authorities in Lisbon, and above all the Dutch on the Guinea coast, react? That an overseas dependency, in this case Brazil, established direct maritime-commercial relations with a foreign region was against the principles of mercantilism which held that a colony could only trade with the mother country. But the authorities in Lisbon bowed to necessity by granting the necessary licences (*alvarás*), although obviously they did so very reluctantly.[44] Hence a bilateral trade system was established instead of the classic triangular one. But the trading link in question did become a permanent source of irritation to the Portuguese government in Lisbon which tried repeatedly to organize and to control it, even at some stage to stop it altogether, especially after Brazilian gold also became an item of that trade in the first decades of the eighteenth century (gold was discovered in Minas Gerais around 1695).[45] It is noteworthy that the representatives of the Portuguese Crown in Brazil sided generally with the local planters and traders, allowing the latter to impose their will in most instances. It is a testimony to the growing importance of the Mina trade to the Brazilian economy.[46]

The WIC authorized the Brazilian Mina trade, since it was a source of revenue to the company, but imposed severe conditions, the principal one being that the traders brought with them only tobacco and paid a heavy tax (in tobacco) at Elmina before proceeding to the few centres where they were permitted (by the Dutch) to buy slaves. In addition, the Brazilians were forbidden to trade with other European nations or to sell European goods.[47] In this way the Dutch got their share, and free of charge so to speak, of the Brazilian third-rate tobacco, a merchandise which turned out to be increasingly indispensable for the purchase of slaves. The tax, which the WIC claimed the right to levy throughout its existence, and more generally the treatment of the Luso-Brazilians on the coast proved to be an endless source of conflict, a three-cornered conflict in fact, between the Dutch authorities, the Portuguese Crown, and the Luso-Brazilians – with the fourth party, the Africans, siding with the last-mentioned. What is certain is that the Luso-Brazilians always preferred to pay the tax if the alternative was the end of the Mina trade.[48]

There was actually a fifth party, the other Europeans, principally the English, who also wanted (and needed) their share of the third-rate Brazilian tobacco, and later of gold. Hence they sided, not surprisingly, with the Portuguese against the Dutch. What we end up with here is another multidimensional conflict, one which generated very complicating situations at times, plus incidentally a huge amount of paper – that is, sources.[49]

It was with the *Provizão* (Provision) of 12 November 1644, probably linked to the reconquest of São Tomé, that the Portuguese government for the first time authorized Bahian ships to sail straight to the Mina coast, by means of licences. The permission was renewed in 1672, and the number of licences granted increased considerably from 1681.[50] Then, in 1689, the Dutch formally relaxed their prohibition against the Portuguese, allowing them to trade in general on the coast, but still on the condition that each Portuguese-Brazilian ship called first at the WIC headquarters at Elmina and paid the famous 10 per cent tax called *recognitie* by the Dutch, and still mostly in tobacco.[51] It was, in sum, in the 1680s that the Mina tobacco trade really took off.

* * *

We must backtrack to note that as far as the Dutch were concerned, it was around the time of their capture of Elmina that they began to traffic on the Slave Coast and to genuinely enter the slave trade. That beginning can apparently be dated with relative precision to 1636–37 when two vessels commissioned by the WIC purchased slaves in the Allada/Offra region.[52] But the Dutch presence, in the sense of resident officials, was for some time discontinuous, with temporary lodges and/or premises occupied seasonally, as with the Portuguese presence earlier.[53] In addition to regular trade, the WIC pursued and captured many Portuguese slave ships at sea, at least before the armistice of 1642.[54]

How were the Europeans welcomed on the Slave Coast? Overwhelmingly, if were are to believe several Dutch documents dating, according to Adam Jones, from the 1640s or 1650s,[55] and referring to Offra. According to the main one:

> When you first come ashore, you are welcomed by at least 1 000 people[56], dancing and playing. There are also the King's noblemen from all the villages that lie within his territory. These noblemen bring you with the suite they have with them a good 10 miles inland to where the King is. There you make your report in Portuguese concerning the trade.[57]

And there you started paying also. This account all squares rather well with our slave-trade-by-invitation thesis. The festive dimension seems to have become something of a tradition, at least in Allada;[58] so also do the other elements mentioned in the manuscripts. First, all the taxes and duties the Europeans had to pay before being allowed to purchase slaves.[59] And second, the central role of the king who had the first pick of the items the Europeans had to offer, and who was also the first seller of slaves, at the prices the king himself fixed.[60] This practice has given rise to the debate already alluded to, as to whether the slave trade was or became a royal monopoly on the African side. We shall return to that subject later.

Whatever the case, we need to stress that the slave trade on the Slave Coast was organized in a very different way from what prevailed in other regions. In Angola, for instance, there existed, we are told,[61] authentic slave markets on more or less neutral ground where the Europeans were relatively free to pick and choose, not being submitted to the kind of official regulations and pressure that the sources indicate were the rule on the Slave Coast. The Slave Coast was always organized in polities which we may call "kingdoms". And it was these "kingdoms" and their rulers the Europeans traded with, not more or less acephalous societies. Hence the necessity to be on as acceptable terms as possible with whoever held power.[62] Note that the organization in kingdoms implied guarantees for the European traders.

In fact, like all trade, the slave trade too needed a certain level of safety and predictability – law and order. That may sound surprising given the nature of the slave trade and the enormous loss of human life it implied. But the fact is that direct attacks on the slave traders were exceptionally rare on the Slave

Coast. The present author knows of only one, the so-called Carlton affair, when a sloop by that name was attacked in 1686 off Grand Popo and the captain and the cook killed.[63] It is true that we know about other cases too where European slave traders were killed and even executed. But this was not necessarily because they were slave traders, rather because they chose the wrong side in local civil wars or in wars between African rulers, or conspired against whoever was in power. European and Luso-Brazilian slave traders who stuck to their trade had a lot to fear from the local physical conditions and from slave revolts, but less so from the authorities. It may explain in part the "success" of the Slave Coast. When in certain regions or certain periods those authorities began acting arbitrarily or "playing tricks" on the traders – as happened, as we shall see, in the polity of Little Popo-Glidji on the Western Slave Coast from early on, and in Dahomey in the second half of the eighteenth century – the slave traders simply went elsewhere. For there was always elsewhere to go.

* * *

We need to return to the chronology regarding the arrival of the Europeans. The first missionaries to set foot on the Slave Coast were some French Capuchins who stayed at Hueda in 1644; this is the first time, to our knowledge, that Hueda appears in the sources.[64]

What were the French Capuchins doing in Hueda in 1644? Their mission was probably an offshoot of the very intermittent French interest in the Commendo/Eguafo region on the western Gold Coast from 1638, linked to the project of Jean-Baptiste Colbert (Louis XIV's powerful minister), quickly abandoned, to crush the quasi-monopoly of the Dutch over the gold trade.[65] French policy with regard to the Guinea coast was in fact, and continued to be, highly erratic.

The Capuchins in Hueda do not seem to have achieved anything, and the chapel they built was rapidly burnt down. Other Capuchin missionaries arrived more than 15 years later, in January 1660, and in Allada this time – eleven Spanish Capuchins. They were sent officially by King Philip IV of Spain (1621–65) who still considered himself to be the king of Portugal.[66] They arrived at a moment when the Dutch were probably absent temporarily. These Spanish Capuchins seemed, and were in a sense, totally out of context. The mission achieved apparently nothing anyway, and lasted only for a little more than year, having been actively combated by the returning Dutch. That being said, the mission is of considerable interest in the internal African context, since the sources it generated throw, as we shall see, an interesting, not to say intriguing light on a number of relevant subjects.

* * *

As noted, the English arrived on the Guinea coast in 1631–32. But the English Civil War (1642–51) curtailed England's overseas expansion in Africa. There followed a strange episode in 1657 when the famous East India Company tried to enter the Guinea trade – it needed bullion for its trade with India,[67] and may not have been active on the Slave Coast. Its intervention did not last, but it was a strange episode, because the shipping lanes between Europe and Asia avoided the Lower Guinea coast. Since the days of Bartolomeo Dias and his rounding of the Cape of Good Hope in 1488, and because of the prevailing winds and currents, the ships stood always far out from the Gulf of Guinea and in fact close to the Brazilian coast on their way southwards.[68]

But then, in September 1663, two English ships reached the region of Allada, where a factory was established.[69] The ships were sent by the Company of Royal Adventurers of England Trading into Africa, a chartered company created earlier the same year, and described as the most distinguished company ever to trade out of England, since it was owned by 31 members of the royal family – the clearest example we have, says Gijs Rommelse, of collaboration between the Crown and the City.[70] Its Director was none other than the Duke of York, the future King James II (1685–88).[71] J.R. Jones argues that it would be an exaggeration to describe it as an aristocratic treasure hunt,[72] implying that it has been so presented.

At Allada the Dutch tried their best to block the English scheme, but they were forced to live with it. Here was the beginning of the peculiar situation which came to characterize the centres of the Slave Coast, with several European nations present at the same site, and frequent clashes between them. The presence of the English and the resulting competition led to a somewhat dramatic rise in the slave trade.[73] What we have here is apparently the first genuine take-off of the slave trade from the Slave Coast.

Did the arrival of the English in Allada cause a major war between England and the Dutch Republic? Or was it just one of many factors? This was in any case a period of considerable tension between England and the Dutch Republic due, in the last instance, to the passing of the first English Navigation Act in 1651, an act directed very much against the Dutch. It led to constant frictions between the rival English and Dutch empires of trade all over the world.

The chronology is interesting. Indeed, in May 1664 (that is, eight months after the English arrived in Allada), an English naval force under the command of Captain Robert Holmes simply drove out the Dutch from the coast, except from Elmina Castle (and Allada). The English took over, in particular, the fort later known as Cape Coast Castle at Fetu,[74] situated within sight of Elmina, and reputedly the best place in Guinea for acquiring gold.[75]

But the Dutch counter-attack did not take long to come: in early 1665 the famous Admiral Michiel de Ruyter carried out a highly successful reprisal raid, sweeping the English out of West African waters, and capturing almost all the English establishments on the Gold Coast, including their headquarters at Cormantin (the English had been "beaten to dirt at Guinea", as Samuel Pepys put it in his famous Diary).[76] But de Ruyter did not try to take Cape Coast Castle, which then remained English, and became in fact the English headquarters.[77] The English factory at Offra was not eliminated either, being situated inland and thus outside of the reach of the Dutch cannon. An interesting detail: the Dutch captured an English ship which carried a letter of thanks from the Duke of York to the King of Allada, together with various objects also destined for the same king; they included a brass crown, which must have been of considerable value, since it ended up on display in the prestigious Rijksmuseum in Amsterdam.[78]

Whether it was the dispute over trading privileges on the West African coast that "became the occasion" for,[79] or the prelude to, or the cause of the Second Anglo-Dutch naval war (waged *de jure* from March 1665 to July 1667), or whether that war was simply the result of English aggression orchestrated by the Duke of York and his interest group of courtiers and naval officers, as J.R. Jones argues,[80] the events of 1664–67 demonstrated that both the English and the Dutch considered the forts and factories on the Guinea coast to be of prime importance.[81] But they also showed that it was impossible to defend those forts and factories against naval forces from Europe[82] – except those of the Slave Coast. The Dutch and the English were thus doomed to some sort of coexistence on the Guinea coast.

With regard to the Slave Coast, the WIC presumably reaped some short-term benefits from de Ruyter's victory. The war of 1665–67 crippled England's trade at Allada, it simply stopped.[83] Conversely, the Dutch presence and slave trade must have grown considerably, for we learn that around 1670 the WIC had a lodge there, so enormous that it looked like a sizeable village.[84]

But competitors arrived quickly, first the English, who must have returned after a short while, and second the French. The latter, having failed on the

Gold Coast, now tried their luck further east. What happened on 4 January 1670 was that two ships belonging to the new French West Indies Company (Compagnie des Indes Occidentales) arrived off Offra/Jakin, where there were five ships already, significantly all Dutch.[85] The French West Indies Company, although formally private, was in reality state-sponsored and state-owned. This was, then, an official mission designed to break into the Dutch-dominated slave trade. In fact, those in charge were naval officers, including the first among them, a certain Louis Delbée (or D'Elbée).[86] But the brain behind it all, and the one in charge of organizing the slave trade, of which the French had little experience, was a foreigner and a civilian, the fascinating Heinrich Caerloff. Caerloff ought not to occupy us too much since he is peripheral to our story, however we may note that Caerloff was probably in his late thirties in 1670 but already an old hand in the Guinea trade. Born in Pillau, presently Baltiysk in what is now the Russian enclave of Kaliningrad, he served with the WIC in many parts of West Africa. After that he switched to the Swedes, being in fact in charge of the Swedish attempt to gain a foothold on the Gold Coast. But in 1657 he went over to the Danes and led the Danish assault against the Swedes in 1658; Sweden and Denmark were at war at that time, a war which turned out to be a resounding disaster for Denmark, except – thanks to Caerloff – in Guinea. Finally Caerloff became naturalised French some time after 1663.[87]

The Delbée-Caerloff mission was relatively successful, at least in the short run, and in spite of inevitable strong Dutch opposition. Delbée, after having consigned to writing his interesting observations on Allada (see the next chapter), left with some 410 slaves, of whom a hundred died on the Middle Passage and the rest arrived in the West Indies in a rather miserable state, owing to the French lack of experience.[88] And Caerloff, left behind in Offra/Jakin, proceeded to establish a French lodge. A second expedition which arrived in October of the same year was designed to reinforce the French position. As for the king of Allada, he responded positively, even sending a certain Matéo Lopez, who could speak Portuguese, as ambassador to France.[89] Lopez was in fact granted audience by king Louis XIV himself on 19 December 1670.[90] Frustratingly, that embassy has not left anything of interest in the archives.

However, in 1671–72 all the protagonists came up against very severe problems, including the king of Allada, whose maritime provinces, Jakin and possibly also Offra, revolted with the aid of neighbouring Hueda. This led Caerloff to relocate his lodge to Glehue, the future Ouidah,[91] about 30 km.

further west. It is at this stage, then, that Ouidah-Glehue and Hueda genuinely enter our story.

As for the Europeans, they were all to suffer from a major conflagration in Europe, the so-called French-Dutch, or simply Dutch war of 1672–78. England under Charles II (1660–85) and France under Louis XIV mounted in 1672 a concerted effort to crush the Dutch Republic. Part of the war was fought at sea, and that part is called the Third Anglo-Dutch naval war (1672–74). The Dutch more than survived, thanks in part to De Ruyter.[92]

There were no hostilities in African waters this time, but the war meant the end of the companies which operated on the Guinea coast. However, in the case of the Dutch and the English, the problems proved to be transitory, and new, although remodelled companies were shortly established. In the case of the English, it took the shape of the Royal African Company of England (hereafter RAC, 1672–1751) which was like its predecessor close to the Stuarts while they reigned.[93] The RAC, which has gone down in history as the largest single slave-trading business of all time, succeeded in September 1674 in sending its first slave ships to Allada.[94] At the same time the English factory, which had probably been abandoned some years earlier, was reoccupied.[95] From then on there was a permanent British presence on the Slave Coast right up to 1812.

In the case of the Dutch, a new WIC reemerged in 1674. But although it was a reorganised and rather modest copy of its predecessor, its capital being only 15 per cent of the old WIC, it turned out to be a success for quite some time.[96]

The third party, the French, were the real losers, disappearing more or less from the scene until 1702, though with the exception, as we shall see, of some rather spectacular expeditions from time to time. The Dutch and the British, although frequently at loggerheads, at times collaborated in order to impede the French from gaining a foothold on the coast.[97] But the Luso-Brazilians with their tobacco began strongly to make their presence felt, although, as noted, without the benefit of any permanent establishment. Finally, Brandenburger-Prussian and Danish companies were also present occasionally in one way or another, especially the former. There is in fact little doubt that the Churfürstlich-Afrikanisch-Brandenburgische Compagnie, to quote its full name, was relatively active at Ouidah-Glehue in the 1680s and 1690s.[98]

* * *

All in all, it is clear that the late 1670s mark the real take-off of the Atlantic slave trade from the Slave Coast. Indeed, and as we have seen, according to the

Database the exports from the Bight of Benin/Slave Coast were multiplied by four in the relevant period (1676–1700), whereas the overall figure for all of Africa did not even double.

But what is the explanation? It is tempting to link it to another "take-off", that which has been described as "the first global industry" – "New World sugar production".[99] That "take-off" is in turn related to the so-called "sugar revolution". What happened was that the sugar plantation complex spread from its original homeland in northeastern Brazil to Barbados,[100] and then to many other Caribbean islands. (Islands – especially small and flat ones like Barbados – can be "ideal" places for plantations based on slavery, since there is nowhere for the slaves to escape to). This development was in part due to the more or less indirect incentives of the WIC. Hence a dramatic surge in the demand for slaves from Africa, and in fact the emergence of what has been called the South Atlantic System (the Atlantic slave trade plus the sugar plantation complex), converting it into what was for the epoch a colossal economic, and in its essence capitalist, circuit.[101] It was a circuit primarily aimed at satisfying the demand for sugar in northwestern Europe and mainly there – sugar never really caught on in Southern Europe, or for that matter in Africa. Possibly it was the supply from America which created the demand in Europe.[102] We note in this context Jan de Vries' point that "The acceleration and broadening of the demand for sugar…was anything but inevitable".[103] Sugar, not exactly an indispensable commodity, set the whole system in motion, thereby contributing powerfully, we repeat, to the economic upsurge of northwestern Europe. Cotton growing and all that was related to it in North America came very much later.[104]

The problem then is one of cause and effect: did the rise of the South Atlantic System provide the rulers and/or the people of the Slave Coast with, say, a golden opportunity? Or was it the supply on the Slave Coast which made possible the sugar revolution and everything that followed?[105] Put differently, was the expansion of the slave trade demand-driven, as Robin Law implies,[106] or was it on the contrary supply-driven, which, in the present author's opinion, it is equally or perhaps even more logical to argue? But if so, how to explain that supply, or in the opposite case, how to explain that the locals were able to satisfy the demand?

The conclusion is in any case that there exists a strong link between the sugar revolution in the Caribbean and the tremendous rise in slave exports from the Slave Coast.

* * *

The slave trade was the only substantial sector of late seventeenth century English colonial commerce subjected to company organization.[107] Hence it was only logical that those who clamoured for "free trade", in the sense of non-monopolistic trade, should target the slave trade and the RAC for special attention. If we add that the slave trade promised huge gains from the 1680s (a promise not always fulfilled), we can go on to present a new personage who now entered the scene: the interloper. We are referring to the freelance traders excluded from the monopolistic charter system who were nevertheless determined to have their share of the slave trade regardless of what the official regulations and laws stipulated.[108] Hence they advocated "free trade". But they were contraband slavers from a formal point of view. It was certainly not an exclusive English phenomenon; Dutch interlopers (called *lorredraayers*) also made their impact felt from an early date.[109] As for the third major protagonist, the Luso-Brazilians, they were not saddled with this problem – the Portuguese slave trade was and remained "free" in the sense indicated above.

Both the RAC and the WIC combated the interlopers actively. For instance, at one stage the Dutch had five heavily armed cruisers on the coast, the largest one with 32 cannon, to pursue them and also the Luso-Brazilians who failed to pay the obligatory tax at Elmina.[110] One imagines that it drained the resources of both companies.

It may be nevertheless that the interlopers (that is, free traders) contributed in the final instance to the "success" of the slave trade. Their great advantage was that they did not have to worry about the expense of maintaining land bases. Theirs was in fact what is called ship trade. But they did not have to worry either about what Willem Bosman, a WIC employee, called the customs of the land, that is, they did not have to respect the prices the companies tried to enforce[111] – they were in fact accused of driving up the prices, which they obviously did. For that reason the interlopers were welcomed with open arms by the local rulers. As the king of Hueda put it, "those that bring the most & best goods, shall have the most & best slaves".[112]

Actually, the interlopers made themselves indispensable for the slave trade more generally, including the Company trade; they provided the necessary flexibility. Indeed, when the rigid system of the Companies failed – that is, when a fort or lodge was left without provisions – one could always turn to the interlopers.[113] More generally speaking, the WIC protected the English interlopers, and the RAC did the same with the Dutch ones, and so on. This was especially the case of the personnel in the outer forts and minor posts, who were often left to their own devices and therefore found it at times expedient to establish trading relations with the interlopers.[114]

Having mentioned the interlopers, we must also add another group which constituted a nuisance for the companies, namely the pirates, corsairs and privateers. The pirates were not exclusively a Caribbean phenomenon then, contrary to what we are at times led to believe.[115] Interlopers, pirates, corsairs, privateers: the categories seem to have been more or less interchangeable and it is not always easy to determine who was who (apart from the fact that corsairs and privateers were in theory official agents of their respective governments). Whatever the case, we know, as indicated earlier, of quite a few slave ships lost to pirates. Outside of the Slave Coast properly speaking, the island of Príncipe was a frequent target.[116]

* * *

One obvious conclusion that can be drawn from the above is that on the Slave Coast at least the Europeans were very much divided among themselves, they never constituted anything resembling a united front. Actually, the impression one has is that the competition on the European side was always very severe. All this was to the advantage of the opposite side. There is then no reason to believe that the Africans were in any way, let us say, "underpaid" for their slaves.

Actually, given the obviously huge expenses slaving on the very complicated Slave Coast implied, and the limited profits the Europeans must have derived from it, one is left to wonder why they bothered at all. Perhaps the ultimate explanation is non-economic, something to the effect that opting out would be damaging to a country's prestige, and worse, would leave the other European competitors with what was perceived to be too great an advantage.

* * *

The Africans were in a sense equally divided. For by the time the slave trade took off once again, Allada became confronted with a competitor and rival, the neighbouring and tiny polity ("kingdom") of Hueda, Savi being its palatial capital (the distance between Savi and Allada town is a mere 30 km). Hueda was in theory a vassal of Allada, but an increasingly rebellious one.[117] However, behind Allada and Hueda other polities lurked: Dahomey in the immediate hinterland, Akwamu and especially Oyo further afield. Caught in between were Eweland and many other regions.

It is time, then, to turn to the African side of the story.

2

THE AFRICAN SIDE

THE EARLY/LEGENDARY PAST

A team of Danish archaeologists under the direction of Klavs Randsborg has recently demonstrated that the inland Abomey plateau, the core land of Dahomey, was settled by what they call "developed" societies from at least the seventh century BCE, and by "advanced" societies from the seventh century AD. According to them, the eleventh and twelfth centuries AD represented a peak period during which a genuine kingdom emerged in the region, a kingdom they link to the name "Dauma" which figures in this area on some European maps of the sixteenth century.[1] It is clear that the material basis of this flourishing was metallurgy. The archaeologists have in fact unearthed traces of ancient iron production on a huge scale, that is, far exceeding local needs and hence destined in part for export. The relevant area comprises not only the Abomey plateau but also the region to the south-west, and the oldest date so far is from the eleventh century AD. But this iron production, which needed enormous quantities of charcoal, must have depleted whatever there may have been of forest, and ceased therefore rather abruptly in the late sixteenth or the early seventeenth century.[2]

What do we make of these rather spectacular finds, and how do they fit in with what we know about the past from other sources? Here we must introduce the town of Tado situated some 40 km west of Abomey, on the other side of the present-day border between the Republics of Benin and Togo. Tado, also called Ajatado (or Adjatado), is to-day a rather insignificant village. But there is reason to believe that it was at some stage in the past, possibly between the fourteenth and seventeenth centuries, an important metropolis which held sway, effectively or ritually, over a relatively large area.³ Tado in fact looms large in the local oral traditions, being the town from which most ethnic groups and relevant dynasties of the Slave Coast claim descent.⁴ Those claims must show that it carried prestige to hail from Tado. But at some stage, the oral traditions tell us, Tado was rocked by severe convulsions, which led to a number of exoduses and the fall from prominence of that once presumably mighty town. Tado remains however a near-blank from an archaeological point of view; those Danish archaeologists were apparently unable to go as far, presumably because of the border. We do know, however, thanks to Alexis Adande, that there are or were vestiges of old walls at Tado. One is supposed to have surrounded the town, and the other the royal enclosure.⁵ We also know that Tado is situated only a few kilometres' distance from some of the known iron-producing sites on the other side of the modern border. We know too what is most important, that blacksmiths occupy a central role in the oral traditions referring to Tado.

Given all this, it is tempting to make a hypothesis: first, that the iron-producing region extended westwards, encircling Tado, and/or that Tado lorded it over the Abomey plateau (Dauma could be Tado); and second, that Tado's fall from prominence is linked to the end of metallurgy on a large scale. It is in any case difficult to avoid the conclusion that there exists some kind of link between the discoveries made by the Danish archaeologists and the traditions concerning Tado. What that link precisely is, only future archaeological excavations can determine.

* * *

Before looking into the oral traditions of Tado, we need to know that blacksmiths were very special people in Africa of old; they were considered to be expert magicians since they had received the ability to manipulate fire. But an important group (kindred) of blacksmiths also creates tension; they have their own divinities and their own "priests" (the "iron-priests", those who control the blacksmith shrines), and are therefore not always likely to respect the ascendancy of an "earth-priest" or an "earth-priest" turned sacred king. "Iron-priests" may, if their following is numerous, as we presume was the case in Tado, aspire to power themselves.⁶ Hence, perhaps, the confusing traditions of Tado, possibly reflecting the struggle between various groups for supremacy.

According to the traditions collected by Roberto Pazzi, the origin of Tado was the result of a pact or alliance between three kindreds and three corresponding neighbourhoods or wards. Two of these wards were inhabited by indigenous people. But the Alu blacksmiths, reputed to have descended from heaven, were more "ancient" than the Azanu or Dome, the other indigenes. The third ward was inhabited by what Pazzi calls the Ayo or Adja immigrants. There was also a fourth ward, for the traders,[7] as befitted a commercial hub of considerable importance which it is evident Tado must have been.[8]

Now, all the versions evolve around the first three groups: the Azanu (the descendants of Aza, -*nu* always meaning people), the Alu and the Ayo/Adja. But they differ as to which group held the kingship and which group or groups controlled the apparently powerful state council. These then constitute the main theme of the traditions as we have them.

Since the Alu were blacksmiths, we assume that their head was an "iron-priest". But given the fact that the majority of the population (the Azanu and the Ayo/Adja) were farmers, the next logical step would be for us to go looking for an "earth-priest". The most likely candidate is one Togbé-Anyi, who is presented as the first "king" of Tado. But it so happens that Togbé means "ancestor" and Anyi, a variant of *aï*, means "earth"[9] – one obvious implication being that we are not dealing with an individual as such. The next point is that this Togbé-Anyi bore the title of *anyigbafio*,[10] a title we have already encountered frequently, and which we have translated as "earth-priest" (as noted *anyi* means earth, *anyigba* means the earth deity and *fio* or *fia* means chief or headman/king). If it means earth-priest, we can imagine that the title was conserved once the "earth-priest" had become sacred king – if, that is, the institution of "earth-priest" grew into that of sacred king. But the troubling point here is that according to one version, the first king, called Togbé-Anyi in this version too, was a prince from Oyo in Yorubaland, which implies that he was of the stock of Pazzi's Ayo.[11] As such he was surrounded by a seven-member council of state composed of the indigenous Azanu. All this implies a "classic" contrapuntal paramountcy-setup. But if so, what happened to the Alu?

In another version[12] we learn that the Alu had to submit to the combined forces of the Ayo/Adja and the Azanu, the Azanu in this version providing the king, and in fact preserving the institution of kingship up to the present. So the Alu were the great losers in this version too? Not quite, since the Pazzi version has it that the kings of Tado actually allied themselves with those who controlled the "mysterious power of the forge".[13] Furthermore, and according to Gayibor, the esoteric power of the Alu manifested itself on the occasion of the enthronement of the kings[14] (exactly how we are not told). What is more, the Alu were considered to be the uterine "uncles" of the king, and as such not required to approach the king crawling on all fours and covering themselves with dust like the rest.[15] In addition the Alu continued to be all-important as soothsayers, magicians, sorcerers and so on.[16] Although all this may not be contrapuntal paramountcy in the classical sense of the term, one may be forgiven for feeling that it does resemble one.

In the last-mentioned version it is therefore the Ayo/Adja who have disappeared. Actually, in none of the versions is there room for all three groups. It leads us to the suspicion that the traditions refer to a never-ending power struggle, implying perhaps that the kingship was not always in the custody of the same group.

We add for good measure that the apparent successor of the king of Tado, the head of the village of Tohoun, was referred to in the colonial era as not only "*chef de la terre*" (that is, *anyigbafio*), but also as a priest, and as such as a rainmaker in charge of fertility cults.[17] It was probably the one whom the French officer D'Albéca encountered in 1895 and whom he presents as a sort of local pontiff.[18]

Whatever the case, the kings of Tado are portrayed by Nicoué Gayibor, the leading authority in these matters, as a typical sacred king.[19] Indeed, the *anyigbafio* lived secluded in his palace and all (except then the Alu in one version) were required to prostrate themselves in his presence, since no-one, not even his wives, could look him in the face. In order to maintain his magical fluid, the fluid which permitted him to control the occult forces of nature, his feet could not enter into contact with the soil.

All this is timeless, as befitting oral traditions.

* * *

We must mention the point made by Suzanne Preston Blier that Tado, apart from being a place-name, is also a common noun meaning "origins". The worrying implication is of course that Tado was not one single place.[20] But if so, why claim foreign origin, if it could be anywhere, and hence not likely to carry much prestige?

As noted, an upheaval occurred in Tado at some stage, linked to the reign of a particularly tyrannical king. One group of people revolted, tried to seize power, but failed in the end and had to flee. They came to be known as the Aja or Agasuvi. They went southeastwards, but not very far, some 40 km, to the region known as Allada, where they established the polity of that name. But others moved (at the same time?) some 70 kilometres southwestwards, where they founded Notsé. From Allada the Aja-Agasuvi branched off in various directions, establishing especially Dahomey in the north and, somewhat later, Porto Novo/Hogbonu in the east.

In Notsé (Nuatja) too there are vestiges from the past, in the shape of some large unfinished walls and a ditch system that enclosed most of the settlement. There is also a smaller inner wall whose purpose may have been to isolate the royal domain – a classic pattern in the region. All this indicates that the town may have been of importance in earlier centuries, as both a religious and an economic centre.[21]

As for the institutional setup at Notsé, what the oral traditions, as presented to us by Nicoué Gayibor and Nii Quarcoopome, have to tell us is intriguing in the extreme. According to those traditions, Eda, the first king, was installed by the *mawuno*, presented as the priest of Mawu (only Mawu, not Mawu-Liisa) who was also the head of the neighbouring village of Tegbe. And the people of that village claim that they have always lived there, that is, since before the arrival of the people from Tado; so they claim indigenous status. Since the *mawuno* continued to play possibly the central role in the enthronement rites of the kings,[22] the temptation is obviously great to imagine the emergence of some sort of contrapuntal paramountcy with the *mawuno* in the role of the indigenous "earth-priest". But the *mawuno* was, as said, the priest of Mawu, and the king, after being installed, assumed the title of *mawufia*, king of Mawu, along with (once more) that of *anyigbafia*.[23] At this juncture it is easy to get lost in all sorts of conjectures and speculations – for instance the possibility that Mawu, later presented as some sort of Supreme God, may have been originally simply the earth spirit – while forgetting that loose ends and crooked lines are inevitable in the type of context with which we are concerned. Whatever the case, what seems beyond doubt is that the king of Notsé was a typical (secluded) sacred king surrounded by the inevitable council of state.[24]

In Notsé too we encounter the archetypical tyrannical king who provoked an exodus, the fourth one in the official king-list. But in the Notsé case he has a name, he is called Agokoli (or Agorkoli); a king whom Gayibor has attempted, it seems to us, to convert into a tragic hero. He was, according to Gayibor, some sort of revolutionary who tried to transform the Notsé polity into something resembling a centralized and authentic state – a positive aim according to Gayibor, who regrets in a sense that Agokoli did not succeed.[25]

As it was, Agokoli failed because of his own excesses, related to the construction of the walls, and also because he found himself confronted with a determined conservative opposition. Gayibor's thesis is that the action of Agokoli inoculated the Ewes, as it were, against the institution of kingship.[26]

In order to forestall a repetition of the Agokoli episode, kingship became rotational, and it was decided that no king could reign more than three years. At the end of those three years the king died a ritual death, as Gayibor puts it laconically.[27] But if so, we imagine that the task of finding a new king every three years must have become a rather arduous one, although the fact that the kingship alternated between several clans[28] may perhaps have made the task somewhat less demanding.

If the Agokoli story has anything to do with what really happened in the past, and if we are correct in believing that it is all about a king trying to liberate himself from the straightjacket of sacred kingship, then that story is reminiscent of cases already referred to, those of Congo, Benin and Oyo. But if so, the outcome was something close to disaster in all four cases. That being said, it is interesting to note that the priest-kingship (if that is what it was) of Notsé has survived more or less to the present, although completely overshadowed since the beginning of the colonial era by the *yovofia*, literally "white man's chief"[29] – *fia* again. In fact, even as late as the 1810s the priest-king of Notsé was still considered to be a great priest throughout the region[30] – but apparently not for very long afterwards.[31]

There is a small community known as the Adele who live in the mountains north of Atakpame, outside Eweland – another group of people speaking Ghana-Togo mountain languages. Pazzi argues that these Adele were the indigenous inhabitants of the Notsé region from whence they fled. Nevertheless, each king of Notsé (before or after Agokoli or both?), had to make, before his enthronement, a three months' journey to the land of the Adele in order to be initiated. Pazzi concludes that the voyage northwards indicates that the kings of Notsé were in a sense subordinate to the Adele.[32] What do we make of it?

As for the second part of what Paul Nugent calls the Notsé meta-narrative,[33] the contention that all the Ewe originated from Notsé and that they spread out over the future Eweland because the region was empty of people, it is, we repeat, a story to which the modern anthropologists and historians do not subscribe.

We also repeat, lest anyone should be in doubt, that we do not know to what extent, if any, anything of the above (and most of the below) relates to what really happened in the past. But the point is that the oral traditions we have summarized provide us with a magnificent glimpse into the world outlook and the structuring of the societies of the Slave Coast of old.

* * *

We now turn to the traditions collected by the first Europeans who interested themselves in the past of the Slave Coast, namely three Spanish churchmen who wrote in the seventeenth century. Two of them we have mentioned fleetingly already, Alonso de Sandoval and Joseph de Naxara (José de Nájera in modern Spanish). Sandoval was an unorthodox missionary who worked among the slaves in Cartagena de Indias (in modern Colombia), a major hotbed of illicit slave trading,[34] from 1605 to his death in 1652. Although he never went to Africa, he published a book in 1627 in which he assigned to paper what he had learned from his African interlocutors in Cartagena.[35] Naxara on the other hand did go to Africa, he was a member of the aforementioned Spanish mission to Allada in 1660–61, and he went prepared since he had read Sandoval.[36] The third of our Spanish clerics was Basilio de Zamora, another of Sandoval's readers, and high up in the Capuchin order. As such he had access to material left behind by the 1660–61 mission, although he himself, like Sandoval, never set foot in Africa.[37]

The three are agreed that the ruler of the kingdom of Popo ("*Reyno de los Popoes*") was at some time in the past a sort of emperor over the whole region in the sense that a great many kings paid allegiance to him, including the king of Allada. The emperor himself lived some seventy "*leguas*" inland, an uncomfortable fact, since it means 250 km, far beyond the Slave Coast as defined in this book (and far beyond Tado). To the east was Fulao, and then Ardaso, which we identify with, respectively, Foulaen in Tori and Allada (on the old polity of Tori, see next chapter). And either the king of Fulao/Tori or the king of Allada (the sources are confusing) had to wage war against the latter to liberate himself. During this war the emperor of Popo was slain by one of his two vassals. But the people of Allada and/or Fulao/Tori conserved a severed hand of the emperor of Popo which became a holy relic for the victors, the object of a fertility cult.

When did all this happen? According to Naxara, some eight generations before his time,[38] and he wrote in the 1660s – so perhaps around or before 1500. A modern author, Nicoué Gayibor, refers to the above as Allada's war of liberation against Popo, and identifies the latter place with present-day Grand Popo, that is, Hulagan.[39] If so, the emperor of Popo could have been none other than the *Hulaholu* of Hulagan mentioned before. This makes some sense, considering the position of the Hula as possibly the indigenous people of the coastal region, and that of the *Hulaholu* as (still possibly) a ruler of some importance in earlier times. Furthermore, in Naxara's time his kingdom of Popo was certainly the western neighbour of Allada (Fulao/Tori having become a vassal of Allada) and still a power to be reckoned with. But one of the problems in this context (there are others) is the name Popo, which seems to have been unknown to the local population in earlier times.[40]

Whatever the case, Gayibor believes that Grand Popo experienced a prolonged period of inexorable decline after its defeat by Fulao/Tori and/or Allada.[41] But if so, as noted, many people of the region, including those of Aneho and Little Popo, continued to acknowledge at least implicitly the religious-ritual authority of the "Master of the Lagoon", that is, the *Hulaholu*.[42]

We cannot leave the matter of Allada-Fulao/Tori versus Popo without mentioning Jakin and Offra, the twin towns which served as Allada's commercial hub and which may correspond, as noted, to modern Godomey. But the relationship between the two is far from clear. Actually, we know very little about Offra. But Jakin was obviously a genuine principality, and a *Hula* principality at that – paying tribute to the king of Allada with loaves of salt, according to Dalzel.[43] Hence it is not surprising that Jakin was a rather unruly vassal, revolting against Allada in 1671–72, as we have seen, and later often going its own way. Actually, Jakin must have been one of many Hula groups or pockets along the coast which made life difficult for the rulers of Allada. What Offra was exactly, we do not know, but certainly it was a rival of Jakin, considering the hostility between the two, hostility which explains in turn why Jakin took part in the destruction of Offra in 1692. That event may have tilted the balance in favour of Jakin's ally Hueda in its struggle with Allada.[44]

***

Allada constitutes the link between the Tado-Notsé and the Popo (or Sandoval-Naxara-Zamora) stories. But even so, it is not easy to reconcile the two. We can at least note that the former refers principally to the interior and the latter to the coast and possibly to an earlier period. What is noteworthy in any case is that the corpus of oral tradition which began to be committed to writing in the early colonial period, more than two centuries after the Spanish mission, is silent about Popo and the Hula. Actually, the Tado-Notsé narrative had become dominant by then, as people claiming descent from Tado and Notsé have assimilated the Hula to a considerable extent. The defeat of the "Emperor of Popo" by the king of Allada may be considered to be paradigmatic-symbolic in this context, whether it actually happened or not. Indeed, so powerful is the Tado-Notsé narrative that even the Hula themselves were contaminated and began, according to one author, to claim such a descent.[45]

* * *

The Tado-Notsé narrative implies that some groups of people, small or not, moved southwards. If so, it may have been because the south was thinly populated, although the Popo narrative seems to imply the contrary. Or it may have to do with the arrival of the Europeans and the new plants and new animals they introduced – in brief, the desire to take part in whatever opportunities the new situation presented the locals with.[46] But in the latter case we are talking about the sixteenth and even the seventeenth century, rather late dates.

Finally, it has been speculated recently that the Black Death from 1347 onwards and some of the subsequent plague epidemics may have reached Guinea, specifically the land of the Akan in present-day Ghana.[47] If that is the case, it may well have affected the Slave Coast too. And if so again, one may wonder what is the relationship with the findings of the archaeologists and with the Tado-Notsé narrative. In this case we are at least dealing with somewhat earlier dates than the ones suggested above.

* * *

What can be concluded? That the Tado-Notsé narrative is not without a certain logic, but that the Popo one complicates everything. It is tempting, therefore, to argue that those Spanish churchmen have got it all wrong. But it is a temptation we believe should be resisted.

One final problem: was Allada established by people coming from Tado, or is it much older, as the Popo narrative seems to imply? It is time, then, to have a closer look at that polity.

3

ALLADA, ITS VASSALS AND NEIGHBOURS, AND THE EUROPEANS

The oral traditions of Allada are, we repeat, difficult to reconcile with the Popo narrative. Or rather, there are in a sense *two* sets of Allada traditions. One constitutes the prologue or introductory chapter, as it were, to the Dahomean ones, the official Dahomean traditions that is, as enshrined partially in Le Hérissé's book[1] – the Allada-Dahomey narrative, in sum. Of the other tradition, only bits and pieces have survived and surface here and there, thanks in part to the labour of the anthropologist Jacques Lombard.[2] (It is incidentally also difficult to reconcile with the Popo story.)

The reputed four versions or variants of the Allada-Dahomey narrative[3] tell basically the same story; a story in which the town of Tado is presented as the cradle of the dynasties which came to rule Allada, Dahomey and Porto Novo/Hogbonu respectively. The story begins with a Tado princess named Aligbonu who bore a son called Agasu with a male leopard (or a spirit in leopard form – the leopard is always associated with royalty and with power).[4] This Agasu became the founding ancestor of a new kindred (clan or lineage) we have met already, that of the Agasuvi (*vi*=sons) – the Leopard sib, as the Herskovits call it.[5] Agasu's son or grandson in turn was Ajahuto (or Adjahouto).[6] Who did exactly what of the two is somewhat obscure. But as noted, the traditions make it clear that the Agasuvi failed in their attempt to seize power in Tado. They had to flee, and Ajahuto led them to a country called Aïzonou-tômè or Aïda-tômè, meaning the land of the Aïzo, also called Aïda (*tô* or *tômè* means place or land).[7] There Ajahuto went on to found the polity we know as Allada. And the Agasuvi then became also the Alladahonu, called after their new ancestral home, Allada, where the remains of Agasu were buried. Indeed, the king of Allada with his residence at Togudo (east of the present-day town of Allada) became the *agasunon* and the *ajahutonun*, that is the high priest of the cults of Agasu and Ajahuto, the two royal ancestors. In a sense the king *was* Ajahuto.[8]

What happened then to the indigenous Aïzo? (*aï*, it should be recalled, means earth/land and Aïzo refers always to "owners of the land"/firstcomers, those who have emerged from holes in the earth as firstcomers often claim to have done).[9] According to the Allada-Dahomey narrative, Ajahuto's "force" (*"génie"*) was so overwhelming that after his death he replaced or supplanted the *vodun* Aïda/Aïzo presented as a snake.[10] He became thus the *vodun* of the earth (*tôvodun*), accumulating as it were several positions, since he was already *vodun* of the royal clan or lineage. The implication here is that the newcomers could present themselves as, and could claim to be, the new "owners of the land".[11] It obviously constitutes a gross attempt at manipulation. By propagating this version, whoever came up with it also tried to justify the (later) attempt by the Dahomean rulers to eradicate the position of the local "owners of the land". Indeed, the general thrust of this and other traditions is that the Aïzo were few and far between, and the newcomers correspondingly numerous, after which the former were more or less assimilated by the latter, and subsequently the Aïzo played only a marginal role. The implication is that no kind of contrapuntal paramountcy was needed or emerged.

Unsurprisingly, the other (non-official) narrative has a rather different story to tell. Although it seems to accept the Tado tale, it says the newcomers acknowledged that the local people had "earth-priests" whose ritual control of the earth was and remained undisputed.[12] One of these was a certain Tè, Teïdo or Tedo, chief of Davié, who after his death was elevated to the rank of divinity. As such he became one of a number of divinities of the indigenous population which continued to be honoured in the Allada of the Ajatadonu.[13] There existed in Allada, at least up to the 1970s, a Te Dono presented by Claude-Hélène Perrot as the priest of Aïzo Tedo, the chief-turned-deity, the former "*Maître du sol*", of whom Te Dono was the direct descendant.[14] More generally, the newcomers did not contest the primacy of the Aïzo, the "*maîtres de terre*" ("owners of the land" or "earth-priests"), who continued to be recruited among them.[15]

This brings us to the question of contrapuntal paramountcy. There is no direct irrefutable evidence that it constituted the institutional setup of

Allada. But there is a lot of indirect or circumstantial evidence that points in that direction.

However, leaving that subject for a while, we wish to summarize what we know with reasonably certainty about the structure and history of the Alladan polity more generally, and from other sources. And here the conclusion is clear: Allada displayed most, possibly all of the ingredients of a polity of the traditional kind. Among them was a sacred king who lived as a recluse in his palace, and who governed the metropolitan area, probably with a council, the rest of the territory being made up of autonomous principalities whose hereditary rulers paid allegiance to the king.[16]

Among the vassal polities we have already mentioned the principal ones, namely Hueda, Jakin and Dahomey – Dahomey is in fact explicitly referred to by the Spanish sources[17] and must thus have been a power of some importance already in the 1650s/60s. But there were others, notably Tori (or Tori-Bossito) situated halfway between the town of Allada and the sea, and Hevie close by. Both clearly have very interesting pasts and equally interesting structures; "earth-priests" and what look like sacred kings figure prominently, and there are also traces of contrapuntal paramountcy.[18] As for Tori, which figures prominently, as we have seen, in the Sandoval-Naxara-Zamora Popo narrative via its (Hula?) "port" of Foulaen or Fulao, it may have been a power of some importance in the seventeenth century, possibly even lording it over Grand Popo for some time, and also over Hueda.[19] By the time of Willem Barbot, Tori had actually become completely independent, if we are to believe him.[20]

Hevie, which pops up frequently in many contexts, is reputed to have been the cradle of no less than a whole family of *vodun*.[21] Then there was Apa on the coast far out east, also a vassal principality,[22] which suggests that the king of Allada controlled (indirectly) the coast for some way eastwards.

Did the rulers of these vassal principalities claim descent from Agasu? Those of Dahomey certainly did (but from when?), but probably not the others, in spite of Le Hérissé's contention that the rulers of Tori too were of the stock of the Agasuvi;[23] it smacks of propaganda. In the case of Jakin for instance, we are dealing, as noted, with a Hula polity, as reflected in its formal name, Pla, a variant of Hula (although the polity is referred to generally as Jakin in our sources, that name is strictly speaking the title of its ruler).[24]

In any case, what we know of the smaller vassal polities (Tori, Hevie, Apa and others) is unfortunately much too fragmentary to allow any detailed reconstruction of their past; we are permitted only a few glimpses.

It is probable that the king of Allada in turn paid tribute to the *oba* (ruler) of the Edo polity of Benin far to the east.[25] We know that Benin expanded westwards to Lagos in its heyday – Lagos originated as a Benin war-camp – and possibly beyond.[26] Lagos, formally a vassal of Benin up until the colonial era,[27] was already a frontier town full of soldiers in 1603–4, according to some German visitors in the service of the WIC.[28] But it was also an important regional trading centre even at that early date, as the hub of a vast inland water system, if we are to believe Sandra Barnes.[29]

The Benin expansion westwards may have begun very early, according to Ryder, who presents evidence that already in the 1540s the Oba held prisoner an ambassador sent to him by the ruler of "Arida", that is, Allada.[30] And according to the Spanish missionaries, in 1660–61 Benin was the neighbour of Allada.[31] But if so, that situation did not last. The Frenchman Louis Delbée noted in 1671 that Allada was often at war with Benin *and* with the Yoruba kingdom of Oyo far inland.[32] If that is correct it suggests that Allada was, by that time, at the very least an undocile vassal of Benin.

How extensive was Allada's regional hegemony at its height? It covered virtually the whole of the Slave Coast, if we are to believe Robert Norris, who wrote in the 1780s, and who made the possibly extravagant claim that Allada's dominance extended from the Volta to Lagos and north to the Lama.[33] If so, it included incidentally the "Kingdom" of Popo.

If we ask next how old Allada was, we run into an unanswerable question, which is also absurd in a sense. It all depends on our definition of Allada. The impression we are left with is that on the central Slave Coast (to take only that example) there existed many centres of considerable antiquity – Allada/Togudo-Awude, Grand Popo/Hulagan, Tori, Hevie, Tado, Abomey, Kana, Jakin, Savi and others. Their history is a sort of ebb and flow, one centre rising to prominence and lording it over the others, or some of the others, before being superseded by a rival centre, which in turn was superseded by a third such centre, and so on. Something of the same may also have happened internally, a local "earth-priest" (or "iron-priest" or "water-priest", etc.) becoming a sacred king for a while, while reverting to his former position as *primus inter pares* when the material basis for the local sacred kingship evaporated. In this context one suspects that especially the past of Tori and Hevie is of particular relevance.

* * *

We must return to the Allada of roughly the second half of the seventeenth century in order to repeat that on the European side the Dutch were dominant

ALLADA, ITS VASSALS AND NEIGHBOURS, AND THE EUROPEANS

(with a sporadic English presence). But as already pointed out, we have the episode of the Spanish Capuchin missionaries in 1660–61 and the French Delbée-Caerloff expedition of 1671–72. Those episodes have left considerable source material, all the more valuable considering the dearth of Dutch (and English) material.[34] And it so happens that the Spanish and French sources throw some interesting light on the nature and structure of Allada. As for the story of the Spanish Capuchins, it is also of interest in its own right, one reason being that it constitutes an instance where local history blends with global history.

It is a remarkable fact that the initiative for the Capuchin mission came from the authorities of Allada, probably the king. The story begins in 1657 when a certain Bans or Vans, accompanied by his servant, arrived in Cartagena de Indias and presented himself as an ambassador sent by the king of Allada to the court of King Philip IV of Spain. The local Spanish officials chose to take him seriously, even though he had no written credentials of any sort. Hence he was quickly despatched to Spain where he arrived in February 1658 and was soon introduced to the court. He was of course also introduced to the Catholic version of Christianity, and both Bans and his servant were duly baptized, Bans becoming Felipe Zapata.[35] Philip IV was enthusiastic,[36] the Papacy apparently also. Indeed, the Sacra Congregatio de Propaganda Fide (usually as simply Propaganda Fide), founded in 1622 to direct missionary activity, issued a decree dated 4 February 1659 formally establishing the mission to the Kingdom of Arda (Allada).[37] It had become then a serious and official business, involving quite a few important people, and it was to generate a lot of correspondence in all directions.[38] It was also a mission which was intended to last, the missionaries being required to send reports every year, and plans were made to replace those who might die. But even before that, the preparation for the mission had generated a remarkable text, a catechism of the Christian religion in Spanish and the (Gbe) language of Allada,[39] compiled thanks to the collaboration of Bans/Felipe Zapata, and published in record time in Madrid in late 1658; this was the earliest written text in any West African language. It was entitled *Doctrina Christiana*.[40]

The eleven missionaries who finally sailed,[41] together with Bans/Felipe and some others, arrived in Allada (at Offra?) on 14 January 1660 after 50 days at sea, and stayed there for little more than a year (during which time no less than five of them died);[42] we do not know when exactly they left. The missionaries' instructions were clear, first to convert the king – in fact, not to convert anyone before the king.[43]

In the beginning everything went well for the Spaniards, they were enchanted by the landscape,[44] and especially by the hearty welcome they received in the capital and from the king. What surprised them most was that they realized that they had come to a very densely populated region, a fact they thought explained the slave trade – the people of Allada sold their own, according to the missionaries.[45]

They had no problem of communication – many people spoke Portuguese[46] ("*ladinos e inteligentes de nuestra lengua*"), among them a group of at least nominal Christians, although in the manner of the country, that is, polygamous and abiding by the local customs and rituals[47] ("*en España, como en España, y en Arda, como en Arda*"[48] [Allada] – "when in Rome as the Romans do", very freely translated). Nothing of this is really surprising considering the earlier strong position of the Portuguese, the vicinity of São Tomé, and previous missions to Warri and Benin (see below for that of Benin). As for the king, he was clearly eager to convert to Christianity, and even considered himself to have done so after the missionaries sprinkled him with holy water. In fact, he made the missionaries understand that his father and predecessor had already thought of converting but had been prevented from doing so by the "dignitaries".[49]

And yet, in spite of all that, everything went wrong after a while. Bans/Vans relapsed.[50] So did also a strange personage who had apparently accompanied the missionaries from Spain, one who had lived for many years in Spain, and who even had a wife and children there.[51] Worse, relations with the king soured rapidly; the missionaries, the six who survived, were after a while kept prisoners in the enormous royal compound forbidden to proselytize and to teach, and in fact reduced literally to begging. Finally, they were more or less expelled and had to leave in Dutch ships – the ultimate humiliation.[52]

The consequences of this short episode, if any, were rather limited. But the central question is, of course, what lay behind it. The explanation which comes immediately to mind is that from the Alladan side it was an attempt to promote trade, to diversify the polity's external contacts – that is, to break the Dutch monopoly – and from the Spanish side, an attempt to get a foothold on the Guinea coast. There is a lot of support for this common sense interpretation, as it may be called, in the sources. But on the other hand, if commercial considerations were paramount on the Alladan side, why choose Spain, a most unlikely trading partner in that part of the world at that time, why not Portugal, England or even France? And why missionaries?

Let us have a look at the broader picture. First, the Allada mission was not the first Spanish Capuchin mission in Guinea. It had been preceded by one to the kingdom of Benin in 1651–52, which was also a failure – possibly because the Spaniards confused Benin with its neighbour to the south, the apparently Christian Warri-Itsekiri polity. Secondly, as noted, Portugal seceded from the Spanish crown in 1640, an act which, as the Spaniards tried to impede it, led to war between the two countries until 1668. The Spanish monarchy was naturally reluctant to let go of the vast Portuguese overseas empire. One of the consequences of this situation was that the slave trade to Spanish America via the famous *asiento* system – the farming out of that trade through contracts (*asientos*) between the Spanish government and private individuals, usually Portuguese traders – was in a state of limbo, and remained so until 1662–63.[53] Spain itself, it should be noted, was formally barred from directly taking part in the slave trade by the treaty of Tordesillas with Portugal, in force from 1494 to 1750, as that treaty, with papal sanction, placed Africa in the Portuguese sphere. But Philip IV still considered himself to be the legitimate king of Portugal, so that the missionaries sent to Allada were instructed to correspond with the Consejo Supremo de Portugal (Supreme Council for Portuguese affairs) in Madrid, which continued to function.[54] On the other hand, officially patronizing a mission to Allada, which was after all in the Portuguese sphere, could lead to all sorts of diplomatic complications. But perhaps not as long as Philip IV had the support of the Papacy; that is, as long as the Spaniards did not enter the slave trade directly. Which leads to a third point: in the conflict between the two Iberian powers, the Papacy sided with Spain, refusing to recognize Portugal's independence.

Hence Ryder's explanation for the first Spanish Capuchin mission (to Benin) in 1651–52, and which may also be valid for the second one to Allada in 1660–61: "Spain did all in its power to foment bad relations between Lisbon and Rome, and tried to derive advantage from the situation by introducing direct Spanish influence into areas where Portugal had hitherto asserted exclusive ecclesiastical authority, hoping thereby to win political and economic as well as spiritual advantages"[55] – but not necessarily direct commercial ones.

The specific situation in the late 1650s should be noted also. In fact, at the time Bans/Vans arrived in Cartagena de Indias there may have been no Dutch factory in Allada, implying that the moment was propitious for an anti-Dutch action. However, the Dutch seem to have hurried to re-establish a new factory there in 1659/60.[56]

On the Spanish side this was a particularly crucial moment. Indeed, in 1659 a long war with France (1648–59) came to an end, with the signing of what was, for Spain, the humiliating peace of the Pyrenees (7 November 1659). It led incidentally to the stepping up of the war against Portugal, the last effort to impede the Portuguese secession.[57] One suspects that the Allada mission was some kind of minor pawn in this complicated context, although in which sense exactly is difficult to determine.

It may be, in sum, that commercial and diplomatic motives were relevant on both sides. Downright political motives may have been important too on the Allada side, since the missionaries noted that no less than four important vassals had rebelled successfully against the king,[58] the implication being that the central authorities in Allada were in dire need of allies.

Nevertheless, the religious dimension strikes us as highly significant. It was Christian missionaries that the king of Allada wanted, and wanted seriously. As proof of this, the missionaries learned that since the king was under the impression that the Vans/Bans embassy would never return, he had sent a second mission, asking for missionaries once more, an embassy which only made it to the Canary Islands[59] (what happened to it there?). There is actually no doubt that the king was eager to convert to Christianity. The trouble was, however, that the king's perception of Christianity clashed radically with that of the missionaries. One could of course argue with Robin Law that the king of Allada, like other local rulers in other circumstances, credited Christian rituals with practical efficiency, aiming at utilizing them for worldly aims.[60] That, however, may not be all there is to it. In our view the aim (which could be seen as a worldly one) could have been to do away with contrapuntal paramountcy.

Here we take as our point of departure the apparent fact that the king was convinced that the missionaries, and the Christians more generally, were capable of taming whoever or whatever it was which produced thunder and especially lightning. Thunder and lightning wrought frequent havoc on the Slave Coast, especially in the dry season, ranking in effect as one of the main local scourges.[61] If the missionaries were able to liberate them from that scourge, he, the king, would give them everything they wanted and even put an end to all local wars.[62] Now thunder and lightning were one or several deities in the world of the locals, including the famous Sakpata of later accounts. We do not know when thunder and lightning became one or several personalized deities and whether the name of Sakpata was known to the people of Allada. But as we have seen, Sakpata, and by extension all the deities linked to thunder and lightning, were associated with the earth deities, actually *were* earth deities. To master thunder and lightning would therefore have important political *and* religious implications, namely to sap the power-basis of the indigenous "owners of the land", hence to do away with the contrapuntal paramountcy setup which we assume to have characterized Allada.

But after the missionaries had made it clear, first, that they were powerless to tame the forces of nature; second, that converting to Christianity was a serious business implying a thorough understanding of the new religion and therefore a prolonged period of instruction; third, that holy water was to no avail against demons; and fourth, that Christianity was incompatible with polygamy (the king had some 2,000 wives); the king changed his mind and bowed, we presume, to the pressure of the Dutch "heretics" and of his own grandees. But he did see to it that whatever power, magical or otherwise, that could be elicited from the missionaries remained out of reach of his subjects. That the missionaries threatened an armed intervention by the king of Spain if the king of Allada did not abide by their wishes may not have helped matters.[63] In brief, the missionaries were not capable of offering what the king wanted.

As an epilogue to the story, after the failure at Allada three of the missionaries, Naxara included, tried their luck for a short while in what they called the kingdom of Popo, which we may identify with Grand Popo.[64] This may have been another fiasco. However, we have in this context, thanks to Ray Kea, an anecdotal but quite extraordinary story. It is the story of a female slave called Marotta, later renamed Magdalena, probably born (says Kea) in the 1650s in Grand Popo (could it be in the 1660s?). What was extraordinary with her was that her father was a Roman Catholic, that she had been baptized by a Spanish priest, and that she grew up in a Catholic community. Nevertheless, she was sold into slavery in the 1690s, but later manumitted, and died as one of the acknowledged leaders of the (Protestant) Moravian church on the Danish Caribbean island of Saint Thomas.[65]

* * *

The Delbée-Caerloff expedition arrived some nine years after the departure of the Spanish missionaries. And Delbée was fascinated by a personage he called the "Grand Marabout".[66] "*Marabout*" in the French literature refers usually to a Muslim, but in the African context also to non-Muslim clerics or priests of high standing.[67] Delbée's "Grand Marabout" held clearly a very important religious position. He was also the second personage of the state, after the king, and as such he decided not only on matters of religion. He was, in addition, the only person who was not required to prostrate himself in front of the king. And Delbée adds: "*il se vante d'avoir un commerce particulier avec le diable*"⁶⁸ (he prides himself in having a special relationship with the devil) – implying, we suppose, that he had privileged access to the supernatural world. Interestingly, Delbée added that the king was heavily influenced by Christianity, and that he would have converted to Christianity, had it not been for his fear of the power of precisely the "Grand Marabout". Actually, the king (not necessarily the same as in 1660–61) had spent some time in his youth in a monastery in São Tomé⁶⁹ – quite an extraordinary background for a sacred king.

Would it be too audacious to argue that Delbée's "Grand Marabout" may have been the head of the state council? In this context one would have liked to know more about another local figure, namely the "Great Captain", who occupied the first place after royalty in Allada some time later, in 1722:⁷⁰ a successor of Delbée's "Grand Marabout"?

If we now make a rather daring jump to recent, in fact post-colonial times, we are presented with the *aplogan*, a personage Claude-Hélène Perrot qualifies as "*Ministre des cultes*", and who plays a leading role in the resurrected Adjahouto festival in Allada⁷¹ (the French re-established the "kingdom" of Allada in 1894 after some 170 years).⁷² Aplogan "*semble avoir partie liée…avec les anciens maîtres du sol*"⁷³ (seems to be connected to the former "owners of the land"). The fact that the king and the *aplogan* mimic a sort of confrontation between the two induces Perrot to wonder whether it reflects the existence of an old conflict between the two powers.⁷⁴ The alternative is of course to imagine that this is a classic type of festival designed to re-enact the founding of the polity.

Could it be that the "Grand Marabout", the "Great Captain" and the *aplogan* represent the same institution at various periods of time? The temptation is in any case overwhelming to conclude that Allada was indeed characterized by a contrapuntal paramountcy.

More generally, the pertinent point about the Spanish mission, the Delbée mission and the Europeans stationed on the coast may perhaps be that the locals had realized that there existed a rival world view compared with the only one known to them till then, a world view which gave some certain ideas.

* * *

Hueda was, apart from being one of Allada's original vassals, also its neighbour to the west. It was a rather Lilliputian polity since it may have measured only some 50 to 75 km east-west and 35 to 41 km north-south.⁷⁵ But Hueda, which enclosed the two towns of Savi and Ouidah, became, we must emphasize, *the* central hub of the slave trade in West Africa. As such, it was characterized by a massive European presence; for this reason Hueda ranks as possibly the best-known of all the precolonial polities of Africa south of the Sahara.

All the European visitors were full of praise for the country. They also noted that it was prodigiously populated, constituting one great town.[76] In this respect Neil Norman argues that Hueda experienced a rapid and steep increase in population from about 1600,[77] that is, over a period coinciding roughly with the beginning of the slave trade. Incidentally, an extremely high population density implies that diseases were more easily transmitted, including smallpox, one of the main scourges on the Slave Coast[78] (and linked to Sakpata).

As for the local oral traditions, they are as usual concerned with who came first, and who came later, and from where the latecomers originated. In this last respect there are at least three versions on offer, one pointing to Yorubaland and the two others to Tado, but one of them indirectly, via Allada. Indeed, although Hueda and Allada became close competitors and in fact enemies, Hueda was for long a vassal of Allada, before gaining effective independence in the 1680s, although remaining in some sense subordinate to that polity at the ritual level, owing, we presume, to the Tado link. In fact, every new ruler of Hueda had to be consecrated by a dignitary sent from Allada.[79]

But if the rulers, or the ruling clan or lineage of Hueda, came from outside, we are confronted, once more, with a number of by now well-known questions. Who were the firstcomers, and did some sort of contrapuntal paramountcy emerge? As for the firstcomers, they were also Aïzo, according to Agbo's traditional *Histoire*. And they were, once more, suitably few, implying once more that one could afford to overlook them.[80] Hence, again, there is apparently no trace of contrapuntal paramountcy – but only apparently so, as we shall see. An obvious question is, whatever happened to the Hula, who, there is reason to believe, were the indigenes of Ouidah? A possible answer is that the oral traditions may refer to the metropolitan area of Savi in particular, which was governed directly by the king. For Hueda, though Lilliputian, came to be divided into no less than (possibly) 26 provinces, the 25 remaining being in effect autonomous principalities whose rulers the king of Hueda could not depose;[81] one of these was, we dare to presume, the Hula ruler of Ouidah, incidentally a place where salt-extracting was and remained an important economic activity even at the height of the slave trade – in the Hula manner.[82] In other words, even Hueda was a polity of the classic or "traditional" indirect type. It was also "traditional" in the sense that the rulers of Hueda were, like those of Allada, of the sacred-kingship type ("*le roi est respecté comme une divinité*").[83] As such they lived more or less secluded, and were rarely seen in public; in fact the king went out only twice a year, and for religious reasons, according to one anonymous source.[84] And those who went to see him, the Europeans excepted, had to do so crawling on all fours.[85] Finally, and as befitting a sacred society, "some of the gains [from the slave trade were] expended on the veneration of cosmological actors", as Neil Norman has put it.[86]

We need to add a number of details which may be useful when making comparisons with Dahomey later. We learn for instance that on the death of a king everything was topsy-turvy and the royal palace was entirely destroyed.[87] Justice was suspended, with the result that many people had to arm themselves in order to avoid being murdered in this period of anarchy. Human sacrifices were also very much part of the scene, and not only on the death of a king.[88]

As for the estimates of the number of royal wives, they vary widely, from 200 according to Barbot[89] to 3,000 according to Phillips. Phillips adds that "when ships are in great strait for slaves…[the king] will sell 3 or 400 of his wives to complete their number".[90] In fact, royal wives and wives of the dignitaries were sold to the Europeans on the slightest suspicion. It did not help much that the wives were sacrosanct and as such could not be touched; for the king, it was in fact part of the problem, as it meant that they could do as they pleased. However, being sacrosanct they could also be useful as the executors of the king's sentences – they stripped and levelled to the ground the houses of offenders;[91] they could also be useful in internecine wars, separating the warring parties with their great "bastions".[92] But since most royal wives were condemned to lifelong celibacy, their fate does not strike one as very enviable. Bosman argues in fact that some (many?) preferred "a speedy death" to such a miserable life (as wives of the king).[93]

The extensive polygamy meant sexual imbalance. Small wonder, then, that prostitution "flourished" in Hueda. The prostitutes paid a tax to the king, and one of his wives functioned as their captain.[94]

As for the question of contrapuntal paramountcy, there is the fascinating figure of the chief priest of Dangbe – Dangbe the snake being the local tutelary deity or totem or ancestor.[95] The snake is a recurrent religious symbol throughout the world, always linked, as in Hueda,[96] to agricultural fertility, that is, to the earth and hence to the "owners of the land". If one asks what was the relationship between Hwesi, the *vodun* of the earth in Hueda according to Robin Law,[97] and Dangbe, the answer could be something to the effect that Hwesi/Hwedanu/Hueda is linked in some sense to the word snake, whereas

Dan/Dangbe refers to one particular serpent or category of snakes (notice the ending *gbe* which means "tongue").

Following Robin Law again, we argue that the chief priest of Dangbe was clearly an independent figure rivalling the king in power,⁹⁸ like the "Grand Marabout" in Allada – as noted, he was actually referred to precisely as the grand marabout of Hueda in one source. In fact, the chief priest of Dangbe was "held in equal reverence with the king himself; nay, sometimes more", says Atkins, who wrote in the 1730s.⁹⁹

In 1688 the king of Hueda discontinued his annual visits to the central shrine or temple of Dangbe, sending his numerous wives instead, according to Bosman.¹⁰⁰ Why would he do so? If we argue that Hueda was in fact a contrapuntal paramountcy, the chief priest of Dangbe being, as the representative of the "owners of the land", the head of the Council of State, we can go on to argue that the king's decision to discontinue his visits to the shrine represents an attempt to erode the position of the indigenous element.

That being said, what about Hu, the *vodun* of the sea, relegated officially to the position of younger brother of Dangbe? Was that position accepted by the Hula who, we suppose, were especially numerous in Ouidah-Glehue and on the coast? Or was there a religious opposition between Savi, the domain of Dangbe, and the south, the domain of Hula, and hence between the Huedanu and the Hula?¹⁰¹

All this makes sense in the light of what we know about the internal affairs of Hueda more generally. It was in fact, as we shall see, a polity torn frequently by internal strife, in which the kings tried time and again to strengthen the position of the monarchy against whoever it may have been, flirting frequently with Christianity like many other rulers we have encountered, and for the same reasons. An alternative worldview rather than the "traditional" one was very much present in Hueda because of the relatively massive European presence.

* * *

The (planned) grand alliance between Allada and the French, which we imagine Caerloff had projected precisely at the time of the real take-off of the slave trade, never got off the ground. In fact the French were, as noted, eliminated as a major actor owing to the problems they experienced in Europe. And the king of Allada ran up against considerable difficulties with some of his own vassals, particularly those of the maritime provinces. Those provinces, led by Jakin we presume, revolted repeatedly, often supported by Hueda,¹⁰² the latter succeeding in replacing Allada little by little as the main centre of the slave trade. Allada fought back, at times even with considerable success, one of the results being a general atmosphere of tension and insecurity degenerating at times into open warfare. It was a conflict over the control of the slave trade and hence also of access to European goods. In this conflict the divided Europeans did their best to make their impact felt in the sense most favourable to whatever may have been in their interests at any time. But the European traders and trading companies, always eager to be on the winning side, had considerable difficulty in deciding who to support. However, in the end only the Dutch of the WIC remained faithful to Allada, with negative consequences for their trade.

The antagonism between Hueda and Allada is in one sense difficult to understand. A look at the map tells us that Hueda was surrounded on two sides by Allada, on the third by the ocean, and on the fourth by lakes and rivers. In other words, if most of the slaves sold to the Europeans in Hueda-Ouidah came from elsewhere, they must have come through Allada. One apparently obvious conclusion is that the only thing the kings of Allada had to do to bring Hueda to submission was to close the paths. This they actually tried to do several times, but always with limited success. Why? Because, it seems, the king of Allada was disobeyed by his own vassals who preferred to keep the paths open and to carry on trading with Hueda. If so, it is tempting to conclude that the rise of Hueda was in part due to a certain disintegration of the Allada polity. Actually, even the king of Allada himself was at times induced to divert his supply of slaves to Ouidah.[103]

Why did Allada's maritime provinces revolt? For Jakin, a Hula principality, it was in a sense only logical: the slave trade and the European presence provided it, we assume, with a golden opportunity to rid itself of the overrule of the king of Allada. Perhaps there was also a strong Hula element in the other provinces. So was it a contest of Hula and Hueda against Allada? More generally, why not keep the profits from the slave trade for oneself instead of sharing them with a king some distance away in the interior? Actually, one of the handicaps of the king of Allada was that he resided further inland than his Huedan counterpart in Savi (40 km, as opposed to 14). And since the kings of Allada insisted on controlling the slave trade and receiving the Europeans, it meant several long and strenuous voyages for the latter. Even the Dutch, in theory staunch allies of the king of Allada, had to admit that the slave trade was organized in a way which made it exceedingly long and complicated.[104] It may also be that the kings of Allada were too greedy and that the kings of Hueda "won" because they accepted lower levels of "customs" for permission to trade. If so, Allada simply lost out in the competition.¹⁰⁵ But if Allada lost out, it seems clear that Jakin did not, and continued to be a hub of some importance in the context of the slave trade.

* * *

We know nothing about the activities of Caerloff and of the lodge the French established at Glehue in Hueda in 1672; so we presume that the lodge disappeared after a short while owing to the difficulties the French experienced after the war of 1672–74 (see above) in organizing their overseas venture on a solid footing. Nevertheless, individual French slave traders obviously remained active in the region.¹⁰⁶

By the time the French returned in 1682, the situation had changed markedly, it had become characterized by intense competition among several European powers, a competition in which the French lost out. The main protagonists had now become the English, both the Royal African Company and interlopers, plus the Portuguese, especially the Portuguese from São Tomé, and of course the Dutch. The latter, although they were reluctant to leave Allada, did not neglect Hueda. They were in fact frequently present at Savi (the exact chronology in respect of the Dutch there is uncertain), but at Savi only, as we have seen. As for the Portuguese, it seems like they tried, but failed, in 1680 to construct a fort at Ouidah.¹⁰⁷ After that they maintained a lodge at Savi for a short while (1681–82).¹⁰⁸ It has all to do, we believe, with a strange event, the ephemeral occupation of the Danish fort of Christiansborg on the Gold Coast (see below) by the Portuguese of São Tomé. So their offensive came to nothing. Those who did make an impact on the local scene were instead the Portuguese from Brazil who began to arrive in number. However, they did not try to establish any land base for the time being.

We need to focus on the English who, according to Robin Law, emerged for the time being as the "winners" in this competition,¹⁰⁹ and especially on the fascinating figure of Petley Wybourne (Law writes Wyburne), who arrived in Ouidah as an interloper in 1680–81. Although his relations with the RAC were originally tortuous,¹¹⁰ he nevertheless ended his career as the Chief Factor (that is, director or governor) of the RAC establishment in Hueda in 1688, a position he held until his death in February 1690.¹¹¹ There is a sense in which the very enterprising Wybourne, who had his own organization and his own contacts, ought to rank as the pioneer of the European activity in Glehue/Ouidah and in Hueda generally, forcing the RAC to follow suit and especially to abandon Allada.¹¹² That happened in 1683, in spite of strong resistance from the "Fidalgo" (ruler) of Offra who did not hesitate to retain the English stationed there in order to hinder it.[113] It even seems possible to argue that Wybourne was, perhaps together with the king of Hueda, Agbangla (c.1671–1703), the real founder of Ouidah-Glehue, transforming the village into a genuine trading entrepôt/mart, and as such the twin of Savi. It may also be that Wybourne was instrumental in establishing what became the highly successful commercial policy of the Hueda polity, that of converting Ouidah-Glehue into a place of free trade for all ships that arrived there.[114] Moreover, Wybourne, originally an interloper, had shown the futility of company trade, thereby paving the way for the future demise of the RAC.

The lodge built by Wybourne was converted gradually into William's Fort, after King William III of Holland, ruler of England and Scotland 1689–1702. It acquired the reputation of being impregnable. It was built near, rather than within the indigenous village, as were the two other forts later.[115]

The Wybourne story does not end with his death. In fact, we are told by Thomas Phillips, the late-seventeenth-century slave-trader whom we have met frequently already, that a local "fetishman" who tried to cure an Englishman knew where Wybourne's tomb was, and made offerings to Wybourne as if he were an ancestor,[116] as if Wybourne were something like the tutelary deity of the English fort, or perhaps the deified ancestor of the English, if not the Europeans in general. Actually, the English fort was considered to be sacred ground by the local people.[117] Whether this was because Wybourne's tomb was situated there, or whether it was a sacred ground already, is not clear; all the European factories were, or became at one stage or another, protected by native fetishes, the English fort having two, and so-called native fetish ceremonies were performed regularly.[118]

But Wybourne and the rise of Glehue-Ouidah notwithstanding, the Hueda authorities – that is, King Agbangla – were able to impose inland Savi, the "King's Town", the "upper town", as the place where all transactions relating to the trade had to take place.[119] It was at Savi that there was "an influx of slaves from all the regions of that country".[120] It remained the rule as long as the Huedan polity existed, that is until 1727. Hence the European companies (including the Dutch WIC at times)[121] had no choice but to establish what they called "trading lodges" at Savi, all of them situated within the series of ditches that marked the boundary of the royal palace complex. This implied that the Europeans were under the constant gaze of the king and/or his representatives;[122] the palace complex was said in 1719 to constitute more than one-fourth of the town.[123] Incidentally, the lodges at Savi are described as very agreeable, all two storeys high with verandas, the Europeans living on the second floor, and the first floor functioning as a warehouse.¹²⁴

The European Chief Factors or governors resided then in Savi, leaving subordinates in charge at Ouidah-Glehue, "the lower town", even after first the English and much later the French lodges there were transformed into forts.¹²⁵ But of course Ouidah-Glehue was where it really happened. However, the Dutch were never permitted to establish themselves in "the lower town".¹²⁶

* * *

A central personage in the story of the rise of Hueda is the above-mentioned Agbangla, the first king of that polity revealed to us by the sources. Actually, we are poorly informed about Agbangla, in the sense that we cannot say whether he was merely a figurehead or was really responsible for the policy pursued by Hueda.

Whatever the case, it seems likely that Agbangla came to the throne through something like a coup d'état, to the detriment of his elder brother, and thanks to the support of the Europeans, especially the French traders.¹²⁷ Since this was in the early 1670s, it is tempting to assume that the expression "French traders" refers to Heinrich Caerloff. In any case, the support offered by the Europeans implied, according to Bosman, that Agbangla was "sensibly inclined to favour (them)".¹²⁸

Was Agbangla supported by the Europeans because he represented something like an "anti-traditionalist" party? If so, the next interesting episode in this context occurred in the central years of 1681–83 and corresponds to a pattern, and a logic, already familiar to us. Another Capuchin mission, a French one this time, composed of two persons (Celestin de Bruxelles and Benoît de Hulst), set sail in 1681, slightly ahead of the re-establishment of the French lodge, and stayed until some time in 1683. Celestin had been hired and functioned as chaplain to the new French company, but concentrated on the local royal court. Agbangla took him under his protection and he was allowed to instruct the children of the king. The mission met originally with considerable success since Agbangla as well as some of his chiefs agreed to be baptized.¹²⁹

But history repeated itself; the day before the baptism the Capuchins' chapel was burned down and the king lost interest in Christianity, owing, not surprisingly, to the opposition of the local (pagan) dignitaries *and* the European Protestants.¹³⁰

However, the Celestin-Hulst mission was only the first of several missions – at least five, all Catholic, three French and two Italian/Portuguese from São Tomé – to arrive in Hueda in the reign of Agbangla and the years immediately afterwards. Although Agbangla at least always proved himself to be positively disposed, the result was always the same.[131] But the consequence must have been a notable Christian (Catholic) presence in Hueda. It may be evidence of "significant internal tensions", as Robin Law believes.[132] Or maybe it was the Christian presence which provoked that tension.

As for the French, the lodge they established in 1682 never really prospered. But it continued to exist (possibly not continuously), and was bolstered by the short visits of a number of official naval expeditions between 1686 and 1701, often accompanied by missionaries. Those expeditions (usually only one man-of-war) are actually of minor interest to us, since they were mainly directed towards the neighbouring Gold Coast where France continued to nourish great plans.[133]. The French eagerness to establish a foothold on the Gold Coast was a constant, and one that turned into an obsession, and a frustrated obsession, as the years and indeed centuries passed by without any success. But we note that the most famous of the French visits is the one by the then Lieutenant Jean Baptiste Ducasse (or Du Casse) which arrived in Glehue on 1 March 1688 during Wybourne's time,[134] and found one survivor in the French factory.[135] During his visit Ducasse accompanied King Agbangla in the latter's annual procession to the principal shrine of Dangbe, the snake deity, donning a leopard's skin – or so says Bosman.[136] It turned out to be, adds Bosman, Agbangla's last participation in that annual procession (Ducasse went on to make a brilliant career in the service of his king).[137]

The main problem for the French was that they were hampered by Louis XIV's aggressive policy in Europe. It led among other things to yet another war, the long-lasting War of the League of Augsburg, also called the Nine Years' War, from September 1688 to September 1697 – France against England and the Dutch Republic.[138] It was a war which proved negative for the French interests in West Africa, among other places.

* * *

The Huedan authorities, we observe again, were remarkably successful on the external front, thanks to their open-door free trade policy. It was a policy not always to the liking of the Europeans, in the sense that each and every European nation tried at some stage or another to evict the others. Indeed, one of the main problems of the Hueda authorities was to prevent infighting among the Europeans.[139] In fact Hueda became the scene of several mini-wars, as they may be called, between Europeans, as in 1692 when the eight

Frenchmen and four Englishmen present, plus their respective fort slaves (50 on the English side), began firing at each other (an echo of the war of the League of Augsburg),[140] and once more in 1716.[141] It is true that in 1692 the matter was somewhat more complicated owing to the involvement of a neighbouring African polity, namely Glidji (see below). In any case, the African authorities had often to step in as arbitrators.

Those authorities also protected the interlopers against persecution by companies; the argument of the companies being as usual that if ships' captains were allowed to deal directly with African suppliers, they were tempted to offer higher prices in order to expedite their dispatch.[142] The Africans on the other hand wanted as much competition as possible among the Europeans, and they got it.

* * *

The remarkable upsurge in the slave trade in especially the 1680s is, as noted, clearly borne out by the Database. But even without that, the evidence at hand is eloquent, testifying to the very considerable activity during that decade, and especially at Ouidah-Glehue. There were frequently seven to eight slave ships at the same time in the Ouidah road.[143] It is also clear that the Europeans' demand became insatiable, so that it was a seller's market. Prices increased perhaps fourfold during the next thirty to forty years or so.[144]

4

DAHOMEY AND ITS NEIGHBOURS

EARLY BEGINNINGS AND AFTER

We now turn to the interesting developments which took place in the interior north of the Lama: the region centred on the Abomey plateau, which had suffered steep eclipse after the collapse of Tado and the local metallurgy at the end of the sixteenth or beginning of the seventeenth century. That region witnessed some time in the (early?) seventeenth century the emergence of a new polity, that of Dahomey, originally a vassal of Allada. The beginning of the reign of the one who is usually presented as its first genuine king (*aho* or *ahosu*), Wegbaja, is dated to the 1640s or 1650s – if, that is, he is a genuine historical personage as opposed to some sort of culture hero.[1] (We know of suspiciously few, indeed only three rulers of Dahomey in the roughly one hundred years between the 1640s and 1740.)

As for the name Dahomey itself, there are many explanations, but none that has acquired any degree of consensus among the specialists. We note, however, at the risk of adding to the confusion (and for whatever it may be worth), that *daho* means "great" or "important" and *me* means "free persons". Dahome is indeed a not infrequent spelling.

Even Le Hérissé's semi-official version of the origins of Dahomey is explicit: those who founded the new polity were a horde of outlaws ("*horde proscrite*") who settled down among, and succeeded later in lording it over, people who considered them to be aliens.[2] These newcomers have been presented variously as slave-hunters, *condottières* (mercenaries), or bandits who thrived on rapine and raiding.[3] Whatever the case, all this implies that we are confronted once more with the type of questions which should be familiar to us by now.

Among the indigenes, those we call Guedevi, the children of Guede, seem to have been predominant. Obviously they too, like Aïzo, were said to have emerged out of the earth itself. And, still unsurprisingly, their leader was, according to C. Raymond Oké, an *aïnon* ("earth-priest") who resided at Kana and whom Oké even provides with a name, Kpahè or Akpahe.[4]

Were the Guedevi Yoruba-speakers, as one tradition asserts?[5] It is certainly possible, considering the fact that the area is close to the border between the Gbe and the Yoruba. But it does smack of propaganda, since the Yoruba came to assume the role of arch-enemies of the Dahomeans.[6]

However, the Guedevi may not have been the only indigenes. The sources refer also to the mysterious Ana – hence, incidentally, the word *anato*, which became the word for commoners in Dahomey.[7] Then there were the Aziza or "little folk", supernatural monkey-like creatures who lived in the forests, and who look suspiciously like the hobgoblins of European folklore, and who may relate to quite a remote past (is it permitted to think of the Pygmies in this context?). They are presented, just like the Pygmies of Equatorial Africa, as the truly original first "owners of the land". They are said to have taught men medicine and to have given them their gods.[8]

As pointed out repeatedly already, the newcomers did not try to establish any kind of *modus vivendi* with the indigenous "earth-priest(s)" of the "owners of the land". Quite the contrary, they set out simply to eliminate them, by either deporting or massacring them or both – or else by assimilating them. Worse, the rulers of Dahomey appropriated for themselves the title of *aïnon*.[9] Hence no contrapuntal paramountcy emerged, in flagrant denial of what we may consider to be the rules of the game at the time.

But were the Guedevi really eliminated *en masse*, as opposed to their leaders only? Opinions vary. The Herskovitses are in no doubt. They conclude from local legends, the way we read them, that the majority of the Guedevi were sold into slavery and that the Dahomean rulers effectuated a genuine ethnic cleansing.[10] Most of the Guedevi apparently ended up in Saint Domingue (Haiti), where one of the most important families of *vodun* is said to be of Guedevi origin.[11] But Melville Herskovits notes nevertheless that there were still clear traces of indigenous people on the Abomey plateau in the twentieth century. He refers to sibs which claimed descent from people who came down from the sky or came out of the ground and/or the mountainsides and had no *tohwiyo* (founding ancestor), and who claim to have been *in situ* before the arrival of the royal clan.[12] As for Félix Iroko, he notes the existence even today of a clan significantly called Aïnon in the Abomey region, a clan whose members have the gift of healing with their hands, according to him.[13] And Danish archaeologists have encountered villagers who claim to be descendants of the Guedevi.[14]

It may be too that many Guedevi fled to the north, to Mahi country, and especially to Savalou north-west of Dassa-Zoumè, originally a small Yoruba polity but increasingly Gbe-speaking, and a place where disgruntled people from the Abomey plateau found refuge from a very early date. We note that the people of Savalou came to be known as Gbéto, and that their traditions revolve around a certain Aïnon, presented (unsurprisingly) as "*maîtresse du sol*" and Ouo, "*maître du sol*" (mistress, master of the soil).[15]

There is furthermore one strange tradition which has it, according to Father Vicente Pires who was in Dahomey in 1797, that the Guedevi still around were confined to some sort of ghetto somewhere inside Dahomey.[16] Yet another tradition asserts that a Guedevi prince survived the debacle, and that this prince and his successors received some sort of ritual payment from the Dahomean kings. The idea is that the rulers of Dahomey purchased the land from the Guedevi, a purchase re-enacted periodically, and that this purchase legitimized their position.[17] Actually, the Dahomeans are said to have purchased regularly "*les grands fétiches*" (the great deities) of the vanquished peoples and brought them to Abomey, thus demonstrating their victories on what we may call the sacred level, and also in order to incorporate the "*fétiches*" in a sort of national pantheon.[18] Since this comes from Le Hérissé's semi-official version, and since the very idea of purchase of land and of rights, not to mention divinities, can safely be considered to be irreconcilable with the then local conceptual worldview, it is tempting to conclude that this is a somewhat puerile attempt at manipulation. Savary's comment[19] that the cults of the "new" divinities were closely watched certainly makes sense in this respect.

The Dahomeans would perhaps not have become a power to reckon with had they not been able to eliminate their local rival and eastern neighbour, the Weme polity. The way they did so certainly strengthens the theory that Dahomey was a polity of a new and revolutionary kind.

The Weme polity (perhaps another vassal of Allada) was in all likelihood loosely structured or organized, that is, in the traditional manner.[20] According to the traditions of Dahomey, our main source, the struggle between Weme and Dahomey turned out to be a fierce and long drawn-out affair. At one stage

Weme even succeeded in ravaging Abomey. And at a crucial moment during the final showdown between the two enemies, the king of Dahomey, Akaba, suddenly died of smallpox (possibly in 1716). But Akaba's death was concealed, and his twin sister, the famous Tassi Hangbe, impersonated him in order to avoid demoralizing the Dahomean warriors. Finally the Dahomeans carried the day and routed the Wemenu completely.[21] The Dahomeans had defeated a worthy enemy after having come within a hair's breadth of catastrophe; this is the stuff that legends and epic tales are made of.

But the death of Akaba and the victory over the Wemenu possibly sparked off some sort of succession dispute and civil war, provoked by the fact that Akaba was followed as king not by one of his sons, but by Agaja, who was apparently a younger brother of the twins Tassi Hangbe-Akaba.[22] But a certain Agbo Sassa, possibly a son of Akaba and possibly also the legitimate successor, revolted, supported by Tassi Hangbe. This Tassi Hangbe has fascinated and divided historians. She appears, in fact, in a number of roles, as regent for Agbo Sassa (who was too young to rule) and even, in her capacity of twin sister, as co-ruler with Akaba.[23] But then there are those, Robin Law most notably, who doubt her very existence, suggesting that she is a late invention since no eighteenth- or nineteenth-century source mentions her.[24] But if so, for what purpose was she invented?[25] Whatever the case, there was some sort of civil war, a great battle said to have been fought between the "two kings of Foay" (that is, Fon = Dahomey).[26] Agaja won, and became the undisputed lord of Dahomey until his death in 1740. Note that the traditions which refer to Tassi Hangbe and Agbo Sassa stress the fact that neither was killed; Agbo Sassa fled and established a small polity somewhere in the north, while Tassi Hangbe lived out her days in confinement in Abomey.[27]

If one wonders how Hueda and Allada reacted to all this, the answer is that this may be the period when Dahomey severed its ties with Allada and tried a rapprochement with Hueda and with the French at Ouidah-Glehue (the French fort there dates from 1704) – a sort of alliance directed against Allada (the anti-Dahomean alliance the king of Allada proposed to Hueda was rejected by the latter). As for the chronology, we know that the Dahomeans and the French were on excellent terms by 1715/16, that is, possibly at the time of the defeat of the Wemenu.[28] Does French aid explain the Dahomean victory?

What happened to the Weme polity once it was defeated? The answer is that it was completely destroyed, erased from the surface of the earth, so to speak. This became the dominant pattern in the treatment the Dahomeans meted out to their vanquished enemies. In this context it is especially noteworthy that they tried increasingly to exterminate the vanquished ruling kindreds/dynasties, down to their last members, if necessary by every ruse or trick in the book[29] (they did not always succeed, as we shall see). After that they installed a headman of their choice who had no family link with the local population and who served at the king's pleasure.[30] This is not the way vanquished polities are treated according to the "traditional" model, which holds that a defeated entity is always permitted to continue to exist, for instance as a vassal of the victor.

As for the defeated Wemenu, those who survived, they migrated en masse south and south-eastwards, towards the vast floodplain formed by the Weme and So rivers and also towards the land situated on the left bank of the Weme – regions until then apparently sparsely populated by small groups of Yoruba- and Gbe-speakers. The migrations were in many instances led by members of the defeated Weme dynasty who established a number of small successor-states in the south, notably at Adjohoun and at Dangbo, the latter village north-east of present-day Porto Novo/Hogbonu. Here the fugitives felt safe, we are told, since the warriors of Dahomey are traditionally considered to have been reluctant to cross water because it jeopardized, it was believed, the "force" they derived from their ancestors.[31]

What about the people the incoming Wemenu encountered? Those who cultivated the land lived apparently in small acephalous communities under the headmanship of "earth-priests" (that is, *aïnon*). Although the small indigenous population submitted to the newcomers from the north, the latter acknowledged their existence and respected the ritual prerogatives of their *aïnon*. For instance, in Adjohoun the incoming Weme prince acknowledged the irremovable rights and prerogatives of the *aïnon* of the local Yoruba, named Tosso.[32] Roughly the same situation obtained in a number of other localities.[33] In other words, the Wemenu abided everywhere by the rules of the game.

The new polities thus created were and remained small, and outside the mainstream, as it were, of the history of the region. And the local society remained remarkably egalitarian, according to Paul Pélissier.[34] But the southeastern part of the Slave Coast continued to serve as a refugee zone, notably after the conquest of Allada by Dahomey in 1724 – a refugee zone protected in the east by the heavily wooded Sakété plateau.[35]

* * *

Since the present author put forward the claim that no "contrapuntal paramountcy" emerged in Dahomey,[36] Edna Bay, Suzanne Preston Blier and

Robin Law have all argued the opposite. Or to be more precise in the case of Edna Bay, she contends that the newcomers "did make the kind of ceremonial accommodations that conquering dynasties typically made in Africa to recognize the rights of autochtonous peoples".[37] The trouble with that statement is that contrapuntal paramountcy involves a lot more than merely "ceremonial accommodations".

More generally, the argument of Bay, Blier and Law revolves around the institutions of the *agasunon*, the *ajahutonun* and the *kpojito*. To begin with the *agasunon*, he is presented as the priest of the dynastic ancestor of the royal sib and as such the one who installed the king. As such, also, he was the king's ritual superior, at least in theory.[38] But if so, this suggests an internal dynastic cult among the newcomers which in no way relates to the indigenous "owners of the land". Furthermore, Maurice Glélé makes it clear first, that the institution was *created* by the king of Dahomey, and second, that the *agasunon* was what we may call a puppet, and as such completely dependent on the king.[39]

As for the *ajahutonun*, who held the traditional title of the kings of Allada, the office was revived as late as 1740–45. As he was presented as "king" of Allada, and as such as the one responsible for the supreme cult in honour of Ajahuto, every new king of Dahomey had to be consecrated by him. Thus "The kings of Dahomey...secured the traditional legitimacy which could be conferred only by a king of Allada", according to Robin Law.[40] But Jacques Lombard has demonstrated the obvious, namely that it was another case of window-dressing, the *ajahutonen* being, as the *agasunon*, a mere puppet. In fact, in Dahomean Allada the royal governor with the title of *akplogan* continued to be the leading local authority.[41]

Robin Law also refers to the custom that every new king of Dahomey "bought" his realm (see above). According to him, this "buying" constitutes another example of contrapuntal paramountcy: a logic we have refuted earlier.

Suzanne Preston Blier for her part contends (as does also Edna Bay) that the first *kpojito*, or queen-mother of Dahomey, was a Guedevi, that is, from the indigenous people of the Abomey plateau.[42] This would make her the "mother" of the royal sib, a situation equivalent, it is suggested, to contrapuntal paramountcy. But even if we assume that the position of *kpojito* existed already in the seventeenth century, and that the first incumbent was a Guedevi, the origin of the first Queen Mother of Dahomey is not particularly relevant to the institutional setup of contrapuntal paramountcy as defined earlier.

It is, in sum, difficult to see what the examples put forward by Bay, Preston and Law have to do with contrapuntal paramountcy. That institutional set-up implies among other things, we repeat, the existence of a more or less powerful state council composed of heads of autonomous lineages representing in some sense the "owners of the land". In fact, there was never, as far as we know, anything even remotely resembling a state council in Dahomey, only a number of officials assisting the king. The two leading ones were the *migan* (the "prime minister") and his deputy the *meu*, holders of offices whose origins and attributes are far from clear. But what is beyond doubt is that those offices were not hereditary, at least not in theory, and that their incumbents, like in fact all royal officials, served at the king's pleasure. Furthermore, no-one has ever suggested that they were in any way linked to the indigenous "owners of the land".[43]

* * *

By refusing to establish contrapuntal paramountcy and by completely obliterating vanquished polities, the monarchs of Dahomey had apparently set out on a revolutionary path. But there was more to come. Indeed, to paraphrase Robin Law again, in Dahomean thought sovereignty came to be equated with rights of ownership, implying that Dahomey was simply considered to be the property of the king. Furthermore, since the king appropriated the title of *aïnon* for himself and infused it with a new meaning, the king became the owner of all land, says Law, and in fact also the owner of everything *on* the land – that is to say, owner in the modern absolute sense of the term. One of the logical consequences was that the king could and did grant land to whoever he wished, grants he could revoke at any time. Those who lived on the land were in fact conceded only usufructuary rights.[44]

All this is based on Le Hérissé who stated simply that not even their very existence "belonged" to the inhabitants of Dahomey – "*leur existence même ne leur appartenait pas*";[45] in essence they were all slaves of the king.

What we are confronted with here looks on the surface of it like an attempt to revolutionize society, to do away with the existing structure. Law has argued in this context that the traditional kinship-based (and decentralized) political structure was replaced by a territorially defined and extremely autocratic system based on effective military force rather than common descent – implying a transition from a "tribal" system to a territorial state and a process of militarization.[46] Indeed, in Dahomey royal authority was explicitly defined, says Law, in terms of territory and not consanguinity, and conceived in patrimonial rather than patriarchal terms. A very "modernizing" approach, in other words.

But what Law refers to may perhaps be best described as the *aim* of the rulers. If that is the case, the impression one is left with is that they did not really succeed – if, that is, they really tried. Put differently, it seems to the present author as if the early kings of Dahomey either failed to make, or stopped very short of making, a clean slate of the past. What those kings did, basically, was, we contend, to manipulate and to subvert, that is, to remodel the old system from within, but not necessarily to do away with its logic. Or if one prefers, in their quest for legitimacy the rulers of Dahomey tried to have it both ways, relying on, while at the same time trying to manipulate, the very logic of the old order they may have aimed at erasing. We are referring here especially to the kinship ideology and the central position of religious beliefs. In this respect the people in power engaged in very extensive and complex spiritual engineering, leading to a dramatic refiguration of the local religion. In particular, they tried to reorder the invisible world, that is, to convert the cult of the royal ancestors, possibly also that of Mawu-Liisa, into the exclusive focus of the religious life of the locals – incidentally bequeathing to posterity an absolutely bewildering religious setup. One Dahomean king, Agonglo, tried in 1789 to cut through it all by adopting Christianity; but it cost him his life, as will be described later.

Let us proceed by stages: first, Le Hérissé's "*horde proscrite*", once in power, went about looking for respectable ancestors, and found them in nearby Allada. Hence the claim that the ruling sib hailed from that of Allada. The inconvenience of that link was that it implied a relationship of vassalage to Allada. The second stage consisted therefore in making a direct link to nearby Tado and to Agasu, and thus bypassing the Alladan connection. In other words, the members of the ruling sib of Dahomey presented themselves as Agasuvi, the children of the leopard, who had migrated directly from Tado to Abomey.[47] Dahomey cultivated, for good measure, relations with Tado,[48] a town the Dahomeans never tried to conquer, strangely enough.

Second, deified ancestors of the royal sib were empowered, while other *vodun*s were ignored or suppressed, in the expectation that their strength would be diminished.[49] Actually, the monarchy tried to suppress the ancestor cults of the component lineages of Dahomey – that is, to concentrate or monopolize ritual, and hence also political and judicial power, in the hands of the monarchy, rupturing the dynastic continuity of the vanquished communities and depriving them of the supernatural support they would normally anticipate from a deceased king or lineage head.[50] In other words, the Dahomeans, regardless of whichever lineage they belonged to, were in theory henceforth to worship only, or at least primarily, the ancestors of the king. The king's ancestors were then supposed to become the ancestors of *all* the Dahomeans, the king, as the descendant of the most powerful of the ancestors, becoming then the undisputed master of all Dahomeans, the "father" as it were of them all.

Put differently, the monarchs distorted the function and meaning of kin, transforming "social and kin relations into devices for the exercise and consolidation of state power".[51] So instead of abolishing the very kinship-foundation of society, they set about transforming the royal sib, the Hwegbonu, into a very numerous and hence very powerful one. They proclaimed that daughters did not relinquish their membership of the clan upon marrying, a nonsense in a patrilineal society, and that the children of both sexes of all the members of the royal sib also belonged to that sib[52] – the excuse being that royal blood could not be permitted to flow into other strains, as Herskovits has expressed it.[53] It resulted obviously in an enormous sib which made up possibly the majority of the population of the capital Abomey. And all the other kindreds were attached to the monarchy, that is to the royal sib, but in subordinate positions, a way of undermining their power and position.[54] The logical corollary was to establish a family connection ("*lien de parenté*") between Agasu and the *voduns* of the subaltern groups. We imagine that Agasu, and his earthly representative the king of Dahomey, became the "father" or "elder brother" in this context: not an unusual procedure in world history (one thinks of the Chinese emperors in this context). In any case, Agasu was represented as much the "strongest" of all the ancestors and all the *voduns*, the one the others had to submit to.[55]

Incidentally, the fact that the monarchs felt it necessary to leave the members of the royal sib idle implied that they came to constitute a parasitic caste which was a burden on the economic and social resources of the country.[56]

It is logical in this context that the monarchs should appropriate for themselves the justice previously in the hands of the kindred-heads. The most common punishment was, also logically enough, to be removed from one's kin and sent as a slave to cultivate one of the royal estates.[57]

But as we have argued repeatedly, it is not at all certain that the Dahomean kings achieved what they aimed at. It may be that many Dahomeans came to internalize the idea that their heads belonged to the king, to paraphrase once more the title of Robin Law's famous article – that they were all slaves of the king. But when Law goes on to argue that the newcomers succeeded "in winning acceptance of the legitimacy of their rule",[58] we beg to dissent. There is in fact ample evidence to the contrary: that the monarchs of Dahomey, by trying to manipulate the logic of the old society, and hence by accepting that logic, if even only in part, left themselves open to decisive counterattacks. For as has been pointed out, Sakpata, the *vodun* which came to symbolize the old order, turned out to be a redoubtable enemy, in spite of active persecution. Sakpata was and remained a focus of opposition to the monarchy, and a powerful one at that. One consequence was, as Paul Mercier has pointed out, that no genuine state religion ever emerged in Dahomey,[59] the implication being that religion escaped the complete control of the Dahomean kings – a very uncomfortable situation in a sacred society. The implication was also that the monarchy had to institute a system of surveillance of religious practices,[60] an unheard-of occurrence in Africa of old.

Rather surprisingly, Edna Bay provides us with considerable ammunition in this context. She argues in fact (somewhat contradictorily considering her stance on the problem of contrapuntal paramountcy) that questions of legitimacy were raised at two levels: the right of the dynasty to rule, and the right of what she calls the state to establish its authority over kin groups. In fact, she goes on to point out that signs of unrest and rebellion expressed at least in part through religious movements and metaphors came to punctuate the history of the polity.[61]

We deduce that the Dahomean rulers had little choice but to continue to resort to terror and attempt to pursue what looks like a totalitarian programme. In this context it certainly makes sense that the rulers tried, and in fact largely succeeded, to convert Dahomey into an essentially militaristic polity. Indeed, as Robin Law has demonstrated, the institutions and ideology of Dahomey came to be permeated by a military ethos far beyond anything which had existed previously.[62] The outcome was what seems to have been a uniquely efficient and professionalized military organisation based on a system of conscription. There was, then, an army which was clearly much better trained than the mass forces raised in Allada and Whydah. But the question is whether the army was designed exclusively for external purposes, or if those who built it also had potential domestic problems in mind. Was there an early totalitarian polity in eighteenth-century Africa?

To return to the army, it is noteworthy that the inland polity of Dahomey became a pioneer in the acquisition and use of firearms. This was moreover not a late development, quite the contrary, since it began already in the reign of the very first genuine king of Dahomey (the one presented as such by the traditions), Wegbaja. Moreover, the Dahomeans could use firearms rather efficiently because of their high standards of discipline and drill. But David Ross points out that they do not seem to have had any concept of rigorous battle training.[63]

The question is just what impact firearms had on the coast of Guinea. We note in this context that Robin Law has questioned the efficiency of firearms at this early stage ("it is possible to argue that too much has been made of the military impact of firearms").[64] He has also expressed the opinion that the transition to firearms was a slow process.[65] To which we may add Edna Bay's point that the arms sold in Africa were at best the weapons of the previous generation of European armies.[66]

We are anyway far from the case of Japan where firearms were adopted immediately following their first appearance in 1543, and the Japanese succeeded very rapidly in manufacturing them.[67] Or is this an unfair comparison?

It remains nevertheless that the export of firearms to the Gold and Slave Coasts increased tremendously from the 1660s onwards. In fact, one tentative estimate has it that some 180,000 guns had found their way to those coasts by the 1730s.[68] They must have made *some* difference.

Obviously, firearms could come only from the Europeans. This begs the question of the relationship between inland Dahomey and those Europeans. But apart from the possible early alliance with the French referred to above, our sources are remarkably silent on the matter. What we have is only the archaeological record which indicates stable contacts with the Europeans from the earliest phases of the Dahomean kingdom.[69] However, logic and common sense tell us, first, that the relations with the Europeans must have been of prime importance to the Dahomeans; second, that it was likely that Dahomey would sooner or later try to eliminate the intermediaries between itself and the coast, that is, Allada and Hueda; and third, that the only way to pay for the firearms was to sell slaves, implying in turn that Dahomey was committed to slave-raiding and the slave trade from its very inception. Is this then a classic case of the guns-slaves cycle (to raid or be raided) dear to some historians?[70] We see in any case, once more, that Akinjogbin's theory that Dahomey was opposed to the slave trade does not make much sense. In this context, Davis Ross's viewpoint, that Dahomey, having exhausted the slave-producing potential of the Abomey plateau, turned to the thickly populated but internally divided southern Aja kingdoms, Allada and Hueda, seems more logical.[71]

Or is it that the people of the Abomey plateau experienced frequent periods of drought, as Newbury argues,[72] and that they were forced to raid in search of supplies?

Firearms may, anyway, not be the whole story. In fact, Dahomey was renowned for its excellent iron-smiths who produced iron weaponry and tools of a high standard. The iron-smiths are said to have had a special relationship with the monarchy,[73] whatever that relationship was. The problem here is that the god of the iron-smiths was Gu, the local counterpart of Ogun,[74] and was presented occasionally, along with Sakpata *et al.*, as one of the oppositional *vodun*s in Dahomey.

5

CONVULSIONS FURTHER WEST

The historical process on the Western (Little) Slave Coast in the 1670s–80s and later was in large part conditioned by what happened further west, on the eastern Gold Coast. But the radical changes that region witnessed may in turn be linked to some extent to occurrences even further west, to the long period of wars of state formation (or wars described as such by many historians)[1] among the Twi-speaking Akan of the Central Gold Coast. The main result was the emergence in 1701–2 of a genuine regional superpower, that of Asante.

On the eastern Gold Coast, the main antagonists in the 1670s and the 1680s were the two polities of Accra in the south and Akwamu, originally an inland polity, in the north. Accra, a polity of the Ga-Adangbe, with its capital at Ayawaso or Great Accra eleven miles inland, was traditionally the central hub of the gold trade. Hence the three European forts (English, Dutch and Danish) at Little Accra on the coast (which is the present-day town of Accra).[2]

As for the ethnically heterogeneous[3] but mainly Twi-speaking Akwamu in the north, it was traditionally an enemy of Denkyira, the leading polity further west on the Gold Coast. Hence it became early on an ally of Asante, Denkyira's rival and eventual successor.[4]

Between 1677 and 1682 (the chronology is uncertain) Akwamu, for reasons unknown, invaded and destroyed the old polity of Accra, levelling the capital Ayawaso to the ground, and becoming thus the first inland polity to reach the coast.[5] But the result was a very complicated situation, due in part to the fact that Akwamu chose to rule the conquered region indirectly, via the many local Ga-Adangbe chiefs, the former vassals of the king of Accra who had now switched allegiance to that of Akwamu. They turned out to be unruly, strongly resentful as they were of Akwamu overlordship,[6] with the result that the kings of Akwamu were obliged, or chose, to invade the former Accra kingdom, Ga-Adangbeland, several times, until at least 1723.[7]

The Europeans were caught in the middle, especially the Danes, who miscalculated and sided for too long with the losers, the Ga-Adangbe.[8] The result was that they lost Christiansborg twice, the first time in 1679, strangely enough to the Portuguese of São Tomé.[9] For the latter it was, we suspect, part of a grand scheme intended to resurrect the Portuguese presence on the coast and in the last resort to reconquer Elmina[10] – witness the previously mentioned Portuguese attempt on the Slave Coast in the 1680s. Hence Christiansborg became São Francisco Xavier, and it had an abnormally, suspiciously large garrison.[11] This was in any case the first genuine official Portuguese foray into the Gold and Slave Coasts since 1642. But the Portuguese had to give up as soon as 1682, presumably because of Dutch opposition, and the Danes returned in February 1683.[12] The second time the Danes lost Christiansborg was in June 1693, for one year, when it was occupied by the Akwamus themselves.[13] To the best of our knowledge, this was the first and only time Africans took over a European fort.

However, the central point about the Akwamu invasions is that they sent succeeding waves of Ga-Adangbe refugees fleeing eastwards across the Volta and into the Western Slave Coast. But before investigating some of the consequences, we must look at what happened inside Akwamu itself in about 1689: a genuine coup d'état according to Ivor Wilks, our principal authority. Apparently the military leaders succeeded in seizing power from the clan heads, the *abusuahenfo*, with the former replacing the latter in the council of state. Thus a certain Basua, who is presented as the *brafo*, or commander-in-chief of the army, became the real head of state in his capacity as regent.[14] What does all this mean? One possible interpretation is that the nature of the Akwamu polity was radically changed, the Akwamu military leaders rejecting or casting off, in a sense, the traditional model. Hence Akwamu became similar to Dahomey later and some of the Congo-Angola polities earlier, that is, a military polity organized for war, specifically for slave-raiding. In fact, Akwamu instigated the transformation of the Gold Coast into another Slave Coast.

But Basua the *brafo* died in 1699, and no further *brafo* is mentioned. What happened next? Here the story is somewhat confusing, since Basua is also referred to as *akwamuhene* or king of Akwamu.[15] He was replaced as *akwamuhene* by Ado, but Ado was precisely the *akwamuhene* from whom Basua had wrested power earlier. If, that is, Wilks, our main source, has got it right. Could it be, for instance, that there were *two* Ados? Whatever the case, the Ado who died in 1702 was in turn succeeded by his brother Akonno.[16] And this Akonno, who died in 1725, was, apart from being a heavy drinker,[17] a monarch who earned himself a terrible reputation, including among the Europeans, as a predatory ruler who surrounded himself with real bandits. Raiding, slave-raiding that is, and warfare more generally became in fact a genuine state enterprise in Akwamu, thanks in part to the huge amount of firearms that the Danes in particular did not hesitate to sell to that dreaded polity.[18]

Apart from his reputation, what is interesting about Akonno is that he was often on the move; he frequently visited, for instance, the European forts at Little Accra, and even wined and dined there. At one stage Akonno and his followers stayed at Christiansborg-Osu more than two months, much to the dismay of the Danes.[19] One of them, Johannes Rask, explicitly compared him with the king of Hueda, since the former "travels wherever he wants to and is often on campaigns", whereas the latter "may not travel outside of his houses or residences",[20] as befitting a genuine sacred king. The conclusion is that the (we presume) originally sacred kingship of Akwamu had been desacralized and that Akonno, whoever he may have been, behaved as if he were the head of a war-band, free of any traditional, including religious, constraints – more or less in the Dahomean manner.

* * *

The Akwamu conquest and invasions of the land of the Ga-Adangbe sent, as noted, successive waves of refugees into the Western (Little) Slave Coast, that is Eweland. Many had little choice but to support themselves as bandits or as mercenaries, thus creating a generalized climate of insecurity. Grand Popo suffered especially,[21] and Keta became a hotbed of banditry.[22] Among the victims were quite a few Europeans involved in a number of rather bloody incidents – incidents of a type that were and continued to be unknown on the Central Slave Coast.[23] Those incidents may also help explain why the slave trade, and more generally trade with the Europeans, never really took off on the Western Slave Coast. Hence the dearth of European sources, and a very uncertain chronology.

But as far as we know, many, possibly most Ga-Adangbe refugees were assimilated over time by the Ewe. In the case of the Anlo-Ewe, if it is correct that the defensive confederation they established dates from the 1680s, it must have been as a response to precisely the fact that they found themselves sandwiched in between the expanding Akwamu and the Ga-Adangbe refugees who founded Little Popo-Glidji[24] (see below). But if so, the confederation turned out to be a success in the sense that the Anlo-Ewe managed (apparently) to maintain their independence, at least for the time being. However, many of the Ga-Adangbe refugees obviously settled down among the Anlo-Ewe where they are believed to have contributed to improving and broadening the maritime skills of the latter.[25] We also know of a new clan, that of the Dzevi, which is considered to be of Adangbe origin. That clan is even credited with imposing a new and important war deity which rose to prominence in the second half of the eighteenth century.[26]

The only place where the Ga-Adangbe refugees apparently converted themselves into genuine conquerors was in the region known today as Aneho or Little Popo. We say "apparently" because the fact is that the Ga-Adangbe were linguistically assimilated by the local Gbe-speaking Ewe, the process giving rise to a new Ewe sub-group (and dialect) that we call Guin.[27] The implication is that the incoming Ga-Adangbe may not have been that numerous after all. Nevertheless, all the sources are agreed that a conquest did take place, that the conquerors were led by a deposed prince from Accra and that they established themselves at Glidji on the northern bank of the lagoon, some kilometres inland. After which they set about to subjugate, apparently with violence, the *dukowo* of the acephalous and reputedly docile Watchi-Ewe, plus some Hula, especially the Bê.[28] In the process they also secured the allegiance of the headman of the Mina of coastal Aneho,[29] and also took the precaution, according to their traditions, of asking none other than the ruler of old Tado for a wife. That ruler also obligingly endorsed their installation and overlordship over a fair slice of territory. The *hulaholu* of Agbanakin was ignored in the process.[30]

This calls for some explanation. There existed a colony of Mina (Fante) canoemen at Aneho-Little Popo long before the arrival of the Ga-Adangbe/Guin. This was because of Aneho's position as the point of trans-shipment of canoes from the lagoon. The canoes were hauled across the sandspit which Aneho-Little Popo constituted, then continuing their voyage by sea westwards, which was possible only in the Harmattan season.[31] Coastal Aneho-Little Popo functioned in short as a way-station where the canoemen waited for the right season to proceed to the Gold Coast; the opening of the lagoon at Little Popo-Aneho is not navigable.

Since the original name of Aneho-Little Popo seems to have been Hulavi, meaning Little Hula, the implication is that there was already a Hula presence there.³² Actually, the Mina-Fante secured the permission of the *hulaholu* of Agbanakin and considered themselves to be his vassals. With the rise of Glidji they changed their allegiance but maintained their very autonomous status.³³ In fact the rulers of Little Popo-Glidji had every reason to cajole their vassals of Little Popo-Aneho since the latter controlled access to the Europeans and hence to the slave trade.

When was all this? We know that warriors from Glidji under the legendary Ofori (the leading general under the king) certainly made their impact felt on the Central Slave Coast from 1692, and that according to the traditions, the real founder of Glidji was the second king, a certain Foli Bébé, who reigned, the historians believe, between approximately 1694 and 1727/33 – unless, that is, several persons/kings hide behind the Foli Bébé of the traditions. Note that Foli Bébé may not have been of royal blood, and may instead have been the son of the aforementioned Ofori³⁴ – the result of another coup d'état? (To avoid any confusion, we refer to the new polity with its inland capital as Little Popo-Glidji, while Little Popo-Aneho is the original coastal settlement which became an autonomous vassal entity within that polity).

The inevitable question is whether Little Popo-Glidji came to be characterized by a contrapuntal paramountcy or not. The evidence is ambiguous. On the one hand Diedrich Westermann, as interpreted by Nicoué Gayibor,³⁵ has argued that the king was surrounded by a powerful council of state. In this council there were four very important members, including the *duto*, a title we have suggested earlier is that of the "earth-priest". And indeed, in Little Popo-Glidji the *duto* was, according to the Westermann/Gayibor version, the "owner of the land" in the ritual sense of the term and as such the descendant of the first mythical settler.³⁶ But then there are the official traditions of Little Popo-Glidji (or what are presented as such) which state flatly that its metropolitan area was empty of people when the newcomers arrived, implying that there were no "owners of the land" with whom to establish a *modus vivendi*. This version is, apart from being incompatible with the Westermann/Gayibor one, absurd from a linguistic point of view. It is in addition hotly disputed by the guardians of the traditions of Agbanakin.³⁷ We conclude that the Glidji version is pure propaganda, something which, according to Gayibor, even the people of Glidji themselves are uncomfortably aware of.³⁸

But whether there was a contrapuntal paramountcy or not, we can deduce from the above that the Ga-Adangbe conquerors were familiar with and respected the rules of the game, although they tried to manipulate them to their advantage. Hence the reference to Tado and the systematic negligence of the *hulaholu*. Little Popo-Glidji was then in a sense a polity of the traditional kind, but a strangely unfinished or incomplete one, if it can be so described.

Whatever the case, the achievements of the people who conquered Little Popo-Glidji and surroundings were rather limited. Little Popo-Glidji was and remained a small second-rate polity poorly structured and lacking in internal cohesion, owing not only to the conflicting traditions but also to the fact that Little Popo-Aneho went frequently on its own way. In addition there was the problem of legitimacy, and in all directions. For if the kings of Little Popo-Glidji were upstarts, not belonging to the royal dynasty of Accra, and their claim to the land spurious, then they really had little going for them. Furthermore, if the aim of the Guin was to dominate or to impose law and order on at least parts of the Western Slave Coast, they were not very successful. In fact, the Guin themselves often behaved like bandits and served as mercenaries throughout the region.[39]

* * *

We must return further west, to Akwamu, and the chronology, and note that the new (military?) rulers of that polity acquired a frightful reputation. They became in fact notorious for their numerous abuses.[40]

After the conquest of Accra, Akwamu turned both eastwards and north-north-eastwards.[41] In the latter case inland Eweland (Ewedome) was conquered, at least in part, plus also the Akan polity of Kwahu, finally subdued in 1710, and Agona, although quite some time later. Eastwards the first victims were the Ladoku or Lampi with their coastal town of Ningo, which was directly incorporated into Akwamu. Then came the turn of Ada (on the Western Slave Coast). Whether Ada's neighbour to the east, the Anlo confederation, was genuinely conquered by Akwamu, or simply suffered from Akwamu raids, the specialists disagree.[42] There is also disagreement about what happened exactly to Keta, the most unruly member of the Anlo confederation.[43] But one of the constants in this region, whether under Akwamu overrule or not, is the animosity between Ada and Anlo, due principally to disagreements over fishing rights.[44]

What we have referred to above is what Sandra Greene calls Akwamu's imperial wars, whose aim, according to her, was to control the trade routes along the coast and between the coast and the interior. Greene adds that Akwamu's control waxed and waned during the next two centuries,[45] the implication being that Akwamu never succeeded in stabilizing the region (if, that is, the Akwamu rulers thought in terms of stabilization).

With regard to the Anlo confederation, it is said that the many wars of the period, and the many defeats that the confederation suffered, led, as noted, to the emergence of a new deity, a war deity called Nyigble or Nyigbla. But on closer inspection this Nyigble/Nyigbla turns out to be simply a personified revelation of Mawu,[46] whatever that may mean exactly.

* * *

The supply of slaves for sale on the Western Slave Coast was and remained intermittent and unreliable.[47] This was in spite of the high hopes the English especially nourished at one stage, dreaming of developing Little Popo-Aneho into a counterweight to Ouidah-Glehue.[48] But in fact the history of the European presence on the Western Slave Coast generally turned out to be that of the establishment and abandonment of ephemeral factories, especially by the smaller European nations which sought to escape from the intense competition in the major marts. A relatively lively trade in ivory developed, but only for a little while.[49]

Perhaps the main reason was in the final analysis the lack of stability in the region, the fact that even the two leading polities, Akwamu and Little Popo-Glidji, were never capable of imposing a minimum of order. Actually, those two polities fuelled the disorder with their depredations and wars and contributed also to the image of near-chaos which the modern historian (or at least this historian) is left with when investigating the rather tortuous history of the Western Slave Coast.

What was lacking was a great inland polity of the Oyo type; that is, a polity serving as a stable purveyor and capable of, let us say, regularizing it all, if that is what Oyo really did. Maybe it is the same role that Asante came to perform later on the Gold Coast.

6

THE 1680s–1720s

AN OVERVIEW

In the preceding chapters we have dealt more or less separately with the past of the polities and historical actors of our region. It is time to connect the various pieces and to present the reader with a chronologically oriented overview of the period between the 1680s and all the way to the 1720s – that is, the first 40–50 years of the epoch when the slave trade was of prime importance on the coast.

* * *

On the Central Slave Coast, the main theme in our period on the political level is the conflict between Hueda – at times a very divided polity – and Allada, whose internal situation, unfortunately, we are poorly informed about. Actually, we are dealing with a multi-dimensional conflict, since many other protagonists also entered the fray, including the Europeans, who in addition fought among themselves.

The trouble was that conflict degenerated frequently into genuine warfare, intermittent or not, as for instance between 1688 and 1693.[1] But if Willem Bosman is correct in arguing that the people of Hueda and Allada were rather unwarlike, the question is, who did the actual fighting? In fact, Bosman himself provides us with the answer: bandits-mercenaries from the west.[2] The superiority of those mercenaries over the local forces became quickly evident, according to Robin Law.[3]

As for the Europeans, at least some of them had not yet learned that certain types of belligerent action, in which they could be permitted to indulge themselves on the Gold Coast and elsewhere, were out of the question on the Slave Coast.[4] The Dutch were particularly slow learners in this respect.

We start with the Dutch who were established, as noted, at Offra in the coastal region of Allada, originally the leading trading centre on the Slave Coast. But the Dutch, as the allies of the king of Allada, often found themselves in rebel territory, since the maritime provinces, some of them autonomous principalities, often revolted against their suzerain. Here we must present a certain Isaac van Hoolwerff who became chief factor at Offra in 1686, replacing Willem de la Palma, a personage we will encounter later on. Hoolwerff and his superiors at Elmina obviously had great plans, to crush the maritime provinces *and* Hueda, thanks, once more, to the recruitment of bandits-mercenaries from the west. But if the brutal van Hoolwerff won the first round,[5] this attempt at a Gold Coast-type European-sponsored war went all wrong, since Hoolwerff himself was killed, possibly executed, in 1690, still in Offra, and the WIC lodge there was burnt down.[6]

But then, in January 1692 the new polity of Little Popo-Glidji entered the fray in grand style. Mercenaries commanded by Ofori, the general mentioned earlier, hired by the king of Allada and hence also by the Dutch, attacked and destroyed Offra, burning down in the process the lodge the WIC had reconstructed after the Hoolwerff affair. The Fidalgo ("king") and principal men of Offra had to flee to Hueda and the surrounding villages were destroyed and burnt.[7] Indeed, the small region of Offra was and remained totally devastated and depopulated, according to a later report.[8]

The fact that Jakin, presented earlier as the twin town and ally of Offra, not only sided with the king of Allada (and hence with the Dutch) but even took an active part in the destruction of Offra is, on the surface, somewhat surprising. Perhaps the Hula of Jakin had no choice, or perhaps they tried to avoid the same fate as their neighbours. Or this was a golden opportunity to get rid of a rival? Whatever the case, there is a sense in which the mini-polity of Jakin came into its own after 1692–93. But Jakin's position must have been, and must have remained, rather precarious.

The next target for Ofori and his men was Hueda and Ouidah-Glehue, no less. In this they met originally with success, since they were able to occupy Ouidah-Glehue for 25 days some time in October/November 1692, burning down the French factory there, but not the English one.[9] Marching northwards, they came within a mile of Savi, laying waste a great part of the country. But then they had, all of a sudden, to abandon their campaign, strangely enough for lack of ammunition – or so says Bosman.[10]

Ofori's withdrawal left relations between Allada and Hueda in a state of effective stalemate. Hostilities between the two petered out into a sort of phoney war, but with the paths remaining open most of the time.[11]

In sum, the events of 1690–93 proved disastrous to the Dutch and the French. Thomas Phillips, who met the French factor and his deputy in 1693–4, noted that they were dejected and poor, "having no livelihood but from the king's bounty".[12] It changed somehow, we imagine, only with the arrival of one of those short occasional missions the French were in a sense known for, that of the Chevalier D'Amon or Damon which stayed in Ouidah/Hueda from 11 December 1698 to 31 January 1699.[13]

But the Dutch fared even worse. Their position, as the so-called allies of Ofori, became untenable; evicted from Offra, they also had to abandon the factory they had maintained at Savi.[14] They were allowed to return only ten years later. In fact, 1693 is presented as a sort of pivotal year in the fortunes of the WIC on the Guinea coast. From then on its revenues sank sharply, never really to recover.[15]

It is true that Willem Bosman, second-in-command at Elmina, tried to sort out matters with the Hueda authorities during various visits between 1697 and 1699, with limited success. In fact Bosman, faithful to the rough behaviour which had become the trade-mark of the Dutch on the Guinea coast (and elsewhere),[16] attempted in 1697 a sort of mini-coup against the English. What Bosman did was simply to hire "Mina Blacks" (Ga-Adangbe mercenaries again) in order to seize the acting English director, a sergeant, and to destroy the English factory, the sergeant barely escaping with his life.[17] Bosman obviously failed; equally obviously, there is no trace of the incident in his book.

Did Akwamu take part in the 1692–93 war? Apparently both sides solicited Akwamu's intervention, paying vast amounts.[18] But although the English director of James Fort in Accra reported that trade there had come to a standstill because all the people of the region, and especially the Akwamus, had gone to fight in Hueda[19] (on both sides?), there is in the final analysis little evidence of any direct Akwamu intervention. That being said, the belligerents considered Akwamu a power to be reckoned with, the Dutch in particular, who were able to secure a treaty with that polity at that very time, in 1693. The treaty, which regulated conditions principally in the Accra region, is said also to have confirmed the Dutch as middlemen with regard to an alliance between Hueda and Akwamu which one presumes came into existence.[20] Hence the always intriguing Dutch assumed in a sense two roles, as both allies and foes of Hueda, trying to ride two horses as it were.

The English tried something of the same. On the one hand, they negotiated with Ofori for military assistance against the French (the War of the League of Augsburg again) – another European mini-war in the making; Agbangla of Hueda considered those negotiations to be treacherous, since Ofori was his enemy.[21] But on the other hand, at one stage (in 1691) the English intervened on the side of Hueda by landing "40 fully armed Mina slaves [mercenaries?] & 3 field-guns" at Offra itself.[22] However, it did not save the English chief factor John Wortley (the successor of Wybourne) from being arrested and deported in April 1692.[23] Agbangla had thus taught the European a lesson and had indicated clearly that there were limits beyond which the Europeans were not allowed to trespass. The lesson was not lost on the English, who emerged in fact as the great beneficiaries of the 1692–93 war on the European side. Indeed, the English of the RAC could take advantage of the fact that slaves turned out to be "very plenty" the following year, so that the slave ships did not have to stay for more than four to five weeks to complete their cargoes – an exceptionally short time[24].

As for Ofori and his men, after the fiasco at Hueda, they tried their luck in the west, turning against the Adangme immigrants in Keta. But here they were even less successful, since Ofori was killed in December 1693 or January 1694.[25] Next, the Ga-Adangbe refugees (called "Alampoes") who controlled Keta struck back, attacking and destroying Little Popo, meaning presumably the "kingdom" of Glidji. However, Ofori's successor, also called Ofori (Ofori Bembeneen), possibly identical with the Folo Bébé or second king of Glidji mentioned earlier, was able to rout the "Alampoes" and to recover Little Popo – or what was left of it – in February 1695.[26] One notes the ease with which villages, towns and forts were destroyed and, in particular, quickly rebuilt.

In the meantime, in 1694, Anlo allied itself with Hueda in a military confrontation with, strangely enough, Grand Popo-Hulagan (and at a time when the powers in between, Keta and Little Popo-Glidji, continued to be occupied with their own war).[27] But another version has it that "Alampoes" from Keta besieged Grand Popo, in support of, or on behalf of, the Hueda king.[28] We even know that the Huedans received assistance and ammunition from French ships (for reasons unknown). In any case, the people of Grand Popo succeeded in repulsing the assailants after a siege lasting a month,[29] not a minor feat for a small polity such as Grand Popo. In brief, this Huedan attempt at expansion, if that is what it was, failed. Hueda did not try again, so that Grand Popo-Hulagan maintained its independence.

* * *

After a few years' apparent lull, what happened in 1698–99 was that Oyo, in conjunction with Hueda, sent its mighty cavalry against Allada, where it committed, it is said, a great slaughter, thus establishing Oyo's ferocious reputation.[30] But was it really a devastating invasion or was it merely a punitive raid? And more generally, what was it all about? To chastise a rebellious vassal, if that is what the king of Allada was, or to force the king of Allada to become a vassal? Or was it to force Allada to keep the paths open and to stop interfering with the movement of the slave caravans from the north? The truth is once more that we do not know. The only thing we can say for certain is that it demonstrates that Oyo took, or continued to take, a keen interest in the affairs of the Slave Coast and that what had happened must have weakened Allada and strengthened Hueda. Our guess is that the Oyo intervention helped to expand the slave trade in and from Hueda, explaining why King Agbangla, incidentally a great lover of sedans,[31] had "grown very haughty and proud since Whidah [Ouidah] has been attended with so many ships".[32] As a result, the slave trade was "almost ruined" from the European point of view, implying that too many ships arrived on the coast.[33]

Then there came a new round in 1700 in the constant antagonism between Little Popo-Glidji and the Ga-Adangme "Alampoes" of Keta. This time the former were victorious since the latter were driven out of Keta. In fact the whole population of Keta fled.[34]

Then, in mid-February 1702 "the king of Aqvambu [Akwamu] unexpectedly rose up with all his might & expelled the whole population of the country, beginning a mile from here [i.e. Christiansborg fort at Accra] & pursuing them as far as...Aguina [Anloga?] on the Slave Coast".[35] This was apparently a new stage of what we have referred to earlier as Akwamu's imperial expansion. The Anlo confederacy was overrun, plus Keta, plus also Little-Popo/Glidji. Its king had to flee once more, to Allada this time. Finally, the Akwamu army arrived in Hueda in May 1702, a rather long way from home (note that there is no mention of Grand Popo-Agbanakin in this account). This time there is no doubt; Akwamu was or had become the ally of Hueda, the riches of Hueda having proved irresistible, we suppose. At Hueda, where the Akwamus rested for a few weeks, the local authorities urged them to continue eastwards, in the direction of Jakin and Allada. But the Akwamus did exactly the opposite, they retreated westwards. Rumour had it that Denkyira and Akyem, as enemies of the new polity of Asante (established in 1701–2) and therefore also of Akwamu, were preparing an attack on the Akwamu heartland.[36] Hence the retreat, which may also have been caused by the fact that Akwamuhene Ado was terminally ill; he died in fact shortly afterwards.[37]

But did the Akwamus return home more or less empty-handed or not? On this subject disagreement is, surprisingly enough, close to total among the specialists. On the one hand, Sandra Greene and Ivor Wilks argue that the rulers of Akwamu succeeded in incorporating the Slave Coast up to Ouidah-Glehue into their polity, Anlo included, and that Hueda became a tribute paying vassal of Akwamu, remaining so until 1727.[38] But on the other, as noted, D.E.K. Amenumey denies flatly that Akwamu ever ruled over Anlo.[39] And Silke Strickrodt and Robin Law doubt very much that Hueda became in any way a subordinate of Akwamu. It may be that the alliance between the two polities was maintained, for which reason Hueda solicited military assistance repeatedly from its ally. But the fact is that no such direct assistance was ever forthcoming.[40]

As for Little Popo-Glidji, another victim of Akwamu in 1702, it seems very much as if it was able to re-establish itself (miraculously?) as an independent polity quickly, continuing in fact to hire out mercenaries in all directions. By 1717 it had even recovered control over Keta.[41] But the rulers of Little Popo-Glidji continued to "put tricks upon all (the Captains)",[42] which did not help the slave trade.

Can we detect behind all these events an attempt on behalf of Lilliputian Hueda to construct some sort of grand coalition composed of Oyo, Akwamu and the English of the RAC, possibly also Jakin, against Allada and Little Popo-Glidji?

* * *

To backtrack slightly, the situation which emerged after 1693 with only the English effectively present on shore may not have been to the liking of the Huedans. But although the English were permitted to transform their factory-lodge at Ouidah-Glehue into a genuine fort[43] (were the local authorities looking for a shelter in case of an emergency?), the Huedans probably welcomed the (timid) French return in 1698–99 (the D'Amon expedition) with some relief.

It is significant in this respect that the Huedan authorities invited, at this very time in 1698, a company of Luso-Portuguese merchants to establish a factory. But the initiative failed because of the negative attitude of the Portuguese crown, more than ever opposed to the Mina trade because of the problem of contraband and the vexations inflicted by the Dutch.[44] One may classify it as another episode in the infighting between the authorities in Lisbon and their supposed subordinates in Salvador da Bahia.

* * *

Also in 1698, a minor revolution took place in the organization of England's African venture. Parliament passed the so-called "ten per cent act", implying the abolition of the Royal African Company's legal monopoly of the English slave trade. England's trade to Africa was then formally thrown open to private traders. The interlopers became the "ten-per cent" traders – they had to pay a ten per cent tax on the merchandise they departed with, for the upkeep of the RAC forts and lodges.[45]

The measure may not have amounted to much at the practical level – most interlopers turned ten per cent traders objected to it anyway, since it implied that they lost their free-rider benefits.[46] In addition, the RAC fought back on the Slave Coast, via another charm offensive directed at the Hueda authorities, promising to enlarge its trade and to increase the number of white people stationed there, also establishing a regular monthly postal service with Cape Coast Castle,[47] the message being that the Huedans did not need to trade with anyone else.[48] The Huedans may not have taken the hint, the African authorities being always in favour of maximum competition on the European side, and hence siding always with the interlopers.

In any case, the "ten per cent act" lapsed in 1712, which meant that the British slave trade had been totally deregulated (but also that there was, for long, no money for the upkeep of the forts).[49] The French and the Dutch did not go quite as far, but to some extent liberalised their respective slave trades anyway in the next decades (the details are very complicated and in any case unnecessary for our purpose).[50]

What is clear, then, is that 1698 inaugurated a new era, the beginning of the slow process of retreat from monopoly and adoption of free trade. In the long run it meant that the forts and lodges became, if not obsolete, even less important than what they had been earlier. However, all the relevant European nations decided to keep them – to the relief of the modern historians. But the problem was how to pay for their upkeep, and the solutions varied. Usually, and logically, the Crown and/or the traders had, directly or indirectly, to foot the bill.[51] The independent traders, however they were organized, and whichever private company they belonged to, were much less interested in internal African affairs, and hence much less prone to dabble in them, than the representatives of the chartered companies. All they wanted was to do their trade as quickly as possible and leave it at that. The implication is that the independent traders were precisely that, independent – vis-à-vis both the African authorities and the European ones.

* * *

In the case of the Slave Coast it is clear that the competition among the Europeans increased considerably, owing not only to the ten per cent traders but also to the massive arrival of the French from 1704 and the increased presence of the Luso-Portuguese from about 1706. They drove up the prices quite spectacularly.[52] It is symptomatic that the Danes complained (in 1713) about what they called "shameful" – meaning much too high – prices.[53] Actually, the demand exceeded the supply to such an extent that many ships had to leave the Ouidah roads empty-handed.[54] It had become very much a sellers' market.

* * *

The arrival of the French is indirectly linked to a major event on the international scene, the accession to the Spanish throne in 1700 of one of Louis XIV's grandsons, Philip V. This dynastic change presented the other European nations with the worrying prospect of a powerful joint French-Spanish realm, with France in the leading role. It led to the outbreak in 1702 of what many historians consider to be the first genuine world war, the War of the Spanish Succession (1702–13/14), which pitted Spain and especially France against most of the rest, led by England, Great Britain from 1707, a country set on the road to being a superpower thanks to its successes in that war.[55]

The French-Spanish rapprochement implied among other things that the French were granted the Spanish *asiento* for ten years (1703–13).[56] In a sense it forced the French authorities to get involved in the slave trade, and they had to start, if not from scratch, at least from a position of inferiority compared with the other slave-trading nations.[57] During those ten years the French were supposed to deliver 36,000 or 48,000 *"pièces d'Inde"* (*"piezas de India"*)[58] to the Spanish territories in America. Their problem was where to find all those slaves and how to pay for them. The French suffered to some extent from the same problem as the Portuguese: they had not much to offer owing to their deficient industries. They had therefore to purchase a fair amount of the merchandise they needed for the slave trade in more or less hostile places such as the Dutch Republic and Hamburg[59] – not very advantageous for the national economy. The French did however come up with a trump card after a while, cheap brandy[60] – although rum from the British colonies became rapidly a tough competitor.[61]

The French started out by simply robbing slaves from the others, and especially the British. In this they were far from unsuccessful.[62] But the French realized that they had to involve themselves directly in the slave trade and on a relatively grand scale. The obvious place to choose was Ouidah-Glehue in Hueda. The French *asiento* turned out to be a fiasco,[63] in the sense that the French managed to deliver only some 13,000 slaves (*pièces d'Inde*) into Spanish America.[64] However, for our purpose the central point is that the *asiento* implied that the French had to catapult themselves to centre stage on the Slave Coast in 1704.

But given the outbreak of the War of the Spanish Succession, would not the French have to deliver and to win battles against the English and the Dutch in order to attain their aim? It is at this stage that the Hueda authorities came to their rescue. Hueda forced the English, the French and the Dutch – the Dutch had made a discreet return to Savi some months earlier[65] – to sign on 25 April 1703 a formal treaty guaranteeing the neutrality of the port of Ouidah-Glehue, the famous Treaty of Neutrality in the history of the Slave Coast.[66] On the face of it, it meant merely the formalizing of what had always been the policy of Hueda and also of Allada. But the formalization was important enough. In the preamble the king declared his determination to maintain "a firm and durable peace throughout his entire realm". The king also threatened to decapitate whoever dared to trouble the neutrality of the Ouidah-Glehue road (Europeans included). All the captains who arrived in the roads had to sign the treaty.[67] Originally stipulated to last for the duration of the war, it remained in fact in force for some 91 years, until 1794, when it became an indirect casualty of the French Revolution, as we shall see. As a result, Ouidah-Glehue acquired quickly the reputation of a sort of safe haven, the only place along the whole Guinea coast where ships from all nations could trade in safety, independently of whichever war went on among European powers elsewhere.[68] It implied among other things the rapid development of the town of Ouidah-Glehue, the "lower town" (as opposed to Savi, the "upper town"). In brief, the case of Ouidah-Glehue illustrates the general point made by Wim Klooster, that in the Atlantic world "The neutral ports, open to flags of all nation, thrived in seasons of war".[69]

* * *

But shortly after the signing of the treaty, the Huedans made life difficult for themselves. The old king Agbangla died in August 1703, *all* his wives were sold to the Europeans (a very unusual occurrence, we suppose), and the – perhaps inevitable – succession dispute degenerated into a full-scale civil war in which the eldest son who had been passed over succeeded in recruiting an army in Allada, whose support (maybe counterproductive) he secured.[70] Finally a youngster by the name of Aisan or Amar/Amat ascended the throne. He was obviously the candidate of the English of the RAC, who, we note again, still held a preponderant position at that time. Was the installation of Amar the price the grandees had to pay for the support of the RAC? Or was it also in the interest of those grandees to put a feeble king on the throne after the probably energetic Agbangla?[71]

But the problem was that the king of Allada, although the enemy of Hueda, continued nevertheless to be considered its ritual overlord, for reasons which remain obscure. This implied that Alladan officials had to "make customs" for the deceased king Agbangla and also had to enthrone the new king.[72] But the king of Allada refused to play his part, logically enough, with – one imagines – negative consequences for the legitimacy of Amar. The seeds of internal discord had been sown in Hueda.

* * *

Next came the massive arrival of the French, in two waves, and obviously against strong opposition from the English of the RAC and the Dutch of the WIC.[73] But naturally the Huedans ignored the English and Dutch recriminations.

The first French wave was a direct consequence of the evacuation of Assini (or Issiny) in July 1703, the last and only French foothold on the Gold Coast (strictly speaking, on the Ivory Coast), in turn a direct consequence of the outbreak of the War of the Spanish Succession.[74] The Danes especially feared that the French fleet (four or five men-of-war and three merchant vessels) would attack them on its way eastwards.[75] But the French sailed directly to Ouidah-Glehue, where they prepared for battle. So did the ships already there. However, after having been informed about the Treaty of Neutrality signed the previous April, all sides desisted.[76] The Treaty had overcome its first and most decisive test.[77]

Obviously the French ships moved on from Ouidah-Glehue, but some of the personnel remained. Then came the second wave, a squadron under the command of a former *corsaire* (privateer) by the name of Jean Doublet, temporarily in the service of the Company of the Asiento, the new name of the Company of Guinea. The squadron, which included a number of enemy ships seized to the west, and which must therefore have been an imposing sight, arrived at Ouidah-Glehue on 27 September 1704, and stayed until 15 November. It was an official military expedition designed to take as many enemy ships as possible as prizes (except in the Ouidah-Glehue roads, where the Treaty of Neutrality prohibited this); to transport slaves to the Americas; and to establish a fort at Ouidah-Glehue.[78]

The French were lavishly treated by the Huedan authorities, the king included, who during a spectacular dinner offered to them was partially hidden in an alcove, as befitted a sacred king. The French were in particular impressed by a certain Captain Assou who, apart from speaking French rather well (*"parle joliment français"*)[79] and being the brother of the great priest (the *grand marabout* in Doublet's terminology), looked to the French like the power behind the throne. In brief, the Doublet mission was a resounding success: for the Huedans, who had acquired a genuine counterweight against the English (and the Dutch), and also for the French, whose fort was constructed in record time (two months) by more than 400 workers called out by the king. It was named Saint Louis de Gregoy (Gregoy being a French version of Glehue), it was equipped with cannon taken from a captured Dutch ship, and it became renowned for its enormous garden outside its gates.[80]

The Doublet mission was also a success in the sense that it left with more than a thousand slaves. But most perished en route. One of the ships caught fire off Cape Lopez and sank, leaving us with another heart-breaking description of slaves in chains trying desperately to save their lives; another met a similar fate in the Caribbean.[81]

But the French fort got off to a depressing start, since the second official mission which arrived on 13 February 1706 found it in a disorderly state, the director having been murdered by the surgeon, with the chaplain playing some sort of central but undefined role. Incidentally, after leaving Ouidah-Glehue the warship went to Príncipe, where it bombarded and captured the Portuguese fort. But as for the murderer, he managed to get away to Martinique.[82]

* * *

The year 1704 also saw the arrival in Ouidah-Glehue of other foreigners, but from the north this time, namely two so-called "Male", a word which refers to Muslim traders, possibly Hausa in this case. But theirs was a terrible fate – they were simply executed, the locals believing them to be spies for Allada.[83] However, other Male traders followed in their footsteps, opening the eyes of the Huedan authorities to the opportunities these newcomers represented; as a consequence they changed their attitude, guaranteeing the traders' security.[84] Regrettably we are poorly informed about the early phase of this link with the north.

The conflict between Allada and Hueda, which had become a constant, flared up again in July 1705, when Allada declared closed all the roads leading to Ouidah-Glehue. This amounted to a declaration of war, and war did in fact erupt some time later, Akwamu supporting Hueda indirectly, some historians believe, by recruiting Anlo troops to fight against Allada.[85] The immediate result was that the supply of slaves fell off.[86]

The always intriguing Dutch seem to have been in part responsible. Having tried, as noted, to persuade the Huedans to expel the French, the Dutch sought a second rapprochement with Allada in April 1705. What exactly the Dutch – or rather the Dutch Governor ("General") at Elmina, Willem de la Palma – had in mind, apart from trying to marginalize the French and English,[87] and how they thought to achieve it, is far from clear. What is clear is that de la Palma, a heavy drinker, threw away whatever it was he aimed at by most undiplomatic behaviour, even provoking an open revolt among his own subordinates. De la Palma, apparently disgusted with the course of events, died in late 1705, after which, in a sort of fitting epilogue, the Dutch lodge at Savi was entirely ruined by fire some time in 1706,[88] although it was rebuilt later. But the Huedan authorities had become wary of the Dutch, so that they were never permitted to build a fort at Ouidah-Glehue.[89]

We have mentioned all this because it illustrates the point made by van Dantzig that the Central Slave Coast had become a hotbed of intrigue among the Europeans, with everybody wanting to expel everybody else.[90] But it also illustrates once more a point made already, that the rough behaviour that often characterized the Europeans on the Gold Coast turned out to be counterproductive on the Slave Coast.

Finally, the intrigues of the Dutch may have signalled to the authorities of Allada that the position of the Europeans was not unshakeable and that a return to Allada was a distinct possibility. But for the time being the war between Hueda and Allada petered out, ending in a sort of unsatisfactory stalemate for both sides.[91] Allada continued nevertheless to impose blockades of Hueda, but, as noted, those blockades always turned out to be inefficient, sabotaged as they were by the king's own vassals.

* * *

Next came the Luso-Brazilians and the Brazilian gold which arrived in Ouidah-Glehue for the first time in 1706.[92] Gold deposits had been discovered in the Minas Gerais region in the interior of southern Brazil in the 1690s. But although there was a formal ban on exporting gold to any region outside of the Portuguese empire (it was even made a capital offence from 1723),[93] a thriving contraband developed nevertheless with considerable quantities of gold finding their way to the Guinea coast, especially to Ouidah-Glehue.[94] So it was that Richard Willis, the local chief factor of the RAC, received in 1707 orders to trade gold for slaves,[95] and the other Europeans followed suit rapidly. So also, and perhaps somewhat more surprisingly, did the local Africans. This was at a time when the gold deposits on the Gold Coast were in the process of becoming exhausted.

Gold and third-grade tobacco proved to be an irresistible combination which propelled the Luso-Brazilians to centre-stage.[96] It triggered intense competition among the others to provide the Luso-Brazilians with slaves in exchange for tobacco and especially for gold; the Europeans, and especially the British, tried in the process to control this new gold trade, something the Luso-Brazilians did not allow to happen.[97] But the latter also bought slaves directly and with considerable success. The result of all this was that the Luso-Brazilians could pick and choose as they wished, going away with the "best" ones. Indeed, "gold slaves" or "Portuguese slaves" became a concept, referring to the most sought after slaves, males in their early twenties, physically strong and with no defects – that is, top quality slaves.[98] Hence "to procure a cargo of choice Negros", to use an expression encountered frequently in the English sources,[99] became close to impossible for the others.[100]

The authorities in Lisbon looked with increasing mercantilist alarm upon the large quantities of gold and tobacco which private traders from Brazil sent to the Costa da Mina in order to purchase slaves,[101] plus in fact a lot of European merchandise, bought often with high-quality tobacco this time (plus sugar); these European goods were then imported illegally into Brazil. The *Costa da Mina* became thus a centre of contraband trade for the Luso-Brazilians, and the Mina trade developed into one of prime economic importance for the region of Bahia especially.[102]

The increasingly severe competition fuelled the climate of intrigue, leading in fact to a round of spectacular, not to say burlesque rows among the Europeans (the Luso-Brazilians excluded), culminating with the expulsion of various European chief factors/governors, especially in 1715.[103] Amusing to read about, they testify to the extreme degree of discord among the Europeans, even inside each camp, the superiors quarrelling with their subordinates.

* * *

But before that Hueda was rocked by a severe succession crisis in 1708, when king Aisan-Amar died, possibly poisoned, on 8 October 1708, after a reign of only five years.[104] The new king, Huffon, was a minor about 13 years old, and as such apparently not suited to execute some of the rituals incumbent upon the king.[105] In addition he too, like his predecessor, had to do without the ritual blessing of the relevant Allada officials. The result was some sort of short civil war, prompting the Europeans to land troops (in fact perhaps sailors from the ships in the roads) to protect their fellow-countrymen; but they did not take part in the fighting.[106]

Was Huffon, like his two predecessors, imposed by the Europeans, as some authors have surmised? But if so, which Europeans and for which purpose? Or was there an attempt by the leading headmen of the realm, Captain Assou included, to weaken the central authorities?[107]

In 1712 the still very young Huffon (or Captain Assou) embarked on what amounted to a genuine revolution, to sidestep the traditional hereditary chiefs in favour of people of his own making.[108] The temptation is great to interpret it as an attempt of those in charge in Hueda to change radically the very basis of the power of the kingship – something, we have suggested, that Agbangla too may have tried. But "the common people were divided", as Snelgrave remarked,[109] which meant that the outcome was internal strife, not to say civil war, with the traditional chiefs appealing for assistance to Huffon's formal overlord, the king of Allada. The civil war may have lasted until 1715, with the result, it is said, that royal power more or less collapsed.[110]

This constituted a golden opportunity for Allada, which was able to impose an unexpectedly effective blockade in February 1714, with the result that Hueda, that is to say Huffon and his mercenaries from Little Popo-Glidji, went to war in April the same year, leading to a sharp drop in trade.[111] But Huffon's army is said to have suffered a particularly humiliating defeat in April 1717.[112]

It was at this precise moment that, as we have seen, Dahomey began to dabble in the affairs of the coast. Having made itself independent of Allada (the traditional date for this, as noted, being 1715), and sought to ally itself with Hueda, Dahomey made finally (apparently) common cause with its former suzerain Allada in 1717.[113] Hence the prospects of the Huedans began to look rather bleak; they had been defeated in war and they were probably facing a formidable alliance between Allada and Dahomey.

But the Huedans were saved by a stroke of good luck, if the death of the old king of Allada in July 1717 can be called that (we know only that he died very old, not even his name has come down to us). This meant, as usual, a prolonged ceremonial-ritual cycle, and hence a halt to all belligerency. And then the succession was disputed between two brothers, Soso (or Sozo), who finally won (1717–24), and Hussar.[114]

Now both sides seemed apparently ready for a rapprochement. The new king of Allada, Soso, certainly played his part, since he agreed to crown king Huffon of Hueda (now of age) as tradition commanded – and the paths were reopened. As a consequence, in January 1718 Soso sent his officials to Hueda to "make custom" for the deceased kings Agbangla and Amar,[115] thus ending the state of dangerous ritual emergency under which the people of Hueda had lived ever since the death of king Agbangla in 1703.

One may surmise that what happened in 1717–18 had the potential of heralding a new era in the history of the Central Slave Coast. But it was not to be. In fact, for reasons unknown, relations soured once more, and very quickly so; the Alladan blockade of Hueda was revived before the end of 1718. At that time Dahomey had problems of its own – if, that is, the civil war which we have referred to earlier did in fact take place around that time. The blockade was maintained for the next six years, until the destruction of Allada itself in 1724.[116] Yet we cannot talk of going back to square one, since the Huedans had succeeded in "normalizing" their ritual-religious situation, which was perhaps their principal aim.

But the internal problems continued in both polities. In Hueda the by now universally hated Huffon made, if we are to believe the Europeans, a bid for absolute power in the early 1720s, thereby setting aside and even alienating the "new men" he himself had brought to power some years earlier.[117] What came out of it we do not know for certain, but probably nothing positive, since according to a French source from 1722 Huffon even asked the king of Allada, of all people, for troops against his own people.[118] As for Allada, its king had to face a revolt by some of his subjects in 1722.[119]

Then, in January 1724, that same king, Soso, died suddenly after a short reign of only seven years. It led to yet another succession dispute, with a certain Hussar, possibly the same as the defeated candidate in 1717, in the role of the leading claimant. But Hussar committed what turned out to be a major tragic blunder, that of soliciting in his favour the intervention of Allada's northern neighbour Dahomey.[120]

* * *

How did the slave trade get into this unpropitious situation? As can be deduced from the Database, it was not at all negatively affected, quite the contrary – it was possibly fuelled by the troubles and wars presented above. What changes we note have to do with the distribution among the participating nations.

About the mid-1710s some 18–19,000 slaves were exported annually from Ouidah-Glehue, according to a contemporary source (figures slightly higher than those of the Database). What was new was that the Luso-Brazilians now rivalled and possibly surpassed the British, the share of each being 6–7,000 slaves, whereas the share of the French had probably declined to 5–6,000, and that of the Dutch had plummeted to 1,500. This implied that some 12 to 14 ships often moored in the Ouidah-Glehue roads at the same time and that 35 arrived every month.[121]

The decline of the French share may perhaps be ascribed to the end in 1713/14 of the War of the Spanish Succession, a war which had not gone well for the French; in particular they lost the Spanish *asiento* to the English in May 1713. After that the Compagnie de l'Asiente went bankrupt, the Crown having to take over, while the superiors in France accused the drastically reduced staff on the spot of debauchery and all sorts of scandals (that reduction, incidentally, was compensated by a steep increase in the number of fort slaves.[122]) Under the new Compagnie des Indes which took over the totality of France's colonial interests in the Atlantic world in 1720, the situation does not seem to have improved markedly.[123] The perennial problem of the French was that they had no forts on the Gold Coast and therefore no easy access to canoemen, the French officials complaining that the canoemen worked for them only when they had nothing else to do, or when they felt like it.[124]

As for the Luso-Brazilians, the problems with the Dutch continued and even escalated, at least apparently. We cannot be sure because it is difficult to see clearly in this instance, the abundant sources notwithstanding, since there was a considerable difference between what went on at the top, the governmental level – the Portuguese authorities becoming increasingly vehement and menacing in their protests,[125] – and what went on locally on the coast. There the Luso-Brazilians had considerable success, as noted, and, according to the Dutch sources, the collection of the 10 per cent tax from the Luso-Brazilians became somewhat lax in the 1710s and especially in the 1720s.[126] But although lax, its mere existence proved increasingly obnoxious to the Portuguese crown in particular.[127]

The increasing importance of the Luso-Brazilians was made concrete and visible in 1721 with the beginning of the construction of their fort in Ouidah-Glehue, the third such fort, very close to the two others (the three forts were located about 300 metres from one another, and practically in a straight line[128]). It is significant that the man in charge on the spot, José Torres, received the necessary go-ahead from the Count of Sabugoza, the Portuguese Viceroy in Salvador da Bahia (1720–35), who acted more or less on his own – in spite of Torres' dubious reputation, which Sabugoza apparently chose to ignore.[129] Clearly Torres and Sabugoza represented the Bahian commercial interests in direct opposition to the authorities in Lisbon which had tried for years to persuade the Bahian traders to take their trade elsewhere. It is also significant that the Portuguese fort which emerged somewhat slowly from the ground,[130] in spite of strong English and French opposition and downright sabotage on behalf of the Dutch, but with the enthusiastic support of Huffon,[131] was put *de facto* under the authority of the viceroy in Salvador da Bahia.[132] And as with the other forts in Ouidah-Glehue, an indigenous quarter (Docomè) grew up rapidly around this one too;[133] the forts, like the castles of the Middle Ages in Europe, attracted people.[134]

The Portuguese also showed their teeth in January 1724 when a Portuguese battleship shot to pieces a Dutch frigate off Elmina. It was supposed to be the beginning of a plan of reprisals, but one which never really got off the ground.[135]

As for the fort, later known as São João Baptista (St John the Baptist), it certainly made a difference to the Portuguese position. This was shown by the complaints of others to the effect that the Portuguese now made the law in Ouidah-Glehue.[136]

Above all, the construction of a third fort in Ouidah-Glehue consolidated that place as the leading slave mart in the region, a position that had been seriously threatened in the second half of the 1710s. The supposed breakdown of central power in Hueda, mentioned above, had led the Europeans to begin thinking about getting out of Hueda, that is, returning to Jakin and Allada and establishing factories in other parts of the coast, such as Little Popo-Aneho. They did so in fact, repeatedly, although temporarily, and without getting to the point of constructing forts.[137] The trouble was that the Western Slave Coast continued to be characterized by near-chaotic conditions, due primarily to the depredations of Akwamu;[138] and that in Allada the king did it all wrong from the European point of view. He doubled the customs duties in 1718, while at the same time enforcing more strictly the requirement for European captains to travel to the Alladan capital far in the inland to trade, which resulted in greatly increased costs.[139] According to the modern historians Isaac Akinjogbin and Robin Law both the kings of Allada and Hueda in fact attempted to shore up royal control of the slave trade, possibly trying to make it a royal monopoly, and in particular to exclude the hinterland traders from direct contact with the Europeans, to make the Huedans and Alladans into obligatory middlemen[140] – to the detriment of Dahomey among others. But although Law argues that Allada had partially recovered its position by 1718,[141] that did not last, for in the end it looks very much as if Hueda and Ouidah-Glehue maintained their position. Apart from the construction of the Portuguese forts, we have all the complaints about the insolence of Huffon, about his enormous wealth, and about all the ships which arrived in the Ouidah-Glehue road, "spoiling" the trade (that is, provoking too much competition);[142] those complaints indicate that the Europeans certainly did not have it their own way.

* * *

We cannot leave Hueda and Ouidah-Glehue in the 1710s and the 1720s without returning to the subject of the pirates who for a short while represented a serious menace. It began in 1719 when some 5–600 pirates, most having been expelled from the Bahamas, descended on West Africa, establishing bases in Sierra Leone and on Annobón, and seizing some 47 slave ships according to the official figures, but probably more, mostly in 1719.[143] Piracy is said to have disrupted trade severely at Ouidah-Glehue in the relevant period, provoking incidentally a rapprochement between Huffon and the European directors.[144] The Portuguese were afraid the pirates might try to seize São Tomé.[145] As related earlier, the pirates were protagonists in a particularly nasty episode in the Ouidah-Glehue roads in January 1722 which resulted in the loss of many hundred lives.

But the European powers reacted relatively quickly, the British dispatched warships, and the Dutch WIC sent its local cruisers in pursuit of the pirates.[146] By February 1722 it was already over, the pirates having been decisively defeated in battle and most of them captured (only by the British). The epilogue was a spectacular trial at Cape Coast Castle, the largest trial of pirates ever held, which began at the end of March 1722. The Court was remarkable for its leniency since of the 160 or so individuals brought to trial, only 52 were sent to the gallows[147] (in trials involving the charge of piracy, normally defendants were either condemned to death or acquitted). Note the central role of Surgeon-Lieutenant John Atkins in this affair, the very same man who went on to write a book which ranks, as we have seen, as one of the main sources for the history of that coast.[148] After 1722 the British appear to have occasionally sent men-of-war to the coast of Guinea to keep it free of pirates.[149]

PART C
CHRONOLOGICAL OVERVIEW
THE 1720s–1850/51

1

THE DRAMATIC AND DECISIVE 1720s

In March 1724 Apocalypse descended upon the people of the metropolitan area of the old polity of Allada. Warriors of Dahomey routed the local army completely on 30 March, carrying out in the process a massive carnage, something probably unheard of until then on the Slave Coast. "Had it rain'd blood, it could not have lain thicker on the ground" was how an unwilling European eyewitness with the uncommon name of Bulfinch Lambe described it.[1] This massacre, a form of what we may call ostentatious brutality,[2] marked a real caesura in the history of the Slave Coast – the beginning of the most spectacular, most dramatic and certainly most bloody phase in the history of that coast. It was a phase, moreover, which saw a major reshaping of the map, since three of the leading protagonists of the previous era disappeared: Allada (in 1724–6), Hueda (in 1727–30/33) and Akwamu (in 1730) – although in the latter case some sort of small successor polity survived east of the river Volta, as an exclusively Slave Coast polity. Allada, Hueda and Akwamu were followed by the Hula polity of Jakin in 1732. From then on the scene was dominated by the new leading power of the Slave Coast, and the conqueror of three of the four polities mentioned above – Dahomey – at the cost of a tremendous number of human lives. But the Dahomean assaults did not go uncontested, the Dahomeans encountering stiff opposition in many instances, both internally and externally. There is in any case no question that the history of the Slave Coast gravitates from the 1720s onwards around Dahomey.

There is a nearly perfect coincidence in time between these events and what happened on the neighbouring Gold Coast. After the death of the first king of Asante, Asantehene Osei Tutu, on the battlefield in 1717, and after a period of interregnum and internal strife, the second Asantehene, Opoku Ware (died 1750), was able to stabilize the situation and to embark upon a very successful expansionist policy, but as far as we know not in the excessively brutal Dahomean manner; Asante eventually became possibly larger than present-day Ghana.[3]

Were king Agaja of Dahomey and his successor Tegbesu inspired by the example of their contemporary Opoku Ware? If so, they did not, in spite of Agaja's several conquests, get anywhere near the achievements (if so they can be described) of the latter – the "traditional" ways of Asante proved to be much more efficient both internally and externally than the "revolutionary" ones of Dahomey. That is in part because the rulers of Asante never had to grapple with the problem which always bedevilled their Dahomean counterparts, the problem of legitimacy.

* * *

The backdrop to what happened in 1724 in Allada concerned an internal conflict which we presume ran deep, and which was personified by the king Soso or Sozo, the one who had tried a rapprochement with Hueda, and his brother Hussar, the losing pretender in 1717. Hussar's party seems to have included the "Great Captain" or "Constable", the highest-ranking dignitary after the king, and as such possibly the successor to Delbée's "Grand Marabout", plus several "governors" (that is, crown vassals).[4] The details are far from clear, one possibility being that Sozo died suddenly in January 1724, and that the election of his son (name unknown) was contested by Hussar. The other (less likely) possibility is that Hussar rose in rebellion against Sozo. But the essential point seems to be in any case that the Dahomean attack originated in a sense as a mercenary venture, the Dahomeans having been hired to support the claims of Hussar. But the victorious Dahomeans betrayed their "employer" since they put a son of Soso (another son?) on the throne instead. After ensuring that the new king paid homage to Agaja, thus converting the former into a puppet of the latter, the main bulk of the Dahomean army went home.[5]

What happened exactly in 1724? Was it the beginning of the conquest of Allada? Or was it a one-time intervention or a raid which because of its success gave Agaja the idea to conquer Allada? The long-term consequences of 1724 are in any case not in doubt; the mortally wounded Allada *was* finally conquered, in 1726, and in fact annexed, that is, swallowed up by

Dahomey and erased from the map as a separate entity. And all the subordinate principalities,[6] having at first simply changed overlord, were equally wiped out in the end, with the temporary exception of Jakin; and their rulers were replaced by Dahomean nominees who owed their allegiance exclusively to Agaja,[7] in the usual Dahomean manner. The Dahomeans demonstrated in fact once more that they had no intention of respecting the indirect-rule model. But how long did it all take, and how many mopping-up actions were necessary? The chronology is far from clear in this respect.

The exception was, as noted, coastal Jakin, whose ruler made his submission to Agaja in April 1724.[8] The Jakin polity was permitted to continue to exist as an autonomous, if not virtually independent entity, and took over from Ouidah-Glehue (that is, recovered more or less its old position) as the leading trade slaving centre.[9] As such it was to play an important role on the local scene for a while.

Incidentally, some sort of tourism occurred in 1724, since many Dahomeans went to see south of Jakin what they had never seen before: the ocean.[10]

As for the many Alladans who fled to Hueda, quite a few were either sold as slaves or left to die from hunger, accused as they were of having killed snakes belonging to the species the Huedans considered to be their totem animal.[11]

What about the few Europeans (we do not know how many) who were present in Allada on 30 March 1724? They were taken prisoners, but all but one were quickly liberated. The one exception was the above-mentioned Bulfinch Lambe who found himself confined to Abomey, the first European to set foot on the Dahomean capital, possibly the first on Dahomean soil generally.

Lambe was a special case. As a RAC employee stationed at Jakin, he had been "panyarred" – another of those words which have disappeared from current English; that is, he had been seized in 1722 by the king of Allada to enforce the payment of a debt that king Soso claimed the RAC owed him (the RAC had reopened a lodge in Jakin in July 1722). And since the RAC did nothing, Lambe languished in captivity in Allada until he passed into the custody of Agaja,[12] together with at least one Luso-Brazilian mulatto (Luso-Brazilian mulattoes pop up everywhere in the history of the Slave Coast, but always in minor roles). Since furthermore (according to Dalzel) "Agaja considered having white men about him a great addition to his grandeur",[13] it became the role of Lambe to sit next to the king whenever he appeared in public: "When (the King) comes out in Publick, the Portuguese and I are call'd to sit all day in the sun". But Lambe added that Agaja "pays us pretty well for it";[14] in fact Lambe was quite lavishly treated by his captors. We shall return to Lambe's life, worthy of a film.

* * *

On 14 April 1726 the redoubtable cavalry of Oyo descended all of a sudden on Dahomey, inflicting an apparently shattering defeat; Abomey is reported to have been burned, and Agaja and Dahomey were believed to have been finished off[15] (incidentally, this was a defeat by cavalry dependent upon *imported* horses, from the north, of infantry equipped with *imported* muskets, from the south).[16] One who seems to have tried to take advantage of the situation was Hussar, the eternal pretender to the throne of Allada, who may even have succeeded in reoccupying Allada for a while, and who even contemplated marching against Dahomey itself.[17]

But to cut a long (and complicated) story short, the strange fact (we consider it so) is that both Agaja and Dahomey survived the debacle, re-emerging more or less unscathed after the Oyo cavalry had been forced to retreat. The outcome was finally a sort of treaty between Oyo and Dahomey; a treaty according to which Agaja submitted to Oyo, and accepted to pay a tribute, but on condition that Oyo gave the Dahomeans a free hand in Allada.[18]

Dahomey thus ceased formally to be an independent polity in 1726 and became instead, still formally, a vassal of Oyo. But although Dahomey remained a vassal of Oyo all the way to 1818, the treaty of 1726 proved in reality to be no more than an unsteady and short-lived truce.

Here a long digression is necessary in order to confront problems which the historians have grappled with for a long time. The Oyo invasion of April 1726 turned out to be but the first of a number of such invasions (exactly how many is not clear). And each time the scenario of 1726 repeated itself; that is, the Dahomeans were defeated, after which the Oyo cavalry retreated, and then the Dahomeans re-emerged from their hiding, carrying on as usual, as it were.[19] The question is why Oyo was unable to fully wipe out Dahomey, why its cavalry always had to retreat after a short while, and what Oyo was up to more generally. But the question is also, and perhaps above all, how the Dahomeans survived.

With regard to Oyo we encounter an annoying blank: we know nothing about the motivations and aims of the Oyo rulers. As Robin Law has put it: "The motives behind [the] Oyo intervention can only be surmised". And he went on to speculate that "The rulers of Oyo may simply have grasped the opportunity presented by the local conflicts in the south-west to strengthen their influence in the area". Or perhaps, "The Dahomian conquest of the coast threatened the commercial interests of Oyo" so that "the *alafin* [king of Oyo] intervened in order to keep open the slave-trade ports for the Oyo traders".[20] If so, this was nothing new, since, as we have noted earlier, Oyo had probably intervened in the south already in the seventeenth century.

It is also possible that there were pre-emptive strikes, of a sort, on behalf of Oyo; that Dahomey, the new aggressive and militaristic polity which had emerged in the south-west, and which obviously did not respect the rules of the game, preoccupied the Alafin and his men. If so, was Oyo the guardian of the traditional order threatened by Dahomey?

But why were all the invasions of Dahomey followed by as many retreats, why was Oyo unable or unwilling to conquer Dahomey – in spite of the fact that Oyo's manpower advantage over Dahomey was overwhelming, according to Stanley Alpern?[21] It may have had to do first, and simply, with the considerable distance between metropolitan Oyo and Dahomey, and the many rivers that had to be crossed in between; and second, with the fact that the people of Dahomey were Fon (Gbe-speakers) and not Yoruba and therefore unlikely to acquiesce gracefully, over time, in Oyo rule, indirect or otherwise. Then there is the problem of the Oyo cavalry, a cavalry relying incidentally on archery and not firearms, and accompanied also by archers on foot.[22] Here the problem is, to return to a theme evoked in the Introduction, the danger represented to horses by trypanosomiasis and the tsetse fly, its vector. Trypanosomiasis is basically a phenomenon of regions covered by rain forest, but it is no stranger to the savanna, at least not to the most humid parts. In fact, the further southwards one gets from the tsetse-free area in northern Yorubaland (situated largely inside the Oyo empire), the greater the danger to horses.[23] This tallies with what we know about horses generally on the Slave Coast in the seventeenth and eighteenth centuries – that they were few, uniformly small, and not bred locally.[24] One consequence was that no-one ever thought in terms of cavalry on that coast. The point here is that the Oyo cavalry was at risk even in the Abomey region, since it was not entirely free of the tsetse fly; the cavalry had in any case to avoid the rainy seasons, when little or no fodder was available.

We may add that cavalry is not always, or by definition, superior to infantry; especially not if the infantry is, contrary to the opposing cavalry, equipped with firearms and artillery. Dahomey did have firearms, but no artillery. No-one was ever capable of mounting genuine artillery on the Slave Coast.

In this context John Thornton has argued that the Dahomean army responded to the Oyo challenge by adopting a close order of fighting, appropriate for dealing with cavalry-using forces, and in constructing field fortifications.[25] This is the kind of statement which leaves the impression that we really know these things. But the heart of the matter is first, that Dahomey only defeated Oyo once, at the very end, when its cavalry was probably no longer operative; and second, that Oyo may not have had the means, or dreaded the consequences, of any prolonged military activity in the south – something which Agaja knew, so that he opted for his famous delaying tactic. Incidentally, the Oyo menace may explain in part why Agaja was apparently bent on conquering the southern Slave Coast. It meant that he and his people had somewhere to go in case of a major onslaught, namely south of the Lama, since to cross that area was impossible for horsemen; to go around it also involved huge practical problems, as it meant much larger rivers to cross than further north. It may be of significance in this context that Agaja moved, in 1730, his secular capital from Abomey to Allada, in fact a new Allada, some three km away, on the other side of the river Auté.[26] But of course, the change of capital was also charged with mythical-religious symbolism, the Agasuvi having come home, in a sense, to the place where Agasu, their mythical ancestor, was buried (the direct link between Tado and Abomey had not yet been established).

As for the Dahomeans' ability to survive the Oyo onslaughts, the standard explanation has been that they disappeared into the bush while waiting for the Oyo cavalry to retreat. But we now have an alternative or supplementary explanation, and a much more convincing one, thanks to the earlier-mentioned team of Danish archaeologists led by Klavs Randsborg and Inga Merkyte. It is that the population simply disappeared underground. Indeed, the Randsborg-Merkyte team has dug out a number of so-called caves ("*sous-terrains*"), in their words beautifully carved and spacious subterranean caves, more than a thousand of which have been located so far.[27] The Danish team believes that there may be no less than between 8,000 and 16,000 of them, and exclusively on the Abomey plateau. The soil of that plateau makes the ground very suitable for durable subterranean structures. The archaeologists add that the town of Abomey was already surrounded by a deep and wide moat from the mid-seventeenth century.[28]

* * *

We must return to the chronological account and note the obvious, namely that the retreat of Oyo freed Agaja's hand and left Hussar and his men in a dramatic situation. In brief, Agaja had no problems in reconquering (or conquering) Allada, massacring Hussar and his men and completing the destruction of Allada in May 1726. This time no puppet ruler was installed; Allada was annexed. The English slave trader William Snelgrave reported seeing "A great ruin'd town" in 1727.[29] Snelgrave, who journeyed from Jakin to Allada, "saw the remains of towns and villages, with a great quantity of (human) bones strewed about the fields", and in the King's camp in the capital heaps of dead men's heads, those of the 4,000 or so Alladans reported to have been sacrificed by the Dahomeans to their gods.[30] One interesting detail is that Agaja, whose countenance much impressed Snelgrave, told him that he was resolved to encourage trade.[31]

In May/June 1726 Bulfinch Lambe was "dismissed by the King of (Dahomey, but) in a very handsome manner", as the English director put it,[32] and allowed to return to Hueda. He returned, according to his account, with a letter containing an unequivocal message: Agaja had every intention of conquering Hueda. What was more, Agaja expected the Europeans to remain neutral: "When I send my forces against Whidah [Hueda]...I shall give orders...to take care not to hurt any of the white men, in goods or persons, if they keep in their Fort & Factory. But if they come in a warlike manner...".[33] Can we deduce that the Huedans and the Europeans had been duly forewarned? The trouble is that Jeremy Tinker, the then RAC director in Hueda, testified later in London that Lambe never showed him any letter from Agaja (or was Lambe too resentful against the RAC to do so?). This is the main reason why the British authorities concluded that the letter Lambe presented to them in 1731 was a forgery, that is, written not by Agaja but by Lambe himself – a conclusion Robin Law disagrees with. We shall return later to the extraordinary adventures of Lambe and the famous letter. But for the moment we must note that Lambe left Ouidah-Glehue after only three months and was thus spared the spectacle of another Dahomean massacre. Note also that Lambe did not mention Oyo's attack on Dahomey on 14 April 1726, an attack we suppose he had witnessed.

However, whether the letter existed or not, did Lambe not have any useful information to share with the people in Hueda, whether European, Luso-Brazilian or African? And did not the rise of Dahomey, and especially what had happened in Allada in 1724 and 1726, constitute a warning serious enough? But if so, it was not heeded; no attempt was made to set aside internal discord and present a united front against the new external enemy – if, that is, Dahomey was perceived as such.

Actually, it looks as if Hueda was already in the midst of a process of more or less complete disintegration with civil war. There was possibly one such war in 1725, and if not a general civil war, at least a several days' fight with many dead in April 1726, coinciding with Oyo's assault on Dahomey.[34] Then, an unmistakeable sign, one vassal of the king of Hueda, the *aplogan* of the border principality of Gome, simply changed sides during the second half of 1726, severing his ties with the king of Hueda and instead paying allegiance to Agaja.[35]

But the authorities of Hueda remained unmoved; it is even said that the king and his leading dignitary Captain Assou laughed at the rumours of a Dahomean invasion[36] (so there were such rumours). How to explain their attitude? Did they have an unlimited faith in their tutelary deity the snake? Or did they believe they could hire enough mercenaries to defeat Dahomey? Or did they believe that Oyo, and possibly also Akwamu, or both, would come to their rescue? As a final possibility, the always intriguing Dutch had promised in November 1726 assistance from Elmina in case of an emergency, on the condition that the king of Hueda agreed to demolish the Portuguese fort and allow them to build a proper lodge at Ouidah-Glehue.[37] Whether the king of Hueda really did so promise is not certain, our sources are somewhat ambiguous. But as we shall see, there certainly were Huedans who believed that the Dutch had promised their help.

* * *

Robin Law's account of the Dahomean conquest of Hueda and the shoreline of the Central Slave Coast[38] makes clear that it turned out to be a long drawn-out affair which lasted until 1730, 1733, 1745 or even to 1775, if not later, depending on one's definition – if, that is, what happened in 1727 was really the beginning of a determined intention on the part of Agaja to conquer Hueda.

Whatever the case, and whether expected or not, the Dahomean assault on Savi, the capital of Hueda, occurred on 9 March 1727.[39] And the same devastation which had taken place in Allada in 1724 and in 1726 was now repeated; the town and the surroundings were laid waste with great, and once more ostentatious, brutality.[40] The assault claimed some 5,000 dead and 10–11,000 prisoners according to the testimony of the Luso-Brazilian Director Francisco Pereyra Mendes,[41] for what that may be worth. The same Pereyra Mendes argues that Agaja told him that he, the king of Dahomey, certainly wanted to trade with the Europeans, and that he had decided to conquer Allada and Hueda because the rulers of those two polities prevented him from doing so.[42] This strikes us as a more logical motive for the conquest of the coast than the one forwarded by Akinjogbin, that Dahomey conquered the coast in order to put an end to the slave trade.

In brief, the Huedan army had been soundly defeated, in spite of the contention made by a French observer that it was far more numerous than the opposing forces. But the Huedans (or the hired mercenaries) declined to fight, according to him.[43]

The European lodges in Savi did not escape the destruction, and were burnt to the ground, never to be rebuilt again. Of the Europeans present, some 38 were made prisoners and taken to Allada where Agaja resided. However, they were released relatively quickly, after three weeks' captivity in rather inhuman conditions, according to themselves. But five Dutchmen, after being freed by the Dahomeans, were then taken prisoner by the Huedans, because the WIC had not honoured its promise to aid Hueda – according to the Huedans. The Dutch arrived finally at Keta on 2 April aboard a Portuguese ship, more dead than alive.[44] Hendrik Hertogh, the Director in Hueda and already an old hand in the Guinea trade, was not among the five; he had escaped to Jakin.

Actually, not all the Europeans in Savi were taken prisoner in March 1727. In the middle of the chaos many managed to escape to Ouidah-Glehue, and even to the nine ships moored in the Ouidah-Glehue roads at that time,[45] incidentally leaving behind a considerable quantity of trade goods.[46] Most of the ships left in a hurry. But in one ship the slaves, who believed (we suppose) that their hour of liberation had arrived, staged a revolt, with a tragic outcome – no-one came to their rescue, and 30 of them were killed.[47] We add in this context the story of an English ship which arrived shortly afterwards, and which decided to stay instead of going to Jakin. It had great success, since people were in starving conditions, selling servants and children etc. in order to buy food from Grand Popo – or so says William Snelgrave.[48]

After the assault on Savi, one version has it that the Dahomeans then moved south to Ouidah-Glehue, laying siege to the European forts[49] and actually demolishing (more or less?) the Portuguese one, possibly as a warning. But the siege of the two others and especially the French fort (where many Europeans had taken refuge) was lifted after only a few days;[50] this was what was left of the French fort, since it had been severely damaged, or burnt down, by an accidental fire, presumably in January-February 1727, and still not repaired completely at the end of February (the French "useing all possible Expedition to get it repaired").[51] What happened next, in April, was that the main part of the Dahomean army simply withdrew, not only from Ouidah-Glehue, which was left by implication under the authority of the European forts, but also from Hueda generally, leaving apparently only a small garrison at Savi.[52]

The explanation provided by Snelgrave is that the Dahomean army had to be despatched against Tofo, to the north in Allada, presumably because the people of Tofo had attacked a Dahomean (slave) caravan. Snelgrave tells us that the campaign against Tofo was entirely successful, since it yielded 1,800 captives, 400 of whom were promptly sacrificed in a ceremony at Allada witnessed by the same Snelgrave.[53] But if the people of Tofo had embarked upon such an action, it was obviously because they thought they could get away with it. And if so, the whole affair alerts us to the possibility that Dahomey's hold over the region which had constituted Allada was still tenuous, that the Dahomeans were perhaps overstretched, that they simply had not the resources and the manpower necessary to pacify Allada, let alone to genuinely conquer Hueda in addition. And in the background Oyo continued to lurk.

* * *

All this lends credit to what a Danish observer in Accra suggested, that what the Dahomeans had carried out was merely a raid, that what interested them was to secure as high a ransom as possible from the Huedans.[54] It may be significant in this context that the Dahomeans allowed, or were unable to hinder, the exodus of a very considerable part of the Huedan population. Among those who escaped were, even more significantly, the king himself, and most of the leading dignitaries, Captain Assou included, the very people capable of paying a ransom – and the very people the Dahomeans would have sought out in the first place if their aim had really been to conquer. It is true that the exiled Huedans had to regroup, especially in the difficult and more or less wetland region to the west, where in theory the Dahomean army was at a considerable disadvantage.[55] But there are indications that many of them considered it to be a temporary inconvenience and expected to return to their land soon. In other words, the Huedans may have believed that they had lost a battle, but not the war.[56] If so, they were not altogether wrong, since a war, which it is tempting to call either the Huedan Three-Years' or even the Huedan Seven Years' War (1727–30/34), was actually the result of the Dahomean attack on 9 March 1727.

Since our sources are occasionally confusing about the details (while some are truly bloodcurdling),[57] we concentrate on the central theme, which is clear enough, namely that the (presumably unofficial) alliance between the exiled

Huedans and Oyo several times enabled the former to reoccupy not only Ouidah-Glehue beach but also more or less the whole of Hueda, Savi included, especially at the beginning of 1730, and even to start reconstructing their land at some stage.[58] All this happened, obviously, with the connivance of the Europeans in Ouidah-Glehue who dreaded the Dahomeans and hoped for the return of their old trading partners, the Huedans.[59] But to repeat, each time the Oyo cavalry had to retreat after a while from Dahomey, leaving the Dahomeans a free hand in the south. The hostilities did not preclude occasional negotiations; at one stage Agaja even offered Huffon to return to Savi, but as a vassal of his.[60]

The Europeans found themselves caught in a very uncomfortable in-the-middle position, due in part to the fact that their forts and their cannon had acquired all of a sudden a vital importance in this war between Africans. Even more vital had become the control of Ouidah-Glehue beach and hence of the slave trade. On top of it all this was intrigue time, even inside the forts, especially the French one.[61] Many Europeans feared for their lives and braced themselves for the worst.[62] In fact, the European community was to pay a high price in lives. It began with the French director Houdoyer Dupetitval who was captured by the Huedans, accused of siding with the Dahomeans. He died in captivity or was killed by the same Huedans, actually betrayed by one of his own subordinates, a certain Étienne Gallot, whom the Huedans then installed as the new director; Gallot was forced to flee soon afterwards but managed somehow to return to France.[63] In this process the French fort was blown up, somewhat accidentally, leaving a great many of the occupants, who happened to be exiled Huedans, dead. As for Dupetitval's English colleague Charles Testefolle, he was accused by the Dahomeans of betraying *their* cause and tortured and executed.[64] Also a Portuguese official by the name of Simão Cardoso was killed, by the Huedans this time.[65]

Both directors were quickly replaced and reinforcements sent, and the French fort in particular was repaired.[66] The Europeans and Luso-Brazilians had then no intention of abandoning Ouidah-Glehue, war or no war. The slave trade was too important. In addition, Agaja encouraged them; he went out of his way, time and again (but after the Testefolle affair), to assure the Europeans that he meant them no harm, that in fact he had every intention of collaborating closely with them.[67] At one stage he even went as far as to threaten with the death penalty anyone who molested the Europeans in any way.[68] Agaja's attitude does not strike one as characteristic of someone bent on ending the slave trade. The same may be said of his appointment in September

1728 of three chiefs to act as liaison officers with the forts, and especially to levy customs from them.[69] They were replaced in 1733 by one official, the *tegan*, title later changed to *yovogan* (unless *tegan* was a name), literally the chief of the white men, governor of Ouidah-Glehue and in fact of coastal Dahomey, and as such a sort of viceroy. The establishment of this institution is generally taken to imply more effective Dahomean control over Ouidah-Glehue.[70] But it should be noted that most Slave Coast polities had this institution, called *yevuga* among the Ewe.[71]

Once more a pertinent question is, given the turbulence of the period, what happened with the slave trade. And the answer is, as we have seen from the Database, that the period 1726–30 marked an all-time high – for reasons all too obvious. It was then very much business as usual. However, the next five years were marked by a steep decline, never to be reversed.

Were there other peoples or groups involved in the war? It seems as if the Mahi, the northern neighbours of Dahomey living in a hilly region difficult to conquer, and organized into a loose confederacy, assisted the Oyos.[72] As for the exiled Huedans, they obviously had contacts with Hendrik Hertogh, the WIC Director who had come to dominate the scene in Jakin, and with Little Popo-Glidji. But if so, nothing concrete came out of those contacts.

What we can risk arguing on the other hand, and more generally, is that what happened in 1724–27 and afterwards sent shock-waves throughout the whole region, implying the spread of disorder and banditry with many paths closed – it might be seen as a general breakdown of law and order, resulting even in the sacking and burning of minor European factories, such as the WIC's at Keta in August 1731.[73] In this field the Ge of Little Popo-Glidji seem to have been particularly notorious – banditry may even have amounted to a state-sponsored enterprise among them, according to one modern historian.[74]

* * *

What changed the situation radically in 1730 was that Oyo opted out, at least for the time being. The result was two more or less formal treaties, thanks apparently to the efforts of the third fort director, the Luso-Brazilian João Basilio, who was actually a Frenchman.[75] The treaty between Dahomey and Oyo contained, it seems, basically the same provisions as the truce-armistice of 1726: Dahomey became, or continued to be a vassal of Oyo and as such had to pay from now on a huge humiliating tribute, including in people, the *ayogban* (load), so called by the Dahomeans.[76] But the counterpart was peace and a free hand in the south, that is, no more wars on two fronts. In the second treaty of August 1730, between Dahomey and the Europeans, the latter promised to give no more support to the exiled Huedans – a promise they were not always able or willing to keep. But this left the exiled Huedans out in the cold, especially since the third treaty which the Europeans had hoped for, between Dahomey and the exiled Huedans, never materialized, simply because Agaja was not interested.[77] The implication was that the exiled Huedans from now on considered the Europeans as their enemies, and were bent on expelling them.[78] The exiled Huedans in fact reacted furiously to the European-Dahomean rapprochement, launching a number of raids on Ouidah-Glehue beach between at least May and August 1731, and later. On one occasion six Europeans were killed.[79] As usual, the Europeans were caught in the middle.[80] The exiled Huedans also concluded, we presume, that they needed a new and solid territorial basis. In short, they turned against their erstwhile ally Grand Popo and tried simply to conquer that polity between 1731 and 1733; but in this they do not seem to have been successful.[81]

The exiled Huedans were also seriously weakened by the deaths of both Captain Assou, the soul of the resistance, and the king himself, Huffon, still not forty years old, in June-August 1733. Huffon's death triggered off a succession dispute, which in turn made a group of exiled Huedans submit to Agaja. The latter even installed a sort of Huedan puppet-king in Savi in 1734, with the obvious hope of enticing more Huedans to return "home". But it turned out to be a fiasco. Anyway, in 1734 Agaja virtually finished off what was left of the Huedans, with what seems like the active assistance of the French who had clearly decided to opt for what they expected to be the winning side.[82]

But the exiled Huedans, or what was left of them, did gain a territorial base of sorts in the end; they established a small polity in the loosely organized region west of Lake Ahémé, at modern Houeyogbe, just 30 km northwest of Savi.[83] And they continued, in spite of everything, to pose a threat to the Dahomeans, resorting increasingly to genuine guerrilla warfare. Or were the exiled Huedans of the sources actually warriors from Little Popo-Glidji?

What is certain, though, is that Agaja had consolidated his position, and that the conquest of what had been Hueda had become irreversible. But it was by now a thoroughly devastated region.[84] For the time being the Dahomeans had anyway nothing to fear from Oyo, which seems to have been immersed in problems of its own, as the removal of three Alafins in quick succession over the next years seems to show.[85]

* * *

SLAVE TRADERS BY INVITATION

Had the decision of Oyo to opt out in 1730 anything to do with the demise of Akwamu on the Gold Coast, possibly Oyo's *de facto* ally? It is tempting to believe so. For that demise all sources agree about the cause – the increasingly sinister reputation of Akwamu. The list of grievances is a rather long one, including the illegal enslavement of freemen and the terrorizing actions of bands of "rascals" and robber barons inside Akwamu itself, whether at the instigation or with the connivance of the Akwamuhene and his men.[86]

The revolt began among the Ga of Little Accra in January 1728.[87] According to one version, the one who took the initiative was a certain Amu, the local Akwamu governor and a member of the royal family. As usual, the Europeans were caught in the middle, not knowing what to do. The Danes bet once more on the loser, Akwamu, with the result that Christiansborg was blockaded between mid-September 1729 and January 1730.[88]

But the decisive event was the intervention of the neighbouring polity of Akyem in May 1730, with the tacit support of Asante.[89] The end result was the defeat and fall of Akwamu in September, described by Fynn as "one of the most decisive victories in Gold Coast History".[90]

But some members of the royal lineage of Akwamu, together with their clients and followers, managed to escape east of the Volta and to subdue many inland Ewe communities, Peki notably.[91] The *de facto* leader was none other than Amu, the one who revolted in Accra in 1728 and who had by now changed sides.[92] This New Akwamu, as it is often called – often in alliance with Anlo on the coast, a former vassal of "Old" Akwamu – proved to be an enduring entity, dominating many inland Ewe *dukowo* for the next hundred years or so.[93]

Incidentally, the collapse of "Old" Akwamu paved the way for the beginning of timid Danish expansion eastwards into the Slave Coast. Indeed, New Akwamu agreed in November 1731 to formally relinquish its authority over the Ada area at the mouth of the river Volta for a substantial payment in goods. It was a payment made by the Danes on behalf of the Ada in return for a Danish trading monopoly over the area.[94]

* * *

If we now ask why the Dahomeans began expanding southwards, a summary of the possible motives (some already noted) may be as follows: they had run out of raiding grounds, and therefore considered the thickly populated south to be a promising alternative. Or they were thinking of opting for a middleman role.[95] Or perhaps, as the Danes believed, the Dahomeans had been systematically robbed by the Huedans on their return trips to Abomey.[96] Or else the Dahomeans needed a place to go, a safe haven south of the Lama, in case of a genuine and successful onslaught by Oyo. Or, alternatively, they needed to secure direct and guaranteed access to the Europeans, and hence to the source of firearms – simply to eliminate the coastal intermediaries, as Akwamu had done some time earlier, and to appropriate for themselves the riches of Hueda. Perhaps all these reasons are pertinent.

* * *

At this point it is necessary to take leave from the affairs of the Slave Coast for a while and to move to a very different place, namely the Court of St. James's in London. On 7 May 1731 (Old style) George II, King of Great Britain and Ireland (1727–60), received in audience Bulfinch Lambe, the one who witnessed the Dahomean assault on Allada in 1724. In the audience Lambe was accompanied by a certain Adomo Tomo, known as Captain Tom, a native of Jakin.[97] The obvious question is what this was all about, and the answer is that the two presented themselves as, and were believed to be, the ambassadors of the king of Dahomey, and were fêted as such in London:[98] ambassadors of a little-known kingdom but a suitably exotic one.

That it had taken the two more than four years to travel from Ouidah-Glehue to London, with numerous adventures on the way, was something no-one seemed to have paid attention to. It is by all accounts an extraordinary story with many ramifications, which it is difficult to summarize quickly. But since it has already been told, at least partially, in a number of publications, we can afford to move to what matters for our purpose, namely the letter allegedly dictated by king Agaja which the two carried with them. Was it genuine, and if so, what is the relevance of its content? The authorities in London took the matter most seriously and organized hearings in which people with first-hand knowledge of the Slave Coast, already mentioned in this work – notably William Snelgrave and above all Jeremy Tinker, the governor of Williams Fort at the time of Lambe's return to Ouidah-Glehue in 1726 – took part. And Tinker made the point which to the present author seems conclusive, that if the letter was genuine, why did Lambe and everybody else, Agaja included, keep quiet about it until 1731?[99] Robin Law has reached, as we have seen, the opposite conclusion. Nevertheless, Law's central point, that the content of the letter is in the final analysis of rather limited interest anyway, seems to us most pertinent. For in the letter Agaja merely stated his wish to see agricultural plantations established in Africa. But there is nothing in the letter which indicates that Agaja considered plantations as an alternative to the slave trade and that he wanted to put an end to that trade. Quite the contrary, in fact: "to carry on a flourishing trade between us, there neither will nor shall be any want of slaves", wrote Agaja or Lambe.[100] However, a long line of authors, from John Atkins to I.A. Akinjogbin, via Basil Davidson and others, has interpreted it as implying that Agaja actually wanted to put an end to the slave trade. Here, then, we have the origin of the myth that Agaja was opposed to, and in fact tried to abolish the slave trade, a myth based on one phrase in a letter which may not even be genuine; a myth which ignores moreover all the declarations Agaja made in the opposite sense, including one in the very same letter. Worse, the myth simply ignores the course of events. But myths never die.

The broader, although counter-factual question is whether establishing plantations in Africa, that is, employing the slaves locally instead of transporting them to America, could have been a feasible alternative. The first answer is that the African solution *was* tried to some extent; the plantation system originated in fact on the islands off the coast of Africa, especially São Tomé,[101] before "migrating" to the Americas. But although the Europeans thought at times about establishing plantations on the African mainland, none of the projects in that sense ever came to fruition. The reason may be that the Europeans were totally in control in America, but certainly not in Africa. Obviously, in Africa the slaves could run away much more easily than in America. Put differently, the Atlantic Ocean constituted simply a gigantic natural moat behind which the plantation sector based on slavery was relatively safe. And it is certain also that the European powers did not want products from Africa to enter into competition with the products of their American colonies.[102]

2

AFTERMATH AND GENERAL CONSIDERATIONS

Having reached the 1730s, we return to the events on the Slave Coast. The question is whether it is possible to detect any long-term trends behind all the skirmishes, battles, plots and intrigues of all sorts during that decade. The first possibility is that the Dahomean "revolutionary-predatory" model was already running out of steam. The second is the restructuring and small-scale societies of the Eastern Slave Coast, until then loosely organized.

With regard to the first trend, it is clear that by the 1730s the days of easy surprise victories for Dahomey were already over. The Dahomeans had showed their hand – they had demonstrated that, in the words of Robin Law, they continued to operate as large-scale bandits rather than empire-builders, seeking to plunder rather than to consolidate, to enslave or kill rather than to subjugate and absorb.[1] Hence, those who felt menaced by Dahomey now knew all too well what was in store for them, especially the ruling elites. They had basically two options, to flee or to fight to the bitter end. A third option, to submit and to become a tribute-paying autonomous vassal, was one that Dahomey did not contemplate. The fact of not respecting the rules of the game was beginning to prove counterproductive.

A proof of sorts is that Agaja failed to expand further. In the north the Mahi put up a stiff enough resistance to force Agaja to give up his attempt to conquer them, after his army is reputed to have suffered tremendous casualties (this in 1731–32). It was an outcome which is said to have dealt a severe blow to Agaja's prestige[2] and which blocked the expansion of Dahomey northwards. Worse, the first cracks (that we know of) in the structure of Dahomey itself appeared. A disgruntled son of Agaja deserted with, it is said, some 4,000 warriors. They joined the Weme successor-polity at Dangbo far in the southeast, thereby joining also, possibly, the anti-Dahomean alliance that Hendrik Hertogh, the WIC official, tried to organize from Jakin.[3]

More quarrels and cracks followed. In June 1733 Agaja ordered the execution of a certain Possu (a title?), described as one of the highest ranking officers of the army. This Possu had planned to flee to Savalu in the north, a village or town which was to become the favourite place of exile for disgruntled Abomey dignitaries who managed to escape.[4] Then, possibly in 1735, no less an official than the Mehu (the third personage of the polity) revolted.[5] His destiny is unknown, but can easily be guessed at. It may have been at the same time that another, and possibly large, section of the Dahomean army deserted, led by a certain Ashangmo. Strictly speaking, we are certain only of the desertion of Ashangmo (or Shampo);[6] but since he was, although a mercenary, high up in the military hierarchy, it is unlikely that he fled alone. To understand what this was all about, we must know that Agaja, owing in part to the terrible losses his army had endured, had recruited large numbers of mercenaries, including some from Little Popo-Glidji and including Ashangmo, who belonged in fact to the local royal sib. He improved his situation shortly afterwards to become (possibly) the third and the by far most reputed king of that polity.

Agaja sent a large detachment in pursuit of the fugitives, but it was cut to pieces at Keta in 1737, in part thanks to the surprisingly self-sacrificing attitude of the Dutch director of the local fort[7] (if it was a genuine fort – its existence does not appear in any of the other sources the present author has had access to). Since the Dahomean attempt at revenge at the end of 1738 or the beginning of 1739 also failed,[8] we can argue that the Dahomeans suffered a resounding setback, which may help explain the state of near-civil war in Dahomey, which Law believes he has detected at that moment.[9] One possible indication of the seriousness of the matter is that Agaja risked imperilling his relations with the Portuguese by throwing into prison the previously mentioned director João Basilio, accused of aiding Ashangmo. Agaja also blamed Basilio for the shortage of gold, since according to Agaja Basilio had attempted to persuade the Luso-Brazilian captains to sell gold exclusively to him – that is, to establish a monopoly.[10] Basilio remained in detention for some eleven months in quite appalling conditions.[11] It is significant that the authorities in Salvador da Bahia and Lisbon did nothing. But Basilio was reinstated in the end, and with honour.[12] Pierre Verger's theory[13] is that Basilio fell victim to the intrigues of fellow-Luso-Brazilian Francisco Nunes, Agaja's

AFTERMATH AND GENERAL CONSIDERATIONS

secretary, whose ambition it was to take over as director, something which he succeeded in doing for a while under Tegbesu, as will be described later.

If what happened in 1737–39 was also an attempt by the Dahomeans to expand westwards, it can only be described as a fiasco. What is also certain is that the 1737–39 events were the beginning of a genuine war between Dahomey and Little Popo-Glidji, a war which was to last for some 58 years, to 1795. What happened in 1737–39 also paved the way for the Danes at Keta.

As for Ashangmo, after becoming king, he made the mistake of blackmailing and threatening the crew of a French slave ship in February 1738.[14] In fact, Ashangmo's commercial acumen turned out to be on a par with that of his predecessors, he was often accused of swindling and offending ("*vexer*") the ship captains, which caused the Europeans and the Luso-Brazilians to remain reluctant to trade at Little Popo.[15]

* * *

We must step slightly back in time and note that Agaja was somewhat more successful with regard to Jakin, although his victory turned out to be, in a sense, a Pyrrhic one. In this context we encounter once more Hendrik Hertogh (originally Herzog, he was born German), one of the few Europeans who has played a central role in the history of the Slave Coast. Hertogh, after having fled from Hueda (in time), as noted, was responsible for setting up, or expanding, the WIC lodge in Jakin, where the Dutch had been preceded or were joined by the English and the Luso-Brazilians, who however both remained present in Ouidah-Glehue as well. The Luso-Brazilians even began to erect a fort at Jakin, but this was in ruins already by the autumn of 1731.[16]

At Jakin Hertogh, who clearly dreamed of a monopolistic position, turned out to be quite a success, especially as a slave trader, and "with God's blessing", as one official report put it.[17] Hertogh's success was in fact such that the central WIC authorities in the Netherlands made him *de facto* independent of the director-general at Elmina (Jan Pranger) – with the title of governor, a title very high up in the WIC hierarchy.[18] He was even put in charge (in 1735) of relations with Benin and the ivory trade there which the Dutch wished to continue, but had to abandon two years later.[19] All this implies, among other things, that the Dutch were henceforth divided among themselves, Pranger at Elmina advocating a rapprochement with Agaja, and indeed negotiating with him, while Hertogh tried to promote a vast anti-Dahomean alliance in collaboration with the king of Jakin, and including the exiled Huedans[20] – all with the active connivance of the central WIC authorities in the Netherlands.

Hertogh was also central in what we may call the mini-war between the WIC and the Portuguese (including the Luso-Brazilians) at that time, even at Jakin itself, the Portuguese having become all too powerful for the taste of the Dutch while they no longer accepted the treatment the Dutch meted out to them.[21] But as usual the Portuguese were also divided among themselves, the Portuguese Crown doing its best to stop the Luso-Brazilians' trade with the Costa da Mina, especially the contraband in gold, believing this would deal a shattering blow to the Dutch; while the Crown's own representatives in Brazil, allied with the local traders and in fact with the Dahomeans, sabotaged the official Portuguese policy and Portuguese laws – as usual. The Luso-Brazilians could, thanks to their tobacco, procure not only slaves but also all sorts of European goods, and goods much cheaper than the merchandise imported from Portugal.[22] Still, the stagnation and decline in the Luso-Brazilian slave trade in the 1730s seem quite evident, considering the complaints of the Luso-Brazilian officials.[23] Perhaps the Luso-Brazilians preferred to charter English ships which transported the slaves for them.[24]

This was, incidentally, roughly at the same time (1728–31) as the relations between the RAC and the WIC reached a very low ebb, the two being virtually at war, according to Johannes Postma.[25] We repeat in this context that the RAC had lost its monopoly in 1712, and the WIC suffered the same fate in 1731–34.[26] But the difference was that whereas the RAC disappeared altogether (in 1750), the WIC did not. Indeed, it maintained certain privileges, in particular its unique position in the trade with the Luso-Brazilians; Dutch free traders were not allowed to trade with ships from Brazil.[27]

But the main theme of the epoch is the antagonism between Agaja and Hertogh, the latter ranking as the most serious opponent of the former. And according to Agaja (as reported by the Luso-Brazilians), Hertogh tried to assassinate him at least four times.[28] That, we imagine, was why Agaja struck out against tiny Jakin in his usual manner in April 1732, just after the Mahi setback; he staged major carnage, as well as taking some 4,500 prisoners, including 20 or so Europeans. But Agaja failed to exploit his opportunity enough, since both Hertogh and the king of Jakin got away, fleeing eastward.[29] Not so Hertogh's five or six Dutch subordinates (not to mention his African ones), who were caught and, unlike the other Europeans, not released immediately, but only a year later[30] (Hertogh was not quite a Captain of the grand tradition[31]). It is significant, considering the atmosphere in the Dutch camp, that the WIC employee sent from Elmina who secured the release of the prisoners, and who then managed to re-establish the factory at Jakin, was dismissed because he was unwilling or unable to collaborate with Hertogh, as he had been ordered to do by his superiors in the Netherlands.[32]

Before pursuing the Hertogh story, we must note that 1732 was not quite the end of Jakin as a commercial hub. Hence the second attack in November 1734 to persuade the Europeans to relocate to Ouidah-Glehue, where Agaja wanted to concentrate the slave trade. The last to comply were the Luso-Brazilians in 1738, after which Jakin disappeared from the map.[33]

The conquest of Jakin may be considered to be the best-known of a number of mopping-up actions against the former vassals of the former kings of Allada and Hueda; the best-known because Europeans were involved. We know of a few others, like one against Gome with its ruler, the *aplogan*, the one who seceded from Hueda in 1726. His territory was burned in December 1733, although the *aplogan* himself narrowly escaped, and burnt a second time the next year.[34]

As for the obviously very enterprising Hertogh, he had no problem in re-emerging as a central figure wherever he took up residence, whether in Apa[35] (1732–36) or in what became Badagry (from 1736), and always strongly backed by his superiors in the Netherlands. Actually Hertogh, under his local name of Huntokonu, ranks simply as the founder of Badagry (more correctly Agbadarigi), a town which came to be settled by refugees from many parts, and hence acquired a distinctly cosmopolitan character.[36] And of course, when in 1737 Hertogh set up a factory at Epe (Ekpe on modern maps, some 22 km east of Jakin), precisely the place to which the former king of Jakin and his followers had fled in 1732, establishing there a sort of successor polity,[37] Hertogh's factory turned out to be quite a success, rivalling Ouidah-Glehue.[38] As one fellow Dutchman put it, Hertogh acted as a sort of independent prince or ruler,[39] possibly in a Kiplingian (*The Man who would be King*) sense.

But as a genuine African prince in a war zone Hertogh had to assume the risks of that position. So in the end Agaja caught up with him; Hertogh was assassinated in Badagry on 29 April 1738 – at the behest of Agaja we are told, but, significantly, by a disgruntled refugee from Hueda, in fact a member of the former ruling sib of Hueda whom Hertogh had declined to make chief or king.[40] After that the WIC and the Dutch simply faded away from the Slave Coast.

* * *

Clearly, Hendrik Hertogh's grand coalition never got off the ground. Was it because it was made up of too many "has-beens"? Or did commercial jealousies and competing claims to political sovereignty ruin Hertogh's efforts, as Robin

Law suggests?⁴¹ Or were the Danes closer to the mark when they argued, already in 1732, that Hertogh had "played the false god among the Blacks" – implying that he was something of an impostor?⁴² It is true that Hertogh came forward with some quite extravagant suggestions, including one to bribe Asante "to come down to fight Dahomme [Dahomey])". It provoked (naturally) the sarcasm of the increasingly anti-Hertogh Dutch of Elmina.⁴³

A third possibility may be that Hertogh was primarily interested in promoting the slave trade, as well as his own fortune and his own career, and that the alleged grand alliance was merely a sort of window-dressing in this context. But if so, the possibly over-confident Hertogh paid the highest prize in the end, in one sense a somewhat redeeming exit.

* * *

The founding of Badagry in the east, and more generally the action of Hertogh, heralded a new general trend: the emergence of articulated polities on the Eastern Slave Coast. It is in this context significant that the rule of the first king of the future leading polity in the east, Hogbonu (Porto Novo),⁴⁴ is usually dated to the 1730s.⁴⁵ The king in question, Te-Agbanlin, claimed to hail from Allada,⁴⁶ and hence the new polity was also called simply Allada, and in fact was considered to be the successor-state to Allada.⁴⁷ The implication is that those who established Porto-Novo were refugees from the west, which may well have been the case. If so, Porto Novo ought to have been characterized by some sort of contrapuntal paramountcy, which is not certain, but cannot be excluded⁴⁸ (the local traditions are highly ambiguous, and no genuinely serious recent studies exist). It is, for instance, possible that the king could be asked to commit suicide.⁴⁹ More certainly, the reigns of the local kings were uniformly short, brothers succeeding brothers in what is called succession in Z.⁵⁰ Actually, central royal authority was so weak that one European visitor claimed that he discerned none at all.⁵¹ Porto-Novo, in sum, was not a polity of the Dahomean kind.

The rise of the new polities and commercial centres in the east played into the hands of Oyo, which was looking for outlets to the Atlantic beyond the reach of Dahomey.

* * *

It is time to focus on a major internal development in Dahomey, the emergence of what turned out to be a regular feature of the life of that polity throughout its existence: a several weeks long annual ritual "festival" called *xwetanu* (also written *xuetanu* or *huetanu* etc.),[52] and known to the Europeans as the "Annual Customs". *Xwetanu* means literally "Yearly Head Business", according to Law.[53] It acquired rapidly a sinister reputation due to the part called the "Watering of the Graves" of the royal ancestors, the "watering" being effected with blood from sacrificial victims. If we follow Robin Law, the first ever "Annual Customs" were celebrated in January 1733, and with the three fort directors in attendance.[54] In fact, the presence of the Directors came to be required, they had to travel to Abomey at least once every year – actually the only time they were allowed to travel outside Ouidah-Glehue – and to stay in Abomey for 18–20 days.[55] Hence we are well informed about the Customs.[56] If one asks why there was this compulsory European/Luso-Brazilian attendance, the answer is first that it was a source of prestige for the king (recall Bulfinch Lambe in 1724–26), and secondly that it was part of the Dahomean monarchy's attempt to redefine the relationship with the Europeans and the Luso-Brazilians. Briefly stated, Agaja and his successors decided, unilaterally, that the fort directors were their subordinates; but as subordinates, though high-ranking ones, they had to pay tribute. Thus the fort Directors were subjected to the king's jurisdiction, as opposed to benefiting from some sort of extra-territoriality. In fact, the kings of Dahomey dismissed and expelled directors not to their liking, as the kings of Hueda had done before them, but also tried at times to appoint their successors,[57] something their Huedan predecessors had never attempted. All the foreigners were also closely watched.[58] In fact, the Dahomeans began early on to monitor the activities of the expatriates, progressively restricting their movements, in the end not even allowing them to move freely between the forts and the ships.

Actually, the Europeans and the Luso-Brazilians came increasingly to look like genuine hostages in their forts, which were, we repeat once more, *inland* forts. As a result, leaving eighteenth-century Ouidah-Glehue undetected became close to impossible.[59] Finally, the three directors were formally required to operate as heads of the African quarters which had emerged around the forts, that is, to be responsible to the king for their good behaviour.

Needless to add, the Europeans and the Luso-Brazilians on the coast, like their superiors at home, never acquiesced formally in any of this. But they found it convenient to play along, up to a point: that is, they served, or pretended to serve, two masters. It turned out to be, unsurprisingly, a rather complicated task.

It is important to understand what all this means: that in Dahomey the expatriates functioned under conditions which were unheard of on the rest of the Guinea coast, if not the coast of Africa generally. Actually, the present author is not aware of a comparable situation anywhere else in the European presence in the non-European world during the relevant centuries.

The trouble was, however, that the Dahomeans did not have the means to fully apply their policy. Perhaps it could have worked if the Europeans and the Luso-Brazilians had had no alternative or if the Dahomeans had been able to control genuinely the whole of the Slave Coast. But they were not so able. As it was, the slave trade from Dahomey dwindled slowly but steadily over the years, for the benefit of the rising trading centres of the Eastern Slave Coast; centres actively supported, if not controlled, by Oyo.

* * *

After this long digression, we need to return to the "Annual Customs" and to argue that to force the three directors to travel and to attend jointly was also a way of trying to smooth out whatever discrepancies may have existed between them. It was necessary, or became in fact imperative, for the Dahomean kings to avoid any serious problems not with, but among the directors, a rather complicated task at times.

Along with the three fort directors and their entourages, a host of other people were required to attend the "Annual Customs",[60] actually all the dignitaries and all the family heads of all of Dahomey – all those who paid taxes, the prostitutes included.

The sinister reputation of the "Annual Customs" is, we repeat, linked to the human sacrifices, the watering of the graves with human blood, considered to constitute the necessary periodic reinforcement of the link with the ancestors. This brings us to the general question of human sacrifice in Dahomey and elsewhere in West Africa. An in-depth treatment of the subject is beyond the scope of the present work. We content ourselves therefore with referring to what looks like some sort of consensus among the historians, namely that human sacrifice was common and widespread throughout the region in the precolonial era, especially in relation to funerals of prominent persons, but that the practice attained quite unprecedented levels in Dahomey – where it was performed in part under the gaze of the Europeans.[61] However, the "Annual Customs" claimed only a proportionally limited number of victims, if that can be said about 20 to 60 or so victims.[62] But human sacrifice seems to have become virtually an everyday occurrence in Dahomey; it was part of daily life, so to speak.[63] The Europeans and the Luso-Brazilians were forced to watch only a minor part of the killings, the public ones.[64] They were also invited to participate as executioners – apparently an honour – but as far as we know, no-one ever accepted,[65] which we may consider fortunate.

What was the logic behind human sacrifice? To show that the king's ancestors were different from those of commoners? Or to provide the dead with a retinue in the after-life, or send messengers to the royal ancestors in order to inform them about what went on in the world of the living? In the last-mentioned case one may reasonably wonder, within the very logic of the local religions, if there were not other ways of communicating with the ancestors. There certainly were, as we have in fact seen earlier. The final explanation we can think of is that human sacrifices served simply, or were thought to reinforce, the prestige of those in power.

But human sacrifices were only one part of the "Annual Customs". This was also a gigantic coming-together which included the exchange of gifts, the payment of taxes, all sorts of reporting about conditions outside the capital, a lot of "palavers" and of course the celebration of military successes (the Dahomean army was by definition always victorious). It involved in addition, and perhaps above all, the distribution of huge quantities of goods from the famous platform. It was finally an occasion during which the monarch distributed wives (recall the sexual imbalance characteristic of the local societies), and of course also slaves, to deserving subjects.

What then were the "Annual Customs" about, in the final instance? In Edna Bay's interpretation, they were in a sense nothing new. In its religious nucleus such a ritual was performed each year by every lineage. However, at the level of the monarchy, the "Annual Customs" imitated but also violated the meaning of ceremonies in honour of the ancestors. Moreover, by requiring the compulsory representation of all tax-payers, the monarchy used the ceremonial cycle as an integrative device for the polity. Actually, the message of the Customs was that the well-being of the royal line and the well-being of the kingdom were synonymous.[66] Or in more direct language, it was an attempt at manipulation on the part of the monarchy, that is, the glorification of the king, the royal sib and the royal ancestors.

Note that there is nowhere any trace in Dahomey of any ritualized rebellion, a useful safety-valve known from many polities.[67] Was it deemed too dangerous by the kings of Dahomey?

But apart from the "Annual Customs", there were also the "Grand Customs" (*ahosu tanu* – *ahosu* meaning king, but also clan), much more infrequent, celebrated only once in each reign. They were lavish ceremonies in honour of the king's immediate predecessor – the final funeral for the deceased monarch as it were, and the final installation ceremony of his successor. They took place at least 18 months after a monarch's death, and only after the new king had demonstrated his command of both visible and supernatural sources of power.[68] If we are to believe two European observers, some eight to nine hundred people were sacrificed after the death of Tegbesu in 1774,[69] and some 1,500 after the death of his successor, Kpengla, in 1789.[70] But since no European ever attended the "Grand Customs", the question is whether we can trust those observers.

* * *

The new Dahomean regime was certainly not to the liking of the Europeans.[71] One can easily understand why, considering all the bloodshed, and considering also Agaja's insistence on more rigorous control of trade conditions. The problem too was that the Dahomeans took only a limited interest in the middleman trade, the implication being that the supply of slaves became exclusively dependent upon the Dahomeans' own slave-capturing activities, and vulnerable therefore to any downturn in their military fortunes. The problem was finally, for the English, French and Dutch, that Agaja demonstrated a clear preference for payment in gold (for reasons unknown), and hence for the Luso-Brazilians.[72] The French in particular continued to hope to take over as middlemen between the Luso-Brazilians and the Africans, selling to the former the merchandise they needed to buy slaves for from the latter, in exchange for tobacco and gold.[73]

Agaja passed away in May or June 1740.[74] What to think of him? Gayibor states that he died entirely worn down by his setbacks and disappointments.[75] David Ross argues that under Agaja Dahomey had been less a functioning state (we prefer the word polity) than a mobile military band and that the establishment of a permanent administration of the conquered territories was seriously undertaken only under his successor.[76] But the institution of the "Annual Customs" indicates that the first rudiments of the elaborate ceremonial life and administrative control which, according to Edna Bay, came to characterize the polity by the nineteenth century[77] were in fact established during the reign of Agaja. As for Akinjogbin, he argues simply that Dahomey had to be rebuilt almost from nothing after the death of Agaja,[78] an assertion which strikes us as somewhat exaggerated.

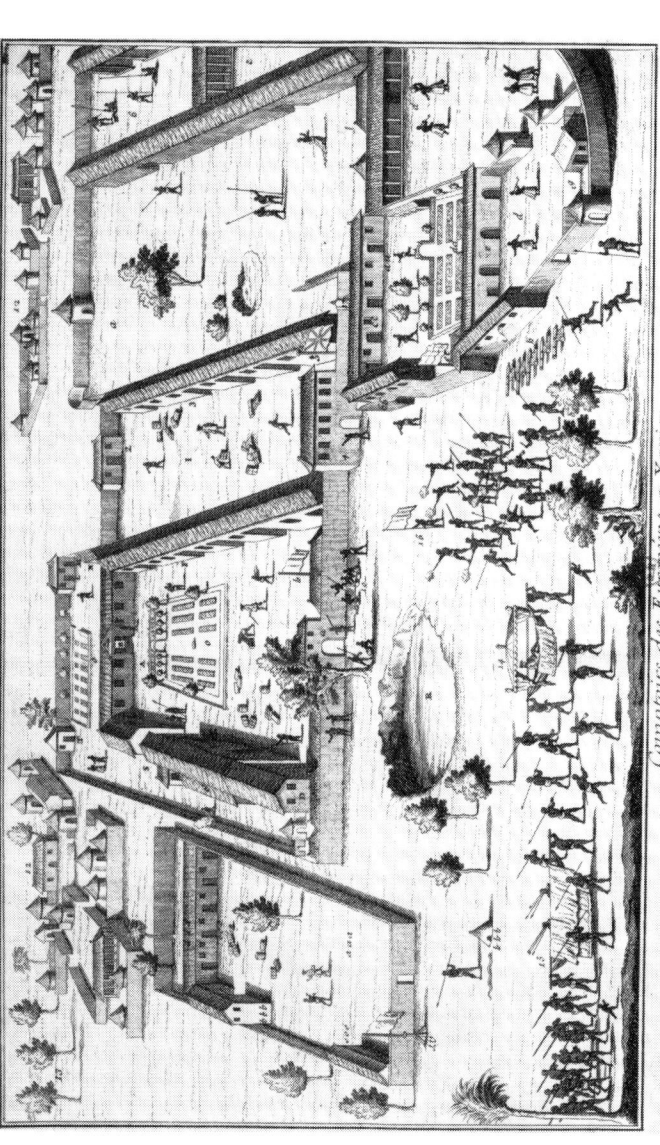

FIGURE 1: European lodges in the inland town of Savi, then the capital of Hueda and hub of the local slave trade (17th century). From the Des Marchais archive, British Library

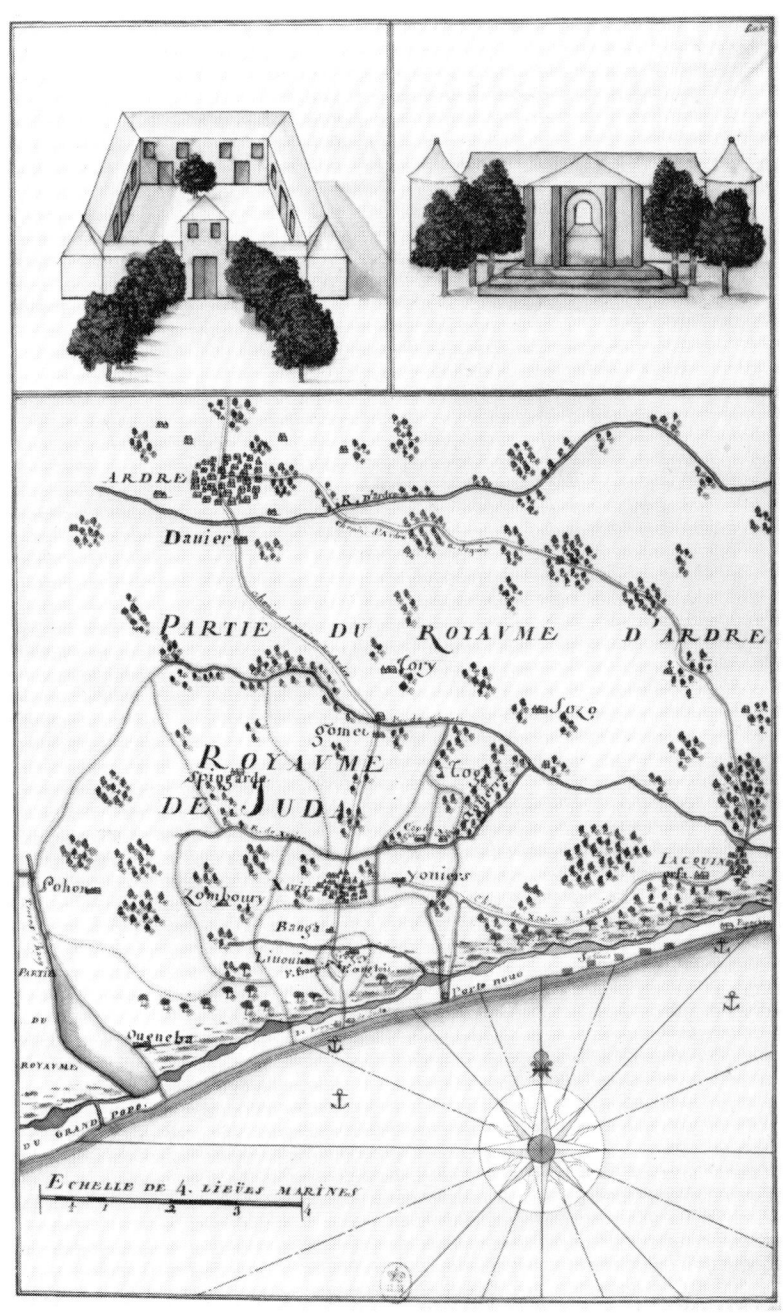

FIGURE 2: Map of the Slave Coast before 1724. From the Des Marchais archive, British Library

FIGURE 3: Restored main building of Ouidah's Portuguese "fort" (2010). Photograph by Finn Fuglestad

FIGURE 4: View of the River Weme at Porto Novo (1980s). Photograph by Finn Fuglestad

3

NEAR DISASTER

THE FIRST YEARS OF THE TEGBESU ERA

After Agaja the conqueror, Tegbesu the consolidator and organizer? This is one possible way of presenting the history of Dahomey and of the Slave Coast in the eighteenth century. What seems reasonably clear is that Agaja's conquests generated quite severe problems and tensions, which is why Tegbesu found himself in 1740 at the helm of a polity on the brink of implosion on the internal front and faced with a number of formidable enemies on the external one.

Tegbesu reacted by resorting to very heavy-handed methods, including recurrent expropriations and even executions of his own dignitaries.[1] Actually, it seems possible to argue that Tegbesu established something akin to a regime of terror, converting Dahomey into the closest thing seen in pre-colonial Africa to a "totalitarian" polity complete with a secret police.[2] (We are aware that the "totalitarian" concept, in the way it is usually defined, may not sit well with Africa of old, which is why we use it in inverted commas).

One could argue that Tegbesu's course of action implied admission of his failure to tackle the monarchy's two basic problems. The first was that of legitimacy, including how to reconcile conquerors and conquered. The latter, the people of the region we may call southern Ajaland, remained clearly hostile.[3] It does not seem to have helped in this respect that Tegbesu tried to settle Ouidah-Gleue (and old Hueda more generally?) with loyal people from the Abomey plateau.[4]

The second problem was that Tegbesu, as the ruler of a polity based on a warrior-ethos, was under an obligation to extend the boundaries of Dahomey, that is, to conquer new territory, something neither he nor his first three successors were really able to do. Tegbesu managed to launch raids eastwards, some of them fairly successful,[5] and to make incursions into the hilly Mahi country in the north. But that was as far as it went. Actually Tegbesu started a war against the Mahi which was to last for some 15–20 years, if not longer.[6] However, although Tegbesu failed to subdue the Mahis,[7] the latter became important suppliers of slaves through Dahomey.[8] They assumed, then, the double role of both perpetrators and victims, a strange but not unusual combination in the era of the slave trade.[9] It was only much later, during the second half of the reign of king Gezo (1818–58), that Dahomey finally managed for a while to live up to its self-proclaimed ethos.

Tegbesu, then, found himself confronted with an impressive array of enemies, both internal and external, as well as some quite serious structural problems. On the external front Tegbesu was faced with a formidable alliance of Oyo and the exiled Huedans (both having been resuscitated in a sense), and especially the Ge polity of Little Popo-Glidji under its energetic king Ashangmo, now a major power in the region. And on the internal front Tegbesu had to deal with widespread unrest, if not real open revolt. This at a time when the slave trade and the revenue derived from it had declined and relations with the Europeans had become problematic.

Yet for all that, the era of Tegbesu may be considered Dahomey's classic age. Furthermore, it could perhaps be argued that Tegbesu, by the very fact of emerging in a sense victorious in the end, and regardless of the price, had demonstrated that he possessed the necessary "luck" or "force" (*mana*); that he had, in sum, the blessing of the gods – a legitimacy of sorts?

Such is the general picture. The problems begin when we try to fill in the details: the link or relationship between them is not always clear; for instance what is cause and what is effect, and who was allied with whom. Hence the difficulty, indeed impossibility, of constructing a coherent narrative in which all the (known) details fall into place.

* * *

But to begin at the beginning: Agaja's death triggered off what looks like something akin to a civil war between some of his sons. One of them, possibly the eldest and legitimate heir, by the name of Aghidisu, was proclaimed king in Allada. But he was rapidly challenged by another son, the one we know as

NEAR DISASTER

Tegbesu. And although it is said that Aghidisu had the support of Oyo, he lost out, but only after three years of infighting, according to Le Hérissé.[10] In the end (in 1743?), Aghidisu was dumped into the ocean (royal blood could not be spilled). His many followers, including quite a few royal princes, suffered a similar fate.[11]

Was this the usual succession quarrel, or was something more afoot? There is the somewhat troubling fact that Aghidisu was proclaimed king in Allada, then the secular capital (Abomey being always the religious capital). If we add that Tegbesu moved the secular capital back to Abomey in September or October 1743,[12] at a decidedly inauspicious moment (and after obtaining, significantly or strangely enough, the permission of Oyo), one may begin to wonder whether some sort of regional-conceptual opposition was involved, and if so whether Allada represented the old pre-Dahomean order ready to re-emerge, and Abomey the opposite.

If so, the question also is whether there is a link between, on the one hand, Aghidisu and his cause and on the other, the disaffection of the people and the challenge to the monarchy apparently characteristic of Tegbesu's reign, possibly also the succeeding ones. This disaffection was led by the followers of local religious cults. It has been noted by many scholars,[13] among them Edna Bay, who argues that there was a broad resurgence of cults, related not surprisingly to Sakpata and more generally to the old "masters of the land".[14] She thus admits implicitly that the accommodations previously made, still according to her, with the local "owners of the land" did not function (the present author believes, as already stated, that no such accommodation was ever made).

The next question is whether there is a link between the developments just mentioned and the fact that Tegbesu had to confront a major external onslaught in 1743, that is, the year in which we presume that Aghidisu was decisively defeated. It is tempting to answer in the affirmative, although the precise nature of that link eludes us. We refer in any case to the alliance between Oyo, Ashangmo's Ge polity of Little Popo-Glidji and the exiled Huedans, as well as, possibly, Aghidisu and his followers. As before, and as usual, Oyo attacked the Dahomean heartland, the Abomey plateau, from the north, whereas the others concentrated on the south, that is, Ouidah and its surroundings, a region they were able to occupy, although only for some three months.[15]

The onslaught was repelled in the end, the familiar pattern from the 1720s repeating itself; that is, Oyo withdrew after a short while, later giving up altogether (in 1747 or 1748), thus leaving Dahomey once more a free hand in the south. However, it did not stop the Ge and the exiled Huedans from returning to the offensive time and again, already later in 1743, and after a four-year lull in August 1747, when most of the Dahomean forces stationed in the south were driven out, but again only for a while.[16] Many more raids or onslaughts followed. The assailants came often close to victory, but never more than close.

Here we have yet another example of the surprising inability of the enemies of Dahomey to coordinate their efforts effectively, an inability already evident in the epoch of Hertogh and earlier. That being said, it is tempting to argue, and to conclude, that Dahomey came very close to total destruction in 1743.

* * *

Why did Oyo once again take the offensive against Dahomey after a very long lull? The answer seems to be that the hard-pressed Agaja had ignored his tributary obligations during his final years, as his successor, whether Aghidisu or Tegbesu, also did. The Dahomeans could get away with it owing to the somewhat troubled state of affairs inside Oyo in the late 1730s and first years of the 1740s. But a new and energetic Alafin by the name of Onisile[17] was not prepared to tolerate the Dahomean affront; hence the attack in 1743. And of course, Tegbesu had in the long run no choice but to accede to most of Oyo's demands. The result was a new peace treaty between the two in 1747 or 1748, with very stiff terms for the Dahomeans – a considerable annual tribute. However, it was a compromise peace, because Oyo had once more been unable to inflict a decisive defeat on the Dahomean forces.[18] It turned out to be the last such treaty. Some years later, beginning possibly in 1754, new and very severe cracks appeared in the Oyo edifice.

As for the exiled Huedans, how to explain what we may call their resurrection after the severe defeats of the 1730s? The answer could be that it was a result of Tegbesu's emerging reign of terror. There are in fact some passing hints here and there to the effect that many of Tegbesu's subjects preferred the precarious life of the exiled Huedans to the dangers at home. The ranks of the exiled Huedans seem in any case to have swelled, encouraging them to take up again their raiding activities, with, we imagine, some hope of success given their powerful allies plus the perturbed state of affairs inside Dahomey.

As for the rise to prominence of Little Popo-Glidji, we can do no more than ascribe it to Ashangmo's personal qualities, as well as his earlier military successes against Dahomey. What is certain in any case is that Little Popo-Glidji played for a while a central role in the history of both the Central and the Western Slave Coast.

NEAR DISASTER

The Europeans were, as usual, caught in the middle. Although none were killed this time, the events resulted in the expulsion of all three directors, the French and Luso-Brazilian ones in 1743, and their English colleague in 1745. The French director was accused of refusing asylum to the defeated Dahomean forces,[19] and the Luso-Brazilian one of collaborating with Dahomey's enemies. As for the English director, what happened is somewhat more obscure; he seems to have fallen victim to some sort of mutiny by his African employees, but apparently instigated by Tegbesu.[20] The case of the Luso-Brazilian director, who was still João Basilio, is the most dramatic and most significant one. It is said that Tegbesu wanted to execute him, but was prevented from doing so through the intervention of the new French director Jacques Levet. Instead he was thrown into jail for the second time, together with some of his subordinates (24 June 1743), and they were left to linger in jail for four months, then emerging more dead than alive.[21] After that they were deported. But back in Salvador da Bahia Basilio was again thrown into prison, for obscure reasons, and in prison he died, on 8 May 1744.[22] The result of this treatment of Basilio at the hand of the Brazilian authorities was that they experienced thereafter great difficulties in recruiting personnel for Ouidah-Glehue.[23]

Less than a month after Basilio's arrest, on 26 July 1743 the Dahomeans stormed the Portuguese fort and levelled it to the ground with, as it turned out, many exiled Huedans inside.[24] Their presence was, we imagine, proof to the Dahomeans of Basilio's connivance with the assailants (the alternative explanation is that the few remaining Portuguese had been forced at pistol-point to let them in). It is true that the Dahomeans repented quickly and promised to rebuild the fort, something they took their time in doing, if they ever completed the task. If we add that the earlier mentioned Luso-Brazilian adventurer Francisco Nunes succeeded in taking possession of the fort (or what was left of it) on 20 March 1746 and to remain in possession of it for some eight months, with the obvious acquiescence of Tegbesu,[25] one can easily understand that the Portuguese authorities had had enough and ruminated about how to punish the king of Dahomey, this "barbarian kinglet" (*bárbaro régulo*) – but (naturally) without jeopardizing the slave trade. They came, unsurprisingly, to the conclusion that it was not possible.[26] However, Dahomey's "otherness" and its heavy militarization were becoming increasingly counterproductive. It was more and more clear that the slave traders no longer enjoyed the relative security and well-functioning organization which characterized the days of the Huedan polity. The Europeans and the Luso-Brazilians were bound to begin to look elsewhere.

But the Dahomeans did try to come to terms with the Luso-Brazilians, and in a rather spectacular way, by sending an embassy to the Viceroy in Salvador da Bahia, an embassy which arrived on 29 June 1750 and stayed for no less than nine and a half months, at the expense of the Portuguese Crown. The details vary from source to source, but it seems that the embassy was composed of two to three officials and a considerable number of servants, plus or including four ten-year old girls (slaves?), some of whom ended up serving in the chambers of the Queen of Portugal. The embassy was correctly received and lodged in the facilities of the Jesuits. But the Portuguese officials made it clear to the Dahomeans the resentment the destruction of the Portuguese fort had provoked in them, and that future relations between Portugal and the Dahomeans depended on the latter's ability to restore the Portuguese fort to its former state.[27] However, the Portuguese authorities quickly backed down from their tough stance. Indeed, already the next year a worried king of Portugal impressed upon his viceroy in Brazil the necessity to maintain cordial relations with the king of Dahomey in order to preserve the fort in Ouidah-Glehue.[28]

What was the Dahomean embassy all about? Probably to try to persuade the Portuguese authorities to revoke their famous decree of 1743, a decree we shall return to very shortly.

But before that we must note that the problems with the Dutch at Elmina continued. In fact, the treatment the Dutch meted out to the Luso-Brazilians shocked even the other Europeans, especially the French. In Brazil the traders heading for the Costa da Mina had to swear that they would not land at Elmina, and that they would pay nothing to the Dutch. But to little avail. In fact, the complaints of the Portuguese authorities against the violence suffered by their subjects at the hand of the Dutch (and the British) became a constant.[29]

The Dahomeans' extreme reaction in the Portuguese case provides us with an introduction to the policy of Tegbesu with regard to the slave trade and the Europeans. Tegbesu's ire was probably provoked in part by the falling off of the Luso-Brazilian trade, which was in turn due, still in part, to the decree the Portuguese authorities had issued in the eventful year of 1743. The decree restricted the number of ships permitted to go to the Costa da Mina each year to 24; in addition, the ships had to sail in groups in strict rotation and at intervals of three months. Whatever the logic of this measure – it resulted in a sort of monopoly operated by only a few traders – the aim seems to have been to control and also to limit the Mina trade, and above all perhaps to protect the ships under the Portuguese flag against the Dutch.[30] But to

Tegbesu it represented clearly an intolerable attempt by Dahomey's leading trading partner to restrict the competition among the participants in the slave trade.[31] It may not have been to the liking of the other Europeans either, as they still needed Brazilian gold and especially tobacco with which to pay for the slaves.[32]

But more generally, what we discern here is the culture clash which came increasingly to characterize the relations between the Dahomeans and the Europeans, and which was perhaps rooted in Dahomey's very special warrior ethos. Briefly stated, it looks as if Tegbesu was intent on establishing a pure command economy[33] in which the Europeans, as his subordinates, were supposed to obey his orders, even in matters exclusively economic, and not orders coming from whoever it might be far away on the other side of the ocean. In fact, Tegbesu even tried to appoint his own men as directors, when he had servile European renegades at hand. Moreover, Tegbesu, who was obviously a stranger to any kind of what we may call rational economic logic, seems to have believed that one way of compensating for the declining revenue was by bullying the local Europeans and squeezing out of them as much as possible; obviously a very counterproductive line of conduct in the long run. Above all, Tegbesu seems to have believed that the European directors had it in their power to direct the slave ships to wherever they pleased, and thus to see to it that the European ships trafficked only at Ouidah-Glehue.[34] Tegbesu had clearly not understood that all the European slave traders were, after the end of the monopolistic companies, independent traders who did not depend in any way on the directors of the forts. The Dahomeans also tried to eliminate the new centres out east by raiding, or even better by trying to destroy them, as had been done with Jakin earlier. But in this the Dahomeans singularly failed.

Here we are back once more to the perennial question of how the slave trade was organized on the African side, whether or not we are dealing with a royal or state monopoly of overseas trade in Dahomey. But whatever the relevant definitions, the obvious point is that the overseas trade was tightly *controlled* by the monarchy, and that the traders, whatever their formal position, were closely watched and supposed to obey the royal will;[35] the commercial profession was considered (naturally) to be ignoble by the Dahomean warrior elite.[36]

However, the Dahomeans did worry if, for instance, it transpired that the Europeans contemplated establishing new posts, or moving elsewhere, as for instance with the French plans to attempt (once more) an installation at

Anomabo-Amoku on the Gold Coast in the early 1750s, after being evicted from there at least twice already;[37] or when it was feared that hostility among the Europeans would prove prejudicial to trade. When the mid-century sequence of wars erupted between Great Britain and France, the king of Dahomey asked the local British director to write to his king "to be Friends with France".[38] And later, during the Seven Years' War (1756–63), the same king donated a cow to each fort "to desire [in the words of the British director] all the whitemen to live in friendship and let all palavers [disputes] die...to desire the English Captains would not mollest the French, desiring that all the gentlemen would eat together and be friends".[39] In fact, war or no war, the three directors apparently dined and wined together once every month. There was also dining and wining with ships' officers, especially those of warships, more or less irrespective of nationality.[40]

The Seven Years' War did actually see some limited warlike actions in Guinean waters, the French attacking. This happened especially in 1756–57, when the French sent a squadron of four ships under the famous Guy-François de Kersaint which arrived at Ouidah-Glehue on 4 February 1757 after capturing eleven English ships, sinking three and taking more than 1,200 slaves. But de Kersaint failed to capture Cape Coast Castle, although there were six British dead, the French suffering three casualties. It is significant that the squadron could not stay at Ouidah-Glehue for lack of food; it had to move on to the island of Príncipe.[41] As for the British, they are reported to have sent two battleships every year to protect the slave trade.[42] Did any of them encounter French men-of-war? Then in January 1762 the French sent a frigate to Guinea where it burned and sank all the English slave ships it came across,[43] with the consequences one can imagine for the slaves on board. Finally, there were also privateers who managed to wreak some havoc.[44]

Incidentally, according to the French (and according to a logic familiar to us), the British tried to persuade Tegbesu to come down on their side, to expel the French – that is, to end the free-trade status of Ouidah-Glehue. According to the French, the Dahomeans had to threaten to blow up William's Fort to make the British desist.[45]

As for the Luso-Brazilians, the system formally established in 1743 was abolished in March 1756, indicating a return to what we may call free trade. There was however an important condition, one very much disliked by the Dahomeans: the ships had to be small, and there was supposed to be only one ship under the Portuguese flag at any time in the Ouidah-Glehue roads. Many Portuguese captains probably avoided Ouidah-Glehue as a consequence,[46] going out east instead. Naturally, Tegbesu was furious. And equally naturally, the then Portuguese director was given three days to decamp and to leave the fort (what was left of it) in the hands of the storekeeper. Equally naturally, the ex-director, once back in Salvador da Bahia, experienced problems with the Brazilian authorities who accused him of abandoning his post, in fact suspecting him of having mounted the whole affair in order to get away from Ouidah-Glehue.[47] After the Basilio story Ouidah-Glehue was no longer a sought-after destination, quite the contrary. It did not help that at least five more directors were expelled over the next years.[48] This trend was not confined to the Portuguese; on the British side, serving at William's Fort under Lionel Abson came to be considered a punishment for misbehaviour.[49] Still, the Luso-Brazilians continued to dominate the local commercial scene – "the Portuguese run away with all the trade here",[50] Brazilian tobacco remaining the commanding article.

The formal return to complete free trade occurred only in 1778, after the fall of the Marquis of Pombal, the *de facto* ruler of Portugal from 1756 to 1777, and as a result of a very heated debate over the organization of the Mina trade, a trade which continued to be vital to the Brazilians.[51]

One way of bullying the Europeans was to demand ever more gifts (*dashee*), including gifts for quite extravagant reasons.[52] We cannot go too much into the details (or offer any kind of statistics). But some extracts from the Account-book of William's Fort provide us with at least some of the flavour of the epoch: "Gave in a dashee [gift] to…Vice-Roy [the *yovogan*] on his receiving advice of a victory…by one of the King's generals over some inland country… Gave a maintenance & dispatch to the king's messenger that came down to shew us the rebels head which he had cut off… Gave in a dashee to the king on his killing a rebel by sending down his head – the other forts doing the like".[53] (How the Europeans reacted to the sending of cut-off heads is not recorded – it occurred with some frequency throughout the history of the European presence.)[54] In addition, "the Vice-Roy & caboceers [local dignitaries] came [often] to dance & play before the fort", also occurrences which required *dashee* by the Europeans.[55]

The general impression is that this was a period when the European presence was progressively reduced, when the forts were beginning to fall apart from lack of repair, and when an unhealthy climate crept into the European camp.[56] Probably those on the spot found it expedient to function to some extent according to the Dahomeans' culture, that is as African dignitaries, while the authorities in Europe looked the other way. A close to perfect example of a European director to the liking of the Dahomeans was Lionel Abson, the English Director 1770–1803, actually the last *de facto* English director, with his plurality of African wives. John Adams described him as "more an [*sic*] Dahomean than a European".[57]

In sum, the Dahomeans, without measuring the counterproductive effects of their policy, and without actually wanting it, provoked the slow disentanglement of the Europeans, the British going out west and the Luso-Brazilians out east. After the demise of the Royal African Company of England in 1750–51, the upkeep of the forts was in charge of the earlier mentioned Company of Merchants Trading in Africa, a so-called regulating company, that is, a company which did not do any trading on its own – it was *de facto* a government agency subsisting thanks to parliamentary grants.[58] It came to be known as the African Company, and is therefore confused at times with the *Royal* African Company.

That leaves the French, who had nowhere else to go (after their attempts at Annamabo had failed), and so clung on, taking slowly over from the Luso-Brazilians as the leading nation in Ouidah-Glehue.[59] It may be symbolic that in 1767 the French fort was removed from the authority of the Compagnie des Indes and placed directly under that of the Crown: The Ministry of the Navy and the Colonies.[60] We see then that on the European side the respective governments increasingly took charge of the affairs on the Slave Coast.

The forts often caught fire, by accident, in this period, especially the British one, which was nearly reduced to ashes several times. What is noteworthy is that all hands always took part in extinguishing the fires and in the rebuilding – the French, the Luso-Brazilians and the African townspeople, whether ordered to do so or not by the king of Dahomey.[61]

*　*　*

After this long digression, we return to the main track and to Tegbesu's regime of terror, or at least that part of it we know about, since it was witnessed more or less by the Europeans. Given the flimsy nature of the evidence, and the unreliable chronological framework, we can do no more than to highlight certain episodes and trends.

Possibly the most spectacular, and certainly the best documented such episode was the execution in 1746 of either all the black merchants or all the official traders in Ouidah-Glehue, apparently because they had become too rich for the taste of Tegbesu, and were therefore perceived as a threat to the monarchy.[62] Whatever the details of the affair, and the exact status of the victims, it is obvious that such heavy-handed action was not conducive to a favourable business climate, or for that matter to the emergence of a proto-capitalist mercantile sector. Such an emergence was obviously out of the question anyway in Tegbesu's Dahomey.

Another aspect of the terror was what looks like a thorough purge in the higher echelons of the state apparatus, especially in the military establishment – a great many army officers were also executed. We note more generally that William Devaynes, director of William's Fort three times and for 12 years altogether between 1747 and 1763 (he was aged 17 in 1747), testified in 1788 to the semi-official African Committee of the Company of Merchants Trading in Africa that he did "not recollect that any of the King's Great Officers during the time he was there, died a natural death".[63] This was admittedly 25 years after he left Dahomey. But it is corroborated by quite a few contemporary documents, many in fact signed by the same Devaynes.[64] The main victims, or the victims we are best informed about (again, because the Europeans were in a sense witnesses) were the successive holders of the office of *tegan/yovogan*, an office which, because of the power it wielded, clearly invited corruption. It began with the *yovogan* appointed in possibly 1743, who revolted two years later. His peculiarity was that he was a eunuch, something which did not stop him from having, we are told, a great many beautiful wives, who were in addition very devoted to him since he allowed them to do as they pleased. That eunuch, by the name of Tanga,[65] planned to seize the English fort and then to proclaim himself king of Ouidah-Glehue (or Hueda?). But in this he failed, owing in part to the determined stance of the English director Isaac Gregory. In the end, Tanga was killed and all his wives decided to die with him – according to Robert Norris, our main source, who wrote in the 1770s,[66] many years after the actual events (those who consider the story about his wives too good to be true may have a point since, as Robin Law has tartly noted, "it lacks explicit coronation from other sources").[67] As for Isaac Gregory, the director of William's fort between 1739 and 1745, he had to face several attacks. The first was in the early 1740s when an attempt was made on the English fort, leading to the stabbing to death, by Dahomeans, of a canoeman and a seaman inside the fort.[68] Then came the Tanga affair. Finally, and as already noted, at the end of 1745 the British fort's African garrison mutinied, with the result that Gregory was expelled.[69]

One may wonder what was the link between Tanga and the other actors of this period, including Aghidisu, the exiled Huedans and their allies. It can be noted for instance that the Tanga affair took place in 1745 and the execution of all the official traders the following year.

Tanga became the first of a long list of *yovogan*s executed, no less than five or six between 1743 and 1763; they were executed generally, it is argued, on the basis of unproved allegations.[70] The execution of the incumbent *yovogan* in 1755 was to the satisfaction of all the whites and all the Africans, if we are to believe a French source.[71] After that, Tegbesu seems to have tried to reduce the power of the *yovogan* through the creation of offices that took over some of his competences.[72]

The year 1754 also witnessed the revolts of the vassal kings of Tori and Ajara or Ajirrah,[73] a fact which demonstrates that what we may call the consolidation of the conquered territories had not yet been completed. Tori was a tiny but well-known polity of considerable antiquity[74] and a renowned religious centre, reasons for which, we suppose, the Dahomeans had permitted it to subsist as an autonomous polity; we have no other references to Ajara.

We note that many of the executions referred to so far, especially of the merchants and the *yovogan*s, took place in Ouidah-Glehue. This is one of the reasons why Edna Bay believes that the terror was especially ferocious in that town. She concludes, logically, that the governing elite in Abomey had difficulties in controlling the recently conquered Ouidah (in fact old Hueda?) and that the relationship between the capital and the main trading centre in the south was and remained problematic, thus reinforcing a point made above already. In this context she argues, credibly, that the people of the latter were contemptuous of the "northerners".[75] But again, the question is the link between those who were executed and all the other actors in this turbulent period.

As a conclusion, one may wonder, as did the French, how Tegbesu was able to get away with it all. Indeed, the French believed at one stage that Tegbesu was digging his own grave.[76] But that did not turn out to be the case.

4

MORE ABOUT THE TEGBESU ERA

Tegbesu carried out what might be called more constructive measures, in particular efforts to legitimate the monarchy's position by trying to manipulate the ideological-religious sphere. In this context we note in particular the institution of an organized cult of Mawu-Liisa, the Supreme Deity, a cult Tegbesu tried to link to the monarchy. The idea was presumably to present the Dahomean hierarchy with the monarch on top as the logical replica of the supranatural world, which was now an ordered world, with an active Mawu-Liisa at the summit – a "creator couple...that mirrored the rulers in the land of the visible".[1]

More generally, the ruling elite attempted to "convince" the Dahomeans that the monarch and his ancestors were much more efficient in providing people with the necessary supranatural protection than the divinities associated with the "owners of the land" and related matters.

The second aspect which needs to be mentioned, already mentioned earlier, is the importance of the direct link with Tado and Agasu, with Agasu linked directly from Tado to Abomey – skipping the Allada connexion, and thus establishing a more direct connection with the presumably very powerful founding ancestor. Tegbesu (or his successor Kpengla) even built temples for Agasu along the fictional "migrational path" from Tado to Abomey.[2]

But this did not stop Tegbesu, somewhat contradictorily, from reviving the cult of Ajahuto in Allada in 1740–45. Indeed, an *ajahutonun*, a "king" of Allada and as such the supreme priest of the cult of Ajahuto, was installed (Ajahuto was the mythical son or grandson of Agasu). It may even be that every new king of Dahomey had to be consecrated by the *ajahutonun*.[3] "The kings of Dahomey thereby secured the traditional legitimacy which could be conferred only by a king of Allada",[4] argues Robin Law. But we repeat what Jacques Lombard has made clear, that in this case, as in that of the *agasunon* mentioned earlier, it was mere window-dressing.

There were other inventions as well, especially at the level of ancestor worship. What we end up with in any case is an increasingly syncretic, not to say labyrinthine official religion; a religion whose at times obscure logic escapes in part the present author, as one suspects it also escaped in part many of the Dahomeans of the time.[5]

In addition, Tegbesu seems to have tried to adopt some of the outer trappings of traditional sacred kingship. For instance, whereas Agaja had been constantly on the move, Tegbesu attempted to isolate himself from public view, in order to distance himself and to mystify the kingship. It became also customary, when approaching the king, to crawl on all fours covering oneself with dust in the classic tradition.[6] And it was said that the king's *mana* resided in his hair and nails, a virtually universal archetype linked to sacred kingship.[7] We note finally that according to Maurice Glélé the king had to submit himself to a purification ceremony, a so-called ritual bath, during which a child of 6–7 years old served as scapegoat, and as such "disappeared" afterwards.[8]

With regard to the Muslim traders coming from the north, the evidence is somewhat contradictory. It is argued on the one hand that they were now fêted by the king as his guests, the king being eager to secure the service of Muslim clerics for their magical-religious acumen.[9] But on the other hand Le Hérissé tells us that Muslims were generally forbidden to enter Dahomey except as slaves.[10]

Was Tegbesu successful in his attempt at manipulating the religious-ideological sphere? As we shall see, probably not.

*   *   *

On a practical level, Tegbesu issued in 1746, the year of the executions of the traders, a proclamation declaring "the paths open and free to all traders" to come to Ouidah-Glehue.[11] It was a proclamation reaffirmed frequently throughout the years. This was perhaps an attempt to change radically Dahomey's approach to the slave trade. For the 1746 proclamation implied the admission of failure of what we may call the Dahomean model, that is, the predatory one – the admission, in sum, that raids and warfare were not the only, not even an adequate means of procuring slaves in the long run. What was necessary was a return to the pre-1724/1727 system when the Slave Coast served principally as an intermediary. This apparently happened to some extent.[12]

But the trouble with Tegbesu's new policy was that there were attempts to prevent the hinterland traders from travelling to the coast to deal directly with the Europeans,[13] and that the main inland supplier, Oyo, had no confidence in Dahomey, as we shall see.

Tegbesu also made (somewhat contradictorily, considering his general policy) a gesture in the direction of the Europeans, by substantially reducing the rates they had to pay to trade, obviously in the hope of stemming the desertion of the slavers.[14] According to David Ross the result was what he has called Ouidah's mid-century prosperity; but if so, Ross adds that it lasted only to the end of the 1760s.[15]

* * *

In the south the trail of violence, the raids of the Ge and the exiled Huedans, continued. There was possibly one raid in 1749 and certainly at least six more in the 1750s,[16] one in November 1755 being particularly disastrous to the Dahomeans and the Europeans (of whom four were taken prisoner).[17] That was after Tegbesu had tried, in 1754–55, a most unusual stratagem: propagating the false news that he had committed suicide, in order to entice his external enemies to take advantage of the interim always following a king's death to attack, the Dahomeans having prepared an ambush.[18] But as far as we know, none of those enemies made any move.

However, a most serious and perhaps decisive attack took place on 12–13 July 1763. Although our sources are (as usual) somewhat contradictory, what seems to have happened was that first the local Dahomean forces were worsted on the 12th, the survivors taking refuge in the French fort where Pruneau de Pommegeorge was in command; and then the French and British forts opened fire with the cannon that still functioned (the Portuguese fort may have had none). This was apparently enough to stall the assailants until the next day, the 13th, when a considerable body of the Dahomean army arrived swiftly on the horizon to rescue the besieged Europeans, who felt they had come close to total disaster ("*a deux doigts*", as Pruneau expressed it[19]). So this was a joint French-British-Dahomean military victory over the exiled Huedans and their allies, certainly a historical first in the annals of the Slave Coast.[20]

The defeat of the exiled Huedans notwithstanding, Pruneau was of the opinion that Tegbesu's cruelty and his looting of his own people had so weakened his position that his days were numbered. Indeed, Pruneau thought it was inevitable that the exiled Huedans would recover their land one day soon.[21] But Pruneau, like other observers before him (see above), was proved wrong in the end.

July 1763 turned out to be an unmitigated disaster for the exiled Huedans and the Ge, with the result that the latter, who were also experiencing problems in the west, began to opt out. They agreed in fact to peace treaties with Dahomey in 1769 and 1772, short-lived certainly, but nevertheless highly significant. It is also significant that the initiative came from Tegbesu and that the successive British Directors (Dalzel and Abson) served as go-betweens.[22]

On the other hand, the 1763 disaster was, surprisingly enough, not the end of the quite incredibly resilient exiled Huedans. In fact their raiding continued (but perhaps less and less destructively), eleven times between 1767 and 1781 according to Akinjogbin (but probably more), the Dahomeans being unable to check the danger.[23] In 1770 the assailants made no less than four incursions, burning every canoe on the beach and at times carrying away Europeans,[24] who we suppose had to be ransomed.

What were the exiled Huedans (and the Ge to the extent that they participated) trying to do now that they had probably no more hope of reconquering old Hueda? Obviously to ruin the slave trade, not because of any abolitionist fervour, but to strike a blow at a vital source of income for Dahomey and especially for the monarchy. For a decline in the slave trade threatened the celebration of the very expensive Annual Customs, and the Customs were considered indispensable for whatever legitimacy the monarchy enjoyed – or so believes, for instance, William Argyle.[25] However, one could perhaps equally well argue that the exiled Huedans and their allies had by now been converted into a gang of brigands without any precise political aims.

The near-definitive end of the exiled Huedans came, it can be argued, in 1774–75, at the time of the death of Tegbesu (in May 1774), and the accession of his successor Kpengla. The king of the exiled Huedans also died, a death which triggered yet another of those incomprehensible succession disputes. One of the contestants petitioned Kpengla for assistance, strange as it may sound, with the final result easily imaginable:[26] briefly, a repeat performance of 1734. Even so, it was not quite the end of the exiled Huedans, since we know of several raids in 1781,[27] though none after that date.

There remained the increasingly weakened Little Popo-Glidji which continued to pose a threat of sorts until 1795.

* * *

MORE ABOUT THE TEGBESU ERA

What was Dahomean society like in the eighteenth century? We have a number of general characteristics and descriptions to which we now turn. But the problem is that we (and often also the authors from whom they have been borrowed) cannot determine always if they apply to the eighteenth century or the next one or both. We have in any case decided to include them in the present chapter, for reasons of convenience, while repeating that their chronological anchoring remains imprecise.

If we begin at the centre, we encounter the enormous royal compound, called the Simboji palace, which an English visitor during the last years of Tegbesu's reign described as having the appearance of an assemblage of farmyards.[28] What is left of it at present, now the Museum of Abomey, has still that appearance. What has disappeared since are all the human skulls which lined the palace walls (that earth mixed with blood from sacrificial victims was used to build those walls[29] is another matter). Of particular importance were the preserved skulls of defeated enemy chiefs or kings – they "played an important role in the transmission of traditional history, since each skull served as a memento of the campaign in which it was taken".[30]

The activities inside the compound were deliberately shrouded in secrecy, says Edna Bay.[31] Those who genuinely resided there were the king and his very numerous dependants, principally his "wives", the *ahosi*, five to eight thousand of them in the nineteenth century (in theory, all female inhabitants of the polity were at the pleasure of the King).[32] The *ahosi* made up about 15 per cent of Abomey's total population, according to Edna Bay whom we continue to follow here;[33] Abomey may have had 24,000 inhabitants and Kana 15,000 (Ouidah-Glehue something in between) in the 1770s. Few of the "wives" were wives in the usual sense of the term – at least a quarter (we suspect more) were in fact warriors composing the royal bodyguard, who came to be known by the Europeans as Amazons. Since they could not divorce, the choice they had was between celibacy or adultery, and adultery was punishable with death. Small wonder then that we have some chilling stories of girls preferring death by suicide to the destiny of royal wives.[34] If we add that all dignitaries, whether in Dahomey or in Allada and Hueda earlier, or anywhere else on the Slave and Gold Coasts for that matter, had a profusion of wives, the next question is what was the status and condition of women in general? From the point of view of modern sensibilities it can only be described as abject, as many observers have argued.[35] The widespread practice of polygamy continued incidentally to produce a very skewed sex balance, which in turn meant that "low-ranking men were deprived of access to resources, and specifically to women",[36] which meant in turn that prostitution proliferated. It was inexpensive and organized more or less by the monarchy as a royal monopoly. But the prostitutes, who were as a general rule war captives, had to pay a heavy annual tax.[37]

What about the spectacular story of Norris that the death of a king provoked a tremendous bloodbath, the *ahosi* in particular beginning to massacre each other and continuing to do so until the successor had taken possession of the palace?[38] As far as we know, it is confirmed only by Dalzel and Dunglas,[39] not necessarily independent sources in this context, but is flatly denied by Maurice Glélé.[40] On the other hand, given the pent-up frustration which we imagine characterized life inside the palace, some sort of common hysteria unleashed by the death of a king does not sound altogether implausible.

* * *

Turning now to the administration, the highly centralized Dahomey presents us with a pyramidal multi-tiered hierarchy,[41] with provincial chiefs (*avogan*), district and village chiefs (*togan* and *tohosu*), plus ward chiefs; the village and ward chief being local people, but very closely watched,[42] those higher up being royal appointees. To make the king's command known throughout his realm, Tegbesu established in possibly 1745 the institution of royal messengers, the famous "halfheads" (*legede* in the local tongue), so called because half of their heads were shaved, thus making them easily recognizable. The model was the equally famous *ilari* of Oyo.[43] Each halfhead carried a baton, called *recade* (from the Portuguese *recado*, "message"), likened to a tomahawk by Stanley Alpern.[44] The presence of a *recade* was equivalent to the presence of the king himself.[45]

The halfheads were men who had distinguished themselves in battle. As such they wore around their necks strings of the teeth of those enemies they had killed with their own hands. The halfheads were "never permitted to walk, but (had to) run at full speed, and (were) relieved at certain distances on the road, by relays of others".[46] "In delivering...the *King's word*, the messenger as well as all those around him fall prostrate on the ground & cover their heads with dust, or with mud if it rains; so that they often display very hideous figures".[47]

In addition there were what Obichere calls "intelligence officers" by the name of *gninouhon*, "spies", located all over the kingdom[48] – the secret police we have referred to earlier.

We repeat that there was no Council of State, and in fact nothing resembling any system of checks and balances, implying that the king wielded unlimited power. Indeed, all wealth in the kingdom was said to belong to the king, his subjects enjoying only its temporary use. Hence, at the death of a dignitary, headman or chief of family, for example, his wealth reverted to the king, who, according to the official version presented by Le Hérissé, restored it to the heir, levying only a fictitious duty.[49] But Robin Law's contention that the king took three-quarters[50] strikes one as much more credible. The king had, among other things, to provide sustenance to his enormous sib, whose members did nothing and were therefore a very onerous charge for the polity.[51]

Actually, many contemporary observers and modern scholars have come to the conclusion that the inhabitants of Dahomey were all slaves of the king – at least in theory. As they were slaves, the king could dispose of them at will: "My head belongs to the king", to quote the title of a Robin Law article we have referred to frequently already, which is in turn an utterance by a servant of the eighteenth century slave trader Robert Norris.[52] In fact, not only his head, but also his whole body, his property, his will, his everything.[53]

What we observe seems to have a distinctly totalitarian flavour. It may be relevant in this context to evoke the *bocio* amulets and sculptures. Whatever the chronological context of the *bocio* art and its diffusion, anyone who has perused, if only superficially, the art historian Suzanne Preston Blier's magnificent book on the subject,[54] and contemplated its many photos, must have been deeply impressed and disturbed by those grotesque, or one might say deliberately provocative and horrid, but at the same time elaborate and sophisticated, works of art which convey tension and anxiety almost to an unbearable degree. They are (to continue to paraphrase Ms Blier) truly objects of fury whose counteraesthetic power literally hits the beholder – the result of a collective trauma which a non-literate society expressed in its own very peculiar way. Regardless of how widespread or significant the *bocio* objects may have been, or when they began to be made, one suspects that Blier is correct in attributing them to "state-induced or supported violence".[55]

Is it possible to be more specific? Although Suzanne Blier is reluctant to do so ("these forms remain...unknowable, resistant to interpretation"[56]), she provides us nevertheless with some relevant clues. She notes in fact that the *bocio* are "closely identified with *vodun* power, religious tenets, and philosophy – (that is) the derivation of the powers which actuate the *bo/bocio* arts are ascribed to *vodun* such as Legba, the Earth gods (that is, Sakpata *et al.* once again), and, most importantly, to the earlier mentioned 'little folk' – the *aziza*, of the forest".[57] In a word, they challenge the status quo,[58] that is, the monarchy, and hence the system established by Agaja and Tegbesu.

What we end up with here is, we suspect, a deeply split Dahomey in which the official ideology of the monarchy was actively challenged and combated by what we presume to be important sections of the population.

* * *

Moving to the Eastern Slave Coast, we note that Oyo began some time in the eighteenth century to establish a sort of thin territorial corridor east of the Yewa river all the way down to Porto Novo and Badagry, both places situated at a distance of a nine-days journey from metropolitan Oyo.[59] It permitted the Oyo traders to travel all the way to the coast, and in fact, given the attitude of the local rulers, to establish direct relations with the Europeans.[60] To the authorities of Porto Novo especially, this development implied riches and also protection against Dahomey, all at the price of a modest tribute to Oyo.[61]

Since we do not really know what happened in and to Badagry after the Hertogh affair, we can go on to note that as far as Porto Novo and its coastal beach "port" of Seme (actually on the coast this time) are concerned, the pioneers on the European side were the Luso-Brazilians. In fact, although the sources are not very eloquent, it seems that the first to open up direct trade with Porto Novo some time in the late 1750s was a shadowy figure by the name of João de Oliveira,[62] a freed slave from Brazil.[63] According to Robin Law, with the Portuguese there also arrived the first Yoruba Muslims.[64] Oliveira was soon followed by "other slave traders anxious to escape the tight control that the king of Dahomey was attempting to impose on the commerce at Ouidah".[65] It is claimed that what contributed to the success of the eastern ports was the surprising thirty per cent lower loading time compared with Ouidah-Glehue[66] (because of fewer regulations?).

What is certain is that the slave trade from the Porto Novo region soared, and that from Ouidah-Glehue declined correspondingly;[67] and that there was a close alliance between Oyo, Porto Novo and the Luso-Brazilians. A token of the alliance between the latter two was the fact that as early as 1774–75 the king of Porto Novo asked the Portuguese to establish a fort in his dominions (it may have been in 1775, since the throne of Porto Novo is reputed to have been vacant for a full ten years between 1765 and 1775[68]). But although the authorities in Salvador da Bahia were favourable, nothing came of it.[69] In fact, no forts were ever constructed in the eastern area, proof that they were not needed in the slave trade.

We note finally that the people of the Porto Novo region, although probably of a rather heterogeneous origin, coalesced into a new ethnic group, the Gbe-speaking Gun or Egun.[70]

MORE ABOUT THE TEGBESU ERA

Porto Novo was accompanied, or possibly preceded, by other polities such as Ekpe/Epe-Ketonou, Badagry (both of Hertoghian fame) and especially Lagos (Awori in Yoruba),[71] where the first recorded loading of slaves is dated to 1765, according to Sandra Barnes.[72] In fact, a slaving port was established at Lagos in the 1760s, when Oba Akinsemoyin (reigned c.1760 to 1775) invited (we repeat: invited) slave traders from Porto Novo to settle there.[73]

The question is how all this fits in with what we know about the internal evolution of Oyo, an internal evolution which presaged momentous changes in Yorubaland and by consequence also on the Slave Coast. The way we interpret the evidence presented by Samuel Johnson, Robin Law and I.A. Akinjogbin[74] is that the internal institutional set-up, the local variant of contrapuntal paramountcy, simply broke down, at least temporarily. What happened was that the *oyo mesi*, the state council and especially its head, the *Basorun* Gaha, forced the suicide of two successive Alafins, and then assumed effective power for some twenty years (c. 1754–74).[75] Although the institution itself was not (perhaps could not be) abolished, three more Alafins were ordered to commit suicide by the *oyo mesi* and Gaha. However, the fourth, by the name of Abiodun, managed to stage a coup (or counter-coup), deposing and executing Gaha, but again without abolishing the relevant institution, that of the *basorun* this time.[76] Possibly it was under Abiodun that the slave trade from Oyo via the Eastern Slave Coast really took off.

The consequences of these internal upheavals (Law insists that they were exclusively internal) were probably a radical weakening of Oyo's might, more concretely the decline of what was the cornerstone of that might, namely the famous but very expensive cavalry. Actually it disappeared altogether at some undetermined time during the last decades of the eighteenth century and the first of the following one.[77] It obviously presaged the slow agony and final fall of Oyo itself, an event we will turn to.

* * *

We now move to the Western Slave Coast and neighbouring regions, where the picture is complicated in the extreme. We can begin by enumerating the leading protagonists. In the middle there was the Anlo confederacy and its ally in the north, New Akwamu, which controlled a fair slice of inland Eweland. But among the member-polities of the Anlo confederacy was unruly Keta which often went its own ways and whose excruciatingly intricate past can defeat even the most obstinate of historians. Anlo/Keta was flanked to the east by Little Popo-Glidji, and to the west by the Ada of the mouth of the river Volta. Ada had in turn a special and close relationship with the Danes of Christiansborg at Accra. The Ada and the Danes, plus Agave or Agavedji north of Keta, became, in a sense logically, the allies of Little Popo-Glidji against Anlo/Keta.

The Danes embarked in this period on an expansionist policy, a regional imperialist drive of sorts – something rather uncommon among the Europeans on the coast of Guinea. What made that drive possible was Akyem's very lax overlordship since 1730 over the eastern Gold Coast, leaving the indigenous Ga-Adangbe more or less to their own devices. And since Ga-Adangbe society had by then reverted to what we presume was its original acephalous state,[78] the result was a sort of power-vacuum which in turn facilitated the expansionist designs of the Danes along the coast eastwards in the direction of the River Volta and the Ada, and beyond, and in spite of English and above all Dutch opposition.[79] The strip of coast between Accra and the Volta estuary, and beyond, attained some importance owing mainly to the revival of Akwamu power in the hinterland (that is, New Akwamu) and the presumably intensive exploitation by New Akwamu of the slave and ivory resources of the Ewe Krepi and their neighbours.

Little Popo-Glidji under Ashangbo was able in 1741, with the collaboration of the Danes, to defeat Anlo/Keta. Keta was in fact occupied and Anlo proper was forced to accept a subordinate position. Significantly enough, Anlo had to accept a Danish monopoly over trade which among other things established a ceiling for the rates at which the Anlo could sell slaves to the Danes.[80] But since the Anlo landscape has been described as a smuggler's paradise,[81] one may reasonably wonder how efficient that monopoly was.

A complicating factor was Asante's defeat of a certain number of southern Akan polities, Akyem very much included, in March 1742.[82] It allowed Asante to reach the sea for the first time, to invade the Eastern Gold Coast and to lay siege to the European forts, leaving the Europeans, the Danes included, with little choice but to accede to the Asante demands.[83] From then on the Europeans had to pay rent to the Asantehene in Kumasi as the new overlord of the Eastern Gold Coast, a region which then became formally part of ever-expanding Asante. But Asante too contented itself with a lax, even absentee overlordship for the next fifteen years or so,[84] implying that little changed on the ground, and hence that the Ga-Adangbe had simply changed overlords.

However, if Asante reached the coast, it also reached the River Volta, meaning contact with New Akwamu on the other bank. In fact New Akwamu acknowledged Asante overlordship, possibly in 1744, in return for the latter's support, an alliance which cowed completely the indigenous Krepi Ewe, we are told.[85] Asante emerged thus as a potential enemy of Little Popo-Glidji, the Ada and the Danes. It complicated matters for the Danes, who were at the same time, in a sense, vassals of the same Asante, in the latter's capacity as overlord of Accra and the European forts there.

As if this were not enough, Akyem, although defeated and having become a tributary polity of Asante, was able to revolt against its overlord and even to emerge as an actor of its own on the Western Slave Coast scene[86] – and obviously as an ally of Little Popo-Glidji, the Ada and the Danes.

Was there also a battle between Asante and either Oyo or Dahomey, possibly in 1764? The case is far from clear-cut. But if there was (what were they fighting over?), it seems to have been an isolated event with negligible consequences.[87]

It would not serve any useful purpose to relate in detail all the skirmishes, battles and wars between the protagonists, especially Ada and Anlo,[88] in the relevant period – plus some changes of alliance. But what was the situation when the smoke began to lift (partially) in the mid-1770s? The most noteworthy difference was that Little Popo-Glidji, whose great king Ashangmo passed away in the late 1760s or early 1770s, had lost out on the Western Slave Coast, as it was also in the process of doing further east, and had begun its slow descent into insignificance.[89] But this did not stop the Danes establishing a lodge at Little Popo in 1772.[90]

As for Akyem, after a show of strength in 1767–70, when its army marched as far east as Little Popo-Glidji, thereafter it disappeared completely from the Slave Coast scene.[91] Ada and Agave too were among the losers, in spite of an early success, thanks in part to Danish support, during the so-called Nonobewa war of 1750–51. But Ada suffered a major defeat in February 1769, when the Danes avoided coming to the rescue of their old ally.[92] However, the Danes, who had in a sense betted on the wrong side (as usual), managed somehow to overcome their apparent handicap, as we shall see.

That leaves us with the "victor", namely the Anlo confederacy which also Keta now joined (or rejoined) after recovering its independence from Little Popo-Glidji in 1772.[93] According to Sandra Greene, Anlo's victory was achieved thanks to, or was accompanied by, a major internal religious-conceptual revolution, the rise of an apparently new divinity, a war divinity in fact, by the name of Nyigba or Nyigbla. We say apparently because the same Sandra Greene has defined Nyigba as a new separate conception or personified revelation of the Supreme Being, namely Mawu.[94]

* * *

Tegbesu died in May 1774, in the same year as the coup against *basorun* Gaha, while in the world at large, in the same year the American Revolution really got under way. It was, then, the beginning of the Age of the Atlantic Revolutions; revolutions which were bound to have a profound impact upon the questions of slave trade and slavery and hence upon the affairs of the Slave Coast.

5

CONTINUATION

We begin by noting, as a curiosity of sorts in the larger context, that the American Revolution (1765/74–1783) led to fears among the British in Guinea of American privateers and suspicion that the rebels might be supplied with gunpowder from that coast. The result was a certain British naval military presence and activity in Guinean waters.[1] The war in North America had also a direct and negative effect on the British (but only the British) slave trade, that is, on the slave traders, as the Database makes clear.

As for the American Declaration of Independence of 1776, a naive reader may be excused for finding it absolutely incompatible with both the slave trade and slavery ("We hold these truths to be self-evident, that all men are created equal..."). The same can be said of another famous declaration of another revolution, the French Declaration of the Rights of Man and of the Citizen on 26 August 1789 (not to mention the revolutionary motto of *Liberté, Égalité, Fraternité*). But as is well known, that conclusion was not commonly drawn then. On the other hand, those declarations indicate that something was afoot in the Western world, which was after all the world of the Enlightenment. And Revolutionary France did at long last, more than four years after the outbreak of the Revolution and the issuing of the Declaration of the Rights of Man, get around to abolishing the slave trade and slavery, on 4 February 1794. Revolutionary France also proceeded immediately to combat that trade actively, including military action extending to the Slave Coast. But Napoleon Bonaparte (ruler 1799–1814/15) decided upon the opposite course and re-legalized both the slave trade and slavery in 1802. At an early stage Revolutionary France lost control of the American slave islands, including Saint-Domingue, where the slaves liberated themselves, starting with the famous revolt of 1791; the formal abolition of slavery in 1794 had then no practical consequences. But the slave trade was another matter.[2]

As it was, it fell to a nation which came to struggle against both the American and French Revolutions, Great Britain, to enact the first concrete measure against the slave trade. The Dolben Act (after Sir William Dolben) of 1788 restricted the number of slaves that could be carried on British slave ships.[3] Then in May 1789 William Wilberforce enacted an historical first, when he began moving resolutions condemning the slave trade in the House of Commons; an initiative which had no possibility of prospering then[4] (it was then that one of Wilberforce's opponents read aloud the earlier mentioned Agaja-Lambe letter from 1726). But only three years later the House of Commons voted a bill to abolish the slave trade, a bill which was, however, defeated in the House of Lords. Nevertheless, the campaign initiated in 1789 did achieve its aim in the end, in 1807, when the British slave trade was outlawed. By then Denmark, or Denmark-Norway, had already abolished the slave trade, in 1792, but with the proviso that it should enter into effect only ten years later (1 January 1803). But the local Danes on the coast refused to enforce the law, which was binding only for the direct subjects of the Danish Crown and ships flying the Danish colours anyway. The illegal Danish slave trade continued at least until the 1830s, if not longer.[5]

In view of all this a well-informed observer of the international scene at the end of the eighteenth century might well have concluded that the tide was turning, that the days of the slave trade, and even of slavery, were numbered. He would have been right of course. But what he might perhaps not have foreseen was that it would take a hundred years and an extraordinarily complicated itinerary – a spiral path full of detours and disappointments, as it has been expressed[6] – to eradicate the evil *legally* in the Western world: that is, if we consider the Dolben Act of 1788 as the first step, and Brazil's effective abolition of slavery in 1888 as the end, with 1807 as the pivotal date.

* * *

The developments in the Western world for the time being (during the period covered in this chapter, 1774–97) had, perhaps somewhat surprisingly, no impact whatsoever on the Transatlantic slave trade. Quite the contrary in fact, since according to the global figures of the Database, that trade experienced an all-time high between 1776 and 1800, 1786–96 being the top ten-year period. Hence Wilberforce and his allies assaulted a trade which was prospering as never before.

Within that general situation, however, the slave trade from the Slave Coast experienced a slight absolute and a somewhat more marked relative decline. But there is reason to believe that the decline was particularly steep on the *Central* Slave Coast, as opposed to the *Eastern* Slave Coast, where the slave trade actually soared. Since the steep decline on the Central Slave Coast corresponds to the beginning of the end of the European and Luso-Brazilian presence – the abandonment of the forts (see below) – it is tempting to postulate a connection. But that temptation should be resisted. The fundamental cause was clearly the continuing erratic, not to say absurd, policy of the Dahomean rulers.

* * *

In the case of Dahomey the 23 years which followed the death of Tegbesu are not easy to define or to categorize. But the expression "more of the same" comes to mind. The "totalitarian" Dahomean regime continued frequently to find itself on the defensive, apparently suffering from a severe defeat at the hands of Oyo in early 1779. We say apparently, because that supposed defeat is mentioned only in one source.[7] But if it did happen, it helps to explain what occurred later the same year: the king of Dahomey was permitted (he had then to ask for permission) by the local British director Lionel Abson to send a messenger all the way to Cape Coast Castle, "in order to lay a state of his wants before the [British] Governor".[8] However, whatever those wants were, apart from being obviously very much needed, this strange Dahomean initiative led to nothing, according to Akinjogbin.[9] But it is tempting to postulate a link between this episode and the fact that Dahomey seems to have experienced the next year (in 1780) a genuine famine, certainly not a frequent phenomenon on the coast.[10] However, if famine there was, we have unfortunately no details about it. But two years later, in 1782, a great scarcity of provisions was reported – "had it not been for the wild...spontaneous productions of the woods, half of the country would have starved", if we are to believe Archibald Dalzel and Lionel Abson.[11] And in 1788 an epidemic (of smallpox?) claimed untold victims.[12]

These, then, are some of the ingredients of the crisis which Dahomey experienced from the 1770s onwards, according to some contemporary observers[13] and some later historians.[14] Another problem was that the two kings we are concerned with here, Kpengla and Agonglo, were, as rulers of a polity imbued with a warrior ethos, utterly unable to conquer any new territory.

Worse, Kpengla's raiding parties were often defeated,[15] although they are reported to have reached as far as Ketu in 1789.[16] An early exception to that rule was the destruction of the small polity of Ekpe/Epe, the successor of Jakin, in 1778. But Ekpe/Epe seems to have risen again shortly afterwards, now with Ketonu as its centre and as a tributary to Porto Novo.[17] As it was, the Dahomeans had great difficulties in acquiring the necessary slaves, according to a French source. Indeed, the same source argues that the king began to sell his own subjects in the 1770s.[18]

On the external front Dahomey was reduced at times to the position of a mere agent of the will of Oyo, to castigate Oyo's recalcitrant vassals when Oyo so ordered (see below). And Kpengla died in April 1789 of the smallpox[19] (related to the epidemic in 1788, perhaps), the redoubtable arm of Sakpata, the oppositional *vodun*.

But all was not uniformly bleak for the Dahomeans. To begin with, the evident decline of Oyo carried hopes for the future for Dahomey, while at the same time boding ill for Oyo's protégés on the Eastern Slave Coast. Furthermore, although the slave trade continued to decline, there were moments when it recovered somehow. And the earlier mentioned return of the Luso-Brazilians to complete free trade in 1778, with the intensified competition among them that it meant, was certainly good news to Dahomey.

There were also signs of more contacts with the interior, resulting among other things in a timid diversification of the economy. For instance, by the end of the eighteenth century a sizeable community of so-called "royal" Muslim clients and artisans (working especially in leather tanning and dyeing) had been established at Abomey and Kana.[20]

The influx of northern Muslims (Malés) from Hausaland in particular had also a religious dimension. For the Dahomean rulers, always on the lookout for supranatural support, petitioned the Malés to pray to their god for Dahomean success. And Islamic amulets, typically consisting of or incorporating written verses from the Quran, enjoyed considerable popularity.[21]

* * *

If one asks if there was any attempt to alter the direction staked out by Agaja and Tegbesu, the answer is that there was: king Agonglo's intention at the very end of the period to convert to Christianity. But it cost him his life, as we shall see, provoking what looks like a coup d'état and a lot of bloodshed.

It is in any case difficult to agree with Robin Law when he argues that "the Dahomians clearly had by [the 1770s] won the consent of many of the conquered to the legitimacy of their rule".[22] Linda Heywood and John Thornton seem to be of the same opinion in a somewhat ambiguous contribution, but then they add an interesting twist which points clearly in the opposite direction. They note that the kingdom of Kongo lived on in the memories of the slaves in America who came from there – many slave societies elected a king of Kongo[23] – but the slaves originating from the Slave Coast were reluctant to identify with the Kingdom of Dahomey; no "king of Dahomey" is known from among the slaves in America.[24]

* * *

As for the details, we begin this time with the region least involved in the slave trade, the Western Slave Coast, where we have already noted that a quite unusual development was taking place: the rise of what may be described as a European power of sorts, the Danes at Christiansborg. And this European power staged something quite unheard-of on the coast, outright military aggression against an African polity, namely Anlo, the leading polity of the region. If it failed in the end, it was not because of African resistance, but because the other Europeans, and especially the British, had the means to persuade the government in Copenhagen to repudiate its local representatives.

The background was the previously noted rise of the Anlo confederacy to a position of prominence. And Anlo succeeded in solidifying its newfound position by a number of successful campaigns between 1774 and 1781 against especially Little Popo-Glidji and Ada, plus other lower Volta riverain communities. Ada was simply destroyed in 1776.[25] In this situation the losers appealed to their old allies the Danes, arguing that the Danes had to protect them with a fortification, otherwise they would seek help from another nation. That other nation could only have been the Dutch of the WIC,[26] but the Dutch were virtually eliminated for a while in the 1780s, by the British, because of the war Great Britain declared on the Dutch Republic in December 1780, blaming the Dutch for becoming much too intimate with the American rebels. What resulted is often called the Fourth Anglo-Dutch Naval War (1780–84), a war which turned out to be an unmitigated disaster for the Dutch.[27] The war was also fought in Guinean waters (it should be remarked that since the days of Samuel Pepys the African facet of wars between European powers is generally treated cavalierly, if at all, in the historical literature). Briefly, the British drove the Dutch from all their positions on the coast, except Elmina. In particular, in April 1782 the British destroyed the Dutch fort Crevecoeur at Accra, with the result that the Dutch lodges to the east had to be abandoned. Since the British were not particularly interested in that region, this gave the Danes a free hand.[28] And it so happened that the Danes, who adopted a suitably neutral stance during the Anglo-Dutch contention, actually leaning on the English side, had clearly expansionist designs. At least the new Danish Governor, Jens Adolph Kiøge (1780–88), had such designs. In fact, and to anticipate later discussion, under Kiøge the Danes established four new forts, including two on the Slave Coast, if we count Ada (in addition to the two earlier ones on the Gold Coast), plus a number of lodges. All this apparently led to a considerable upsurge in the Danish slave trade.[29]

It all began in earnest in October 1783 when the Danes constructed Fort Kongensten at Ada to support the Ada polity, or what was left of it, against Anlo. "The Adas were heartily pleased" with the construction of Kongensten, says Isert, since now they had a safe refuge in case of attack.[30] It was the prelude to the so-called Sagbadre war from February to June 1784,[31] a blatant war of aggression, the Danes organizing an expeditionary force of some 2,000 Africans which marched against Anlo, plus an imposing contingent from Little Popo-Glidji[32] (Gayibor calls it "*la guerre anlo-danoise*").[33] Only three Danes actually took part in the military operations, Governor Kiøge himself, a sergeant, and the famous Paul Erdmann Isert mentioned earlier, whose book contains all the necessary details.[34] On the other side we note that New Akwamu as well as Keta, that very special member of the Anlo confederacy, decided to remain neutral.[35] As for mighty Asante, our sources are silent, implying that Asante remained aloof. The reason may be that the death of Asantehene Osei Kwadwo in 1777 triggered off a civil war which lasted until the 1790s. Osei Kwadwo was succeeded by a minor, Osei Kwame, and the regency of the Queen-Mother provoked strong negative internal reactions, according to John Fynn.[36]

Isert's testimony leaves no doubt that the Sagbadre war was fought with great cruelty, claiming a considerable number of casualties. Anlo, and especially the capital Anlogan, was devastated.[37] The excuse of the Danes, the way we read Isert, is that they lost control of their troops.

The war ended with a complete victory for Ada, the Danes and their allies, in spite of indirect British aid to Anlo.[38] As a result the Danes, who had already tried earlier to control Anlo's trade, imposed what one may call an economic protectorate on Anlo, prohibiting the local people from trading with other European nations. But this new Danish trade monopoly was probably no more effective than the previous one.[39] In addition, the Danes compelled the people of Keta, who (as noted) had remained ostensibly neutral, to accept the construction (from June 1784) of a fort, Fort Prindsensten, in their midst. It was, as is often pointed out, the only fort ever erected on the Guinea coast against the will of the local population. It could be done because the king of Little Popo-Glidji took upon himself the task of protector of the fort and in fact of governor of Keta;[40] in other words, Keta was occupied once more by Little Popo-Glidji. However, the Danish hold of the area was and remained shaky – precisely because the Danish involvement in African affairs did not have the favour of the local people.[41]

It is probable that the Danes nourished a much grander design. The central character here is Paul Isert. Shortly after the end of the Sagbadre war he went to Ouidah and stayed there for some five months, from November 1784 to April 1785, as the head of a sort of factory.[42] Although Isert himself is not very eloquent about what he was doing in Dahomey,[43] the British were probably correct in believing that something serious was afoot,[44] especially since there are hints that the Danes had also their eyes set on regions even further east, Porto Novo in particular,[45] where the "Lagoon War" (see below) had just ended with Porto Novo (and Dahomey) on the winning side.

But whatever the Danish designs were, they were cut short by developments on the international scene. The American War of Independence ended for practical purposes in April 1783, and the war between Great Britain and the Dutch Republic in May 1784; this meant the return of the Dutch (and the British) to the Guinean scene, both uncomfortable with the Danish expansionism.[46] And as a sign of the times, in 1785 some leading dignitaries in Little Popo-Glidji asked the British to establish a factory in their polity to protect them against the Danes.[47]

In fact, the determined joint opposition of the Dutch and the British to the Danish designs, plus the resistance of the locals, meant that the whole Danish set-up fell rapidly apart. The details are again somewhat obscure. But there is no question that the situation on the ground deteriorated quickly for the Danes between 1786 and 1790. Several Danish lodges were destroyed, trade in the Keta-Popo area came to a standstill and individual Danes were attacked, one even killed.[48] Worse, the death of the king of Little Popo-Glidji in 1788 led to the usual succession dispute, the Danes supporting (again) the losing party,[49] with the negative consequences one can imagine.

There followed a quite spectacular (and frankly incomprehensible) change of alliances, the Danes allying themselves with Anlo (plus New Akwamu) against Little Popo-Glidji, and the latter emerging as the new enemy.[50] There also followed a new round of skirmishes, including the so-called Keta war in

1792, the outcome of which was that Anlo and the Danes lost, principally to Little-Popo and its allies, actively supported by both the British and the Dutch.[51] In this context we note that the Danes crossed a red line by appealing to successive African polities, namely Akyem, Asante, Akwamu and even Dahomey, to intervene militarily in their favour, an absolute historical first. No one did intervene, of course, but the Dutch and the British were outraged.[52] It fell to Archibald Dalzel, now governor of Cape Coast Castle and of the British establishments, temporarily in alliance with the Dutch,[53] to initiate the diplomatic activity which led in the end to the recall of the very belligerent Danish governor, Andreas Riegelsen Biørn (1789–93), followed by the effective retreat of the Danes from the land to the east, that is, the final collapse of the Danes' grand scheme. However, Anlo and its neighbours continued, strangely enough, to be considered part of the Danish sphere of influence, and the Danish-Anlo alliance was maintained in a sense, possibly because of Anlo's fears of Little Popo-Glidji.[54]

* * *

Kpengla began his reign by announcing his intention to liberate Dahomey from Oyo,[55] and by celebrating the defeat and death of the last effective king of the exiled Huedans. But Kpengla got nowhere with Oyo, and in fact Oyo demanded more tribute, and Kpengla had no choice but to give in.[56] It has been argued that Kpengla tried to establish Dahomey in a middleman position. But if so, that attempt may not have lasted very long (depending on one's definition of what a middleman position implies[57]). What seems certain in any case is that the Dahomean monarchy's commercial acumen had not improved in any way. In fact, Kpengla sought even greater regulation of trade; he established fixed (that is, artificially high) prices; he and his agents resorted to compulsory purchases, that is, confiscations; he expelled all foreigners except those of Oyo, and he enacted a number of other oppressive restrictions, the whole amounting to an attempt to establish a monopoly of trade.[58] Such actions, added to European wars and the French anti-slavery measures, as well as the severe surveillance and very limited freedom of movement to which the Europeans continued to be subjected,[59] inevitably had negative consequences. But there was a measure which pointed in the opposite direction – the granting of the status of *caboceers* (chiefs or dignitaries) to the traders in Dahomey in 1779.[60]

Kpengla's role as an auxiliary of Oyo came into evidence with the so-called "Lagoon War" between 1780 and 1784 (coinciding with the Fourth Anglo-

Dutch naval war on the international scene). It was, as usual, a complicated affair in which it is easy to get lost in the details. But as far as this author has been able to ascertain, what we may call Oyo's "imperial" system on the Eastern Slave Coast broke down. Oyo's local vassals began to quarrel among themselves, and some even with Oyo itself:[61] Badagry, Ketu, Porto Novo, Ketonu, the Weme successor polities (not directly involved in the slave trade) and also finally Lagos with its famous war canoes,[62] although that polity was still formally a vassal of Benin. The disputes may have had something to do with the increased revenue from the slave trade, as well as conflicting pretentions to local hegemony. In particular, the fact that Porto Novo had become possibly the leading centre of the slave trade on the whole of the Slave Coast in the 1780s[63] provoked the enmity of the others, Badagry especially, which became Porto Novo's irreconcilable enemy. In this situation Oyo enlisted the assistance of some of its vassals, Dahomey most notably – perhaps Kpengla was more than happy to comply. The result was that the Weme successor polities, plus Badagry and Ketonu, were defeated, the latter two being destroyed outright in the process.[64] Lagos, which had taken part on Oyo's side, emerged considerably reinforced. As for Porto Novo, although also among the winners, it seems nevertheless to have been left in a somewhat fragile position, and for that reason looked for, or intensified its search for European allies, the French in particular, possibly also the Danes. Note that by then a colourful local trader by the name of Tamata, but better known as Monsieur Pierre, had become its *de facto* ruler.[65] Monsieur Pierre, a Hausa by origin, was in a sense the first of a new brand of people who was to put their mark on the Slave Coast.

As for Oyo, it suffered at the same time as the "Lagoon War" a severe reverse in the north; the Bariba freed themselves from Oyo overrule in July 1783. Oyo's apparent attempt to reverse the situation, by attacking the Bariba polity of Kaiama, ended in disaster for the attackers.[66] It certainly boded ill for the future.

Oyo had been weakened and Dahomey strengthened. This new balance of forces may be said to be reflected in the apparent fact that the tribute Dahomey had to pay to Oyo was substantially reduced in 1784 (unless this was simply an expression of gratitude for Dahomey's assistance in the "Lagoon War"). Dahomey was also strengthened because the slave trade from Ouidah revived somewhat, owing, we imagine, to the Lagoon War, but also to the timid return of British ships now that both the war against the Dutch and the war in America had ended.[67] In addition, the Luso-Brazilian trade on the Costa da Mina in general continued to be considerable, thanks to the continuing success of the third-rate tobacco,[68] and also thanks, as noted, to the continuing success of the third-rate tobacco,[68] and also thanks, as noted, to the dissolution of the WIC, in 1791. That dissolution meant, we repeat, the formal end of the ten per cent tax imposed on the Luso-Brazilians.

The French slave trade from Ouidah expanded too,[69] the French having discovered that it was possible to acquire the third-rate Brazilian tobacco directly in Lisbon by bribing the local officials there.[70] To give an idea, in 1787 eight ships flying the Portuguese colours, three French but only one British, traded for slaves at Ouidah.[71] However, the French were being increasingly attracted to Porto Novo-Seme, while continuing incidentally also to be interested in the Gold Coast.[72] On the latter coast, the French finally succeeded in 1786 to establish a permanent lodge, at the site of Amoko between Anomabo and Winneba,[73] and placed under the authority of the director of Ouidah (why the British allowed it this time we do not know). That director was between 1786 and 1789 the famous Monsieur Gourg (so referred to in the sources, we do not know his first name), a one-armed war veteran. Incidentally, to send a one-armed ex-officer to the Slave Coast, that is, to a region where tradition has it that all headmen and rulers were supposed to be without physical blemish, does not strike one as particularly fortunate.

As noted, the rulers of Porto Novo had come to realize that they could no longer count on the protection of Oyo. Instead they turned to the French, asking for the construction of no less than three forts.[74] That led the French authorities, those in Versailles that is, plus the slave-traders of La Rochelle in particular to begin to toy with rather grand plans for the future. The idea seems to have been to transform Porto Novo into a dependency of France, or at the very least some sort of central base for French activity in the whole of the Bight of Benin, with ramifications both eastwards and westwards. The idea seems also to have been to abandon Ouidah altogether in the process.[75] Monsieur Gourg, who was originally opposed to those plans, thought nevertheless in terms of an alliance between the French, Oyo, Porto Novo and Little Popo-Glidji against Dahomey, complete with an embargo on the trade at Ouidah[76] – regardless of the Luso-Brazilians.

However, all that was counting without Kpengla and his heavy-handed methods, which paid off for once. What happened was that Kpengla decided to act on his own, that is, without the permission of Oyo. So he staged in July 1787 a massive attack not on Porto Novo as such, but on the Europeans, principally the French, in Seme, Porto Novo's beach "port", some 60 km east of Ouidah.[77] It was very much in line with Dahomey's policy of trying to eliminate the competitors of Ouidah physically. The attack on Seme implies that the Dahomeans had got used to what was earlier off limits to them: the very watery landscape out east. At the time of the assault there were eleven French ships in the roads, and a few Luso-Brazilian ones, but no British – which indicates clearly that Porto Novo had far surpassed Ouidah as a centre for the slave trade (by comparison with the 12 ships which called at Ouidah during the whole of 1787, see above). The Dahomeans took as prisoners 14 Frenchmen and one Luso-Brazilian, as well as some 80 canoemen from the Gold Coast and of course an unknown number of slaves. Many of the prisoners were sent inland and treated harshly.[78] Monsieur Gourg had a very difficult time ransoming them, especially since the ship-owners were reluctant to pay their share.[79] Whether he succeeded completely and exactly how many died, we do not know. What we do seem to know is first, that the French did not consider what had happened as quite the end of the game, and second, that peace certainly did not return to the Eastern Slave Coast; the Dahomeans carried out a second raid against Porto Novo-Seme in 1791,[80] this time apparently with the permission of Oyo, while Badagry was destroyed once more, in 1793, by Lagos in fact, possibly with the assistance of Porto Novo.[81] But the long-term consequences are clear – first, the French scheme fell apart, and second, the alarmed authorities of Porto Novo understood that they could not count on the French either and had therefore to come to terms with Dahomey, which they did to some extent[82] (the details are obscure). As for the Dahomean authorities, they felt entitled to take as hostages crew members of any slavers or canoes they could lay their hands on which they suspected of having avoided Ouidah at one stage or another, or were driven ashore in Dahomey; this was called piracy by the British. And also as usual, the ship-owners were reluctant to pay the ransoms demanded.[83]

By then, in order to drive home their point, the Dahomeans expelled Monsieur Gourg, together with the fort's surgeon, in November 1789 (shortly after the accession of Agonglo). According to Lionel Abson, an eye-witness in a sense, they were severely mistreated in the process, that is, "bound and carried...to the beach, where [Gourg] was obliged to remain all night [no mention of the surgeon], exposed to the mosquitos and sand flies, till five o'clock next morning, when he was thrown into a canoe".[84] Both Gourg and the surgeon survived, thanks possibly to the British at Cape Coast Castle,[85] but their ordeal was, we presume, not lost on the others.

What may have irked in particular the Dahomeans in the case of Monsieur Gourg was that he represented obviously a new type of director, personifying an attempt by the superior authorities in Europe to choose directors less subservient to the Dahomeans than, for instance, Gourg's notoriously lax predecessor Ollivier de Montaguère (director 1775–86)[86] or the Briton Lionel Abson, or for that matter the Luso-Brazilians.[87] As for Abson, he was accused in this period of "shameful and scandalous negligence", no less, by his superiors,[88] – but, significantly, not replaced. The question is if he *could* have been replaced, if the Dahomeans would have permitted it, and the likely answer is no.

Gourg's exit meant in reality that the French presence had lapsed. It is true that the fort's storekeeper, Deniau de la Garenne, took over as acting director. But he spent the next eight years as a sort of hostage of the Dahomeans before being able to leave[89] (no director was permitted to leave as long as his successor had not arrived, unless, that is, one was expelled). Anyway, Gourg's departure was followed by the French Revolution, by the first abolition of the French slave trade in 1794, and finally, and symbolically, by the surrender (to the British) of the last and sole Frenchman in Amoko in 1804.[90] It meant that from then on the Luso-Brazilians had it all to themselves.

But the Dahomean action aroused the ire of Oyo, certainly a decaying power by then but still one to be reckoned with. In fact, it is believed that the Alafin managed to force Kpengla to share at least the spoils of the 1787 raid with him.[91] In addition, the Oyos either devastated or occupied or conquered Mahi country in early 1788, neither of which Dahomey had ever really been able to do.[92] What exactly happened in 1788 is (as so often) far from clear. But if conquest there was, it is not certain what Oyo rule involved. What is certain is that the presence of Oyo in Dahomey's very backyard was perceived by the Dahomeans as potentially threatening – it provoked panic, if we are to believe the French and Abson,[93] perhaps precisely the effect Oyo had been pursuing, dissuading Dahomey from following the example of the Bariba. It seems also that Oyo explicitly forbade Dahomey from trying to conquer Porto Novo and the Eastern Slave Coast.[94] But Kpengla's action paid off, at least in the short term, in the sense that the slave trade from Porto Novo did slow down, whereas that from Ouidah surged somewhat and continued to remain at a reasonably high level during the first years of the reign of Agonglo.[95] But the problems remained, that is, the tolls and impediments of all sorts that had been put in place.[96] The end result was that the epicentre of the slave trade moved further east, to Lagos.

* * *

We need to focus on the year 1789, that is the year of the beginning of the French Revolution, and locally that of the deaths of Kpengla of Dahomey and Abiodun of Oyo (in the latter case the presumed year).

Abiodun, the man who overthrew Basorun Gana, and is generally presented as the last strong Alafin of Oyo, was poisoned in possibly April 1789. His successor Awole was overthrown and had to commit suicide in 1796 (again, the presumed date). The reason may have been the revolt of Nupe, the second vassal of Oyo (after Bariba) to secede. In fact Nupe not only revolted but also defeated Oyo in war, and was able to impose a tribute on its former overlord[97] – Dahomey becoming thus an indirect tributary of far-away Nupe. After which two further *Alafins* suffered the same fate as Awole, possibly in the space of one year. After that the province of Ilorin revolted in its turn.[98] It was at long last the real beginning of the final agony of Oyo, but an agony which took an excruciatingly long time. What is remarkable is that the warrior-polity of Dahomey was utterly unable to follow the examples of Bariba and Nupe and end its vassalage of the now radically weakened Oyo.

As for Kpengla, who died, as noted, of smallpox – another blow to the monarchy – he was followed by his son Agonglo, a young man in his early twenties. But his reign turned out to be the shortest of all the Dahomean kings, a mere eight years.[99]

Although Agonglo began his reign by expelling Monsieur Gourg, he is usually presented in a comparatively favourable light.[100] That is, he is credited with having removed some, but apparently only some, of the oppressive restrictions imposed on the traders, including the internal trading community in Dahomey itself which was beginning to emerge – somewhat miraculously, one is tempted to add.[101]

What complicated matters for Agonglo was the complete *volte-face* of Revolutionary France, which not only abolished the slave trade in 1794 but also decided to combat it, sending in the autumn of 1794 a squadron of no less than six ships and 1,040 crew to the coast of West Africa (this was after the beginning of the war with Great Britain in 1793). After sweeping the coast between Sierra Leone and Grand Popo, a long stretch, the French squadron attacked the ships in the Ouidah roads, capturing all the slavers there (all apparently Luso-Brazilians). The Dahomeans protested, seized all the forts and confined the few European staff still within the fort walls. Next, over three days (6–8 December 1794), the squadron took eight Luso-Brazilian slavers between Ouidah and Porto Novo.[102] The usual question is what happened to the slaves on board; there is no mention of this squadron or of Ouidah in the standard works on the French Revolution the present author is familiar with. The French had thus put an end to the position of Ouidah as a free trade centre open to all, and they were to return in 1797.

As for Agonglo's efforts to procure slaves and to demonstrate that he was a worthy successor of Agaja, raiding Mahi country and eastwards as usual, they were at best only moderately successful, also as usual[103] (was there any Oyo presence?). But Agonglo did meet with success in relation to Little Popo-Glidji. After he opened the hostilities in 1793, according to Nicoué Gayibor,[104] Little Popo-Glidji then attacked Grand Popo (which now re-emerges once more in the sources) *and* Dahomey in 1795, but apparently was soundly defeated at a place called Adame, the king of Little Popo-Glidji himself being among the casualties. It is said that this was the end of the war between Little Popo-Glidji which had begun some 58 years earlier, in 1737.[105] It may be, as Silke Strickrodt has argued,[106] that the consequences were not in any way dramatic for Dahomey in the short run. But 1795 was the beginning of the end of the polity we have called Little Popo-Glidji (or Genyi), that is, the end of one of Dahomey's main enemies.

Here we must pause for a moment and note that the next year, in 1796, the Dahomean army was, according to Yves Person, virtually annihilated by the acephalous Watchi Ewe, the neighbours and possibly vassals of Little Popo-Glidji.[107] The problem with Person's contention is that it is not corroborated (nor for that matter refuted) by any other source and so ought perhaps not to be taken into consideration. On the other hand, if Person is correct, it throws a sharp light on the weakness of Dahomey; it helps to explain Agonglo's fate, plus the fact that Dahomey was never able to expand westwards, even after the weakening of Little Popo-Glidji.

But to return to 1795, it was also the year when a second Dahomean embassy was sent to Brazil, an embassy which also travelled all the way to Portugal. The embassy, which was away for no less than two years, has left abundant sources, but as usual one-sided.[108] They are also ambiguous since some of them seem to imply that the embassy was in part the result of obscure intrigues among the few Portuguese in Ouidah. There is, however, little doubt that the aim of the Dahomeans was, as before, to persuade the Luso-Brazilians to trade exclusively with Dahomey, and more generally to step up their commercial activity at Ouidah. There is, furthermore, no doubt that the authorities in Brazil had no intention of acceding to the Dahomean demands. The whole mission, and especially the behaviour of the ambassadors, left their hosts with a starkly negative impression of Dahomey and the Dahomeans. But what is interesting is what happened in Dahomey as a consequence of this mission. On their return trip the Dahomeans were accompanied by the new Portuguese director and notably by two missionaries, Vicente Ferreira Pires and Cypriano Pires Sardinha. Their task, as set out by the Prince-Regent of Portugal, the future João VI, was to convert the king of Dahomey and his entourage to Christianity. They arrived in Ouidah on 8 April 1797.

The two missionaries were, according to the account of Pires, our only genuine (reliable?) source,[109] received by Agonglo with what sounds like enthusiasm. In fact, like many rulers on the Slave Coast before him, Agonglo expressed his desire to convert to Christianity. If it is correct, as Edna Bay believes, that Agonglo had already established a shrine in his palace in honour of Christianity, a shrine attended by a "wife" of his reputed to be of Afro-Dutch ancestry,[110] then Agonglo's attitude begins to make some sense. Anyway, Agonglo received the two priests in audience for apparently the second time on 23 April 1797, an audience during which he expressed his desire to convert on the spot.[111] But eight days later, on 1 May, he was dead, murdered by one of his "wives". It was part of a genuine coup, but was opposed by a counter-coup by Agonglo's "party" which prevailed in the end.[112] It was all accompanied, according to Pires, by scenes of horror which the same Pires has described in frightening detail.[113]

But if the leading figures on Agonglo's side "won", the Christianity element disappeared out of sight. The new king was a younger son of Agonglo, known as Adandozan. He must have been a teenager at that time, possibly about 15 years old, which suggests that others ruled in his name.

His companion having died, Pires was able to leave on 29 October 1797 in the middle of another French attack. In the confusion the last (acting) French director, and the last Frenchman around, the previously mentioned Deniau de la Garenne, managed to get on board one of the French warships and to escape – or so says Pires. But the problem is that we know that Deniau left on 17–20 August, whatever this chronological confusion may mean.[114]

What is in any case interesting is that Pires left with three letters for the Portuguese authorities ostensibly dictated by Adandozan. But only one is believed to reflect Adandozan's will and wishes (or the will and wishes of whoever ruled in his name), the other two being inventions of Pires. That third letter is a very large shopping-list of all that Adandozan wanted. And Adandozan wanted quite a lot. How would he pay for it all? As usual, with slaves, even good slaves (*boms captivos*).[115] Many of the losers in this power struggle were sold to the slave-traders, including a royal princess by the name of Agontime, of whom more in the next chapter.

* * *

How to conclude? Perhaps with the impression of a rather fluid situation, in which whoever wielded power in Dahomey did not really control the course of events, contrary to what had been the case to some extent under Agaja and Tegbesu. Or one might suggest that this was a regime unable to change a very counterproductive policy, a regime whose principal aim seems to have been simply to survive. But if so, we will have to admit that the regime proved, when all is said and done, surprisingly resilient – a resilience that is in a sense hard to explain. It survived at what price, paid by whom?

6

THE LONG GOODBYE

It is tempting to conclude, on the basis of what has been argued in the preceding chapter, that by the turn of the century the slave trade and slavery were doomed, Napoleon Bonaparte notwithstanding, and whatever the Database and the statistics may tell. It is true that the Revolutionary and Napoleonic wars contributed to the delaying of the inevitable. Resistance there certainly was also, including a number of rearguard actions, some on a grand scale and some long-lasting. But in the end they were just that: rearguard actions.

If one asks about the deeper causes of this sea change, the present author is among the possibly naive historians who *believe* (as opposed to knowing) that it was all about ending an anomaly, a protuberance of sorts, within what is often called Western (Christian) Civilization.[1] Or put differently, in the case of especially Great Britain, the emerging superpower of the nineteenth century, and the champion of what goes under the names of liberalism and human rights, the gulf between the officially proclaimed ideals and the practice of the slave trade and slavery had become unbearably wide. It is in any case tolerably clear that Britain, once a leading slave trading nation, did not stand to benefit from its outlawing, not to mention the abolition of slavery, quite the contrary.[2] The word "econocide" has indeed been used. Put differently, if Great Britain stood for Liberal Capitalism, a point had been reached where in one specific field the two components of that expression had become incompatible. At that crossroad and in that specific field Britain chose liberalism, sacrificing capitalism.

There is however a theory that the humanitarians convinced the capitalists that abolition would be good for business in the (very) long run (never mind the not-so-short run). The argument is that slavery is in the final analysis incompatible with capitalism, for the simple reason that capitalism needs consumers and slaves consume very little.[3] Is this too *recherché* to be convincing? But perhaps there were, let us say more or genuinely "powerful economic forces" (in the Marxist sense) at work behind the disintegration of the slave system? However, if so, those forces are "extremely difficult to ascertain clearly", as Franklin W. Knight, a believer in that theory, once admitted. He added that "there is no longer a consensus as to why slavery ended during the nineteenth century".[4] That consensus will elude us, we believe, as long as Knight and co. keep searching for those same forces.

We repeat and stress the distinction between the abolition of the *slave trade* on the one hand and *slavery* on the other, the latter being formally outside the scope of the present work. The abolition of the slave *trade* always came first, that of slavery much later. For instance, Great Britain outlawed the slave trade in 1807, but slavery only in 1833; the United States also outlawed the slave trade in 1807 but slavery in 1865; and France abolished the slave trade a second time in 1818 but slavery in 1848 (Denmark also abolished slavery in 1848, or more correctly, was forced to do so because of a successful slave revolt in that year[5]). In addition there is often a considerable time-lag between the *de jure* and the *de facto* abolition of the slave trade, in the Brazilian case no less than 19 years (1831 and 1850 respectively).[6]

Those who thought that the abolition of the slave trade would inevitably lead to the more or less rapid disappearance of slavery overlooked one fundamental point: a slave population, if treated relatively leniently as was the case in the US (thanks to the relatively less onerous labour requirements of cotton compared with sugar-cane), could continue indefinitely. We all know what it took to abolish slavery in the US.

* * *

The first three decades or so of the nineteenth century constitute, somewhat paradoxically, the least known period in the recent past of the Slave Coast covered in this work.[7] The reason is clear enough: the permanent European/Luso-Brazilian presence on land was progressively reduced, and came to a complete end by 1812 at the latest. The Europeans/Luso-Brazilians abandoned their forts at Ouidah, much to the disapproval of the Dahomean authorities (there remained the Danish fort Prindsensten at Keta, but a fort whose irrelevance had already become manifest). Hence our principal informants about the affairs of the Slave Coast disappeared from the scene. There is no way around that handicap, which means that any kind of in-depth analysis is even more hazardous for this period than for the earlier one. We have then little choice but to remain at a rather superficial level, and to take refuge at times in some well-known global trends.

The dearth of sources is especially annoying because the period we are entering presents us with an intriguing enigma already referred to, the reign and especially the deposition, possibly in 1818, of king Adandozan of Dahomey. The strange point is that Adandozan was not killed, and in fact was permitted to live out his days in apparent tranquillity.[8] An ex-king living thus is, as far as the present author is aware, a very rare figure indeed in the history of Sub-Saharan Africa. In this respect we have to lament the fact that our research has not resulted in any significant breakthrough, and does not permit us to come up with any convincing explanation.

But to return to the theme of Europeans as residents, and to anticipate: they did return to Ouidah, in the 1840s. The "new" Europeans were, however, not government employees or slave traders, but missionaries and especially private merchants engaged in what is usually called "legitimate trade". It is true that officials (although mostly non-resident) also made their appearance after a while, but officials whose mission was to try to persuade the Dahomeans to put an end to the slave trade and human sacrifice. In the meantime all the European slave trading nations had outlawed the slave trade. So had the American ones, except that in the case of Brazil (independent from 1822) the formal outlawing of the slave trade (in 1831) was a measure no-one respected, or even had to respect, given the openly pro-slave trade attitude of the authorities; the same was the case with Spain. The wider point is that the formal outlawing of the slave trade did not mean the end of that ignominious trade. Indeed, the legal slave trade was replaced by what we may call smuggling, usually referred to as the illegal slave trade.[9]

The international community split over the issue of the slave trade. On the one hand there were those, especially Great Britain, but also increasingly France after the end of the Napoleonic wars, Denmark and other European nations, which were determined to put an end to the slave trade. And on the other those equally determined to carry on with that trade, the Luso-Brazilians in particular, as well as Spain (because of Cuba and Puerto Rico), plus for a while the slave states of the southern USA; and, last but not least, many peoples and/or rulers in Africa, the Slave Coast very much included. So although it is reasonable to hypothesize that British abolition may have caused severe economic dislocation at least in the short run,[10] the continuous existence of both a demand for slaves and a supply meant opportunities for those willing to carry on with the slave trade.

Why were the Luso-Brazilians especially determined to do so, whatever the rest of the world might think or say and also regardless of whatever laws and treaties they may have signed? And why did the British display initially, although only initially, considerable leniency in their case – even agreeing to a treaty with the Portuguese in 1810 which actually opened the way for the continuation of the slave trade from Ouidah? According to that treaty the Portuguese agreed officially to abandon the slave trade in areas outside its claimed dominions on the African coast, except at Ouidah.[11]

Here it should be recalled that Portugal is Britain's oldest ally, and that the Portuguese court and government, faced with an imminent French invasion, fled in the autumn of 1807 to Brazil, Portugal's main overseas possession, where they remained right up to July 1821, despite the liberation of Portugal in March 1811 and the end of the Napoleonic wars in 1814–15.[12] As a Portuguese statesman once put it, "without Brazil Portugal is an insignificant power".[13] The Portuguese crown was then in dire straits from 1807 onwards, a fact which may explain a good deal. But it had long been the policy of the local authorities to facilitate the slave trade, including with the Costa da Mina, as much as possible[14] (that the share of slaves imported from that coast declined steadily compared with the total amount of slaves imported to Brazil from Africa generally is another matter). The Portuguese court and government, once installed in Rio de Janeiro in March 1808, simply continued the same policy. Those in command in Brazil, whether Portuguese or later Brazilians, stressed time and again, and in no uncertain terms, that slavery and hence the slave trade were absolutely essential to the economy and development of the land.[15] Perhaps understandable during the Napoleonic wars, this article of faith, in our opinion absurd and never really justified, began to make less and less sense afterwards. Hence, since it was decided to rely basically on slavery, little effort was made to attract genuine free settlers from Europe.

As for the British authorities, they were left after 1807–8 with the task of enforcing the new legislation, that is, to put an effective end to the participation, directly or indirectly, by British subjects in the slave trade. To that effect Parliament enacted increasingly restrictive laws, especially the famous Felony Act of 14 May 1811 (no Briton could assist vessels in the slave trade), and closed all possible loopholes, of which there were originally a good many.[16] To that effect also the British government organized from 1810 the equally famous West African squadron (often called the Anti-Slave Trade squadron), designed to seize British ships suspected of slave-trading.[17] But at the same time British diplomacy began to try to persuade, pressure, bully or threaten other nations to abolish the slave trade and especially to sign treaties allowing the British men-of-war to search and seize the ships of those nations if they carried slaves, or (from 1839) even if they were simply equipped to carry slaves; the latter measure was a severe blow to the illicit trade.[18] It is a story in which the guns of the Royal Navy hovered increasingly in the background, thanks in the last analysis to the British taxpayer. For instance, the British more or less forced the Portuguese government (still in Rio de Janeiro) to sign a second treaty in January 1815, a treaty according to which the Portuguese slave trade was banned north of the Equator, Ouidah included this time, from 1817.[19] They also tried to persuade the local African rulers to end the slave trade, with no success at all in the case of Dahomey and the Slave Coast (the West African squadron got nowhere at Ouidah, that very special place[20]).

This action did not end the slave trade, but it drove it underground, so to speak. Or one might say that the slave trade continued with the difference that it had become illegal from a European and American *de jure* point of view, but not from a *de facto* one, and certainly not from an African one. That is, the slave trade went rapidly from something close to respectability to widespread opprobrium, and those who continued the practice were considered increasingly as little better than criminals. Thus theirs became an increasingly risky business. The situation changed, only in 1850, though the change then was radical, as we shall see.

*　*　*

Was the illegal slave trade from the Slave Coast/Bight of Benin a success? The British thought so and long despaired of being able to stop it.[21] But the figures tell a somewhat different story. It is true that the Slave Coast/Bight of Benin exported up to five hundred thousand slaves during the half-century between 1800 and 1850[22] (though this included the last years of the legitimate slave trade), a fairly "respectable" figure. But it was only one-seventh of the African total during that period, and, of course, far behind the figures of the "golden era" (1701–30). Note that of those five hundred thousand slaves or so, about 75 per cent went to Brazil and 20 per cent to the Spanish islands of the Caribbean. As for the ports of embarkation, we note the continuing rise of

Lagos and the corresponding depressed state of affairs on the Central Slave Coast.[23] (With regard to the slave trade from the Western Slave Coast, principally Anlo, our ignorance is close to total.) As for the profits, the British believed that those of the slave traders were substantial.[24] Maybe they were, but at the macroeconomic level the picture looks somewhat different. Indeed, according to recent research, prices, which had risen steadily since the 1760s, experienced a sudden collapse after the British abolition in 1807–8, and recovered only from about 1846, that is, at the very end.[25]

The question one feels like asking in this context, and especially in the case of the Central Slave Coast and Dahomey, is whether it was really worth it. A possible answer is that it was a *faute-de-mieux* situation – the local elite was unable to come up with an alternative, slave trade and raiding being in a sense their raison d'être. The only other possibility was the export of palm-oil, but that only began in the late 1830s. Can we deduce that the Dahomey of especially Adandozan was an impoverished polity confronted with a rather complicated situation?

* * *

The global context until 1814/15 was that of the French Revolutionary and Napoleonic wars. And as usual with regard to wars between European powers, the fighting which took place in Guinean waters has not attracted the attention of the historians. We know however that the French targeted the Portuguese in 1799–1800. In fact the island of Príncipe was occupied for a month (29 December 1799 to 30 January 1800), and the French captured and burned an unknown number of Portuguese ships on the *Costa da Mina*.[26] The perennial question is whether there were slaves on board, and, if so, what happened to them.

We also know about a number of naval skirmishes between the French and the British between 1803 and 1806. In fact, the British complained about the "very extensive and ruinous Depredations" committed upon the African trade by French privateers.[27] The more global consequences of all this activity seem, however, to have been rather limited, since neither nation was heavily involved in the slave trade at that time.[28]

* * *

On the local scene, we recall that the last acting French director fled rather precipitately in 1797. He argued, following an already familiar pattern, that it was the only way he could leave, since according to him the king of Dahomey would never have given him permission to depart.[29] The fort was left in the custody of a local person described as a free mulatto.

The French were followed by the Luso-Brazilians who simply gave up their fort in 1805 after the expulsion of no less than four directors in quick succession between 1797 and 1804, the Dahomean way of protesting against the sharp drop in the Portuguese trade. In 1805 the incumbent director died and was not replaced.[30] But the Portuguese Prince-Regent pressed for the reoccupation of the fort of Ouidah even as late as 1816,[31] and the Portuguese never gave up their claim to the fort.

The British were the last to depart. Here we must return to the case of Lionel Abson, who died in June 1803. As he had become a Dahomean chief, that is, considered as such by the Dahomean authorities, the king seized his estate, including his (local) wives and children. Among the latter was his well-known daughter Sally, who was taken to the royal seraglio, very much against her will. There she became, according to a visiting Briton who met her, "a prey to grief, (reason for which she) sunk broken hearted to the grave".[32]

Since the British hauled down the flag only in 1812,[33] the question is what became of William's Fort after Abson's death and especially after the abolition of the British slave trade in 1807–8. Actually, the authorities at Cape Coast Castle alleged in February 1807 that there was no longer any genuine British fort at Ouidah.[34] The fort seems to have been converted into a sort of penal colony.[35] Anyway, the few Britons present, perhaps intermittently, did not indulge in any trade and endured, generally speaking, a "subjection utterly disgraceful to the English flag".[36] But perhaps those stationed there took part in the great civilizing scheme A.G. Hopkins has argued the British tried to put into practice with the abolition of the slave trade,[37] that is, to convince the Dahomean authorities to focus on agriculture instead of raids and the slave trade.

We repeat that the abandonment of the forts had nothing to do as such with the effective end of the slave trade which occurred roughly half a century later. It did not imply either, we also repeat, that the Dahomean authorities desired the Europeans and Luso-Brazilians to leave or to sever their ties with them. The impression the sources convey is in fact exactly the opposite. Hence for instance the two embassies Dahomey sent to Brazil as late as 1805 and 1811 (the third and fourth altogether); they were no more successful than the earlier ones. It is also significant that after the Euro-American withdrawal the Dahomeans tried at times to persuade or force Europeans who chanced to pass by, so to speak, to take over as directors and/or to reoccupy the forts[38] (the rest of the time local people with some connection with the Europeans served as "directors"). It seems in fact that the forts were maintained, as was also the fiction that the European presence continued.[39]

What is certain is that Dahomey did not feel like going it alone, so to speak, once the Europeans and Luso-Brazilians had departed, and felt it impossible to take over the organization and administration of the slave trade, actually a much more complicated trade now that it had become illegal. Hence the emergence of a new category of people which did the job, but probably at a far higher price than what the Europeans had exacted; a new category of brokers, what we may call anything from merchant princes to mafia bosses. These were people like the previously mentioned Monsieur Pierre in Porto Novo, possibly the prototype, and above all Francisco Félix de Souza, known as the Chacha, a personal nickname which became a title,[40] in Ouidah. De Souza, who probably had a rather murky past, was perhaps the brother of the last official Portuguese director, and may have begun his career as the *de facto* director after the death of his brother in 1805, before setting out on his own.[41] A group of people helped found a community called Brazilians, though quite a few were actually of French or Spanish origin (Monsieur Pierre was of course neither French nor Brazilian). That the Brazilian connection carried prestige, we see from the fact that the French Ollivier family changed its name to Oliveira.[42] These Brazilians, generally mulattos, also included former slaves returning from Brazil; they developed a very peculiar and original culture which set them apart from the Africans *and* the Europeans.[43]

* * *

The teenager Adandozan became nominal king of Dahomey in 1797; a regency seems to have ruled in his name until about 1804.[44] Adandozan was, as noted, the one who has been left out from what we may call the official king-list of Dahomey, and continues to be so left out (as not even a casual visitor to the region can fail to notice since that list is on display everywhere). It is a list which conveys the impression that the Dahomean throne was vacant between 1797 and 1818. But Adandozan does figure in the oral traditions, including in the ones collected by Auguste Le Hérissé. Those traditions represent Adandozan as something like the quintessential cruel and evil king, accused of the most heinous atrocities and cruelties one can imagine. But he was also considered to be a great magician, if not a sorcerer, who could cast spells[45] – to the extent that it was reported to be perilous even to pronounce his name, even up to the 1970s,[46] if not later.

The modern historian cannot exclude the possibility that there is some grain of truth in the accusations levied against Adandozan. But they are so massive and so one-sided that one may be excused for being somewhat sceptical,[47] especially since the historian is familiar with the well-known archetypical tyrannical kings in the past of Africa, as in the Tado and Notsé narratives. And is it true that, as the traditions insinuate, Adandozan was not very successful in war? If so, this was a sort of supreme sin for a king of a warrior polity. But if so also, Adandozan's two, possibly three, predecessors were equally unsuccessful. Why did they not suffer the same opprobrium?

Then there is the fact that Adandozan was unable, although he tried, to end Dahomey's status as a tribute-paying vassal of the by now tottering Oyo[48] (it would be a long totter, however). But again, his predecessors had been equally unsuccessful.

Now, if Adandozan was and still is depicted in a most negative way, perhaps much more negative than the facts warrant, the question is why, and the answer is far from obvious. However, if we consider Adandozan as the classic scapegoat, one consequence is that his predecessors, and especially his immediate successor Gezo, necessarily appear in a much more favourable light. More generally, if one is left with the impression that Adandozan, by perhaps pushing the system established by Agaja and Tegbesu to its uttermost logical and/or absurd end, including a very active secret police,[49] took upon himself all the evil which the collectivity we may call the kings of Dahomey may be charged with, he then exonerated the others to some extent. His successor Gezo in particular needed all the favourable light he could get, being a distant relative of Adandozan[50] and as such not really legitimate, *and* seizing power through a coup d'état, presumably in 1818 ("presumably", because, as noted, we are far from certain about the precise date of the coup; there was no Father Pires present this time).

Another question is, why was Adandozan simply deposed, but not killed?[51] Was it to avoid turning Adandozan into a martyr – if so, why? Or was it to avoid for as long as possible Adandozan, the magician, being converted into a genuine *vodun*? There are those who argue that Adandozan became a *vodun* in life, and that in fact he never died.[52] It is in any case clear that the magical aura surrounding Adandozan needs to be explored.

***

So what did Adandozan do exactly? He seems to have tried what one may describe as the usual methods, that is, first to raid the neighbouring Mahi country, but with, as always, limited success (the question here is again what was exactly Oyo's relationship with the Mahi); second, to disrupt the trade of the neighbouring ports, that is, to raid Badagry and Porto Novo, and hence to force the slave traders to concentrate on Ouidah (in this he was somewhat more successful); third, to send missions to Brazil and Portugal; and fourth, to liberate Dahomey from the tutelage of Oyo. But then there is a fifth point hinted at by certain historians – that Adandozan tried to impose some genuinely revolutionary changes, that he was in fact an innovative king, desiring to break with the traditional slave trade.[53] In this context one may note that Yves Person has argued that Adandozan inaugurated in 1808 a sort of grand harvest festival, the implication being that he tried, encouraged possibly by the British, to convert Dahomey into a polity focusing on agriculture. But if so, he was again unsuccessful, according to Person.[54] To this we must add Adandozan's clearly tortuous relations with the Brazilians, and especially with the future Chacha.

If these speculations come anywhere near the truth – they, including the works of Person and Elisée Soumonni, are based on somewhat flimsy evidence – then Gezo's coup against Adandozan begins to make some sense, since it led to a reversal of the latter's presumed policy.

With regard to the first point above, many Mahi had to seek refuge in the region of Atakpamé.[55] As for the second point, it is clear that there was intermittent warfare between Dahomey and Porto Novo during at least the first half of Adandozan's reign. It is also clear that the aggressor was at times Porto Novo.[56] However, the rulers of Porto Novo came to the conclusion that the best way to stop the Dahomean raids was perhaps not to fight but to dig, that is, to eliminate the short strip of land at present-day Cotonou which blocked the opening of the lagoon to the sea and permitted the Dahomean raiding parties to move out east. To this effect they even asked the authorities in Brazil to send out an engineer. But as with so many other local initiatives, nothing came of this.[57] That said, the conflict between Dahomey and Porto Novo was finally to the advantage of the slave trading polities further east, Lagos especially.

Regarding the embassies to Brazil and Portugal, the central fact about them is that as usual the Dahomeans achieved nothing. Since Adandozan had expelled several directors, he suffered from a severe problem of credibility vis-à-vis the Luso-Brazilian authorities. Anyway, what the Dahomeans wanted, that the Portuguese should trade only at Ouidah, was again roundly rejected.

The abundant sources for the two embassies, especially the one in 1805,[58] contain some astonishing details. First, Adandozan tried to entice the Portuguese by arguing that there were gold mines in his realm, gold mines which had so far remained a secret, but which he was now prepared to exploit for the benefit of the Portuguese. The Luso-Brazilians did not believe him, and for good reason.

Second, whoever penned the letter destined for the Luso-Brazilian authorities added a few sentences of his own in which he described Adandozan as a cruel man. He also stated that he had been a captive for no less than 23 years – that is, since 1782 – and finished by saying that he dared not go on for fear of awaking suspicions. So much for the faith we can put in letters penned by Europeans and Luso-Brazilians (compare the case of Bulfinch Lambe mentioned earlier). But here one asks oneself what happened to the unknown person who penned the letter. How many Luso-Brazilian captives were there really in Abomey, and were they ever liberated? We doubt that they were, considering the attitude of the Luso-Brazilian authorities in these matters.

Third, Adandozan, presumably in order to demonstrate that he was serious, made a point of indicating to the Luso-Brazilian authorities the number of people he had sacrificed in order to assure the success of the embassies, and also in order to inform his ancestors about what was going on. It may not have cut any ice with the addressees.

Fourth, the interpreter of the embassy was a certain Innocencio Marquès, a Brazilian mulatto and a slave trader at Porto Novo whom the Dahomeans had captured during one of their raids eastwards. Although he had sworn to return to Dahomey, he remained in Bahia where he became a militia captain and a sort of counsellor for the affairs of the Costa da Mina.

We note finally that Dahomey was not the only African polity to send an embassy to Brazil in this period. Lagos did the same in 1807–8, an embassy described by Pierre Verger as absurd[59] (and not even mentioned by Kristin Mann). But here also there are some interesting details. First the ambassador of Lagos offered a Pygmy as a gift to the Portuguese Prince-Regent, presumably a Pygmy slave (what happened to him or her?). The second detail worth mentioning is that the ship which carried the ambassadors from Lagos on the return trip was captured first by the French and then by the British (this was the epoch of the Napoleonic Wars) and forced to return to Salvador da Bahia before heading for the Slave Coast a second time.

The third Slave Coast polity which sent an embassy to Brazil was Porto Novo. Its embassy arrived in Salvador da Bahia in December 1810 and thus coincided with the fourth Dahomean one which arrived in January 1811, and was still there in September 1812.⁶⁰ The Brazilian authorities considered the coincidence of the two embassies as embarrassing, as they pursued mutually incompatible aims.⁶¹ In any case, 1811–12 marks the last direct contact between the polities of the Slave Coast and the authorities in Brazil.

* * *

If all this suggests a rather negative trend in the internal developments of Dahomey in this period, we can add two factors which we believe point in the same direction. The first is the frightening *bocio* art referred to earlier, which there is reason to believe flourished in this period. The second is that famine seems to have struck in 1809–10, and the country experienced a number of natural disasters to 1812. There is, in addition, the cryptic but possibly revealing statement made by Herskovits that Sakpata and the Sakpata priests were quite simply expelled from Abomey by Adandozan.⁶² To expel a deity is obviously an impossible task. But the point here is that, as we have argued repeatedly, Sakpata was considered to represent a threat to royal authority. Hence the deity's "expulsion" may be interpreted as a new round in the struggle between the monarchy and its opponents. Or put differently, the perennial problem of the monarchy's legitimacy resurfaced once again.

In this context we need to mention some strange and cryptic hints made by Maurice Glélé.⁶³ He argues that under Adandozan the descendants of a certain Awesu Dokonou, until then integrated into the ranks of the conquerors (that is, the supporters of the monarchy), had begun to detach themselves from Abomey and instead made allegiance to a certain Josu, chief of Munyon in the suburb of Abomey. That is all Glélé has to say. And of course we have really no idea who Awesu Dokonou and Josu were or represented. But we note that Glélé gives the impression that Josu was some sort of autonomous prince or vassal close to the very centre of the polity. However, assuming that Glélé can be trusted, it is tempting to argue that what he has to say points in the same direction as the expulsion of Sakpata and its priests: to severe cracks in the very fabric of Dahomey. This may correspond with Edna Bay's evaluation of nineteenth-century Dahomey in general, that "In retrospect, one senses a certain desperation at the center, a fear that control was being lost… the monarchy was responding to the decline of resources by moving toward greater coercion".⁶⁴ If so, it all began under Adandozan, if not earlier. But if so also, were the heavy-handed methods of Adandozan indispensable for maintaining the Dahomean regime?

THE LONG GOODBYE

When was Adandozan dethroned? The conventionally given date is 1818. But as noted, that date is quite uncertain. It may have been earlier or (more probably) later. But what we do know is first that it was a genuine coup, second that the new king, Gezo, belonged to another lineage than the one which had provided Dahomey with its kings until then,[65] and third that the Chacha played a leading, possibly determining role – he financed the coup.[66] Gezo was in other words a usurper, and in fact doubly so if one considers, as we do, that the legitimacy of the very monarchy was dubious. As for the Chacha, since he owed his position to the withdrawal of the Europeans and the Luso-Brazilians, one may reasonably wonder if a coup such as this could have been possible if the forts had remained operative. The counterfactual argument is then that if Adandozan had adopted a less counterproductive policy towards the Europeans and the Luso-Brazilians he might have saved his throne. We assume here that the new brokers, the Brazilians, had, unlike their predecessors, no scruples in intervening directly in the internal affairs of Dahomey.

The final point in this context is that the active support of the Chacha may have given Gezo little choice but to carry on with, and in fact to opt for, the illegal slave trade.

* * *

On the Western Slave Coast the situation had been changed by the defeat of Little Popo-Glidji in 1795 and the *de facto* withdrawal of the Danes. This implied the "liberation" of Anlo and Keta, the two having established peace at long last in 1802. The situation was modified once more from 1807 when Asante on the neighbouring Gold Coast (also opposed to the ending of the slave trade[67]) embarked upon a new round of expansion, this time southwards, at the expense of the coastal Fante especially. This was reminiscent of the Dahomean southward drive of 1724–27. By 1817 the Asante had annihilated all resistance, its overlordship being recognized all the way to the River Volta, but possibly not beyond.[68] However, the polities of the Western Slave Coast, Ada and New Akwamu plus Anlo-Keta and Little Popo-Glidji, were or became clients or vassals to varying degrees of Asante. The question is to what degree. Both New Akwamu and Anlo, but especially the first, were, we learn, firmly within the orbit of Asante, having lent assistance and collaborated in the crushing of the Fante. As for little Ada and its riverain neighbours, mighty Asante does not seem to have succeeded in subduing them,[69] if indeed Asante really tried. Regarding Little Popo-Glidji, by now seriously weakened but too far away, opinions vary.[70]

As for Anlo, having "freed" itself from Little Popo-Glidji and the Danes, and now enjoying the protection of Asante, it attracted a number of traders of various origins who established close relations with the local authorities.[71] The result was an era of prosperity based on the illegal slave trade which its ally New Akwamu fuelled. Anlo continued in fact to be the leading slave trading polity (if not the only one) on the Western Slave Coast, and remained so until the 1860s. Hence it found itself pitted against first the Danes (theoretically overlords until 1850, but legally obliged to combat the slave trade since 1803) and then the British.[72]

Regarding Little Popo-Glidji, the defeat at the battle of Adame in 1795 heralded the disintegration of that polity. That disintegration was in a sense written into the very fabric of the polity. The central monarchy had been completely discredited because of the defeat at Adame.[73] Hence the autonomous town of Aneho, the genuine Little Popo, distanced itself more and more from Glidji. But in Aneho itself tension rose between the two leading clans, the one that traditionally wielded power and a new one on the rise known under the name of Lawson, and linked to the trade with the Europeans and the Luso-Brazilians. In fact, the heads of that clan belonged to the same category as Monsieur Pierre in Porto Novo and the Chacha and the Brazilians in Ouidah, the new merchant-princes. The difference is that the Lawson clan was clearly of indigenous origin, although claiming close ties to the Europeans, as the name suggests. But the result of it all was some sort of civil war which meant the end of the polity of Little Popo-Glidji as it had been known till then.[74]

* * *

On the Eastern Slave Coast this period saw the continuing rise to prominence of the previously insignificant Lagos. Lagos shared with the two other leading polities, Porto Novo and Badagry, three significant features. The first was a weak monarchy (none at all for most of the time in Badagry) and one torn by internal strife, especially in Lagos from at least the mid-eighteenth century[75] (perhaps because no genuine contrapuntal paramountcy had been allowed to emerge); this was very far from the "totalitarian" model of Dahomey. Secondly, there were, as noted, no European or Luso-Brazilian forts, and Badagry and especially Lagos did without any non-indigenous brokers. And thirdly, they all opted for the illegal slave trade.

As for Lagos, its slave exports soared dramatically between 1786 and 1790, owing probably to the "Lagoon War" of 1780–84 and its sequels. But then it returned to a much more modest level between 1784 and 1801, before soaring to unprecedented heights during the next fifty years, dwarfing Badagry and Porto Novo and also Ouidah, in spite of all the internal conflicts. In addition to the elements already mentioned (such as the counterproductive policy of Dahomey) to explain it all, we must not forget Lagos's very position, too far to the east for the army of Dahomey, and in any case inaccessible, situated on an island in the vast Lagos lagoon.

Then, in about 1811–12 or about 1817, depending on one's definition, the notorious Yoruba wars erupted. They came to fuel powerfully the illegal slave trade.

* * *

It is time to investigate briefly a famous and fascinating myth from the reign of Gezo, namely that of Agontime. She was a royal princess belonging to Agonglo's family, that is, to the losing party in the power struggle in 1797. For that reason she was sold into slavery. But it so happened that Gezo chose as his *kpojito* ("queen-mother") a woman with precisely the same name, Agontime, said to have returned from overseas. Was she the same woman? That is, had she been found by one of the search parties ostensibly sent to the New World by Gezo to bring home someone who was, it is claimed, none other than his old wetnurse? The modern historian is suitably sceptical, although he does know of examples of members of the royal sib who were redeemed after spending years as slaves in the Americas.[76] But perhaps the central point about Agontime is, as Edna Bay has argued, that she became, as a high-ranking individual sold out of Dahomey at the time of Adandozan's succession, an emblem of opposition to the same Adandozan, and in the process contributed to legitimate Gezo's usurpation. To the believers she was in fact living proof of Adandozan's excesses since members of the royal sib were, they argued, not supposed to be sold into slavery.[77] However, as Edna Bay has also pointed out, "being traded overseas was one of several documented punishments for losers in political struggles at court".[78]

Another prominent figure in the reign of Gezo, and much more famous, is of course the Chacha. If we ask what exactly was his role or position after the coup, the answer is that it is far from clear, the relatively large literature about him notwithstanding. The problem begins already with his title, *the* Chacha, that is, the first Chacha – a nickname converted into a title, but a title with very unclear attributes. However, let us follow David Ross who argues that de Souza was made a Dahomean chief, was given the monopoly of the sale of slaves from Ouidah, and was put in charge of, or controlled all Dahomean relations with the Europeans. In fact, Ross alludes to the "monarch's dependence on an outsider", something he considers to be "a new development in Fon politics".[79] All of this is rather vague, however, as Ross himself admits. What then about the Chacha's relations with the Brazilian community in Dahomey, a community he is considered to have founded in some way, but which became genuinely prominent only after 1835, according to Elisée Soumonni?[80] The date here refers to the great urban revolt among the slaves in Salvador da Bahia in Brazil which goes under the name of Malês (that is, Muslim-inspired).[81] Many of the rebels caught were forced to leave Brazil and several ended up on the Slave Coast, some even as slave traders.[82] That former slaves became active in the slave trade is a fact which should not surprise us by now, we have seen that the past is full of examples of this.

So was the Chacha, besides being by far the most important slave trader, the head, unofficial or otherwise, of the local Brazilians? And/or was he some sort of Viceroy of Ouidah, as the title of a well-known novel implies?[83] Was he also the power behind the throne, with Gezo in some sense his hostage? If so, does it explain why Dahomey stuck to the illegal slave trade to the end? Or was it the other way around, was the Chacha a mere useful subordinate of Gezo? Was furthermore the Chacha a sort of ruffian, godfather or nabob, as portrayed by among others Captain Canot,[84] himself not a very commendable individual? And if so, can we risk arguing that we are in the world of organized crime?

The first Chacha is presented on the one hand as a gentleman, or a tropical *fidalgo*, with exquisite manners,[85] and on the other as a ruthless, insensitive slave trader with many vices – he had some 302 wives according to Elisée Soumonni[86] – and who turned out in the end to be a rather poor businessman (he was probably illiterate). He died in fact heavily in debt (in 1849), possibly courtesy of the British anti-slave trade squadron.[87] Hence, and although de Souza was followed by one of his sons, the position of the Chacha seems to have lost progressively much of its importance and relevance, whatever it was. This may also have been due to the rise of other Brazilian traders to prominence[88] – the emergence of a genuine merchant community, and an affluent one, according to Robin Law.[89] If so, does this mean that Gezo was in the process of liberating himself from the grip of the Chachas, assuming that he had been in such a grip, and does it explain the fact that Gezo put an end after the 1840s to the relatively liberal tax regime the Ouidah merchant community had, according to Robin Law, enjoyed under him until then?[90]

THE LONG GOODBYE

What we can say for certain, and as a conclusion, is that the Chacha personified the illegal slave trade; a trade without which the Chacha and his likes would have been inconceivable.

* * *

We must move backwards in time once more, to the accession of Gezo the usurper. It looked as if it might herald in a new era for Dahomey, because the very conditions that determined the life and existence of the polity were being profoundly modified, and positively so, seen from the point of view of the Dahomean elite.

First, Dahomey's old local enemy Little Popo-Glidji entered, as noted, into a process of disintegration, a process more or less complete by 1834. Aneho had become by then a completely independent mini-polity under the Lawsons.[91]

Second, and obviously more fundamental, the Yoruba wars, which erupted some time in the 1810s,[92] resulted in the long-expected collapse of Oyo. They were completed in possibly 1836–37, with the abandonment of the old capital of Oyo Ile. Gezo and Dahomey had their share in all this, defeating the Oyo army twice in 1823.[93] This was certainly not a major feat, considering the weakness of that army by then. But Gezo did free Dahomey from its vassalage to Oyo, a fact which may explain Gezo's position in the traditions as Dahomey's most revered king (along with Agaja).[94] And Dahomey could begin raiding again.

The disappearance first of Little Popo-Glidji and later of the Oyo empire meant that Dahomey had no longer any serious external enemies. The collapse of Oyo and the long period of warfare which was the result in Yorubaland meant in addition a huge number of refugees and war prisoners, fuelling the slave trade, and not only at Lagos.[95] Hence the external slave trade experienced a clear recovery (again mostly on the Eastern Slave Coast) all the way to 1850/51, when it virtually stopped all of a sudden, as the Database makes very clear.

The removal of Dahomey's enemies opened the way to the first significant aggrandisement of Dahomey since the days of Agaja. Although the chronology is unclear, it may have begun with the occupation of what we have presented earlier as the Adja-Mono plateau west of Lake Ahémé, which had strangely enough remained independent until then.[96] It continued with the subjugation of most of Mahi country and of Sabe, a Yoruba polity close by.[97] And further east both Ketu and Porto Novo, which could no longer count on the protection of Oyo, were forced to come to terms with Dahomey, although they did manage to conserve their autonomy.[98] Porto Novo, which probably fell away from Oyo even before 1823, had to wage war with Badagry for many years, until 1830.[99]

Third, the economy and especially the external trade of Dahomey were diversified. In addition to slaves, Dahomey and in fact the whole of the Slave Coast began to export a mundane vegetable oil derived from a palm fruit which grew wild in the region. This was palm oil, for which there turned out to be a considerable demand in Europe.[100] Its export, however, began in earnest relatively late, in 1838, after Gezo had been king for quite some time. It was then that the Gold Coast-based mulatto merchant Thomas Hutton opened a factory for the oil trade at Ouidah, reoccupying in the process the old William's Fort, although only temporarily.[101] Hutton was followed in 1842 by the French firm of Victor Régis of Marseille which set up shop in the French fort, the second of the forts thus to be reoccupied[102] (the firm also lent for some time what may be called "a helping hand" to the slave traders[103]). The Régis firm turned out to be the most active European commercial presence in the place.

In the minds of many Europeans palm oil was supposed to represent an alternative to the illegal slave trade; it was "legitimate". Recent research has made clear, however, that the locals did not perceive the two branches of the export-economy as antagonistic or mutually exclusive, but rather as complementary. Indeed, the leading slave-traders also took up palm oil production and export. As for the production part, the question is whether and to what extent slave labour was involved – that is, whether genuine plantations emerged – or whether most of the oil was processed by independent small-scale producers. The question is also the role of the monarchy in all this, whether and to what extent the monarchy was able to benefit from the income from this new resource. The way we interpret the existing literature is that it was not necessarily a question of either-or, but of both, the problem being the relative importance of the respective alternatives. But palm-oil could only be produced on or close to the coast because of the problem of transport.[104] And on the import side, the nations involved in the oil trade, principally Britain and France, could boast much more advanced economies than those of Spain-Cuba and Portugal-Brazil, and had therefore more to offer than the countries involved in the illegal slave trade:[105] a new variant of an old story. It should be noted finally, and most importantly, that the collection and selling of the palm oil, by its very nature, did not and could not provoke any fundamental change in the organization of economic production.

In addition to the palm oil traders, a stream of visitors, especially British, also arrived, after 1843. Among them were missionaries (well received as always),[106] explorers, and government officials, the latter sent to persuade Dahomey to end the slave trade.[107] Those visitors have left abundant sources, many of them even wrote books – the exotic nature of Dahomey continued to intrigue and attract readers. We have in short a considerable number of eye-witness accounts. Hence, the history of nineteenth-century Dahomey from the second half of the 1840s is well known.

Conditions were in short favourable for Dahomey. But the Dahomean leaders seem to have been unable to genuinely benefit from this new situation. In fact, when Dahomey was brought to the test, it signally failed. The main problem was the tremendously fragile foundation of the illegal slave trade as one of the main pillars of the Dahomean economy. It was dramatically demonstrated once the British began to put genuine pressure on the demand side. Indeed, in 1850 the British, by threatening to bombard Brazilian ports, gave the Brazilian authorities no choice but to enact at long last effective legislation against the slave trade. A law voted by the Brazilian Congress on 4 September 1850 defined the import of slaves to Brazil as an act of piracy and, as such, punishable with death.[108] The illegal slave trade to Brazil collapsed almost immediately. With that collapse our story ends, in a sense.

* * *

To return to a theme evoked above, the present historian may be excused for wondering what would have happened, or rather would not have happened, had Great Britain not decided to launch what may be considered to be a veritable crusade against the slave trade. What if one had left everything to the market forces? After all, Africans were determined to continue supplying slaves, and the Brazilians in particular equally determined to import those same slaves. But this was a field in which the British government, certainly a capitalist one, was prepared to infringe on all existing international conventions and laws, *and* to use violence or at least the threat thereof, to stop the law of supply and demand from functioning. We repeat that it was in the end the demand which was eliminated, not the supply.

In order to underscore their point, the British blockaded at various moments in 1851–52 the coast of the Bight of Benin, including that of Dahomey, and bombarded Lagos in December 1851. The consequence was the establishment of a *de facto* protectorate over the latter polity, with the result that all the slave traders fled.[109] It heralded the beginning of the colonial era. But Dahomey, which could not be touched by sea, hung on, thus becoming the last stronghold of the illegal slave trade on the Guinea coast, as it tried to benefit from the fact that the (small) Spanish-Cuban market still remained open, although not for long (to 1862 or a little later).[110] In conclusion, Dahomey persisted doggedly, stubbornly, with the slave trade, and to the very bitter end.

More surprising, Dahomey, as the quintessential warrior polity, was unable to take advantage of the golden opportunity for easy conquest which the Yoruba wars presented it with, that is, to establish itself as the dominant polity in the wider area. In fact, out of the chaos in Yorubaland there arose in the 1820s and 1830s two new polities, the result of the regrouping of refugees, namely Ibadan and especially Abeokuta. Neither was, as far as we know, particularly well articulated or structured, although both benefited from the indirect support of the British;[111] and neither was particularly militarized or militaristic. Yet the upstart polity of Abeokuta proved to be far too formidable for Dahomey. It began in 1844 when Abeokuta forces ambushed successfully an important Dahomean military detachment. And it continued in March 1851 and March 1864 (in the latter year under Gezo's successor Glélé) when Abeokuta inflicted on Dahomey two resounding and humiliating defeats.[112] To Gezo, who sought to legitimize his usurpation by presenting himself as a successful warrior king, reasserting in the process the Dahomean militaristic values,[113] the defeat of 1851 must have been a major blow, occurring as it did at the same time as the collapse of the illegal slave trade.

On the internal front Gezo is said to have tried to put through "an economic and political revolution which might have made Dahomey a model of what, in English eyes, an African state ought to have been".[114] But if so, that attempted revolution, which was not at all evident to the British authorities of the time (nor is it evident to the present author), also failed. One may call attention in this context to the readiness with which the historians attribute reforming intentions to successive Dahomean kings. As it is, Gezo is principally known for the doubling of "inside" and "outside" officials,[115] a measure the historians are not certain how to interpret. It is tempting, however, to argue that it is a sign of a king who did not feel altogether safe, fearing perhaps the same fate as Adandozan, and who, by making the government machine somewhat more collective (and outsized), tried to avoid any undesired concentration of power. It is in any case tempting to relate this doubling to the dramatic growth of the unproductive palace population.[116]

If we are correct in diagnosing a certain feeling of insecurity (as suggested by the comments of Edna Bay above), that feeling may also explain the many ritual innovations associated with Gezo, amounting to more spiritual engineering. They led to a significant extension of the ceremonial cycle, an extension which proved in turn negative to commerce in Edna Bay's view.[117] We note in this context especially the new emphasis on the increasingly popular Fa geomancy and the corresponding elevation of Fa diviners (*bokonon*) to central political positions. The other innovations consisted in enhancing once again the importance of the ancestor cult, in order, says Edna Bay, to weaken once again the appeal of the so-called popular *vodun*, that is, Sakpata and Hevioso.[118] It should be noted in this context that Gezo could not honour his predecessor Adandozan with the usual elaborate funeral ceremonies, for the very simple reason that Adandozan was still alive[119] (it is even possible that he outlived Gezo who passed away in 1858, perhaps killed by his own[120] if he too did not fall victim to Sakpata's smallpox[121]). What the above indicates in any case is that Sakpata was still very much around, in spite of its "expulsion" under Adandozan. In fact, Gezo too "banned" the cult of Sakpata.[122] But more generally, why ritual innovations if the existing rituals functioned well? Obviously they did not, and we deduce that Gezo continued to be beset by the perennial problem of legitimacy.

Gezo, always on the lookout for supernatural support like all Dahomean kings, obtained a number of Christian religious statues, and with great ceremony installed them in a specially constructed house. It is said that Gezo attributed his success against Oyo to those statues.[123] What happened then to the Muslim influence noted earlier?

It is also believed that Gezo streamlined the military structure, reorganizing the famous female guard, the Amazons,[124] and considerably increasing the standing army (if that is what it was).

* * *

If the testimony of European visitors in the 1840s is anything to go by, very little if anything had changed in Dahomey by then (unless we suffer from an optical illusion, in the sense that those testimonies either colour or constitute the basis for our perception of Dahomey also in earlier times). For instance, Blaise Brue, the local agent of the Régis company, incidentally invested solemnly with the command of the French fort and the adjoining village by none other than Gezo himself in May 1843,[125] maintained that the Dahomean regime was of the despotic kind, the king having the right of life and death over his subjects ("*droit de vie & de mort sur ses sujets*"), and that the custom of human sacrifice continued unabated. In fact, Brue noted the oppressive display of human skulls virtually everywhere.[126]

Then there is Brodie Cruickshank, a British official, who visited Dahomey in 1848. Cruickshank echoed earlier writers by describing Dahomey, or at least the region of Kana (he wrote Canna), as nothing less than a "beautiful Eden", endowed with what he qualified as "a superior system of agriculture". He was especially impressed by the (probably recently constructed[127]) royal road between Kana and Abomey, and noticed also the "most respectable appearance" of the royal palaces. But then there were the skulls to be seen everywhere. And the general atmosphere was one of "fanaticism and blind obeyance" in this "very despotic and extremely warlike" land.[128]

The observant Cruickshank added that "Nothing prevents an increase of wealth among the people but the King's policy in seizing upon the property of deceased persons – it renders (the ordinary Dahomean) contented with the simple supply of his few wants".[129] The moral was that there was no incentive to work.

* * *

It remains for us to say a few words about the Western (Little) Slave Coast, where the general trend noticed in the preceding chapter was the ending of external interference. One cause was the previously mentioned disintegration of Little Popo-Glidji, which obviously affected the Western Slave Coast as well. Another, equally external cause was the beginning of the confrontation on the Gold Coast between on the one hand Asante, weakened by the end of the slave trade, and on the other the British and their allies the Fante. After the Crown assumed direct control of the forts in 1821 (only until 1828, but again, and permanently, from 1843, thus heralding in the colonial era on that coast), the stage was set in 1823 for the first of the four Anglo-Asante wars which eventually spelled the end of Asante. Hence Asante's indirect and ill-defined dominance of the Western Slave Coast came to an end.[130] The main beneficiaries were the inland Ewe and the main loser New Akwamu. First, New Akwamu liberated itself from Asante, even fighting against Asante on the side of the British; but secondly, the inland Ewe polities (*dukowo*) united under the leadership of Peki and waged what it is tempting to call a successful wars of liberation against New Akwamu between 1829 and 1834. After which New Akwamu, which had at one stage appealed to the Danes for assistance, disappeared from the scene.[131] This does not seem to have affected the Anlo confederacy in any negative way, however. Indeed, Anlo continued to practice the illegal slave trade to the very end; among the victims were not infrequently its own inhabitants.[132]

THE LONG GOODBYE

We note finally that Anlo had become by then a thoroughly maritime-oriented polity. It was reflected in a subtle ongoing religious change, the god of the sea Yewe, the local variant of Hu, became ever more important, appealing especially to the many foreigners who had settled in the polity, to the detriment of Nyigble associated with the *Awoamefia*. In short, there was a religious transition to the maritime world.[133]

* * *

As we have noted, the fight against the illegal slave trade turned out to be the prelude to the colonial era on the coast of Guinea. Indeed, although Dahomey – or what was left of it – fell to French (and not British) invaders only in 1892–94 (and Asante to the British only in 1896), the writing on the wall was clear for everyone to see already by the 1850s, if not earlier.

EPILOGUE

The main themes evoked in this work, especially the one summarized in its very title, plus the themes of the origins and nature of the Dahomean polity, and the conclusions they have generated, have been stated – we hope – with sufficient clarity. They do not need therefore to be further elaborated upon in the following. But they lead us to reflections of a theoretical-global character.

In this day and age of Global History, in which Africa appears as the marginalized "loser" in a sense (it is mostly about the so-called Western world and Asia), the balance has to be corrected, which is what we have had in mind when writing this work. Can we in fact imagine the modern world without the consequences of slavery and the slave trade? And what would that trade have been without that small place we call the Slave Coast?

We have also tried to show that, apart from Dahomey and possibly Akwamu, the polities of the Slave Coast were in no way unique, but very similar to many polities elsewhere in the world before and outside the regions where so-called revealed religions came to dominate. Even the exception to the rule, the militaristic-"totalitarian" Dahomey (plus Akwamu), is of course no exception at all in a broader comparative context. Hence the Slave Coast, and West Africa south of the Sahara more generally, ought to constitute a fertile ground for comparative studies. The study of the past of that region alerts us in particular to the central role of what we may call religion in so-called "pagan" societies. The word "pagan" may shock but is not used, we repeat, in any pejorative sense, only for lack of a suitable alternative – such terms as the often-used "ethnic religions" strike us as inadequate, if not misleading. So we are dealing with that we call sacred ("pagan") societies, as defined earlier in this work. It is the world of Mother-Earth, of ritual "control" of the land, of earth-priests, of kindreds or sibs, of sacred kingship, of contrapuntal paramountcy, of *mana*, of ritual king-slaying, and so on.

If pressed, we would be inclined to argue that the sacred societies constituted for very long the norm in the past of humanity. In fact, we believe that one way of conceptualizing a very fair slice of that past is to argue for a dichotomy between, on the one hand, the sacred "pagan" societies, and on the other, societies in which forces pointing in a quite different direction were at work: forces which would lead in the long run to a growth economy, secularization, industrialization and so on – though this dichotomy does leave us, we readily admit, with a very large rest-category, including notably most of the Graeco-Roman world of Antiquity. There is anyway no question about who "won", or who is in the process of "winning", since the sacred "pagan" societies are fast disappearing from the surface of the earth. Actually, they began to disappear very early in what is called the West, the Muslim world included, that is, the part of the world where the science of history emerged. For that reason they have remained to a considerable extent outside the gaze of historians.[1] Or put differently, most historians are familiar with the exception, the West, not necessarily with the rule.

We think, furthermore, that the revealed religions, by propagating a linear concept of time and also, in the case of Christianity especially, by postulating an incipient distinction between the secular and religious spheres ("Render unto Caesar the things that are Caesar's, and unto God the things that are God's"[2]), contributed powerfully in the long run, and somewhat paradoxically, to the marginalization of the sacred – once what we may perhaps call the sacred-totalitarian-fundamentalist pretensions of the medieval Catholic church had been definitively defeated by the men and women of the Renaissance, by Martin Luther and a few others, and by the Enlightenment, which left as legacy a diversity of more or less irreconcilable truth claims. In the case of Africa, and singularly in the case of the region and the period studied above, we have unveiled several attempts at breaking out of the straightjacket that one may consider, or some have considered, the sacred societies to constitute. One such attempt may have been made in Dahomey, whether consciously or not. But if so, it failed, since the rulers of Dahomey were unable to come up with a genuinely functioning alternative – if they ever really tried – relying finally on little more than brute force, the result being that they found themselves saddled with an unresolvable problem of legitimacy. Hence the increasingly militaristic and "totalitarian" deviation of the Dahomean regime (whether or not the case of Dahomey really fits the usual definitions of "totalitarianism" is a moot but irrelevant point in this context). If so, we cannot exclude, incidentally, the possibility that the imperialist conquest in the 1890s, whatever its excesses, was perceived as some sort of liberation by the people of the Slave Coast. Casimir Agbo certainly hints as much in the case of Ouidah.[3]

But how does the slave trade fit into all this? We must note that the first polities which entered the slave trade, Allada and Hueda, were of the "traditionalist" (sacred-"pagan") kind. What Dahomey did was simply to break into, and to take over, an already well-established trade. Actually, Dahomey almost "spoiled" it all through its lack of commercial acumen. But more to the point, sacred societies are also kinship-type societies, and, as noted, in that kind of society whoever belongs to another kindred than one's own does not count for very much. Besides, the slave trade proved to be the easy way out, the easy way to procure a number of desired goods, many of them generating prestige, including in the religious sense, without jeopardizing the basic structure of the society and its world outlook (this is not to deny the strain provoked by the slave trade on that structure and that world-view). There is, in sum, something non-revolutionary, something deeply conservative about the slave trade on the supply-side; nothing in the way of radical changes in what the Marxists call the mode of production. The point is that the slave trade, including the capture of slaves, belongs in the final instance to the most basic and "primitive" of all economic activities, that of hunting and gathering. Or if one prefers, it is based on the extraction of what we may presumptuously call "natural resources". And as is well known, the extraction of, and especially dependency on, such resources can be very perilous in the long run.

That being said, the present author has to admit that the slave trade, that most absurd of the occurrences in the past, belongs in his mind to the same category as many central events and occurrences which the same author would be grateful if someone could explain satisfactorily to him. Among them are the Greek "miracle" (the first genuinely massive breakout from the sacred ["pagan"] societies model), the emergence of revealed religions, the rise and especially the fall of the Roman Empire,[4] the First World War, the rapid Nazification of Germany after January 1933, the Spanish Civil War of 1936–39 – the latter two being personal, not to say existentialist problems – and so on. We believe we know a lot about those events or occurrences, and others, and we believe we also understand to a considerable extent what they were all about. But as for genuinely *explaining* them, there is always something missing, an element which eludes us, the question which surfaces after the last answer one has been able to come up with. The conclusion is that history cannot explain what it is supposed to explain, namely the past. But perhaps we are asking for too much.

In this context we feel like adding a point which has become embarrassingly clear to us, and which is reflected, we believe, in the preceding chapters: how hopelessly little we really know, when all is said and done, about the past of the Slave Coast. And what we do know, or at least what the present author has tried to demonstrate, clashes uncomfortably often with the seductive concepts and theories elaborated by impatient historians eager, very understandably, to incorporate the past of the Slave Coast into more general contexts, theoretical or otherwise.

So what is left? Perhaps something called insight...

* * *

A personal note: in the late 1980s whoever drove along the narrow and (in theory) tarred road along the coast between Lomé in Togo and Cotonou in the present-day Republic of Benin could easily have missed the town of Ouidah. Only a rather worn road-sign which had fallen down indicated where one had to turn to the right. However, once the centre of the town was reached, the conclusion which imposed itself upon the visitor was that the town was a melancholy, not to say depressing one, belonging to the infamous "hole-in-the-middle-of-nowhere" category. There was, even with the best of intentions, nothing of interest to be seen. The town was, to be quite honest, rather repulsive. What I witnessed was the result of many decades of decay and neglect. As for the access to the beach it was impossible with a car, there were simply no roads. I made it down to the seaside after a terrible ride on a rented motorcycle – all that sand – including across a bridge of sorts over the lagoon. It was an overwhelming experience to wander absolutely alone along that enormous beach, and contemplate the mighty Atlantic (no boats on the horizon), while trying to imagine the unimaginable, the sufferings and deaths of so many fellow-humans on that precise spot not so long ago.

Crossing the Atlantic some time later, I had the opportunity to travel to the famed town of Salvador da Bahia de todos os Santos (to quote its full name) in the traditionally poor north-eastern part of Brazil. Salvador's close relations

EPILOGUE

with the coast of West Africa have been an important theme in this work. Salvador and its bay are the centre of a region called the Recôncavo. And on the other side of that bay, some way inland, I visited another equally melancholy backwater-town: Cachoeira (present population: less than 40,000), known principally today – according to Wikipedia – as the centre of *candomblé*, a so-called Afro-Brazilian religion, and *capoeira*, a dance and martial art. Yet those two backwater-towns, Cachoeira and Ouidah, were intimately linked in the past, since most of the famous third-class rejected or *refugado* tobacco consumed on the Slave Coast came from the region of Cachoeira (B.J. Barickman tells us that Cachoeira prospered well into the nineteenth century but then declined precipitously, along with tobacco[5]). The question is why – why some regions prospered in the past but were later turned into backwaters, while others experienced exactly the opposite. I believe I know some of the answers. All the same, contemplating first Ouidah and then Cachoeira in the 1980s can only be described as an impacting, thought-provoking experience.

The next and last time I visited Ouidah was some twenty years later (by then Cachoeira was out of my reach). In the meantime the town had changed radically, and for the better. There had in particular been erected, with the financial assistance of various international organizations, some monuments – one even imposing, and on the beach itself – which were supposed to indicate that this was indeed a major centre of the slave trade (it is no longer possible to be alone on that beach now complete with a hotel and restaurants). But the aim seems to have been principally to attract what is called "ethnic tourism" in the wake of the "finding-one's-roots" movement triggered by Alex Haley's famous *Roots*.[6] And the problem is that the direct relationship between those monuments and the historical reality they are supposed to symbolize is unfortunately very spurious.[7] It is all the more embarrassing since at the same time a Slave Route Project with clear intellectual ambitions was launched.[8]

To quote Elisée Soumonni, a native son who has appeared frequently in the preceding pages, "The not always explicitly avowed intention of [it all] is to generate revenue through external assistance and to stimulate the development of tourist activities".[9] The so-called first *voodoo* (and not *vodu*) festival organized in 2004[10] was part of the same tourist offensive.

But the "ethnic tourism" has not really taken off, so that the monuments had already by the time I contemplated them a certain worn-out aspect, suffering obviously from poor maintenance.

The problem is that the majority of slaves from the Slave Coast were exported to Brazil and the French islands, and the descendants of slaves in those parts of the New World do not yet have the same purchasing power as those of the US. And although the Slave Coast was by far the leading epicentre of the slave trade in West Africa, and is to-day probably one of the safest places on the continent, the Afro-Americans of the US head for Ghana, the former Gold Coast, and Senegal, believing rightly or wrongly that that is where their ancestors came from, not for the Slave Coast (the historians only know that relatively few slaves ended up in British North America, later the US – possibly about 6 per cent of the total). It is telling in this context that President Obama himself chose to go, during his two visits to West Africa, to Ghana and Senegal, not to Benin-Togo and the Slave Coast. The two former places display what the latter does not: old buildings – forts, European forts that is, and on the sea-shore – which to the layman constitute concrete evidence of the slave trade.

NOTES

LIST OF ABBREVIATIONS

1. Portuguese orthography has changed frequently in the last centuries.
2. See the preceding footnote.
3. England did not adopt the Gregorian calendar from 1582 until 1751, by which time the old Julian calendar lagged 10 days behind the Gregorian one. In addition, the civil year officially began on 25 March rather than on 1 January.

INTRODUCTION

1. Unless otherwise indicated, all figures and dates with regard to the slave trade are from the monumental Trans-Atlantic Slave Trade Database, Emory University, National Endowment for the Humanities, and the W.E.B. Du Bois Institute, University of Harvard (http://www.slavevoyages.org/tast/assessment/estimates. faces. Retrieved at various times since December 2011). The scholars responsible are David Eltis, David Richardson, Stephen D. Behrendt, and Manolo Florentino.
   A version destined for a larger audience is David Eltis and David Richardson, *Atlas of the Transatlantic Slave Trade* (Yale University Press, 2010)
2. According to Robin Law, *Ouidah. The Social History of a West African Slaving 'Port' 1727–1892* (Ohio University Press and Oxford, James Currey, 2004a). The book is in fact dedicated "To the memory of the more than one million enslaved Africans who passed through Ouidah on their way to slavery in the Americas or death in the Middle Passage".
3. Justly Watson, "A Report on the Survey of William's Fort Whydah [Ouidah]", 1755 (NA, CO 267/11).
4. "Un triple barre de brisants épouvantables", E. Bouët-Willaumez, *Commerce et traite des noirs aux côtes occidentales d'Afrique. 1er janvier 1848* (Paris, 1848; reprinted Geneva, 1978), 122; "trois rouleaux de barre", Simone Berbain, *Le comptoir français de Juda (Ouidah) au XVIIIe siècle. Études sur la traite des noirs au golfe de Guinée* (Dakar, IFAN, 1942), 70, referring to Joseph Crassous' experience in 1772–74.

NOTES p. [2]

See also, for instance, Robert Harms, *The Diligent: A Voyage through the Worlds of the Slave Trade* (New York, 2002), 199 (based on an unpublished manuscript by the slave trader Robert Durand from 1731–32); and "Relation du Royaume de Judas en Guinée. De son gouvernement, des moeurs de ses habitants, de leur Religion. Et du Negoce qui s'y fait", ca. 1715 (CAOM-DFC, carton 75, doc.104).

5. In addition to the above: Père Dieudonné Rinchon, *Pierre-Ignace-Liévin Van Alstein, capitaine négrier. Gand 1733-Nantes 1793* (Dakar, IFAN, 1964), 339; Robert Norris, *Memoirs of the Reign of Bossa Ahádee, King of Dahomey. To which are Added, the Author's Journey to Abomey, the Capital; and a Short Account of the African Slave Trade* (1789, reprinted London [Frank Cass] 1968), 61-2.

6. See, for instance, *Barbot on Guinea. The Writings of Jean Barbot on West Africa 1678–1712*, 2 volumes, P.E.H. Hair, Adam Jones and Robin Law (eds) (London [The Hakluyt Society], 1992), 631; J.A. Skertchly, *Dahomey as it is* (London, Chapman and Hall, 1874), 7; Antoine Edmé Pruneau de Pommegeorge, PDP, *Description de la Nigritie* (Amsterdam and Paris, Chez Maradan, 1789), 199; Law (2004a), 135.

7. See, for instance, letters from Whydah [Ouidah] in March 1687 signed John Carter, in Robin Law (ed.), *Further Correspondence of the Royal African Company of England Relating to the 'Slave Coast'. Selected Documents from Ms. Rawlinson C.745–747 in the Bodleian Library, Oxford* (African Studies Program, Univ. of Wisconsin-Madison, 1992a), 45; and in Robin Law (ed.), *The English in West Africa, 1691–1699. The Local Correspondence of the Royal African Company of England 1681–1699*, Part 3 (Oxford University Press/British Academy, 2006), 340-41. See also William (Willem) Bosman, *A New and Accurate Description of the Coast of Guinea* (first published in Dutch in 1704; new English edition London [Frank Cass], 1967), 337; William Smith, *A New Voyage to Guinea* (1744, reprinted [Routledge] 1967), 166-7.

A certain Jean Papineau became famous because he survived miraculously a ten-hour stint in the sea, possibly because he had a long knife with him. See Captain John Adams, *Remarks on the Country extending from Cape Palmas to the River Congo* (London, 1823, reprinted 1966), 57-60.

8. Patrick Manning, *Slavery, Colonialism and Economic Growth in Dahomey, 1640–1960* (Cambridge University Press, 1982), 332.

9. See, for instance, Law (2004a), 18; and "Mémoire de Jacques Proa, dit Proa des îles", 1806, 94 (AD-Charente Maritime, La Rochelle, 4J2318).

Even so, ships must have been driven ashore during storms especially. One spectacular episode in 1705, in which a ship was smashed to pieces, is recorded in Nigel Tattersfield, *The Forgotten Trade. Comprising the Log of the "Daniel and Henry" of 1700 and Accounts of the Slave Trade from the Minor Ports of England, 1698–1725* (London, Jonathan Cape, 1991), 105-7.

10. In addition to the ones already cited, cf. for instance "Inspection", 1755 (NA, T70/176); John M'Leod, *A Voyage to Africa. With Some Accounts of the Manners and Customs of the Dahomian People* (1820, reprinted London [Frank Cass] 1971), 7-8; N***, *Voyage aux côtes de Guinée et en Amerique* (Amsterdam, 1719), 57; J.F. Landolphe, *Mémoires du Capitaine Landolphe rédigés sur son manuscrit par J.S. Quesné* (2 vols., Paris,1823), II, 27-8; Richard F. Burton, *Wanderings in West Africa, from Liverpool to Fernando Po*, vol. II (London, Dover Publications, 1863), 189.

p. [3]

Note finally what the official *Western Coast of Africa*, published by the Hydrographer of the Navy, counselled in 1849: "nothing ought to induce an attempt to land anywhere [on the Slave Coast] in other than local canoes and surf boats, and even these require much skill in handling" (12th edition published in London 1967 under the title *Africa Pilot*, and prepared by Lieut. Commander J.F. Gruning, vol. I, 472).

There is a particularly vivid description in Frederick E. Forbes, *Dahomey and the Dahomans. Being the Journals of Two Missions to the King of Dahomey and Residence at his Capital in the years 1849 and 1850* (London, Longman etc., 1851), vol.I, 11-14 & 45; vol.II, 127-9, 200-1.

11. André Guilcher, "La région côtière du Bas-Dahomey occidental. Étude de géographie physique et humaine appliquée", *Bulletin de l'IFAN*, série B, vol. XXI, 3-4 (1959), 357-424 (386-7).

12. Excellent description in "Mémoire pour servir d'Instruction au Directeur qui me succedera au comptoir de Juda, par Mr. Gourg" 1791 (CAOM-DFC, carton 75, doc. 118). Published under the title *Ancien mémoire sur le Dahomey* in *Mémorial de l'artillerie de Marine*, vol. XX (1892), 747-76. See also Thomas Phillips, "A Journal of a Voyage Made in the Hannibal of London, Ann. 1693,1694 (etc)", in Awnsham Churchill and John Churchill (eds), *Collection of Voyages & Travels*, vol. VI (1732), 171-239 (214); Law (2004a), 26.

There are some splendid illustrations, in a cartoon of all places, one actually based in part on genuine primary sources: François Bourgeon, *Le Comptoir de Juda* (vol. 3 of *Les Passagers du Vent*) (Jacques Glénat, Grenoble, 1981).

13. See, for example, Smith (1744/1967), 169; Alexandre L. D'Albéca, one of the first colonial administrators in the region: "Voyage au pays des Éoués", I, *Le Tour du Monde*, no. 8, 23.2.1895, 85-92 (88). Pruneau (1789), 170. *Les hamacaires*, i.e. those who transported the hammocks, were considered to be the aristocracy among the porters.

14. Although trypanosomiasis is basically a phenomenon of regions covered by rain forest, the Slave Coast was and is not free of it. In fact, the closer one gets to the coast, the more the tsetse fly becomes numerous. (Information deduced from a superficial perusal of the relevant websites of the World Health Organization.)

For an interesting historical angling, see A. Norman Klein, "Toward a New understanding of Akan origins", *Africa*, 2, 66 (1996), 248-73.

15. Pruneau (1789), *Description*, 242-4.

16. See, for instance, *Journal du Corsaire Jean Doublet, Lieutenant de frégate sous Louis XIV*, edited by Charles Bréard (Paris 1883), 253; Vicente Ferreira Pires and Clado Ribeiro de Lessa (ed.), *Crónica de uma Embaixada Luso-Brasileira à Costa d'África em fins do século XVIII, incluindo o texto da Viagem de África em o Reino de Daomé escrita pelo Padre Vicente Ferreira Pires no ano de 1800 e até o presente inédita* (São Paulo, 1957), 26-8; Skertchly (1874), 5.

17. Reported in Johannes Rask, *En kort og sandferdig reisebeskrivelse til og fra Guinea* (Trondhjem [Trondheim], 1754). English version by Selena Axelrod Winsnes: *Two Views from Christiansborg Castle*, vol. I, *A Brief and Truthful Description of a Journey to and from Guinea* (Accra, Sub-Saharan Publishers, 2009), 49.

18. Kenneth G. Kelly, "Using Historically Informed Archaeology: Seventeenth and Eighteenth Century Hueda/European Interaction on the Coast of Bénin", *Journal of Archaeological Method and Theory*, vol. 4, nos. 3/4 (1997), 353-66.
19. It has been completely dwarfed by the rise of a number of new towns, Cotonou in particular.

    No one seems to know for certain how many people live in Ouidah at present. The estimates range widely, from 25,000 to 90,000. In the 1860s the British believed that the town had about 25,000 inhabitants (Rear Admiral Henry Keppel to the Secretary of the Admiralty, 16.7.1860; NA, ADM/123/183).
20. Its destiny is curious. After the French conquest, it became a Portuguese enclave, in fact the world's smallest colony, since it measured little more than two hectares. It was annexed by the Republic of Dahomey, now Benin, on 1 August 1962, without any resistance. It was converted into a museum in 1967. See Edmundo Correia Lopes, *São João Batista de Ajudá* (Lisbon, Edições Cosmos, Coll. Cadernos coloniais no.58, 1939); J. Anacoreta Correia, "O forte português de Ajudá na Costa do Benim (subsídios para a sua historia)", *Boletim da Sociedade de Geografia de Lisboa*, ser. 180a 7.12.1996, 23-86.

    On the Portuguese fort generally, see also Pierre Verger, *Le Fort St. Jean-Baptiste d'Ajuda* (Mémoire de l'Institut de Recherches Appliquées du Dahomey, 1966).

    The French fort was razed to the ground in 1908, much to the chagrin of the local population, if we are to believe Casimir Agbo dit Alidji, *Histoire de Ouidah du XVIe au XXe siècle* (printed in Avignon, 1959), 25 & 300. As for the English fort, it rather faded away over the years (Law, 2004a, 33).
21. Point discussed in Finn Fuglestad, "Le questionnement du 'port' de Ouidah (Côte des Esclaves)", in Øystein Rian, Finn Erhard Johannessen, Øystein Sørensen and Finn Fuglestad (eds), *Revolusjon og resonnement. Festskrift [Festschrift] til Kåre Tønnesson på 70-årsdagen den 1. januar 1996* (Oslo 1995), 125-36.
22. Law talks of the "conventional image of a land cut off from the sea"; Robin Law, "Between the Sea and the Lagoons: The Interaction of Maritime and Inland Navigation on the Precolonial Slave Coast", *Cahiers d'Études Africaines*, XXIX, 2 (1989a), 209-37 (209). See also Jean-Pierre Chauveau, "Une histoire maritime africaine est-elle possible? Historiographie et histoire de la navigation et de la pêche africaine à la côte occidentale depuis le XVe siècle", *Cahiers d'Études Africaines*, XXVI, 1-2 (1986), 173-235.

    There were, then, no local "navigational nurseries" in John Hargreaves' felicitous expression. Quoted in Emmanuel Kwaku Akyeampong, *Between the Sea & the Lagoon. An Eco-social History of the Anlo of Southeastern Ghana, c.1850 to Recent Times* (Ohio University Press/James Currey, Oxford 2001), 30.
23. Landolphe said in 1786 (p. 28): "en considérant cette foule de difficultés pour arriver au pays des noirs, n'est on pas tenté de croire que la nature a voulu les soustraire à l'esclavage des Blancs?"
24. Joseph E. Inikori, "The Unmeasured Hazards of the Atlantic Slave Trade: Sources, Causes and Historiographical Implications", in Doudou Diène (ed.), *From Chains to Bonds. The Slave Trade Revisited* (Paris/UNESCO and New York/Oxford, Berghahn, 2001), 22-35.

25. To be correct, we must add that there was at times a fourth (small) fort, at Keta in the west, the short-lasting Dutch one of Singelenburg to 1737, and the Danish fort of Prindsensten erected in 1784, of which ruins are still visible to-day. But those forts were always of quite marginal relevance in the broader picture. Note that Keta is situated on a reef of soft rock and constitutes as such some sort of exception on the Slave Coast. Cf. A.W. Lawrence, *Trade Castles & Forts of West Africa* (London, Jonathan Cape, 1963), 364.

    Another late Danish fort, at Ada, was situated right on the border between the Slave and Gold Coasts.

26. Watson's report from 1755, *op. cit*; Adams (1823/1966), 51. Here is an early description of the English fort: "100 yards square, 21 good guns mounted- a trench 20 foot deep & 18 foot wide, commonly guarded with about 20 white men & 100 gromettoes [=slaves?]". Charles Davenant, *Reflections upon the Constitution and Management of the Trade to Africa* (etc.) (London 1709), part 2, 34.

27. This at the beginning of the nineteenth century (13 Dutch, 9 or 10 English and 3 Danish forts). There were, in addition, about 20 other trading stations. Cf. Ivor Wilks, "The Mossi and Akan states, 1400 to 1800", in J.F. Ade Ajayi and Michael Crowder (eds), *History of West Africa*, vol. one (third ed., Harlow/Essex, Longman, 1985), 465-502; based on J.D. Fage, "A New Check List of the Forts and Castles of Ghana", *Transactions of the Historical Society of Ghana*, IV (1959).

    There was one fort every 10 to 15 miles, according to Rebecca Shumway, *The Fante and the Transatlantic Slave Trade* (University of Rochester Press, 2011a), 3.

28. Cf. among others: John Atkins (Surgeon in the Royal Navy), *A Voyage to Guinea, Brasil, and the West Indies; in His Majesty's Ships, the Swallow and Weymouth* (1735, new impression London [F. Cass, 1970), 172; Abraham Du Port from Whydah [Ouidah], 12.11.1727 [O.s.], in Robin Law (ed.), *Correspondence of the Royal African Company's Chief Merchants at Cabo Corso Castle with William's Fort, Whydah, and the Little Popo Factory, 1717-1728. An Annotated Transcription of Ms. Francklin 1055/1 in the Bedfordshire County Record Office* (African Studies Program, University of Wisconsin-Madison, 1991), 12; M'Leod (1820/1967), 14-15.

29. *Ibid.*, 14-16; Bourgeon (1981), 57-8; based on authentic archival documents, in particular "Deux plans de Juda, avec commentaires, par l'Abbé Bullet, 1776" (AN, C6-27, d.11).

30. A good example is found in Accounts-William's Fort Nov-Dec.1752 (NA, T70/1158).

31. Law (2004a), 163; Harms (2002), 158.

32. Tattersfield (1991), 81. For instance, the English clung to the belief that in the larger sense they were essential for the preservation of their interests in Africa. K.G. Davies, *The Royal African Company* (London, Longmans etc., 1957), 262.

    Says Rebecca Shumway (referring only to the Gold Coast forts): "The forts had to do with reasons that made more sense in the broader context of European empire building in the Atlantic than in the local context of Guinea" (Shumway [2011a], 62).

33. Albert van Dantzig, *Les Hollandais sur la Côte de Guinée à l'époque de l'essor de l'Ashanti et du Dahomey 1680-1740* (Paris, SFHOM, 1980).

34. There is a good example in a letter signed E. Jackline, Whydah [Ouidah], 13.10.1692 [O.s.] in Law (1992a), 55.

35. Peter C.W. Gutkind, "The Canoemen of the Gold Coast (Ghana). A Survey and an Exploration in Precolonial Labour History", *Cahiers d'Études Africaines*, XXIX, 3-4 (1989), 339-76; Jane Martin, "Krumen 'down the coast': Liberian Migrants on the West African Coast in the 19th and 20th Centuries", *International Journal of African Historical Studies*, 18, 3 (1985), 401-23; Akyeampong (2001), 30.

    The most recent works on Fante are those of Rebecca Shumway (2011), and Rebecca Shumway, "The Fante Shrine of Nananom Mpow and the Atlantic Slave Trade in Southern Ghana", *International Journal of African Historical Studies*, 44, 1 (2011b), 27-44; and Robin Law, "The Government of Fante in the Seventeenth Century", *Journal of African History*, 54, 1 (2013), 31-51. Neither refers to the canoemen.

36. Phillips (1732), 228 ; Johann Peter Oettinger's account from 1692–93 in Adam Jones (ed.), *Brandenburg Sources for West African History 1680–1700* (Stuttgart/Wiesbaden, 1985), 189.

37. The correct present Portuguese spelling is *remadores*. The relationship between the Europeans and the canoemen constitutes a frequently recurring theme in the sources.

38. "Relation du Royaume de Judas en Guinée" (op. cit.); Letter from Whydah [Ouidah] 24.12.1729/30 [O.s.] (NA T70/1466); Phillips (1732), 228; Law (1989), 226-7; Rincon (1964), 338.

39. Even the British Methodist missionary Freeman's horse in 1843. Thomas Birch Freeman, *Journal of Various Visits to the Kingdoms of Ashanti, Aku, and Dahomi, in Western Africa* (London, second ed. 1844, third ed., 1968), 242.

40. "Bom sera que vão confesados com os olhos serados, e o Credo na boca" – not easy to translate, but the gist of it is that one should be at peace with the Almighty, and profess one's faith in Him before confronting the surf. Jozé Antonio Caldas, "Noticia geral de toda esta capitania da Bahia desde o seu descobrimento até o prezente anno de 1759" [i.e. written in 1759], *Revista do Instituto Geographico e Historico da Bahia*, 57 (1931), 287-315 (301).

41. No statistics are available. Our own list of individual cases is a very long one, but does not lead us anywhere.

42. See documents reproduced in Robin Law (ed.), *The English in West Africa, 1685–1688. The Local Correspondence of the Royal African Company of England, 1681–1699*, Part 2 (Oxford University Press/British Academy, 2001a), 339-43; and Law (1992a), 43 & 429.

43. "On every occasion a fetish man, covered from head to foot with gris-gris stands in the boat invoking the spirit of the waters to be propitious & quell the raging of the sea (on reaching the shore) thanks are immediately returned to the water-divinity". James Fawckner, *Narrative of Captain James Fawckner's Travels to the Coast of Benin, West Africa* (London 1837),120. See also Richard Lander, *Records of Captain Clapperton's Last Expedition to Africa* (London, 1830, 2nd ed. 1967), vol. I, 42; Paul Isert, *Letters on West Africa and the Slave Trade. Paul Erdmann Isert's Journey to Guinea and the Caribbean Islands in Columbia (1788)*, Selena Winsnes (ed.) and trans. (British Academy/Oxford University Press, 1992), 28; Réflexions sur Juda, par le sieur De Chenevert et l'abbé Bulet, à Juda [Ouidah] le 1.6.1776, 12 (CAOM-DFC, carton 75, doc. 111); Akyeampong (2001), 108; Bosman (1704/1967), 368a.

From all this we learn that rough seas were attributed to the sea goddess (Hu), considered to be the meanest of the divinities.

44. See, for instance, "Journal de navigation du sieur Joseph Crassous de Médeuil, Lieutenant en premier 'Le Roy Dahomey' 1772-74" (AM La Rochelle, série EE, carton 282-3).
45. Law (1989), 228-9; Journal kept at Christiansborg 23.12.1698-1.9.1703, in Ole Justesen (ed.), *Danish Sources for the History of Ghana 1657–1754*, 2 volumes (Copenhagen 2005), 128-9.
46. Inspired by Robin Law, "West Africa's Discovery of the Atlantic", *International Journal of African Historical Studies*, 44, 1 (2011), 1-25.
47. Phillips (1732), 228. Or as a Frenchman noted, one had to treat the canoemen well, for disgruntled canoemen were not above "losing" merchandise and slaves in the surf: "Mémoire concernant la Compagnie de Judas", 1722 (AN C6-25).
48. Pires (1957), 138.
49. David Eltis, *Economic Growth and the Ending of the Transatlantic Slave Trade* (Oxford University Press, 1987), 92 & 162; and by the same author, *The Rise of African Slavery in the Americas* (Cambridge University Press, 2000), 149 & 182-3.
50. For a general overview, see Robin Law, *The Slave Coast of West Africa 1550–1750. The Impact of the Atlantic Slave Trade on an African Society* (Oxford University Press, 1991b).
51. "Réflexions sur Juda" 1776 (op.cit.), 12; Law (1989), 211.
52. Olfert Dapper, *Description de l'Afrique* (Amsterdam, 1686), 306 [Originally published in Dutch under the title *Naureurige Beschrijvinge der Afrikaenesche Gewesten* (etc) (Amsterdam 1668)] (the French translation of Dapper has an unfavourable reputation, but it is the only version I have had access too); Silke Strickrodt, "Afro-European Trade Relations on the Western Slave Coast, 16th to 19th centuries" (unpublished PhD thesis, University of Stirling, 2003), 129ff (Strickrodt's thesis has been superseded recently by her book on the same subject: *Afro-European Trade in the Atlantic World: The Western Slave Coast, c.1550–c.1885*, published by James Currey in early 2015. But it appeared after the completion of the present work). See also Bouët-Willaumez (1848/1978), 123.
53. On Anlo, see Akyeampong (2001).
54. That is, 21 years before Columbus crossed the Atlantic. Note that Columbus made at least one voyage, possibly more, to the Guinea coast, to São Jorge da Mina, present-day Elmina, in the 1480s. P.E.H. Hair, "Columbus from Guinea to America", *History in Africa*, 17 (1990), 113-29.
55. But the latter sold out between 1717 and 1720 according to Albert van Dantzig and Barbara Priddy, *A Short History of the Forts and Castles of Ghana* (Accra, 1971), 37-9. It was in 1603 that the Elector of Brandenburg acquired Prussia, and in 1701 that he took the title of king of Prussia.
56. They were eliminated very early on, by the Danes in fact. See György Nováky, *Handelskompanier och kompanihandel. Svenska Afrikakompaniet 1649–1663. En studie i feodal handel* (Acta Universitatis Upsaliensis, Uppsala, 1990). Summarized in György Nováky, "Small Company and the Gold Coast: the Swedish African Company, 1650–1663", *Itinerario*, 16, 1 (1992), 57-76.

57. On the forts in general, see Lawrence (1963); Dantzig and Priddy (1971).
58. See for instance, letter signed E.N. Boris et al., 14.11.1739 (Justesen [2005], 558); Isert (1788/1992).
59. On the Danish activity in Guinea, the leading work is Per O. Hernæs, *Slaves, Danes, and African Coast Society. The Danish Slave Trade from West Africa and Afro-Danish Relations on the Eighteenth-Century Gold Coast* (Department of History, University of Trondheim, 1995). An older but still useful work is Georg Nørregaard, *Guldkysten. De danske etablissementer i Guinea* (København [Copenhagen] 2nd ed. 1968) [the English translation is reputed unreliable].
60. Paul Roussier (ed.), *L'établissement d'Issiny 1687-1702. Voyages de Ducasse, Tibierge et d'Amon à la côte de Guinée publiés pour la première fois et suivis de la Relation du Voyage du Royaume d'Issiny du P. Godefroy Loyer* (Paris 1935); Gérard Chouin, *Eguafo: un royaume africain 'au coeur françois' (1637–1688). Mutations socio-économiques et politique européenne d'un État de la Côte de l'Or (Ghana) au XVIIe siècle* (Paris, AFERA éd., 1998), esp. 166-9; Shumway (2011a), 45-6.
61. The main work on the Portuguese on the coast of Guinea remains Pierre Verger, *Flux et reflux de la traite des nègres entre le Golfe de Bénin et Bahia de Todos os Santos du XVIIe au XIXe siècle* (Paris/The Hague, Mouton, 1968).
62. "Description nautique de la Côte d'Afrique etc.", no date, but probably 1780s (AN Marine, 2/JJ/95); Robert Smith, "The Canoe in West African History", *Journal of African History*, XI, 4 (1970), 515-33; *Africa Pilot* (1967), 452; Lawrence (1963), 30.

    At Elmina, the oldest and largest European fort, landing could be effected in ship's boats.
63. In addition to the above, see Hans Christian Monrad's testimony from his stay on the Gold Coast between 1805 and 1809, published in 1822. English version by Selena Axelrod Winsnes in *Two views from Christiansborg Castle, vol. II: A Description of the Guinea Coast and its Inhabitants* (Accra, Sub-Saharan Publishers, 2009), 103 & 242.
64. *Africa Pilot* (1967), 450-51; "Description nautique" (op. cit.).
65. Ludewig Ferdinand Rømer, *A Reliable Account of the Coast of Guinea (1760)*, Selena Axelrod Winsnes (ed.) and trans. (British Academy/Oxford University Press, 2000); 192; *Africa Pilot*, (1967), 441; Bouët-Willaumez (1848/1978), 122.
66. Erick Tilleman, *En kort og enfoldig beretning om det landskab Guinea og dets beskaffenhed (1697). A Short and Simple Account of the Country Guinea and its Nature*; Selena Axelrod Winsnes (ed.) and trans. (University of Wisconsin-Madison, 1994), 34.
67. The main work on Benin is A.F.C. Ryder, *Benin and the Europeans 1485–1897* (London, Longmans, 1969).
68. Armando Cortesão and A. Teixeira da Mota, *Portugaliae Monumenta Cartographica*, vol. II (Lisbon, 1960), 212.
69. Duarte Pacheco Pereira, *Esmeraldo de Situ Orbis*, George H.T. Kimble (ed.) and trans. (London, The Hakluyt Society 1937; first published in 1892, but probably written in 1505–8). See J.D. Fage, "A Commentary on Duarte Pacheco Pereira's Account of the Lower Guinea Coastlands in his *Esmeraldo de Situ Orbis*, and on Some Other Early Accounts", *History in Africa*, 7 (1980), 47-80 (65); A.F.C. Ryder,

"Dutch Trade on the Nigerian Coast during the Seventeenth Century", *Journal of the Historical Society of Nigeria*, III, 3 (1966), 195-210 (196).

70. The first time some of the story appeared in print may have been in Blaise Brue, "Voyage fait en 1843 dans le royaume de Dahomey", *Revue Coloniale*, VII (1845), 55-68; except that Brue argued that the first Europeans were Frenchmen, not Portuguese. Brue was followed by Sir Richard F. Burton, *A Mission to Gelele, King of Dahomey (etc)* (second ed. 1864; new ed. with an Introduction and Notes by C.W. Newbury; London [Routledge and Kegan Paul], 1966), vol. II, 297 (this time the Portuguese were the first); and then by a host of other writers, especially Portuguese. See for instance Pupo Correia, "Subsídios para a história de S. João Baptista de Ajudá. A chegada dos Portugueses ao Dahomey", *O Mundo Português*, VI, 63 (1939), 105-7. The story was enshrined as part of the local tradition in Agbo (1959), 15, 48, 67, 132 & 194.

See Robin Law's extensive treatment and interpretation of the subject in *Ouidah* (2004a), 14, 21-2, 93-4 & 106.

We note finally that, although some locals became divinities, the first Portuguese did not. This may be considered to be somewhat strange, since according to Sandra Barnes the "conventional pattern for dealing with extraordinary ideas, culture heroes, or anomalies in nature was to deify them". See her "Introduction: The Many Faces of Ogun", in the book edited by her, *Africa's Ogun: Old World and New* (Indiana University Press, 1989), 5.

71. Édouard Foà, *Le Dahomey* (Paris 1895), 224; Paul Marty, "Études sur l'Islam au Dahomey", *Revue du Monde Musulman*, LX (1925), 109-88 (129). Note that Kpatè and Kpassè, the king of Hueda at the time of the event according to the traditions, even had streets named after them in the colonial era (Agbo [1959], 298-9).

72. Underlined in Dapper (1686), 304.

For a quick overview, see Colleen E. Kriger, "'Guinea cloth'. Production and Consumption of Cotton Textiles in West Africa before and during the Atlantic Slave Trade", in Giorgio Riello and Prasannan Parthasarath (eds), *The Spinning World. A Global History of Cotton Textiles, 1200–1850* (Oxford University Press, 2009), 105-26.

Cotton was apparently a commodity produced and prized also in Dahomey much later.

73. "Description des Roiaumes ou l'on fait le commerce en Afrique, avec le Journal du voyage fait en Guinée avec trois vaisseaux du Roy; Le Capitaine du vaisseau "La Tempête" [i.e. Du Casse and hence from 1687–88] (AN Marine 3/JJ/252).

74. The same applies to the Gold Coast, where "the native population…did not appreciate the philanthropy of the abolition act" of 1807. Eveline C. Martin, *The British West African Settlements 1750–1821. A Study in Local Administration* (London, Longmans etc., 1927), 152.

75. J.D. Fage, "Slaves and Society in Western Africa, c.1445–c.1700", *Journal of African History*, 21, 3 (1980), 289-310 (309).

76. The theme is much in evidence in many of Fage's works, and in fact already in his famous article "Slavery and the Slave Trade in the Context of West African History", *Journal of African History*, X, 3 (1969), 393-404.

77. Seymour Drescher, "White Atlantic? The Choice for African Slave Labor in the Plantation Americas", in David Eltis, Frank D. Lewis and Kenneth L. Sokoloff (eds), *Slavery in the Development of the Americas* (Cambridge University Press, 2004), 31-69.
78. Two letters from Ouidah, both dated 14.10.1713 (NA, T70/3 & 5), one of them signed Charles Greene. Also J. Tinker and Humfreys from Whydah [Ouidah] 10.5.1724 (NA, T70/7)[all O.s. dates].
79. The standard work remains Herbert S. Klein, *The Middle Passage. Comparative studies in the Atlantic slave trade* (Princeton University Press, 1978). But see also Eltis and Richardson (2010), 159-96.
80. For a discussion, see Finn Fuglestad, *The Ambiguities of History. The Problem of Ethnocentrism in Historical Writing* (Oslo Academic Press, 2005).
81. We consider it pertinent in this respect to refer to the astonishment expressed by the prominent Conservative MP Charles B. Adderley in the House on Commons on 3 April 1865: "How, then, along such a coast can slaves be exportable?" It is true that he reacted to a testimony which depicted the conditions on the Guinea coast generally in the era of the so-called illegitimate slave trade. But that trade was at its most intense on the Slave Coast. See *Parliamentary Papers: Report from the Select Committee on Africa (Western Coast). Ordered, by the House of Commons, to be Printed, 26 June 1865*, 53. Adderley, the chairman of that committee, was Cabinet minister twice, in 1858–59 and 1874–78.

    One feels that Adderley's astonishment ought to have been shared by most modern historians.
82. To refer only to what has filtered down to the in a sense non-specialized literature: we know that African slaves comprised the vast majority of the migrants to the Americas before 1800. But high death rates and low birth rates meant that they did not generate a proportionate number of descendants. Cf. James Belich, *Replenishing the Earth: The Settler Revolution and the Rise of the Anglo-World 1783–1939* (Oxford University Press, 2009), 26 (in fact based on several articles by David Eltis). We also know that "The West Indian slave population was far smaller than the total number of slaves shipped there, indicating that very high levels of slave mortality required constant slave inflows to replenish supply". (Ronald Findlay and Kevin H. O'Rourke, *Power and Plenty. Trade, War, and the World Economy in the Second Millenium* [Princeton University Press, 2007], 231). This strikes us as a polite way of saying that some sort of "soft" genocide occured.

    Note furthermore that many slaves, after arriving wherever it may have been in the Americas, were submitted to the extra hardship of being resold, re-exported or smuggled to other places on that continent. Cf. for instance Wim Klooster, "Inter-Imperial Smuggling in the Americas, 1600–1800", in Bernard Bailyn and Patricia L. Denault (eds), *Soundings in Atlantic History. Latent Structures and Intellectual Currents, 1500-1830* (Harvard University Press, 2009), 141-80.

    Only 5 per cent of the slaves ended up in North America. Although perhaps they should not be seen as the lucky few, most of them were set to work growing cotton as opposed to the much more demanding sugar-cane. Hence, "Life expectancy and reproductive potential were much poorer in the Caribbean than on the North

American mainland" (Eltis and Richardson, *Atlas*, 161). What is true for the Caribbean is also true for Brazil.

83. To the best of our knowledge, the study of that trade has not progessed very far since the pioneering contribution by Ralph A. Austen in 1979. Cf. his "The Trans-Saharan Slave Trade: A Tentative Census", in Henry A. Gemery and Jan S. Hogendorn (eds), *The Uncommon Market. Essays in the Economic History of the Atlantic Slave Trade* (New York 1979), 23-76.

84. Even today it is difficult not to be repelled by the classic argument that the Africans were better off as slaves in America than as freemen in Africa, and that as slaves in America they were offered the possibility to "see the light" and thus presumably to avoid eternal damnation. A notorious example is the foreword by Bishop Erik Pontoppidan (1698-1764) dated 1760 in Rømer (1760/2000), 5-12. Pontoppidan was a leading figure in the Lutheran church of Denmark-Norway. His name may still ring a bell among the older generation of Danes and Norwegians, owing to his famous catechism whose lifetime spanned several centuries.

85. Inspired in part by David Brion Davis, *The Problem of Slavery in Western Culture* (Oxford University Press, 1966).

86. Pruneau (1789), 207-8, 216-7 & 262. He went on to argue that "les partisans [de la traite] veulent rendre la religion complice de leurs crimes" (ibid. 263-4).
There also comes to mind in this context the experience of John Newton (1725–1807), a captain of slave ships who became an Anglican cleric and wrote the hymn "Amazing Grace" (point made to the present author by Edna Bay).

87. We are referring to the Slave Trade Act of that year. For a discussion, see Eltis (1987).

88. The historian in question is Arif Dirlik, and the comments above are inspired by a recent review of his in *American Historical Review*, 5 (2010), 1445-7.

89. *Parliamentary Papers. Correspondence with British Ministers and Agents in Foreign Countries, and with Foreign Ministers in England, relating to the Slave Trade. From April 1, 1849, to March 31, 1850 (Presented to both Houses of Parliament by Command of Her Majesty. 1850)*, 6 (also published by Irish University Press in the series Slave Trade, vol. 37, Shannon, 1969).

90. It is true that Denmark (or, if one prefers, Denmark-Norway) abolished the slave trade in 1792, but with effect only from 1802-3 – before Britain. But that prohibition concerned only Danish subjects, with the result that the slave trade went on as before from the Danish establishments. Cf. Ole Feldbæk and Ole Justesen, *Kolonierne i Asien og Afrika* (Copenhagen, 1980), last chapter.

We find it significant that there existed absolutely no abolitionist movement in the eighteenth century in the reputedly most tolerant and most humanitarian of the European countries, namely the Dutch Republic, in contrast to Britain and France. The Netherlands was in fact among the last European states to abolish the slave trade and slavery. Cf. Ernst van den Boogaart, "Books on Black Africa. The Dutch Publications and their owners in the seventeenth and eighteenth centuries", in Beatrix Heintzle and Adam Jones (eds), *European Sources for Sub-Saharan Africa before 1900: Use and Abuse. Paideuma*, vol. 33 (Wiesbaden, 1987), 115-26; Seymour Drescher, "The Long Goodbye: Dutch Capitalism and Antislavery in Comparative Perspective", *American Historical Review*, 1, 99 (1994), 44-69.

91. Tapan Raychaudhuri, *Jan Company in Coromandel 1605–1690: A Study in the Interrelations of European Commerce and Traditional Economies* (The Hague, Martinus Nijhoff, 1962), 164-7.
    The Portuguese apparently had a somewhat similar experience in India. Cf. King/ secretário de Estado, to Viceroy Brazil, Lisbon, 29.5.1731 (OR, vol. 27, doc. 79; reproduced in *Anais/Annaes do Archivo Público da Bahia/Arquivo do Estado da Bahia*, vol.42 [1976], 81).
92. Law (2004a), 14. Other historians who have done field work on the Slave Coast, notably Edna Bay, have come away with the same impression (personal communication, 3 January 2015).
93. *Ibid.*, 148-9. And the treatment of slavery and the slave trade in Agbo's *Histoire*, the – we repeat – leading local traditional history, cannot be described as anything but a gross attempt at falsification. This is the book which has become canonical locally, according to Law (2004a), 66.
94. Notably Robert M. Baum, *Shrines of the Slave Trade. Diola Religion and Society in Precolonial Senegambia* (Oxford University Press, 1999), 97 & 178; Shumway (2011b), 133.
95. Law (2004a), 50.
96. *Ibid.*, 153.
97. See her books *Et si l'Afrique refusait le développement?* (Paris, L'Harmattan, 1991); and *Comment l'Afrique en est arrivée là* (Paris, L'Harmattan, 2011); plus a famous interview with her in *Paris-Match*, 20.8.1992, under the title "L'Afrique serait-elle incurable?"
98. From authors quoted in Jeffrey Gunn, "Creating a Paradox: Quobna Ottobah Cugoano and the Slave Trade's Violation of the Principles of Christianity, Reason, and Property Ownership", *Journal of World History*, vol. 21, 4 (2011), 629-56 (631). Gunn's article provides us with an illuminating account of the arguments in favour of and against slavery and the slave trade in the eighteenth century and earlier.
99. It means having filled up half the expected cargo of slaves. Expression encountered in document 814, dated 1.3.1686 [O.s.] in Law (2001a).
100. Quoted in Emilia Viotti da Costa, "The Portuguese-African Slave Trade. A Lesson in Colonialism", *Latin American Perspectives*, 12, 1 (1985), 41-61 (47).
101. The word is used systematically in the Ordens Régias, as in for instance the one signed in Lisbon on 27 May 1716 (vol. XI, doc. 54). Published in *Anais/Annaes do Archivo Público/do Arquivo do Estado da Bahia, Brazil,* vol. XXI (1949), 314.
    The verb is obviously a hangover from the period when the Portuguese (and other Europeans) did in fact ransom Christian captives in Muslim countries.
102. "Les Nègres…si necessaires pour la culture des sucres, tabacs, cottons, indigos & autres denrées", *Édit du Roy du mois de Mars 1696* (printed). Consulted in AD Loire Atlantique, Nantes (C739).
103. "J'en demande pardon à l'humanité, mais les nègres sont aux cultures de nos colonies ce que les boeufs et les chevaux sont aux cultures d'Europe", Mémoire anonyme ca. 1775 (AN, Colonies F/2a/11).

104. "Este triste, mas necessario commercio"; Conde do Funchal & Linhares to the British Government, Rio 16.11.1811 (OR, vol. 112, doc. 299C, Arquivo (Público) do Estado da Bahia, Brazil).
105. Peter Novick, *That Noble Dream: the "Objectivity Question" and the American Historical Profession* (Cambridge University Press, 1988).
106. Or at the least carry connotations which are not necessarily applicable to Africa of old. Among those who argue the contrary, at least in the case of Dahomey, is Robin Law (1991b), 70-104. Linda Heywood and John Thornton agree with him. See their "Kongo and Dahomey, 1660–1815: African Political Leadership in the Era of the Slave Trade and Its Impact on the Formation of African Identity in Brazil", in Bernard Bailyn and Patricia L. Denault (eds), *Soundings in Atlantic History. Latent Structures and Intellectual Currents, 1500–1830* (Harvard University Press, 2009), 86-111.

A1
THE SLAVE COAST: A GENERAL PRESENTATION

1. The Lower Guinea Coast is usually defined as the region between Cape Mesurado in Liberia and Cameroon or Gabon. The name Guinea was for long synonymous with Black Africa. The English coin known as Guinea was first struck in 1668 by the Royal African Company from gold imported from that coast.
2. Robin Law, *The Slave Coast of West Africa 1550–1750. The Impact of the Atlantic Slave Trade on an African Society* (Oxford University Press, 1991b), 13.
3. James Fairhead and Melissa Leach, *Misreading the African Landscape. Society and Ecology in a Forest-savanna Mosaic* (Cambridge University Press, 1996); Law (1991b), 19.
4. On the climate and the geography in general of the region, cf. in particular Alfred Comlan Mondjannagni, *Campagnes et villes du sud de la République Populaire du Bénin* (Paris/The Hague, Mouton, 1977); André Guilcher, "La région côtière du Bas-Dahomey occidental. Étude de géographie physique et humaine appliquée", *Bulletin de l'IFAN*, série B, XXI, 3-4 (1959).
5. See, for instance, Strikrodt (2003), 28.
6. Excellent map in Larry W. Yarak, *Asante and the Dutch, 1744–1873* (Oxford University Press, 1990), 5.
7. Valentin A. Agbo and Pierre Bediye, "Le plateau Adja", in Jon Daane, Mark Breusers and Erik Frederiks (eds), *Dynamique paysanne sur le plateau Adja du Bénin* (Paris, Karthala, 1997), 29-48, especially 32-9.
8. Robin Law argues that it appeared in print for the first time in the book by the Dane Erich Tilleman published in 1697 and referred to above. See his *The Kingdom of Allada* (Leiden, Research School CNWS, 1997c), 1. Earlier it was called Costa Darida or Costa Arda, Arda being another name for Allada. Cf. Armando Cortesão and A. Teixeira da Mota, *Portugaliae Monumenta Cartographica* (Lisbon, 1960), vol. II, 266 & III, 362.
9. The central work on Oyo remains Robin Law, *The Oyo Empire c.1600–c.1836. A West African Imperialism in the Era of the Atlantic Slave Trade* (Oxford University Press, 1977).

If Law's and my own calculations are anything to go by, Oyo at its greatest extent, in the 1780s, covered a territory one and a half time that of the whole Slave Coast. At that time Oyo embraced roughly half the land area and half the population of Yorubaland, according to J.D.Y. Peel, *Religious Encounter and the Making of the Yoruba* (Notre Dame: Indiana University Press, 2000), 28-9.

10. Main work: Ivor Wilks, *Akwamu 1640–1750. A Study of the Rise and Fall of a West African Empire* (University of Trondheim, 2001), the printed version of a thesis of 1958.

11. The pioneering work on the past of Ketu is E.G. Parrinder, *The Story of Ketu. An Ancient Yoruba Kingdom* (Ibadan University Press, 1956).

    On the Yoruba inside the Slave Coast generally, see Paul Mercier, "Notice sur le peuplement Yoruba au Dahomey-Togo", *Études Dahoméennes*, IV (1950), 29-40.

12. Hounkpatin C. Capo, "Le Gbe est une langue unique", *Africa*, 53, 2 (1983), 47-57. See also his "Elements of Ewe-Gen-Aja-Fon dialectology", in François de Medeiros (ed.), *Peuples du golfe du Bénin. Aja-Ewe* (Paris, Karthala, 1984), 167-78.

13. But if so, one is left with, for instance, the problem of translating the phrase "our Gbe language". Cf. E.Y. Egblewogbe, "The language(s) of the Lower Volta and Yewa area, a problem of classification and terminology", in N.L. Gayibor (ed.), *Toponymie historique et glossonymes actuels de l'ancienne Côte des Esclaves (XVe-XIXe siècle)* (Lomé, Presses de l'Université du Benin, 1990), 103.

14. See the excellent maps in Irene Quaye, "The Ga and their Neighbours 1600–1742" (unpublished PhD thesis, University of Ghana, 1972).

15. Law (1991b), 14.

16. Robert S. Smith, *Kingdoms of the Yoruba* (London, Methuen, 2nd ed., 1976), 77. See also the excellent map in Patrick Manning, *Slavery, Colonialism and Economic Growth in Dahomey, 1640–1960* (Cambridge University Press, 1982), 23.

17. Peel (2000), 29.

18. Dassa-Zoumé, also called Idàìsà, and Savè, Sabi or Sabe. See Abiodun Adediran, "The Formation of the Sabe Kingdom in Central Benin Republic", *Africana Marburgensia*, 16, 2 (1983), 60-74; Bíódún Adédìrán, "Ìdàìsà: The Making of a Frontier Yorùbá State", *Cahiers d'Études Africaines*, XXIV, 1 (1984), 71-85.

19. For a discussion, see the classic work of Robin Horton, "Stateless Societies in the History of West Africa", in Ajayi and Crowder, *History of West Africa*, 87-128.

20. Smith (1978), 78.

21. Jessie Gaston-Mulira, "A History of the Mahi peoples from 1774 to 1920 (Benin)" (PhD thesis, UCLA, 1984); Barbara F. Grimes (ed.), *Ethnologue. Languages of the World* (11th edit., Dallas, 1988), 149-53; Sylvain C. Anignikin, "Histoire des populations mahi. À propos de la controverse sur l'ethnonyme et le toponyme 'Mahi'", *Cahiers d'Études Africaines*, XLI, 2 (2001), 243-65.

22. Paul Nugent, "A Regional Melting Pot: The Ewe and Their Neighbours in the Ghana-Togo Borderlands", in Benjamin Lawrance (ed.), *A Handbook of Eweland: The Ewe of Togo and Benin* (Accra, Woeli, 2005), 29-43 (32); Jean-Claude Froelich, "Les problèmes posés par les refoulés montagnards de culture paléonigritique", *Cahiers d'Études Africaines* V, 3 (1964), 383-99.

See the small, but illustrative map in Lynne Brydon, "Rice, Yams and Chiefs in Avatime: Speculations on the Development of a Social Order", *Africa*, 51, 2 (1981), 659-77 (660).

23. Paul Nugent, "'A Few Lesser Peoples': the Central Togo Minorities and their Ewe Neighbours", in Carola Lentz and Paul Nugent (eds), *Ethnicity in Ghana: The Limits of Invention* (Basingstoke/London, Macmillan, 2000), 162-82 (164).
24. Nicoué Lodjou Gayibor and Angele Aguigah, "Early Settlements and Archaeology of the Adja-Tado Cultural Zone", in Lawrance (2005), 1-14; Brydon (1981).
25. Paul Nugent, *Myths of Origin and the Origin of Myth: Local Politics and the Uses of History in Ghana's Volta Region* (Berlin, Das Arabische Buch, 1997), 2.
26. Egblewogbe (1990), 100.
27. Nugent (2000), 164.
28. Examples in M.A. Kwamena-Poh, *Government and Politics in the Akuapem State 1730–1850* (London, Longman and Evanston: Northwestern University Press, 1973), 46 & 151-4; Quaye (1972), 28 & 93.
29. Inspired by Stephan Bühnen, "Place Names as an Historical Source: An Introduction with Examples from Southern Senegambia and Germany", *History in Africa*, 19 (1992), 45-101. It is the only work of its kind that we know of. Bühnen's pioneering effort has certainly not been followed up as far as the Slave Coast is concerned.
30. I.A. Akinjogbin, *Dahomey and its Neighbours 1708–1818* (Cambridge University Press, 1967) esp. p. 72.
31. Law (2004a), 21-2; R.P. Thomas Moulero, "Histoire et légendes des Djêkens", *Études Dahoméennes* (NS), 8 (1966), 39-56 (43).
32. Law (2004a), 19.
33. *Djè* means salt. But even so the toponym of Djèkin is uncertain. Cf. Josette Rivallain, "Le sel dans les villages côtiers et lagunaires du Bas-Dahomey: sa fabrication, sa place dans le circuit du sel africain", *West African Journal of Archaeology*, 7 (1977), 143-69; A. Félix Iroko, "Le sel marin de la Côte des Esclaves durant la période précoloniale", *Africa* (Rome), XLVI, 4 (1991), 520-40.
34. A. Félix Iroko, *Les Hula du XIVe au XIXe siècle* (Cotonou, 2001), esp. 49; Claude Savary, *La pensée symbolique des Fô. Tableau de la société et étude de la litterature orale d'expression sacrée dans l'ancien royaume du Dahomey* (Geneva, 1976), 150; Roberto Pazzi, "Recherche sur le vocabulaire des langues Evè, Aja, Gèn et Fòn" (Première partie: Lexique des noms) (mimeogr., Lomé, 1976), 75; Strickrodt (2003), 52.
35. William Bosman, *A New and Accurate Description of the Coast of Guinea* (first published in Dutch in 1704; new English edition [Frank Cass], 1967), 368a.
36. Iroko (2001, p. 283) argues that the first Hula villages were among the most ancient human settlements on the coast. And according to Montserrat Palau-Martí, the Hula dominated the coast from the river Volta to Badagry. See her *Le Roi-Dieu au Bénin (Sud Togo, Dahomey, Nigeria occidental)* (Paris, Berger-Levrault, 1964), 96-7. See more generally Luis Nicolau Parés, "The Hula 'Problem': Ethnicity on the Pre-Colonial Slave Coast", in Toyin Falola and Matt D. Childs (eds), *The Changing Worlds of Atlantic Africa. Essays in Honor of Robin Law* (Durham, 2009), 323-46.
37. Salt came from the lagoons whose water was salty, but also from the soil which contained an impressive level of salinity, higher than that of the ocean. Salt extraction

is incidentally very hard work. See Rivallain (1977); Iroko (2001), 253; Strickrodt (2003), 53.
38. A. Félix Iroko, *Mosaïques d'histoire béninoise*, vol. I (Tulle, 1998), 13.
39. Law (2004a), 23.
40. In the colonial period a certain Dagbo Hounon, presented as the priest of Hou (i.e. Hu) was considered to be the chief priest ("*chef supérieur*") of all the local priests ("*féticheurs*") of Ouidah (Agbo, 1959).
41. On Hulagan-Great Popo, see Robin Law, "Les toutes premières descriptions de Petit-Popo par les européens: des années 1680 aux années 1690", in N.L. Gayibor (ed.), *Le tricentenaire d'Aneho et du pays guin*, vol.I (Lomé, Presses de l'Université du Bénin, 2001), 33-58 (34); Strickrodt (2003), 48; Law (1991b), 15-16.
42. Iroko (2001), 106.
43. Paul Isert, *Letters on West Africa and the Slave Trade. Paul Erdmann Isert's Journey to Guinea and the Caribbean Islands in Columbia (1788)*, Selena Winsnes (ed.) and trans. (British Academy/Oxford University Press, 1992), 93-4.
44. Sacred king, according to Iroko (2001), 117-22.
45. Law (1991b), 30.
46. Dahomey had very imprecise and constantly fluctuating borders, like most polities in Africa of old. Exactly which area the kings of Dahomey controlled effectively at any period of time is in fact impossible to determine (50-85 km east-west and 135 km north-south?). Its population has been estimated by various authors as between 150,000 and 200,000 inhabitants. But none offers any supporting evidence, and none indicates with any precision the relevant period.
47. Sandra E. Greene, "Notsie Narratives: History, Memory, and Meaning in West Africa", *South Atlantic Quarterly*, 101-4 (2002), 1015-41, esp. 1016-22.
48. Nugent (2005), 29.
49. Meera Venkatachalam, "Between the Devil and the Cross: Religion, Slavery, and the Making of the Anlo-Ewe", *Journal of African History* 53, 1 (2012), 45-64 (49).
50. *Ibid*.
51. Michel Verdon, *The Abutia Ewe of West Africa. A Chiefdom that Never Was* (Berlin etc., Mouton, 1983), 23; Kate Skinner, "Local Historians and Strangers with Big Eyes: The Politics of Ewe History in Ghana and its Global Diaspora", *History in Africa*, 37 (2010), 125-58 (131).
52. Paul Nugent, "Putting the History Back into Ethnicity: Enslavement, Religion, and Cultural Brokerage in the Construction of Madinka/Jola and Ewe/Agotime Identities in West Africa, c.1650–1930", *Comparative Studies in Society and History*, 50, 4 (2008), 920-48 (935); Ray A. Kea, "Akwamu-Anlo Relations c.1750-1813", *Transactions of the Historical Society of Ghana*, 10 (1969), 29-63 (33).
53. Venkatachalam (2012), 53.
54. See for instance Manning (1982), 24.
55. On Genyi/Glidji, see Nicoué Lodjou Gayibor, "Les origines du Royaume de Glidji", *Annales de l'Université du Bénin, Togo*, III (1976), 75-102; plus many other works by the same author. See also Strickrodt (2003).
56. One of those who believes (or believed?) so is Nicoué Lodjou Gayibor. He has argued that the Benin Gap is the result of human activity. Cf. his "Écologie et histoire: les

origines de la savane du Bénin", *Cahiers d'Études Africaines*, XXVI, 1-2 (1986), 13-41; and "Les origines de la savane du Bénin: une chasse gardée?", *Cahiers d'Études Africaines*, XXXIX, 1 (1989), 137-8.

But Chantal Blanc-Pamard and Pierre Peltre argue that it is at least 20,000 years old. Cf. their "Remarques à propos de 'Ecologie et histoire: les origines de la savane du Bénin'", *Cahiers d'Études Africaines*, XXVII, 3-4 (1987), 419-23. However, Lawrence Barham and Peter Mitchell (*The First Africans. African Archaeology from the Earliest Toolmakers to most Recent Foragers* [Cambridge University Press, 2008], 358) state that what they call the Benin Gap savanna corridor was abruptly reopened some 4,500 to 4,100 years ago.

For a general overview of the question, see Fairhead and Leach (1996), 288.

57. *Ibid.*
58. Stanley B. Alpern, "On the Origins of the Amazons of Dahomey", *History in Africa*, 25 (1998), 9-25; and by the ame author, *Amazons of Black Sparta. The Women Warriors of Dahomey* (New York University Press and London, C. Hurst, 1998).
59. Blanc-Pamard and Peltre (1987), 421.
60. Work by Sharon Nicholson and G.Brooks, quoted in Emmanuel Kwaku Akyeampong, *Between the Sea and the Lagoon. An Eco-Social History of the Anlo of Southeastern Ghana, c.1850 to Recent Times* (Ohio University Press/Oxford, James Currey, 2001), 32; Fairhead and Leach (1996), 50.
61. Verena Pfeiffer, *Agriculture au Sud-Bénin: Passé et perspectives* (Paris, L'Harmattan, 1988), 78; Mondjannagni (1977).

    On the ravages of the thunderstorms in Ouidah in the eighteenth century, cf. for example: "à M. Gourg, Versailles 8 Xbre [December] 1787" (AN Colonies, B-196).
62. Hans Christian Monrad, *Bidrag til en Skildring af Guinea-kysten og dens Indbyggere* (etc) (Copenhagen, 1822). English version by Selena Axelrod Winsnes in *Two views from Christiansborg Castle, vol. II: A Description of the Guinea Coast and its Inhabitants* (Accra, Sub-Saharan Publishers, 2009), 178 & 200-1. There is a long description in Robert Norris, *Memoirs of the Reign of Bossa Ahádee, King of Dahomey. To which are added, the Author's Journey to Abomey, the Capital; and a Short Account of the African Slave Trade* (1789, reprinted London [Frank Cass] 1968), 112-18.
63. J.A Skertchly, *Dahomey as it is* (London, Chapman and Hall, 1874), 40. See also M'Leod (1820/1971), 21; etc.
64. Letters signed Carter from Whidah [Ouidah] 28.12.1685, 1.3.1686 & 6.1.1686/7 [O.s.], in Robin Law, (ed.), *The English in West Africa, 1691–1699. The Local Correspondence of the Royal African Company of England 1681–1699*, Part 3 (Oxford University Press/British Academy, 2006), documents 813, 814 & 822; Law, "West Africa's Discovery of the Atlantic", *International Journal of African Historical Studies*, 1, 44 (2011), esp. p. 8.
65. Bosman (1704/1967), 328; E.N. Boris et al. from Christiansborg, 14.11.1739, in Ole Justesen (ed.), *Danish Sources for the History of Ghana 1657–1754*, 2 volumes (Copenhagen, 2005), 558.
66. Guilcher (1959), 362 & 413.
67. B.K. Drake argues that they did not care anyway. See his "The Liverpool-African Voyage c.1790–1807: Commercial Problems", in R.Anstey & P.E.H. Hair (eds),

Liverpool, the Atlantic Slave Trade, and Abolition. Essays to Illustrate Current Knowledge (Historic Society of Lancashire and Cheshire, Occasional Series, vol. 2, 1976), 126-56 (132).

68. To state the obvious, and in the words of Postma, "the slave trade was a very complex and risky business with a variety of unpredictable forces that could influence its outcome"; Johannes Menne Postma, *The Dutch in the Atlantic Slave Trade 1600-1815* (Cambridge University Press, 1990), 253.

   But the slave traders knew well the timetable of it all, as demonstrated by Bosman (1704/1967, 748). He advised to leave Europe not later than 10-15 Sept, because then it was possible to reach the Americas by the end of April – the sugar-making season – and to leave before the hurricane season set in. The problem is whether they were able to keep to that timetable.

69. Gayibor (1986), 17.
70. Akyeampong (2001), 1; G.K. Nukunya, "The Land and the People", in Francis Agbodeka (ed.), *A Handbook of Eweland vol. I: The Ewes of Southeastern Ghana* (Accra, Woeli, 1997), 8-13.
71. For a general discussion, see Law (1991b), 13-32; Strickrodt (2003), 32-4; Jean M. Grove and A.M. Johansen, "The Historical Geography of the Volta Delta, Ghana, during the period of Danish Influence", *Bulletin de l'IFAN*, série B, XXX, 4 (1968) 1376-1421.
72. Guilcher (1959), 410.
73. "A sandy, swampy island of only about two square miles in size": Kristin Mann, *Slavery and the Birth of an African City. Lagos, 1760–1900* (Indiana University Press, 2007), 23. Mann's is the standard work on the history of Lagos.
74. Ryder (1969), 158. More generally, see Sandra T. Barnes, "The Economic Significance of Inland Coastal Fishing in Seventeenth-Century Lagos", in Falola and Childs (2009), 51-66 (53).
75. Blocked by a sand bank which was there in the eighteenth century (and earlier) and which has not moved since. See "Description nautique de la Côte d'Afrique" (op. cit.); Edward Bold, *The Merchant's and Mariner's African Guide; Containing an Accurate Description of the Coast, Bays, Harbours, and Adjacent Islands of West Africa (etc)* (London, 1819, republished in Salem, US, 1823), 64-5.

   Little Popo is often called Pichaninee Popo in the English sources, from the Portuguese *pequeno*, meaning precisely "little".

76. Guilcher (1959), 384-5 & 412.
77. Note that "Wetlands and shallow lakes are among the most productive ecosystems in the world per unit of surface area. The more productive an ecosystem, the more biomass humans can appropriate from it for food, fiber, fuel, construction materials, and medicines without negatively affecting the system's function". Quotation from Vera Candiani, "The Desagüe Reconsidered: Environmental Dimensions of Class Conflict in Colonial Mexico", *Hispanic American Historical Review*, 92, 1 (2012), 5-39 (21).
78. Robin Law, "Between the Sea and the Lagoons: The Interaction of Maritime and Inland Navigation on the Precolonial Slave Coast", *Cahiers d'Études Africaines*, XXIX, 2 (1989a), 222.

79. *Ibid.*, 214; Robert S. Smith, "The Canoe in West African History", *Journal of African History*, XI, 4 (1970), 518; Thomas Birch Freeman, *Journal of Various Visits to the Kingdoms of Ashanti, Aku, and Dahomi, in Western Africa* (London, second ed. 1844, third ed., 1968), 278.
80. Nicoué Lodjou Gayibor, "Esquisse d'une histoire économique des Ewe de l'ère précoloniale", *Annuaire de l'Université du Bénin, Togo*, V (1978), 129-44 (131).
81. Norris (1789/1968), 80-81; Law (1991b), 19-20; Édouard Dunglas, *Contribution à l'histoire du Moyen-Dahomey* (2 vols. of *Études Dahoméennes*, 1957), 84; A. Aubréville, "Les forêts du Dahomey et du Togo", *Bulletin du Comité d'Études Historiques et Scientifiques de l'Afrique Occidentale Française*, XX, 1-2 (1937), 1-112.
82. Mondjannagni (1977), 211.
83. "...a more fertile soil [than the one in Hueda/Ouidah], and one more abounding in rich and healthy plantations, I have never seen", one European commented. B. Cruickshank: report on a Mission to the King of Dahomey, 19.11.1848 (*Parliamentary Papers*, 1850, IX, 534-5). See also Pruneau de Pommegorge (1789), 204 & 236.
84. Pfeiffer (1988), 63.
85. "The country being very populous & till the ground three times every year for corn for their subsistance" (Ambrose Baldwyn & co. from Whydah [Ouidah], 28.3.1723 [O.s.] [NA T70/7]).
86. James Houstoun, *Some New and Accurate Observations, Geographical, Natural and Historical, Containing a True and Impartial Account of the Situation, Product, and Natural History of the Coast of Guinea (etc)* (London, 1725), 26.
87. William O. Jones quoted in Stanley B. Alpern, "Exotic Plants of Western Africa: Where They Came from and When", *History in Africa*, 35 (2008), 63-102 (64).
88. Nadia Lowell, "The Watchi-Ewe: Histories and Origins", in Lawrance (2005), 90-114.
89. Jouke S. Wigboldus, "Trade and Agriculture in Coastal Benin c.1470–1600: an Examination of Manning's Early-growth Thesis", *Afdeling Agrarische Geschiedenis. Bijdragen* (Agricultural University of Wageningen), vol. 28 (1986), 299-383 (337-8).
90. São Tomé has been qualified by Stanley Alpern as "a veritable agricultural experiment station". See his "The European Introduction of Crops into West Africa in Precolonial Times", *History in Africa*, 19 (1992), 13-43. See also Wigboldus (1986), 353.
91. Alpern (2008), 69; Bosman (1704/1967), letter 2 & page 645; Wigboldus (1986), 330-53; etc.
92. Bosman (1704/1967), 31-2. As for Alexis Adande, he argues that there was a great famine on the Central Slave Coast in 1682 (before the real take-off of maize?). See his "Togudo-Awude, capitale de l'ancien royaume d'Allada. Étude d'une cité précoloniale d'après les sources orales, écrites et les données de l'archéologie" (Thesis Université de Paris, Panthéon-Sorbonne, 1984) 312.
93. See especially, Journal de navigation du sieur Joseph Crassous de Médeuil (op. cit.); Gourg, "Mémoire", Juda [Ouidah] 12.5.1785 (AN, Colonies C6-26, d.63).
94. Phillips (1732), 215-16; Bosman (1704/1967), 390; Pires (1957), 29; Johann Peter Oettinger's account of his voyage to Guinea 1692-93, in Jones (1985), 180-98; Adams (1823/1966), 67; *Barbot on Guinea*, 634; Abraham Du Port from Whydah (Ouidah) 11.11.1727 (O.s.), in Law (1990a), 12.

95. Especially Archibald Dalzel – see the many letters from him in the Edinburgh University Library, Dk.7 52, some quoted in I.A. Akinjogbin, "Archibald Dalzel: Slave Trader and Historian of Dahomey", *Journal of African History*, VII,1 (1966), 67-78. See also Isert (1788/1992), 2.
96. Smith (1744/1967, 194-5): "the real beauty of this country...All who have ever been here, allow this to be one of the most delightful countries in the world". Bosman (1704/1967, 339): "the most charming place that imagination can represent".

    See also Isert (1788/1992), 104-5; William Snelgrave, *A New Account of some Parts of Guinea, and the Slave Trade (etc)* (London 1734, new impression, F. Cass, 1971), 3; Phillips (1732), 214; Dralsé de Grand-Pierre, *Relation de divers voyages faits dans l'Amérique et aux Indes occidentales* (Paris, 1718), 164-71; Relation du Royaume de Judas en Guinée (op. cit.); and many others.
97. Houstoun (1725), 26-7.
98. *Ibid.*, 34.
99. The quotation is from Tattersfield (1991), 107. Other examples in Per O. Hernæs, "Den Balstyrige Bergenser på Gullkysten", *Norsk Sjøfartsmuseum. Årsberetning 1995* (Oslo, 1996), 127-38; Davies (1957); document 819 dated 22.11.1686 [O. s.] in Law (2001a); Monrad (1822/2009), 202-3; letter from William's Fort 25.5.1715 [Old style] (NA T70/3).
100. Postma (1990), 65.
101. Tattersfield (1991), 85-107; A.F.C. Ryder, "The re-establishment of Portuguese factories on the Costa da Mina to the mid-eighteenth century", *Journal of the Historical Society of Nigeria*, II, 3 (1958), 157-83.
102. So called by Monrad (1822/2009), 264.
103. Davies (1957), 83 & 97-8. Davies adds that between 1684 and 1732, among the shore-based English personnel in West Africa, well over half died in the first year and only one in ten got back to England.
104. Various letters from 1680-81 in Robin Law (ed), *Correspondence from the Royal African Company's Factories at Offra and Whydah on the Slace Coast of West Africa in the Public Record Office, London 1678-93* (Centre of African Studies, Edinburgh Univerity, 1990a) 14-18 & 26-7; Carter, Whiddah [Ouidah], 11.11.1686 & 16.3.1687, in Law (2006), 333 & 342.
105. Postma (1990), 65.
106. Both titles are used in the sources, also that of chief. They seem to have been interchangeable.
107. Akinjogbin (1967), 70-71; Examination of William Devaynes by the African Committee, 22.3.1788 (NA BT 6/9).
108. Akinjogbin (1967), 218-9.
109. Hernæs (1996).
110. For example, David Henley and Ian Caldwell (eds), *Stranger-kings in Indonesia and Beyond*. Special issue of *Indonesia and the Malay World* (vol. 36, No. 105, July 2008).
111. Law (2011), 10ff.

A2
HISTORIOGRAPHY, SOURCES AND EPISTEMOLOGY

1. Philip D. Curtin, *The Atlantic Slave Trade. A Census* (University of Wisconsin Press, 1969).
2. See footnote 1 in the Introduction.
3. It is true that "the facts speak only when the historian calls on them: it is he who decides to which facts to give the floor and in what order" (E.H. Carr, *What is History?* [London, 1990], 11). Yes, but Carr refers here to a situation where there is an abundance of facts and where the role of the historian becomes to pick and choose. It is a luxury denied to many.
4. Manning (1982).
5. Wigboldus (1986), 299-383.
6. *The History of Dahomy, an Inland Kingdom of Africa. Compiled from Authentic Memoirs* (London 1793, 2nd edition, with a new introduction by J.D. Fage, Frank Cass, 1967), XI. The title is rather strange, since Dahomey was no longer exclusively an inland polity in Dalzel's time.
7. Patrick Manning, "The Slave Trade in the Bight of Benin, 1640–1890", in H. Gemery and J. Hogendorn (eds), *The Uncommon Market. Essays in the Economic History of the Atlantic Slave Trade* (New York, 1979), 107-41 (129).
8. Nadia Lowell, "The Watchi-Ewe: Histories and Origins", in Benjamin Lawrance (ed.), *A Handbook of Eweland: The Ewe of Togo and Benin* (Accra, Woeli, 2005), 97.
9. Lionel Abson from Whydah [Ouidah] 24.10.1770 (NA T70/31).
10. Rank list 1795 (NA T70/1606); Law (2004a), 75. Abson was one of the very few Europeans who became fluent in Gbe.
11. James A. Rawley, "Further Light on Archibald Dalzel", *International Journal of African Historical Studies*, 17, 2 (1984), 317-23; Loren K. Waldman, "An Unnoticed Aspect of Archibald Dalzel's the History of Dahomey", *Journal of African History*, VI, 2 (1965), 185-92.
12. I.A Akinjogbin, "Agaja and the Conquest of the Coastal Aja States 1724–30", *Journal of the Historical Society of Nigeria*, II, 4 (1963), 74-6.
13. See, for instance, Dalzel's sober testimony to the African Committee in April 1788: "The Examination of A.Dalzel. by the Committee of the Company of Merchants trading to Africa" (often called the African Committee) 5-8.4.1788 (NA, BT 6/10).
14. Including those in the Birmingham Central Library (the Galton Family Papers) and, as already noted, in the Edinburgh University Library.
15. An excellent summary of the controversy in Thomas Constantine Maroukis, "Warfare and Society in the Kingdom of Dahomey: 1818–1894" (unpublished PhD Thesis, Boston University 1974), 2.
16. Pruneau (1789).
17. I.A Akinjogbin, *Dahomey and its Neighbours 1708–1818* (Cambridge University Press, 1967).
18. *Ibid.*, 15-17.
19. P.C. Lloyd, "Sacred Kingship and Government among the Yoruba", *Africa*, 30, 3 (1960), 221-37 (225).

20. Theory first put forward in Akinjogbin's, "Agaja and the Conquest of the Coastal Aja States 1724–30", *Journal of the Historical Society of Nigeria*, II, 4 (1963), 545-66. Akinjogbin admitted at least that Dahomey took part in the slave trade, whereas Dov Ronen states flatly (and absurdly) that "Dahomey was *not* a slave trading state". See his "On the African Role in the Trans-Atlantic Slave Trade in Dahomey", *Cahiers d'Études Africaines*, XI, 1 (1971), 5-13 (13).
21. Akinjogbin (1967), 34.
22. Lisa A. Lindsay, "Extraversion, Creolization, and Dependency in the Atlantic Slave Trade", *Journal of African History*, 55, 2 (2014), 133-45.
23. Based on three articles by Robin Law: "King Agaja of Dahomey, the Slave Trade, and the Question of West African Plantations: the Mission of Bulfinch Lambe and Adomo Tomo to England, 1726–32", *Journal of Imperial and Commonwealth History*, 19, 2 (1991), 137-63; "Further Light on Bulfinch Lambe and the 'Emperor of Pawpaw': King Agaja of Dahomey's Letter to King George I of England, 1726", *History in Africa*, 17 (1990), 211-26; "An Alternative Text of King Agaja of Dahomey's Letter to King George I of England, 1726", *History in Africa*, 29 (2002), 257-71.
24. John Atkins (*A Voyage to Guinea, Brasil, and the West Indies; in His Majesty's Ships, the Swallow and Weymouth*, 1735, London, new impression [F. Cass], 1970, 122), argued that Agaja's aim was to stop raids on his own people. Atkins and Pruneau de Pommegeorge were the only convinced Abolitionists among the early writers.
25. See for instance Rodney's famous book *How Europe Underdeveloped Africa* (London, 1972); and Basil Davidson's *Black Mother* (Boston, 1961).
26. Akinjogbin (1967), 26-37.
27. First formulated in his review of Akinjogbin's book in *Journal of the Historical Society of Nigeria*, IV, 2 (1968), 344-7; and elaborated upon in his "The Fall of Allada, 1724 – an Ideological Revolution?", *ibid.*, V, 1 (1969), 157-63. It is true that Law expressed himself somewhat more cautiously in his 1991 book.
28. A.I. Asiwaju and Robin Law, "From the Volta to the Niger, c.1600–1800", in Ajayi & Crowder (1985), 412-64 (455). The hypothesis of continuity between Allada and Dahomey especially has been defended by such authors as Montserrat Palau-Martí, Dov Ronen and W.J. Argyle.
29. According to her, "what seems to have been unique in Dahomey will often be found to be an intensification of common practices, or subtle alterations in institutions known elsewhere (in West Africa)": Edna G. Bay, *Wives of the Leopard. Gender, Politics, and Culture in the Kingdom of Dahomey* (University of Virginia Press, 1998), 4.
30. Robin Law, "Warfare on the West African Slave Coast, 1650-1850", in R. Brian Ferguson and Neil L. Whitehead (eds), *War in the Tribal Zone: Expanding States and Indigenous Warfare* (Santa Fe, 1992), 103-26; Law (1991b), 347-8.
31. *Ibid.*, 349.
32. *Ibid.*, 330-31.
33. J. Cameron Monroe, "Building the State in Dahomey: Power and Landscape in the Bight of Benin", in J. Cameron Monroe and Akinwurai Ogundiran (eds), *Power and Landscape in Atlantic West Africa. Archaeological Perspectives* (Cambridge University Press, 2012), 191-221 (192).

34. "Banditti" according to Frederick E. Forbes (*Dahomey and the Dahomans. Being the Journals of two Missions to the King of Dahomey and Residence at his Capital in the Years 1849 and 1850*, [London, 1851]), I, 19. David Ross agrees. See his "The Anti-Slave Trade Theme in Dahomean History: An Examination of the Evidence", *History in Africa*, IX (1982), 263-71; and "European Models and West African History: further Comments on the Recent Historiography of Dahomey", *History in Africa*, X (1983), 293-305.
35. A central thesis in Akinjogbin (1967).
36. Theme discussed in Finn Fuglestad, "Quelques réflexions sur l'histoire et les institutions de l'ancien royaume du Dahomey et de ses voisins", *Bulletin de l'IFAN*, 39, 2 (1977), 493-517.
37. Jacques Lombard, "The Kingdom of Dahomey", in D. Forde and P.M. Kaberry (eds), *West African Kingdoms in the Nineteenth Century* (London, 1967), 70-92 (81).
38. As Edna Bay (1998, 130) has put it: "the Dahomean armed forces were beaten ignominiously and more than once, when they faced foes of roughly equal strength" – and even, in our opinion, of inferior strength.
39. Richard F. Burton, *A Mission to Gelele, King of Dahomey (etc)* (1864/1966), II, 231. Dahomey's limited achievements have also been underlined by Thomas C. Maroukis, "Dahomian Warfare and the Slave Trade", paper presented at the African Studies Association Convention, New Orleans 22-26.11.1985, 5.
    Or as a French official argued already in 1777, the Dahomeans "n'ont jamais été puissants, quelques actions éclatantes du grand-père de ce roy [i.e. Agaja and Kpengla respectively] leur ont donné une réputation qui fait toute leur force" (Levet de Juda [Ouidah] 6.10.1777 [AN C6-26]).
40. Lombard (1967), 89.
41. Matt D. Childs and Toyin Falola, "Introduction: Robin Law and African Historiography", Falola & Childs (2009), 1-28 (1).
42. Law (1991b), 11.
43. Law, *ibid.*, 8.
44. Examples mentioned in Albert van Dantzig (1986), 257; Justesen (2005), 354-5, 361 & 369; and Stephen D. Behrendt, "The Journal of an African Slaver, 1789-1792, and the Gold Coast Slave Trade of William Collow", *History in Africa*, 22 (1995), 61-71.
45. Albert van Dantzig, "Willem Bosman's *New and Accurate Description of the Coast of Guinea*: How Accurate is it?" *History in Africa*, 1 (1974), 101-8.
46. Ernst van den Boogaart, "Books on Black Africa. The Dutch Publications and their owners in the seventeenth and eighteenth centuries", in Beatrix Heintze and Adam Jones (eds), *European Sources for Sub-Saharan Africa before 1900: Use and Abuse. Paideuma*, vol. 33 (Wiesbaden, 1987), 117.
47. Selena Axelrod Winsnes, "P.E. Isert in German, French, and English: A Comparison of Translations", *HA*, 19 (1992), 401-10.
48. See the pertinent discussion in David Henige, "The Race is not Always to the Swift. Thoughts on the Use of Written Sources for the Study of Early African History", in Heintzle & Jones (1987), 53-79.
49. In Sandoval's case the slaves he worked among in Cartagena de las Indias. Alonso de Sandoval (1576–1652), *De Instauranda Aethiopum Salute* (Seville, 1627). New

edition: *Un tratado sobre la esclavitud* (Introducción, transcripción y traducción de Enriqueta Vila Vilar), (Madrid, Alianza Editorial, 1987).

50. Editors' Introduction to *Barbot on Guinea*, pp. XIV & XLIII.
51. See her "On the Trail of the Bush King: A Dahomean Lesson in the Use of Evidence", *History in Africa*,, 6 (1979), 1-15 (2).
52. Quoted in Editors' Introduction, *Barbot on Guinea*, p. XCVIII.
53. In our case, especially those of Argyle and Herskovits, as we shall see.
54. Robin Law, "'Legitimate' Trade and Gender Relations in Yorubaland and Dahomey", in the book edited by him: *From Slave Trade to 'Legitimate' Commerce. The Commercial Transition in Nineteenth-century West Africa* (Cambridge University Press, 1995), 195-214 (195).
55. An idea of the problem is given by Suzanne Preston Blier, "Field Days: Melville J. Herskovits in Dahomey", *History in Africa*, 16 (1989), 1-22.
56. It has resulted in his monumental *Flux et Reflux...* (1968).
57. Many of these duplicates, and other documents in Lisbon, have been printed, although often in abridged form, in *Inventario dos documentos relativos ao Brasil existentes no Archivo de Marinha e Ultramar de Lisboa* (organisado para a Biblioteca Nacional do Rio de Janeiro por Eduardo de Castro e Almeida), five volumes (1913–1918). Quite a few relevant documents have also been printed in the *Anais/Annaes do Archivo Público/do Arquivo do Estado da Bahia*.
58. See for instance Kenneth G. Kelly, "The Archaeology of African-European Interaction: Investigating the Social Roles of Trade, Traders, and the Use of Space in the Seventeenth- and Eighteenth-Century Hueda Kingdom, Republic of Bénin", *World Archaeology*, 28, 3 (1997b), 351-69; and Kelly (1997a); Neil L. Norman, "Hueda (Whydah) Country and Town: Archaeological Perspectives on the Rise and Collapse of an African Atlantic Kingdom", *International Journal of African Historical Studies*, 42, 3 (2009), 387-410.
59. Main work: Klavs Randsborg and Inga Merkyte et al., *Bénin Archaeology. The Ancient Kingdoms*, 2 vols (Oxford, Wiley-Blackwell, 2009 [*Acta Archaeologica* Vols.80-1 & 2 & *Acta Archaeologica* Supplementa XI).
60. Robert Durand, "Journal de bord d'un négrier, 1731–1732"; in Beinecke Library, Yale, Gen. Mss. vol. 7; as indicated in Harms (2002). But Harms has unfortunately not deemed it necessary so far to follow in the footsteps of Law, that is, to present us with a scholarly published edition of the document.
61. According to Justesen (2005, p. V), those who do not have a thorough knowledge of the Danish language in the period, and who have not the opportunity to take a crack course in palaeography, are faced with an impossible task.
62. The Dutchman Albert van Dantzig tells us comfortingly that the Dutch archives are unreadable for those of us who have not had a Dutch upbringing. Cf. his "The Furley Collection. Its Value and Limitations for the Study of Ghana's History"; in Heintzle & Jones (1987), 423-32 (428).
63. Albert van Dantzig, *The Dutch and the Guinea Coast, 1674–1742: A Collection of Documents from the General State Archive at the Hague* (Accra, Academy of Arts and Sciences, 1978); Justesen (2005). Adam Jones has done the same for a number of relevant German sources.

64. The quotation is from Bulfinch Lambe, reproduced in William Smith, *A New Voyage to Guinea* (1744/1967), 182.
65. Karl Polanyi, with Abraham Rotstein, *Dahomey and the Slave Trade. An Analysis of an Archaic Economy* (Seattle, University of Washington Press, 1966), page XX.
66. "Literacy was...viewed with grave suspicion by the Asante state", according to T.C. McCaskie, *State and Society in Pre-Colonial Asante* (Cambridge University Press, 1995, paperback edit. 2002), 9. And McCaskie added that the introduction of unauthorized use of a foreign fashion, in thought or behaviour, was a capital offence (*ibid.*, 100).

    This recalls the Dane H.C. Monrad's famous point about the two gifts that the Africans and the Europeans received, according to the people of the Gold Coast: "The gift...which fell to the Whites contained books (etc) [whereas the gift which fell to the Africans did not]. Nonetheless, by no means do (the Negroes) envy (the Europeans this gift) – they do not...covet it, but exist, in general, very happy in their own sphere" (Monrad [1822/2009], 33).
67. Edouard Foà, *Le Dahomey* (1895), 173.
68. Underlined by Dalzel in his examination by the African Committee in April 1788 (*op. cit.*).
69. Réflexions sur Juda, 1776 (*op. cit.*), 15; M'Leod (1820/1971), 29; Isert (1788/1992), 104.
70. The best-known case is that of the Merina kingdom of Madagascar in the nineteenth century. Cf. Solofo Randrianja and Stephen Ellis, *Madagascar: A Short History* (London & Chicago, 2009).
71. Verger (1966), 60. The many Portuguese prisoners the kings of Dahomey came to keep do not seem to have been employed in any concrete or practical way.
72. Throughout the eighteenth century not one Dahomean was trained in Europe or in São Tomé, according to Akinjogbin (1967), 210.
73. Kenneth Kelly, "Indigenous Responses to Colonial Encounters on the West African Coast: Hueda and Dahomey from the Seventeenth through Nineteenth Centuries", in Claire L. Lyons and John K. Papadopoulos (eds), *The Archaeology of Colonialism* (Los Angeles, Getty Research Institute, 2002), 96-120 (115).
74. If something was not tried, or was not known to his father or grandfathers, our African will reject it, it was said: Aarestrup, Biørn, J.M. Kjøge, J. Gjønge, Rasmussen: "Nogle bidrag til Kundskab om den danske strækning på Guinea Kysten. Christiansborg 8.6.1774", in *Arkiv for Statistik, politik og Huusholdningsvidenskaber* (Udgivet af [edited by] Prof. Friderik Thaarup), vol. III (Kjøbenhavn/Copenhagen, 1797–8), 161-92 (191).

    Or as Monsieur Gourg, Director of the French fort in Ouidah-Glehue in the 1780s, expressed it rather crudely: they believe that the spirits (*fétiches*) will kill them if they innovate (Gourg de Juda, 24.1.1789 [AN C6-26, d.111]).
75. Short story from 1888, made into a film by John Huston in 1975.
76. According to Tom McCaskie who talks about the staggering wealth and diversity of Denkyira and Asante traditions, possibly unrivalled in West Africa. See his "Denkyira in the Making of Asante c.1660–1720", *Journal of African History*, 48, 1 (2007) 1-25 (4 & 25).

77. Compare this with Fanteland and John Kofi Fynn's seven-volume *Oral Traditions of Fante States*, published 1974–76, according to Shumway (2011a), 210.
78. Samuel Johnson, *The History of the Yorubas, from the Earliest Times to the Beginning of the British Protectorate* (London, G. Routledge, 1921; but written in 1897).
79. Manning (1979), 112.
80. David Henige talked already in his 1987 article (p. 74) of "the impending demise of much oral historiography because of the impossibility of testing its conclusions". Another central article which abounds impactingly in the same sense is Donald R. Wright, "Requiem for the Use of Oral Tradition to Reconstruct the Precolonial History of the Lower Gambia", *History in Africa*, 18 (1991), 399-408.
81. Bay (1998), 38.
82. Robin Law, "History and Legitimacy: Aspects of the Use of the Past in Precolonial Dahomey", *History in Africa*, 15 (1988), 431-56 (437).
83. Auguste Le Hérissé, *L'Ancien Royaume du Dahomey. Moeurs, religion, histoire* (Paris, E. Larose, 1911).
84. Bay (1998), 38.
85. Law (1988), 434.
86. On Le Hérissé, see Bay (1998), 32; Stanley B. Alpern, "On the Origins of the Amazons of Dahomey", *History in Africa*, 25 (1998a), 11, footnote 14.
87. Le Hérissé (1911), 3 & 273; Law (1988), 431.
88. *Kpo*=leopard, *ji*= to give birth or to engender, *to*= agent; according to her (1998), 72).
89. *Ibid.*, 71-80.
90. Edna G. Bay, "Belief, Legitimacy and the *Kpojito*: An Institutional History of the 'Queen Mother' in Precolonial Dahomey", *Journal of African History*, 35, 1 (1995), 1-27 (1).
91. Inspired by Claude-Hélène Perrot, "La fête d'Adjahouto à Allada (Dahomey) et ses enseignements historiques", *Annales de l'Université d'Abidjan*, série I, t.I (1972), 132-49.
92. Finn Fuglestad, "The Trevor-Roper Trap or the Imperialism of History. An Essay", *History in Africa*, 19 (1992), 309-26.
93. Paul Nugent, "Putting the History Back into Ethnicity: Enslavement, Religion, and Cultural Brokerage in the Construction of Madinka/Jola and Ewe/Agotime Identities in West Africa, c.1650–1930", *Comparative Studies in Society and History*, 50, 4 (2008), 934.
94. So also does Ross (1983).
95. Akinjogbin (1967), 25.
96. *Ibid.*, 118.
97. Robert Norris, *Memoirs of the Reign of Bossa Ahádee, King of Dahomey. To which are added, the Author's Journey to Abomey, the Capital; and a Short Account of the African Slave Trade* (1789/1968), 1-2.
98. Maurice Ahanhanzo Glélé, *Le Danxome du pouvoir aja à la nation fon* (Paris, 1974) 166-80.
99. John C. Yoder, "Fly and Elephant Parties. Political Polarization in Dahomey, 1840-1870", *Journal of African History*, 15, 3 (1974), 417-43.

100. J. Cameron Monroe, "Continuity, Revolution or Evolution on the Slave Coast of West Africa? Royal Architecture and Political Order in Precolonial Dahomey", *Journal of African History*, 48, 3 (2007), 349-73. See also his "Dahomey and the Atlantic Slave Trade. Archaeology and Political Order on the Bight of Benin", in Akinwumi Ogundiran and Toyin Falola (eds), *Archaeology of Atlantic Africa and the African Diaspora* (Indiana University Press, 2007), 10. But Monroe may well be correct when he argues that Dahomey significantly expanded state control throughout its territory during the eighteenth and nineteenth centuries.
101. Law (1991b), 330.
102. Point elaborated upon in Fuglestad, *The Ambiguities of History. The Problem of Ethnocentrism in Historical Writing* (Oslo Academic Press, 2005).
103. Joyce Appleby, "The Power of History", *American Historical Review*, 103, 1 (1998), 1-14.
104. Inspired by the works of the Austrian historian Otto Brunner as summarized in Steffen Patzold, "Le 'premier âge féodal' vu d'Allemagne. Essai sur les historiographies française et allemande", in Dominique Iogna-Prat, Michel Lauwers, Florian Mazel and Isabelle Rosé (eds), *Cluny. Les moines et la société au premier âge féodal* (Presses Universitaires de Rennes, 2013), 19-29.
105. Notably Peter Charles Hoffer, *The Historians' Paradox: The Study of History in Our Time* (New York University Press, 2008).
106. The classic extreme example of the contrary is Renaissance Italy. See Paula Findlen, "Possessing the Past: The Material World of the Italian Renaissance", *American Historical Review*, 103, 1 (1998), 83-114.
107. Here we have allowed ourselves to plagiarize E.P. Thompson's famous *The Making of the English Working Class* (first publ. 1963, Penguin ed., 1991), 257 & 542.
108. Igor Kopytoff, "The Internal African Frontier: The Making of African Political Culture", in the book edited by him: *The African Frontier. The Reproduction of Traditional African Societies* (Indiana University Press, 1987), 3-84 (78).

A3
SOCIETAL, RELIGIOUS AND POLITICAL STRUCTURES: A MODEL

1. Dalzel (1793/1967), VI.
2. Examination of A. Dalzel/Dalzell by the African Committee 5-8.4.1788 (*op. cit.*).
3. "Ce pays sans ombre de religion"; Lettre de Juda, 17.1.1734 (AN C6-25, d.152)- a typical utterance.
4. "The Negroes recognize, without exception, a Supreme Being" (Monrad [1822/2009], 32); "ils croient tous à...l'existence d'un être suprême, immense, infini, créateur de tout (mais) trop grand pour se mêler de regir le monde" ("Réflexions sur Juda", 1776 [*op. cit.*], 73-4).
5. See his, "For Marx but with Reservations about Althusser: A Comment on Bernstein and Depelchin", *History in Africa*, 8 (1981), 247-51; and "In Search of a Marxist Perspective on Pre-Colonial Tropical Africa", *Journal of African History*, 19, 3 (1978), 441-52.
6. We have tried to substantiate this point in a number of works: "A Reconsideration of Hausa history before the Jihad", *Journal of African History*, XIX, 3 (1978), 319-

7. Madeline Manoukian, *The Ewe-speaking Peoples of Togoland and the Gold Coast* (London, IAI Ethnographic Survey of Africa, 1952), 46 (based on the works of Jacob Spieth).

   (continuing note 6): 39; "Earth-priests, 'Priest-Chiefs', and Sacred Kings in Ancient Norway, Iceland and West Africa. A Comparative Essay", *Scandinavian Journal of History*, IV, 1 (1979), 47-74; "The 'tompon-tany' and the 'tompon-drano' in the History of Central and Western Madagascar", *History in Africa*, IX (1982), 61-76 (written with the assistance of Stephen Ellis); "Precolonial Subsaharan Africa and the Ancient Norse World: Looking for Similarities", *History in Africa*, vol. 33, (2006), 179-203. Plus the 1977 and 2005 works, and some works in Norwegian.
8. Gaston Mulira (1984), 17.
9. O.B. Lawuyi, "The Obatala Factor in Yoruba History", *History in Africa*, 19 (1992), 369-75 (373).
10. Roberto Pazzi, "Recherche sur le vocabulaire des langues Evè, Aja, Gèn et Fòn" (Première partie: Lexique des noms) (1976), 78.
11. Bay (1998), 132-3; Paul Hazoumé, *Le pacte de sang au Dahomey* (Paris, Institut d'Ethnologie, 1937; reprinted 1956), 19-26, 57; Suzanne Preston Blier, "Razing the Roof: The Imperative of Building Destruction in Danhomè (Dahomey)", in Tony Atkin and Joseph Rykwert (eds), *Structure and Meaning in Human Settlements* (Philadelphia, 2005), 165-84 (180).
12. Brodie Cruickshank, *Eighteen Years on the Gold Coast of Africa* (London, 1853; 2nd ed., Frank Cass, 1966), 173. And of course competition for power (in Anlo) was waged in part on a spiritual battlefield: Sandra E. Greene, *Gender, Ethnicity, and Social Change on the Upper Slave Coast. A History of the Anlo-Ewe* (Portsmouth, NH and London, Heinemann and J. Currey, 1996), 55.
13. Bay (1998), 60 & 131-3; W.J. Argyle, *The Fon of Dahomey. A History and Ethnography of the Old Kingdom* (Oxford University Press, 1966), 83.

    Significantly, according to the French officer Alexandre D'Albéca the locals believed that the French could conquer their land in the 1890s because they had much closer relations with Mawu than the Africans. (See his "Voyage au pays de Éoués".)
14. Édouard Dunglas, "Origine du Royaume de Porto-Novo", *Études Dahoméennes* (ns), 9-10, 1967), 29-62 (31); Alfred Comlan Mondjannagni, *Campagnes et villes du sud de la République du Bénin* (Paris/The Hague, Mouton, 1977), 275.
15. Sandra Barnes' Introduction to the book edited by her (*Africa's Ogun*), 4.
16. See footnote 45 in the Introduction; Monrad (1822/2009), 178.
17. The famous *fa*-divination consists in finding out the will of the gods; Melville J. and Frances S. Herskovits, *Dahomean Narrative. A Cross-cultural Analysis* (Northwestern University Press, 1958), 177.
18. Monrad (1822/2009).
19. "Oddly enough, as [the] new African history was developing, little attention was paid to the history of African religions", Robert M. Baum, *Shrines of the Slave Trade. Diola Religion and Society in Precolonial Senegambia* (Oxford University Press, 1999), 10.
20. Winston King, "Religion", in Mircea Eliade (ed.), *The Encyclopedia of Religion*, vol. 12 (New York, Macmillan, 1987), 282-93 (282).

21. What precedes and follows constitute a personal interpretation of the following works: Suzanne Preston Blier, *African Vodun. Art, Psychology and Power* (University of Chicago Press, 1995); Roger Brand, *Ethnographie et vocabulaire religieux des cultes vodoun* (Munich, LINCOM Europa, 2000); Melville J. Herskovits, *Dahomey. An Ancient West African Kingdom*, 2 vols (New York 1938, Northwestern University Press, 1967); Judy Rosenthal, "Religious Traditions of the Togo and Benin Ewe", in Benjamin Lawrance (ed), *A Handbook of Eweland. The Ewe of Togo and Benin* (Accra, Woeli, 2005), 183-96; Christian R. Gaba, "The Religious Life of the People", in Francis Agbodeka, *A Handbook of Eweland vol. I: The Ewes of Southeastern Ghana* (Accra, Woeli, 1997), 85-104; Claude Savary, *La pensée symbolique des Fõ. Tableau de la société et étude de la litterature orale d'expression sacrée dans l'ancien royaume du Dahomey* (Geneva, 1976).
22. Reputed closeness to supernatural forces was used to legitimize all positions of authority, according to Sandra E. Greene, "Conflict and Crisis: a Note on the Workings of the Political Economy and Ideology of the Anlo-Ewe in the Precolonial Period", *Rural Africana*, 17 (1983), 83-96 (88).
23. Louis Brenner, "'Religious' Discourse in and about Africa", in Karen Barber and P.F. de Moraes Farias (eds), *Discourse and Its Disguises: The Interpretation of African Oral Texts* (Birmingham, Centre of West African Studies, 1989), 87-105 (87). See also Baum (1999), 35.

    The Malagasy language did not have separate words for "politics" and "religion" (Randrianja & Ellis (2009), 62).
24. At least according to Rodney Stark, *One True God: Historical Consequences of Monotheism* (Princeton University Press, 2001), 108.
25. Winston King (1987) again: "what the West calls religions is...an integral part of the total ongoing way of life" (282), it cannot be separated from the rest, cannot be defined as a separate sphere. Or if one prefers, "the religious is scarcely distinguishable from the sociocultural" (283).
26. Chris Abotchie, "Legal Processes and Institutions", in Francis Agbodeka (ed.), *A Handbook of Eweland vol. I: The Ewes of Southeastern Ghana* (Accra, Woeli, 1997) 73-84 (75).
27. *Ibid.*, 74; Savary (1976), 188 & 375; Brand (2000), 54; Pazzi (1976), 285; etc.; plus personal communication from Edna Bay dated 11 April 2015.
28. "Les morts existent à l'état de forces spirituelles" (Savary [1976], 188).
29. Paul Pélissier, *Le pays du Bas Ouémé: une région témoin du Dahomey méridional* (Dakar, Faculté des Lettres et Sciences Humaines, 1963), 56; Marie-Josée Pineau-Jamous, "Porto-Novo: royauté, localité et parenté", *Cahiers d'Études Africaines*, XXVI, 4 (1986), 547-76; Herskovits (1938/1967), I, 171-83; Manoukian (1950), 22-40; etc.
30. Pazzi (1976), 302.
31. J.D.Y. Peel, *Religious Encounter and the Making of the Yoruba* (Indiana University Press, 2000), 30.
32. John Pemberton III and Funso S. Afolayan, *Yoruba Sacred Kingship. "A Power Like That of the Gods"* (Washington and London, Smithsonian Institution Press, 1996).
33. Robert Smith, *Kingdoms of the Yoruba* (London, Methuen, 1976), esp. 129-31; Peter Morton-Williams, "An Outline of the Cosmology and Cult Organization of the

Oyo Yoruba", *Africa*, XXXIV, 3 (1964), 243-61; Peter C. Lloyd, *The Political Development of Yoruba Kingdoms in the Eighteenth and Nineteenth Centuries* (Royal Anthropological Institute of Great Britain and Ireland, 1971); etc.

34. Peter C. Lloyd, "Sacred Kingship and Government among the Yoruba", *Africa*, 30, 3 (1960), 227. For a comparison with the Akan, see Michelle Gilbert, "The Person of the King: Ritual and Power in a Ghanaian State", in David Cannadine and Simon Price (eds), *Rituals of Royalty. Power and Ceremonial in Traditional Societies* (Cambridge University Press, 1987), 298-330 (esp. 319).

35. Robert J. Wenke, *The Ancient Egyptian State. The Origins of Egyptian Culture (c.8000–2000 BC)* (Cambridge University Press, 2009), 271-3.

36. This is a theme we have treated in all but two of the works of ours listed in the Bibliography.

37. Basile Kossou, "La notion de pouvoir dans l'aire culturelle aja-fon", in *Le concept de pouvoir en Afrique* (UNESCO, 1981), 84-106 [name of editor not indicated]; Edna G. Bay, *Iron Altars of the Fon People of Benin* (catalogue, exhibition, Emory Museum of Art and Archaeology, October 2–December 21, 1985), "Introduction"; Pierre Verger, *Note sur le culte des Orisa et Vodun à Bahia, la Baie de tous les saints au Brésil, et à l'ancienne Côte des Esclaves en Afrique* (Mémoire de l'IFAN, no.51, Dakar, 1957); Pineau-Jamous (1986), 547; Brand (2000), 8; Savary (1976), 165; etc.

38. Morton-Williams (1964), 253; Montserrat Palau-Martí, *Le Roi-Dieu au Bénin (Sud Togo, Dahomey, Nigeria occidental)* (Paris, Berger-Levrault, 1964), 158-69.

39. We are referring of course to Sir James Frazer and his multivolume *The Golden Bough* (1890, third edition 1906-15, plus later abridged editions).

40. Gilbert (1987), 323.

41. A.F.C. Ryder, *Benin and the Europeans 1485-1897* (London, Longmans, 1969), 71.

42. Palau-Martí (1964), 11. We consider the title of her book unfortunate.

43. Lucien Scubla, "Sacred King, Sacrificial Victim, Surrogate Victim *or* Frazer, Hocart, Girard", in Declan Quigley (ed.), *The Character of Kingship* (Oxford/New York, Berg, 2005), 39-62 (40).

44. Nii Otokunor Quarcoopome, "Notse's Ancient Kingship: Some Archaeological and Art-historical Considerations", *African Archaeological Review*, 11 (1993), 109-28 (126).

45. Lloyd (1960), 225.

46. *Ibid.*, 236.

47. Ade M. Obayemi, "The Yoruba and Edo-speaking Peoples and their Neighbours before 1600 A.D.", in Ajayi & Crowder (1985), 255-322; Johnson (1897/1921), esp. 143.

48. Andrew H. Apter, *Black Critics and Kings: the Hermeneutics of Power in Yoruba* (University of Chicago Press, 1992), 22-3; Lawuyi (1992), 369-75; R. Smith (1976), 60.

49. Mondjannagni (1977), 162.

50. Again the reference is to the works of the present author. See footnote 6 above.

51. Mondjannagni (1977), 162; Jacques Lombard, "Contribution à l'histoire d'une ancienne société politique du Dahomey: la royauté d'Allada", *Bylletin de l'IFAN*, XXIX, 1-2 (1967), 40-66; Montserrat Palau-Martí, *L'Histoire de Sàbe et de ses rois*.

(*République du Bénin*) (Paris, Maisonneuve et Larose 1992); and by the same author: *Société et religion au Bénin (les Sàbè-Opara)* (Paris, Maisonneuve et Larose, 1993).

52. Igor Kopytoff, "The Internal African Frontier: The Making of African Political Culture", in Igor Kopytoff (ed.), *The African Frontier. The Reproduction of Traditional African Societies* (Indiana University Press, 1987).

53. On this and the following see, in a comparative context, for instance Fuglestad with Ellis (1982); Martha Kaplan, *Neither Cargo nor Cult. Ritual Politics and the Colonial Imagination in Fiji* (Duke University Press, 1995); Ian Caldwell, "Power, State and Society Among the Pre-Islamic Bugis", *Bijdragen tot de Taal-, Land-en Volkenkunde*, 151, 3 (1995), 394-421; possibly also David Johnson, *Spectacle and Sacrifice: The Ritual foundations of Village Life in North China* (Harvard University, Asia Center, 2009). The heads of the *shê* territorial units look to us rather like "earth-priests".

As far as Cambodia is concerned, there are the very interesting observations made by the Chinese diplomat and traveller Zhou Daguan (1266–1346) in the late thirteenth century called *A Record of Cambodia: the Land and its People* (translated and edited by Peter Harris, Silkworm Books, 2007).

54. Some references in Fuglestad (1979), 53, footnote 24.

55. We have been told that the earlier Bamileke, Tikar and other societies of Cameroon before the emergence of the *fon* chieftainchips are relevant examples in this context. But it is a point we have been unable to investigate so far.

56. As in Anlo: Greene (1983), 86.

57. B.A. Agiri, "Early Oyo History Reconsidered", *History in Africa*, II (1975); Robin Law, *The Oyo Empire c.1600–c.1836. A West African Imperialism in the Era of the Atlantic Slave Trade* (Oxford University Press, 1977a), 29.

58. See for instance David Henley and Ian Caldwell, "Kings and Covenants. Stranger-kings and social contract in Sulawesi", *Indonesia and the Malay World*, vol. 36, no. 105 (2008), 269-91.

59. Jack Goody in the "Introduction" to the book edited by him, *Succession to High Office* (Cambridge University Press, 1966), 1-56 (5).

60. Fuglestad (1979), and many of the works referred to in the preceding.

61. Interesting illustration of many of the themes referred to above (although not from the perspective adopted in the present work) in Alfred Adler, *Le pouvoir et l'interdit. Royauté et religion en Afrique noire* (Paris, Albin Michel, 2000).

62. The most famous case world-wide is that of the Incas: Geoffrey W. Conrad & Arthur A. Demarest, *Religion and Empire. The Dynamics of Aztec and Inca Expansionism* (Cambridge University Press,1984). In Africa, the book by Adler (preceding footnote) seems to us to refer to a similar case.

The book by Conrad and Demarest constitutes incidentally a powerful argument in favour of our sacred-society thesis.

63. Robin Law, who may not be in agreement with our interpretation here, notes nevertheless that the political system of Oyo involved an uneasy balance between the *alafin* and the *oyo mesi* which was bound to give rise to recurrent tensions, not to say bitter strife, between the two. Cf. Law (1977a), 76; and by the same author, "Making Sense of a Traditional Narrative: Political Disintegration in the Kingdom of Oyo", *Cahiers d'Études Africaines*, XXII, 3-4 (1982), 387-401 (esp. 399).

64. Inspired by Henley and Caldwell (2008).
65. Speculation based on Sandra T. Barnes and Paula Girshick Ben-Amos, "Ogun, the Empire Builder", in Barnes (ed.), *Africa's Ogun*, 39-64 (42); Apter (1992), 21-5.
66. See for instance R. Smith (1976); and for the case of Asante: Larry W. Yarak, *Asante and the Dutch, 1744–1873* (Oxford University Press, 1990), 12.
67. For instance, the cases of Anlo and Glidji on the Slave Coast, as we shall see.

A4
SOME CONCRETE, PRACTICAL IMPLICATIONS

1. "Le monde surnaturel est intégré au monde des vivants et forme avec lui un tout cohérent" (Savary [1976], 143).
2. *Ibid.*; Pazzi (1976), 284; Pierre Verger, "Oral Tradition in the Cult of the Orishas and its Connection with the History of the Yoruba", *Journal of the Historical Society of Nigeria*, I (1956), 61-3: Morton-Williams (1964a), 252; Manoukian (1950), 45; Akyeampong (2001), 33.
3. Pazzi (1976), 286.
4. Savary (1976), 149 & 164; Law (1991b), 105-6; Bernard Maupoil, *La Géomancie à l'ancienne Côte des Esclaves* (Paris, Institut d'Ethnologie, 1943), 35-8; etc.
5. Le Hérissé (1911), 158-60; Hazoumé (1937/1956), 160-61.
6. For instance Pazzi (1976), 302.
7. Note in any case that Legba is a very complex deity and has in fact many roles. Brand (2000), 65; Savary (1976), 161; Foà (1895), 223; etc.
8. Rosenthal (2005), 184; Savary (1976), 156 & 211-12; Bay (1998), 23; Herskovits (1938/1967), I, 209-10 (note that the "love thy neighbour as thyself" theme is not much in evidence).
9. Barnes (1989), 3.
10. Blier (1995a), 4.
11. Brand (2000*)*, 1-2.
12. Joan Dayan: "Vodou practices must be viewed as ritual reenactments of Haiti's colonial past, even more than as retentions from Africa". Cf. her *Haiti, History and the Gods* (University of California Press, 1995), XVII-XX, 35-6.
13. Pierre Verger, "Le culte des Vodoun d'Abomey aurait-il été apporté à Saint-Louis de Maranhon par la mère du roi Ghézo?", *Études Dahoméennes*, 8 (1952), 19-24; Bay (2001), 42-60; Brand (2000), 41.
14. Argyle (1966), 176-7; Marty (1925), I, 125-6; Herskovits (1958), 12; Maupoil (1943), 69; and many others.
15. Nicoué Lodjou Gayibor, "Migrations-société-civilisation: les Ewe du sud-Togo" (thèse-3e cycle, Paris I, 1975), 396.
16. Gaba (1997), 47.
17. Herskovits (1958), 132-4. Hence similar to Olorun or Olodumare among the Yoruba (Lloyd [1960] 223) and Onyame among the Akan (Emmanuel Akyeampong and Pashington Obeng, "Spirituality, Gender, and Power in Asante History", *International Journal of African Historical Studies*, 28, 3 [1995], 481-508 [483]).

18. Note that the same family pattern, with the lesser deities emanating from the supreme one, has been proposed for other parts of West Africa, notably the Fante and the Ga of the Gold Coast and the Diola of Senegambia. Cf. T.C. McCaskie, "Nananom Mpow of Mankessim: An Essay in Fante History", in David Henige and T.C. McCaskie (eds), *West African Economic and Social History. Studies in Memory of Marion Johnson* (African Studies Program, University of Wisconsin, Madison, 1990), 133-50 (139); Irene Quaye, "The Ga and their Neighbours 1600-1742" (PhD thesis, University of Ghana, 1972), 269; Baum (1999), 38-42 & 105-7.
19. Herskovits (1958), 132-4.
20. According to a person in Ouidah interviewed by Bosman, the number of their gods was endless and innumerable – "we make and break our gods daily", he added (Bosman [1704/1967], 367a-368).
21. Maupoil (1943), 68.
22. Herskovits (1958), 135.
23. See footnote 45 in the Introduction.
24. Maupoil (1943); Blier (2005), 175.
25. Verger (1957), 141; Barnes (1989); Herskovits (1958), 133-4.
26. Wording by Greene (2002), 1019.
27. Le Hérissé (1911), 128.
28. Pazzi (1976), 60; Brand (2000), 1; Argyle (1966), 183.
29. Herskovits (1958), 37.
30. *Ibid.*, 35; Verger (1957), 141 & 157.
31. Atkins (1735/1970), 180; "Relation du Royaume de Judas (ca. 1715)" (*op. cit.*), 90; Hender Molesworth and Rowland Powell to the RAC, Jamaica 24.1.1680/1 (O.s), in Elizabeth Donnan (ed.), *Documents Illustrative of the History of the Slave Trade to America*, vol. I, 1441-1700 (Washington DC, Carnegie Institution, 1930), 271; Robert Elwes, off Cape Lopez 31.1.1686 (O.s); & Georges Nantes, from Barbados 10.5. 1686 (O.s); both in Law (2006), 379; Mondjannagni (1977), 121 & 162.
32. Savary (1976), 153-61; Brand (2000), 3 & 77; Herskovits (1938/1967), II, 135-7; Argyle (1966), 185-6; Herskovits (1958), 17; Edna G. Bay, *Asen, Ancestors, and Vodun: Tracing Change in African Art* (University of Illinois Press, 2008), 56 (in addition to her *Wives of the Leopard*, especially 115-18).
33. For instance Catherine Coquery-Vidrovitch, "De la traite des esclaves à l'exportation de l'huile de palme et de palmistes au Dahomey: XIXe siècle", in C. Meillassoux (ed.), *The Development of Indigenous Trade and Markets in West Africa* (Oxford University Press, 1971), 107-23 (112).
34. For instance: Jan Vansina, *Kingdoms of the Savanna* (University of Wisconsin Press, 1966); Georges Balandier, *Daily Life in the Kingdom of Kongo* (translated from the French, London and New York, 1968) and *Political Anthropology* (Penguin ed., 1970); John K. Thornton, *The Kingdom of Kongo. Civil War and Transition 1641–1718* (University of Wisconsin Press, 1983); Susan Herlin Broadhead, "Beyond Decline: the Kingdom of the Kongo in the Eighteenth and Nineteenth Centuries", *International Journal of African Historical Studies*, 12, 4 (1979), 615-50; John Thornton, "The Origins and Early History of the Kingdom of Kongo, c. 1350–1550", *International Journal of African Historical Studies*, 34, 1 (2001), 89-120; Louis Jadin

and Mireille Dicorato (eds), *Correspondance de Dom Afonso, roi du Congo 1506–1543* (Brussels, Académie Royale des Sciences d'Outre-Mer, 1974); John K.Thornton, "The Kingdom of Kongo, ca.1390–1678. The Development of an African Social Formation", *Cahiers d'Études Africaines*, XXII, 3-4 (1982), 325-42.

35. The dates used by John K. Thornton in "Afro-Christian Syncretism in the Kingdom of Kongo", *Journal of African History*, 54, 1 (2013), 53-77.
36. A.F.C. Ryder, "Missionary Activities in the Kingdom of Warri to the Early Nineteenth Century", *Journal of the Historical Society of Nigeria*, vol. 2, 1 (1960), 1-26; William A. Moore, *History of Itsekiri* (1936; 2nd edit. Frank Cass 1970, with a new Introd. by P.C. Lloyd), 30-33; P. Mateo de Anguiano (1649–1726), *Misiones Capuchinas en África, vol. II, Misiones al Reino de la Zinga, Benín, Arda, Guineà, y Sierra Leona* (Madrid, 1685; modern edition: vol. VII of *Missionalia Hispanica* [con introducción y notas del P. Buenaventura de Carrocera], Madrid [Consejo Superior de Investigaciones Cientificas & Instituto Santo Toribio de Mogrovejo, 1957]), 251-66.
37. Personal interpretation of, among other works, Ryder (1969), 4-21, 107, 202 & 313; R.E. Bradbury, *Benin Studies*, Peter Morton-Williams (ed.) (Oxford University Press/ International African Institute, 1973), esp. 138-40; Dmitri M. Bondarenko, "Advent of the Second (Oba) Dynasty: Another Assessment of a Benin History Key Point", *HA*, 30 (2003), 63-85; Dmitri M. Bondarenko and Peter M. Roese, "Between the *Ogiso* and *Oba* Dynasties: An Interpretation of Interregnum in the Benin Kingdom", *ibid.*, 31 (2004), 103-15; Paula Ben-Amos Girshick and John Thornton, "Civil War in the Kingdom of Benin, 1689–1721: Continuity or Political Change?", *Journal of African History*, 42, 3 (2001), 353-76.
38. Pemberton III (1989), 105-46 (138).
39. Robert Smith, "The Lagos Consulate, 1851-1861: An Outline", *Journal of African History*, XV, 3 (1974), 393-416 (esp. 394); Mann (2007), 27-9, 36 & 49.
40. Adédirán (1984), 80; Aimé Sègla and Adékin E. Boko, "De la cosmologie à la rationalisation de la vie sociale. Ces mots idààcha qui parlent ou la mémoire d'un type de calendrier yoruba ancien", *Cahiers d'Études Africaines*, XLVI, 1 (2006), 11-50.

    As for Savè/Chabe, there are apparently clear traces of contrapuntal paramountcy: R.P. Thomas Mouléro, "Histoire et légende de Chabe (Save)", *Études Dahoméennes* (ns), 2 (1964), 51-92 (61-2).
41. Parrinder (1956), 14-22; Palau-Martí (1964), 56-8 & 195; Iroko (1998),155.
42. As usual, personal interpretation of: Jacques Lombard, "La vie politique dans une ancienne société de type féodal: les Bariba du Dahomey", *Cahiers d'Études Africaines*, XXII, 3 (1960), 5-45; Marjorie Helen Stewart, "The Kisra legend as oral history", *International Journal of African Historical Studies*, 13, 1 (1980), 51-70.
43. Kwame Yeboa Daaku, *Trade and Politics on the Gold Coast 1600 to 1720. A Study of the African Reaction to European Trade* (Oxford at the Clarendon Press, 1970), 159-60. According to A. Norman Klein, there is interestingly a rough "correlation between the distribution of forest-living, yam-growing, Kwa-speaking populations and an abnormal blood type, haemoglobin S (HbS, the sickle cell gene), which offers resistance to malarial parasites" (Klein [1996], 250). Kwa is a very broad linguistic category englobing all the languages of the coast of Guinea.

44. *Ibid.*, 253; Yarak (1990), 4-16; McCaskie (1995/2002), 275-85. Another interesting work on Asante is Pescheux (2003).
45. Klein (1996), 254; Gérard Pescheux, *Le royaume asante (Ghana). Parenté, pouvoir, histoire, XVIIe–XXe siècles* (Paris, Karthala, 2003), 52; Peter Shinnie, "Early Asante: Is Wilks Right?", in John Hunwick and Nancy Lawler (eds), *The Cloth of Many Colored Silks. Papers on History and Society Ghanaian and Islamic in Honor of Ivor Wilks* (Northwestern University Press, 1996), 195-203.
46. Pescheux (2003), 534; Gilbert (1987), 303; Captain R.S. Rattray, *The Tribes of the Ashanti Hinterland* (2 volumes, Oxford at the Clarendon Press, 1932), vol. I, p.XIX.
47. Ivor Wilks, "Aspects of Bureaucratization in Ashanti in the Nineteenth Century", *Journal of African History*, VII, 2 (1966), 215-32 (215).
48. Fynn (1971), 40.
49. Ivor Wilks, "Ashanti Government" in Daryll Forde and P.M. Kaberry (eds), *West African Kingdoms in the Nineteenth Century* (International African Institute/Oxford University Press, 1967), 206-38 (221).
50. Underlined especially in Per O. Hernæs, "Dansk-Norske handelsutposter på Gullkysten i slavehandelens æra", *Norsk Sjøfartsmuseum. Årsberetning 1997* (Oslo, 1998), 129-41 (135).
51. The classic work is Rattray (1932). See also David Tait, "The Political System of Konkomba", *Africa*, XXIII, 3 (1953), 213-23; Jack Goody, "The Over-Kingdom of Gonja" in Forde & Kaberry (1967), 179-205; Goody (1966), 142-76.
52. Michel Izard, *Introduction à l'histoire des royaumes mossi* (2 volumes, Paris/Ouagadougou-CNRS/CVRS, 1970), and many other works by the same author; Wilks (1985), 466-72.
53. Shumway (2011a), 154 & 164. The ultimate authority in these matters is John Kofi Fynn whose works on the Fante we have been unable to consult.
54. Madeline Manoukian, *Akan and Ga-Adangme Peoples of the Gold Coast* (Oxford University Press/International African Institute, 1950), 66 & 86; Quaye (1972), 94-5.
55. Everything on the Akwamu constitutes my personal interpretation of Wilks (2001).
56. Nicoué Lodjou Gayibor (ed. but Gayibor wrote most chapters), *Histoire des Togolais, vol. I: Des origines à 1884* (Presses de l'Université du Bénin, 1997), 326.
57. Including Nugent (2005), 38.
58. Greene (2002a), 1022; D.E.K. Amenumey, *The Ewe in Pre-Colonial Times. A Political History with Special Emphasis on the Anlo, Ge and Krepi* (Accra, Sedco, 1986), 11-12; Laumann in *ibid.*, 14-28 (17).
59. The matter may be apparently somewhat more complicated. For a discussion see Michel Verdon, *The Abutia Ewe of West Africa. The Chiefdom that Never Was* (Berlin etc., Mouton, 1983); Benjamin N. Lawrance, "Bankoe v. Dome: Traditions and Petitions in the Ho-Asogli Amalgamation, British Mandated Togoland, 1919-39", *Journal of African History*, 46, 2 (2005), 243-67; Nicoué Lodjou Gayibor, "L'aire culturelle Ajatado des origines à la fin du XVIIIe siècle" (Thesis, Paris I University, 1985), 439-40.
60. Manoukian (1952), 34; Laumann (2005), 18.
61. Gayibor (1997), 327; Gaba (1997), 36.
62. Paul Nugent, "Putting the History Back into Ethnicity: Enslavement, Religion, and Cultural Brokerage in the Construction of Madinka/Jola and Ewe/Agotime Identities

in West Africa, c.1650–1930", *Comparative Studies in Society and History*, 50, 4 (2008), 935.
63. Gayibor (1975), 382.
64. Amenumey (1986), 15.
65. Nukunya (1997), 63-4; Gaba (1997), 36-8; etc.
66. Abotchie (1997), 81.
67. Nukunya (1997), 48-9.
68. *Ibid.*
69. Greene (1996), 2 & 27-8.
70. Sandra E. Greene, "The Past and Present of an Anlo-Ewe Oral Tradition", *History in Africa*, 12 (1985), 73-87 (79); Akyeampong (2001), 106.
71. Greene (1983), 88.
72. Nii Otokunor Quarcoopome's short but informative study (1993), 109-28, does not pretend to be one.
73. Law (1991b), 14.
74. Gaba (1997), 38.
75. McCaskie (1995/2002), 144-242; Pescheux (2003), 181 & 539.
76. Pemberton (1989), 138; Apter (1992), 21-5; Agiri (1975), 75-9; Law (1977a), 66-73.
77. McCaskie (1995/2002), 147.
78. Fuglestad (2005), 107-20.
79. Our thinking in these matters has been influenced in particular by the reading of Nancy M. Farriss' magnificent "Remembering the Future, Anticipating the Past: History, Time, and Cosmology among the Maya of Yucatan", in Diane Owen Hughes and Thomas R. Trautmann (eds), *Time. Histories and Ethnologies* (University of Michigan Press, 1995), 107-38.
80. Here we part company with David Henige when he says that he believes "that oral societies do not forget their past so much as they reject...the need for its memory to be factual". David Henige, "Impossible to Disprove yet Impossible to Believe: the Unforgiving Epistemology of Deep-time oral tradition", *History in Africa*, 36 (2009), 127-234 (231).
81. Savary (1976), 374-5. Baum (1999, 58-9) argues the same for parts of Senegambia.
82. Skertchly (1874), 13.
83. Adams (1823/1966), 203. In the case of the Gold Coast, we note what H.C. Monrad (1822/2009, 43 & 80) has to say: "In general, it is not essential for the Negroes to know when this or that happened... Time is never precious for the Negro". See also *ibid.*, 89 & 227).
84. Law (1988), 433.
85. *Ibid.*, 436.
86. Lombard (1967a), 80.

A5
A FEW COMMENTS ON CERTAIN ECONOMIC MATTERS

1. A reputation based primarily on his classic work *The Great Transformation. The Political and Economic Origins of our Time*, first published in 1944.

2. Polanyi (1966); and by the same author: "Sortings and the 'Ounce Trade' in the West African Slave Trade", *Journal of African History*, V, 3 (1964), 381-93.
3. Law (2004a), 147.
4. Georg Elwert,*Wirtschaft und Herrschaft von 'Dāxome' (Dahomey) im 18. Jahrhundert: Ökonomie des Sklavenraubs und Gesellschaftsstruktur 1724 bis 1818* (Munich, 1973). For an evaluation, cf. Agneta Pallinder-Law's review entitled, "The Slave Trade Economy in Dahomey", *Journal of African History*, 2 (1975), 306-7.
5. Roberta Walker Kilkenny, "The Slave Mode of Production: Precolonial Dahomey", in Donald Crummey and C.C. Stewart (eds), *Modes of Production in Africa: the Precolonial Era* (Beverly Hills/London, 1981), 157-73 (160).
6. Jack Goody, *Technology, Tradition, and the State in Africa* (Oxford University Press/ International African Institute, 1971).
7. David Eltis and Lawrence C. Jennings: "Trade between Western Africa and the Atlantic World in the Pre-colonial Era", *American Historical Review*, XLIII, 4 (1988), 936-59.
8. Joseph E. Inikori, "The Economic Impact of the 1807 British Abolition of the Transatlantic Slave Trade", in Toyin Falola and Matt D. Childs (eds), *The Changing Worlds of Atlantic Africa. Essays in Honor of Robin Law* (Durham, NC, 2009), 163-82 (176).
9. *Ibid.*, 177.
10. Robin Law, "The Gold Trade of Whydah in the Seventeenth and Eighteenth Centuries", in David Henige and T.C. McCaskie (eds), *West African Economic and Social History: Studies in Memory of Marion Johnson* (University of Wisconsin, Madison, 1990), 105-18; Robin Law, "Computing Domestic Prices in Precolonial West Africa: a Methodological Exercise from the Slave Coast", *History in Africa*, 18 (1991), 239-57; Robin Law, "Cowries, Gold, and Dollars: Exchange Rate Instability and Domestic Price Inflation in Dahomey in the Eighteenth and Nineteenth Centuries", in Jane I. Guyer (ed.), *Money Matters. Instability, Values and Social Payments in the Modern History of West African Communities* (Heineman/James Currey, 1995), 53-73; Robin Law, "Finance and Credit in Pre-Colonial Dahomey", in Endre Stiansen and Jane I. Guyer (eds), *Credit, Currencies and Culture. African Financial Institutions in Historical Perspective* (Uppsala, 1999), 15-37.
11. M'Leod (1820/1971), 93.
12. Inspired by Belich (2009), 96.
13. In the case of the Slave Coast, see in particular Norman (2009b), 187-218; and another article by the same author (2009a), esp. 408.
14. Underlined in *ibid.*, 402, and in Greene (1996b), 39-40, among other works, including in some rather unexpected ones, such as for instance Daniel Hopkins, "Peter Thonning's Map of Danish Guinea and its Use in Colonial Administration and Atlantic Diplomacy 1801-1890", *Cartographica*, 35, 3-4 (1998), 99-122 (108).
15. Apart from *The Ambiguities of History*, we have exposed our views on the course of European and Global History in several works in Norwegian. Among the latter, *Vekstøkonomi. Et globalhistorisk essay* (Oslo, Unipub, 2010).

Of the vast literature on the origins and rise of capitalism, one of the most pertinent works remains in our opinion Jean Baechler's "Essai sur les origines du système capitaliste", *Archives Européennes de Sociologie*, IX, 2 (1968), 205-63.

16. Law (1991b), 56.
17. *Ibid.*, 220. See also Arnold below (footnote 36).
18. Jan S. Hogendorn and Marion Johnson, *The Shell Money of the Slave Trade* (Cambridge University Press, 1986).
19. *Ibid.*, 6 & 92.
20. Jan S. Hogendorn and Henry A. Gemery: "Abolition and its Impact on Monies Imported to West Africa", in David Eltis and James Walvin (eds), *The Abolition of the Atlantic Slave Trade. Origins and Effects in Europe, Africa, and the Americas* (University of Wisconsin Press, 1981), 99-115 (108).
21. Its importance has been exaggerated according to Eltis (2000), 184, footnote 59.
22. Polanyi (1966), 187.
23. Hogendorn and Johnson (1986), 2.
24. Gayibor (1997), 229.
25. Marion Johnson, "The Ounce in Eighteenth-century West African Trade", *Journal of African History*, VII, 2 (1966), 197-214; and by the same author, "The Atlantic Slave Trade and the Economy of West Africa", in R. Anstey and P.E.H. Hair (eds), *Liverpool, The African Slave Trade, and Abolition* (Historic Society of Lancashire and Cheshire, 1976), 14-38.
26. Postma (1990), 228.
27. *Ibid.*, 211.
28. David Northrup, "New Evidence of the French Slave-Trade in the Bight of Benin", *Slavery and Abolition*, 24, 3 (2003), 61-81 (64).
29. A.G. Hopkins, *An Economic History of West Africa* (London, Longman, 1973), 111.
30. Long lists in Stanley B. Alpern, "What Africans Got for Their Slaves: A Master List of European Trade Goods", *History in Africa*, 22 (1995), 5-43; *Barbot on Guinea*, 657-8; Northrup (2003), 66-7; Johnson (1976), 15-8; Davies (1957), 170-5; Law (1991b), 199-205.
31. Inga Merkyte and Klavs Randsborg, "Graves from Dahomey: Beliefs, Ritual and society in Ancient Bénin", *Journal of African Archaeology*, VII, 1 (2009), 55-77 (61-3).
32. The French director at Ouidah noted in 1734, and complained about "*les révolutions continuelles en goût de ce pays*" (Levet de Juda 17.1.1734, *op. cit.*). See also Justesen (2005), XXVI; etc.
33. The only work we know about regarding cross-cultural trade is Philip D. Curtin's *Cross-cultural Trade in World History* (Cambridge University Press, 1984). But its perspective is distinct from the one adopted in the present book.
34. "The circulation of objects...is not merely a physical process but is also a movement and displacement of competing conceptions of things": Nicholas Thomas, *Entangled Objects: Exchange, Material Culture, and Colonialism in the Pacific* (Harvard University Press, 1991). Or as Kenneth Kelly has expressed it (Kelly (1997b): "trade items...were assigned values and meanings consistent with the (local) cultural system".
35. Well illustrated in Harms (2002), 248-9.
36. For a discussion, cf. Rosemary Arnold, "A Port of Trade: Whydah on the Guinea Coast", in Karl Polanyi, Conrad Arensberg and Harry W. Pearson (eds), *Trade and Markets in the Early Empires. Economies in History and Theory* (New York, The Free

37. Polanyi (1964), 384.
38. E.W. Evans and David Richardson, "Hunting for Rents: the Economics of Slaving in Pre-colonial Africa", *Economic History Review*, XLVIII, 4 (1995), 665-86 (667-71).
39. *Ibid.*, 676.
40. Johnson (1976), 32-3. Additional concrete examples in Alain Yacou, *Journaux de bord et de traite de Joseph Crassous de Médeuil. De La Rochelle à la côte de Guinée et aux Antilles (1772–1776)* (Paris, Karthala, 2001), 137; Harms (2002), 232.
41. Law (1992b); and by the same author, "Horses, Firearms, and Political Power in Precolonial West Africa", *Past & Present*, no. 72 (1976), 112-32.
42. *Ibid.*, 114-15.
43. Eltis (2000).
44. Anonymous: *Certain Considerations Relating to the RAC of England* (etc), printed 1680 (Harley MS 7310; British Library-Department of Manuscripts).
45. Mémoire des Negociants de Nantes etc. 25.11.1777 (AD-Loire Atlantique, Nantes, C738).
46. Indeed, the Royal African Company, which for long had a monopoly of the English slave trade, encouraged English merchants and manufacturers to compete with the Dutch, and with success (underlined in Davies [1957] 174).
47. Inspired in the last resort by Nuala Zahedieh, "Regulation, Rent-seeking, and the Glorious Revolution in the English Atlantic Economy", *Economic History Review*, 63, 4 (2010), 865-90.
48. Findlay and O'Rourke (2007), 533.

A6
THE DATABASE AND THE SLAVE TRADE FROM THE SLAVE COAST

1. See the Introduction, footnote 1.
2. Elaborated in Stephen D. Behrendt, "The Annual Volume and Regional Distribution of the British Slave Trade, 1780–1807", *Journal of African History*, 38, 2 (1997), 187-211.
3. R.E. Bradbury, *The Benin Kingdom and the Edo-Speaking Peoples of South-Western Nigeria* (London, International African Institute, 1957), together with a section on *The Itsekiri*, by P.C. Lloyd, 20.
4. Landolphe (1823), I; Ryder (1969), 33, 125, 212 & 229.
5. Ryder (1966), 203; Ryder (1969), 41-5 & 65; "Relation du voyage de Guynée fait en 1687 sur la frégate 'La Tempeste' par le Sr. Du Casse", in Roussier (1935), 1-47 (15).
6. But note that between 1780 & 1807 the number of slaves embarked from the Benin kingdom made up 19.4 per cent of all slaves embarked on British ships, only British ships, in the Bight of Benin. Figures from Behrendt (1997), 205.
7. Ryder (1969), 45.
8. *Ibid.*, 198.

9. Benin cloth, not necessarily made in Benin itself but exported through Benin, was sold on the Gold Coast and later even in Brazil. However, it began to lose out in the competition with Indian and European textiles already in the seventeenth century.
    The *akori* beads came originally from Ife before those from Venice took over. Cf. Ryder (1966), 203-4; Daaku (1970), 24; Merkyte and Randsborg (2009), 61; Tilleman (1697/1994), 153; O. Euba, "Of Blue Beads and Red: the Role of Ife in the West African Trade in Kori Beads", *Journal of the Historical Society of Nigeria*, 11, 1-2 (1982), 109-27.
10. M. de Mithon de Legoma, Haiti, 15.2.1717 (AN Marine B/1/20, f.134-). General reputation of Benin slaves: "*les moins estimés- se chagrinent et meurent promptement*"; Pruneau (1789), 244.
11. David Eltis, Paul E. Lovejoy and David Richardson, "Slave-trading Ports: Towards an Atlantic-Wide Perspective, 1676–1832", in R. Law and Silke Strickrodt (eds), *Ports of the Slave Trade (Bights of Benin and Biafra)* (Centre of Commonwealth Studies, University Of Stirling, 1999), 12-34 (20-21).
12. See for instance Northrup (2003), 62-3.
13. This began very early: Thomas Clarke & Hugh Elliott to the RAC, Orphra [Offra] in Arda [Allada], 17.9.1678 [O.s.], in Donnan (1930), 236-7.
14. As expressd by Joseph Blaney in a letter from Whydah (Ouidah), and referring specifically to that place, 1.3.1715 [O.s.] (PRO C.113/276).
15. Hernæs (1998). Among the many other examples: Edwyn Stede and Stephen Gascoigne to the RAC, Barbados, 27.1.1682/3 [O.s.] (Donnan [1930], 304).
16. "Return from the Commissioners for Trade and Plantations, to the Honourable House of Commons, in consequence of the address of the said House to His Majesty of the 29th Day of January 1777 (etc)", printed 1777, p. 6 (NA, T70/177); Dantzig and Priddy (1971), 17-18; many documents in Justesen (2005), 112-29, 261 & 328; G. Aguirre Beltran, "Tribal Origins of Slaves in Mexico", *Journal of Negro History*, 31-3 (1946), 269-352 (315).
17. Ray A. Kea, *Settlements, Trade, and Politics in the Seventeenth-Century Gold Coast* (Johns Hopkins University Press, 1982), 105-6.
18. Law (2004a), 39; etc.
19. E. Jackline from Whydah [Ouidah], 13.10.1692 [O.s.], in Law (1992a), 55.
20. Ryder's book from 1969 is, once more, the obvious reference.
21. Note that the early Atlantic slave trade (exclusively Portuguese) was far from negligible, it may have involved from 900 to 2,200 slaves a year. Cf. Ivana Elbl, "The Volume of the Early Atlantic Slave Trade, 1450–1521", *Journal of African History*, 38, 1 (1997), 31-75.
22. Eltis & Richardson (2010), 197.
23. A slightly earlier date cannot be ruled out. See the interesting discussion in David Wheat, "The First Great Waves: African Provenance Zones for the Transatlantic Slave Trade to Cartagena de Indias, 1570–1640", *Journal of African History*, 52, 1 (2011), 1-22. The first slaves from the future Slave Coast were perhaps sent to Cartagena de Indias in present-day Colombia.
24. Robin Law, "The Evolution of the Brazilian Community in Ouidah", *Slavery and Abolition*, 22, 1 (2001), 22-41; also published in Kristin Mann and Edna G. Bay

(eds), *Rethinking the African Diaspora: the Making of a Black Atlantic World in the Bight of Benin and Brazil* (London, Frank Cass, 2001).
The African population in Brazil increased from nearly two million in 1798 to 5.8 million in 1872: Inikori (2009), 171.

25. The Gold Coast "became fully integrated into the Atlantic slave trade suddenly, between roughly 1700 and 1725", according to Shumway (2011a), 54.
26. Documents quoted in Yacou (2001), 139.
27. Useful summary of existing statistics in Mann (2007), 33.
28. For instance, the RAC at its fullest extent (in 1689) employed all told more than 300 white men in Africa, three-fourths of whom were foreigners (Davies [1957], 251-4).
29. Inikori (2001); and by the same author: "The Known, the Unknown, the Knowable, and the Unknowable: Evidence and the Evaluation of Evidence in the Measurement of the Trans-Atlantic Slave Trade", in Toyin Falola (ed.), *Ghana in Africa and the World: Essays in Honor of Adu Boahen* (Trenton, NJ & Asmara, Eritrea, 2003), 535-65.
30. J.E. Inikori, "The Volume of the British Slave Trade, 1655-1807", *Cahiers d'Etudes Africaines*, XXXII, 4 (1992), 643-88 (685).
31. Source material published in Donnan (1930), I, 355-6.
32. Inikori (2001), 89 & 96-7.
33. Norris (1789/1968), 69-70; Dalzel's testimony in the meeting of the Committee of the African Association on 2.8.1804, in Robin Hallett (ed), *Records of the African Association 1788–1831* (London/Edinburgh, Thomas Nelson & Sons, 1964), 194; Robin Law, "Further Light on John Duncan's Account of the 'Fellatah Country'", *History in Africa*, 28 (2001), 129-38; etc.
34. Lander (1830/1967), 35.
35. Theory of Evans and Richardson (1995), 675. It may be significant that we do not know on the Slave Coast of any trading network or trading community like the one that there is reason to believe the famous and somewhat mysterious Akani of the Gold Coast constituted, especially in pre-Asante times. The Akani are however primarily associated with the gold and not the slave trade. Cf. Albert van Dantzig, "The Akanists: A West African Hansa", in Henige and McCaskie (1990), 205-16; Kea (1982), 30 & 248-87; Shumway (2011a), 37-40.
36. Manning (1979, 125) does point out that the evidence is – unsurprisingly – scattered and quite impressionistic. See also, by the same author, "Contours of slavery and social change in Africa", *American Historical Review*, 88, 4 (1983), 835-57 (847).
37. Law (1991b), 222-3.
38. Robin Law, "Ethnicities of Enslaved Africans in the Diaspora: On the Meanings of 'Mina' (Again)", *History in Africa*, 32 (2005), 247-67.
39. Law (1977a), esp. p. 219.
40. Robin Law, "A West African Cavalry State: the Kingdom of Oyo", *Journal of African History*, 16 (1975), 1-15.
41. On Borgu see Robin Law and Paul E. Lovejoy, "Borgu in the Atlantic Slave Trade", *African Economic History*, 27 (1999), 69-92.
42. Messrs Miles and Dalzel (both old Guinea hands) considered that the slave trade was carried by a chain of merchants from the Coast indefinitely in many directions towards the interior (Meeting of the Committee of the African Association 2.8.1804;

in Hallet [1964], 193-5). Pruneau (1789), 151: some slaves came from 50 or 60 days' march in the interior having been *"vendus à dix marchés différens en route"*. See also the testimony of Oettinger from 1692-3 in Jones (1985), 195-6; and that of P. Labarthe, *Voyage à la Côte de Guinée, ou description des Côtes d d'Afrique depuis le cap Tagrin jusqu'au cap de Lopez-Gonzalves* (Paris, Debray, an XI [1803]), 104-5; plus finally M. (Xavier) Béraud, "Note sur le Dahomé" (dated Whydah [Ouidah] 26.3.1866), *Bulletin de la Société de Géographie*, 5e série, vol.12 (1866), 371-86 (374).

43. Studies of ethnic origins of slaves in America, based on data from shipping and plantation records, are inconclusive, and at times flawed, in our opinion, and have therefore not been further pursued recently. We have decided to abstain from providing references to them.

44. Kenneth G. Kelly, "Change and Continuity in Coastal Bénin", in Christopher R. DeCorse (ed.), *West Africa during the Atlantic Slave Trade: Archaeological Perspectives* (Leicester University Press, 2001), 81-100 (96). We have to do with an "extrapolation of remarkable audacity", to use a famous expression by David Henige, a type of extrapolation uncomfortably common in the field of the history of the slave trade according to him (and I agree). See David Henige, "Measuring the Immeasurable: the Atlantic Slave Trade, West African Population and the Pyrrhonian Critic", *Journal of African History*, 27, 2 (1986), 295-313.

45. Fr Joseph de Naxara (modern: José de Nájera), *Espejo mystico en que el hombre interior se mira practicamente ilustrado para los conocimientos de Dios, y el exercicio de la virtudes (etc)* (Madrid 1672), 239 [consulted in BNA, sección impresos no. 3/63664].

46. In addition to Naxara, see van Hoolwerff from Offra 2.4.1687 in Dantzig (1978), 29-30; and "The Examination of A. Dalzel by the African Committee", 5.4.1788 (*op. cit.*). Then there is the case of the many Huedan fugitives in 1727 and later which we will encounter in Part B.

47. Phillips (1732), 219; Pruneau (1789), 165-6; Bosman (1704/1967), 344-5.

48. *Idem*; Dalzel (1793/1967), 211; Lombard (1967), 89; etc.

49. Bay (2001), 52; Herskovits (1938/1967), II, 32.

50. A. Félix Iroko, "Condamnations pénales et ravitaillement en esclaves de la traite négrière", in Elisée Soumonni, Bellarmin C. Codo and Joseph Adande (eds), *Le Bénin et la route de l'esclave* (Cotonou, ONEPI, 1994), 93-5; Bay (2001), 45; Chenevert and Bulet, "Réflexions sur Juda" (op. cit.), 52.

51. Robin Law, "On Pawning and Enslavement for Debt in the Pre-Colonial Slave Coast", in Toyin Falola and Paul E. Lovejoy (eds), *Pawnship in Africa: Debt Bondage in Historical Perspective* (Boulder, Westview, 1994), 55-69.

52. Law (1991b), 185-8.

53. Kelly (1997a), 362-3.

54. Harms (2002), 250.

55. Phillips (1732), 218; "Relation du Royaume de Judas", ca. 1715 (*op. cit.*), 86; Bosman (1704/1967), 364; Law (2004a), 132.

56. Again Phillips (1732), 218.

57. *Barbot on Guinea*, 635; Bay (1998), 47. See also Aubrey Burl, *Black Barty: Bartholomew Roberts and his Pirate Crew 1718-1723* (first publ., 1997; Sutton Publishing, 2006), 219.

58. Oettinger in Jones (1985), 196.
59. Postma's contention (based on Ratelband) that slaves were initially kept in *leggers*, floating ships "in a lagoon", and later in corrals on the beach, until a company slave ship arrived, refers presumably to Offra, since it is difficult to reconcile with the rest of the evidence for Ouidah. What is certain is that there were, in contrast to the Gold Coast, no facilities like warehouses or dungeons (Postma [1990], 96).
60. The whole process is remarkably well described in "Instructions pour la coste de Guinée", ca. 1722 (AN Marine 3/JJ/252).
61. In 1773 (Yacou [2001], 122).
62. Isert (1788/1992), 98.
63. Law (2004a), 129-34.
64. Pruneau (1789), 209-13.
65. Houstoun (1725), 35.
66. Examination by R. Norris of the African Committee, 27.2.1788 (NA BT 6/9).
67. Law (2004a), 141.
68. Minutes of Council, Elmina, 11.1.1706, in Dantzig (1978), 127.
69. Lander (1830/1967), II, 250-51.
70. Postma (1990, 236) is, as far as we can see, the only one to make this point.
71. Snelgrave (1734/1971), 107; Herskovits (1938/1967), I, 55; Argyle (1966), 142; Alpern (1998b), 135; Honorat Aguessy, "Le Dan-Home du XIXe siècle était-il une société esclavagiste?", *Revue Française d'Études Politiques Africaines*, 50 (1970), 71-91 (75); Edna G. Bay, "Servitude and Wordly Success in the Palace of Dahomey", in Claire C. Robertson and Martin A. Klein (eds), *Women and Slavery in Africa* (University of Wisconsin Press, 1983), 340-67 (345); etc.
72. See for instance Compte rendu Le Phoenix, Petit Popo, 30.3.1738 (AD Charente Maritime, B.5729 d/p 79); Phillips (1732), 219 etc. (Relevant passages from Phillips also in Donnan [1930], 402-3).
73. Yacou (2001) and Harms (2002) provide good examples.
74. Bosman (1704/1967), 364a.
75. Documents in Justesen (2005), 189 & 770-73.
76. A good description of this practice in Gov. Wellemsen from Christiansborg, 23.1.1728; *ibid.*, 373.
77. Information (occasionally contradictory) and discussion: Letter from Whidah [Ouidah] 3.12.1707 [O.s.] (NA T70/2); N. Dubois, memorandum dated 10.11.1710 (ex-Zentrales Staatsarchiv, Merseburg; R.65.32 vol.I, ff.30-36 -courtesy of Adam Jones); "Relation du Royaume de Judas" c.1715 (*op. cit.*), p. 86; Pruneau (1789), 206; Yacou (2001), 137, 241-4; Gourg, "Mémoire 1791" (*op. cit.*); Northrup (2003); Postma (1990), 141 & 162; Klein (1978); Eltis & Richardson (2010), 159-96; Harms (2002); Conde de Sabugosa from Bahia 20.5.1734, reproduced in Verger (1968), 86.
78. Stephen D. Behrendt, David Eltis and David Richardson, "The Cost of Coercion: African Agency in the Pre-modern Atlantic World", *Economic History Review*, LIV, 3 (2001), 454-76 (459).
79. *Ibid.*, 466.
80. Examination of Dalzel by the African Committee, 5-8.4.1788 (*op. cit.*). See also Pruneau (1789), 206.

81. Tattersfield (1991), 114.
82. Example: letter from Lisbon 22.8.1719, OR, vol.XIV, doc.134; reproduced in *Anais/Annaes do Archivo Público/do Arquivo do Estado da Bahia*, XXXII (1952), 35.
83. For instance, no less than four English captains died at Ouidah between March and May 1686: Law (2006*)*, 331-3. Other examples from Law (1991a), 37-8; plus a letter from Jaquin (Jakin) in 1722 (NA T70/7).
84. Bouët-Willaumez (1848/1978, 195) reports of cases of cannibalism among the waiting slaves, due to inadequate feeding.
    At one stage the Danes, because of shortage of food, sold off their slaves to the Portuguese and others "so that they would not die" (Frantz Boye et al., from Christiansborg, 3.4.1714; in Justesen [2005], 246). Our guess is that they did anyway.
85. C.A. Syndermann from Christiansborg, 29.12.1723 (*ibid.*, 300).
86. *Barbot on Guinea*, 639-40 & 774-5; Atkins (1735/1970), 175; Pruneau (1789), 207.
87. Editors in *Barbot on Guinea*, 46.
88. Tattersfield (1991), 112.
89. Law (1992a), 29-33; Letter from Whydah [Ouidah] 6.6.1686 [O. s.] (NA T70/11).
90. Burl (1997/2006), 223 (referring to the original documents in NA: High Court of Admiralty Papers-HCA 49/Bundle 104 – a source we have not been able to consult). Roberts and his men figure in Robert Louis Stevenson's *Treasure Island* (1883). Most of them were either killed in action or hanged. John Atkins, whose earlier mentioned book (1735/1970) ranks as a major source for the history of the Slave Coast, played, in his capacity of naval surgeon, a central role in the trial of the pirates at Cape Coast Castle in 1722–23 (*ibid.*, 186-94; Burl [1997/2006], 223-87).
    Unsurprisingly "pirates cared nothing about the slaves": Arne Bialuschewski, "Black People under the Black Flag: Piracy and the Slave Trade on the West Coast of Africa, 1718-1723", *Slavery and Abolition*, 29, 4 (2008), 461-75 (469).
    A French view of it all can be read in "Mémoire de la course des forbains", 6.2.1722 (AN C6-25).
91. Guy-François de Kersaint, Journal de navigation 1757, 5.5.1757 (AN Marine B/4/77, doc.20); Report signed Marseille, 11.10. 1762 (AN Marine B/4/103, doc.183). Portuguese version of these events in OR, vol. 56, doc.17; Viceroy Bahia 10.5.1757 (APEB: Arquivo (Público) do Estado da Bahia).
92. Behrendt, Eltis and Richardson (2001), 459 & 462-3.
    Some sources: Rask (1754/2009), 53; Bosman (1704/1967), 365a; *Barbot on Guinea*, 775-82; Phillips (1732), 219; Bouchel de Juda, 30.4.1722 (AN C6-25, f.47).
93. See for instance, Phillips (1732), 229.
94. Tattersfield (1991), 121.
95. Phillips (1732), 229-30.
96. The most explicit on this point was a Frenchman by the name of Jacques Proa in 1777–8 who noted that "*[les Négresses] ont…une manière de faire jouir qui vaut bien celle des Européennes*". He did not add that to them is was a question of life or death ("Mémoire de Jacques Proa, dit Proa des îles", *op. cit.*).
97. See for instance, "Instruction pour la Coste de Guinée", ca.1722" (*op. cit.*); Harms (2002), 273. There is an excellent illustrative map in Eltis and Richardson (2010), 8.
98. "Instructions pour la Coste de Guinée" - ca. 1722 (*op. cit.*).

99. See, for instance, the description by Sir Henry Huntley, *Seven Years' Service on the Slave Coast of Western Africa* (London, Thomas Cautley Newby, 1850), 125-7. See also Tony Hodges and Malyn Newitt, *São Tomé and Príncipe. From Plantation Colony to Microstate* (Boulder, Westview, 1988), esp. 25; Robert Garfield, *A History of São Tomé Island, 1470-1655. The Key to Guinea* (Mellen Research University Press, 1992).
100. Bosman (1704/1967), 415.
101. Letter from R. Miles, Governor of the Cape Coast Castle; date missing, but must be early 1780s (NA T70/32) (among the many descriptions of the islands at the time of the slave trade, see Pruneau [1789], 249-60).
102. Tattersfield (1991), 117.
103. The *Diligent* in 1731 needed only 12 days on the crossing to Príncipe, but another ship arrived at São Tomé four and a half months after having left the Guinea coast (Harms [2002] 277). Three weeks' crossing is recorded in Aarestrup et al. (1797–8), 192.
104. (2001), 464.
105. Hernæs (1995), 251-2.
106. Example from Caldas (1759/1931), 298.
107. Pires (1800/1957), 140. See also Memorandum-1770s (AN Marine 3/JJ/247, doc.6); *Barbot on Guinea*, 722; Yacou (2001), 249-51.
108. According to Phillips (1732), 221.
109. In *Barbot on Guinea* (772-3) we have a close to rosy description of the Middle Passage – no more than 50 days and with quite adequate food, owing to the abundance of fish, birds and all sorts of sea-creatures, especially in the area of the island of Ascension.
110. For instance, in the period 1707–11 "56 slave ships owned by British merchants (were) lost, largely to enemy privateers (i.e.) over a quarter of all the ships estimated to have cleared British ports for Africa in this period" – including those on the home run. David Richardson, "The Eighteenth-century British Slave Trade: Estimates of its Volume and Coastal Distribution in Africa", *Research in Economic History. A Research Annual*, vol. 12 (Greenwich, CT 1989), 151-96 (158).
111. Most clearly expressed in a letter signed Baldwin & Humphreys, Whydah [Ouidah] 30.6.1722 [O.s] (NA T70/7).
112. "*On perd 1/6e des esclaves dans la traversée. Et après la vente à l'Amérique il en meurt au moins le quart, avant qu'ils soient accoutumés au climat*" (Mémoire 1714, AN C6-25 doc. 6).
113. "Africans who survived the Middle passage had dramatically different experiences when they landed, depending on where their voyage took them"; Eltis and Richardson (2010), 161.
114. From about the 1710s the slave trade to Bahia was supplying more labour to the mineral regions of the Brazilian hinterland than to the sugar-producing areas of the northeast. Cf. Alexandre Vieira Ribeiro, "The Transatlantic Slave Trade to Bahia, 1582–1851", in David Eltis and David Richardson (eds), *Extending the Frontiers. Essays on the New Transatlantic Slave Trade Database* (New Haven, Yale University Press, 2008), 130-54 (136).
115. For an amusing account of how the Europeans tried to evade those customs whenever they could, see J. Blythe from Whidah [Ouidah] 7.8.1687 [O. s.], in Law (2006), 399.

116. Law (2004a), 147.
117. Rinchon (1964), 342-3.
118. Phillips (1732), 216.
119. Law (2004a), 36-7; Gilles Soglo, "Notes sur la traite des esclaves à Glexwe (Ouidah)", in Soumonni, Codo & Adande (1994), 66-72 (67).
120. That is, if our French sources can be trusted. Cf. Mémoire sur le fort de Juda [Ouidah], postérieur à 1763-7 (CAOM-DFC, carton 26, c.75, d.109); Baud-Duchiron de Juda [Ouidah], 1.9.1778 (AN C6-26).
121. *Idem*; Williams Fort, Day book, March-April & Nov-Dec. 1763, signed Goodson (NA T70/1159); Williams Fort, Day book, July-Sept.1781, signed Abson (NA T70/1162); Gourg, "Mémoire pour servir d'instruction", 1791 (French archival source), p. 5; Per O. Hernæs, *Palaver: Peace or "problem"? A Note on the "Palaver-system" on the Gold Coast in the 18th Century based on Examples drawn from Danish Sources* (working papers 1-1988, Centre for African Studies, University of Copenhagen), 24; various documents in Law (2001a), 208-10 & 242.
122. Report of a Select Committee - no date - probably 1776 (NA, BT 6/3).

B1
FOCUS ON THE EUROPEAN SIDE

1. C.R. Crone (ed. and trans.), *The Voyages of Cadamosto, and other documents on Western Africa in the second half of the fifteenth century* (The Hakluyt Society, 1937), 114-25; John Vogt, *Portuguese rule on the Gold Coast 1469–1682* (Athens, University of Georgia Press, 1979), 1-92.
2. Or as Bosman put it (1704/1967, 334), the Portuguse were "loaded with...sorry goods". See also Ryder (1969), 43. On the history of Portugal, cf. Joaquim Romero Magalhães (ed.), *No alvorecer da modernidade (1480–1620)* and António Manuel Hespanha (ed.), *O Antigo Regime (1620–1807)*, respectively volumes III & IV of José Mattoso [gen. editor] *História de Portugal* (Lisbon, Ed. Estampa, 1997 & 1998).
3. It was built, "not because of fear of the local African polities, but because of fear of...a rival European power", namely Castile (Hair, "Columbus", 117).
4. Hair (*ibid.*) adds that Elmina was the first fortress in the history of the world to be built and maintained several thousand miles from the homeland. And Lawrence notes that it was the earliest European building in the Tropics (Lawrence [1963], 25).
    Monrad points out that the first Portuguese forts were built at the best sites, "where the surf breaks against rocky promontories", those being the safest places for landing along the coast (Monrad [1822/2009], 253 & 258).
5. Chauveau (1986), 196.
6. There is some disagreement among the specialists as to the precise definition of the *Costa da Mina* (See Law, 2005). It is true that the Capitania (Captaincy) of Mina covered formally only the region to the Volta river, the region east of that river "belonging" to the Captaincy of São Tomé. But the limits of the official Captaincies may not be relevant in this context. In fact *Costa da Mina* was a loose and primarily geographic term which no-one ever bothered to define properly, but in common parlance the *Costa da Mina* was routinely considered to englobe the coast both west

and especially east of Elmina, in fact all the way to Cape Formosa in present-day southern Nigeria.

7. "*Paños de algodon* [cloth], *y aceite de palma y muchas legumbres, como iñame y otros mantenimientos*". Cf. "Relação de Garcia Mendes Castelo Branco, começando da Mina atee o Cabo Negro (1620)", in Padre António Brásio (coligida e anotada pelo), *Monumenta Missionaria Africana*, vol. VI (*África Ocidental [1611-1621]*) (Lisbon, Agência Geral do Ultramar, 1955), 468-78 (470).

   The king of Allada was "our friend" according to the same Castello Branco. See also Pieter de Marees, *Description and Historical Account of the Gold Kingdom of Guinea (1602)* (translated from the Dutch and edited by Albert van Dantzig and Adam Jones; publ. for the British Academy by Oxford University Press, 1987), 225.

   The cloth was resold on the Gold Coast. Cf. K. Ratelband (uitgegeven door), *Vijf dagregisters van het kasteel São Jorge da Mina (Elmina) aan de Goudkust (1645–1647)* ('s-Gravenhage [the Hague], Linschoten Vereeniging, Martinus Nijhoff, 1953), 37-9, 158 & 381.

8. J.D. Fage, "More about Aggrey and Akori beads", in *2000 ans d'histoire africaine. Le sol, la parole et l'écrit. Mélanges en hommage à Raymond Mauny*, tôme I (Paris, SFHOM, 1981), 205-211; Law (1990b), 105. The beads of African origin were, as noted, later replaced by beads from Venice.

9. Robin Law, "The Slave Trade in Seventeenth-century Allada: a Revision", *African Economic History*, 22 (1994d), 59-92 (62-6).

10. 1593 is the date given in Ryder (1969), 84.

11. Underlined in a rather unlikely publication, G.F. Zook's *The Company of Royal Adventurers Trading into Africa* (originally published in *The Journal of Negro History* in 1919. Reprinted New York, Negro Universities Press, 1969), 45.

12. Postma (1990), 14-22.

13. Of the many works it is possible to refer to regarding the events related in this section, the ones we are most familiar with are C.R. Boxer, *The Dutch Seaborne Empire 1600–1800* (Hutchinson 1965; Pelican 1973); and Jonathan I. Israel, *The Dutch Republic. Its Rise, Greatness, and Fall 1477–1806* (Oxford University Press, 1995).

14. Garfield (1992), 251-79.

15. On this, and the next point, see, for a discussion: Postma (1990), 76; Verger (1968), 42; Dantzig (1978), 225-7; Israel (1995), 935-46; Hespanha (1997/8); Ernst van den Boogaart and Pieter C. Emmer, "The Dutch Participation in the Atlantic Slave Trade, 1596–1650", in Henry A. Gemery and Jan S. Hogendorn (eds), *The Uncommon Market. Essays in the Economic History of the Atlantic Slave Trade* (New York, 1979), 353-75.

16. Dantzig (1978), 225-7.

17. Boxer (1965/1973), 94-125.

18. "We cannot carry on trade without war nor war without trade", as one Dutch official in Java expressed it in 1614 (*ibid.*, 107).

19. See for example, Klooster (2009).

20. The official Dutch policy was that the Director-General of the WIC at Elmina "should try to convince the natives, with sweetness or with harshness…that once they belong to our trading-stations they should not trade with foreign ships" (Document from 1675 in Dantzig [1978]12).

21. African Committee to the Lords of the Treasury, 9.4.1812; *British Parliamentary Papers. Report from the Select Committee on papers relating to the African Forts* (ordered, by the House of Commons, to be Printed, 26.6.1816) (published by the Irish UP in the series Colonies Africa, vol. 1 – Shannon, 1968), 104.
22. The only reference we have found to that company is Margaret Makepeace, "English Traders on the Guinea Coast, 1657-1668: An Analysis of the East India Company Archive", *History in Africa*, 16 (1989), 237-84.
23. J.R. Jones, *The Anglo-Dutch Wars of the Seventeenth Century* (Longman, 1996), 178.
24. Jan de Vries and Ad van der Woude, *The First Modern Economy. Success, Failure, and Perseverance of the Dutch Economy, 1500–1815* (Cambridge University Press, 1997).
25. Postma (1990), 1-25.
26. Say Findlay and O'Rourke (2007), 178.
27. According to Boxer (1965/1973), 26.
28. Findlay and O'Rourke (2007), 187. See also Postma (1990), 23; & Documents from 1730 in Dantzig (1978), 238-9.
29. Klooster (2009), 154.
30. Postma (1990), 26-55.
31. Ryder (1958), 157.
32. Note the role of Italian Capuchins in this respect: Padre António Brásio (coligida e anotada), *Monumenta Missionaria Africana,* vol. XIV *(África Ocidental [1686–1699])* (Lisbon, 1985).
33. According to Justesen's "Introduction" (2005), XI.
34. Hernæs (1988), 20-34; Shumway (2011a), 66.
    The word *cassare* is one the Europeans of the epoch and modern scholars insist on deriving, curiously enough, from *casa*, i.e. house, whereas it is much more logical to conclude that it comes from the verb *casar*, meaning to marry. It appears in fact always in the context of matrimony.
35. "Luso-" comes from Lusitania, the Latin name for Portugal.
36. The main work on the Brazilian tobacco is of course Verger (1968).
37. Rae Jean Dell Flory, "Bahian Society in the Mid-Colonial Period: the Sugar Planters, Tobacco Growers, Merchants, and Artisans of Salvador and the Recôncavo, 1680–1725" (PhD thesis, University of Texas, 1978). Flory points out (158-9) that tobacco was not grown on plantations and can therefore be characterized as a smallholder crop.
38. John Edward Philips, "African Smoking and Pipes", *Journal of African History*, 24, 3 (1983), 303-19. The popularity of tobacco and pipe-smoking is even confirmed by archaeology (Kelly [2002], 105).
39. The theme is a constantly recurring one in the sources and the literature. In addition to Verger (1968), see for instance Isert (1788/1992), 139; Neil L. Norman, "From the Shadow of an Atlantic Citadel: An Archaeology of the Huedan Countryside", in J. Cameron Monroe and Akinwumi Ogundiran (eds), *Power and Landscape in Atlantic West Africa. Archaeological Perspectives* (Cambridge University Press, 2012), 142-66 (156-8).
40. See for instance T. Edward Bowdich, *A Mission from Cape Coast Castle to Ashantee (etc)* (London, John Murray, 1819; 3rd ed. F.Cass, 1966, ed. by W.E.F. Ward), 337.

41. Norris (1789/1968), 146-7; Gourg, "Mémoire 1791" (*op.cit.*), 7-9: "L'essai que j'en avais fait [to cultivate de tobacco plant] avoit surpassé mon attente...tabac superbe, d'une qualité de beaucoup supérieure à celui du Bresil".
42. Verger (1968), 37; A.P. Wærøe et al., from Christiansborg 30.4.1734 (Justesen [2005], 497); Levet de Juda [Ouidah] 2.3.1791 (AN C6-27, d.89).
43. Flory (1978), 246.
44. The royal decree of 12.11.1644 allowed slave traders to carry third-rate tobacco directly from Salvador to Bight of Benin to buy slaves (Verger [1968], 29). That is, only two years after the loss of the last Portuguese fort to the Dutch.
45. A.J.R. Russell-Wood, "Colonial Brazil: the Gold Cycle. c.1690–1750", in Leslie Bethell (ed.), *The Cambridge History of Latin America*, vol. II (Colonial Latin America) (1984), 547-600 (547-8).
46. On the abundant literature on the subject, we retain: Flory (1978), 161-2; and Carl A. Hanson, "Monopoly and Contraband in the Portuguese Tobacco Trade, 1621–1702", *Luso-Brazilian Review*, XIX, 2 (1982), 149-68.

    As for the stream of regulations, many of them figure in *Inventario*, vol. II (1914), esp. pages 166, 195 & 241; and in *Anais*, vol. 31 (1949), pages 95, 119 & 126, & vol. 32 (1952), pages 15 & 23.
47. Verger (1968), 28.
48. Flory (1978), 246; Hanson (1982), 159; Dantzig (1980), 161; Conde de Sabugosa [Viceroy 1720-35], Bahia 20.5.1734 (OR, vol. 30, doc. 30 - reproduced in *Anais* for 1977).
49. Some references (apart from the OR): Caldas (1759/1931), 292; Dantzig (1978), 9; Verger (1968), 224; Entry-journal Christiansborg 28.2.1704 (Justesen [2005], 194); Agreement Sir Dalby Thomas & Dutch General, 30.6 (o. s.), 11.7. (new style) 1708 (NA, T70/1516); Governor Cape Coast Castle 27.7 & 26.10.1781 (NA, T70/33); Anonymous, "Discurso Preliminar, Historico, Introductivo com naturaleza de Descripção Economica da Comarca e Cidade da Bahia" [no date, but later than 1789], *Annaes da Bibliotheca Nacional do Rio de Janeiro*, vol. XXVII (1905), 281-348 (341).
50. Summary in OR, vol. 71 (1761), page 259 (APEB). See also Verger (1968), 29; Lopes (1939), 6.
51. Postma (1990), 76-7.
52. Law (1994d), 66; Ernst van den Boogaart, "The Trade between Western Africa and the Atlantic World, 1600–1690: Estimates of Trends in Composition and Value", *Journal of African History*, 33, 3 (1992), 369-85 (373).
53. Law (1997c), 6; Strickroth (2003), 70. It must be remembered that the archives of the WIC for this early period have been lost.
54. Boogaart and Emmer (1979), 358.
55. Adam Jones (transcribed, translated and edited), *West Africa in the Mid-Seventeenth Century. An Anonymous Dutch Manuscript* (African Studies Association Press, 1995), 3.
56. But only 2-300 people according to another source (*ibid.*, 38, fn.3).
57. *Ibid.*, 37. It has been copied, it seems to us, by Dapper (1686, 306).
58. See for instance Buenaventura de Carrocera, OFM Cap., "Misión Capuchina al Reino de Arda", *Missionalia Hispanica*, VI, no. 18 (1949), 523-46 (534). Later, at least, the

installation of a new European Director in Ouidah continued to be a pompous affair, including, very much, in the epoch of Dahomey (Pruneau [1789], 170-74).
59. Northrup (2003) gives an idea of the situation in 1789/90; nothing had changed. See also Yacou (2001), 128-33; Law (2004a), 118; etc.
60. According to Thomas Phillips (1732, 218), the slavers could not refuse to buy the slaves of the king, usually the worst of the lot; they were *Reys Cosa* (Portuguese for "things of the king"). See also (Louis) Delbée (or D'Elbée), "Journal du voyage du Sieur Delbée, Commissaire general de la Marine, aux Isles, dans la coste de Guynée", in J. de Clodoré (ed.), *Relation de ce qui s'est passé dans les isles et terre-ferme de l'Amérique pendant la dernière guerre avec l'Angleterre et depuis en exécution de Traitté de Breda*, vol. II (Paris, G. Clouzier, 1671/microfilm edition Hachette 1972), 347-558 (438-9); *Barbot on Guinea*, 365; Law (2004a), 117; etc.
61. By Rinchon (1964), 337.
62. As one RAC official expressed it, "trade of Whydah [Ouidah] differs from...the rest of the coast..it depends upon the pleasure of the king (therefore necessary to) humour him" (RAC to Capt. Willis, London 21.8. 1705 [O. s.] [NA, T70/52]). Reason for which the RAC provided the king with "a very strong fashionable SEDAN" (*idem*. 12.2. 1706/7 [O.s.] (NA T70/52).
63. Robert Elwes, off Cape Lopez 31.1.1686; in Law (2006), 379.
64. P. Rocco da Cesinale, *Storia delle missioni dei Cappuccini*, tomo III (Roma, Tipografia Barbèra, 1873), 487; "Relation du Royaume de Judas, ca. 1715" (*op. cit.*); Akinjogbin (1967), 28.
65. Chouin (1998), 124.
66. Summary in Buenaventura de Carrocera (OFM Cap.), "Misión Capuchina al Reino de Arda", *Missionalia Hispanica*, VI, no. 18 (1949), 523-46.
67. Makepeace (1989).
68. Bailey W. Diffie & George D. Winius, *Foundations of the Portuguese Empire 1415–1580* (Un. of Minnesota Press, 1977), 160-2, 179 & map after page 192; Garfield (1992), 291.
69. Law (1994d), 73.
70. Gijs Rommelse, "The Role of Mercantilism in Anglo-Dutch Political Relations, 1650-74", *Economic History Review*, 63, 3 (2010), 591-611 (601).
71. Zook (1919/1969), 13.
72. Jones (1996), 150.
73. Law (1997c), 88.
74. Zook (1919/1969), 47. Holmes' original journals from his African expeditions are at Pepys Library, Magdalene College, Cambridge (PL 2698).
75. Makepeace (1989), 244.
76. Quoted in Zook (1919/1969), 61.
77. J.J. Crooks (ed.), *Records Relating to the Gold Coast Settlements from 1750 to 1874* (first ed. Dublin 1923, 2nd ed. Frank Cass, 1973), 3.
78. Kroon van Ardra met Bijbehorend Dokument-inventory number NM 816 a & b. Koper en glas, perkament.
    The crown was exposed as destined for Allada on the *Gold Coast*, that is, until the present writer took it upon himself to point out the error in a letter to the

museum, and received a letter of thanks from Dr. W.H. Vroom, Director of the "Afdeling Nederlandse Geschiedenis", dated 30 July 1987. The Duke of York's letter was published in R. van Luttervelt, "Herrinneringen aan Michiel Adriaenszoon de Ruyter in het Rijksmuseum", *Bulletin van het Rijksmuseum*, vol. 5, 2 (1957), 27-71 (53).
79. Zook (1919/1969), 62.
80. Jones (1996), 154-5.
81. "It is very probable that both England & the United Provinces greatly overestimated the value of the African forts & factories, but, at that time, the possession of them seemed very important", Zook (1919/1969), 62.
82. So argues at least Davies (1996), 12.
83. Law (1997c), 88. In sum, "the promising beginnings of the Royal Adventurers were wrecked by the Dutch wars": C.W. Newbury, *The Western Slave Coast and its Rulers. European Trade and Administration among the Yoruba and Adja-speaking Peoples of South-Western Nigeria, Southern Dahomey and Togo* (Oxford at the Clarendon Press 1961, reprinted 1973), 19.
84. Document ca. 1670 in Dantzig (1978), 11. See also another document p. 20.
85. Delbée (1671/1972), 384.
86. Abdoulaye Ly, *La Compagnie du Sénégal* (Paris, Présence Africaine, 1958), 101.
87. *Ibid.*, 21 & 94-5; Garfield (1992), 274; Quaye (1972), 37, 49, 94, 98 & 104; Nováky (1992), 57-69; Postma (1990), 75; Dantzig (1980), 38-46; Victor Granlund, *En svensk koloni i Afrika eller Svenska Afrikanska kompaniets historia* (Stockholm, 1879), 13-14.
88. Ly (1958), 103.
89. Carrocera (1949), 534.
90. Berbain (1942), 38.
91. *Barbot on Guinea*, 635-6.
92. Jones (1996), 179ff.
93. Davies (1957); Zahedieh (2010), 878.
94. Law (1994d), 76.
95. Law (1997c), 7.
96. Postma (1990), 36-8 & 110.
97. *Ibid.*, 74.
98. Ouidah-Glehue pops up frequently in Justesen (2005). See also Strickrodt (2003), 111; A. Jones (1985), 6-7 & 164-99; letters from Josiah Pearson Whydah 22.4. 1694 & 8.4.1695 (O.s.); in Law (1992a), 58-60 (the Brandenburgers sold the slaves at Danish Saint Thomas).
99. Belich (2009), 21. He adds: "A borrowed Asian crop was grown on expropriated Native American land by coerced African labour for the benefit of Europe" (21-2).
100. B.W. Higman, "The Sugar Revolution", *Economic History Review*, LIII, 2 (2000), 213-36.
101. The obvious reference is Philip D. Curtin, *The Rise and Fall of the Plantation Complex. Essays in Atlantic History* (Cambridge University Press, 1990).
102. Sidney W. Mintz insinuates as much in his classic *Sweetness and Power. The Place of Sugar in Modern History* (first publ. 1985, Penguin ed. 1986).

103. Jan de Vries, *The Industrious Revolution. Consumer Behaviour and the Household Economy, 1650 to the Present* (Cambridge University Press, 2008), 155.
104. Note also that cultivating and processing cotton was much less demanding (which meant less deadly) than sugar cane.
105. David Eltis is one who does not see a problem here, since he denies any active agency to the people of the Slave Coast. Says Eltis: "The foundations of the eighteenth century Carribean plantation economies based on African slave labour were laid in the 1650s and 1660s. The key factors...were probably the restoration of peace in England, and declines in both emigration from and population in England that began in the later 1650s. Strong productivity growth in the slave shipping business also helped. Above all, however, Europeans were unable to contemplate chattel slavery and slave trade-like shipping conditions for Europeans. African participation in transatlantic migration was much larger than European before the nineteenth century, but it was...driven by the refusal of voluntary migrants (or non-prisoners) [from Europe] to work on sugar estates, and the apparent inability of the European capitalists to overcome this aversion either by force or inducement... [Thus] seventeenth-century merchant capitalism was subject to ethnocentric blinkers, and was not quite as unbridled as it is often portrayed" (Eltis [1997], 108). In sum, all the relevant factors were European: a questionable assertion.
106. Law (2004a), 13.
107. Zahedieh (2010), 873.
108. See, for instance, "Instructions to Captain Samuel Kempthorne", London, 4.5.1686 (Donnan [1930], I, 354-5), and various documents from 1690 (*ibid.*, 377-85); Anonymous, "Certain considerations" (*op. cit.*).
109. Postma (1990), 78-83.
110. Revealing comments in Knud Rost and Claus Fedders from Christiansborg, 31.10.1718 (Justesen [2005], 272-3).
111. Bosman (1704/1967), 363a). At one stage the Danes accused the interlopers of abducting free Negroes (Thrane, 27.3.1702, in Justesen [2005], 123).
112. Josiah Pearson from Whydah [Ouidah], 8.4.1695 [O. s.], in Law (1992a), 59-60.
113. Most clearly expressed in Ligaard, 7.1.1707 (Justesen [2005], 204).
114. Dantzig (1978), 9; M. Johnson (1976), 22.
115. Tattersfield (1991), 84; Kris E. Lane, *Pillaging the Empire: Piracy in the Americas 1500-1750* (Armonk, NY/London; M.E. Sharpe, 1998).
116. Documents in Law (2006), 388. Also documents in Salvatore Saccone, *Il viaggio di Padre Domenico Bernardi in Brasile ed in Africa nel quadro dell'attività missionaria dei Cappuccini agli inizio dell 'età moderna. Con il testo della Relazione del "Viaggio"* (Bologna, Pàtron Editore, 1980) [mainly reproduction of documents 1713–1726], 168-72.
117. According to Law, Hueda became independent some time in the seventeenth century, but continued in some sense to acknowledge the overlordship of Allada. Cf. his "'The Common People were Divided': Monarchy, Aristocracy and Political Factionalism in the Kingdom of Whydah, 1671-1727", *International Journal of African Historical Studies*, 23, 2 (1990), 201-29 (213).

B2
THE AFRICAN SIDE: THE EARLY/LEGENDARY PAST

1. Randsborg & Merkyte (2009), I, 24-32 & 268.
2. *Ibid.*, 198-264 & 271.
3. Gayibor & Aguigah (2005), 7.
4. We are dealing here with a well-known worldwide archetype, places which the traditions point to as cradles for dynasties and/or peoples and which conserved some sort of mythical-historical status.
5. Adande (1984), 81.
6. Cf. the case of Kongo mentioned earlier.
7. Pazzi (1976), 229-33. See also his "Aperçu sur l'implantation actuelle et les migrations anciennes des peuples de l'aire aja-tado", in François de Medeiros (ed.), *Peuples du golfe du Bénin. Aja-Ewe* (Paris, Karthala, 1984), 11-19.
8. Gayibor and Aguigah (2005), 7; Wigboldus (1986), 312.
9. Gayibor (1997), 155.
10. *Ibid.*, 160.
11. Palau-Martí (1964), 96-7. Palau-Martí adds that when the king became very old, the earth opened itself under him and engulfed him. Does this imply a claim to indigenous status?
12. Agbo and Bediye (1997), 32-3.
13. Pazzi (1976), 230.
14. Gayibor (1997), 156-7.
15. *Ibid.*, 160.
16. Pazzi (1976), 230.
17. Dunglas (1957), 76; Gayibor (1997), 160-61.
18. D'Albèca, "Voyage", IV, *Le Tour du Monde*, no.11. 16.3.1895, 121-8 (124).
19. The reference is again to the relevant chapters in Gayibor (1997).
20. Suzanne Preston Blier, "The Path of the Leopard: Motherhood and Majesty in Early Danhomè", *Journal of African History*, 36, 3 (1995), 391-417 (408).
21. Gayibor (1997), 46-68; Quarcoopome (1997); Greene (2002a), 1061-7; Kelly (2001), 869.
22. Gayibor (1997), 170-78.
23. Quarcoopome (1997), 124.
24. Gayibor (1975), 119-20; Greene (2002a), 1024.
25. N.L. Gayibor, "Le remodelage des traditions historiques: La légende d'Agokoli, roi de Notse", in Claude-Hélène Perrot (ed.), *Sources orales de l'histoire de l'Afrique* (Paris, 1989), 209-14.
26. Gayibor (1997), 326.
27. *Ibid.,* 180-81 & 187.
28. Quarcoopome (1997), 110.
29. *Ibid.*, 110-11.
30. G.A. Robertson, *Notes on Africa; Particularly those Parts which are Situated between Cape Verd and the River Congo; (etc)* (London, Sherwood, Neely, and Jones, 1819), 236-8.

31. Sandra E. Greene, *Sacred Sites and the Colonial Encounter: A History of Meaning and Memory in Ghana* (Indiana University Press, 2002), 15-17.
32. Pazzi (1984); and Pazzi (1976), 238.
33. Nugent (2008), 935.
34. Klooster (2009), 153.
35. Sandoval (1627/1987), esp. 123 & 139.
36. Naxara (1672), 202.
37. R.P.F. Basilio de Zamora: "Cosmographia, o descripcion del mundo", dated 1675, p. 46 (Colección de MSS Borbón-Lorenzana, no. 244, consulted in the Biblioteca Provincial de Toledo, now part of the Biblioteca Pública del Estado en Toledo).
38. Naxara (1672), 204-5.
39. N.L. Gayibor, "Toponymie et toponymes anciens de la Côte des Esclaves", in the book edited by him: *Toponymie historique et glossonymes actuels de l'ancienne Côte des Esclaves (XVe-XIXe siècle)* (Lomé, Presses de l'Université du Benin, 1990), 25-42 & I-VIII (41).
40. André Pognon, "Le problème 'Popo'", *Études Dahoméennes*, XIII (1955), 13-14.
41. Gayibor (1985), 264-7; Gayibor (1997), 340.
42. Strickroth (2003), 80-81; Isert (1788/1992), 95.
43. Dalzel (1793/1967), 11.
44. Law (2004a), 46.
45. Iroko (2001), 17-34.
46. This is the theory of Yves Person, "Les monarchies africaines" [mainly about Dahomey], *Le Mois en Afrique*, 200 (July-Sept. 1982) 161-176 [167] & 202-3 (Oct.-Dec. 1982), 104-121.
47. Gérard L. Chouin and Christopher R. Decorse, "Prelude to the Atlantic Trade: New Perspectives on Southern Ghana's Pre-Atlantic History (800–1500)", *Journal of African History*, 51, 2 (2010), 123-45.

B3
ALLADA, ITS VASSALS AND NEIGHBOURS, AND THE EUROPEANS

1. Le Hérissé (1911).
2. See especially Lombard (1967b).
3. According to Herskovits (1938/1967), I, 167-9.
4. Argyle (1966), 5.
5. Herskovits (1933/1964), 35.
6. Argyle (1966), 195-6; Herskovits (1938/1967), I, 158; Paul Mercier, "The Fon of Dahomey", in D. Forde (ed.), *African Worlds. Studies in the Cosmological Ideas and Social Values of African Peoples* (Oxford University Press/International African Institute, 1954), 210-34 (225-6); Le Hérissé (1911),10.
7. *Ibid.*, 273; Adande (1984), 238; Hazoumé (1937/1956), 140.
8. Lombard (1967b), 50-52; Asiwaju and Law (1985), 432; Perrot (1972), 136-8.
9. In addition to earlier references, see especially C. Raymond Oké, "L'ancien Danhome des origines à la formation territoriale du royaume" (thesis, Université de Paris I-Sorbonne, 1972). Extracts published under the title "Les siècles obscurs du royaume

aja du Danxome", in François de Medeiros (ed.), *Peuples du golfe du Bénin. Aja-Ewe* (Paris, Karthala, 1984), 46-66.
10. Adande (1984), 238.
11. Le Hérissé, (1911), 100-3, 106-12 & 275-6; Argyle (1966), 4-5.
12. Summarized in Lombard (1967b), 57.
13. *Ibid.*, 57; Adande (1984), 292-3. Herskovits (1958, 358) adds the interesting detail that none of the Adjahuto ever entered the temple of Tedo.
14. Perrot (1972), 144.
15. Adande (1984), 127; Oké (1984), 51.
16. Bouchel de Juda, 30.4.1722 (*op. cit.*); Lombard (1967), 50-51.
17. Zamora, "Cosmographia" (*op. cit.*), 47.
18. Mondjannagni (1977), 137-63; Oké (1972), 46-66; Iroko (1998), 13-15.
19. Wigboldus (1986), 322; Robin Law, "Jean Barbot as a Source for the Slave Coast of West Africa", *History in Africa*, 9 (1982), 155-73 (159). Wigboldus believes Tori's "port" of Foulaen/Fulao was the place where the French established themselves in 1671, and that there is more generally a confusion between Foulaen and Ouidah. He may have a point.
20. *Barbot on Guinea*, 621.
21. Mondjannagni (1977), 88 & 121; Argyle (1966), 182.
22. What we know of Apa is summarized in Law (1997c), 16 (and map facing page 1).
23. Le Hérissé (1911), 273.
24. Mouléro (1966), 43-4.
25. Document from ca. 1670 in Dantzig (1978), 11.
26. Ryder (1969), 14.
27. Bradbury (1957), 21.
28. Ulsheimer in Adam Jones (ed.), *German Sources for West African History 1599-1669* (Wiesbaden, F. Steiner, 1983), 24.
29. Barnes (2009).
30. Ryder (1969), 73.
31. "Misiones del Congo y Etiopia" (BNE Ms. 18 178, folios 211-3) – a summary of the Capuchin mission to Allada written after its ending. See also Ryder (1969), 312.
32. Delbée (1671/1972), 558. Oyo and Benin were irreconcilable enemies of those of Allada, according to Barbot (*Barbot on Guinea*, 639).
33. Norris (1789/1968), XI.
34. Ryder (1969), 87; Law (1991b), 354.
35. After his godfather, Pedro Zapata, the governor at Cartagena de las Indias [or was he the interpreter encountered in Cartagena?]. His servant became Antonio, but he died on the return trip to Allada: "Misiones del Congo y Etiopia" (*op. cit.*); Carrocera (1949), 526.
36. *Ibid.*, 532-3; King's Instructions 28.6.1659 for the Prefect P. Luis Antonio de Salamanca (BNE Ms. 3818, f. 74-5), reproduced in Anguiano (1685/1957), II, 240-42.
37. Cód. 3818, folios 65-65v (BNE); also in Padre António Brásio (ed.), *África Ocidental (1656–1665)*, vol. XII of his *Monumenta Missionaria Africana* (Lisbon, Academia Portuguesa da História, 1981), 216-17.

38. The original documents in the Vatican Archivio della Sacra Congregazione per l'Evangelizzazione dei Popoli o "de Propaganda Fide"; especially the series Scritture originali Congregazioni Generali and Acta Sacrae. But most have been reproduced in Brásio (1981).
39. But the text in Gbe is very clumsy according to Gayibor (1997, 226).
40. The easiest available version is the French one. Cf. Henri Labouret and Paul Rivet, *Le Royaume d'Arda et son évangélisation au XVIIe siècle* (Paris, Institut d'Ethnologie, 1929). The Spanish version is in Anguiano (1685/1957), II, 251-66.

    There are two known extant copies of the original 1658 edition of the *Doctrina Christiana*, one in the Biblioteca del Palacio Real de Madrid (sign.IX-5.051), and the other in the Biblioteca del Instituto de San Isidro, also in Madrid.
41. The Provincial of the Capuchins of Castile to Propaganda Fide, 20.7.1659; in Brásio (1981), 254-5.
42. The really genuine primary sources are the two letters written by Padre Luís de Salamanca, as noted the head of the mission (but possibly penned by someone else, since Salamanca fell sick relatively quickly). They are dated Zima (Allada) 26 & 28.5.1660 and were sent to Propaganda Fide – reproduced in Brásio (1981), 285-8.

    There is in addition a very useful summary of the mission with the title "Relación de lo que sucedió a los Padres misionarios del reino de Arda (etc)", and written evidently very shortly after the end of the mission – possibly by some of the participants. Reproduced in Anguiano (1685/1957) (original in BNE, Ms.6170, ff. 120-5).
43. King's Instructions 28.6.1659 (*op. cit.*).
44. Underlined especially in Zamora, "Cosmographia" (*op. cit.*), 48.
45. *Ibid.*, 62-4; in addition to Naxara's observation (1672, 239) already referred to.
46. *Ibid.*, 204 & 238-9.
47. Carrocera (1949), 538.
48. Anguiano (1685/1957), 247.
49. *Ibid.*, 245.
50. Misiones del Congo y Etiopia (*op. cit.*).
51. Anguiano (1685/1957), 247-8.
52. *Ibid.*, 248-50; Naxara (1672), 35.
53. Reyes Fernández Durán, *La corona española y el tráfico de negros. Del monopolio al libre comercio* (Ecobook, Editorial del Economista, Madrid, 2011). There is also a lot of general interest in Paul Lokken, "From the 'Kingdoms of Angola' to Santiago de Guatemala: The Portuguese Asientos and Spanish Central America, 1595–1640", *Hispanic American Historical Review*, 93, 2 (2013), 171-203. See also Postma (1990), 31-47.
54. King's Instructions 28.6.1659 (*op. cit.*).
55. Ryder (1969), 99.
56. Possibility deduced from Strickroth (2003), 70.
57. On Spanish history in this period, the possible references are of course legion, one being Henry Kamen, *Spain 1469–1714. A Society of Conflict* (Longman, 1983).
58. Zamora, "Cosmographia" (*op. cit.*), 47.
59. Padre Luís de Salamanca's letter of 26.5.1660 (*op. cit.*)

60. Robin Law, "Religion, Trade and Politics on the 'Slave Coast': Roman Catholic Missions in Allada and Whydah in the Seventeenth Century", *Journal of Religion in Africa*, XXI, 1 (1991), 42-77 (especially 63-4 & 70); and by the same author, "Islam in Dahomey: a Case Study of the Introduction and Influence of Islam in a Peripheral area of West Africa", *Scottish Journal of Religious Studies*, VII, 2 (1986), 95-116 (113).
61. Some scattered examples: Versailles à M. Gourg, 8.12.1787 (*op. cit.*); Zamora, "Cosmographia" (*op. cit.*), 47; A. Félix Iroko, "Les hommes et les incendies à la Côte des Esclaves durant la période précoloniale", *Africa* (Rome), XLVIII, 3 (1993), 396-423.
62. A recurring theme: Misiones del Congo y Etiopia (*op. cit.*); Carrocera (1949), 535; "Relación de lo que sucedió a los Padres misionarios" (*op. cit.*), 245.
63. References in the preceding footnote, and in Carrocera (1949), 535-40, plus in the whole of the "Relación" (Spanish archival source).
64. Naxara (1672) does not mention directly his Popo experience, although Grand Popo looms relatively large in his account (pp. 202-3). What we have comes from Carrocera (1949, 541-2) for whatever it may be worth.
65. Ray A. Kea, "From Catholicism to Moravian Pietism. The World of Marotta/Magdalena, a Woman of Popo and St. Thomas", in Elizabeth Mancke and Carole Shammas (eds), *The Creation of the British Atlantic World* (Johns Hopkins University Press, 2005), 115-36.
66. Delbée (1671/1972), 434.
67. Another Frenchman, Jean Doublet (1883, p. 253), used the same title for the great priest of Hueda in 1704.
68. Delbée (1671/1972), 427-34 (the quotation from p. 434).
69. *Ibid.*, 443.
70. Bouchel de Ouidah, 30.4.1722 (*op. cit.*).
71. Perrot (1972), 136-42.
72. D'Albéca (1895), I, 86.
73. Perrot (1972), 142.
74. *Ibid.*, 148.
75. Norman (2009a), 339.
76. Des Marchais, "Journal de Navigation du voyage en Guinée, Iles d'Amérique, Indes Espanoles, fait en 1704" (British Library, Department of Manuscripts, Additional Manuscripts Add.19560), VII/75; Bosman (1704/1967), 339.
77. Norman (2009a), 394 & 402.
78. Law (2004a), 81.
79. Marcel Gavoy, "Note historique sur Ouidah par l'administrateur Gavoy (1913)", *Études Dahoméennes*, 13 (1955), 47-78; Agbo (1959), 12-16; Des Marchais, "Journal de Navigation" (*op. cit.*), 79-81; Robin Law, "Ideologies of Royal Power: the Dissolution and Reconstruction of Political Authority on the 'Slave Coast', 1680–1750", *Africa*, 57, 3 (1987), 321-44 (321); and by the same author (1990c), 214.

Finally, there is a curious tradition, which may or may not square with the above, which has it that the first settlers in Hueda were people who had been ousted from their original homeland and were then permitted to settle down in their new habitat by the king of Allada. What happened next was that the local Alladan governor

turned over the power to the head of the newcomer with, that is, the assent of the king of Allada (Relation du Royaume de Judas en Guinée [*op. cit.*], 21).
80. Agbo (1959), 12-16.
81. Des Marchais, "Journal" (*op. cit.*, 75-6; Norman (2012), 150-51.
82. "Relation du Royaume de Judas en Guinée" (*op. cit.*), 75.
83. Des Marchais, "Journal" (*op. cit.*, 77).
84. N****, *Voyage aux côtes de Guinée et en Amerique* (Amsterdam, 1719), 42-3.
85. Des Marchais, "Journal" (*op. cit.*), 77; Phillips (1732), 216.
86. Norman (2009a), 402. He adds (p. 408) that nails were associated with magico-religious power, another classic feature of sacred societies and sacred kingship, together with long hair (remember Samson).
87. Des Marchais, "Journal" (*op. cit.*), 87-8.
88. "Relation du Royaume de Judas en Guinée" (*op. cit.*), 34-5 & 42; Law (1990c), 205; Smith (1744/1967), 206.
89. *Barbot on Guinea*, 638.
90. Phillips (1732), 219.
91. Bosman (1704/1967), 344-5 & 367; Smith (1744/1967), 206. But note that Smith may not be an independent source. Cf. Harvey M. Feinberg, "An Eighteenth-century case of plagiarism: William Smith's *A New Voyage to Guinea*", *History in Africa*, 6 (1979), 45-50.
92. "Relation du Royaume de Judas en Guinée" (*op. cit.*), 83.
93. Bosman (1704/1967), 345.
94. "Relation du Royaume de Judas en Guinée" (*op. cit.*), 47-8.
95. Note that Huedanu/Hwedanu, meaning the people of Hueda, is also said to mean the people of the snake. Cf. Herskovits (1933/1964), 76.
96. Robin Law, "'My Head Belongs to the King': On the Political and Ritual Significance of Decapitation in Pre-colonial Dahomey", *Journal of African History*, 30, 3 (1989), 399-415 (413); Law (1991b), 112-15.
97. Law (2004a), 81.
98. Law (1991b), 112.
99. Atkins (1735/1970), 110-33.
100. Bosman (1704/1967), 371.
101. The priest of Hu was, according to Agbo, very much the chief priest in Ouidah in the colonial era (Agbo [1959], 138 & 257).
102. *Barbot on Guinea*, 635; Law (1991b), 238-41.
103. Law (1991b), 127-8.
104. Albert van Dantzig, "Les hollandais sur la Côte des esclaves: parties gagnées et parties perdues", in *Études Africaines Offertes à Henri Brunschwig* (Paris, EHE Sciences Sociales, 1982), 79-89 (80).
105. This is the opinion of Law (2004a), 46.
106. Including, between 1675 and 1679, a private French trader by the name of Jean Oudiette (Ly [1958], 128, footnote 16).
107. Verger talks about "la tentative malheureuse (en 1680) faite depuis São Thomé pour construire une forteresse à Ajuda" (Ouidah): Verger (1966), 4-5. See also Correia (1996).

108. Robin Law (ed.), *The English in West Africa, 1681–1683. The Local Correspondence of the Royal African Company of England, 1681–1699*, Part 1 (Oxford University Press/British Academy, 1997) 241, footnote 58.
109. Law (1991b), 130-31.
110. Wybourne described the RAC officials as "horne mad, Brandy mad, boy mad, Treacherous & foole mad men", and accused them of intriguing against their own colleagues; Wybourne, Guydah [Ouidah], 8.12.1682 [O.s.], in Law (1992a), 25.
111. Phillips (1732), 226.
112. The sources for Wybourne, the RAC, and the other actors in the 1680s/90s in Hueda and Allada are quite abundant, making possible a detailed reconstruction, something which will not be attempted here, however. Most have been reproduced in the collections of primary sources published by Robin Law (*Further Correspondence* and *The English in West Africa*, Parts 1, 2 & 3).
113. Letter from John Winder 23.3.1681/2 [O.s.]; in Law (1992a), 10.
114. The locals "will have all ships trade that comes" (Thorne from Ophra in Arda 4.12.1681 [O.s.], but referring to Hueda; *ibid.,* 5.
115. Law (2004a), 32-3.
116. Phillips (1732), 226.
117. According to Dalzel "The spot on which William's Fort stands, was formerly dedicated to religious purposes...the governors...have permitted a house within the walls...to be appropriated to Nabbakou, the titular god of the place...the reason why the English fort has escaped the disasters which befell the other forts" (Dalzel [1793/1967], 92-3; repeated in Law [2004a], 93). But Law adds that the French fort too had a shrine.
118. Burton (1864/1966), I, 64.
119. Many documents in NA T70/3 & T70/1474.
120. Dubois, Memorandum, 10.11.1710 (*op. cit.*)
121. The Dutch established a lodge in 1687, as noted earlier.
122. Neil L. Norman and Kenneth G. Kelly, "Landscape Politics: The Serpent Ditch and the Rainbow in West Africa", *American Anthropologist*, 106, 1 (2004), 98-110 (101 & 108); Kelly (1997b), 356.
123. N*** (1719),42-3. The palace was "the meanest I ever saw", stated Phillips (1732, 216). And Atkins agreed with him (1735/1970, 110).
124. Smith (1744/1967), 192-3.
125. Law (2004a), 44.
126. Des Marchais, "Journal" (*op. cit.*), 52.
127. Summary of the evidence in Law (1991c), 52.
128. Bosman (1704/1967), 366-366a.
129. We possess two letters (in Latin) written by Celestin de Bruxelles, one signed Dieppe 19.9.1681, and the other signed Juidae [Ouidah] in Guineâ 2.11.1682, both published in *Analecta Ordinis Minorum Capuccinorum*, vol. XXXI (Rome, 1915), 328-30 & 357-8. See also Louis Jadin, "L'oeuvre missionnaire en Afrique noire" in J. Metzler (ed.): *Sacrae Congregationis de Propaganda Fide. Memoria rerum 1622–1972 (350 anni a servizio delle Missioni)* (Rome/Freiburg/Vienna, 1972), vol. I/2, 413-546 (457).

130. "Relation du Royaume de Judas en Guinée" (*op. cit.*), 69-70. Hulst set out into the interior (did he reach Dahomey?) and died there in November 1683.
131. R. Père Godefroy Loyer (1660-1715), *Relation du voyage du royaume d'Issyny, Côte d'Or, Païs de Guinée, en Afrique (etc)* (Paris, 1714), esp. 14-15 & 296-7; Bosman (1704/1967), 368, 385-7; Père Gonzalez François, "Relation abrégée du voyage des Frères Prêcheurs, missionaires en Afrique et en Guinée (etc)", in "La Mission du V.P. Gonzalez François en Guinée, sur les côtes d'Afrique (1688)", *Année Dominicaine (etc)* (vol. 14, Sept. 1702, new edit. 1900), 461-75 (472-4); Cardeal Fabrício Spada ao Núncio Apostólico em Portugal, 8.2.1699, Brásio, XIV (1985), 187; N*** (1719), 52-4; Raymond J. Loenertz OP, "Dominicains français missionnaires en Guinée au XVIIe siècle", *Archivum Fratrum Praedicatorum* (Rome), vol. XXIV (1954), 240-68 (254); Law (1991c), 55-7.
132. Law (1991c), 52.
133. See Roussier (1935), which also contains most of the relevant primary sources, including Loyer's *Relation*.
134. Ducasse's "Relation" is reproduced in *ibid.*, 1-47. For Wybourne's reaction, see his letter of 18.2.1688 [O.s.] in Law (2006), 346-7.
135. According to the English. See Thomas James from Whydah [Ouidah] 29.12.1687 [O.s.] in Law (1992a), 49.
136. Bosman (1704/1967), 371.
137. Robert Du Casse, *L'Amiral Du Casse (1646–1715)* (Paris, Berger-Levrault, 1876). For the voyage to Guinea in 1687-8, see pp. 59-69.
138. John A. Lynn, *The Wars of Louis XIV 1667–1714* (Longman, 1999), 191-265.
139. See for instance Law (1990c), 203-12.
140. The relevant sources in Law (1991a), 29-30 & 74; and Law (1992a), 51-3, 90-91.
141. On the French side: "Mémoire sur la Guinée" 1716 (CAOM-DFC, c.75 d.113-4; Lettre de Du Colombier, ca. 1716 (AN Marine B/3/236).
142. Documents in Law (1991a), 29-30.
143. See for instance: "Description des Roiaumes ou l'on fait le commerce en Afrique" [written by Ducasse] (*op. cit.*); and many documents in the file NA T70/11; letter from Ouidah dated 21.6.1688, in A. Jones (1985), 164-5.
144. Robin Law, "Dahomey and the Slave Trade: Reflections on the Historiography of the Rise of Dahomey", *Journal of African History*, 27 (1986a), 237-67 (240); Eltis (2000), 153.

B4
DAHOMEY AND ITS NEIGHBOURS: EARLY BEGINNINGS AND AFTER

1. Cf. Law (1988), 446-7; Law (1997c), 65.
2. Le Hérissé (1911), esp. 273 & 289. See also Dunglas (1957), 90.
3. Pruneau & Guestard de Juda [Ouidah], 18.3.1750 (AN C6-25); Chenevert & Bullet, "Réflexions sur Juda" (*op. cit.*); Pruneau (1789), 153-4; Law (1992b), 116. It is above all a recurrent theme in the many works of David Ross, the way we read him.
4. Oké (1984), 61-3.
5. Anignikin (2001), 256.

6. Lombard (1967b), 86.
7. Blier (1995a), 18-27; Aguessy (1970), 76.
8. [R.P.] Jacques Bertho, "La parenté des Yoruba aux peuplades du Dahomey et du Togo", *Africa*, vol. 19 (1949), 121-32 (126); Alexandre Adandé, "Le maïs et ses usages dans le Bas-Dahomey", *Bulletin de l'IFAN*, XV, 1 (1953), 220-82 (269); Herskovits (1958), 217; etc.

    Note the role of "little people" clad as apes in the reception of a new European Director at Ouidah-Glehue (Pruneau [1789], 170-74).

    On the Pygmies more generally, see Kairn A. Klieman, *"The Pygmies Were our Compass." Bantu and Batwa in the History of West Central Africa, Early Times to c. 1900 C.E.* (Portsmouth, NH, Heinemann, 2003).
9. Le Hérissé says as much (1911, 243), as does also Glélé (1974, 67), both "officialists". The king was in addition *dokunnò*, which Glélé translates as *"maître et possesseur de toutes les richesses"*.
10. Herskovits (1933/1964), 35.
11. Verger (1952), 22; Bay (2001), 54.
12. Herskovits (1938/1967), I, 172-8.
13. Iroko (1993), 412.
14. Merkyte & Randsborg (2009), 70.
15. J.A.M.A.R. Bergé, "Étude sur le pays Mahi (1926–1928). (Cercle de Savalou-Colonie du Dahomey) AOF", *Bulletin du Comité d'Études Historiques et Scientifiques de l'Afrique Occidentale Française* XI, 4 (1928), 708-55 (esp. 739-45); Robin Law, "Dahomey and the North-West", in Claude-Hélène Perrot (ed.), *Cahiers du CRA (Centre de Recherches Africaines): Spécial Togo-Benin*, no. 8 (1994c), 149-67 (152); Herskovits (1938/1967), I, 172; Le Hérissé (1911), 278; Dunglas (1957), 94.
16. Pires (1800/1957), 88-9.
17. This purchase was ceremonially re-enacted at the installation of each new king, who symbolically "bought Dahomey" by a distribution of cowries, implying incidentally a very low price. (Law [1989b], 407; Glélé [1974], 111).
18. Le Hérissé (1911), 102-3 & 243-4; Law (1987), 334.
19. Savary (1976), 144.
20. Pélissier (1963), 44.
21. Le Hérissé (1911), 291-5; Oké (1972), 90; Dunglas (1957), 97-9 & 143; Law (1991b), 265-6.
22. Le Hérissé (1911), 294-5. Twins were greatly valued traditionally, to the point of being worshipped. Cf. Foà (1895), 193; Amélie Degbelo: "Les Amazones du Danxomè 1645-1900" (mémoire de maîtrise, Université Nationale du Bénin, 1979), 35.
23. Dunglas (1957), 96-9; Anatole Coissy, "Un règne de femme dans l'ancien royaume d'Abomey", *Études Dahoméennes*, 2 (1949), 5-8.
24. Robin Law, "The 'Amazons' of Dahomey", *Paideuma*, vol. 39 (1993), 245-60 (250). This echoes Mercier (1954), 232 .
25. Among those who believe in Tassi Hangbe's existence are Edna Bay (1998, 54-6) and Stanley Alpern. The latter argues that "The long silence on Ahangbé [Tassi Hangbe] may well have been due not to her non-existence but to a dynastic policy of suppressing her memory" (Alpern, 1998b, 10), as happened with Adandozan later.

26. According to Thomas Baillie from Cape Coast Castle 17.3. 1717/18 [O.s.] (PRO C113/262).
27. Bay (2001), 54.
28. Conseil de la Marine 5.1.1717, referring to a letter from Bouchel, Ouidah, 22.6.1716, (AN Marine B/1/19, f.1-3). Law (1997c), 110-11.
29. Apart from the case of Weme, examples in M'Leod (1820/1971), 66-71; Adande (1984), 91.
30. Le Hérissé (1911), 246-7; Argyle (1966), 82.
31. Based mostly on Pélissier (1963), 43-5. But see also Dunglas (1957), 57-66; and R.P. Thomas Mouléro, "Histoire des Wémenous ou Dékanmènous", *Études Dahoméennes* (NS), no.3 (1964), 51-76. Mouléro's work is, however, hard to decipher.
32. Dunglas (1957), 65.
33. Mouléro (1964), 65-73; and in many parts in Pélissier (1963). See also Georges Edouard Bourgoignie, *Les hommes de l'eau. Ethno-écologie du Dahomey lacustre* (Paris, Éditions Universitaires, 1972), 71-2.
34. Pélissier (1963), 55.
35. *Ibid.*, 46.
36. Fuglestad (1977).
37. Bay (1995), 11.
38. Law (1989b), 408.
39. "*Il tient tout du roi*", Glélé (1974), 66.
40. Law (1991b), 331. See also Law (1997a), 328.
41. Lombard (1967), 55-6. See also Glélé (1974), 65.
42. Blier (1995b).
43. Argyle (1966), 71; Glélé (1974), 127; Herskovits (1938/1967), I, 108-11; etc.
44. Law (1989b), 405-7; Law (2004a), 85.
45. Le Hérissé (1911), 243 & 248.
46. Law (1992b), 106-7.
47. As all our authors point out.
48. D'Albéca (1895), IV, 124.
49. Herskovits (1938/1967), I, 228; Bay (1998), 23.
50. Law (1989b), 401 & 413-14.
51. Expression from Bay (1998), 16.
52. *Ibid.*, 35 & 52-3; Michael Houseman, Blandine Legonou, Christiane Massy and Xavier Crepin: "Note sur la structure évolutive d'une ville historique. L'exemple d'Abomey (République populaire du Bénin)", *Cahiers d'Études Africaines*, XXVI, 4 (1986), 527-46 (535-6 & 543).
53. Herskovits (1938/1967), II, 38 (footnote).
54. Houseman et al., (1986), 542.
55. Le Hérissé (1911), 102-7.
56. *Ibid.*, 32-7; Argyle (1966), 60-63; Herskovits (1938/1967), II, 38-9.
57. Argyle (1966), 89-92.
58. *Ibid.*, 399.
59. Mercier (1954), 214.
60. Herskovits (1933/1964), 36.

61. Bay (1998), 319-20.
62. Law (1992b); Law (1991b), esp. 269-71; and many of his other works.
63. David Ross, "Dahomey", in Michael Crowder (ed.), *West African Resistance* (2nd ed., London, 1978), 144-69 (154).
64. Law (1976), 123.
65. Law (1991b), 227.
66. Bay (1998), 202.
67. Findlay & O'Rourke (2007), 171.
68. According to Ray A. Kea, "Firearms and Warfare on the Gold and Slave Coasts from the Sixteenth to the Nineteenth Centuries", *Journal of African History*, XII, 2 (1971), 185-213 (191).
69. Merkyte and Randsborg (2009), 76.
70. Examples: Ray A. Kea, "Administration and trade in the Akwamu empire, 1681–1730", in B.K. Swartz Jr & R.E. Dumett (eds), *West African Culture Dynamics. Archaeological and Historical Perspectives* (The Hague etc. Mouton, 1980), 371-92; W.A. Richards, "The Import of Firearms into West Africa in the Eighteenth Century", *Journal of African History*, 21, 1 (1980), 43-59.
71. David Ross, "Robert Norris, Agaja, and the Dahomean Conquest of Allada and Whydah", *History in Africa*, 16 (1989), 311-24 (314-5). The same viewpoint was in fact expressed by the Chenevert and Bullet in 1776 ("Réflexions sur Juda", *op. cit*).
72. Newbury (1961/1973), 27.
73. Barnes & Ben-Amos (1989), 48; Lombard (1967), 80; Burton (1864/1966), I, 291; Forbes (1851), 69.
74. Barnes & Ben-Amos (1989), 48.

B5
CONVULSIONS FURTHER WEST

1. Including Akyeampong (2001, 39).
2. Quaye (1972), 85.
3. Because of the presence of many Ga, according to Gilbert (1987), 311.
4. Fynn (1971), 37-9.
5. Quaye (1972), 117; Wilks (2001), 107-13.
6. According to Tilleman (1697/1994, 28).
7. *Ibid.*; Quaye (1972), 109-58, 274-5; documents in Justesen (2005), 216-17, 298, 318, 329.
8. The English and the Dutch either changed sides several times or supported both, not the Danes. (Quaye [1972], 109-58).
9. Justesen (2005), 54-5; Wilks (2001), 12.
10. Carta de Paulo Freire de Noronha ao Príncipe Regente D. Pedro (c.1671), in Brásio (1982), XIII, 153-8. Freire de Noronha was Governor of São Tomé 1668–71. The one who took over in 1673, Julião de Campos Barreto, was the one who conquered Christiansborg (Carta de um religioso a El-Rei, 17.10.1678; *ibid.*, 446-52).
11. Vogt (1979), 203-4.
12. Tilleman (1697/1994), 456; Sandra E. Greene, "Land, Lineage and Clan in Early Anlo", *Africa*, vol. 51 (1981), 451-64 (456).

13. Phillips (1732), 211-13; Wilks (2001), 24-5.
14. Wilks (2001), 55.
15. Quaye (1972, 158) argues that Basua and Ado were joint kings from 1680/81 to 1699.
16. *Ibid.*, 122.
17. Frantz Boye et al. from Christiansborg, 3.4.1714 (Justesen [2005], 248).
18. Quaye (1972), 155; Wilks (2001), 66 ff (based in part on Rømer [1760/2000]); Ray A. Kea, "'I Am Here to Plunder on the General Road'- Bandits and Banditry in the Pre-nineteenth Century Gold Coast", in Donald Crummey (ed.), *Banditry, Rebellion and Social Protest in Africa* (London, 1986), 109-32; plus a number of Danish sources reproduced in Justesen (2005), 136-8, 173-6, 199-200, 204-5, 232-3, 326, 361-3, 369-70.
19. Governor Herrn from Christiansborg, 1.7.1722, *ibid.*, 295.
20. Rask (1754/2009), 153.
21. Strickrodt (2003), 72, Law (2001c), 39; Akyeampong (2001), 39-40.
22. Kea (1986), 118.
23. Relevant documents (pages 41 & 50-1) in Law (2001c); and in Law (1992a), 36-7 & 42. See also Law (1991b), 243; Strickrodt (2003), 108-11.
24. Gayibor (1997), 378-83.
25. Greene (1988), 76.
26. Greene (1996b), 64; and by the same author: "Sacred Terrain: Religion, Politics, and Place in the History of Anloga (Ghana)," *International Journal of African Historical Studies*, 30, 1 (1997), 1-22.
27. Alain Mignot, *La terre et le pouvoir chez les Guin du sud-est du Togo* (Paris, Publications de la Sorbonne, 1985).
28. *Ibid.*, 70-74; N.L. Gayibor, "Origines et formation du Genyi", in N.L. Gayibor (ed.), *Le tricentenaire d'Aného et du pays guin*, I (Lomé-Presses de l'Université du Bénin, 2001), 19-31; N. Lowell (2005).
29. Mignot (1985), 185-7.
30. *Ibid.*, 29-53 & 76-86.
31. Strickrodt (2003), 79.
32. Law (2001c), 34.
33. Nicoué Lodjou Gayibor, "Recueil des sources orales du pays Aja-Ewe" (mimeogr., Institut Pedagogique National, Lomé, March 1977), 52; and by the same, "Recueil des sources orales de la region d'Aneho" (mimeogr., same Institute, same place, Oct. 1977), 19.
34. For a discussion, cf. Letters from Carter in Whydah [Ouidah] 10.5.1687 [O.s.] and from Pearson, same place, 8.4.1695 [O. s.], both in Law (1992a), pages 47-8 & 60 respectively; plus many of the works of Nicoué Gayibor, especially his "Les rois de Glidji: une chronologie revisée", *History in Africa*, vol. 22 (1995), 197-222 (217); and Gayibor (2001), 27.
35. Diedrich Westermann, *Die Glidyi-Ewe in Togo* (Berlin, 1935), 216 (a book we have been unable to consult); Gayibor (1985), 882-9.
36. "Le propriétaire du sol...en principe le descendant du premier occupant du sol... chargé d'accomplir certains rites propitiatoires liés au culte de la terre en tant que divinité"; (Gayibor [1985], 889).

37. Summary in Mignot (1985), 35-42 & 52-3; Gayibor (Mars 1977), 48-58.
38. Or as Mignot has expressed it (1985, 81) "dans la tradition des Guin tout est manipulation".
39. See for instance Gayibor (1997), I, 25.
40. For instance Fynn (1971), 67-9.
41. What follows is based on Justesen (2005), 214-15; 229,550; Wilks (2001), 19, 28, 33-4; Nørregaard (1968), 112; Daaku (1970), 155; Rask (1754/2009).
42. Amenumey argues that "there is no truth in the claim that Akwamu imposed its authority over Anlo", whereas most others argue the opposite. Cf. D.E.K. Amenumey, "A Brief History", in F. Agbodeka, *A Handbook of Eweland, volume I: The Ewes of Southeastern Ghana* (Accra, Woeli,1997), 14-27 (18).
43. See, for instance, Akyeampong (2001), 17.
44. Isert (1788/1992), 41; Grove and Johansen (1968), 1383-92.
45. Greene (2002b), 16.
46. Greene (1983), 90; Greene (1997), 10-11.
47. Law (1991b), 141-8; Strickrodt (2003), 117.
48. Pearson from Whydah [Ouidah], 8.4.1695 [O. s.], in Law (1992a), 60; RAC to W. Hicks at Whydah [Ouidah], 13.11.1711 [O. s.] (NA T70/52).
49. M' Leod (1820/1971), 139-40; Newbury (1961/1973), 29; Gayibor (1978), 138; Strickrodt (2003), 179-80; etc.

B6
THE 1680s–1720s: AN OVERVIEW

1. Adande (1984), 312.
2. Bosman (1704/1967), 395-8.
3. Law (1992b), 115.
4. A good example from the Gold Coast was the so-called Komenda wars. Cf. Dantzig (1980), 102-14; Chouin (1998), 166-81; Robin Law, "The Komenda Wars, 1694-1700: A Revised Narrative", *History in Africa*, 34 (2007), 133-68.
5. Hoolwerff himself provides us with examples in a letter of his from Ouidah 31.1.1687 (Dantzig [1978], 29).
6. Summary of the events in letter from Valentyn Gros, Hoolwerff's short-stay successor, 21.12.1690 *(ibid.,* 34-5).
7. Information from Valentyn Gros, summarized by him in document dated 18.2.1692 *(ibid.,* 62).
8. By de la Palma 31.3.1705 *(ibid.,* 109).
9. "We had much adoe to keep (Ofori) from plundering the factory. The French director was panyarred...and would me too if he could gett me. (Ofori is) very desireous to knock us all on the head". All the Europeans wanted to leave, but only the Dutch were permitted to do so. Cf. E. Jackline from Whydah [Ouidah], 25.12.1692 [O.s.] in Law (1992a), 56, and footnotes 374 & 378 on p. 92.
10. As interpreted and discussed by Strickrodt (2003), 105. See also Jackline from Whydah in Law (1992a).
11. Law (1991b), 246-7.

12. Phillips (1732), 222. See also Tattersfield (1991), 87-8.
13. Roussier (1935), 84.
14. Dantzig (1980), 74.
15. A. Jones (1985), 10.
16. Their action in Indonesia has been qualified by Findlay and O'Rourke (2007,199) as nothing less than "genocidal".
17. Pearson from Whydah [Ouidah], 15.4.1697 [O.s.] in Law (1992a), 60-61; Dantzig (1980), 74-5.
18. Jackline from Whydah [Ouidah], 13.10.1692 [O. s.], in Law (1992a), 56; Strickroth (2003), 104.
19. John Bloome from James Fort, Accra 10.10 & 11.12. 1692 [O.s.]; in Law (1992a), 56 & 69.
20. Wilks (2001), 33.
21. Several letters from John Wortley and Edward Jackline in 1692 (Law [1992a], 51-5 & 90-91); Phillips (1732), 215.
22. According to the Dutch (letter signed V. Gros, 7.8.1691, in Dantzig [1978], 35).
23. Edward Jackline from Whydah [Ouidah], 10.5.1692 [O.s.], in Law (1992a), 52-4: "here is no resisting the Country", Jackline concluded, a conclusion Robin Law has used as the title of one of his articles. Cf. Robin Law, "'Here is No Resisting the Country': The Realities of Power in Afro-European Relations on the West African 'Slave Coast'", *Itinerario*, 18 (1994e), 50-64.
24. Francis Smith from Whydah [Ouidah] 20.9.1693 [O.s.], in Law (1992a), 57.
25. Strickrodt (2003), 105. Thomas Phillips argues that he was poisoned by members of his entourage who had been bought by the king of Hueda (Phillips [1732], 220).
26. Strickrodt (2003), 106.
27. Law (1991b), 60-61; Akyeampong (2001), 38.
28. Strickrodt (2003), 106.
29. Pearson from Whydah [Ouidah], 3.4.1694 [O. s.], in Law (1992a), 58; Bosman (1704/1967), 335-6; Law (1992b), 109.
30. Bosman (1704/1967), 396-7; Law (1977a), 157.
31. Willis from Whydah [Ouidah] 23.3.1703/4 [O.s.] (NA T70/28).
32. Capt. Matthew Wilson to the RAC, from King's Town, Whydah [meaning Savi], 26.6.1699; in Donnan (1930), I, 436.
33. "There are so many ships here at the Coast that they might have rained down from the clouds...also much sickness of smallpox among the Negroes this year" (Thrane from Christiansborg, 27.7.1700; in Justesen [2005], 118).
34. Bosman (1704/1967), 329-30; Law (1991b), 241.
35. Thrane from Christiansborg, 27.3.1702 (Justesen [2005], 123).
36. Wilks (2001), 28.
37. On Ado's retreat, there are many relevant documents in Justesen (2005), 154-8. The Danes monitored closely the events in the east and the retreat of the Akwamus.
38. Greene (1981), 459; Wilks (2001), 29. See also Dantzig (1980), 220.
39. See the preceding chapter.
40. For instance, in 1722 ounces of gold were delivered by Hueda to Akwamu via Dutch commies. The idea was to attack Jakin. But as the Akwamu did nothing, the king of

41. Strickrodt (2003), 119.
42. Expression in letter from E. Jackline, Whydah [Ouidah], 13.10.1692 [O. s.] in Law (1992a), 55. Silke Strickrodt makes it clear throughout her dissertation that the rulers of Little Popo-Glidji never mended their ways.
43. Law (2004a), 33.
44. "Carta determinado ouvir os homens de negócio sôbre consentir o rei de Ajudá-Hueda que se faça na sua terra uma feitoria ou fortaleza, e informar dos meios que se oferecem para edificar e sustentar o seu presídio" (Lisbon 2.12.1698); OR, vol. 5, doc.80; in *Anais*, vol. 31 [1949], 97. Also several more documents of the OR, vols. 8 & 11 in the same volume of the *Anais*. See also Verger (1966), 5-8; & Ryder (1958), 159, for slightly different versions.
45. Davies (1957), 79 & 135. It had to do with the Glorious Revolution, according to Zahedieh (2010), 883.
46. Zahedieh (2010), 883.
47. RAC to King of Widah [Hueda], London 12.8.1701 [O. s.] (NA T70/51).
48. There is a significant letter from the RAC, signed 14.8.1713 [O.s.] to Joseph Blaney at Ouidah: "You must endeavour to get the French & Dutch agents to join with you in giving effectual disappointment to interlopers and constantly use your utmost interest & skill with the natives to do the same" (NA T70/52) (same argument in other documents from 1713 in the same file).
49. Davies (1957), 134-6 & 151-2. The RAC's role and position in the context of English politics have recently been re-examined in William A. Pettigrew, *Freedom's Debt: the Royal African Company and the Politics of the Atlantic Slave Trade, 1672–1752* (University of North Carolina Press, 2013).

David Eltis argues that the RAC accounted for just over 17 per cent of British slaving voyages between 1699 and 1703–4 (and later?), as opposed to 75 per cent in the 1680s (Eltis [2000], 153, fn.63).
50. Philippe Haudrere, *La compagnie française des Indes au XVIIIe siècle* (Paris, Librairie de l'Inde éditeur, 1989), 124 & 392. See also documents 172, 175 & others in AN C6-27. Note that the French slave trade, in contrast to the English, remained heavily subsidized. Dantzig (1980), 17; Postma (1990), 115-16.
51. On the English case, see Davies (1957), 344-5; Martin (1927), 8-27; Parliamentary Papers, "Reports...relating to the African Forts" (*op. cit.*), 3-4.
52. Manning (1983), 844.
53. Frantz Boye from Christiansborg, 30.5.1713 & 3.4. 1714 (Justesen [2005], 243 & 249).
54. Many documents in *ibid.*, pp. 197, 205, 209-15.
55. A possible reference is once more Lynn (1999); to which we may add Joaquím Albaredo Salvadó, *La Guerra de Sucesión de España (1700–1714)* (Barcelona, Crítica, 2010).
56. Treaty signed in Madrid in August 1701 by none other than Jean-Baptiste Ducasse, the one who is reputed to have donned a leopard's skin in Hueda in 1688. The relevant documents in AN Colonies F/2a/7.

57. Note that "The French Americas actually took in fewer slaves than any of the major European empires in the Americas"; David Eltis and David Richardson, "Prices of African Slaves Newly Arrived in the Americas, 1673–1865: New Evidence on Long-Run Trends and Regional Differentials", in David Eltis, Frank D. Lewis and Kenneth L. Sokoloff (eds), *Slavery in the Development of the Americas* (Cambridge University Press, 2004), 181-218 (190).
58. See Chapter V in part A.
59. Lettres de la Chambre de Commerce de Nantes, 9.7.1718 & 24.2.1720 (AN Marine B/3/251 & B/6/264).
60. Berbain (1942), 83; M. Johnson (1966), 208-9.
61. Eltis (2000), 127-8.
62. *Ibid.*, 125-6; Davies (1957), 207. Relevant documents in NA T70/14 and AN Colonies F/2a/7.
63. Something the French realized already in 1706: Mémoire sur le commerce de l'asiente et les moyens de remedier aux abus-1706 (AN Colonies F/2a/7).
64. Mémoire de la Compagnie de l'Assiente 27.6.1716 (AN Colonies, F/2a/8).
65. Law (1991b), 133-4.
66. Original draft reproduced in Dantzig (1978), 115-16.
67. Des Marchais, "Journal de Navigation" (*op. cit.*), 29-30 & 52-4; Dantzig (1980), 149.

   Some details regarding the treaty's practical application are presented by the Dane Johannes Rask: "at Fida (Ouidah-Glehue), the one enemy will not attack the other for a distance of 2 miles above and two miles below. If two ships belonging to nations at war with each other are anchored there for trade and they both become ready to sail at the same time, they are not allowed to weigh anchor at the same time, but one of them must leave at least 24 hours before the other one. Therefore, ships for all the countries head for Fida [Ouidah-Glehue]" (Rask [1754/2009], 72).
68. The contrast with the Gold Coast was underlined by the neutral Danes. See for example letter from Lygaard, 14.7. 1708 (Justesen [2005], 214).
69. Klooster (2009), 172.
70. N*** (1719), 41-3; Law (1991b), 252.
71. Letters from Whydah [Ouidah] 25 & 26.8. 1703 [O.s.] (NA T70/13); Akinjogbin (1967), 35; Law (1990c), 217.
72. N*** (1719), 111; Law (1991b), 252-4.
73. RAC to Peter Duffield at Widah [Ouidah], London 23.2.1702 [O. s.] (NA T70/51); RAC to W. Hicks at Whidah [Ouidah], 13.11.1711 [O. s.] (NA T70/52). Also many documents in NA T70/14; Dantzig (1980), 149.
74. Roussier (1935), XXXIII.
75. Gov. Hartwig Meyer to the Directors, Christiansborg 23.9.1703 (Justesen [2005], 168-9).
76. N*** (1719), 40-41; Letter from Whydah [Ouidah] 25.8.1703 (archival source).
77. Not all parts of Guinea were equally fortunate. We have already referred to the situation on the Gold Coast. And São Tomé suffered a devastating attack by the French in April-May 1709 (Garfield [1992], 294).
78. Doublet (1883), 250-57.
79. *Ibid.*, 258.

80. *Ibid.*, 253-6; Berbain (1942), 39 & 56.
81. Doublet (1883), 262-3.
82. Lettres de Martinique 6.7.1706 & 8.2.1707 (AN Colonies C/8a/16, f.160 & C/8b/2, f.86).
83. Law (1997c), 5; Marty (1925), 113.
84. Law (1986b), 99.
85. Law (1991b), 250-51; Greene (1996b), 33.
86. Letters from van der Broucke, 26.8.1705 & 10.11.1705 (Dantzig [1978], 111 & 125).
87. Relevant documents in *ibid.*, 113-19.
88. Postma (1990), 75.
89. Dantzig (1980), 168.
90. *Ibid.*, 214-21.
91. *Ibid.*, 148-57; Law (1991b), 139-40 & 253-4.
92. Richard Willis from Whydah [Ouidah], 8.12.1706 [O. s.] (NA T70/5).
93. Documento 3, Lisbon 1.3.1723, OR vol. XVIII 1722-3 (*Anais*, vol. 32 [1952], 124).
94. Verger, *Flux*, 47.
95. Willis originally proposed this type of trade in a letter from Ouidah dated 18.2.1707 [O. s.] (NA T70/5). But the RAC authorities in London were dead set against it: "We strictly forbid you to trade with the Portugueze, or in the least to encourage them. Your notion of tradeing with the Portugueze is very destructive to the English interests...should the Portugueze by your encouragement fix themselves in the Whiddah [Ouidah] trade, you will bring irreparable injury to the English nation" (from the RAC to Capt.Willis, 26.6.1707 [O. s.] [NA T70/52]).

    However, those same authorities effectuated a complete volte-face in a very short time. Cf. RAC to Capt. R.Willis, 19.9.1707 [O.s.] (NA T70/52). And in 1712 the question was how "the Portugueze trade at Whidah [Ouidah] may be made advantageous and subservient to ours" (African House to Whydah, 17.3.1712 [O. s.] [NA T70/52]).
96. Tobacco exports to West Africa multiplied seven times between 1700 and 1750, before stagnation set in. Cf. B.J. Barickman, *A Bahian Counterpoint. Sugar, Tobacco, Cassava and Slavery in the Recôncavo, 1780–1860* (Stanford University Press, 1998), 29. Gold we know much less about.
97. As Joseph Blaney, the English director at Ouidah, admitted in 1714: "There is no way to make the Portuguese trade subservient to the Company's interests", (Blaney from Whydah [Ouidah], 22.4.1714 [O. s.][NA T70/5]).
98. Platfue et al., from Christiansborg 16.1.1751 (Justesen [2005], 813); Harms (2002), 148 & 247; David Henige and Marion Johnson, "Agaja and the slave trade: another look at the evidence", *History in Africa*, III (1976), 57-67 (63).
99. Example: RAC to Ambrose Baldwyn, African House, 14.12.1720 (NA T70/53).
100. Bitter complaint from for instance William Baillie Williams Fort, 20.11.1716 [O.s.] (T70/22).
101. Ryder (1958), 158.
102. Flory (1978), 189-91 & 218.
103. RAC to Whydah (Ouidah) 4.10.1711 [O. s.] (NA T70/52); Randall Logan from Whidah (Ouidah) 14.2.1714 [O. s.] (NA T70/6: the same to Joseph Blaney, Whydah

(Ouidah) 15.3.1715 [O. s.] (NA T70/3); from Cape Coast Castle, 2.5.1715 [O. s.] (NA T70/6); J. Blaney from Whydah (Ouidah) 10.12.1715 [O.s.] (NA; T70/6); Bouchel: Mémoire…pour le rétablissement du commerce de Juda et Ardre, 20.8.1718 (AN C6-25, d.38); Mémoire sur la Guinée, 1716 (*op. cit.*). Law (1990b), 108; Verger (1968), 47-51; Harms (2002), 209-10.

104. Relation du Royaume de Judas, c.1715 (*op. cit.*), 33.
105. Du Coulombier, "Mémoire de la suite des affaires du pays de Juda", 14.12.1715 (AN C6-25, d.25).
106. Relation du Royaume de Judas (*op. cit.*); Akinjogbin (1967), 40.
107. For a discussion, see Dralsé de Grand-Pierre (1718), 168-9; Akinjogbin (1967), 39-40; Law (1991b), 150-53.
108. According to Akinjogbin (1967), 47.
109. Snelgrave (1734/1971), 5. See also Norman (2012).
110. Lettre de Juda 29.5.1714 (AN C6-25, d.17); Du Coulombier, Mémoire de la suite des affaires de Juda, 14.2.1715 (*op. cit.*); Akinjogbin (1967), 42; Oké (1972), 99-105.
111. Law (1987), 321; Law (1990c), 222-3.
112. *Ibid.*, 224; Strickrodt (2003), 120.
113. Letter from W. Green, late factor at Jakin, 2.10.1717 (NA T70/22; Law (1997c), 110; Asiwaju and Law (1985), 440.
114. Law (1991b), 259-60; Law (1997c), 59 & 108.
115. Law (1990c), 224-5.
116. Law (1997c), 59-61.
117. Example: letter from Williams Fort 10.5.1720 [O. s.] (NA T70/54). More generally: Law (1990c), 227.
118. Bouchel, de Juda, 30.4.1722 (*op. cit.*).
119. *Ibid.*; Law (1987), 321.
120. Law (1997c), 107-10.
121. Mémoire de l'Estat du pays de Juda et de son négoce, 1716 (AN C6-25, d.31).
122. Projet d'instruction du Conseil de la Marine au Sieur Bouchel, Louvre, 10.10.1716 (AN Marine B/1/9, f.431); Berbain (1942), 57.
123. *Ibid.*, 36; Haudrere (1989), 57.
124. Mémoire de Lisbonne, 20.3.1717 (AN C6-25); Mémoire concernant la Cie de Juda, 1722 (*op. cit.*).
125. In 1719 the Portuguese government threatened to prohibit the trade with the Dutch, to expel them and to confiscate their ships in Brazil. Cf. OR, vol. 52, doc. 71, Lisbon 5.5.1719 (reproduced in *Anais* no. 47 [1983] 73). Ryder (1958, 158) talks of the "exactions" committed by the Dutch which were regularly "supplemented by barely-disguised piracy".
126. Dantzig (1980), 24.
127. There were occasionally discussions about sending Portuguese warships to the Costa da Mina for protection against the Dutch (de Lisboa, 16.6.1726 [AHU, São Tomé, caixa 5, doc. 21]).
128. Kelly (2002), 109 & map page 111.
129. Various documents in *Anais*, vol. 32 (1952), 88-9 & 112 ff. There is a catalogue of all the grievances of Portuguese, but not necessarily Luso-Brazilian officialdom,

against Torres in Conde de Sabugosa to the King, 16.6.1730 (APEB OR, vol. 27, Doc.25a, folha 81).

130. But the English noted already in 1722 that the Portuguese had built a fort and factory at Ouidah (letter from William's Fort 25.1. 1721/2 [O. s.] [NA T70/7]).
131. Anonymous document (no date) in AN C6-25, d.40; Dantzig (1980), 199; Verger (1968), 139-44.
132. (Correia Lopes [1939], 7).
133. Law (2004a), 10 & 37-8.
134. Point made by Davies (1957), 279.
135. Lopes Correia (1939), 6.
136. "Les portugais font la loy à présent"; Levesque de Whydah [Ouidah], 4.4.1723 (AN C6-25, d.47).
137. Conseil de Marine, 29.9.1718 (AN C6-25, d.37); Bouchel de Juda 30.4.1722 (*op. cit.*); William Baillie from Sabee [Savi], April 1719 (PRO C113/262); Strickrodt (2003), 128; Akinjogbin (1967), 52-6; Law (1991d), 140.
138. Rost et al. from Christiansborg 11.3 & 15.6,1719 (Justesen [2005], 274-5).
139. See especially William Baillie from Sabee [Savi] 30.4.1718 [O. s.] (NA T70/1475); Akinjogbin (1967), 56.
140. Akinjogbin (1967), 51-2; Law (1977a), 220-21.
141. Law (1991b), 140-41.
142. Levesque de Ouidah, Sept? 1717 (AN C6-25, d.35); Bouchel de Xavier [Savi?] 6.6.1717 (AN C6-25, d.33); William Baillie from Sabee [Savi], April 1719 (*op. cit.*).
143. Mémoire de la course des forbains, 6.2.1722 (*op. cit.*); Mémoire concernant la Cie de Judas 1722 (*op. cit.*); Snelgrave (1734/1971), 193-220; Bialuschewski (2008), 469; Lane (1998), 189; etc.
144. According to Akinjogbin (1967), 58.
145. De Lisboa 22.9.1724; OR, vol. XX (*Anais*, 32 [1952], 188).
146. Atkins (1735/1970), 190-4; Postma (1990), 79.
147. Burl (1997/2006), 245-61.
148. Atkins (1735/1970).
149. As noted by the Danes. Cf. Waerö from Christiansborg 24.12.1730 (Justesen [2005], 433).

C1
THE DRAMATIC AND DECISIVE 1720s

1. Lambe's letter of 27.11.1724, in Smith (1744/1967), 186.
2. Expression borrowed from Law (1991b), 286.
3. Fynn (1971), 46-68, and map on p. 125 (but is the map acceptable?).
4. Law (1997c), 109.
5. Among the Europeans who wrote about these events, the one who comes closest to the status of eye-witness, apart from Lambe, is William Snelgrave. But even Snelgrave seems to have got lost at times in the details.
6. There were at least nine of them, according to Law ([1997c], 109) - the nine who acknowledged the king of Dahomey as their new suzerain.

7. Or so argues Adande ([1984], 228).
8. According to Snelgrave ([1734/1971], 20).
9. A central testimony in this context is that of the French slave-trader Robert Durand who did business at Jakin for some months in 1731–32. When he arrived on board *Le Diligent*, he counted 15 ships there, eight of them flying the Portuguese colours (Harms [2002], 227). According to Durand, the town was prodigiously rich (*ibid.*, 236).
10. Or so argues Snelgrave (1734/1971, 98).
11. Ringard/Law (1727/1988b), 326.
12. This from Snelgrave (1734/1971), 7-9; Smith (1744/1967), 70; Dunglas, (1957), 150.
13. Dalzel (1793/1967), 10.
14. As reported by William Smith (1744/1967), 177.
15. *Ibid*. Elaborations in Akinjogbin (1967), 82; Law (1977a), 160; etc.
16. A point made by Law (1976), 123.
17. Letter from the Luso-Brazilian Director Francisco Pereyra Mendes, 22.5.1726 (*op. cit.*), quoted in Verger (1966), 25; Pruneau and Guestard, 18.3.1750 (*op. cit.*); Law (1997c), 118.
18. Or this is what Pruneau & Guestard argued in a letter dated 18.3.1750 (archival source). See also Law (1997c), 118.
19. See for instance Law (1977a), 160-3
20. *Ibid.*, 158.
21. Alpern (1998a), 37.
22. Peter Morton-Williams, "The Oyo Yoruba and the Atlantic Trade, 1670-1830", *Journal of the Historical Society of Nigeria*, 3, no.1 (1964), 25-45; Law (1977a), 186.
23. Deduced from a superficial perusal of World Health Organization websites. There are some illuminating pages on the problem in general in Robin Law, *The Horse in West African History. The Role of the Horse in the Societies of Precolonial West Africa* (International African Institute/Oxford University Press, 1980), 76-82. See also Klein (1996), 251.
24. Although extremely well proportioned, according to M'Leod (1820/1971), 29. See also Bay (1998), 115.
25. John Thornton, "Warfare, Slave Trading and European Influence: Atlantic Africa 1450–1800", in Jeremy Black (ed.), *War in the Early Modern World, 1450–1815* (London, UCL Press, 1999), 129-46 (137).
26. Law (1997c), 121.
27. There are modern parallels in the Rif war in Northern Morocco in the 1920s and the Vietnam war ending in 1975. Recalled by María Rosa de Madariaga, *Abd-el-Krim el Jatabi. La lucha por la independencia* (Madrid, Alianza Editorial, 2009), 20.
28. Randsborg and Merkyte (2009), vol. 2, 3-31, 57-97 & 269; Merkyte and Randsborg (2009), 61.
29. Snelgrave (1734/1971), 28.
30. *Ibid.*, 26 & 31-2.
31. *Ibid.*, 61-4 & 75.
32. Jeremy Tinker & co. from William's Fort, 28.5.1726 [O.s.] (NA T70/7).

33. Law (2002), 267.
34. Letter from Pereyra Mendes, 22.5.1726 (*op. cit.*).
35. Snelgrave (1734/1971), 9 & 20-21; Akinjogbin (1967), 68-9.
36. Ringard/Law (1727/1988b), 326.
37. Dantzig (1980), 220.
38. Law (2004a), 52-70.
39. Ringard/Law (1727/1988b), 328.
40. This is confirmed by the archeologists. The site was resettled only in the nineteenth century. Cf. Norman (2009a), 393.
41. Letter 4.4.1727, quoted in Verger (1966), 26.
42. *Ibid.*
43. Ringard/Law (1727/1988b), 327.
44. Dantzig (1982), 86.
45. Ringard/Law (1727/1988b), 326-8.
46. According to a member of the *Diligent*'s crew who claimed to have been present in Hueda on 9 March 1727 (Harms [2002], 152).
47. *Ibid.*, 153; Jean Mettas, *Répertoire des expéditions négrières françaises au XVIIIe siècle* (Paris, SFHOM, 1978), 116-19.
48. Snelgrave (1734/1971), 86.
49. Dantzig (1980), 227.
50. Duport from William's fort, 20.3.1726/7 [O. s.] (NA T70/7); Verger (1966), 27.
51. Thomas Wilson from Ouidah, 27.2.1728 [O.s.], in Law (1991a), 19-21.
52. Snelgrave (1734/1971), 115; Law (2004a), 52.
53. Snelgrave (1734/1971), 120; Law (1991b), 287.
54. Pahl et al. from Christiansborg, 10.9.1727 (Justesen [2005], 363).
55. Snelgrave (1734/1971), 27.
56. See, for instance, Thomas Wilson from William's Fort 24.2 1727/8 & 29.4.1728 [O. s.] in Law (1991a), 19-20 & 25; H. Dupetitval de Juda [Ouidah] 20.5., 15.8, 19.8 & 13.9.1728 (AN C6/25); Charles Testefolle from Whydah [Ouidah] 30.10.1729 [O. s.] (NA T70/7); Snelgrave (1734/1971), 115-19; etc.
57. The details in many of the sources printed in Law (1991a).
58. Wilson from William's Fort, 24.2.1727/8 (*op. cit.*); Law (2004a), 56-7.
59. Thomas Wilson (in letter from Whydah/Ouidah 29.4.1728 [O.s.) called Dahomey "the enemy" and noted that trade was impossible as long as "the enemy is master of the country one day and the Whydahs [Huedans] the other". And he added that the Huedans sold each other in order to maintain themselves (in Law [1991a], 25-9).
60. Huffon refused anyway, having still not lost faith in the final victory of Oyo (Dupetitval de Ouidah, 20.5. 1728 [*op.cit.*]). Dupetitval was the one who tried to negotiate.
61. There was in fact a very complicated plot against Dupetitval, the French Director, according to the same Dupetitval. The (strange?) idea was to deliver the fort to the warriors of Little Popo-Glidji, who (still according to Dupetitval) counted on the collaboration of the Dutch (Hertogh) in Jakin, the English Director and some of Dupetitval's own subalterns, plus – we imagine – the exiled Huedans; all directed against Dahomey. (Dupetitval de Juda [Ouidah] 15.8, 19.8 & 13.9.1728 [*op.cit.*]).

62. As the English director Abraham Du Port put it, "I'm fully resolved to blow up the fort before I'll go a prisoner a second time to Ardah" (Du Port was among the Europeans captured by the Dahomeans on 9.3.1727). Cf. Du Port from William's Fort, 23.10.1727 [O. s.] (Law [1991a], 14-15). His successor Thomas Wilson, who arrived in February 1728, was equally determined: "I am resolved to defend [William's Fort] to the last minute" (Wilson from William's Fort 24.2.1727/8 [*op.cit.*]).

    In the English fort, possibly the best manned and equipped of the three, there were in April 1728 some 40 Europeans and 400 lightly armed but possibly unreliable Africans: not a very imposing force by any standard (Wilson from William's Fort 29.4.1728 [O.s.], *ibid.*, 25-9).
63. Mémoire de la Compagnie des Indes, 8.11.1730 (AN C6-25, d.144); Hertogh to Praeger/Pranger, 8.8.1730 (Dantzig [1978], 250); Harms (2002), 221.
64. John Brathwaite from William's Fort, 20.5.1730 [O. s.] (NA T70/4).
65. Verger (1966), 31.
66. Edward Deane/Deanes from William's Fort, 26.6.1731 [O. s.] (NA T70/7).
67. In fact, on 30.4.1728 [O. s.] Agaja sent ambassadors (to the three forts) "assuring us that they had no designe against the white men- they were only come against those Whydahs that had revolted against the king of Dahomey whilst the Ayous [Oyos] had come on him" (Thomas Wilson from William's Fort 12.7.1728 [O.s.], in Law [1991a], 32-8).
68. Relevant documents in Verger (1968), 145; and in Law (2004a), 52-4.
69. *Ibid.*, 55.
70. But according to the French director of the Fort St. Louis de Gregory (lettre 26.8.1733, AN C6-25 d.146), it came about because the European directors complained about the three captains. The Director added "Ce changement a amené beaucoup de tranquilité. Ce Tegan a ordre de ne point importuner les Directeurs des Forts". In other words, it was a concession to the Europeans. Law's thesis, in 1991b, 335-6; repeated in 2004a, 57 & 109.
71. Manoukian (1952), 35.
72. Adédirán (1984), 75; Dantzig (1980), 232.
73. Elmina Journal 8.1.1732 (Dantzig [1978], 273).
74. Strickrodt (2003), 125-34. See also Law (1991b), 315.
75. (Correa) Lopes (1939), 29.
76. Summary and discussion in Akinjogbin (1967), 68; Law (1977a), 161; Herskovits (1958), 167.
77. "King of Dahomey will hear of no accomodation with the King of Whydah [Hueda]" (John Brathwaite, Whydah/Ouidah 16.8.1730 [O.s.]; NA T70/7).
78. Mémoire sur le commerce de Nantes, 30.1.1732 (AD-Loire Atlantique C.740); Harms (2002), 221; Gayibor (1985), 906.
79. Directeur du Fort St. Louis (Ouidah) 26.8.1733, d.146); Deane/Deanes, William's Fort 26.6.1731; Mémoire sur le commerce de Nantes, 30.1.1732 (all *op. cit.*).
80. Cf. the very informative instructions to Julien Du Bélay, the new French director, in 1733: "Cette troupe de Judaïques [exiled Huedans] fait des courses et occasionne bien les désordres; ils demandent souvent des emprunts ou des gratifications au comptoir de la Compagnie, sur lesquels il faut que M. Dubellay soit bien réservé. Il

doit craindre surtout de ne pas faire penser à Dada [the king of Dahomey] qu'il favorise ces réfugiés...D'un autre côté, il est nécessaire qu'il n'indispose pas les Judaïques au point qu'ils l'empèchent de passer la barre" (Instructions pour...Julien Du Bélay, 27.6.1733 [AN C6-25, doc. 28]).

81. Directeur Fort St.Louis, 26.8.1733 (*op. cit.*).
82. This was the reason for which three Frenchmen had their throats slit by the exiled Huedans in September 1733. See lettres de Juda (Ouidah) 26.8.1733, 20.9.1733 (AN C6/25) & 7.1. 1734 (all *op. cit.*).
83. Law (2004a), 52.
84. Norman (2012), 160.
85. S. Johnson (1921), 174-6; Law (1991b), 295.
86. Wilks (2001), 73-4 & 83-6; Rømer (1760/2000), 136-7; and a great many other Danish sources (in Justesen [2005], 357, 361, 374-5 etc.).
87. Quaye (1972), 165.
88. Wilks (2001), 85-6.
89. *Ibid.*, 81-98; Daaku (1970), 181; Quaye (1972), 175-8.
90. Fynn (1971), 71.
91. *Ibid.*, 108.
92. Wilks (2001), 105-8.
93. C.K. Welman, *The Native States of the Gold Coast. History and Constitution I. Peki* (London, Dawsons of Pall Mall, 1924, reprinted 1969), 7-8; Sandra E. Greene, "Cultural Zones in the Era of the Atlantic Slave Trade: Exploring the Yoruba Connection with the Anlo-Ewe", in Paul E. Lovejoy (ed.), *Identity in the Shadow of Slavery* (London/New York, Continuum, 2000), 86-101 (93-4); Gayibor (1985), 874; etc.
94. Wilks (2001), 109.
95. Inspired by the discussion in David Ross, "The Dahomean Middleman System, 1727-c.1818", *Journal of African History*, 28, 3 (1987), 357-75 (esp. 384).
96. Pahl et al. from Christiansborg, 10.9.1727 (Justesen [2005], 363).
97. Law (1991d), 144-5. Note that before the audience they conferred with William Snelgrave, who was in London at that time, and who advised against returning to Dahomey, given the fate of Testefolle (Snelgrave [1734/1971], 68-71).
98. *Ibid.*, 71; Law (1991d), 146.
99. *Journal of the Commissioners for Trade and Plantations from January 1728–9 to December 1934, preserved in the Public Record Office* (London, HMSO, 1928), 199-203. See also African House (RAC Headquarters) to the R.H. Lords Comissioners for Trade and Plantations 10.6 & 7.10. 1731 (T70/172).
100. Law (2002), 261-70.
101. Garfield (1992).
102. Examination of William Devaynes by the African Committee, 22.3.1788 (*op. cit.*); Letter from the African Committee to the Lords of the Treasury, 9.4.1812 (*Parliamentary Papers*, "Report – Select Committee", 1816/1968 [*op. cit.*], 105); Stefan Halikowski Smith, "'Profits Sprout like Tropical Plants': a Fresh Look at what Went Wrong with the Eurasian Spice Yrade c. 1550–1800", *Journal of Global History*, vol. 3, 3 (2008), 389-418.

C2
AFTERMATH AND GENERAL CONSIDERATIONS

1. Law (1991b), 329.
2. *Ibid.*, 294; Examination of Robert Norris by the African Committee, 27.2.1788 (*op. cit.*).
3. Dantzig (1980), 232.
4. Akinjogbin (1967), 105.
5. Robin Law, "The Slave Trader as Historian: Robert Norris and the History of Dahomey", *History in Africa*, 16 (1989c), 219-35 (226).
6. On Ashangmo (and on Little Popo-Glidji, which he calls Genyi) the leading authority is Nicoué Lodjo Gayibor. See his 1985 thesis, 908; plus Gayibor (1997), 260-61; Gayibor (2001), 27; and above all *Le Genyi. Un royaume oublié de la Côte de Guinée au temps de la traite des noirs* (Lomé, Editions Haro, 1990), esp. 104-13.
7. Declaration of the Soldier Johan Joost Steirmark, made at Elmina, 4.12.1737, in Dantzig (1978), 327-32; Strickrodt (2003), 134.
8. According to the traditions of Little Popo-Glidji. Cf. Gayibor (1990), 109.
9. Law (1987), 322.
10. Law (1990b), 110.
11. Verger (1966), 60.
12. Verger (1968), 169-71.
13. *Ibid.*, 167-8.
14. Compte-rendu, Le Phoenix, Petit Popo 30.3. 1738 (*op. cit.*).
15. "Cet endroit est à fuir" was the message of a French "Mémoire" dated 13.12.1740 (CAOM-DFC); Rømer (1760/2000), 176; Platfues et al. from Christiansborg, 12.4.1749 (Justesen [2005], 763); Strickrodt (2003), 150-51.
16. Harms (2002), 230.
17. From WIC 3.1.1729 (Dantzig [1978], 229).
18. The factual dimension of the Hertogh story is based on Dantzig (1980), 229-42, which is in turn based on the collection of Dutch documents published by the same Dantzig: (1978), 242-342.
19. See also Ryder (1969), 192.
20. See also Verger (1966), 38.
21. Postma (1990), 77.
22. Most clearly expressed – much later – in Carta de José da Silva Lisboa, advogado da Bahia, 18.10.1781 (*Inventario* II, 504-5).
23. De Bahia, 22.4.1733, OR, vol. 29, doc. 74 (reproduced in *Anais*, 43 [1977], 25); Vicerei Brazil ao Rei de Portugal (sobre) o estado decadente dos negócios e navegação na Costa da Mina (Bahia, 20.5.1734; OR, vol. 30, doc. 30; both reproduced in *ibid*, 43 [1977], 25 & 65); VR ao rei Port.: decadência do comércio com à Costa da Mina (Bahia 30.8.1736, OR, vol.32, doc.82; ibid., 44 [1979], 30); Flory (1978), 256; etc.
24. Or so argued the Danes: E.N. Boris de Christiansborg, 3.5.1738 (Justesen [2005], 537).
25. Postma (1978), 75.
26. Dantzig (1980), 232.

27. Postma (1978), 78.
28. Letter from Antonio Pinto, Portuguese factor in Jakin, n.d. (AHU, São Tomé caixa 4); also communication from the same quoted in Pranger to Hertogh 11.7.1733 (Dantzig [1978], 291).
29. For a summary of the relevant sources, and a discussion, see Law (1997c), 4; Dantzig (1980), 232-4; Robin Law, "A Lagoonside Port of the Eighteenth-Century Slave Coast: The Early History of Badagry", *Canadian Journal of African Studies*, 28, 1 (1994b), 32-59 (38).
30. Hoffmester from Jaquin, 1.8.1732 & Carstares from Ardah, 7.8.1732, in Dantzig (1978), 279-80.
31. He took very little care of his subordinates, according to the General at Elmina (Minutes, Elmina, 21.5.1732, in *ibid.*, 271-2).
32. Chamber of Amsterdam to Director-General at Elmina, 20.4.1734, in *ibid.*, 307-9; Dantzig (1980), 235.
33. Postma (1990), 99; Akinjogbin (1967), 100.
34. *Ibid.*, 105.
35. Hertogh to Pranger, 16.4.1732 (archival source).
36. Law (1994b), 32-3 & 38-43; T. Ola Avoseh, *A Short History of Badagry* (Lagos, 1938).
37. Law (1994b), 38.
38. Even according to a French source; "Mémoire" dated 13.12.1740 (*op. cit.*).
39. J. Elet from Jaquin [Jakin], 8.11.1733, in Dantzig (1978), 304.
40. Robin Law, "Trade and Politics behind the Slave Coast: the Lagoon Traffic and the Rise of Lagos 1500-1800", *Journal of African History*, 24, 3 (1983), 321-48 (342).
41. Law (1991b), 313.
42. A.P. Wærøe et al. from Christiansborg 26.5.1732 (Justesen [2005], 460). Note the date, back in 1732.
43. Pranger to Hertogh 9.8.1732; 25.12.1732; & 15.1.1734, in Dantzig (1978), 266-7, 269-70 & 304.
44. Hogbonu, also written Xogbonu (Adjatchè in Yoruba), means "great house". Cf. Alexis Bancole & Gilles Raoul Soglo, "Porto-Novo et la traite negrière", in Elisée Soumonni, Bellarmin C. Codo and Joseph Adande (eds), *Le Bénin et la route de l'esclave* (Cotonou, ONEPI, 1994), 76-8. The Portuguese name Porto-Novo was applied originally to modern Sèmè on the seashore, i.e. the "port" of Hogbonu (Law [2004a], 201).
45. Mercier (1950), 31-3.
46. Dunglas (1967), 29.
47. Law (1997c), 1-2.
48. Dunglas tells us that the king and his "Prime Minister", the Zounon, the latter being qualified as "Chef de la Terre", could not see each other. The king reigned during the day and the Zounon during the night (Dunglas [1967], 58-9). There was a state council, the *Mito*, which elected the king (Palau-Marti [1964], 188-91).
49. Admittedly, this is based on a source that cannot be considered reliable: the guide of the contemporary royal palace of Porto-Novo, who showed the present author the entry of the room where according to him the king retreated when he had to commit suicide.

50. A. Akindélé and C. Aguessy, *Contribution à l'étude de l'histoire de l'ancien royaume de Porto Novo* (Dakar, IFAN, 1953); Yves Person, "Chronologie du royaume gun de Hogbonu (Porto-Novo)", *Cahiers d'Études Africaines*, XV, 2 (1975), 217-38.
51. Adams (1823/1966), 82.
52. Brand (2000), 93; Bay (1983), 345.
53. Law (1989b), 402.
54. Law (1989c), 225. Agaja had to insist in order to make them attend. A French report talks of "les sollicitations reiterées de Dada [Agaja] pour assister": Directeur de Juda [Ouidah] 26.8. 1733 (AN C6-25, doc. 148).
55. "The journey is always made in perfect safety, & travellers accomodated with Eastern hospitality...there are a kind of caravanseras in the towns through which (the Europeans) pass, allotted for their reception"; Dalzel (1793/1967), XIX. Cf more generally: Pruneau (1789), 178-83; Norris (1789/1968), 69-70; Herskovits (1938/1967), I, 3-4.
56. Among the many eye-witness accounts, the perhaps most informative, apart from that of Dalzel, is one from as late as 1789 by Monsieur Gourg: Journal de mon voyage pour assister aux coutumes, Juda [Ouidah] 22.1.1789 (AN C6-26, d.110).
57. Akinjogbin (1967), 190; Law (2004a), 107-8.
58. Example: Examination of Dalzel by the African Committee, 5-8.4.1788 (*op. cit.*).
59. M'Leod (1820/1971), 100-2; Ross (1987), 366.
60. In addition to the sources and works already referred to, see also Foà (1895), 285-94; Lombard (1967b), 85; Coquery-Vidrovitch (1971), 712; etc.
61. Relation du Royaume de Judas [Hueda], c.1715 (*op. cit.*), 53; S. Johnson (1921), 143; McCaskie (1995/2002), 215-6; Robin Law, "Human Sacrifice in Pre-colonial West Africa", *African Affairs*, vol. 84, no. 334 (1985), 53-87.
62. M'Leod (1820/1971), 59-60. Dalzel argued that the victims of the executions were resigned to their fate, and without fear (The Examination of A.D. Dalzell by the African Committee 5-8.4.1788). William Devaynes argued more or less the same, also during an examination by the African Committee 22.3.1788; as did Chenevert and Bullet in "Réflexions sur Juda", 1776 (all *op. cit.*), 73. See also some interesting comments in *Captain Canot; or, Twenty Years of an African Slaver (etc)*- written down and edited by Brantz Mayer (New York and London,1854, new edition by Arno Press and the New York Times, 1968), 266-8. Were the victims doped?
63. Testimony of Robert Norris: "I never saw less than six decollated heads placed in the passage leading to the King's [Tegbesu's] apartment, when I have been there" (Examination of Norris by the African Committee, 27.2.1788 [*op. cit.*]).
64. Pruneau (1789), 190-94.
65. However, the only recorded refusal this author is aware of is that of Captain Canot (1854/1968, 268).
66. Bay (1998), 21.
67. Including Asante (McCaskie [1995/2002], 215-16).
68. Argyle (1966), 112-16; Bay (2008), 27; Savary (1976), 190.
69. Landolphe (1823), II, 30.
70. Testimony of Lionel Abson as reproduced in Dalzel (1793/1967), 204-30.

71. Law argues (1991b, 305-6) that their attitude changed to pessimism in the 1730s. But had it ever been optimistic?
72. *Ibid.*, 306-8.
73. Lettre de Annamabou 31.5.1744 (AN C6-25, doc. 168/170).
74. Verger (1966), 66.
75. Gayibor (1985), 914.
76. Or this is, to be precise, how Robin Law (1989c, 220) interprets Ross (1987, 362-4).
77. (1998, 64). The present author is less certain.
78. Akinjogbin (1967), 110

C3
NEAR DISASTER: THE FIRST YEARS OF THE TEGBESU ERA

1. Lists and summary in the files NA T70/1157 & 1158 (see below); Law (1991b), 327-8; Bay (1998), 109.
2. On the last point, see the interesting elaborations in Boniface I. Obichere, "Change and Innovation in the Administration of the Kingdom of Dahomey", *Journal of African Studies*, vol. 1, 3 (1974), 235-51 (241).
3. For instance, Agbo (1959) refers consistently to the post-1727 period as one of Dahomean "domination" and "occupation". See also Ross (1989), 318.
4. Agbo (1959), 44-5.
5. Details and summary in Law (1994b), 47; and Law (1991b), 314.
6. Norris (1789/1968), 19-20; Foà (1895), 17.
7. Even Le Hérissé (1911, 132) admits that the wars against Mahi were unsuccessful.
8. Gaston-Mulira (1984), 48; Law (1989b), 54.
9. Deduced from Joseph C. Miller, *Way of Death: Merchant Capitalism and the Angolan Slave Trade* (University of Wisconsin Press, 1988). There are also cases of liberated slaves becoming slave traders. A classic example is that of João Oliveira which will be evoked later. See in addition, for instance: from Sierra Leone to Earl of Clarendon, 2.9.1857 (NA ADM, 123/177).
10. Le Hérissé (1911), 300.
11. Law's interpretation (1989c, 225) based on the relevant pages in Norris (1789/1968).
12. Law (1987), 326.
13. Including the Herskovitses (1933/1964, 35; & 1938/1967, II, 104); endorsed by Law (1991b), 327.
14. Bay (1998), 91-2.
15. The main source for the events referred to in this section is: Jacques Levet [the new French Director] de Juda [Ouidah] 20.8.1743 (AN C6-25; d.156-61). See also Law (1991b), 321-2.
16. Overview in Law (1991b), 322; and in Law (2004a), 61.
17. S. Johnson (1921), 176.
18. For a discussion – Law discussing with himself – see Law (1977a), 165, & (1991b), 323; and finally Asiwaju and Law (1985), 444.
19. Levet de Juda [Ouidah] 25.2.1744 (AN C6-25). There is some confusion in the literature as to the identity of the director expelled in 1743, because the one expelled

and his replacement had very similar names. The latter was apparently also expelled in the end.

20. According to the French. The English director had to seek refuge in the Portuguese fort (Levet de Juda [Ouidah] 13.10 1746, AN C6-25, doc. 180).
21. Verger (1966), 71. However, some of those who were captured with Basilio, presumably Africans, were apparently liberated only ten years later, in 1753. See Tenente Theodosio Rodrigues, Fortaleza de S. João de Ajudá, 27.5.1753 (*Inventario* I [1913], 60]).
22. On the second Basilio affair the fundamental source are the letters from Jacques Levet de Juda dated 16.8.1743 doc.158; 13.10.1746 & 1.10.1747, the two first from Ouidah, the last from Bahia (all in AN C6-25). See also Verger (1966), 68-81.
23. Lopes (1939), 29-30.
24. Levet de Juda [Ouidah] 16.8.1743 (*op. cit.*). For more details, Verger (1966), 69; and Ryder (1958), 172.
25. Lopes (1939), 35-7; Carta-Conde das Galvêas, André de Mello e Castro, para o Rei Dogme (Dahomey) queixando-se de sua deslealdade para com o Rei de Portugal, consentindo que Francisco Nunes Pereira arbitrariamente usurpasse o logar de Director da Fortaleza portugueza, Bahia 2.9.1746 (*Inventario*, I [1913], 37).
26. King of Portugal to Viceroy of Brazil, 25.10.1749 (OR, vol. 76, doc. 73, folha 168, APEB). As for Nunes, he is reported to have ended his days in the penal colony of Benguela (Lopes [1939], 38).
27. Extensive quotations from the relevant sources in Verger (1969), 86-109.
28. Carta Secretario (do Rei) Belém, 21.10.1751 (OR vol. 48, Doc. 79; in *Anais*, 46 [1982], 125).
29. See the many documents in *Inventario*, II (1914), 165-7. Also some interesting information in "Journal de..Crassous" (*op. cit.*), 111.
30. Again the relevant sources are reproduced in part in Verger (1966), 88-109. See also Ryder (1958), 171.
31. Information from T.R. da Costa in Ajudá [Ouidah] contained in letter from Viceroy Conde dos Arcos, Bahia 23.5.1758 (*Inventario*, I [1913] 277).
32. See, for instance, Instructions to Governor Thomas Melvil by the Company of Merchants trading to Africa, 17.4.1751 (in Crooks [1923/1973], 18).
33. A list of the monarchy's many economic monopolies in Lombard (1967a), 89.
34. Most clearly expressed in letters from the French director in Ouidah, 6.6.1759; and from his English colleague (William Devaynes) 8.6. 1759. Both in a Portuguese collection, namely OR, vol. 61, Documents 155B & 155D (APEB).
35. On Law's position, see especially his "The Origins and Evolution of the Merchant Community in Ouidah", in Robin Law and Silke Strickrodt (eds), *Ports of the Slave Trade (Bights of Benin and Biafra)* (University of Stirling, 1999b), 55-70 (57). See also Law (2004a), 115.
36. At least according to Dalzel (and Abson) (1793/1967), 213.
37. The second and bloodiest French attempt was in 1744–46 and cost the lives of about 60 Frenchmen and 250 of their African auxiliaries - the number of British casualties is unknown (de Annamabou, 31.5.1744 [*op. cit.*], and: Levet de Juda [Ouidah],

12.10.1746 [doc. 179]). The third attempt was in 1752, but lasted for only 16 days (Perier de Salvent à Brest, 8.5.1752 [AN-Marine B/4/65, f.194 ff]).

The British were always determined to foil the French attempts (see for instance: from Cape Coast Castle, 30.1.1751 [NA T70/68]). In fact they considered it their right to open fire on French ships which headed for their establishments, and told the French so in no uncertain terms (Documents translated from English, 1750 [AD-Loire Atlantique, C687]). The British doctrine in these matters was very clearly expressed in 1814:"The French have at all times evinced the greatest anxiety to erect Forts, & to obtain a share of the trade upon the Gold Coast, while this Country has uniformly refused to grant to them any establishment there; and even in time of peace has driven off their ships and excluded them from all participation in that trade" (Committee of the Company of Merchants trading to Africa, to Earl Bathurst, 21.6.1814, in *Parliamentary Papers*, 1850/1968 [*op. cit.*], 118). Lord Bathurst was Secretary of State for War and the Colonies.

38. William's fort, Accounts for July & August 1754 (NA T70/1158).
39. Daybook-William's fort, Sept-Oct. 1762, signed William Goodson (NA T70/1159).
40. Accounts-William's Fort Nov-Dec.1752 (*op. cit.*); & Sept-Oct. 1758, signed William Devaynes (NA T70/1158).
41. Instruction du Roy à de Kersaint, Fontainbleau le 5 9bre/Novembre 1756 (AN Marine B/4/73, doc.4); Kersaint: Journal de navigation 1757, 5.5.1757 (*op. cit.*). On these events also an unexpected source: Viceroy Bahia 10.5.1757 (*op. cit.*).
42. According to a French report. Levet de Juda [Ouidah] 13.6.1758 (AN-C6-25).
43. "Épopée glorieuse", according to the author of an official document dated Marseille, 11 8bre/Octobre 1762 (*op. cit.*).
44. Example: London to Mr. Devaynes at Whydah [Ouidah], 22.7.1758 (NA T70/29).
45. Mémoire de Juda [Ouidah] 20.2.1763 (AN C6-25).
46. Verger (1966), 66-7 & 103-10.
47. De Bahia 22.5.1758 & 28.8.1759 (OR, vol. 60, folha 153 & vol. 61, doc. 97, 155 & 155 A-G, APEB); Vice-Rei Conde dos Arcos, Bahia 23.5.1758 (*Inventario*, I [913], 277); Officio do Governo interino, Bahia, 30.9.1761 (*ibid.*, 475).
48. Deduced from especially Verger (1968), 240 (most Portuguese directors were in fact temporarily promoted subalterns).
49. Council, Cape Coast Castle, 11.12.1788 (in Crooks [1923/1973], 75-6).
50. Captain Jenkins from Whydah [Ouidah], 28.7.1762 (NA T70/31).
51. "Este importantíssimo ramo de comércio" [this very important branch of trade]. Expression used in the protests from the "Oficiais da Câmara desta cidade" [the members of the Municipal Council of Bahia] and others in documents annexed to memorandum from King of Portugal, Lisbon 30.3. 1756 (OR vol. 55, doc. 39 & 39A). More protests in *ibid.*, vol. 71, doc. 110A (no date). Earlier protests in for instance: Mesa de Inspeção, Bahia 27.7.1754 (*ibid.*, vol. 73, doc. 38A).
52. In general, see for instance, Guestad et al., de Juda [Ouidah] 11.5.1753 (AN C6-25).
53. Accounts, Sept-Oct.1758, signed William Devaynes, William's Fort (*op. cit.*).
54. Many examples in the Account books to 1764 (NA T70/1158-9), and in those for Oct-Nov-Dec. 1784 (NA T70/1162); plus Daybook Jan-Feb-March 1785 (NA T70/1162).

55. For instance: Accounts-William's Fort, signed William Devaynes July-Aug.1752 (NA T70/1158).
56. Pruneau de Pommegeorge was of the opinon (in 1764) that the French fort did not look like one, but instead like a worn-down farmstead ("métairie de Beauce") (Mémoire par M. Pruneau, Juda [Ouidah] 1764 [AN C6-25]).
    William's Fort was reputed "very much out of repair" in 1766 and "in bad repair" in 1776. There were four Europeans in William's Fort in the 1760s, and only two in the 1770s, one of them being obviously Lionel Abson, plus from 54 to 80 fort slaves. (Return from the Commissioners for trade and plantations..1777 [*op. cit.*]).
57. Adams (1823/1966), 52-5. His French colleague Monsieur Gourg added that Abson was "aussi dangereux pour sa nation que pour la nôtre, étant entièrement vendu aux nègres, avec qui il a une très grande affinité" (Gourg de Juda [Ouidah] 1.2.1789 [AN C6-26, doc. 116]).
58. Martin (1927), 10-32.
59. A snapshot of the situation in 1768 according to the then British director Archibald Dalziel (he had not yet changed his name to Dalzel): "The English traders have now for four years abandoned this Port, while the French carry [on] as before. [They have] no less than three ships now in the Road. The King...often demands the reason why [the English traders no longer come]...it would be impolitic [for] me to give the true reasons...namely the vileany [*sic*] and the thievish [*sic*] of his subjects...the French finding they have no competitors, are gradually introducing worse manufactures". Dalziel went on to lament "the wretched state" of William's Fort (A. Dalziel from William's Fort, 27.9.1768 [NA T70/31]).
60. Berbain (1942), 35.
61. Examples: William Goodson from Whydah [Ouidah], 10.11.1764 (NA T70/31); William's fort, Daybook Sept-Oct.1765, signed William Goodson (NA T70/1160); A. Dalziel from Whydah [Ouidah] 18.2.1770 (NA T70/31); William's Fort, Daybook, May-June 1773, signed Lionel Abson (NA T70/1161).
62. The many letters from the French Director Jacques Levet de Juda constitute the main source in this matter, especially the one dated Ouidah 1.2.1746 (*op. cit.*). Elaborations and discussions are found in Robin Law, "Slave-Raiders and Middlemen, Monopolists and Free-Traders: the Supply of Slaves for the Atlantic Trade in Dahomey, c.1715–1850", *Journal of African History*, 30,1 (1989d), 45-68 (esp. 52); and by the same author (1999b), 57.
63. The Examination of William Devaynes by the African Committee, 22.3.1788 (*op. cit.*).
64. See the relevant files in NA T70/1157, 1158 and 1159. Apart from those signed by Devaynes, many bear the signature of William Goodson. A summary is in Law (1991b), 327-8.
65. Unless Tanga is simply a variant of *tegan*, as Edna Bay argues (1998, 108).
66. Norris (1789/1968), 40-44. The story was repeated by many subsequent authors, including Dalzell, Burton and Dunglas.
67. Law (1989c), 229.
68. Henry Turner from William's Fort 20.2.1740 [O. s.] (NA T70/4).
69. Law (1989c), 229.

70. Summary in Akinjogbin (1967), 120; and Elisée Akpo Soumonni, "The Administration of a Port of the Slave Trade: Ouidah in the Nineteenth Century", in R. Law & Silke Strickrodt (eds), *Ports of the Slave Trade (Bights of Benin and Biafra)* (University of Stirling, 1999), 48-54 (50) (notice the word "port" in the title).
71. Levet de Juda (Ouidah), 25 9bre (November) 1755 (AN C6-25).
72. Opinion of Akinjogbin (1967), 121.
73. According to sources consulted by David Ross (1989, 314) and Robin Law (1991b, 328).
74. The main source seems to be Le Hérissé (1911), 273-5. But note that Tori pops up in many places and in many works, for instance in *Barbot on Guinea*, 621, and in Wigboldus (1986), 322.
75. Bay (1998), 107-8. See also Law (2004a), 120-21.
76. "Tegbesu...semble travailler à sa destruction"; Mémoire pour servir à l'intelligence de Juda (etc), Conseil de Directeurs de la Compagnie de Judas [Ouidah], 18.3.1750 (AN C6-25).

C4
MORE ABOUT THE TEGBESU ERA

1. Bay (2008), 24. But Bay also argues that Mawu and Lisa reigned supreme in Dahomey in the eighteenth century, which is less certain. She goes on to argue that Mawu and Lisa were introduced by *kpojito* ("Queen Mother") Hwanjile under Tegbesu, who then became their priest, and as such the head of the religious life in Dahomey, outranking the *agasunon* (Bay [1995], 15). If by "religious life", she means the official religion, she has probably a point.
2. Blier (1995b), 414-15.
3. Law (1987), 328.
4. Law (1991b), 331.
5. But one who has tried, and with success for all we know, to penetrate the logic of the new ancestor cults centred on the royal dynasty is Edna Bay (1998, 318-19). See also Houseman et al. (1986), 543.
6. The Examination of A. Dalzel, 5-8.4.1788 (*op. cit.*); and especially Pruneau (1789), 159-63.
7. Underlined especially by Kossou, (1981), 90.
8. Glélé (1974), 66).
9. Norris (1789/1968), 103; Mahdi Adamu, *The Hausa Factor in West African History* (Zaria, Ahmadu Bello University Press and Oxford University Press, 1978), 114-15; Law (1986b), 112.
10. Le Hérissé (1911), 303.
11. According to the British sources referred to in Law (2004a), 111.
12. Opinion of Law (1986b), 100.
13. *Ibid.*, 102; Law (1991b), 341-2.
14. Robin Law, "Royal Monopoly and Private Enterprise in the Atlantic Trade: the Case of Dahomey", *Journal of African History*, XVIII, 4 (1977b), 555-77 (560).
15. Ross (1987), 369.

16. The relevant evidence is presented in Gayibor (1985), 914-15; Law (1991b), 323.
17. Levet de Juda [Ouidah] 9bre(Novembre), 1755 (*op. cit.*).
18. Jacques Guestard, de Juda [Ouidah] 10.7.1754 & 31.3.1755 (AN C6-25).
19. In a Mémoire, Juda [Ouidah] 1764 (*op. cit.*).
20. Apart from *ibid.*, the main source on the French side is Pruneau (1789), 223-34. On the British side we have another eyewitness account by William Goodson in the Daybook of William's Fort, July-August 1763 (*op. cit.*).
21. The source is again Pruneau's Mémoire of 1764 (*op. cit.*).
22. Here we follow Strickrodt (2003), 142.
23. Akinjogbin (1967), 148-9; Gayibor (1985), 919-20.
24. Abson from Ouidah, 24.10.1770 (*op. cit.*).
25. Argyle (1966), 42-3.
26. The most informative source we have encountered on these events is perhaps a somewhat strange one: Governor & Council for transacting the affairs of the committee of the Companyy of Merchants trading to Africa...to examine the Public Accounts 1.1.1770-31.12.1776 (NA BT 6/16).
27. On raids in 1781, see Daybook Williams Fort, April-June 1781 (NA T70/1162).
28. Norris (1789/1968), VII.
29. Monroe (2007b), 356-7.
30. Law (1988a), 444. The same was to some extent also the case in Asante. See McCaskie (1995/2002), 217.
31. Bay (1998), 357.
32. Herskovits (1938/1967), II, 45.
33. This section is in fact based on two works of hers: 1983 and 1998.
34. *Ibid.*; M'Leod (1820/1971), 50; Herskovits (1938/1967), II, 45; Foà (1895), 192.
35. But consider the following statement: "African studies is replete with some of the most trenchant critiques of the universal woman-as-victim model of historical explanation, in which modernization or colonialism is seen as the singular agent of change rescuing women from the timeless exploitative patriarchy of non-Western societies". Akinwumi Ogundiran, "The End of Prehistory? An African Comment", *American Historical Review*, June 2013, 788-801 (794). Where does this leave the *ahosi*?
36. Bay (1998), 150.
37. *Ibid.*, 149; Norris (1789/1968), 98-9; Pires (1800/1957), 114.
38. Norris (1789/1968), 128-30.
39. Dalzel (1793/1967), 150-52; Dunglas (1957), II, 26-7.
40. Glélé (1974), 108.
41. Obichere (1974), 239-41.
42. To give an example of how the local administrators were treated in Dahomey: "During the time I was in the country, the chief magistrate of a district, for some iniquitous transaction, was ordered by the king not to shave his beard, pare his nails, or wash himself for a certain number of moons, and in this dirty state to sit daily at the palace-gate several hours for public inspection" (M'Leod [1820/1971], 48).
43. Pruneau (1789), 168; Bay (1998), 25-6.
44. Alpern (1998a), 124.

45. Alexandre Adandé, *Les récades des rois du Dahomey* (Dakar, IFAN, 1962), 13-9; Foà (1895), 172.
46. M'Leod (1820/1971), 42-3.
47. *Ibid.*, 46.
48. Obichere (1974), 241.
49. Le Hérissé (1911), 85.
50. Law (1999a), 31.
51. Herskovits (1938/1967), II, 39.
52. "My head belongs to the king, not to myself; if he pleases to send for it..." (Norris [1789/1968], 8).

    Or as French observers put it: "chaque particulier est élevé dans l'idée que la tête appartient au Roy, aussi n'est-il point étonné quand il est condamné à la perdre" (Chenevert and Bullet, "Réflexions sur Juda" [*op. cit.*], 51).
53. All contemporary observers that we know of, including Robert Norris, Monsieur Gourg, William Devaynes, Pruneau de Pommegeorge, Chenevert and Bullet etc., are agreed on this point. And modern scholars such as Melville Herskovits, Stanley Alpern, Suzanne Preston Blier, David Ross etc. certainly abound in the same sense.

    However, Robin Law has argued that "Part of the appeal of submission to the kings of Dahomey may well have been the belief that, with their more highly centralised and autocratic administration, and indeed their greater personal ruthlessness, they might be better able to restore and maintain political order" (Law [1987], 337-8).

    Law also insists on the strict regulations of pawning and enslavement in Dahomey — the idea being that the people of Dahomey, even the slaves, enjoyed a degree of protection not existing before or elsewhere (Law [1994a], 65-6; and by the same author, "Legal and Illegal Enslavement in West Africa, in the Context of the Trans-Atlantic Slave Trade", in Toyin Falola (ed.), *Ghana in Africa and the World: Essays in Honor of Adu Boahen* (Trenton, NJ, Africa World Press, 2003, 513-33 [516]). But Ross has argued that those regulations applied basically only to the members of the Abomey area warrior community and their descendants and slaves (Ross [1989], 323). Whatever the case, we find Law's position difficult to reconcile with the evidence as it stands. As for Akinjogbin (1967, 140), he has argued that Tegbesu created "an orderly contented community". Balderdash, in our opinion.
54. Blier (1995a).
55. *Ibid.*, 26-7.
56. *Ibid.*, 1.
57. *Ibid.*, 5.
58. *Ibid.*, 13.
59. Law (1977a), 89-96; R. Smith (1976), 100-1 & 128; Akinwumi Ogundiran, "Material Life and Domestic Economy in a Frontier of the Oyo Empire During the Mid-Atlantic Age", *International Journal of African Historical Studies*, 42, 3 (2009), 351-65 (357-64).
60. Chenevet and Bullet, "Réflexions sur Juda" (*op. cit.*), 42.
61. Adams (1823/1966), 79-80.

62. On Oliveira, the only genuine source we have found is a summary in *Inventario*, II (1914, no. 8245). It refers to a document with the title: "Attestado de commerciantes da Bahia, em que affirman os serviços prestados pelo preto João de Oliveira ao commercio da Costa da Mina" (Bahia 30.5.1770). From this and subsequent summaries (referring to a document dated Bahia 18.7.1770, *ibid.* nos. 8244-8247) we can deduce that Oliveira opened up two ports for the trade but that he later experienced problems with the law in Salvador da Bahia. We have been unable to locate the documents these summaries refer to.
63. On João de Oliveira, see also Verger (1966), 112; and (Vieira) Ribeiro (2008), 143.
64. Law (1986b), 109.
65. The quotation is from Mann (2007), 34.
66. *Ibid.*, 34-5, based, according to Ms Mann, on calculations of David Eltis. But no references are provided.
67. Some figures and a discussion in Dalzel (1793/1967), 166 & 194; Akinjogbin (1967), 140; Strickrodt (2003), 155 (there is also an interesting, but undated and unsigned French document in AN C6-29).
68. At least according to the official list in what is presented as the Royal Palace in Porto Novo.
69. Officio do Governador, Bahia 16.10.1775 & Carta do Rei de Ardra [Porto Novo], undated. (*Inventario* II [1914, nos. 8941 & 8942], 307-8).
70. Dunglas (1967).
71. In fact, the local inhabitants are known as Awori Yoruba (R. Smith [1976], 105).
72. Barnes (2009), 53.
73. Olatunji Ojo, "The Organization of the Atlantic Slave Trade in Yorubaland, ca.1777 to ca. 1856", *International Journal of African Historical Studies*, 41, 1 (2008), 77-100 (79). Incidentally, Ojo's article and Mann's book (2007, 23-83) make it clear that the Oba of Lagos was little more than a *primus inter pares*, and hence in no way comparable to the king of Dahomey.
74. Law (1982b), esp. 390; Law (1977a), esp. 201; S. Johnson (1921), 178-86; Akinjogbin (1967), 145 ff.
75. Dating due to Dalzel (1793/1967), 156-7.
76. See especially Law (1977a), 201-2.
77. Law (1975).
78. Inspired by Quaye (1972); and by Hernæs (1988), 13-14.
79. The sources and scholarly works are particularly abundant on this subject. Some relevant references: Justesen (2005), 505, 528, 533, 600-2, 608-9, 797, 813; Ray A. Kea, "Ashanti-Danish Relations 1780-1831" (MA thesis, Institute of African Studies, University of Ghana, Legon, 1967), 69-108; Hernæs (1998), 136-7; Akyeampong (2001), 42-6; Nukunya (1997), 69; etc.
80. Greene (1996b), 56-7.
81. By Akyeampong (2001), 4.
82. *Ibid.*, 45; Yarak (1990), 123.
83. For the Danes, see Christian Glob Dorph, Christianshavn, to the Directors, 4.5.1745 (Justesen [2005], 668).
84. Kea (1967), 67; Fynn (1971), 74-5.

85. *Ibid.*, 76; Amenumey (1986), 71-3.
86. Deduced from Ronald R. Atkinson, "Old Akyem and the Origins of Akyems Abuakwa and Kotoku 1675–1775", in B.K. Swartz Jr. and Raymond E. Dumett (eds), *West African Culture Dynamics: Archeological and Cultural Perspectives* (The Hague etc., Mouton, 1989), 349-69 (365-7); Kwamena-Poh (1973), 31-44; Fynn (1971), 108-10.
87. The sources are based on hearsay and are in fact somewhat confusing. The principal ones are William Mutter (from Ouidah?) to African Committee, 27.5.1764 (NA T70/31); Bowdich (1819/1966), 234; and especially Joseph Dupuis, *Journal of a Residence in Ashantee* (1st ed. 1824, second ed., by W.E.F. Ward, London, Frank Cass 1966), 238-49. But since the matter is rather sensational, many scholars have felt the need to comment on it. Among them is Adu Boahen who has argued that there was a full-scale war between Dahomey and Asante from 1760 to 1764 (see his "Asante-Dahomey contacts in the nineteenth century", *Ghana Notes and Queries*, 7 [1965], 1-3). However, most other scholars are far more sceptical. A useful summary and discussion in Law (1994c), 160.
88. Details in Greene (1996b), 56-8 (1997); plus in the many works of Ray Kea.
89. Gayibor (1990), 176-201.
90. Nørregaard (1968), 228.
91. Fynn (1971), 109-10; Kea (1967), 64-5.
92. Nørregaard (1968), 198.
93. Greene (1996b), 82 & 153-7. See also Akyeampong (2001), 7.
94. Greene (2002a), 1019; and Nukunya (1997), 48-9.

C5
CONTINUATION

1. African Office to Cape Coast Castle, 5.9.1775 & 30.12.1778 (both NA T70/69).
2. The details of this tortuous history in Jean Meyer, Jean Tarrade, Annie Rey-Goldzeiguer and Jacques Thobie, *Histoire de la France coloniale. Des origines à 1914* (Paris, Armand Colin, 1991), 277-314.
3. See the excellent short exposé in Drake (1976), 139.
4. Allow us to refer in this respect to a formally non-scientific but nevertheless illuminating book about the fight against the slave trade, Eric Metaxas' *Amazing Grace. William Wilberforce and the Heroic Campaign to End Slavery* (New York, HarperCollins, 2007), esp. 91-102. The book is in a sense the companion to a film, with the same title, of 2006.
5. Nørregaard (1968), 276; Feldbæk and Justesen (1980), 409-29; Sandra E. Greene, "The Individual as Stranger in Nineteenth-Century Anlo: the Politics of Identity and Social Advancement in Precolonial West Africa", in John Hunwick and Nancy Lawler (eds), *The Cloth of Many Colored Silks* (Evanston, Northwestern University Press, 1996), 91-127 (94).
6. By the authors of a comment in the *Camden Review* of 7 November 2013.
7. William's Fort-Daybook, January-March 1779 (NA T70/1162).
8. William's Fort, Daybook July-Sept. 1779, signed Lionel Abson (NA T70/1162).

9. Akinjogbin (1967), 156-9.
10. *Ibid.*, 160-61.
11. Dalzel (1793/1967), 178.
12. De Juda [Ouidah], 16.7.1788 (AN C6-26, doc. 94).
13. De Juda [Ouidah] 6.10.1777 (*op. cit.*). Chenevert and Bullet in "Réflexions sur Juda" (1776 – *op. cit.,* 19-20 & 31) depict a lamentable picture of Ouidah which had less than 2,000 inhabitants, and was situated in the midst of "un pays dévasté où l'on cultive peu".
14. Especially Ross (1987), and Person (1982), part II.
15. Akinjogbin (1967), 155; Dunglas (1957), 69-70.
16. Parrinder (1956), 34.
17. Dunglas (1967), 32.
18. De Juda [Ouidah] 6.10.1777 (*op. cit.*).
19. De Juda [Ouidah], 25.4.1789 (AN C6-26, doc. 132).
20. Pires (1800/1957), 135; Adamu (1978), 114-16.
21. Pires (1800/1957), 135; Dalzel (1793/1967), VI.
22. Law (1991b), 330.
23. An interesting case-study is Marina de Mello e Souza, *Reis negros no Brasil escravista: História da festa de coroação de Rei Congo* (Belo Horizonte, Editora UFMG, 2002).
24. Heywood and Thornton (2009), 106-10.
25. Amenumey (1986), 46-7.
26. Kea (1967), 38 & 69 ff.
27. Opinion of Israel (1995), 1097.
28. Lise Merete Johannesen, "Jens Adolph Kiøge's administrasjonspolitik over for afrikanerne i Guinea 1766–1788" (unpublished dissertation, Københavns Universitet/University of Copenhagen, c. 1966), 44-5; Crooks (1923/1973), 50.
29. Johannesen (c. 1966), 4-11; Hernæs (1998), 137-8. As for the more general picture, cf. Feldbæk and Justesen (1980).
30. Isert (1788/1992), 42-3; Johannesen (c. 1966), 56.
31. Sagbadre is supposed to mean "swallow" in the Ewe tongue and was apparently what Kiøge and/or a certain Danish trader were called by the Anlo (Isert [1788/1992], 2 & 31, fn.1; Gayibor [1985], 937).
32. 1,100 men strong, according to Gayibor (1997*)*, 260-61.
33. Gayibor (1985), 935.
34. Isert (1788/1992*)*, esp. p. 51.
35. According to Gayibor (1985), 937-9.
36. Fynn (1971), 124-6.
37. Isert (1788/1992), 55-65.
38. According to Fynn (1971), 129-30.
39. Akyeampong (2001), 8 & 43.
40. Isert (1788/1992), 74; Lawrence (1963), 361.
41. Fynn, (1971), 128. See also Grove and Johansen (1968), 1377.
42. Isert (1788/1992), 96, including fn. 15.
43. He noted incidentally, and rather surprisingly, that "The Fidas are a very industrious nation, they weave & make cloth out of grass" (*ibid.*, 108-9).

44. From Governor & Council, Cape Coast Castle, 9.7.1785 (NA T70/33); Fynn (1971), 127.
45. According to Monsieur Gourg, cf. his "Mémoire", 12.5.1785 (*op. cit.*).
46. Feldbæk and Justesen (1980), 394-5.
47. Fynn (1971), 127.
48. Kea (1967), 42; Greene (1996b), 85; Amenumey (1986), 54; Gayibor (1985), 941.
49. Gayibor (1990), 131-2.
50. To the point of inciting the Dahomeans in July 1791 to ask the Danes to set up a factory at Ouidah as a protection against Little Popo-Glidji. Or so argues Ray Kea (1967), 42-4.
51. For the details, see Monrad (1822/2009), 76-7; Gayibor (1985), 944; Akyeampong (2001), 7 & 47; Greene (1996b), 85-9; Strickroth (2003), 163-5, etc.
52. Fynn (1971), 132-6; Strickroth (2003), 165, etc.
53. Although he was, at the same time, virtually at war with the same Dutch for trying to protect the Portuguese against what he considered to be the abuses of precisely the Dutch. See a number of letters signed by Archibald Dalzel, October-November-December 1792 & January 1793 (NA T70/33).
54. Amenumey talks of the 1792 fiasco (1986, 60-61). See also Nørregaard (1968), 247-9; Fynn (1971), 133-5, etc. Relevant primary-sources are letters from Dalzel dated 2.5.1792 & 7.2.1793 (NA T70/1565 & T70/33 respectively).
55. Law (1977a), 174.
56. Or so argues Akinjogbin (1967, 162-3).
57. Discussion in Ross (1987, 373-4).
58. See for instance, Gourg de Juda [Ouidah], 2.2.1789 (AN C6-26, doc. 118).
59. M. de Flotte à bord de la frégate "La Junon"[?] en rade du Benin 25.5.1787 (AN-Marine B/4/274); M'Leod (1820/1971), 99-100.
60. How many or how few they were, and what their status was exactly (plus how it changed over time), is a subject many historians have tried to see clear in, but so far with rather limited success in our view. For instance, even private traders were in a sense officials, that is permitted to trade by royal authority. Cf. Dalzel (1793/1967), 170 & 213-24; Akinjogbin (1967), 156-9; Law (2004a), 112-17, etc.
61. On this and what follows, cf. Dalzel (1793/1967), 207; Dunglas (1957), II, 192; Law (1977a), 177-9; Akinjogbin (1967), 165-8; Law (1994b), 47-9; Ojo (2008), 79, etc.
62. Mann (2007), 66-7.
63. "Mémoire contenant des observations sur quelque pointe de la côte de Guinée, visités en 1786 par la corvette le Pandora et sur la possibilité d'y faire des établissements," 6.9.1786 (AN C6-27, doc. 203).
64. The Weme polities only in 1786, according to Yves Person (1975, 227). Dalzel and Abson were indignant that Kpengla slaughtered so many prisoners of war instead of selling them to the Europeans (Dalzel [1793/1967], 181-91).
65. Juge & Consuls de Nantes à Mgr. 28.2.1789 (AN C6-26, doc. 126); Person (1975), 223; Adams (1823/1966), 83-7.
66. Law (1977a), 245 & 262-3.
67. As noted by Lionel Abson in several letters of his, autumn of 1783 (NA T70/1545). See also Akinjogbin (1967), 163-4.

68. As evidenced by British sources from the Gold Coast, the British continued a beneficial barter with the Luso-Brazilians, a barter the Dutch tried as usual to prevent. See for instance Governor & Council, Cape Coast Castle, to African Office, London, 31.10.1780 (NA T70/32); African Office to Cape Coast Castle, 26.6.1782 (NA T70/69).
69. Mémoire...le Pandora, 6.9.1786 (*op. cit.*).
70. Mémoires de Jacques Proa (*op. cit.*), 84; Hardy (?) de Ardres [Porto Novo] 22.6.1786 (Archives de la Chambre de Commerce de la La Rochelle, c.XIX, d.1-pièce 6523); Catherine Lugar, "The Portuguese Tobacco Trade and Tobacco Growers of Bahia in the Late Colonial Period", in Dauril Alden and Warren Dean (eds), *Essays Concerning the Socioeconomic History of Brazil and Portuguese India* (Gainesville, Florida, 1977), 26-70 (47-8).
71. Documents contained in Versailles to M. Gourg, 25 7bre (September) 1788 (in AN Colonies B-198). According to those documents, in the late 1780s 10-12,000 slaves were exported every year from Dahomey, the English share being 7-800, the Portuguese one about 3,000, while the French took the rest.
72. See, for instance, Versailles à M. Gourg, 23.11.1786; & other documents in AN Colonies B-192.
73. J.N. Matson, "The French at Amoku", *Transactions of the Historical Society of the Gold Coast and Togoland*, vol. I, part 2 (1953), 47-60. On the French side there are abundant sources in AN-Colonies B-192 (French archive), Marine B/4 & BB/4/2.
74. Lettre du roi de PNovo signé Monsieur Pierre, 1786 (AN C6-26, doc. 205).
75. How serious those plans were is borne out by the voluminous sources they have generated. They appear in a number of files in the Archives Nationales in Paris: C6/26, Colonies B-192, 196 & 198 (the latter two including in particular the correspondence between Monsieur Gourg and Versailles in 1787-88), Marine B/4/272, 274 & 277.
76. Or that is at least what he argued *a posteriori*. See his letter from Judas [Ouidah] 7.3.1789 (AN C6-26, doc. 128).
77. Exhaustive report by M. Gourg dated 17.7.1787 (AN C6-26). See also letter (from Hardy?) dated Ardres [Porto Novo] 25.9.1787 (Archives de la Chambre de Commerce de La Rochelle, C.XIX, d.11-pièce 6694).
78. Chambre de Commerce de La Rochelle au Ministre, 26.9.1788 (Archives de la Chambre de Commerce de La Rochelle, C.XIX, d.11-pièce 6704).
79. Versailles à M. Gourg, 25 Xbre [December] 1788 (AN Colonies B-198).
80. Capitaine du navire "La Cigogne" de La Rochelle, Porto Novo 27.9.1791; de Juda [Ouidah] 30.9.1791, au Capitaine de "La Cigogne" (both AN C6-27, doc.91).
81. Law (1994b), 50-51; Law (1977a), 268.
82. Monsieur Pierre, de Ardres [Porto Novo] 22.7.1788, aux capitaines français (Archives de la Chambre de Commerce de La Rochelle, carton XIX, doc. 11-pièce 6705); M. Gourg de Juda, 28.2.1789 (AN C6-26, doc.125); Mémoire/Instruction (pour le) commandant de la station à la côte d'Afrique, Versailles 23.11.1788 (AN-Marine, B/4/277, fol.127 ff.).
83. State & conditions of Williams Fort, Whydah [Ouidah], signed Lionel Abson, 27.3.1788 (NA BT 6/7); Africa House to Cape Coast Castle 11.10.1788 (NA

84. In Dalzel (1793/1967), 227-8.
85. When Gourg and Cazeneauve (the surgeon) arrived at Cape Coast Castle "every possible attention [was] shewn them" (Governor & Council, Cape Coast Castle to Africa House 20.11.1789 [NA T70/33]).
86. On Montaguère, see, for instance, Versailles à M. Gourg 13.3.1788 (AN Colonies B-198); and quite a few documents in AN Colonies B-196.
87. Pierre Verger (1966, 123-4) has described in some detail the deplorable state of the Portuguese fort and of its personnel in the 1780s.
88. Africa Office to Cape Coast Castle, 3.12.1795 (NA T70/71).
89. Garenne's story in his "Mémoire concernant l'inutilité du Comptoir de Juda [Ouidah]", Juda 31.7.1789 (CAOM-DFC carton 75-doc. 116).
90. Governor, Cape Coast Castle, to E. Dickson 19.7.1804 (NA T70/34).
91. Dunglas (1957), II, 21-2.
92. De Juda [Ouidah] 16.7.1788 (*op. cit.*); Norris (1789/1968), 139; Law (1977a), 181-2.
93. De Juda [Ouidah], 24.1.1788 (AN C6-26); Dalzel (1793/1967), 198.
94. Dalzel (1793/1967), 168-9, 192-3 & 207; Édouard Dunglas, "Adjohon: étude historique", *Études Dahoméennes* (NS), 8, (1966), 57-73; Ross (1987), 371-2, etc.
95. That at least was the impression of the British on the Gold Coast: from Governor & Council, Cape Coast Castle, 20.8.1789 (NA T70/33). See also Akinjogbin (1967), 170-73.
96. Gourg's "Mémoire" from 1791 (*op. cit.*) is in this respect quite illustrative.
97. De Juda [Ouidah] 8.6.1789 (AN C6-26, d.134); and especially for the events after 1789: Law (1977a), 263-5.
98. *Ibid.*, 250-77.
99. Unless we count the last one, Behanzin, who gave himself up to the French.
100. By, for instance, Akinjogbin (1967), 178-9.
101. Or so argues Dalzel (1793/1967, 223-4), in fact Lionel Abson speaking through Dalzel.
102. From Governor & Council, Cape Coast Castle, 9.5.1795, (NA T70/33); document dated 29.4.1795 (AHU Bahia, caixa 47, no.16045); other Portuguese documents reproduced in Verger (1968), 228, and in Verger (1977), 128-32; (Vieira) Ribeiro (2008), 145; etc.
103. According to Akinjogbin (1967), 180-81.
104. Gayibor (1985), 921-2.
105. *Ibid.*, 922; Law (2004a), 65; some British reports, especially one dated 3.6.1795 in NA T70/33.
106. (2003), 169-71.
107. Person (1982), II, 107.
108. Carta do Rei do Dahomé, 20.3.1795 & letter from Fonseca Aragão, n.d. (*Inventario*, III [1914], 354-5, nos 16.145 & 16.146); "Dois Embaixadores Africanos mandados a Bahia pelo Rei Dagomé" (Carta de D. Fernando Jozé de Portugal, Bahia 21.10.1795), *Revista Trimensal do Instituto Historico e Geographico Brazileiro*, LIX, parte 1 (1896), 413-16; "Regresso do Embaixador do Rei Dagomé para a costa d'Africa" (Carta de

D. Fernando Jozé de Portugal, Bahia 31.12.1796), *ibid.*, 417-19; Luiz Pinto de Souza Coutinho ao Governador Bahia, Queluz 3.4.1796 (Ordens Régias, vol. 81, doc. 7, APEB); Verger (1968), 229 & 265; etc.

109. Pires (1800/1957). A ferocious critic of Pires is Verger (1968, esp. p. 236).
110. Bay (1995), 18.
111. The cause, as given by Pires, was that during the first audience the missionaries had been asked by Agonglo to pray for Dahomean victory over the Mahis, which they said they did, with the result that the Dahomeans emerged victorious... (Pires [1800/1957], 62 & 108).
112. Edna Bay's interpretation (1995, 18) of basically Pires (1800/1957), 77-80.
113. *Ibid.* (i.e. Pires), 70-71 & 119-20.
114. *Ibid.*, 138-40; Verger (1968), 236 & 241; Berbain (1942), 54.
   The French seized the only two ships in the Ouidah roads. There was also an attack on Porto Novo-Seme (Akinjogbin [1967], 183; Verger [1968], 227).
115. The originals in OR, vol. 89, doc. 131B (APEB). For French translations and a very extensive discussion, see Verger [1968], 229-36.

C6
THE LONG GOODBYE

1. "A great shift in moral consciousness in the West", to quote Kristin Mann (2007, 1). There comes to mind David Abulafia's remark that "Europe was [and is?] an idea and an ideal rather than a place" (*The Great Sea. A Human History of the Mediterranean* [Oxford University Press, 2011], 546). We add: had it not been for the slave trade and slavery.
2. This may not be exactly the position of David Eltis, but his arguments can be so interpreted (Ellis [1987] 7-16 & [1997], 105-37).
3. We do not claim paternity for that thesis. Again our thinking may have been inspired by Eltis (1987). But does Eltis agree with us?
4. Knight (1997), 340.
5. See the next footnote.
6. The obvious textbook on the subject is Curtin (1990). The very special Danish case has been studied in depth by Neville A.T. Hall (ed. by B.W. Higman), *Slave Society in the Danish West Indies. St. Thomas, St. John, and St. Croix* (University of the West Indies Press, 1992, 1994), 208-28.
7. "An exceedingly lean period for printed and archival sources", Alpern (1998a), 23.
8. Dunglas (1957), II, 35-47; Bay (1995), 19.
9. We repeat that the fundamental work on the end of the slave trade remains David Eltis' *Economic Growth* (1987). A large part of what precedes and follows is based on that book. But see also Verger [1968], 287-562; and Robin Law, "An African Response to Abolition: Anglo-Dahomian Negotiations on Ending the Slave Trade, 1838-77", *Slavery and Abolition*, 16, 3 (1995), 281-310; and of course many other works by a host of historians.
10. Paul E. Lovejoy and David Richardson, "The Initial 'Crisis of Adaptation': the Impact of British Abolition on the Atlantic Slave Trade in West Africa", in Robin Law (ed.),

From Slave Trade to 'Legitimate' Commerce. The Commercial Transition in Nineteenth-century West Africa (Cambridge University Press, 1995), 32-56.

11. Besides Verger (1968), 294-303, see also William Ernest Frank Ward, *The Royal Navy and the Slavers* (New York, 1969), 58 & 78, and David A. Ross, "The First Chacha of Wydah: Felix Francis De Souza", *Odu* (n.s.), 2 (1969), 19-28 (esp. 21).

12. The best works on the history of Portugal and Brazil in this period are in our opinion Emília Viotti da Costa, *The Brazilian Empire: Myths and Histories* (University of North Carolina Press, 2000); and Gabriel Paquette, *Imperial Portugal in the Age of Atlantic Revolutions: the Luso-Brazilian World, c.1770–1850* (Cambridge University Press, 2013).

13. Quoted (p. 161) in Leslie Bethell "The Independence of Brazil", *The Cambridge History of Latin America*, III (1985, edited by the same Bethell), 157-96. Hence what Bethell calls the metropolization of the colony (*ibid.*, 171).

14. See for example Príncipe ao Gov. da Capitania da Bahia, 22.8.1799 (OR vol. 88, doc. 34, APEB).

15. Prince-regent to Governor of Bahia, Rio de Janeiro, 13.4.1808 (OR, vol.105, doc 15A); Conde de Galvêas (Secretary of State for the Colonies and the Navy) to Conde dos Arcos, Governor of Bahia, 2.8.1811 (OR, vol. 112, doc. 299F); Conde de Galvêas to the British Government; Rio de Janeiro 24.4.1812 (OR, vol. 112, doc.299A); Conde/Marquês de Aguiar (Chief Minister) to Conde dos Arcos, Rio de J. 9.9.1812 (OR, vol. 114, doc. 247); Marquês de Aguiar to Conde dos Arcos, Rio de J. 27.11.1815 (OR, vol. 117, doc. 434; all APEB).

16. One of the consequences was that on the coast of Guinea the local Britons, plus also the Danes and the Dutch, more or less unwittingly gave assistance to the Luso-Brazilian slave traders, before the naval commanders called them to order. See for instance: Capt. Paul Irby to Secretary of the Admiralty, HMS Amelia at Sierra Leone, 4.3.1812 (NA ADM 1/1996); E. White from Cape Coast Castle, to Commodore (Paul) Irby, 9.7.1812 (NA ADM 1/1996 & 123/177).

    The ADM 1/1996 file contains particularly rich material on the fight against the illegal slave trade.

17. The main work remains Ward (1969).

18. In addition to Eltis (1987), see for instance Robin Law, "Francisco Felix de Souza in West Africa, 1800-1849", in José C. Curto and Paul E. Lovejoy (eds), *Enslaving Connections: Western Africa and Brazil during the Era of Slavery* (Prometheus/Humanity Books, Amherst, NY 2004), 187-211; and Law (1995b), 283.

19. Verger (1968), 445.

20. Report - slave trade, no date, 1811? (NA CO 267/29).

21. "The fight against the Slave Trade has signally failed". Report (and conclusion) of HM's Commissioner of Inquiry, R.R. Madden or Marsden 31.7.1841 (NA CO 267/170-1).

22. There is a strange discrepancy between Kristin Mann's figures (2007, 33) and those of the Database, even though Ms Mann refers to precisely that base as her source.

23. According to David Ross, Ouidah's trade declined steadily between 1770 and 1812 (Ross [1987], footnote 70).

24. Cf. for instance letter from Sir James Yeo 7.11.1816 in *Parliam. Papers*, 1968, 6.

25. Lovejoy & Richardson (1995), 33-9.
26. Carta, Officio do Gov. D. Fernando José de Portugal, Bahia 12.5.1800 (*Inventario*, IV [1916] 246).
27. African Company: Minute/Petition to Admiralty, 7.5.1805 (NA BT 6/19).
28. Hamilton from Whydah [Ouidah] 21 & 22.2.1806 (NA T70/1583); M'Leod (1820/1971), 72-3.
29. Denyau de la Garenne, Paris 25 nivôse, an [year] VII/1799 (AN C6-27 doc. 105).
30. Akinjogbin (1967), 187-90; Verger (1968), 239.
31. Marquês de Aguiar (minister) ao Conde dos Arcos, Rio de J. 6.2.1816 (OR, vol. 118,doc. 43; APEB). The Prince-Regent became king the following month.
32. M'Leod (1820/1971), 122-4.
33. It can be deduced from the file T70/1606 (NA) that the last director of William's Fort in 1812, resident or not, was John Hope Smith, aged 25. He became governor at Cape Coast Castle in 1817, and of the British Gold Coast Settlements 1821-22, under the Crown.
34. From Cape Coast Castle 1.2.1807 (NA T70/55).
35. "Mr.D.B...has by no means given me satisfaction, & by way of punishment I sent him to Whydah [Ouidah]." (From Cape Coast Castle to the African Committee, 19.5.1806 [NA T70/1584]). See also Monrad (1822/2009), 261.
36. *Parliamentary Papers*, 1968, 136.
37. A.G. Hopkins, "The 'New International Economic Order' in the Nineteenth Century: Britain's First Development Plan for Africa", in R. Law (ed.), *From Slave Trade to 'Legitimate' Commerce* (Cambridge University Press, 1995), 240-64.
38. For instance, a former British purser "fell into the hands of the people of Whydah [Ouidah], by whom he is retained & put in command of the Fort" (from Cape Coast Castle 14.8.1816 [NA T70/36]).
39. See in addition Robin Law, "Madiki Lemon, the 'English Captain' at Ouidah, 1843-1852: An Exploration in Biography", *History in Africa*, 37 (2010), 107-23.
40. Law (2004a), 167. *Chacha* means "maid" in Spanish, which does not make much sense.
41. Verger (1966), 161 ff; Law (2004b), 190-92. On the Chacha, see also J. Michael Turner, "Les Bresiliens - the Impact of Former Brazilian slaves upon Dahomey" (PhD-thesis, University of Boston 1975).
42. Paul Hazoumé (1937/1956), 30-31.
43. Olabiyi Babalola Yai, "The Identity, Contributions, and Ideology of the Aguda (Afro-Brazilians) of the Gulf of Benin: A Reinterpretation", *Slavery and Abolition*, 22, 1 (2001), 72-82; Robin Law, "The Evolution of the Brazilian Community in Ouidah", *ibid.*, 22-41; David A. Ross, "The Career of Domingo Martinez in the Bight of Benin 1833-64", *Journal of African History*, VI, 1 (1965), 79-90.
44. Person (1982), II, 108.
45. Le Hérissé (1911), 311-8; Dunglas (1957), II, 47; Hazoumé (1937/1956), 27, footnote 1.
46. Glélé (1974), 121.
47. Among the more sceptical historians is David Ross, who has argued that the tales of Adandozan's cruelties may be safely ignored. Cf. his "The Autonomous Kingdom of Dahomey 1818-1894", (Ph.D-thesis, University of London, 1967), 8.

48. Person argues that in 1808 Adandozan was forced once more to pay tribute to Oyo, but probably for the last time. Cf. Person (1982), II, 108.
49. Dunglas (1957) II, 37.
50. Ross (1967), 1.
51. If he died in 1861, as Akinjogbin argues ([1967, 207), then he outlived his successor Gezo.
52. Alfred Burdon Ellis, *The Ewe-speaking Peoples of the Slave Coast of West Africa. Their Religion, Manners, Customs, Laws, Languages, etc.* (1890, reprinted 1966), 89 (the title of the book is misleading, it is not limited to the Ewe).
53. Elisée Soumonni, "The Compatibility of the Slave and Palm Oil Trades in Dahomey, 1818-1858", in Robin Law (ed.), *From Slave Trade to 'Legitimate' Commerce* (Cambridge University Press, 1995), 78-92 (esp. 81).
54. Person (1982) II, 108.
55. Anignikin (2001), 248-9.
56. For a discission, see Person (1975), 225 & 237; Law (1977a), 269-73.
57. Verger (1966), 166.
58. *Ibid.*, 163-5 & 187-8; Verger (1968), 267-81; *Inventario*, V, 1918.
59. What follows is based on Verger (1966), 166-70.
60. Conde de Aguiar ao Conde dos Arcos, Rio de J. 9.9.1812 (*op. cit.*).
61. Conde das Galveas ao Conde dos Arcos, 2.8.1811 (*op. cit.*).
62. Herskovits (1938/1967), II, 131; Verger (1957), 240.
63. Glélé (1974), 117.
64. Bay (1998), 315.
65. Gezo was at best a distant cousin, according to Maroukis (1974, 12).
66. Law (1995b), 284.
67. Fynn (1971), 145-6.
68. *Ibid.*, 145-51; Yarak (1990), 123; E. Martin (1927), 151-3.
69. Kea (1967), 49-54.
70. Strickrodt (2003), 167-8; Amenumey (1986), 41-2.
71. Greene (1996a), 95-6.
72. Akyeampong (2001), 48-57 & 215-16. He characterizes Danish rule as "evanescent" (p. 55).
73. Amenumey (1986), 90-93.
74. Gayibor (1990), 176-201.
75. Mann (2007), 21 & 44.
76. Dalzel (1793/1967), 222-3; Bay (2001), 56.
77. *Ibid.*, 56-7; Glélé (1974), 109; Verger (1952), 21-2.
78. Bay (2001), 52. See also Snelgrave (1734/1971), 98-106.
    Another extraordinary female life story from this epoch is that of Sarah Forbes Bonetta (1843–80). She was a Yoruba, intended by her Dahomean captors in 1850 to be a human sacrifice. She became instead a goddaughter of Queen Victoria. Her story is recorded Walter Dean Myers', *At Her Majesty's Request. An African Princess in Victorian England* (Scholastic Press, 1999) – actually not a scientific work but apparently a book for children.
79. Ross (1967), 18-19; Ross (1969), 20-21.

80. Elisée (Akpo) Soumonni, "Some Reflections on the Brazilian Legacy in Dahomey", *Slavery and Abolition*, 22, 1 (2001), 61-71.
81. João José Reis, *Rebelião escrava no Brasil: A história do levante dos malês 1835* (São Paulo, Editora Brasiliense, 1986).
82. *Ibid.*, 87; Law (2001d), 26-7.
83. Bruce Chatwin, *The Viceroy of Ouidah* (Picador/Pan edition, 1980). Werner Herzog turned it into a film called *Cobra Verde* in 1987, starring Klaus Kinski.
84. *Captain Canot* (1854/1968), 263-4.
85. Ross (1967), 30-31.
86. Soumonni (2001), 67.
87. Ross (1967), 33-4; Law (2004a), 196.
88. See for instance Ross (1965), 79-80.
89. Law (2004a), 147.
90. *Ibid.*, 178-9.
91. Gayibor (1985), 966; Gayibor (1995), 208; Mignot (1985), 196-7.
92. Robert Smith's chronology, dating those wars to the 1820s, is no longer accepted. Still, Smith's well-known article remains a valid introduction to the subject. We refer to his "The Yoruba Wars, c. 1820–93. A General Study", in J.F. Ade Ajayi and Robert Smith, *Yoruba Warfare in the Nineteenth Century* (Cambridge University Press, 1964), 9-55.
93. Law (1977a), 272. For what appears to be an eyewitness account of the fall of Oyo, see H.F.C. Smith, D.M. Last and Gamba Gubio, "Ali Eisami Gazirmabe of Bornu" in P. Curtin (ed.), *Africa Remembered. Narratives by West Africans from the Era of the Slave Trade* (University of Wisconsin Press, 1967), 199-216.
94. Lombard (1967b), 73.
95. Ouidah's position of dominance was progressively eroded by Lagos, says Law (2004a), 160.
96. Agbo and Bediye (1997), 29-48.
97. Anignikin (2001), 248-51; Ross (1967), 44-7.
98. Law (1977a), 273; Ross (1978), 147.
99. R. Law, "The Career of Adele at Lagos and Badagry, c.1807–c.1837", *Journal of the Historical Society of Nigeria*, IX, 2 (1978), 35-59 (46-7).
100. What follows is based mostly on the various contributions, many of which have been referred to already, in R. Law (ed.), *From Slave Trade to 'Legitimate' Commerce* (Cambridge University Press, 1995).
101. Law (1995b), 284.
102. Berbain (1942), 54.
103. Serge Daget, *Répertoire des expéditions négrières françaises à la traite illégale* (Nantes, Centre de Recherche sur l'Histoire du Monde Atlantique etc., 1988), 558.
104. Law (1995b), 284. See also Robin Law, "The Transition from the Slave Trade to 'Legitimate' Commerce", in Doudou Diène (ed.), *From Chains to Bonds. The Slave Trade Revisited* (Paris/UNESCO and New York/Oxford, Berghahn Books, 2001), 22-35.
105. Stressed by Law (2004a), 209.
106. See, for instance, Harrison M. Wright's "Introduction" to Freeman (1844/1968), vii-xxxix (esp. p. xi).

107. Law (1995b), 281-2.
108. Verger (1968), 431. Integral text of the law in Braz do Amaral, *Fatos da Vida do Brazil* (Bahia, Tip Naval, 1941), 166-7. Many other laws related to the slave trade and slavery have also been reproduced in that book.
109. Mann (2007), 95.
110. Law (2004), 236-8.
111. S.O. Biobaku, *The Egba and their Neighbours 1842–1872* (Oxford University Press, 1957); Ross (1967), 91-3 & 101-2; Agneta Pallinder-Law, "Aborted Modernization in West Africa? The Case of Abeokuta", *Journal of African History*, XV, 1 (1974), 65-82.
112. R. Smith (1964), 11.
113. According to Robin Law, "The Politics of Commercial Transition: Factional Conflict in Dahomey in the Context of the Ending of the Atlantic Slave Trade", *Journal of African History*, 38, 2 (1997), 213-33 (219).
114. Ross (1967), 129.
115. Law (1993), 255.
116. Bay (1998), 199.
117. *Ibid.*, 214.
118. Bay (2008), 56.
119. Bay (1995), 19; Bay (1979), 11.
120. Bay (1998), 155.
121. Law's theory (1997b, 227).
122. Le Hérissé (1911), 128-9.
123. Law (1986b), 113.
124. The fame of that guard is inversely proportional to its role, which was rather marginal until the 1840s when the depletion of the male population, due to the many wars, forced Gezo to rely more heavily on his female warriors. The best works on the Amazons are in our opinion Alpern (1998b), and Law (1993).
125. Brue (1845), 67.
126. *Ibid.*, 64-8.
127. Stanley B. Alpern, "Dahomey's Royal Road", *History in Africa*, 26 (1999), 11-24.
128. See his letter of 25.10.1848 in B. Cruickshank, "Letters from the Gold Coast and Slave Coast with an Account of a Mission to the King of Dahomey"- Gold Coast papers, 1848, 52a (MS 173088; Library of the School of Oriental & African Studies, London).
129. *Ibid*; letter dated 3.11.1848.
130. Marion Johnson, "Ashante East of the Volta", *Transactions of the Historical Society of Ghana*, VIII (1965), 33-40.
131. *Ibid.*, 36; Nugent (2008), 935; Welman (1924/1969), 7-8; Amenumey (1986), 74.
132. Akyeampong (2001), 54.
133. *Ibid.*, 106-7. See also Greene (1996b), 94-6.

EPILOGUE

1. Discussed somewhat more in depth, we repeat, in Fuglestad (2005 & 2010).
2. Mark 12:17.
3. Agbo (1959), 74-5.
4. With regard to the last point, the illuminating and intriguing work of Aldo Schiavone, *The End of the Past. Ancient Rome and the Modern World* (English translation, Harvard University Press, 2000) explains part of it.
5. Barickman (1998).
6. Alex Haley, *Roots: The Saga of an American Family* (New York, Doubleday, 1976).
7. Bay (2001), 43; Gaetano Ciarcia, "Restaurer le futur. Sur la *Route de l'Esclave* à Ouidah (Bénin)", *Cahiers d'Etudes Africaines*, XLVIII, 4 (2008) 687-705 (689-91).
8. Soumonni, Codo and Adande (1994).
9. Elisée Soumonni, "From a Port of the Slave Trade to an Urban Community: Robin Law and the History of Ouidah", in Toyin Falola and Matt D. Childs (eds), *The Changing Worlds of Atlantic Africa* (Durham, Carolina Academic Press, 2009), 223-31 (230).
10. The only direct reference I have seen was in an article in the French newspaper *Le Monde*; an article which has since unfortunately disappeared from my collection.

BIBLIOGRAPHY

ARCHIVAL SOURCES

Brazil

Arquivo Publico do Estado da Bahia (Salvador da Bahia):
Ordens Regiaes/Régias: volumes 27 to 118
Colônia volume 197

France

Archives de la Chambre de Commerce de La Rochelle:
Carton XIX, documents 1-11
Archives Départementales de Charente Maritime, La Rochelle:
B.5729 & 4J2318 ("Mémoire de Jacques Proa, dit Proa des iles", 1806)
Archives Départementales de Loire Atlantique, Nantes:
C687-C740
Archives Municipales de La Rochelle:
série EE, carton 282-3 ("Journal de navigation du sieur Joseph Crassous de Médeuil, Lieutenant en premier 'Le Roy Dahomey' 1772-74")

Archives Nationales, Paris
Archives des Colonies:
Colonies B-192, 196 & 198
Colonies C6 (Sénégal ancien)-25 à 29
Colonies C/8a/16
Colonies C/8b/2
Colonies F/2a/7 à 11

Archives de la Marine:
Marine B/1/9, 19 & 20

BIBLIOGRAPHY

Marine B/3/236, 251 & 264
Marine B/4/65, 73, 77, 103, 272, 274 & 277
Marine BB/4/2
Marine 2/JJ/95 ("Description nautique de la Côte d'Afrique [etc].", no date, but probably 1780s)
Marine 3/JJ/247 & 252 ("Description des Roiaumes ou l'on fait le commerce en Afrique, avec le Journal du voyage fait en Guinée avec trois vaisseaux du Roy; Le Capitaine du vaisseau "La Tempête" [i.e. Du Casse, and hence from 1687–8])

Centre des Archives d'Outre-Mer, Aix-en-Provence (Dépôt des Fortifications des Colonies. Côtes d'Afrique):
carton 26, c.75, d.109: Mémoire sur le fort de Juda [Ouidah], postérieur à 1763–7
carton 75, doc. 104: "Relation du Royaume de Judas en Guinée. De son gouvernement, des moeurs de ses habitants, de leur Religion. Et du Negoce qui s'y fait", ca. 1715
carton 75, doc.106: "Mémoire" dated 13.12.1740
carton 75, doc. 111: Réflexions sur Juda, par le sieur De Chenevert et l'abbé Bulet, à Juda [Ouidah] le 1.6.1776
carton 75, doc. 113-4: "Mémoire sur la Guinée" 1716
carton 75, doc. 116: Deniau de Garenne, Mémoire concernant l'inutilité du Comptoir de Juda [Ouidah], Juda 31.7.1789
carton 75, doc. 118: "Mémoire pour servir d'Instruction au Directeur qui me succedera au comptoire de Juda, par Mr. Gourg" (1791), Published under the title "Ancien mémoire sur le Dahomey", in *Mémorial de l'artillerie de Marine*, vol. XX (1892), 747–76

Germany

Ex-Zentrales Staatsarchiv of the former German Democratic Republic, Merseburg [now possibly in Berlin]; R.65.32 vol.I, ff.30-36: N. Dubois, memorandum dated 10.11.1710) – courtesy of Adam Jones

Portugal

Arquivo Histórico Ultramarino, Lisbon:
Bahia, caixa 47
São Tomé, caixas 4 & 5

Spain

Bibliote ca Nacional de España (Madrid):
MSS 3818, f.74-5 King's Instructions 28.7.1659
MSS 18 178 Misiones del Congo y Etiopia, f.211, 212, 213 – a summary of the Capuchin mission to Allada written after its ending (on Naxara, see below)
Biblioteca Provincial de Toledo (now possibly Biblioteca Pública del Estado en Toledo):

BIBLIOGRAPHY

R.P.F. Basilio de Zamora: "Cosmographia, o descripcion del mundo", manuscript dated 1675 (Colección de MSS Borbón-Lorenzana, no.244)

United Kingdom

Birmingham Central Library: The Galton Family papers

British Library, London, Department of Manuscripts:

Anonymous: *Certain Considerations Relating to the RAC of England* (etc), printed 1680 (Harley MS 7310)

Des Marchais, "Journal de Navigation du voyage en Guinée, Iles d'Amérique, Indes Espanoles, fait en 1704" (Additional Manuscripts Add.19560)

Edinburgh University Library:

Dk.7 52, letters from Archibald Dalzel (also written Dalzell)

Library of the School of Oriental and African Studies:

MS 173088: B. Cruickshank: Letters from the Gold Coast and Slave Coast with an Account of a Mission to the King of Dahomey; Gold Coast papers, 1848, 52a

National Archives (formerly Public Record Office), Kew:

Admiralty records:
ADM 1/1996
ADM 123/177
ADM 123/183

Board of Trade records:
BT 6/3 to 6/19

Colonial records:
CO 267/11 (Justly Watson, "A Report on the survey of William's Fort Whydah [Ouidah]", 1755)
CO 267/29
CO 267/170-71

Treasury records:
T70: Records of the African Companies (especially the Royal African Company, 1672-1750; and the Company of Merchants trading to Africa, 1750-1821)
T70/2 to T70/1606

Public Record Office, Chancery Lane, London (later transferred to the National Archives): C113/262 & 276

Printed Presumed Primary Sources (including Travellers' Accounts)

Aarestrup, Biørn, J.M. Kjøge, J. Gjønge, Rasmussen, "Nogle bidrag til Kundskab om den danske strækning på Guinea Kysten. Christiansborg 8.6.1774", in *Arkiv for Statistik, politik og Huusholdningsvidenskaber* (Udgivet af [edited by] Prof. Friderik Thaarup), vol. III (Kjøbenhavn [Copenhagen], 1797–8), 161–92

BIBLIOGRAPHY

Adams, Captain John, *Remarks on the Country extending from Cape Palmas to the River Congo* (London, 1823, reprinted 1966)

Africa Pilot (published originally as *Western Coast of Africa*; first edition 1849; 12th edition London 1967; published by the Hydrographer of the Navy and prepared by Lieut. Commander J.F. Gruning), vol. I

Anais/Annaes do Archivo Público/do Arquivo do Estado da Bahia

Anguiano, P. Mateo de (1649–1726), *Misiones Capuchinas en Africa, vol. II, Misiones al Reino de la Zinga, Benín, Arda, Guineá, y Sierra Leona* (Madrid, 1685; modern edition: vol. VII of *Missionalia Hispanica* [con introducción y notas del P. Buenaventura de Carrocera], Madrid [Consejo Superior de Investigaciones Cientificas & Instituto Santo Toribio de Mogrovejo, 1957]), 251-66

Anonymous, "Discurso Preliminar, Historico, Introductivo com naturaleza de Descripção Economica da Comarca e Cidade da Bahia" [no date, but later than 1789], *Annaes da Bibliotheca Nacional do Rio de Janeiro*, vol. XXVII (1905), 281-348

Atkins, John (Surgeon in the Royal Navy), *A Voyage to Guinea, Brasil, and the West Indies; in His Majesty's Ships, the Swallow and Weymouth* (1735, London, new impression [F. Cass], 1970)

Barbot on Guinea. The Writings of Jean Barbot on West Africa 1678-1712, 2 volumes (ed. by P.E.H. Hair, Adam Jones & Robin Law; London [The Hakluyt Society], 1992)

Beraud, M. (Xavier), "Note sur le Dahomé" (dated Whydah [Ouidah] 26.3.1866), *Bulletin de la Société de Géographie*, 5e série, vol.12 (1866), 371-86

Bold, Edward, *The Merchant's and Mariner's African Guide; Containing an Accurate Description of the Coast, Bays, Harbours, and Adjacent Islands of West Africa (etc)* (London, 1819, republished in Salem, US, 1823)

Bosman, William (Willem), *A New and Accurate Description of the Coast of Guinea* (first published in Dutch in 1704; new English edition London [Frank Cass], 1967)

Bouët-Willaumez, E., *Commerce et traite des noirs aux côtes occidentales d'Afrique. 1er janvier 1848* (Paris, 1848; reprinted Geneva 1978)

Bowdich, T. (Thomas) Edward, *A Mission from Cape Coast Castle to Ashantee (etc)* (London, John Murray, 1819; 3rd ed. W.E.F. Ward [ed.] [F. Cass, 1966])

Brásio, Padre António (coligida e anotada pelo), *Monumenta Missionaria Africana* vol. VI (*África Ocidental [1611–1621]*) (Lisbon, Agência Geral do Ultramar, 1955) vol. XIII (*África Ocidental (1666–1885)* (Lisbon, Academia Portuguesa de Historia, 1982) vol. XIV (*África Ocidental [1686–1699]*) (Lisbon 1985)

Brue, Blaise, "Voyage fait en 1843 dans le royaume de Dahomey", *Revue Coloniale*, VII (1845), 55-68

Burton, Richard F., *Wanderings in West Africa, from Liverpool to Fernando Po* (2 volumes, London, Dover Publications, 1863)

———, *A Mission to Gelele, King of Dahomey (etc)* (second ed. 1864; new ed. with an Introduction and Notes by C.W. Newbury; London [Routledge and Kegan Paul], 1966), two volumes

BIBLIOGRAPHY

Caldas, Jozé Antonio, "Noticia geral de toda esta capitania da Bahia desde o seu descobrimiento até o prezente anno de 1759" [i.e. written in 1759], *Revista do Instituto Geographico e Historico da Bahia* (no. 57, 1931), 287-315

Canot, Captain; or, Twenty Years of an African Slaver (etc); written out and edited by Brantz Mayer (New York & London 1854; new edition by Arno Press and the New York Times, 1968)

Celestin of Bruxelles (letters 1681–82) in *Analecta Ordinis Minorum Capuccinorum*, vol.XXXI (Rome, 1915), 328-30 & 357-8

Cortesão, Armando and A. Teixeira da Mota, *Portugaliae Monumenta Cartographica*, volumes II & III (Lisbon, Imprensa Nacional-Casa da Moeda, 1960)

Crone, C.R. (ed. & translated by), *The Voyages of Cadamosto, and other Documents on Western Africa in the Second Half of the Fifteenth Century* (The Hakluyt Society, 1937)

Crooks, J.J. (ed.), *Records Relating to the Gold Coast Settlements from 1750 to 1874* (first ed. Dublin 1923, 2nd ed. Frank Cass, 1973)

Cruickshank, Brodie, *Report on a Mission to the King of Dahomey*, 19.11.1848 (*Parliamentary Papers*, 1850, IX)

———, *Eighteen Years on the Gold Coast of Africa* (London, 1853; 2nd ed., F.Cass, 1966)

———, (see also u/Library of the School of Oriental and African Studies)

Dalzel, Archibald, *The History of Dahomy, an Inland Kingdom of Africa. Compiled from Authentic Memoirs* (London 1793, 2nd edition, with a new introduction by J.D. Fage, F. Cass, 1967)

Dantzig, Albert van (ed.), *The Dutch and the Guinea Coast, 1674–1742: A Collection of Documents from the General State Archive at the Hague* (Accra, Academy of Arts and Sciences, 1978)

Dapper, Olfert, *Description de l'Afrique* (Amsterdam, 1686). Originally published in Dutch under the title *Naureurige Beschrijvinge der Afrikaenesche Gewesten (etc.)* (Amsterdam, 1668)

Davenant, Charles, *Reflections upon the Constitution and Management of the Trade to Africa (etc.)* (London, 1709)

Delbée (or D'Elbée), Louis, "Journal du voyage du Sieur Delbée, Commissaire general de la Marine, aux Isles, dans la coste de Guynée", in J. de Clodoré (ed.), *Relation de ce qui s'est passé dans les isles et terre-ferme de l'Amérique pendant la dernière guerre avec l'Angleterre et depuis en exécution de Traitté de Breda*, vol. II (Paris, G. Clouzier, 1671/microfilm edition Hachette 1972), 347-558

Des Marchais, "Journal de Navigation du voyage en Guinée, Iles d'Amérique, Indes Espanoles, fait en 1704" (Additional Manuscripts Add.19560)

Doctrina Christiana (Madrid 1658). Cf. Labouret, Henri and Paul Rivet, *Le Royaume d'Arda et son évangélisation au XVIIe siècle* (Paris, Institut d'Ethnologie, 1929); Anguiano, P. Mateo de (1649-1726), *Misiones Capuchinas en Africa*, vol. II, *Misiones al Reino de la Zinga, Benín, Arda, Guineà, y Sierra Leona* (Madrid,

1685; modern edition: vol. VII of *Missionalia Hispanica* [con introducción y notas del P. Buenaventura de Carrocera], Madrid [Consejo Superior de Investigaciones Científicas & Instituto Santo Toribio de Mogrovejo, 1957]), 251-66

Donnan, Elizabeth (ed.), *Documents Illustrative of the History of the Slave Trade to America*, vol. I, 1441–1700 (Washington DC, Carnegie Institution, 1930)

Doublet, Jean, *Journal du Corsaire Jean Doublet, Lieutenant de frégate sous Louis XIV*, edited by Charles Bréard (Paris 1883)

Dralsé de Grand-Pierre, *Relation de divers voyages faits dans l'Amérique et aux Indes occidentales* (Paris 1718)

Dupuis, Joseph, *Journal of a Residence in Ashantee* (1st ed. 1824, second ed., by W.E.F. Ward, London, Frank Cass 1966)

Durand: Robert Durand's manuscript from 1731–32, see under Robert Harms

Fawckner, James, *Narrative of Captain James Fawckner's Travels to the Coast of Benin, West Africa* (London, 1837)

Forbes, Frederick E., *Dahomey and the Dahomans. Being the Journals of two Missions to the King of Dahomey and Residence at his Capital in the Years 1849 and 1850* (2 volumes, London, Longman etc., 1851)

François, Père Gonzalez, "Relation abrégée du voyage des Frères Prêcheurs, missionaires en Afrique et en Guinée (etc)", in "La Mission du V.P. Gonzalez François en Guinée, sur les côtes d'Afrique (1688)", *Année Dominicaine (etc.)* (vol. 14, Sept. 1702, new edit. 1900), 461-75

Freeman, Thomas Birch, *Journal of Various Visits to the Kingdoms of Ashanti, Aku, and Dahomi, in Western Africa* (London, second ed. 1844, third ed., 1968)

Hallett, Robin (ed.), *Records of the African Association 1788–1831* (London/Edinburgh, Thomas Nelson & Sons, 1964)

Houstoun, James, *Some New and Accurate Observations, Geographical, Natural and Historical, Containing a True and Impartial Account of the Situation, Product, and Natural History of the Coast of Guinea (etc.)* (London, 1725)

Huntley, Sir Henry, *Seven years' Service on the Slave Coast of Western Africa* (London, Thomas Cautley Newby, 1850)

Inventario dos documentos relativos ao Brasil existentes no Archivo de Marinha e Ultramar de Lisboa (organisado para a Biblioteca Nacional do Rio de Janeiro por Eduardo de Castro e Almeida), five volumes (1913-1918) - consulted in the Arquivo Histórico Ultramarino de Lisboa, as it is now called.

Isert, Paul (ed. & translated by Selena Winsnes), *Letters on West Africa and the Slave trade. Paul Erdmann Isert's Journey to Guinea and the Caribbean Islands in Columbia (1788)* (British Academy/Oxford University Press, 1992)

Jadin, Louis and Mireille Dicorato (eds), *Correspondance de Dom Afonso, roi du Congo 1506–1543* (Brussels, Académie Royale des Sciences d'Outre-Mer, 1974)

Jones, Adam (ed.), *German Sources for West African History 1599–1669* (Wiesbaden, F. Steiner, 1983)

BIBLIOGRAPHY

———, *Brandenburg Sources for West African History 1680–1700* (Stuttgart/Wiesbaden, 1985)

———, (transcribed, translated & edited by), *West Africa in the Mid- Seventeenth Century. An Anonymous Dutch Manuscript* (Atlanta, Georgia, African Studies Association Press [Emory University], 1995)

Journal of the Commissioners for Trade and Plantations from January 1728–9 to December 1934, Preserved in the Public Record Office (London, HMSO, 1928)

Justesen, Ole (ed.), *Danish Sources for the History of Ghana 1657–1754*, 2 volumes (Copenhagen, Kgl. Danske Videnskabernes Selskab, 2005)

Labarthe, P., *Voyage à la Côte de Guinée, ou description des Côtes d'Afrique depuis le cap Tagrin jusqu'au cap de Lopez-Gonzalves* (Paris, Debray, an XI [1803])

Lander, Richard, *Records of Captain Clapperton's Last Expedition to Africa* (London, 1830, 2nd ed. 1967), 2 volumes

Landolphe, J.F., *Mémoires du Capitaine Landolphe rédigés sur son manuscript par J.S. Quesné* (2 vols., Paris, 1823)

Law, Robin (ed.), *Correspondence from the Royal African Company's Factories at Offra and Whydah on the Slave Coast of West Africa in the Public Record Office, London, 1678–93* (Occasional Papers no.24, Centre of African Studies, Edinburgh Univerity, 1990a)

——— (ed.), *Correspondence of the Royal African Company's Chief Merchants at Cabo Corso Castle with William's Fort, Whydah, and the Little Popo Factory, 1717–1728. An Annotated Transcription of Ms. Francklin 1055/1 in the Bedfordshire County Record Office* (African Studies Program, University of Wisconsin-Madison, 1991a)

——— (ed.), *Further Correspondence of the Royal African Company of England Relating to the 'Slave Coast'. Selected Documents from Ms. Rawlinson C.745–747 in the Bodleian Library, Oxford* (African Studies Program, University of Wisconsin-Madison, 1992a)

——— (ed.), *The English in West Africa, 1681–1683. The Local Correspondence of the Royal African Company of England, 1681–1699*, Part 1 (Oxford University Press/British Academy, 1997a)

——— (ed.), *The English in West Africa, 1685–1688. The Local Correspondence of the Royal African Company of England, 1681–1699*, Part 2 (Oxford University Press/British Academy, 2001a)

——— (ed.), *The English in West Africa, 1691–1699. The Local Correspondence of the Royal African Company of England 1681–1699*, Part 3 (Oxford University Press/British Academy, 2006)

Loyer, R. Père Godefroy (1660–1715), *Relation du voyage du royaume d'Issyny, Côte d'Or, Païs de Guinée, en Afrique (etc)* (Paris, 1714)

Marees, Pieter de, *Description and Historical Account of the Gold Kingdom of Guinea (1602)* (translated from the Dutch, and edited by Albert van Dantzig and Adam Jones; publ. for the British Academy by Oxford University Press, 1987)

BIBLIOGRAPHY

M'Leod, John, *A Voyage to Africa. With Some Accounts of the Manners and Customs of the Dahomian People* (1820, reprinted London [Frank Cass] 1971)

Monrad, Hans Christian, *Bidrag til en Skildring af Guinea-kysten og dens Indbyggere* (etc)(Copenhagen 1822). English version by Selena Axelrod Winsnes in *Two views from Christiansborg Castle, vol. II: A Description of the Guinea Coast and its Inhabitants* (Accra, Sub- Saharan Publishers, 2009)

N***, *Voyage aux côtes de Guinée et en Amerique* (Amsterdam, 1719)

Naxara, Fr. Joseph de (modern: José de Nájera), *Espejo mystico en que el hombre interior se mira practicamente ilustrado para los conocimientos de Dios, y el exercicio de la virtudes (etc.)* (Madrid 1672) [consulted in Biblioteca Nacional de España, Madrid, sección impresos no.3/63664]

Norris, Robert, *Memoirs of the Reign of Bossa Ahádee, King of Dahomey. To which are added, the Author's Journey to Abomey, the Capital; and a Short Account of the African Slave Trade* (1789, reprinted London [Frank Cass] 1968)

Parliamentary Papers. *Report from the Select Committee on papers relating to the African Forts* (ordered, by the House of Commons, to be Printed, 26.6.1816) (published by the Irish University Press in the series Colonies Africa, vol. 1 – Shannon, 1968)

Parliamentary Papers. *Correspondence with British Ministers and Agents in Foreign Countries, and with Foreign Ministers in England, relating to the Slave Trade. From April 1, 1849, to March 31, 1850* (Presented to both Houses of Parliament by Command of Her Majesty. 1850)[also published by the Irish University Press in the series Slave Trade, vol. 37 – Shannon, 1969]

Parliamentary Papers: *Report from the Select Committee on Africa (Western Coast). Ordered, by the House of Commons, to be printed, 26 June 1865*

Pereira, Duarte Pacheco, *Esmeraldo de Situ Orbis*, translated and edited by George H.T. Kimble, (London, The Hakluyt Society, 1937; first published in 1892, but probably written in 1505–8)

Phillips, Thomas, "A Journal of a Voyage made in the Hannibal of London, Ann. 1693, 1694 (etc)", in Awnsham Churchill and John Churchill (eds), *Collection of Voyages & Travels*, vol. VI (1732), 171-239

Pires, Vicente Ferreira (Clado Ribeiro de Lessa ed.), *Crónica de uma Embaixada Luso-Brasileira à Costa d'África em fins do século XVIII, incluindo o texto da Viagem de África em o Reino de Daomé escrita pelo Padre Vicente Ferreira Pires no ano de 1800 e até o presente inédita* (São Paulo, Companhia Editora Nacional, 1957)

Pruneau de Pommegeorge, PDP Antoine Edmé, *Description de la Nigritie* (Amsterdam & Paris, Chez Maradan, 1789)

Rask, Johannes, *En kort og sandferdig reisebeskrivelse til og fra Guinea* (Trondhjem [Trondheim], 1754). English version by Selena Axelrod Winsnes: *Two Views from Christiansborg Castle*, vol. I, *A Brief and Truthful Description of a Journey to and from Guinea* (Accra, Sub- Saharan Publishers, 2009)

Ratelband, K. (uitgegeven door), *Vijf dagregisters van het kasteel São Jorge da Mina*

BIBLIOGRAPHY

(Elmina) aan de Goudkust (1645–1647) ('s-Gravenhage [the Hague], Linschoten Vereeniging, Martinus Nijhoff, 1953)

Revista Trimensal do Instituto Historico e Geographico Brazileiro, LIX, parte 1 (1896), 413-19 (contains official letters from 1795)

Ringard, Sieur (1727), see under Robin Law (ed.), "A Neglected Account"

Robertson, G.A., *Notes on Africa; Particularly those Parts which are Situated between Cape Verd and the River Congo; (etc.)* (London, Sherwood, Neely, and Jones, 1819)

Rømer, Ludewig Ferdinand, *A Reliable Account of the Coast of Guinea (1760)*, translated and edited by Selena Axelrod Winsnes (British Academy/Oxford University Press, 2000)

Roussier, Paul (ed.), *L'établissement d'Issiny 1687–1702. Voyages de Ducasse, Tibierge et d'Amon à la côte de Guinée publiés pour la première fois et suivis de la Relation du Voyage du Royaume d'Issiny du P. Godefroy Loyer* (1714) (Paris, Larose, 1935)

Saccone, Salvatore, *Il viaggio di Padre Domenico Bernardi in Brasile ed in Africa nel quadro dell'attività missionaria dei Cappuccini agli inizio dell'età moderna. Con il testo della Relazione del "Viaggio"* (Bologna, Pàtron Editore, 1980) [mainly reproduction of documents 1713-26]

Sandoval, Alonso de, *De Instauranda Aethiopum Salute* (Seville, 1627) [also known under the title *Naturaleza, policía, sagrada i profana, costumbres i ritos, disciplina i catecismo evangélico de todos los etíopies*] Modern edition: *Un tratado sobre la esclavitud* (Introducción, transcripción y traducción de Enriqueta Vila Vilar; Madrid, Alianza Editorial, 1987)

Skertchly, J.A., *Dahomey as it is* (London, Chapman and Hall, 1874)

Smith, William, *A New Voyage to Guinea* (1744, reprinted London, Routledge, 1967)

Snelgrave, William, *A New Account of some parts of Guinea, and the Slave Trade (etc.)* (London 1734, reprint, Frank Cass, 1971)

Tilleman Erick, *En kort og enfoldig beretning om det landskab Guinea og dets beskaffenhed (1697). A Short and Simple Account of the Country Guinea and its Nature*; translated and edited by Selena Axelrod Winsnes (University of Wisconsin, Madison, 1994)

Vilar, Enriqueta Vila (see under Sandoval)

Yacou, Alain, *Journaux de bord et de traite de Joseph Crassous de Médeuil. De La Rochelle à la côte de Guinée et aux Antilles (1772–1776)* (Paris, Karthala, 2001) [the printed, not quite identical version of a manuscript referred to above]

Zhou Daguan (1266–1346), *A Record of Cambodia: the Land and its People* (translated and edited by Peter Harris, Silkworm Books, 2007)

Secondary Sources (including collections of presumed oral traditions)

Abotchie, Chris, "Legal Processes and Institutions", in Francis Agbodeka (ed.), *A Handbook of Eweland vol. I: The Ewes of Southeastern Ghana* (Accra, Woeli, 1997), 73-84

BIBLIOGRAPHY

Abulafia, David, *The Great Sea. A Human History of the Mediterranean* (Oxford University Press, 2011)

Adamu, Mahdi, *The Hausa Factor in West African History* (Zaria, Ahmadu Bello University Press and Oxford University Press, 1978)

Adandé, Alexandre, "Le maïs et ses usages dans le Bas-Dahomey", *Bulletin de l'IFAN*, XV, 1 (1953), 220-82

———, *Les récades des rois du Dahomey* (Dakar, IFAN, 1962)

Adande, Alexis, "Togudo-Awude, capitale de l'ancien royaume d'Allada. Étude d'une cité précoloniale d'après les sources orales, écrites et les données de l'archéologie" (thesis, Université de Paris, Panthéon-Sorbonne, 1984)

Adediran, Abiodun, "The Formation of the Sabe Kingdom in Central Benin Republic", *Africana Marburgensia*, 16, 2 (1983), 60-74

Adédìrán, Biódún, "Ìdáìsà: The Making of a Frontier Yorùbá State", *Cahiers d'Études Africaines*, XXIV, 1 (1984), 71-85

Adler, Alfred, *Le pouvoir et l'interdit. Royauté et religion en Afrique noire* (Paris, Albin Michel, 2000)

Agbo, Casimir dit Alidji, *Histoire de Ouidah du XVIe au XXe siècle* (printed in Avignon, 1959)

Agbo, Valentin A. and Pierre Bediye, "Le plateau Adja", in Jon Daane, Mark Breusers and Erik Frederiks (eds), *Dynamique paysanne sur le plateau Adja du Bénin* (Paris, Karthala, 1997), 29-48

Agiri, B.A., "Early Oyo History Reconsidered", *History in Africa*, II (1975), 1-16

Aguessi, Honorat, "Le Dan-Home du XIXe siècle était-il une société esclavagiste?", *Revue Française d'Études Politiques Africaines*, 50 (1970), 71-91

Aguirre Beltran, G. "Tribal Origins of Slaves in Mexico", *Journal of Negro History*, 31-3 (1946), 269-352

Akindélé, A. and C. Aguessy, *Contribution à l'étude de l'histoire de l'ancien royaume de Porto Novo* (Dakar, IFAN, 1953)

Akinjogbin, I.A., "Agaja and the Conquest of the Coastal Aja States 1724- 30", *Journal of the Historical Society of Nigeria*, II, 4 (1963), 545-66

———, "Archibald Dalzel: Slave Trader and Historian of Dahomey", *Journal of African History*, VII,1 (1966), 67-78

———, *Dahomey and its Neighbours 1708-1818* (Cambridge University Press, 1967)

Akyeampong, Emmanuel Kwaku, *Between the Sea and the Lagoon. An Eco-Social History of the Anlo of Southeastern Ghana, c.1850 to Recent Times* (Ohio University Press/Oxford, James Currey, 2001)

Akyeampong, Emmanuel and Pashington Obeng, "Spirituality, Gender, and Power in Asante History", *International Journal of African Historical Studies*, 28, 3 (1995), 481-508

Albaredo Salvadó, Joaquím, *La Guerra de Sucesión de España (1700-1714)*, (Barcelona, Crítica, 2010)

BIBLIOGRAPHY

Alpern, Stanley B., "The European Introduction of Crops into West Africa in Precolonial Times", *History in Africa*, 19 (1992) 13-43

———, "What Africans Got for Their Slaves: A Master List of European Trade Goods", *History in Africa,* 22 (1995), 5-43

———, "On the Origins of the Amazons of Dahomey", *History in Africa,* 25 (1998a), 9-25

———, *Amazons of Black Sparta. The Women Warriors of Dahomey* (New York University Press & London, C. Hurst, 1998b)

———, "Dahomey's Royal Road", *History in Africa*, 26 (1999), 11-24

———, "Exotic Plants of Western Africa: Where They Came from and When", *History in Africa*, 35 (2008), 63-102

Amaral, Braz do, *Fatos da Vida do Brasil* (Bahia, Tip Naval, 1941)

Amenumey, D.E.K., *The Ewe in Pre-Colonial Times. A Political History with Special Emphasis on the Anlo, Ge and Krepi* (Accra, Sedco, 1986)

———, "A Brief History", in F. Agbodeka, *A Handbook of Eweland, Volume I: The Ewes of Southeastern Ghana* (Accra, Woeli, 1997), 14-27

Anignikin, Sylvain C., "Histoire des populations mahi. À propos de la controverse sur l'ethnonyme et le toponyme 'Mahi'", *Cahiers d'Études Africaines*, XLI, 2, (2001), 243-65

Appleby, Joyce, "The Power of History", *American Historical Review*, 103, 1 (1998), 1-14

Apter, Andrew H., *Black Critics and Kings: the Hermeneutics of Power in Yoruba* (University of Chicago Press, 1992)

Argyle, W.J., *The Fon of Dahomey. A History and Ethnography of the Old Kingdom* (Oxford University Press, 1966)

Arnold, Rosemary, "A Port of Trade: Whydah on the Guinea Coast", in Karl Polanyi, Conrad Arensberg and Harry W. Pearson (eds), *Trade and Markets in the Early Empires. Economies in History and Theory* (New York, The Free Press, 1957), 154-76

Asiwaju, A.I. and Robin Law, "From the Volta to the Niger, c.1600-1800", in J.F. Ade Ajayi and Michael Crowder (eds), *History of West Africa*, I (3rd edition, Harlow, Essex, Longman, 1985), 412-64

Atkinson, Ronald R., "Old Akyem and the Origins of Akyems Abuakwa and Kotoku 1675–1775", in B.K. Swartz Jr. and Raymond E. Dumett (eds), *West African Culture Dynamics: Archeological and Cultural Perspectives* (The Hague etc., Mouton, 1989), 349-69

Aubréville, A., "Les forêts du Dahomey et du Togo", *Bulletin du Comité d'Études Historiques et Scientifiques de l'Afrique Occidentale Française* XX, 1-2 (1937), 1-112

Austen, Ralph A., "The Trans-Saharan Slave Trade: A Tentative Census", in Henry A. Gemery and Jan S. Hogendorn (eds), *The Uncommon Market. Essays in the Economic History of the Atlantic Slave Trade* (New York, Academic Press, 1979), 23-76

BIBLIOGRAPHY

Avoseh, T. Ola, *A Short History of Badagry* (Lagos, Ife-Olu Printing Works, 1938)

Baechler, Jean "Essai sur les origines du système capitaliste", *Archives Européennes de Sociologie*, IX, 2 (1968), 205-63

Balandier, Georges, *Daily Life in the Kingdom of Kongo* (translated from the French, London & New York, George, Allen & Unwin, 1968)

———, *Political Anthropology* (Penguin ed., 1970)

Bancole, Alexis and Gilles Raoul Soglo, "Porto-Novo et la traite negrière", in Elisée Soumonni, Bellarmin C. Codo and Joseph Adande (eds), *Le Bénin et la route de l'esclave* (Cotonou, ONEPI, 1994), 76-8

Barham, Lawrence and Peter Mitchell, *The First Africans. African Archaeology from the Earliest Toolmakers to Most Recent Foragers* (Cambridge University Press, 2008)

Barickman, B.J., *A Bahian Counterpoint. Sugar, Tobacco, Cassava and Slavery in the Recôncavo, 1780–1860* (Stanford University Press, 1998)

Barnes, Sandra T. (ed.), *Africa's Ogun: Old World and New* (Indiana University Press, 1989)

Barnes, Sandra T. and Paula Girshick Ben-Amos, "Ogun, the Empire Builder", in Sandra T. Barnes (ed.), *Africa's Ogun: Old World and New* (Indiana University Press, 1989), 39-64

Barnes, Sandra T., "The Economic Significance of Inland Coastal Fishing in Seventeenth-Century Lagos", in Toyin Falola and Matt D. Childs (eds), *The Changing Worlds of Atlantic Africa. Essays in Honor of Robin Law* (Durham, Carolina Academic Press, 2009), 51-66

Baum, Robert M., *Shrines of the Slave Trade. Diola Religion and Society in Precolonial Senegambia* (Oxford University Press, 1999)

Bay, Edna G., "On the Trail of the Bush King: A Dahomean Lesson in the Use of Evidence", *History in Africa*, 6 (1979) 1-15

———, "Servitude and Wordly Success in the Palace of Dahomey", in Claire C. Robertson and Martin A. Klein (eds), *Women and Slavery in Africa* (University of Wisconsin Press, 1983), 340-67

———, *Iron Altars of the Fon People of Benin* (catalogue of exhibition, Emory Museum of Art and Archaeology, October 2-December 21, 1985)

———, "Belief, Legitimacy and the *Kpojito*: An Institutional History of the 'Queen Mother' in Precolonial Dahomey", *Journal of African History*, 35, 1 (1995), 1-27

———, *Wives of the Leopard. Gender, Politics, and Culture in the Kingdom of Dahomey* (University of Virginia Press, 1998)

———, "Protection, Political Exile, and the Atlantic Slave-Trade: History and Collective Memory in Dahomey", *Slavery and Abolition*, 22, 1 (2001), 42-60

———, *Asen, Ancestors, and Vodun: Tracing Change in African Art* (University of Illinois Press, 2008)

Behrendt, Stephen D., "The Journal of an African Slaver, 1789–1792, and the Gold Coast Slave Trade of William Collow", *History in Africa*, 22 (1995), 61-71

———, "The Annual Volume and Regional Distribution of the British Slave Trade, 1780-1807", *Journal of African History*, 38, 2 (1997), 187-211

Behrendt, Stephen D., David Eltis and David Richardson, "The Cost of Coercion: African Agency in the Pre-modern Atlantic World", *Economic History Review*, LIV, 3 (2001), 454-76

Belich, James, *Replenishing the Earth: The Settler Revolution and the Rise of the Anglo-World 1783-1939* (Oxford University Press, 2009)

Berbain, Simone, *Le comptoir français de Juda (Ouidah) au XVIIIe siècle. Études sur la traite des noirs au golfe de Guinée* (Dakar, IFAN, 1942)

Bergé, J.A.M.A.R., "Étude sur le pays Mahi (1926–1928). (Cercle de Savalou- Colonie du Dahomey) AOF", *Bulletin du Comité d'Études Historiques et Scientifiques de l'Afrique Occidentale Française*, XI, 4 (1928), 708-55

Bertho, [R.P.] Jacques, "La parenté des Yoruba aux peuplades du Dahomey et du Togo", *Africa*, vol. 19 (1949), 121-32

Bethell, Leslie, "The Independence of Brazil", *The Cambridge History of Latin America*, III (Cambridge University Press, 1985, edited by Leslie Bethell), 157-96

Bialuschewski, Arne, "Black People under the Black Flag: Piracy and the Slave Trade on the West Coast of Africa, 1718–1723", *Slavery and Abolition*, 29, 4 (2008), 461-75

Biobaku, S.O., *The Egba and their Neighbours 1842–1872* (Oxford University Press, 1957)

Blanc-Pamard, Chantal and Pierre Peltre, "Remarques à propos de 'Ecologie et histoire: les origines de la savane du Bénin'", *Cahiers d'Études Africaines*, XXVII, 3-4 (1987), 419-23.

Blier, Suzanne Preston, "Field Days: Melville J. Herskovits in Dahomey", *History in Africa*, 16 (1989), 1-22

———, *African Vodun. Art, Psychology and Power* (University of Chicago Press, 1995a)

———, "The Path of the Leopard: Motherhood and Majesty in Early Danhomè", *Journal of African History*, 36, 3 (1995b), 391-417

———, "Razing the Roof: The Imperative of Building Destruction in Danhomè (Dahomey)", in Tony Atkin and Joseph Rykwert (eds), *Structure and Meaning in Human Settlements* (Philadelphia, University of Pennsylvania Museum of Archaeology and Anthropology, 2005), 165-84

Boahen, Adu, "Asante-Dahomey Contacts in the Nineteenth Century", *Ghana Notes and Queries*, 7 (1965), 1-3

Bondarenko, Dmitri M., "Advent of the Second (Oba) Dynasty: Another Assessment of a Benin History Key Point", *HA*, 30 (2003), 63-85

Bondarenko, Dmitri M. and Peter M. Roese, "Between the *Ogiso* and *Oba* Dynasties: An Interpretation of Interregnum in the Benin Kingdom", *HA*, 31 (2004), 103-15

Boogaart, Ernst van den, "Books on Black Africa. The Dutch Publications and their owners in the seventeenth and eighteenth centuries", in Beatrix Heintze and

BIBLIOGRAPHY

Adam Jones (eds), *European Sources for Sub-Saharan Africa before 1900: Use and Abuse. Paideuma*, vol. 33 (Wiesbaden, Steiner, 1987), 115-26

Boogaart, Ernst van den and Pieter C. Emmer, "The Dutch Participation in the Atlantic Slave Trade, 1596–1650", in Henry A. Gemery and Jan S. Hogendorn (eds), *The Uncommon Market. Essays in the Economic History of the Atlantic Slave Trade* (New York, Academic Press, 1979), 353-75

Bourgoignie, Georges Edouard, *Les hommes de l'eau. Ethno-écologie du Dahomey lacustre* (Paris, Éditions Universitaires, 1972)

Boxer, C.R., *The Dutch Seaborne Empire 1600-1800* (Hutchinson, 1965; Pelican, 1973)

Bradbury, R.E., *The Benin Kingdom and the Edo-Speaking Peoples of South-Western Nigeria* (London, International African Institute, 1957), together with a section on *The Itsekiri*, by P.C. Lloyd

———, *Benin Studies*, Peter Morton Williams (ed.) (Oxford University Press/ International African Institute, 1973)

Brand, Roger, *Ethnographie et vocabulaire religieux des cultes vodoun* (Munich, LINCOM Europa, 2000)

Brenner, Louis, "'Religious' Discourse in and about Africa", in Karen Barber and P.F. de Moraes Farias (eds), *Discourse and Its Disguises: The Interpretation of African Oral Texts* (Birmingham, Centre of West African Studies, 1989), 87-105

Broadhead, Susan Herlin, "Beyond Decline: the Kingdom of the Kongo in the Eighteenth and Nineteenth Centuries", *International Journal of African Historical Studies*, 12, 4 (1979), 615-50

Brydon, Lynne, "Rice, Yams and Chiefs in Avatime: Speculations on the Development of a Social Order", *Africa*, 51, 2 (1981), 659-77

Bühnen, Stephan, "Place Names as an Historical Source: An Introduction, with Examples from Southern Senegambia and Germany", *History in Africa*, 19 (1992), 45-101

Burl, Aubrey, *Black Barty: Bartholomew Roberts and his Pirate Crew 1718- 1723* (1st publ., 1997; Sutton Publishing, 2006)

Caldwell, Ian, "Power, State and Society Among the Pre-Islamic Bugis", *Bijdragen tot de Taal-, Land-en Volkenkunde*, 151, 3 (1995), 394-421

Candiani, Vera, "The Desagüe Reconsidered: Environmental Dimensions of Class Conflict in Colonial Mexico", *Hispanic American Historical Review*, 92, 1 (2012), 5-39

Capo, Hounkpatin C., "Le Gbe est une langue unique", *Africa*, 53, 2 (1983), 47-57

———, "Elements of Ewe-Gen-Aja-Fon Dialectology", in François de Medeiros (ed.), *Peuples du golfe du Bénin. Aja-Ewe* (Paris, Karthala, 1984), 167-78

Carr, E.H., *What is History?* (London, Vintage, 1990)

Carrocera, Buenaventura de (OFM Cap.), "Misión Capuchina al Reino de Arda", *Missionalia Hispanica*, VI, no. 18 (1949), 523-46

Chauveau, Jean-Pierre, "Une histoire maritime africaine est-elle possible?

BIBLIOGRAPHY

Historiographie et histoire de la navigation et de la pêche africaine à la côte occidentale depuis le XVe siècle", *Cahiers d'Études Africaines*, XXVI, 1-2 (1986), 173-235

Childs, Matt D. and Toyin Falola, "Introduction: Robin Law and African Historiography", in Toyin Falola and Matt D. Childs (eds), *The Changing Worlds of Atlantic Africa. Essays in Honor of Robin Law*, (Durham, NC, Carolina Academic, 2009), 1-28

Chouin, Gérard, *Eguafo: un royaume africain 'au coeur françois' (1637–1688). Mutations socio-économiques et politique européenne d'un État de la Côte de l'Or (Ghana) au XVIIe siècle* (Paris, AFERA éd., 1998)

Chouin, Gérard L. and Christopher R. Decorse, "Prelude to the Atlantic Trade: New Perspectives on Southern Ghana's Pre-Atlantic History (800–1500)", *Journal of African History*, 51, 2 (2010), 123-45

Ciarcia, Gaetano, "Restaurer le futur. Sur la *Route de l'Esclave* à Ouidah (Bénin)", *Cahiers d'Études Africaines*, XLVIII, 4 (2008) 687-705

Coissy, Anatole, "Un règne de femme dans l'ancien royaume d'Abomey", *Études Dahoméennes*, 2 (1949), 5-8

Conrad, Geoffrey W. and Arthur A. Demarest, *Religion and Empire. The Dynamics of Aztec and Inca Expansionism* (Cambridge University Press, 1984)

Coquery-Vidrovitch, Catherine, "De la traite des esclaves à l'exportation de l'huile de palme et de palmistes au Dahomey: XIXe siècle", in C. Meillassoux (ed.), *The Development of Indigenous Trade and Markets in West Africa* (Oxford University Press, 1971), 107-23

Correia, J. Anacoreta, "O forte português de Ajudá na Costa do Benim (subsídios para a sua historia)", *Boletim da Sociedade de Geografia de Lisboa*, ser. 180a 7.12.1996, 23-86

Correia, Pupo, "Subsídios para a história de S. João Baptista de Ajudá. A chegada dos Portugueses ao Dahomey", *O Mundo Português* (VI, 63, Lisboa, 1939), 105-7

Correia Lopes (see Lopes)

Curtin, Philip D., *The Atlantic Slave Trade. A Census* (University of Wisconsin Press, 1969)

———, *Cross-cultural Trade in World History*, (Cambridge University Press, 1984)

———, *The Rise and Fall of the Plantation Complex. Essays in Atlantic History* (Cambridge University Press, 1990)

Daaku, Kwame Yeboa, *Trade and Politics on the Gold Coast 1600 to 1720. A Study of the African Reaction to European Trade* (Oxford at the Clarendon Press, 1970)

Daget, Serge, *Répertoire des expéditions négrières françaises à la traite illégale* (Nantes, Centre de Recherche sur l'Histoire du Monde Atlantique etc., 1988)

D'Albéca, Alexandre L., "Voyage au pays des Éoués", I & IV, *Le Tour du Monde*, no.8, 23.2.1895, 85-92; & no. 11, 16.3.1895, 121-8

Dantzig, Albert van, "Willem Bosman's *New and Accurate Description of the Coast of Guinea*: How Accurate is It?", *History in Africa*, 1 (1974), 101-8

———, *Les Hollandais sur la Côte de Guinée à l'époque de l'essor de l'Ashanti et du Dahomey 1680-1740* (Paris, SFHOM, 1980)

BIBLIOGRAPHY

———, "Les hollandais sur la Côte des esclaves: parties gagnées et parties perdues", in *Études africaines offertes à Henri Brunschwig* (Paris, EHE Sciences Sociales, 1982), 79-89

———, "The Furley Collection. Its Value and Limitations for the Study of Ghana's History", in B. Heintze and A. Jones (eds), *European Sources for Sub-Saharan Africa before 1900: Use and Abuse. Paideuma*, 33 (Wiesbaden, Steiner, 1987), 423-32

———, "The Akanists: A West African Hansa", in David Henige and T.C. McCaskie (eds), *West African Economic and Social History. Studies in Memory of Marion Johnson* (Madison, African Studies Program, University of Wisconsin, 1990), 205-16

Dantzig, Albert van and Barbara Priddy, *A Short History of the Forts and Castles of Ghana* (Accra, Ghana Museums and Monuments Board, 1971)

Davidson, Basil, *Black Mother* (Boston, Little, Brown & Company, 1961)

Davies, K.G., *The Royal African Company* (London, Longman, 1957)

Davis, David Brion, *The Problem of Slavery in Western Culture* (Oxford University Press, 1966)

Dayan, Joan, *Haiti, History and the Gods* (Berkeley: University of California Press, 1995)

Degbelo, Amélie: "Les Amazones du Danxomè 1645–1900" (mémoire de maîtrise, Université Nationale du Bénin, 1979)

Dirlik, Arif, review of Joyce Appleby's, *The Relentless Revolution: A History of Capitalism* in *American Historical Review*, 5 (2010), 1445-7

Drake, B.K., "The Liverpool-African Voyage c.1790–1807: Commercial Problems", in R. Anstey and P.E.H. Hair (eds), *Liverpool, the Atlantic Slave Trade, and Abolition.Essays to Illustrate Current Knowledge* (Historic Society of Lancashire and Cheshire, Occasional Series vol. 2, 1976) 126-56

Drescher, Seymour, "The Long Goodbye: Dutch Capitalism and Antislavery in comparative perspective", *American Historical Review*, 1, 99 (1994), 44-69

———, "White Atlantic? The Choice for African Slave Labor in the Plantation Americas", in David Eltis, Frank D. Lewis and Kenneth L. Sokoloff (eds), *Slavery in the Development of the Americas* (Cambridge University Press, 2004), 31-69

Du Casse, Robert, *L'Amiral Du Casse (1646-1715)* (Paris, Berger- Levrault,1876)

Dunglas, Édouard, *Contribution à l'histoire du Moyen-Dahomey* (2 vols. of *Études Dahoméennes*, 1957)

———, "Adjohon: étude historique", *Études Dahoméennes*, (ns), 8, (1966), 57-73

———, "Origine du Royaume de Porto-Novo", *Études Dahoméennes*, (ns), 9-10 (1967), 29-62

Egblewogbe, E.Y., "The Language(s) of the Lower Volta and Yewa Area, a Problem of Classification and Terminology", in Nicoué L. Gayibor (ed.), *Toponymie historique et glossonymesactuels de l'ancienne Côte des Esclaves (XVe-XIXe siècle)* (Lomé, Presses de l'Université du Bénin, 1990)

BIBLIOGRAPHY

Elbl, Ivana, "The Volume of the Early Atlantic Slave Trade, 1450–1521", *Journal of African History*, 38, 1 (1997), 31-75

Ellis, Alfred Burdon, *The Ewe-speaking peoples of the Slave Coast of West Africa. Their Religion, Manners, Customs, Laws, Languages, etc.* (first published in 1890, reprinted 1966)

———, *Economic Growth and the Ending of the Transatlantic Slave Trade* (Oxford University Press, 1987)

———, "The Slave Economies of the Caribbean: Structure, Performance, Evolution and Significance", in Franklin W. Knight (ed.), *The Slave Societies of the Caribbean*, vol. III of *General History of the Caribbean* (UNESCO Publishing-Macmillan, 1997), 105-137

———, *The Rise of African Slavery in the Americas* (Cambridge University Press, 2000)

Eltis, David and Lawrence C. Jennings: "Trade between Western Africa and the Atlantic world in the Pre-Colonial era", *American Historical Review*, XLIII, 4 (1988), 936-59

Eltis, David and David Richardson, "Prices of African Slaves Newly Arrived in the Americas, 1673-1865: New Evidence on Long-Run Trends and Regional Differentials", in David Eltis, Frank D. Lewis and Kenneth L. Sokoloff (eds), *Slavery in the Development of the Americas* (Cambridge University Press, 2004), 181-218

———, *Atlas of the Transatlantic Slave Trade* (Yale University Press, 2010)

Eltis, David, Paul E. Lovejoy and David Richardson, "Slave-trading Ports: Towards an Atlantic-Wide Perspective, 1676-1832", in R. Law and Silke Strickrodt, *Ports of the Slave Trade (Bights of Benin and Biafra)* (Centre of Commonwealth Studies, University of Stirling, 1999), 12-34

Elwert, Georg, *Wirtschaft und Herrschaft von 'Dāxome' (Dahomey) im 18. Jahrhundert: Ökonomie des Sklavenraubs und Gesellschaftsstruktur 1724 bis 1818* (Munich, Klaus Renner, 1973)

Euba, O., "Of Blue Beads and Red: the Role of Ife in the West African Trade in Kori Beads", *Journal of the Historical Society of Nigeria*, 11, 1-2 (1982), 109-27

Evans, E.W. and David Richardson, "Hunting for Rents: the Economics of Slaving in Pre-colonial Africa", *Economic History Review*, XLVIII, 4 (1995), 665-86

Fage, J.D., "A New Check List of the Forts and Castles of Ghana", *Transactions of the Historical Society of Ghana*, IV, 1 (1959)

———, "Slavery and the Slave Trade in the Context of West African History", *Journal of African History*, X, 3 (1969), 393-404

———, "Slaves and Society in Western Africa, c.1445–c.1700", *Journal of African History*, 21, 3 (1980), 289-310

———, "A Commentary on Duarte Pacheco Pereira's Account of the Lower Guinea Coastlands in his *Esmeraldo de Situ Orbis*, and on some Other Early Accounts", *History in Africa*, 7 (1980), 47-80

———, "More about Aggrey and Akori Beads", in *2000 ans d'histoire africaine. Le sol, la parole et l'écrit. Mélanges en hommage à Raymond Mauny*, tôme I (Paris, Société Française d'Histoire d'Outre-Mer, 1981), 205-211

Fairhead, James and Melissa Leach, *Misreading the African Landscape. Society and Ecology in a Forest-savanna Mosaic* (Cambridge University Press, 1996)

Farriss, Nancy M., "Remembering the Future, Anticipating the Past: History, Time, and Cosmology among the Maya of Yucatan", in Diane Owen Hughes and Thomas R. Trautmann (eds), *Time: Histories and Ethnologies* (University of Michigan Press, 1995), 107-38

Feinberg, Harvey M., "An Eighteenth-century Case of Plagiarism: William Smith's A New Voyage to Guinea", *History in Africa*, 6 (1979), 45-50

Feldbæk, Ole and Ole Justesen, *Kolonierne i Asien og Afrika* (København [Copenhagen], Politiken, 1980)

Fernández Durán, Reyes, *La corona española y el tráfico de negros. Del monopolio al libre comercio* (Madrid, Ecobook, Editorial del Economista, 2011)

Findlay, Ronald and Kevin H. O'Rourke, *Power and Plenty. Trade, War, and the World Economy in the Second Millenium* (Princeton University Press, 2007)

Findlen, Paula, "Possessing the Past: The Material World of the Italian Renaissance", *American Historical Review*, 103, 1 (1998), 83-114

Flory, Rae Jean Dell, "Bahian Society in the Mid-Colonial Period: the Sugar Planters, Tobacco Growers, Merchants, and Artisans of Salvador and the Recôncavo, 1680–1725" (unpublished PhD thesis, University of Texas, 1978)

Foà, Édouard, *Le Dahomey* (Paris, 1895)

Frazer, Sir James, *The Golden Bough* (multivolume, 1890; third edition 1906- 15, plus later abridged editions)

Froelich, Jean-Claude, "Les problèmes posés par les refoulés montagnards de culture paléonigritique", *Cahiers d'Études Africaines*, V, 3 (1964), 383-99

Fuglestad, Finn, "Quelques réflexions sur l'histoire et les institutions de l'ancien royaume du Dahomey et de ses voisins", *Bulletin de l'IFAN*, 39, 2 (1977) 493-517

———, "A Reconsideration of Hausa History before the Jihad", *Journal of African History*, XIX, 3 (1978), 319-39

———, "Earth-priests, 'Priest-Chiefs', and Sacred Kings in Ancient Norway, Iceland and West Africa. A Comparative Essay", *Scandinavian Journal of History*, IV, 1 (1979), 47-74

——— (with the assistance of Stephen Ellis), "The 'tompon-tany' and the 'tompon-drano' in the History of Central and Western Madagascar", *History in Africa*, vol. 9 (1982), 61-76

———, "The Trevor-Roper Trap or the Imperialism of History. An Essay", *History in Africa*, 19 (1992), 309-26

———, "Le questionnement du 'port' de Ouidah (Côte des Esclaves)", in Øystein Rian, Finn Erhard Johannessen, Øystein Sørensen and Finn Fuglestad (eds), *Revolusjon og resonnement. Festskrift [Festschrift] til Kåre Tønnesson på 70-årsdagen den 1. januar 1996* (Oslo, Universitetsforl, 1995), 125-36

———, *The Ambiguities of History. The Problem of Ethnocentrism in Historical Writing* (Oslo Academic Press, 2005)

———, "Precolonial Subsaharan Africa and the Ancient Norse World: Looking for Similarities", *History in Africa*, vol. 33 (2006), 179-203

———, *Vekstøkonomi. Et globalhistorisk essay* [Growth economy. An Essay in Global History] (Oslo, Unipub, 2010)

Fynn, John Kofi, *Asante and its Neighbours 1700–1807* (Northwestern University Press, 1971)

Gaba, Christian R., "The Religious Life of the People", in Francis Agbodeka (ed.), *A Handbook of Eweland vol. I: The Ewes of Southeastern Ghana* (Accra, Woeli, 1997), 85-104

Garfield, Robert, *A History of São Tomé Island, 1470-1655. The Key to Guinea* (Mellen Research University Press, 1992)

Gaston-Mulira, Jessie, "A History of the Mahi Peoples from 1774 to 1920 (Benin)" (unpublished PhD thesis, UCLA, 1984)

Gavoy, Marcel, "Note historique sur Ouidah par l'administrateur Gavoy 1913", *Études Dahoméennes*, 13 (1955), 47-78

Gayibor, Nicoué Lodjou, "Migrations-société-civilisation: les Ewe du sud-Togo" (thèse-3e cycle, Paris I, 1975)

———, "Les origines du Royaume de Glidji", *Annales de l'Université du Bénin, Togo*, III (1976), 75-102

———, "Recueil des sources orales du pays Aja-Ewe" (mimeogr., Institut Pédagogique National, Lomé, March 1977)

———, "Recueil des sources orales de la région d'Aneho" (mimeogr., Institut Pédagogique National, Lomé, Oct. 1977)

———, "Esquisse d'une histoire économique des Ewe de l'ère précoloniale", *Annuaire de l'Université du Bénin, Togo*, V (1978), 129-44

———, "L'aire culturelle Ajatado des origines à la fin du XVIIIe siècle" (thèse, Université de Paris I-Panthéon-Sorbonne, 1985)

———, "Écologie et histoire: les origines de la savane du Bénin", *Cahiers d'Études Africaines*, XXVI, 1-2 (1986), 13-41

———, "Les origines de la savane du Bénin: une chasse gardée?", *Cahiers d'Études Africaines*, XXXIX, 1 (1989), 137-8

———, "Le remodelage des traditions historiques: La légende d'Agokoli, roi de Notse", in Claude-Hélène Perrot (ed.), *Sources orales de l'histoire de l'Afrique* (Paris, CNRS, 1989), 209-14

———, *Le Genyi. Un royaume oublié de la Côte de Guinée au temps de la traite des noirs* (Lomé, Editions Haro, 1990)

———, "Toponymie et toponymes anciens de la Côte des Esclaves", in N.L. Gayibor (ed.), *Toponymie historique et glossonymes actuels de l'ancienne Côte des Esclaves (XVe-XIXe siècle)* (Lomé, Presses de l'Université du Bénin, 1990), 25-42 & I-VIII

BIBLIOGRAPHY

———, "Les rois de Glidji: une chronologie revisée", *History in Africa*, 22 (1995), 197-222

Gayibor, Nicoué Lodjou (ed.), *Histoire des Togolais, vol.I: Des origines à 1884* (Lomé, Presses de l'Université du Bénin, 1997)

———, "Origines et formation du Genyi", in N.L. Gayibor (ed.), *Le tricentenaire d'Aného et du pays guin* (Lomé, Presses de l'Université du Bénin, 2001), 19-31

Gayibor, Nicoué Lodjou and Angele Aguigah, "Early Settlements and Archaeology of the Adja-Tado Cultural Zone", in Benjamin Lawrance (ed.), *A Handbook of Eweland: The Ewe of Togo and Benin* (Accra, Woeli, 2005), 1-14

Gilbert, Michelle, "The Person of the King: Ritual and Power in a Ghanaian State", in David Cannadine and Simon Price (eds), *Rituals of Royalty. Power and Ceremonial in Traditional Societies* (Cambridge University Press, 1987), 298-330

Girshick, Paula Ben-Amos and John Thornton, "Civil War in the Kingdom of Benin, 1689–1721: Continuity or Political Change?", *Journal of African History*, 42, 3 (2001), 353-76

Glélé, Maurice Ahanhanzo, *Le Danxome du pouvoir aja à la nation fon* (Paris, Nubia, 1974)

Goody, Jack, "Introduction", in Jack Goody (ed.), *Succession to High Office* (Cambridge University Press, 1966), 1-56

———, "Circulating Succession among the Gonja", in Jack Goody (ed.), *Succession to High Office* (Cambridge University Press, 1966), 142-76

———, "The Over-Kingdom of Gonja" in D.Forde and P.M. Kaberry (eds), *West African Kingdoms in the Nineteenth Century* (Oxford University Press/International African Institute, 1967), 179-205

———, *Technology, Tradition, and the State in Africa* (Oxford University Press/International African Institute, 1971)

Granlund, Victor, *En svensk koloni i Afrika eller Svenska Afrikanska kompaniets historia* (Stockholm, 1879), 13-14

Greene, Sandra E., "Land, Lineage and Clan in Early Anlo", *Africa*, vol. 51 (1981), 451-64

———, "Conflict and Crisis: a Note on the Workings of the Political Economy and Ideology of the Anlo-Ewe in the Precolonial Period", *Rural Africana*, 17 (1983), 83-96

———, "The Past and Present of an Anlo-Ewe Oral Tradition", *History in Africa*, 12 (1985), 73-87

———, "Social Change in Eighteenth-century Anlo. The Role of Technology, Markets and Military Conflict", *Africa*, 58 (1), 1988, 70-86

———, "The Individual as Stranger in Nineteenth-Century Anlo: the Politics of Identity and Social Advancement in Precolonial West Africa", in John Hunwick and Nancy Lawler (eds), *The Cloth of Many Colored Silks. Papers on History and Society Ghanaian and Islamic in Honor of Ivor Wilks* (Evanston, Northwestern University Press, 1996a), 91-127

BIBLIOGRAPHY

———, *Gender, Ethnicity, and Social Change on the Upper Slave Coast. A History of the Anlo-Ewe* (Portsmouth, NH & London, Heinemann & J. Currey, 1996b)

———, "Sacred Terrain: Religion, Politics, and Place in the History of Anloga (Ghana)," *International Journal of African Historical Studies*, 30, 1 (1997), 1-22

———, "Cultural Zones in the Era of the Atlantic Slave Trade: Exploring the Yoruba Connection with the Anlo-Ewe", in Paul E. Lovejoy (ed.), *Identity in the Shadow of Slavery* (London/New York, Continuum, 2000), 86-101

———, "Notsie Narratives: History, Memory, and Meaning in West Africa", *South Atlantic Quarterly*, 101, 4 (2002a), 1015-41

———, "*Sacred Sites and the Colonial Encounter: A History of Meaning and Memory in Ghana* (Indiana University Press, 2002b)

Grimes, Barbara F. (ed), *Ethnologue. Languages of the World* (11th edit., Dallas, Summer Institute of Linguistics, 1988)

Grove, Jean M. and A.M. Johansen, "The Historical Geography of the Volta Delta, Ghana, during the period of Danish Influence", *Bulletin de l'IFAN*, série B, XXX, 4 (1968), 1376-1421.

Guilcher, André, "La région côtière du Bas-Dahomey occidental. Étude de géographie physique et humaine appliquée", *Bulletin de l'IFAN*, série B, vol. XXI, 3-4 (1959), 357-424

Gunn, Jeffrey, "Creating a Paradox: Quobna Ottobah Cugoano and the Slave Trade's Violation of the Principles of Christianity, Reason, and Property Ownership", *Journal of World History*, 4 (2011), 629-56

Gutkind, Peter C.W., "The Canoemen of the Gold Coast (Ghana). A Survey and an Exploration in Precolonial Labour History", *Cahiers d'Études Africaines*, XXIX, 3-4 (1989), 339-76

Hair, P.E.H., "Columbus from Guinea to America", *History in Africa*, 17 (1990), 113-29

Hall, Neville A.T. (ed. by B.W. Higman), *Slave Society in the Danish West Indies. St. Thomas, St. John, and St. Croix* (University of the West Indies Press, 1992, 1994)

Hanson, Carl A., "Monopoly and Contraband in the Portuguese Tobacco Trade, 1621-1702", *Luso-Brazilian Review*, XIX, 2 (1982), 149-68

Harms, Robert, *The Diligent: A Voyage through the Worlds of the Slave Trade* (New York, Perseus, 2002; based on an unpublished manuscript by the French slave-trader Robert Durand: "Journal de bord d'un négrier, 1731–1732" (Beinecke Library, Yale, Gen. Mss, vol.7)

Haudrere, Philippe, *La compagnie française des Indes au XVIIIe siècle* (Paris, Librairie de l'Inde éditeur, 1989)

Hazoumé, Paul, *Le pacte de sang au Dahomey* (Paris, Institut d'Ethnologie, 1937; reprinted 1956)

Henige, David, "Measuring the Immeasurable: the Atlantic Slave Trade, West African Population and the Pyrrhonian Critic", *Journal of African History*, 27, 2 (1986), 295-313

———, "The Race is not Always to the Swift. Thoughts on the Use of Written

Sources for the Study of Early African History", in Beatrix Heintze and Adam Jones (eds), *European Sources for Sub-Saharan Africa before 1900: Use and Abuse. Paideuma*, vol. 33 (Wiesbaden, Steiner, 1987), 53-79

———, "Impossible to Disprove yet Impossible to Believe: the Unforgiving Epistemology of Deep-time Oral Tradition", *History in Africa*, 36 (2009), 127-234 (231)

Henige, David and Marion Johnson, "Agaja and the Slave Trade: Another Look at the Evidence", *History in Africa*, III (1976), 57-67

Henley, David and Ian Caldwell (eds), *Stranger-kings in Indonesia and Beyond*, special issue of *Indonesia and the Malay World* (vol. 36, No. 105, July 2008)

Henley, David and Ian Caldwell, "Kings and Covenants. Stranger-kings and Social Contact in Sulawesi", special issue of *Indonesia and the Malay World* (vol. 36, No. 105, July 2008)269-91

Hernæs, Per O., *Palaver: Peace or "Problem"? A Note on the "Palaver- system" on the Gold Coast in the 18th Century based on Examples drawn from Danish Sources* (working papers 1, Center for African Studies, University of Copenhagen, 1988)

———, *Slaves, Danes, and African Coast Society. The Danish Slave Trade from West Africa and Afro-Danish Relations on the Eighteenth-Century Gold Coast* (Department of History, University of Trondheim, 1995)

———, "Den Balstyrige Bergenser på Gullkysten", *Norsk Sjøfartsmuseum. Årsberetning 1995* (Oslo, 1996), 127-38

———, "Dansk-Norske handelsutposter på Gullkysten i slavehandelens æra", *Norsk Sjøfartsmuseum. Årsberetning 1997* (Oslo, 1998), 129-41

Herskovits, Melville J., *Dahomey. An Ancient West African Kingdom*, 2 vols (New York, 1938, Northwestern University Press, 1967)

Herskovits, Melville J. and Frances S., *Dahomean Narrative. A Cross-Cultural Analysis* (Northwestern University Press, 1958)

———, *An Outline of Dahomean Religious Belief* (Mem. of the American Anthropological Association, no.41/Menasha-Wisc./New York 1933/1964)

Hespanha, António Manuel (ed.), *O Antigo Regime (1620-1807)* (volume IV of José Mattoso [gen. editor] *História de Portugal* [Lisbon, Ed. Estampa, 1998])

Heywood, Linda and John Thornton, "Kongo and Dahomey, 1660-1815: African Political Leadership in the Era of the Slave Trade and Its Impact on the Formation of African Identity in Brazil", in Bernard Bailyn and Patricia L. Denault (eds), *Soundings in Atlantic History. Latent Structures and Intellectual Currents, 1500–1830* (Harvard University Press, 2009), 86-111

Higman, B.W., "The Sugar Revolution", *Economic History Review*, LIII, 2 (2000), 213-36

Hodges, Tony and Malyn Newitt, *São Tomé and Príncipe. From Plantation Colony to Microstate* (Boulder, Westview, 1988)

Hoffer, Peter Charles, *The Historians' Paradox: The Study of History in Our Time* (New York University Press, 2008)

Hogendorn, Jan S. and Henry A. Gemery: "Abolition and its Impact on Monies Imported to West Africa", in David Eltis and James Walvin (eds), *The Abolition of the Atlantic Slave Trade. Origins and Effects in Europe, Africa, and the Americas* (University of Wisconsin Press, 1981), 99-115

Hogendorn, Jan S. and Marion Johnson, *The Shell Money of the Slave Trade* (Cambridge University Press, 1986)

Hopkins, A.G., *An Economic History of West Africa* (London, Longman, 1973)

———, "The 'New International Economic Order' in the Nineteenth Century: Britain's First Development Plan for Africa", in Robin Law (ed.), *From Slave Trade to 'Legitimate' Commerce. The Commercial Transition in Nineteenth-century West Africa* (Cambridge University Press, 1995), 240-64

Hopkins, Daniel, "Peter Thonning's Map of Danish Guinea and its Use in Colonial Administration and Atlantic Diplomacy 1801-1890", *Cartographica*, 35, 3-4 (1998), 99-122

Horton, Robin, "Stateless Societies in the History of West Africa", in J.F. Ade Ajayi & Michael Crowder (eds), *History of West Africa*, Vol. One (Harlow, Essex, Longman, 3rd edition 1985), 87-128

Houseman, Michael, Blandine Legonou, Christiane Massy and Xavier Crepin, "Note sur la structure évolutive d'une ville historique. L'exemple d'Abomey (République populaire du Bénin)", *Cahiers d'Études Africaines* XXVI, 4 (1986), 527-46

Inikori, Joseph E., "The Volume of the British Slave Trade, 1655–1807", *Cahiers d'Études Africaines* XXXII, 4 (1992), 643-88

———, "The Unmeasured Hazards of the Atlantic Slave Trade: Sources, Causes and Historiographical Implications", in Doudou Diène (ed.), *From Chains to Bonds. The Slave Trade Revisited* (Paris, UNESCO & Oxford & New York, Berghahn, 2001), 22-35

———, "The Known, the Unknown, the Knowable, and the Unknowable: Evidence and the Evaluation of Evidence in the Measurement of the Trans-Atlantic Slave Trade", in Toyin Falola (ed.), *Ghana in Africa and the World: Essays in Honor of Adu Boahen* (Trenton, NJ & Asmara, Eritrea, Africa World Press, 2003), 535-65

———, "The Economic Impact of the 1807 British Abolition of the Transatlantic Slave Trade", in Toyin Falola and Matt D. Childs (eds), *The Changing Worlds of Atlantic Africa. Essays in Honor of Robin Law* (Durham, Carolina Academic, 2009), 163-82

Iroko, A. Félix, "Le sel marin de la Côte des Esclaves durant la période précoloniale", *Africa* (Rome), XLVI, 4 (1991) 520-40

———, "Les hommes et les incendies à la Côte des Esclaves durant la période précoloniale", *Africa* (Rome), XLVIII, 3 (1993), 396-423

———, "Condamnations pénales et ravitaillement en esclaves de la traite négrière", in Elisée Soumonni, Bellarmin C. Codo and Joseph Adande (eds), *Le Bénin et la route de l'esclave* (Cotonou, ONEPI, 1994), 93-5

———, *Mosaïques d'histoire béninoise*, vol. I (Tulle, Corrèze Buissonière, 1998)

BIBLIOGRAPHY

———, *Les Hula du XIVe au XIXe siècle* (Cotonou, Nouvelles éditions du Bénin, 2001)

Israel, Jonathan I., *The Dutch Republic. Its Rise, Greatness, and Fall 1477–1806* (Oxford University Press, 1995)

Izard, Michel, *Introduction à l'histoire des royaumes mossi*, 2 volumes (Paris/Ouagadougou, CNRS/CVRS, 1970)

Jadin, Louis, "L'oeuvre missionnaire en Afrique noire" in J.Metzler (ed.), *Sacrae Congregationis de Propaganda Fide. Memoria rerum 1622–1972 (350 anni a servizio delle Missioni* (Rome/Freiburg/Vienna, Herder, 1972), vol. I/2, 413-546

Johannesen, Lise Merete, "Jens Adolph Kiøge's administrasjonspolitik over for afrikanerne i Guinea 1766–1788" (unpublished dissertation, Københans Universitet/University of Copenhagen, c. 1966)

Johnson, David, *Spectacle and Sacrifice: The Ritual Foundations of Village Life in North China* (Harvard University Asia Center, 2009)

Johnson, Marion, "Ashante East of the Volta", *Transctions of the Historical Society of Ghana*, VIII (1965), 33-40

———, "The Ounce in Eighteenth-century West African Trade", *Journal of African History*, VII, 2 (1966), 197-214

———, "The Atlantic Slave Trade and the Economy of West Africa", in R. Anstey and P.E.H. Hair (eds), *Liverpool, The African Slave Trade, and Abolition* (Historic Society of Lancashire and Cheshire, 1976), 14-38

Johnson, Samuel, *The History of the Yorubas, from the Earliest Times to the Beginning of the British Protectorate* (London, G. Routledge, 1921; but written in 1897)

Jones, J.R., *The Anglo-Dutch Wars of the Seventeenth Century* (Longman, 1996)

Kabou, Axelle, *Et si l'Afrique refusait le développement?* (Paris, L'Harmattan, 1991)

———, *Comment l'Afrique en est arrivée là* (Paris, L'Harmattan, 2011)

———, "L'Afrique serait-elle incurable?", interview with Ms Kabou in *Paris-Match*, 20 August 1992

Kamen, Henry, *Spain 1469–1714. A Society of Conflict* (Longman, 1983)

Kaplan, Martha, *Neither Cargo nor Cult. Ritual Politics and the Colonial Imagination in Fiji* (Durham, NC: Duke University Press, 1995)

Kea, Ray A., "Ashanti-Danish Relations 1780–1831" (unpublished MA thesis, Institute of African Studies, University of Ghana, Legon, 1967)

Kea, Ray A., "Akwamu-Anlo Relations c.1750–1813", *Transactions of the Historical Society of Ghana*, 10 (1969), 29-63

———, "Firearms and Warfare on the Gold and Slave Coasts from the Sixteenth to the Nineteenth Centuries", *Journal of African History*, XII, 2 (1971), 185-213

———, "Administration and Trade in the Akwamu Empire, 1681-1730", in B.K. Swartz Jr & R.E. Dumett (eds), *West African Culture Dynamics. Archaeological and Historical Perspectives* (The Hague etc., Mouton, 1980), 371-92

———, *Settlements, Trade, and Politics in the Seventeenth-Century Gold Coast* (Johns Hopkins University Press, 1982)

BIBLIOGRAPHY

———, "'I Am Here to Plunder on the General Road' – Bandits and Banditry in the Pre-nineteenth Century Gold Coast", in Donald Crummey (ed), *Banditry, Rebellion and Social Protest in Africa* (London, Heinemann Educational, 1986), 109-32

———, "From Catholicism to Moravian Pietism. The World of Marotta/Magdalena, a Woman of Popo and St. Thomas", in Elizabeth Mancke and Carole Shammas (eds), *The Creation of the British Atlantic World* (Johns Hopkins University Press, 2005), 115-36

Kelly, Kenneth G., "Using Historically Informed Archaeology: Seventeenth and Eighteenth Century Hueda/European Interaction on the Coast of Bénin", *Journal of Archaeological Method and Theory*, vol. 4, nos. 3/4 (1997a), 353-66

———, "The Archaeology of African-European Interaction: Investigating the Social Roles of Trade, Traders, and the Use of Space in the Seventeenth- and Eighteenth-century Hueda Kingdom, Republic of Bénin", *World Archaeology*, 28, 3 (1997b), 351-69

———, "Change and Continuity in Coastal Bénin", in Christopher R. DeCorse (ed.), *West Africa during the Atlantic Slave Trade: Archaeological Perspectives* (Leicester University Press, 2001), 81-100

———, "Indigenous Responses to Colonial Encounters on the West African Coast: Hueda and Dahomey from the Seventeenth through Nineteenth Centuries", in Claire L. Lyons and John K. Papadopoulos (eds), *The Archaeology of Colonialism* (Los Angeles, Getty Research Institute, 2002), 96-120

Kilkenny, Roberta Walker, "The Slave Mode of Production: Precolonial Dahomey", in Donald Crummey and C.C. Stewart (eds), *Modes of Production in Africa: the Precolonial Era* (Beverly Hills/London, Sage, 1981) 157-73

King, Winston, "Religion", in Mircea Eliade (ed.), *The Encyclopedia of Religion*, vol. 12 (New York, Macmillan, 1987), 282-93

Klein, A. Norman, "Toward a New Understanding of Akan Origins", *Africa*, 66, 2 (1996), 248-73

Klein, Herbert S., *The Middle Passage. Comparative Studies in the Atlantic Slave Trade* (Princeton University Press, 1978)

Klieman, Kairn A., *"The Pygmies Were our Compass." Bantu and Batwa in the History of West Central Africa, Early Times to c. 1900 C.E.* (Portsmouth, NH, Heinemann, 2003)

Klooster, Wim, "Inter-Imperial Smuggling in the Americas, 1600–1800", in Bernard Bailyn and Patricia L. Denault (eds), *Soundings in Atlantic History. Latent Structures and Intellectual Currents, 1500–1830* (Harvard University Press, 2009), 141-80

Knight, Franklin W., "The Disintegration of the Caribbean Slave Systems, 1772–1886", in Franklin W. Knight (ed.), *The Slave Societies of the Caribbean*, vol. III of *General History of the Caribbean* (UNESCO Publishing/Macmillan, 1997), 322-45

Kopytoff, Igor, "The Internal African Frontier: The Making of African Political

Culture", in Igor Kopytoff (ed.), *The African Frontier. The Reproduction of Traditional African Societies* (Indiana University Press, 1987) 3-84

Kossou, Basile, "La notion de pouvoir dans l'aire culturelle aja-fon", in *Le concept de pouvoir en Afrique* (UNESCO, 1981), 84-106 [name of editor not indicated]

Kriger, Colleen E., "'Guinea cloth'. Production and Consumption of Cotton Textiles in West Africa before and during the Atlantic Slave Trade", in Giorgio Riello and Prasannan Parthasarath (eds), *The Spinning World. A Global History of Cotton Textiles, 1200-1850* (Oxford University Press, 2009), 105-26

Kwamena-Poh, M.A., *Government and Politics in the Akuapem State 1730–1850* (London, Longman and Northwestern University Press, 1973)

Labouret, Henri and Paul Rivet, *Le Royaume d'Arda et son évangélisation au XVIIe siècle* (Paris, Institut d'Ethnologie, 1929)

Lane, Kris E., *Pillaging the Empire: Piracy in the Americas 1500–1750* (Armonk, NY/London, M.E. Sharpe, 1998)

Laumann, Dennis, "The History of the Ewe of Togo and Benin from Pre- Colonial to Post-Colonial Times", in Benjamin Lawrance (ed.), *A Handbook of Eweland: The Ewe of Togo and Benin* (Accra, Woeli, 2005), 14-28

Law, Robin, book review in *Journal of the Historical Society of Nigeria*, IV, 2 (1968), 344-7

———, "The Fall of Allada, 1724 - an Ideological Revolution?", *Journal of the Historical Society of Nigeria*, V, 1 (1969), 157-63

———, "A West African Cavalry State: the Kingdom of Oyo", *Journal of African History*, 16 (1975), 1-15

———, "Horses, Firearms, and Political Power in Precolonial West Africa", *Past & Present*, no. 72 (1976), 112-32

———, *The Oyo Empire c.1600–c.1836. A West African Imperialism in the Era of the Atlantic Slave Trade* (Oxford University Press, 1977a)

———, "Royal Monopoly and Private Enterprise in the Atlantic Trade: the Case of Dahomey", *Journal of African History*, XVIII, 4 (1977b), 555-77

———, "The Career of Adele at Lagos and Badagry, c.1807-c.1837", *Journal of the Historical Society of Nigeria*, IX, 2 (1978), 35-59

———, "In Search of a Marxist Perspective on Pre-Colonial Tropical Africa", *Journal of African History*, 19, 3 (1978), 441-52

———, *The Horse in West African History. The Role of the Horse in the Societies of Precolonial West Africa* (International African Institute/Oxford University Press, 1980)

———, "For Marx but with Reservations about Althusser: A Comment on Bernstein and Depelchin", *History in Africa*, 8 (1981), 247-51

———, "Jean Barbot as a Source for the Slave Coast of West Africa", *History in Africa*, 9 (1982), 155-73

———, "Making Sense of a Traditional Narrative: Political Disintegration in the Kingdom of Oyo", *Cahiers d'Études Africaines*, XII, 3-4 (1982b), 387-401

———, "Trade and Politics behind the Slave Coast: the Lagoon Traffic and the Rise of Lagos 1500-1800", *Journal of African History*, 24, 3 (1983), 321-48

———, "Human Sacrifice in Pre-colonial West Africa", *African Affairs*, vol. 84, no. 334 (1985), 53-87

———, "Dahomey and the Slave Trade: Reflections on the Historiography of the Rise of Dahomey", *Journal of African History*, 27 (1986a), 237-67

———, "Islam in Dahomey: a Case Study of the Introduction and Influence of Islam in a Peripheral Area of West Africa", *Scottish Journal of Religious Studies*, VII, 2 (1986b), 95-116

———, "Ideologies of Royal Power: the Dissolution and Reconstruction of Political Authority on the 'Slave Coast', 1680–1750", *Africa*, 57, 3 (1987), 321-44

———, "History and Legitimacy: Aspects of the Use of the Past in Precolonial Dahomey", *History in Africa*, 15 (1988a), 431-56

Law, Robin (ed.), "A Neglected Account of the Dahomian Conquest of Whydah (1727): The 'Relation de la Guerre de Juda' of the Sieur Ringard of Nantes", *History in Africa*, 15 (1988b), 321-38

Law, Robin, "Between the Sea and the Lagoons: The Interaction of Maritime and Inland Navigation on the Precolonial Slave Coast", *Cahiers d'Études Africaines*, XXIX, 2 (1989a), 209-37

———, "'My Head Belongs to the King': On the Political and Ritual Significance of Decapitation in Pre-colonial Dahomey", *Journal of African History*, 30, 3 (1989b), 399-415

———, "The Slave Trader as Historian: Robert Norris and the History of Dahomey", *History in Africa*, 16 (1989c), 219-35

———, "Slave-Raiders and Middlemen, Monopolists and Free-Traders: the Supply of Slaves for the Atlantic Trade in Dahomey, c.1715–1850", *Journal of African History*, 30,1 (1989d), 45-68

———, "Further Light on Bulfinch Lambe and the 'Emperor of Pawpaw': King Agaja of Dahomey's Letter to King George I of England, 1726", *History in Africa*, 17 (1990b), 211-26

———, "The Gold Trade of Whydah in the Seventeenth and Eighteenth Centuries", in David Henige and T.C. McCaskie (eds), *West African Economic and Social History: Studies in Memory of Marion Johnson* (African Studies Program, University of Wisconsin, Madison, 1990b), 105-18

———, "'The Common People were Divided': Monarchy, Aristocracy and Political Factionalism in the Kingdom of Whydah, 1671–1727", *International Journal of African Historican Studies*, 23, 2 (1990c), 201-29

———, "Computing Domestic Prices in Precolonial West Africa: a Methodological Exercise from the Slave Coast", *History in Africa*, 18 (1991) 239-57

———, *The Slave Coast of West Africa 1550–1750. The Impact of the Atlantic Slave Trade on an African Society* (Oxford University Press, 1991b)

———, "Religion, Trade and Politics on the 'Slave Coast': Roman Catholic Missions in Allada and Whydah in the Seventeenth Century", *Journal of Religion in Africa*, XXI (1991c), 42-77

———, "King Agaja of Dahomey, the Slave Trade, and the Question of West African Plantations: the Mission of Bulfinch Lambe and Adomo Tomo to England, 1726–32", *Journal of Imperial and Commonwealth History*, 19, 2 (1991d), 137-63

———, "Warfare on the West African Slave Coast, 1650–1850", in R. Brian Ferguson and Neil L. Whitehead (eds), *War in the Tribal Zone: Expanding States and Indigenous Warfare* (Santa Fé, School of American Research Press, 1992b), 103-26

———, "The 'Amazons' of Dahomey", *Paideuma*, vol. 39 (1993), 245-60

———, "On Pawning and Enslavemenet for Debt in the Pre-Colonial Slave Coast", in Toyin Falola and Paul E. Lovejoy (eds), *Pawnship in Africa: Debt Bondage in Historical Perspective* (Boulder, Westview, 1994a), 55-69

———, "A Lagoonside Port of the Eighteenth-Century Slave Coast: The Early History of Badagry", *Canadian Journal of African Studies*, 28, 1 (1994b), 32-59

———, "Dahomey and the North-West", in Claude-Hélène Perrot (ed.), *Cahiers du CRA (Centre de Recherches Africaines): Spécial Togo-Bénin*, no. 8 (1994c), 149-67

———, "The Slave Trade in Seventeenth-century Allada: a Revision", *African Economic History*, 22 (1994d), 59-92

———, "'Here is No Resisting the Country': The Realities of Power in Afro-European Relations on the West African 'Slave Coast'", *Itinerario*, 18 (1994e), 50-64

———, "Cowries, Gold, and Dollars: Exchange Rate Instability and Domestic Price Inflation in Dahomey in the Eighteenth and Nineteenth Centuries", in Jane I. Guyer (ed.), *Money Matters. Instability, Values and Social Payments in the Modern History of West African Communities* (Heinemann/J.Currey, 1995), 53-73

———, "An African Response to Abolition: Anglo-Dahomian Negotiations on Ending the Slave Trade, 1838-77", *Slavery and Abolition*, 16, 3 (1995b), 281-310

———, "'Legitimate' Trade and Gender Relations in Yorubaland and Dahomey", in Robin Law (ed.), *From Slave Trade to 'Legitimate' Commerce. The Commercial Transition in Nineteenth-Century West Africa* (Cambridge University Press, 1995c), 195-214

———, "The Politics of Commercial Transition: Factional Conflict in Dahomey in the Context of the Ending of the Atlantic Slave Trade", *Journal of African History*, 38, 2 (1997b), 213-33

———, *The Kingdom of Allada* (Leiden, Research School CNWS, 1997c)

———, "Finance and Credit in Pre-Colonial Dahomey", in Endre Stiansen and Jane I. Guyer (eds), *Credit, Currencies and Culture. African Financial Institutions in Historical Perspective* (Uppsala, Nordic Africa Institute, 1999a) 15-37

———, "The Origins and Evolution of the Merchant Community in Ouidah", in Robin Law and Silke Strickrodt (eds), *Ports of the Slave Trade (Bights of Benin and Biafra). Papers from a Conference of the Centre of Commonwealth Sudies, University of Stirling June 1998* (Centre of Commonwealth Studies, University of Stirling; Occasional Paper Number 6, October 1999b), 55-70

———, "The Transition from the Slave Trade to 'Legitimate' Commerce", in Doudou Diène (ed), *From Chains to Bonds. The Slave Trade Revisited* (Paris, UNESCO & New York/Oxford, Berghahn Books, 2001b), 22-35

———, "Les toutes premières descriptions de Petit-Popo par les européens: des années 1680 aux années 1690", in N.L. Gayibor (ed.), *Le tricentenaire d'Aneho et du pays guin*, vol. I (Lomé, Presses de l'Université du Bénin, 2001c), 33-58

———, "Further Light on John Duncan's Account of the 'Fellatah Country'", *History in Africa*, 28 (2001), 129-38

———, "The Evolution of the Brazilian Community in Ouidah", *Slavery and Abolition*, 22, 1 (2001d), 22-41; also published in Kristin Mann and Edna G. Bay (eds), *Rethinking the African Diaspora: the Making of a Black Atlantic World in the Bight of Benin and Brazil* (London, Frank Cass, 2001)

———, "An Alternative Text of King Agaja of Dahomey's Letter to King George I of England, 1726", *History in Africa*, 29 (2002), 257-71

———, "Legal and Illegal Enslavement in West Africa, in the Context of the Trans-Atlantic Slave Trade", in Toyin Falola (ed.), *Ghana in Africa and the World: Essays in Honor of Adu Boahen* (Trenton, NJ, Africa World Press, 2003), 513-33

———, *Ouidah. The Social History of a West African Slaving 'Port' 1727–1892* (Ohio University Press & Oxford, James Currey 2004a)

———, "Francisco Felix de Souza in West Africa, 1800–1849", in José C. Curto and Paul E. Lovejoy (eds), *Enslaving Connections: Western Africa and Brazil during the Era of Slavery* (Amherst, New York, Prometheus/Humanity Books, 2004b), 187-211

———, "Ethnicities of Enslaved Africans in the Diaspora: On the Meanings of 'Mina' (Again)", *History in Africa*, 32 (2005), 247-67

———, "The Komenda Wars, 1694–1700: A Revised Narrative", *History in Africa*, 34 (2007), 133-68

———, "Madiki Lemon, the 'English Captain' at Ouidah, 1843-1852: An Exploration in Biography", *History in Africa*, 37 (2010), 107-123

———, "West Africa's Discovery of the Atlantic", *International Journal of African Historical Studies*, 1, 44 (2011), 1-25

Law, Robin and Paul E. Lovejoy, "Borgu in the Atlantic Slave Trade", *African Economic History*, 27 (1999), 69-92

Lawrance, Benjamin N., "Bankoe v. Dome: Traditions and Petitions in the Ho-Asogli Amalgamation, British Mandated Togoland, 1919–39", *Journal of African History*, 46, 2 (2005), 243-67

Lawrence, A.W., *Trade Castles & Forts of West Africa* (London, Jonathan Cape, 1963)

Lawuyi, O.B., "The Obatala Factor in Yoruba History", *History in Africa*, 19 (1992), 369-75

BIBLIOGRAPHY

Le Hérissé, Auguste, *L'Ancien Royaume du Dahomey. Moeurs, religion, histoire* (Paris, E. Larose, 1911)

Lindsay, Lisa A., "Extraversion, Creolization, and Dependency in the Atlantic Slave Trade", *Journal of African History*, 55, 2 (2014), 133-45

Lloyd, Peter C., "Sacred Kingship and Government among the Yoruba", *Africa*, 30, 3 (1960), 221-37

Lloyd, Peter C., *The Political Development of Yoruba Kingdoms in the Eighteenth and Nineteenth Centuries* (Royal Anthropological Institute of Great Britain and Ireland, 1971)

Loenertz, Raymond J., OP, "Dominicains français missionnaires en Guinée au XVIIe siècle", *Archivum Fratrum Praedicatorum* (Rome), vol. XXIV (1954), 240-68

Lokken, Paul, "From the 'Kingdoms of Angola' to Santiago de Guatemala: The Portuguese Asientos and Spanish Central America, 1595–1640", *Hispanic American Historical Review*, 93, 2 (2013), 171-203

Lombard, Jacques, "La vie politique dans une ancienne société de type féodal: les Bariba du Dahomey", *Cahiers d'Études Africaines*, XXII, 3 (1960), 5-45

———, "The Kingdom of Dahomey", in D. Forde and P.M. Kaberry (eds), *West African Kingdoms in the Nineteenth Century* (Oxford University Press/ International African Institute, 1967a), 70-92

———, "Contribution à l'histoire d'une ancienne société politique du Dahomey: la royauté d'Allada", *Bulletin de l'IFAN*, XXIX, 1-2 (1967b), 40-66

Lopes, Edmundo Correia, *São João Batista de Ajudá* (Lisbon, Edições Cosmos, Coll. Cadernos Coloniais no. 58, 1939)

Lovejoy, Paul E. and David Richardson, "The Initial 'Crisis of Adaptation': the Impact of British Abolition on the Atlantic Slave Trade in West Africa", in Robin Law (ed.), *From Slave Trade to 'Legitimate' Commerce. The Commercial Transition in Nineteenth-century West Africa* (Cambridge University Press, 1995), 32-56

Lowell, Nadia, "The Watchi-Ewe: Histories and Origins", in Benjamin Lawrance (ed.), *A Handbook of Eweland: The Ewe of Togo and Benin* (Accra, Woeli, 2005), 90-114

Lugar, Catherine, "The Portuguese Tobacco Trade and Tobacco Growers of Bahia in the Late Colonial Oeriod", in Dauril Alden and Warren Dean (eds), *Essays Concerning the Socioeconomic History of Brazil and Portuguese India* (Gainesville, University Presses of Florida, 1977), 26-70

Luttervelt, R. van, "Herrinneringen aan Michiel Adriaenszoon de Ruyter in het Rijksmuseum", *Bulletin van het Rijksmuseum*, vol. 5, 2 (1957), 27-71

Ly, Abdoulaye, *La Compagnie du Sénégal* (Paris, Présence Africaine, 1958)

Lynn, John A., *The Wars of Louis XIV 1667–1714* (Longman, 1999)

Madariaga, María Rosa de, *Abd-el-Krim el Jatabi. La lucha por la independencia* (Madrid, Alianza Editorial, 2009)

Magalhães, Joaquim Romero (ed.), *No alvorecer da modernidade (1480–1620)* (vol. III of José Mattoso [gen.editor] *História de Portugal* [Lisbon, Ed. Estampa, 1997])

BIBLIOGRAPHY

Makepeace, Margaret, "English Traders on the Guinea Coast, 1657–1668: An Analysis of the East India Company Archive", *History in Africa*, 16 (1989), 237-84

Mann, Kristin, *Slavery and the Birth of an African City. Lagos, 1760–1900* (Indiana University Press, 2007)

Manning, Patrick, "The Slave Trade in the Bight of Benin, 1640–1890", in H. Gemery and J. Hogendorn (eds), *The Uncommon Market. Essays in the Economic History of the Atlantic Slave Trade* (New York, Academic Press, 1979), 107-41

———, *Slavery, Colonialism and Economic Growth in Dahomey, 1640–1960* (Cambridge University Press, 1982)

———, "Contours of Slavery and Social Change in Africa", *American Historical Review*, 88, 4 (1983), 835-57

Manoukian, Madeline, *Akan and Ga-Adangme Peoples of the Gold Coast* (Oxford University Press/International African Institute, 1950)

———, *The Ewe-speaking Peoples of Togoland and the Gold Coast* (London, IAI Ethnographic Survey of Africa, 1952)

Maroukis, Thomas Constantine, "Warfare and Society in the Kingdom of Dahomey: 1818–1894" (unpubl. PhD thesis, Boston University, 1974)

———, "Dahomian Warfare and the Slave Trade", paper presented at the African Studies Assoc. Convention, New Orleans, 22-26 November 1985

Martin, Eveline C., *The British West African Settlements 1750–1821. A Study in Local Administration* (London, Longmans etc., 1927)

Martin, Jane, "Krumen 'down the Coast': Liberian Migrants on the West African Coast in the 19th and 20th Centuries", *International Journal of African Historical Studies*, 18, 3 (1985), 401-23

Marty, Paul, "Études sur l'Islam au Dahomey", *Revue du Monde Musulman*, LX (1925), 109-88

Matson, J.N., "The French at Amoku", *Transactions of the Historical Society of the Gold Coast and Togoland*, vol. I, part 2 (1953), 47-60

Maupoil, Bernard, *La Géomancie à l'ancienne Côte des Esclaves* (Paris, Institut d'Ethnologie, 1943)

McCaskie, T.C., "Nananom Mpow of Mankessim: An Essay in Fante History", in David Henige and T.C. McCaskie (eds), *West African Economic and Social History: Studies in Memory of Marion Johnson* (University of Wisconsin, Madison, 1990), 205-16

———, *State and Society in Pre-Colonial Asante* (Cambridge University Press, 1995, paperback edit. 2002)

———, "Denkyira in the Making of Asante c.1660–1720", *Journal of African History*, 48, 1 (2007), 1-25

Mello e Souza, Marina de, *Reis negros no Brasil escravista: História da festa de coroação de Rei Congo* (Belo Horizonte, Editora UFMG, 2002)

Mercier, Paul, "Notice sur le peuplement Yoruba au Dahomey-Togo", *Études Dahoméennes*, IV (1950), 29-40

———, "The Fon of Dahomey", in D. Forde (ed.), *African Worlds. Studies in the cosmological ideas and social values of African peoples* (Oxford University Press/ International African Institute, 1954), 210-34

Merkyte, Inga and Klavs Randsborg, "Graves from Dahomey: Beliefs, Ritual and Society in Ancient Bénin", *Journal of African Archaeology*, VII, 1 (2009), 55-77

Metaxas, Eric, *Amazing Grace. William Wilberforce and the Heroic Campaign to End Slavery* (New York, HarperCollins, 2007)

Mettas, Jean, *Répertoire des expéditions négrières françaises au XVIIIe siècle* (Paris, SFHOM, 1978)

Meyer, Jean, Jean Tarrade, Annie Rey-Goldzeiguer and Jacques Thobie, *Histoire de la France coloniale. Des origines à 1914* (Paris, Armand Colin, 1991)

Mignot, Alain, *La terre et le pouvoir chez les Guin du sud-est du Togo* (Paris, Publications de la Sorbonne, 1985)

Miller, Joseph C., *Way of Death: Merchant Capitalism and the Angolan Slave Trade* (University of Wisconsin Press, 1988)

Mintz, Sidney W., *Sweetness and Power. The Place of Sugar in Modern History* (1985, Penguin edition 1986)

Mondjannagni, Alfred Comlan, *Campagnes et villes du sud de la République du Bénin* (Paris/The Hague, Mouton, 1977)

Monroe, J. Cameron, "Dahomey and the Atlantic Slave Trade. Archaeology and Political Order on the Bight of Benin", in Akinwumi Ogundiran and Toyin Falola (eds), *Archaeology of Atlantic Africa and the African Diaspora* (Indiana University Press, 2007)

———, "Continuity, Revolution or Evolution on the Slave Coast of West Africa? Royal Architecture and Political Order in Precolonial Dahomey", *Journal of African History*, 48, 3 (2007b), 349-73

———, "Building the State in Dahomey: Power and Landscape in the Bight of Benin", in J. Cameron Monroe and Akinwurai Ogundiran (eds), *Power and Landscape in Atlantic West Africa. Archaeological Perspectives* (Cambridge University Press, 2012), 191-221

Moore, William A., *History of Itsekiri* (1936; 2nd ed. Frank Cass 1970, with a new Introd. by P.C. Lloyd)

———, "An Outline of the Cosmology and Cult Organization of the Oyo Yoruba", *Africa*, XXXIV, 3 (1964a), 243-61

———, "The Oyo Yoruba and the Atlantic Trade, 1670-1830", *Journal of the Historical Society of Nigeria,* 3, no. 1 (1964b), 25-45

Mouléro, R.P. Thomas, "Histoire et légende de Chabe (Save)", *Études Dahoméennes* (NS), 2 (1964), 51-92

———, "Histoire des Wémenous ou Dékanmènous", *Études Dahoméennes* (NS), no. 3 (1964), 51-76

———, "Histoire et légendes des Djêkens", *Études Dahoméennes* (NS), 8 (1966) 39-56

BIBLIOGRAPHY

Myers, Walter Dean, *At Her Majesty's Request. An African Princess in Victorian England* (New York: Scholastic Press, 1999)

Newbury, C.W., *The Western Slave Coast and its Rulers. European Trade and Administration among the Yoruba and Adja-speaking Peoples of South-Western Nigeria, Southern Dahomey and Togo* (Oxford at the Clarendon Press 1961, reprinted 1973)

Norman, Neil L., "Hueda (Whydah) Country and Town: Archaeological Perspectives on the Rise and Collapse of an African Atlantic Kingdom", *International Journal of African Historical Studies*, 42, 3 (2009a), 387-410

———, "Powerful Pots, Humbling Holes, and Regional Ritual Processes: Towards an Archaeology of Huedan Vodun ca. 1650–1727", *African Archaeological Review*, 26, 3 (2009b), 187-218

———, "From the Shadow of an Atlantic Citadel: An Archaeology of the Huedan Countryside", in J. Cameron Monroe and Akinwumi Ogundiran (eds), *Power and Landscape in Atlantic West Africa. Archaeological Perspectives* (Cambridge University Press, 2012), 142-66

Norman, Neil L. and Kenneth G. Kelly, "Landscape Politics: The Serpent Ditch and the Rainbow in West Africa", *American Anthropologist*, 106, 1 (2004), 98-110

Nørregaard, Georg, *Guldkysten. De danske etablissementer i Guinea* (København [Copenhagen] 2nd ed. 1968) [the English translation is reputed unreliable]

Northrup, David, "New Evidence of the French Slave-Trade in the Bight of Benin", *Slavery and Abolition*, 24, 3 (2003), 61-81

Nováky, György, *Handelskompanier och kompanihandel. Svenska Afrikakompaniet 1649–1663. En studie i feodal handel* (Acta Universitatis Upsaliensis, Uppsala 1990)

———, "Small Company and the Gold Coast: the Swedish African Company, 1650–1663", *Itinerario*, 16, 1 (1992), 57-76

Novick, Peter, *That Noble Dream: the "Objectivity Question" and the American Historical Profession* (Cambridge University Press, 1988)

Nugent, Paul, *Myths of Origin and the Origin of Myth: Local Politics and the Uses of History in Ghana's Volta Region* (Berlin, Das Arabische Buch, 1997)

———, "'A Few Lesser Peoples': the Central Togo Minorities and their Ewe Neighbours", in Carola Lentz and Paul Nugent (eds), *Ethnicity in Ghana: The Limits of Invention* (Basingstoke/London, Macmillan, 2000), 162-82

———, "A Regional Melting Pot: The Ewe and Their Neighbours in the Ghana-Togo Borderlands", in Benjamin Lawrance (ed.), *A Handbook of Eweland: The Ewe of Togo and Benin* (Accra, Woeli, 2005), 29-43

———, "Putting the History Back into Ethnicity: Enslavement, Religion, and Cultural Brokerage in the Construction of Madinka/Jola and Ewe/Agotime Identities in West Africa, c.1650–1930", *Comparative Studies in Society and History*, 50, 4 (2008), 920-48

Nukunya, G.K., "The Land and the People", in Francis Agbodeka (ed.), *A Handbook of Eweland, vol.I: The Ewes of Southeastern Ghana* (Accra, Woeli, 1997), 8-13

Obayemi, Ade M., "The Yoruba and Edo-speaking peoples and their neighbours before 1600 A.D," in J.F. Ade Ajayi and Michael Crowder (eds), *History of West Africa I* (3rd ed., Harlow, Essex, Longman, 1985), 255-322

Obichere, Boniface I., "Change and Innovation in the Administration of the Kingdom of Dahomey", *Journal of African Studies*, vol. 1, 3 (1974), 235-51

Ogundiran, Akinwumi, "Material Life and Domestic Economy in a Frontier of the Oyo Empire During the Mid-Atlantic Age", *International Journal of African Historical Studies*, 42, 3 (2009), 351-65

Ogundiran, Akinwumi, "The End of Prehistory? An African Comment", *American Historical Review*, June 2013, 788-801

Ojo, Olatunji, "The Organization of the Atlantic Slave Trade in Yorubaland, ca. 1777 to ca. 1856", *International Journal of African Historical Studies*, 41, 1 (2008), 77-100

Oké, C. Raymond, "L'ancien Danhome des origines à la formation territoriale du royaume" (unpubl. thesis, Université de Paris I-Sorbonne, 1972)

———, "Les siècles obscurs du royaume aja du Danxome", in François de Medeiros (ed.), *Peuples du golfe du Bénin. Aja-Ewe* (Paris, Karthala, 1984), 46-66

Pallinder-Law, Agneta, "Aborted Modernization in West Africa? The Case of Abeokuta", *Journal of African History*, XV, 1 (1974), 65-82

———, "The Slave Trade Economy in Dahomey", book review in *Journal of African History*, 2 (1975), 306-7

Palau-Martí, Montserrat, *Le Roi-Dieu au Bénin (Sud Togo, Dahomey, Nigeria occidental)* (Paris, Berger-Levrault, 1964)

———, *L'Histoire de Sàbe et de ses rois. (République du Bénin)* (Paris, Maisonneuve et Larose 1992)

———, *Société et religion au Bénin (les Sàbé-Opara)* (Paris, Maisonneuve et Larose, 1993)

Paquette, Gabriel, *Imperial Portugal in the Age of Atlantic Revolutions: the Luso-Brazilian World, c. 1770–1850* (Cambridge, Cambridge University Press, 2013)

Parés, Luis Nicolau, "The Hula 'Problem': Ethnicity on the Pre-Colonial Slave Coast", in Toyin Falola and Matt D. Childs (eds), *The Changing Worlds of Atlantic Africa. Essays in Honor of Robin Law* (Durham, NC, Carolina Academic, 2009), 323-46

Parrinder, E.G., *The Story of Ketu. An Ancient Yoruba Kingdom* (Ibadan University Press, 1956)

Patzold, Steffen, "Le 'premier âge féodal' vu d'Allemagne. Essai sur les historiographies française et allemande", in Dominique Iogna-Prat, Michel Lauwers, Florian Mazel and Isabelle Rosé (eds), *Cluny. Les moines et la société au premier âge féodal* (Presses Universitaires de Rennes, 2013), 19-29

Pazzi, Roberto, "Recherche sur le vocabulaire des langues Evè, Aja, Gèn et Fòn" (Première partie: Lexique des noms) (mimeogr., Lomé, 1976)

———, "Aperçu sur l'implantation actuelle et les migrations anciennes des peuples de l'aire aja-tado", in François de Medeiros (ed.), *Peuples du golfe du Bénin. Aja-Ewe* (Paris, Karthala, 1984), 11-19

Peel, J.D.Y., *Religious Encounter and the Making of the Yoruba* (Indiana University Press, 2000)

Pélissier, Paul, *Le pays du Bas Ouémé: une région témoin du Dahomey méridional* (Dakar, Faculté des Lettres et Sciences Humaines, 1963)

Pemberton III, John, "The Dreadful God and the Divine King", in S. Barnes (ed.), *Africa's Ogun. Old World and New* (Indiana University Press, 1989), 105-46

Pemberton III, John and Funso S. Afolayan, *Yoruba Sacred Kingship. "A Power Like That of the Gods"* (Washington & London, Smithsonian Institution Press, 1996)

Perrot, Claude-Hélène, "La fête d'Adjahouto à Allada (Dahomey) et ses enseignements historiques", *Annales de l'Université d'Abidjan*, série I, t. I (1972), 132-49

Person, Yves, "Chronologie du royaume gun de Hogbonu (Porto-Novo)", *Cahiers d'Études Africaines*, XV, 2 (1975), 217-38

———, "Les monarchies africaines", *Le Mois en Afrique*, no. 200 (July- Sept. 1982) 161-76 & nos 202-3 (Oct.-Dec. 1982), 104-21

Pescheux, Gérard, *Le royaume asante (Ghana). Parenté, pouvoir, histoire, XVIIe-XXe siècles* (Paris, Karthala, 2003)

Pettigrew, William A., *Freedom's Debt: The Royal African Company and the Politics of the Atlantic Slave Trade, 1672–1752* (University of North Carolina Press, 2013)

Pfeiffer, Verena, *Agriculture au Sud-Bénin: Passé et perspectives* (Paris, L'Harmattan, 1988)

Philips, John Edward, "African Smoking and Pipes", *Journal of African History*, 24, 3 (1983), 303-19

Pineau-Jamous, Marie-Josée, "Porto-Novo: royauté, localité et parenté", *Cahiers d'Études Africaines*, XXVI, 4 (1986), 547-76

Pognon, André, "Le problème 'Popo'", *Études Dahoméennes*, XIII (1955), 13-14

Polanyi, Karl, *The Great Transformation. The Political and Economic Origins of our Time*, first published New York, Farrar and Rinehart in 1944.

———, "Sortings and the 'Ounce Trade' in the West African Slave Trade", *Journal of African History*, V, 3 (1964), 381-93

Polanyi, Karl with Abraham Rotstein, *Dahomey and the Slave Trade. An Analysis of an Archaic Economy* (Seattle, University of Washington Press, 1966)

Postma, Johannes Menne, *The Dutch in the Atlantic Slave Trade 1600–1815* (Cambridge University Press, 1990)

Quarcoopome, Nii Otokunor, "Notse's Ancient Kingship: Some Archaeological and Art-historical Considerations", *African Archaeological Review*, 11 (1993), 109-28

Quaye, Irene, "The Ga and their Neighbours 1600–1742" (PhD thesis, University of Ghana, 1972)

Randrianja, Solofo and Stephen Ellis, *Madagascar: A Short History* (London & Chicago, University of Chicago Press, 2009)

Randsborg, Klavs, Inga Merkyte et al., *Bénin Archaeology. The Ancient Kingdoms*, 2 volumes (Oxford, Wiley-Blackwell, 2009 [*Acta Archaeologica* Volumes 80-1 & 2 & *Acta Archaeologica* Supplementa XI])

Rattray, Captain R.S., *The Tribes of the Ashanti Hinterland*, 2 volumes (Oxford at the Clarendon Press, 1932)

Rawley, James A., "Further Light on Archibald Dalzel", *International Journal of African Historical Studies*, 17, 2 (1984), 317-23

Raychaudhuri, Tapan, *Jan Company in Coromandel 1605-1690: A Study in the Interrelations of European Commerce and Traditional Economies* (The Hague, Martinus Nijhoff, 1962)

Reis, João José, *Rebelião escrava no Brasil: A história do levante dos malês 1835* (São Paulo, Editora Brasiliense, 1986)

Ribeiro, Alexandre Vieira, "The Transatlantic Slave Trade to Bahia, 1582-1851", in David Eltis and David Richardson (eds), *Extending the Frontiers. Essays on the New Transatlantic Slave Trade Database* (New Haven, Yale University Press, 2008), 130-54

Richards, W.A., "The Import of Firearms into West Africa in the Eighteenth Century", *Journal of African History*, 21, 1 (1980), 43-59

Rinchon, Père Dieudonné, *Pierre-Ignace-Liévin Van Alstein, capitaine négrier. Gand 1733-Nantes 1793* (Dakar, IFAN, 1964)

Richardson, David, "The Eighteenth-century British Slave Trade: Estimates of its Volume and Coastal Distribution in Africa", *Research in Economic History. A Research Annual*, vol. 12 (Greenwich, CT, 1989), 151-96

Rivallain, Josette, "Le sel dans les villages côtiers et lagunaires du Bas-Dahomey: sa fabrication, sa place dans le circuit du sel africain", *West African Journal of Archaeology*, 7 (1977) 143-69

Rocco da Cesinale, P., *Storia delle missioni dei Cappuccini*, tomo III (Rome, Tipografia Barbèra, 1873)

Rodney, Walter, *How Europe Underdeveloped Africa* (London, Bogle-L'Ouverture Publications, 1972)

Rommelse, Gijs, "The Role of Mercantilism in Anglo-Dutch Political Relations, 1650-74", *Economic History Review*, 63, 3 (2010), 591-611

Ronen, Dov, "On the African Role in the Trans-Atlantic Slave Trade in Dahomey", *Cahiers d'Études Africaines*, XI, 1, 41 (1971), 5-13

Rosenthal, Judy, "Religious Traditions of the Togo and Benin Ewe", in Benjamin Lawrance (ed.), *A Handbook of Eweland. The Ewe of Togo and Benin* (Accra, Woeli, 2005), 183-96

Ross, David A., "The Career of Domingo Martinez in the Bight of Benin 1833-64", *Journal of African History*, VI, 1 (1965), 79-90

Ross, David A., "The Autonomous Kingdom of Dahomey 1818-1894", (unpubl. PhD thesis, University of London, 1967)

———, "The First Chacha of Whydah: Felix Francis De Souza", *Odu* (n.s.), 2 (1969), 19-28

———, "Dahomey", in Michael Crowder (ed.), *West African Resistance* (2nd ed.: London, Hutchinson, 1978), 144-69

———, "The Anti-Slave Trade Theme in Dahomean History: An Examination of the Evidence", *History in Africa*, IX (1982), 263-71

———, "European Models and West African History: further Comments on the Recent Historiography of Dahomey", *History in Africa*, X (1983), 293-305

———, "The Dahomean Middleman System, 1727–c.1818", *Journal of African History*, 28, 3 (1987), 357-75

———, "Robert Norris, Agaja, and the Dahomean conquest of Allada and Whydah", *History in Africa*, 16 (1989), 311-24

Russell-Wood, A.J.R., "Colonial Brazil: the Gold Cycle. c. 1690–1750", in Leslie Bethell (ed.), *The Cambridge History of Latin America*, vol. II (Colonial Latin America) (Cambridge University Press, 1984), 547-600

Ryder, A.F.C., "The Re-establishment of Portuguese Factories on the Costa da Mina to the Mid-eighteenth Century", *Journal of the Historical Society of Nigeria*, II,3 (1958), 157-83

———, "Missionary Activities in the Kingdom of Warri to the Early Nineteenth Century", *Journal of the Historical Society of Nigeria*, vol. 2, 1 (1960), 1-26

———, "Dutch Trade on the Nigerian Coast during the Seventeenth Century", *Journal of the Historical Society of Nigeria*, III, 3 (1966), 195-210

———, *Benin and the Europeans 1485-1897* (London, Longmans, 1969)

Savary, Claude, *La pensée symbolique des Fō. Tableau de la société et étude de la litterature orale d'expression sacrée dans l'ancien royaume du Dahomey* (Geneva, Éditions Médecine et hygiène, 1976)

Schiavone, Aldo, *The End of the Past. Ancient Rome and the Modern World* (English translation, Harvard University Press, 2000)

Scubla, Lucien, "Sacred King, Sacrificial Victim, Surrogate Victim or Frazer, Hocart, Girard", in Declan Quigley (ed.), *The Character of Kingship* (Oxford/New York, Berg, 2005), 39-62

Sègla, Aimé and Adékin E. Boko, "De la cosmologie à la rationalisation de la vie sociale. Ces mots idààcha qui parlent ou la mémoire d'un type de calendrier yoruba ancien", *Cahiers d'Études Africaines*, XLVI, 1 (2006), 11-50

Shinnie, Peter, "Early Asante: Is Wilks Right?", in John Hunwick and Nancy Lawler (eds), *The Cloth of Many Colored Silks. Papers on History and Society Ghanaian and Islamic in Honor of Ivor Wilks* (Northwestern University Press, 1996), 195-203

Shumway, Rebecca, *The Fante and the Transatlantic Slave Trade* (University of Rochester Press, 2011a)

———, "The Fante Shrine of Nananom Mpow and the Atlantic Slave Trade in Southern Ghana", *International Journal of African Historical Studies*, 44, 1 (2011b), 27-44

Smith, H.F.C., D.M. Last and Gamba Gubio, "Ali Eisami Gazirmabe of Bornu" in P.

Curtin (ed.), *Africa Remembered. Narratives by West Africans from the Era of the Slave Trade* (University of Wisconsin Press, 1967), 199-216

Smith, Robert S., "The Canoe in West African History", *Journal of African History*, XI, 4 (1970), 515-33

———, "The Lagos Consulate, 1851-1861: An Outline", *Journal of African History*, XV, 3 (1974), 393-416

———, *Kingdoms of the Yoruba* (London, Methuen, 2nd ed., 1976)

———, "The Yoruba Wars, c. 1820–93. A General Study", in J.F. Ade Ajayi and Robert Smith, *Yoruba Warfare in the Nineteenth Century* (Cambridge University Press, 1964), 9-55

Smith, Stefan Halikowski, "'Profits Sprout like Tropical Plants': a Fresh Look at What went Wrong with the Eurasian Spice Trade c. 1550-1800", *Journal of Global History*, vol. 3, 3 (2008), 389-418

Soglo, Gilles, "Notes sur la traite des esclaves à Glexwe (Ouidah)", in Elisée Soumonni, Bellarmin C. Codo and Joseph Adande (eds), *Le Bénin et la route de l'esclave* (Cotonou, ONEPI, 1994), 66-72

Soumonni, Elisée Akpo, "The Administration of a Port of the Slave Trade: Ouidah in the Nineteenth Century", in R. Law and Silke Strickrodt (eds), *Ports of the Slave Trade (Bights of Benin and Biafra)* (Centre of Commonwealth Studies, University of Stirling, Occasional Paper 6, Oct. 1999), 48-54

———, "The Compatibility of the Slave and Palm Oil Trades in Dahomey, 1818–1858", in Robin Law (ed.), *From Slave Trade to 'Legitimate' Commerce. The Commercial Transition in Nineteenth-century West Africa* (Cambridge University Press, 1995), 78-92

———, "Some Reflections on the Brazilian Legacy in Dahomey", *Slavery and Abolition*, 22, 1 (2001), 61-71

———, "From a Port of the Slave Trade to an Urban Community: Robin Law and the History of Ouidah", in Toyin Falola and Matt D. Childs (eds), *The Changing Worlds of Atlantic Africa. Essays in Honor of Robin Law* (Durham, Carolina Academic Press, 2009), 223-31

Stark, Rodney, *One True God: Historical Consequences of Monotheism* (Princeton University Press, 2001)

Stewart, Marjorie Helen, "The Kisra Legend as Oral History", *International Journal of African Historical Studies*, 13, 1 (1980), 51-70.

Strickrodt, Silke, "Afro-European Trade Relations on the Western Slave Coast, 16th to 19th centuries" (unpublished PhD thesis, University of Stirling, 2003).

———, A revised version of this thesis (with the title *Afro-European Trade in the Atlantic World: The Western Slave Coast, c.1550–c.1885*), was published by James Currey in February 2015, that is, too late for its content to be taken into consideration in the present work)

Tait, David, "The Political System of Konkomba", *Africa*, XXIII, 3 (1953), 213-23

Tattersfield, Nigel, *The Forgotten Trade. Comprising the Log of the "Daniel and Henry" of 1700 and Accounts of the Slave Trade from the Minor Ports of England, 1698–1725* (London, Jonathan Cape, 1991)

Thomas, Nicholas, *Entangled Objects: Exchange, Material Culture, and Colonialism in the Pacific* (Harvard University Press, 1991)

Thompson, E.P., *The Making of the English Working Class* (first publ. 1963, Penguin ed., 1991)

Thornton, John K., "The Kingdom of Kongo, ca. 1390–1678. The Development of an African Social Formation", *Cahiers d'Études Africaines*, XXII, 3-4 (1982), 325-42

———, *The Kingdom of Kongo. Civil War and Transition 1641–1718* (University of Wisconsin Press, 1983)

———, "Warfare, Slave Trading and European Influence: Atlantic Africa 1450–1800", in Jeremy Black (ed.), *War in the Early Modern World, 1450–1815* (London, UCL Press, 1999), 129-46

———, "The Origins and Early History of the Kingdom of Kongo, c. 1350–1550", *International Journal of African Historical Studies*, 34, 1 (2001), 89-120

———, "Afro-Christian Syncretism in the Kingdom of Kongo", *Journal of African History*, 54, 1 (2013), 53-77

Turner, J. Michael, "Les Bresiliens - the Impact of Former Brazilian Slaves upon Dahomey" (unpublished PhD thesis, University of Boston 1975)

Vansina, Jan, *Kingdoms of the Savanna* (University of Wisconsin Press, 1966)

Venkatachalam, Meera, "Between the Devil and the Cross: Religion, Slavery, and the Making of the Anlo-Ewe", *Journal of African History*, 53, 1 (2012), 45-64

Verger, Michel, *The Abutia Ewe of West Africa. The Chiefdom that Never Was* (Berlin etc., Mouton, 1983)

Verger, Pierre, "Le culte des Vodoun d'Abomey aurait-il été apporté à Saint-Louis de Maranhon par la mère du roi Ghézo?", *Études Dahoméennes*, 8 (1952), 19-24

———, "Oral Tradition in the Cult of the Orishas and its Connection with the history of the Yoruba", *Journal of the Historical Society of Nigeria*, I (1956), 61-3

———, *Note sur le culte des Orisa et Vodun à Bahia, la Baie de tous les saints au Brésil, et à l'ancienne Côte des Esclaves en Afrique* (Mémoire de l'IFAN, no. 51, Dakar, 1957)

———, *Le Fort St. Jean-Baptiste d'Ajuda* (Mémoire de l'Institut de Recherches Appliquées du Dahomey, 1966)

———, *Flux et reflux de la traite des nègres entre le Golfe de Bénin et Bahia de Todos os Santos du XVIIe au XIXe siècle* (Paris/The Hague, Mouton, 1968)

Viotti da Costa, Emilia, "The Portuguese-African Slave Trade. A Lesson in Colonialism", *Latin American Perspectives*, 12, 1 (1985), 41-61

———, *The Brazilian Empire: Myths and Histories* (University of North Carolina Press, 2000)

Vogt, John, *Portuguese Rule on the Gold Coast 1469–1682* (Athens, University of Georgia Press, 1979)

BIBLIOGRAPHY

Vries, Jan de, *The Industrious Revolution. Consumer Behavior and the Household Economy, 1650 to the Present* (Cambridge University Press, 2008)

Vries, Jan de and Ad van der Woude, *The First Modern Economy. Success, Failure, and Perseverance of the Dutch Economy, 1500–1815* (Cambridge University Press, 1997)

Waldman, Loren K., "An Unnoticed Aspect of Archibald Dalzel's the History of Dahomey", *Journal of African History*, VI, 2 (1965), 185-92

Ward, William Ernest Frank, *The Royal Navy and the Slavers* (New York, Pantheon Books, 1969)

Welman, C.K., *The Native States of the Gold Coast. History and Constitution I. Peki* (London, Dawsons of Pall Mall, 1924, reprinted 1969)

Wenke, Robert J., *The Ancient Egyptian State. The Origins of Egyptian Culture (c.8000–2000 BC)* (Cambridge University Press, 2009)

Wheat, David, "The First Great Waves: African Provenance Zones for the Transatlantic Slave Trade to Cartagena de Indias, 1570–1640", *Journal of African History*, 52, 1 (2011), 1-22

Wigboldus, Jouke S., "Trade and Agriculture in Coastal Benin c.1470–1600: an Examination of Manning's Early-growth Thesis", *Afdeling Agrarische Geschiedenis. Bijdragen* (Agricultural University of Wageningen), vol. 28 (1986), 299-383

Wilks, Ivor, "Aspects of Bureaucratization in Ashanti in the Nineteenth Century", *Journal of African History*, VII, 2 (1966), 215-32

———, "Ashanti Government" in Daryll Forde and P.M. Kaberry (eds), *West African Kingdoms in the Nineteenth Century* (International African Institute/Oxford University Press, 1967), 206-38

———, "The Mossi and Akan states, 1400 to 1800", in J.F. Ade Ajayi and Michael Crowder (eds), *History of West Africa*, Vol. One (third ed., Harlow/Essex, Longman, 1985), 465-502

———, *Akwamu 1640–1750. A Study of the Rise and Fall of a West African Empire* (University of Trondheim, 2001); the printed version of a thesis of 1958

Winsnes, Selena Axelrod, "P.E. Isert in German, French, and English: A Comparison of Translations", *History in Africa*, 19 (1992), 401-10

Wright, Donald R., "Requiem for the Use of Oral Tradition to Reconstruct the Precolonial History of the Lower Gambia", *History in Africa*, 18 (1991), 399-408

Yai, Olabiyi Babalola, "The Identity, Contributions, and Ideology of the Aguda (Afro-Brazilians) of the Gulf of Benin: A Reinterpretation", *Slavery and Abolition*, 22, 1 (2001), 72-82

Yarak, Larry W., *Asante and the Dutch, 1744–1873* (Oxford University Press, 1990)

Yoder, John C., "Fly and Elephant Parties. Political Polarization in Dahomey, 1840-1870", *Journal of African History*, 15, 3 (1974), 417-43

Zahedieh, Nuala, "Regulation, Rent-seeking, and the Glorious Revolution in the English Atlantic Economy", *Economic History Review*, 63, 4 (2010), 865-90

Zook, G.F., *The Company of Royal Adventurers Trading into Africa* (originally published in *The Journal of Negro History* in 1919. Reprinted New York, Negro Universities Press, 1969)

Online sources

Blench, Roger (maintained by), "Ghana-Togo mountain languages homepage"

Trans-Atlantic Slave Trade Database. Emory University, National Endowment for the Humanities, and W.E.B. Du Bois Institute (University of Harvard). Scholars responsible: David Eltis, David Richardson, Stephen D. Behrendt and Manolo Florentino.

http://www.slavevoyages.org/tast/assessment/estimates.faces. Retrieved at various times since December 2011

World Health Organization – websites on trypanosomiasis.

Museum exhibits

Kroon van Ardra met Bijbehorend Dokument – inventory number NM 816 a & b. Koper en glas, perkament (Rijksmuseum, Amsterdam)

Works of fiction

Bourgeon, François, *Le Comptoir de Juda* (vol. 3 of *Les Passagers du Vent*) (Jacques Glénat, Grenoble, 1981) (cartoon)

Chatwin, Bruce, *The Viceroy of Ouidah* (Picador/Pan edition, 1980)

Haley, Alex, *Roots: The Saga of an American Family* (New York, Doubleday, 1976)

Kipling, Rudyard, *The Man Who Would be King* (short story 1888, film by John Ford 1975)

Stevenson, Robert Louis, *Treasure Island* (1883)

INDEX

Abiodun, King: death of (1789), 260–1
Abson, Lionel: 36, 39–40, 49, 234, 251, 259–60; death of, 271
Ada: 176, 212, 245–7, 277; political relationships of, 246
Adande, Alexis: 33, 130
Adandozan: 267, 272–6, 284; dethroning of, 276–7; expulsion of deities by, 276; family of, 263; narratives of, 273–4
Ado: 172–3; family of, 173
Agaja, King: 41, 200, 204, 209–11, 213–15, 217–18, 224–5, 243, 264; death of (1740), 162, 224, 226–7; family of, 216; movement of secular capital (1730), 204
Agasu: 139, 204; family of, 237
Agbangla, King: 154–6; death of (1703), 187–8, 193
Agbidinukun: 51
Aghidisu: 226–7; death of, 227; followers of, 227
Agonglo, King: 251, 259; family of, 263
Aido-Hwedo (deity): 70–1
Aisan-Amar: death of (1708), 192
Aïzo (ethnic group): 24, 149; depictions of, 139–40
Ajahuto: cult of, 237; family of, 237

Akaba, King: death of, 162
Akan (ethnic group): 176; active opposition to literacy, 48; territory inhabited by, 74, 171
Akinjogbin, Isaac A.: 40, 47, 53, 169, 195, 207, 214; concept of Ebi social theory, 41–2, 68; original rupture theory of, 43
Akonno: death of (1725), 173; family of, 173
Akwamu: 23, 177, 181–4, 199, 206, 212, 289; conquest of Accra, 176; fall of (1730), 212; invasions led by, 172–3, 176, 184; ruling strategies of, 171–2
Allada, Kingdom of: 8, 34, 100, 120, 122, 133, 136, 139–43, 146, 148, 151–3, 169, 179–80, 183, 188–90, 192–3, 195, 291; conquered by Kingdom of Dahomey (1724), 163–4, 193, 199–200; destruction of (1726), 205; English arrival in (1663), 123; Spanish missionaries in, 143–5; vassals of, 128, 136, 148, 159, 166
Alu: myths focusing on, 131–2
Amu: revolt led by (1728), 212
Angola: 120; Dutch rule of Luanda (1641–8), 115

435

INDEX

Anlo (ethnic group): 24, 247
Anlo Confederation: 177, 253–4; members of, 176
Asante, Kingdom of: 48, 74, 78, 177, 200, 246–7, 256, 277, 287
Ashangmo: 216; shortcomings of, 217
Assou, Captain: 206, 208; death of, 211
Atkins, John: 42, 196
Awole: suicide of (1796), 261

Barbot, Willem: 141, 150
Bariba (ethnic group): 260
Basilio, João: 210, 216, 229
Basua: death of (1699), 172–3
Bay, Edna: 42, 46, 50–2, 163–4, 168, 241, 279, 284–5
Béhanzin, King: family of, 51
Behrendt, Stephen: 107
Belize: Boca del Rio, 117
Benin: 15–16, 21, 28, 34, 72–3, 91–3, 100, 129, 134, 142, 145, 217, 292, 294; Abomey, 142; Allada, 23, 28; borders of, 22; Cotonou, 292; Grand Popo, 27, 32, 65, 135, 141–2, 147, 173, 182–3, 207, 211, 261; Grand Popo-Agbanakin, 183; Grand Popo-Hulagan, 182–3; Ketu, 23, 257, 281; Notsé (Nuatja), 48, 76–7, 133–4, 137–8, 273; Porto Novo, 117, 133, 139, 163, 220, 244–5, 255, 257–9, 261, 272, 274–5, 278–9, 281–2; vassals of, 257
Benin Gap: 22, 29–30
Bight of Benin: 8, 92, 98, 126, 258, 269; coast of, 283; concept of, 91; slaves taken from, 94–5
Blier, Suzanne Preston: 70, 132, 163–4; writings on *boico* art and sculpture, 243; writings on *kpojito*, 164
Bonaparte, Napoleon: 265; re-legalisation of slave trade and slavery (1802), 249–50

Bosman, Willem: 33, 46, 105–6, 127, 156, 179, 181
Branco, Garcia Mendes Castello: 114
Brandenburg-Prussia: 6, 9, 98
Brazil: 14, 47, 94, 98, 106, 114, 153, 244, 262, 267–9, 271, 274, 276, 280, 282, 294; Cachoeira, 293; Costa da Mina, 191, 218, 230, 257–8, 268, 270, 275; gold mining in, 118–19, 190–1; Independence of (1822), 267; Minas Gerais, 118, 191; Rio de Janeiro, 268–9 Salvador da Bahia, 47, 94, 105, 185, 195, 216, 229–30, 233, 275, 292–3
Brenner, Louis: 60
de Bruxelles, Celestin: 155
Burkina Faso: 74; Kana, 100, 142, 286

Caerloff, Heinrich: 151, 153, 155; background of, 124
Cape Coast Castle: 9, 40, 92, 123, 185, 232, 251, 271; piracy trials held at (1722), 196
capitalism: 15, 83, 89–90; Liberal, 265; Western Europe, 85
Capo, Hounkpatin: 23–4
Cardoso, Simão: death of, 209
Catholicism: 85, 145; missionaries, 156
Celestin-Hulst Mission: 155–6
Central Slave Coast: 13–14, 33, 39, 97, 173, 179, 190, 193, 206, 228, 251, 270; languages spoken in, 64; territory of, 22
Charles II of England, King: 125
Christianity: 14–16, 59–60, 68, 148, 151, 265, 285, 290; conversion to, 147, 252–3; missionaries, 50, 72–3, 136, 142–4, 146–7, 156, 262–3; Protestantism, 155; spread of, 70–2, 263
Christiansborg (fort): 9, 36, 92, 153, 246, 253; as São Francisco Xavier, 172; blockading of (1729–30), 212

INDEX

Christiansborg-Osu: 173
Churfürstlich-Afrikanisch-Brandenburgische Compagnie: 125
Colombia: 135; Cartagena, 135
Compagnie de l'Asiente: bankruptcy of, 194
Compagnie des Indes: 194
Company of Guinea: as Company of the Asiento, 188–9
Company of Merchants (African Company): 234; African Committee, 235; personnel of, 38
cotton: growing of, 126
Crevecoeur (fort): 253
Cruickshank, Brodie: 58, 286
Cuba: 267, 282, 284

Dahomean religion: 57, 77
Dahomey, Kingdom of: 25, 38, 40–1, 43–4, 49, 52, 54, 68, 72, 78–9, 97, 100, 103–4, 109, 128, 139–41, 150, 159–69, 192–3, 196, 200, 207–8, 210–11, 215–17, 220–2, 224, 228–9, 231–5, 238, 241, 244, 251, 253, 256, 258, 261, 264, 269–72, 274, 276, 281, 283–4, 289–91; Abomey, 204–6, 213, 227, 237, 241, 286; Abomey plateau, 48, 129–30, 159–61, 204, 225; Allada, 204, 237; as vassal of Kingdom of Oyo, 202; conquest of Slave Coast, 3, 96–7; depicted by historians, 41–4, 50–3; economy of, 81–3, 88, 283; expansion of, 3, 28–9, 101, 103, 163–4, 193, 199–201; French conquest of (1892–4), 39; Oyo conflict with (1726), 202, 206; political systems of, 242–3; Simboji Palace, 241; weaponry produced in, 169–70; *Xwetanu* (Annual Customs), 220–4
Dalzel, Archibald: 35–6, 39–40, 46, 104–5, 251, 256; background of, 38; writings of, 38, 40–1, 57–8, 136

D'Amon Expedition (1698–9): 184–5
Dangbe the python (deity): 27; priests of, 150–1; shrines of, 156
Davidson, Basil: 42, 214
Delbée, Louis: 142, 147; background of, 124; theory of 'Grand Marabout', 147–8, 200
Delbée-Caerloff Mission (1671–2): 142, 147–8; success of, 124
Denmark: 267
Denmark-Norway: 98; abolition of slave trade (1792), 250
Devaynes, William: background of, 36; Director of William's Fort, 235
Dias, Bartolomeo: rounding of Cape of Good Hope (1488), 122
Duchasse, Jean-Baptiste: 36, 156
Dupetival, Houdoyer: 209
Dutch Republic (United Provinces): 98, 115, 122, 156, 186, 253, 255; as slave trade nation, 98; Independence of (1640), 115
Dutch West Indies Company: death of personnel of, 35

earth-priest: 71, 76, 130, 142; as king, 65–6, 130; concept of, 65
Eastern Slave Coast: 22, 97, 215, 244, 251, 257, 259, 278; languages spoken in, 29
Edo (ethnic group): 73, 142
Eighty Years' War (1568–1648): 114
Eltis, David: criticisms of, 82
Elwert, Georg: 82
English Navigation Act (1651): political impact of, 122
Evans, E.W.: macroeconomic definition of slave-raiding, 87
Ewe (Vhe)(ethnic group): Peki, 212; spiritual beliefs of, 61, 71; territory inhabited by, 28–9, 75–7; Watchi-Ewe, 33, 39, 262; *yevuga*, 210

437

INDEX

Fante (ethnic group): 6–7, 277, 286; territory inhabited by, 74–5
Findlay, Roland: 89
First World War (1914–18): 291
Foli Bébé: founder of Glidji, 175
Fon (ethnic group): 203; spiritual beliefs of, 61
Fongbe (language): 24
Fourth Anglo-Dutch Naval War (1780–4): 253, 255–7
France: 144, 156, 209, 232; as slave trade nation, 98; colonies of, 194, 232; Declaration of the Rights of Man and of the Citizen (1789), 249; La Rochelle, 258; Marseille, 282; navy of, 232; Revolution (1789–99), 98, 187, 249–50, 260–1, 265, 270; Versailles, 258
Franco-Dutch War (1672–8): belligerents of, 125
Franco-Spanish War (1635–59): Peace of the Pyrenees (1659), 145–6
French West Indies Company: fleet of, 124

Ga (ethnic group): 6; revolt led by (1728), 212
Ga-Adangbe: 175–6; refugees ('Alampoes'), 173–4, 182–3; societal structure of, 246
de la Garenne, Deniau: 260, 263
Gayibor, Nicoué: 175; writings of, 31, 76, 131–6
Gbe (language): 24–5, 143, 163, 203, 244
Gbetome: concept of, 69
George II, King: audience with Bulfinch Lambe, 213
Gezo of Dahomey, King: 15, 226, 273, 281, 284–5; rise to power (1818), 273, 279–80
Ghana, Republic of: 21, 25, 138, 294; Accra, 9, 23, 29, 171, 176, 181; Anlo, 31, 182, 254, 270, 277–8, 287
Ghana-Togo Mountain Languages (GTML-Togo): 25
Glélé, Maurice: 53–4, 164, 238, 242, 276, 284
Gold Coast (region): 4–5, 8–10, 23, 29, 34, 49, 74–5, 92, 96, 124, 153, 156, 171, 199–200, 212, 241, 258–9, 282; Accra, 36, 246–7, 253; Amoko, 258; Anomabo-Amoku, 231–2, 258; Danish slave trade in, 93; Eastern, 246; movement of slaves via, 104; Winneba, 258
Gourg, Monsieur: 258–60
Greene, Sandra: 184; definition of Nyigba, 247
Gu (deity): 71, 170
Guedevi: 160–1; claimed descendets of, 161
Guin (Ge/Gen) (ethnic group): 24, 226–7; banditry activity of, 210; exiled, 239–40
Guinea: 3, 11, 107, 115–16, 121, 144, 232, 249, 255, 287; Elmina, 92, 119, 190, 217, 253; Jakin, 26–8, 31, 103, 114, 124, 136, 141–2, 151–3, 180, 183–4, 199, 201, 218–19; Keta, 8; Little Popo-Ancho, 8, 29, 32, 174–6; Little Popo-Glidji, 174–7, 210–11, 216–17, 226, 240, 245–7, 254–6, 258, 262, 277–8, 281, 286; Offra, 1, 8, 10–11, 22, 26, 28, 34, 114, 123–4, 181; Shama, 7
Guinea Company: 116
Gulf of Guinea: 22
Gun (ethnic group): 24; origins of, 244
Gur (language): 24–5, 74

Haiti: 160; *voodoo* culture of, 70
Haley, Alex: *Roots*, 293
Hangbe-Akaba, Tassi: 162

INDEX

Harmattan (weather phenomenon): impact on maritime navigation, 30–1
Hertogh, Hendrik: 36, 207, 210, 217–20, 244; assassination of (1738), 219
Hevie: 141–2
Hevioso (deity): 71, 285
Hopkins, A.G.: 86, 271
Houstoun, James: 33, 104
Hu (deity): 27, 71, 287
Hueda (ethnic group): 24, 27, 41, 152; exiled, 239–40
Hueda, Kingdom of: 3, 8, 26, 44, 48–9, 89, 100, 136, 141, 148–53, 156–7, 169, 173, 179, 181–3, 188–9, 195, 199, 205–6, 208, 213, 229, 291; as vassal of Allada, 148; Dahomean conquest of, 41, 206, 208, 229; French Capuchins in, 121; Glehue, 153, 156; living standards in, 89–90; polygamy in, 150; population of, 34, 44; succession crisis (1708), 192
Huedan Seven Years' War (1727–30/34): 208
Huffon: revolution led by (1712), 192–3
Hula (ethnic group): 24, 26–7, 136–7, 152; Bê, 22, 174; territory inhabited by, 22, 180
Hussar: 193; death of, 204; family of, 200

Ife: *oni*, 63
Inikori, Joseph: 4, 82, 98–9
Iroko, Félix: 27, 161
iron-priest: 142; concept of, 130
Isert, Paul Erdmann: 27–8, 46, 103, 254–5
Islam: 60, 68; Quran, 252
Italy: 85; Rome, 145

James II of England, King: as Duke of York, 122–3

Japan: spread of firearms in, 169
Jennings, Lawrence C.: criticisms of, 82
Johnson, Samuel: *History of the Yoruba*, 50

Kabou, Axelle: 16
Kelly, Kenneth: 49, 101
de Kersaint, Guy-François: 232
Keta: 176, 184, 207, 216, 247, 254–5, 266–7, 277; Alampoes in, 183
Keta War (1792): 255–6
Kiøge, Jens Adolph: forts constructed by, 254
Kipling, Rudyard: *Man Who Would Be King, The*, 49, 219
Klooster, Wim: 116–17, 187
Knight, Franklin W.: 266
Kongensten (fort): construction of (1783), 254
Kongo, Kingdom of: 67, 72
Kopytoff, Igor: 55–6
Kpengla, King: 240, 251, 260; death of (1789), 260; liberation efforts of, 256; raiding parties ordered by, 252
Kpesi (ethnic group): territory inhabited by, 75
Krepi (ethnic group): 24
Kru (ethnic group): territory inhabited by, 6
Kutome: concept of, 69
Kwadwo, Asantehene Osei: death of, 254

Lagoon War (1780–4): 256–8, 278–9
Lambe, Bulfinch: 205, 221; audience with King George II, 213
Law, Robin: 114, 146, 150, 156, 164–8, 179, 184, 195–6, 202–3, 215, 235, 243, 252–3, 280; observations of economy in Slave Coast, 81–2, 85, 87–8, 90, 102; observations of Dangbe worship, 150–1; writings of,

INDEX

15–16, 21, 26, 38, 42–5, 47, 54, 58, 78–9, 82–3, 206, 213, 219–21

Le Hérissé, Auguste: 47, 51, 139, 141, 165, 238, 243, 272; background of, 51; concept of *horde proescrite*, 166; writings on Kingdom of Dahomey, 159–60

Legba (deity): 69, 71, 243

Lombard, Jacques: 79, 139, 238

Louis XIV of France: 121, 124; family of, 186; foreign policy of, 156; view of role of slave trade, 17

Lower Guinea: 113

Luther, Martin: 290

Mahdi (ethnic group): 24

Mahi (ethnic group): 260, 281

Male: 268; arrival in Ouidah-Glehue (1704), 189–90

Manding (language family): 74

Manning, Patrick: 2, 37–9, 50, 83, 101; observations of slave trade, 100

Marxism: 58, 266, 291; concept of mode of production, 82

Mawu-Liisa (deity): 70–1, 177, 237; priests of, 133; variant names of, 71, 76

McCaskie, Tom: 78

Middle Passage: 12, 37, 107

Mina (ethnic group): 24, 184

Mono, River: 22, 75

Monroe, J. Cameron: 43, 54

de Montaguère, Ollivier: 260

de Nájera, José: 135

Napoleonic Wars (1803–15): 98, 265, 267, 270, 275

Naxara: 101

Netherlands: 217–19; Amsterdam, 123

New Akwamu: 212, 245–6, 277, 286

Niger Delta: 10, 72

Nigeria: 15, 21; Apa, 219; Badagry, 219, 244, 257, 259, 278; Lagos, 41, 95, 117, 142, 257, 259, 270, 275, 278, 281, 283; Lagos State, 21–2; Warri, 144

Nonobewa War (1750–1): 247

Norman, Neil: 149–50

Norris, Robert: 53, 104, 242–3

Nugent, Paul: 25, 28, 53; concept of 'Notsé meta-narrative', 134

Nunes, Francisco: 49, 216–17, 229

Nupe: revolt of, 261

Nyigble/Nyigbla (deity): 177, 247, 287

Oduduwa: cultural importance of, 64

Ofori: 175; mercenaries led by, 180–1; territory occupied by, 180–1

de Oliveira, João: role in opening direct trade with Porto Novo, 244

Opoku Wae: death of (1750), 200

Order of Friars Minor Capuchin: French, 121, 155; presence in Kingdom of Hueda, 121; Spanish, 121, 143–5

O'Rourke, Kevin: 89

Ouidah: 1–3, 5–6, 11, 15, 22, 26, 118, 148–9, 183, 186, 261–3, 266, 278–80, 292–3; Brazilian presence in, 278; European lodges at, 124, 262; local traditions of, 10; oil trade in, 282; Ouidah fort, 36, 153, 266, 271; slave trading in, 7–8, 152, 257–61, 268, 274, 280

Ouidah-Glehue/Whydah: 26–7, 29, 31–2, 34, 40, 81, 83, 86, 105, 124–5, 155, 168, 177, 196, 201, 205, 207, 209, 211, 213, 217–18, 221, 225, 229, 233–4, 236; Brazilian gold trade in, 190–1; development of, 180, 184, 187, 232; drinking water problems in, 106; European factory-lodges/lodges at, 184, 206; forts, 36, 39, 42, 102, 108, 162, 189, 190, 194–5, 230; founding of, 154; Hula population

INDEX

of, 27; piracy in, 196; slave trade in, 103, 105, 107, 157, 193, 244
Oyo, Kingdom of: 23, 66–7, 100–1, 131, 134, 142, 177, 183–4, 202, 209–10, 212, 220, 222, 226–7, 239, 244–6, 260, 274, 282; *alafin*, 63, 228, 261; Oyo Ile, 281; *oyo mesi*, 64; conflict with Kingdom of Dahomey (1726), 202, 206; *ilari*, 242; vassals of, 44, 97, 202–3, 261

Palau-Martí, Montserrat: 63
de la Palma, Willem: 180, 190
Pazzi, Roberto: 69, 131, 134
Pereyra Mendes, Francisco: 206
Perrot, Claude-Hélène: 140, 148
Philip IV of Spain, King: 121, 145; court of, 143
Philip V of Spain, King: family of, 186
Phillips, Thomas: 7, 150, 181; observations of slave ships, 106
Pierre, Monsieur: 257, 272, 278
Pires, Father Vicente Ferreira: 7, 161, 262–3
Polanyi, Karl: studies of Dahomey Kingdom, 81–2, 87
Popo, Kingdom of: 135, 147
Portugal: 90, 98, 113, 144–5, 218, 233, 262, 274, 282; as slave trade nation, 98, 113–14; handicraft industry of, 114; Lisbon, 48, 114, 119, 145, 185, 216
Portuguese Creole (language): use in trade, 117
Postma, Johannes: 35, 218
Prindensten (fort): 266–7; construction of (1784), 255
Pruneau de Pommegeorge, Antoine: 35–6, 40, 46, 103, 239–40; background of, 14–15

Quarcoopome, Nii: 63, 133

Randsborg, Klavs: 129, 204
Régis, Victor: 282, 285
Richardson, David: macroeconomic definition of slave-raiding, 87
Roberts, Bartholomew: attacks on slave ships, 105
Roman Empire: fall of, 291
Ross, David: 169, 224, 239, 279
Royal African Company of England (RAC): 127–8, 153, 182, 184, 188, 218; decline of (1750–1), 154, 234; fleet of, 127; forts and lodges of, 185; personnel of, 38, 153, 191, 201; slave trading activity of, 125
de Ruyter, Michiel: 36, 123
Ryder, A.F.C.: 92, 117, 142, 145

Sacra Congregatio de Propaganda Fide: founding of (1622), 143
Sagbadre War (1784): 254
Saint Louis de Gregoy (fort): construction of, 189
Sakpata (deity): 70–2, 168, 227, 243, 276, 285; priests of, 276
de Sandoval, Alonso: 46, 135
São João Baptista (fort): 195
São Tomé and Príncipe: 33, 49, 73, 93, 106, 128, 153, 156, 172, 232; Dutch capture of (1641), 115; harbours of, 106; Portuguese re-conquest of (1644), 119
Sardinha, Pires: 263
Sassa, Agbo: 162
Saudi Arabia: Mecca, 78; Medina, 78
Savary, Claude: 78
Savi: 3, 102, 128, 142, 148, 151–2, 180, 206, 209, 211; archaeological focus on, 48; Dutch factory in, 181; European lodges at, 42, 155, 190, 207; European trading establishments, 41–2, 155; governance of, 149; Portuguese

INDEX

presence in, 153; slave trade in, 103, 107, 154
Second Anglo-Dutch Naval War (1665–7): 116, 123
Second Franco-Dahomean War (1892–4): political impact of, 39
Seven Years' War (1756–63): 232
Sierra Leone: 196, 261
Slave Coast: 1–2, 4, 6–13, 16–18, 25, 28–30, 33–4, 37, 41, 44, 47–50, 52–3, 55, 57–8, 60–1, 69–70, 72–3, 75, 79, 91–5, 100, 109, 113–14, 116–17, 119–22, 126, 130, 135, 142, 146, 149, 163, 180, 185–7, 199, 203–4, 210, 215, 217, 219, 221, 234, 241, 266–7, 269, 275–6, 289, 291–2, 294; agriculture in, 83; economy of, 81, 83–4, 86, 96; Eweland, 27, 29, 61, 75–6, 134, 173, 176, 245; Hula population of, 27; kindred cultures in, 62, 84, 131, 167; languages spoken in 23–5; origin of term, 22–3; religious cultures of, 57–60; territory of, 21–2
slave trade: 1–2, 12–16, 33–4, 38, 41–2, 89, 100, 102–3, 108–9, 117, 119–20, 122, 150, 177, 191, 193–4, 214, 238–9, 265, 267, 270, 283, 291; abolition of, 250, 266; American, 266; British, 185, 265–6; Danish, 93, 250; French, 187, 249–50, 266; illegal (1807–8), 7, 98, 280, 286; local collaboration in, 4; Portuguese, 127, 269; role in Slave Coast economy, 100–2, 127; *sklavenraub* (robbery of slaves), 82, 87; slave caravans, 30, 208; slave ships, 12–13; Trans-Atlantic, 1–2, 14, 34, 82, 91, 93–4, 104–5, 125–6
Smith, Adam: *Wealth of Nations*, 84
Snelgrave, William: 205, 207–8, 213
Soso/Sozo: 193, 201; death of (1724), 193, 200; family of, 200

Soumonni, Elisée: 274, 293
South Atlantic System: concept of, 126
de Souza, Francisco Félix (Chacha): 272, 277, 279–81
Spain: 98, 114–15, 144, 267, 282, 284; Civil War (1936–9), 291; Madrid, 143
Strickrodt, Silke: 184, 262
Sweden: 124

Tanga: 235–6
Tattersfield, Nigel: observations of slave ships, 105–6
Tegbesu, King: 43, 200, 225–6, 229–31, 234–7, 239–40, 243, 264; death of (1774), 240, 248, 251; military campaigns of, 226–8; proclamations issued by (1746), 238
Testefolle, Charles: 209
Third Anglo-Dutch Naval War (1672–4): 125
Thomas, Nicolas: concept of 'Entangled Objects', 86–7
Thornton, John: 203–4, 253
tobacco: 118–19, 191; *soca* (*refugado*), 117–18; use in taxation, 119
Tofinu (ethnic group): 24
Togo, Republic of: 21, 24–5, 28, 34, 76, 100, 129, 294; borders of, 22; Lomé, 292; Tado, 48, 129–33, 135, 137–8, 149, 166, 174, 176, 204, 237, 273
Tori: 135, 141–2; as vassal of Allada, 136
Trans-Atlantic Slave Trade Database: 91–2, 98–9, 114, 157, 193–4, 210, 250–1; aims of, 37, 99–100; West-Central region, 72
Treaty of Neutrality (1703): 189; provisions of, 188
Treaty of Tordesillas (1494): provisions of, 113
Trevor-Roper, Prof Hugh: 57–8; criticisms of, 54–5

442

INDEX

Tsardom of Russia: Pillau, 124
Tsetse fly: cause of fatalities due to trypanosomiasis, 3, 203
Tutu, Asantehene Osei: death of (1717), 200

Ultramarino, Arquivo Histórico: 48
United East India Company (VOC): 116–17
United Kingdom (UK): 98, 144, 232, 253, 261, 265, 269; as slave trade nation, 98; Civil War (1642–51), 122; Dolben Act (1788), 250; Felony Act (1811), 268–9; House of Commons, 36, 41, 250; House of Lords, 250; London, 36, 213; Parliament, 39, 268; Royal Navy, 7, 269
United States of America (USA): 48, 98–9, 266–7, 294; Revolutionary War (1765/75–83) 248–50, 255

Verger, Pierre: 47, 216–17
Volta, River: 6–7, 21–2, 24, 75, 91, 142, 212, 246, 277

War of the League of Augsburg (1688–97): 157, 182; belligerents of, 156, 182
War of the Spanish Succession (1702–14): 194; belligerents of, 186–7; political impact of, 97–8
Wegbaja, King: 159, 168–9
Weme (polity): 161–2, 216, 257; destruction of, 162–3

Weme, River: 27, 31–2, 161; flood plain of, 29, 163
Wemenu (Oueneou) (ethnic group): 24; migration of, 163
West Indies Company (WIC): 116–17, 119, 123–5, 142, 152, 154, 180–1, 188, 210, 217–18; authorization of Brazilian Mina trade, 118–19; dissolution of (1791), 258; establishment of, 116; fleet of, 127, 196; personnel of, 127, 210, 218–19; pursuit and capture of Portuguese slave ships, 120
Western Slave Coast: 22, 171–3, 176, 195, 228, 245–7, 277, 286; Ada, 176, 254; Ewe population of, 75–6; ivory trade in, 29; slave trade in, 177
Wilberforce, William: 250–1
Wilks, Ivor: 75, 172–3, 184
William III of Holland, King: 154
William's Fort: 154, 232–3, 271; personnel of, 235
Wybourne, Petley: 36, 153–4, 182

Yoder, John: 53–4
Yoruba (ethnic group): 25, 73, 279; language of, 24, 29, 65, 160, 163, 245; religion of, 58, 71; territory inhabited by, 21, 23, 73–4, 281
Yorubaland: 23, 42, 62, 73, 78, 131, 245, 284

Zapata, Felipe (Bans): 145–6; *Doctrina Christiana*, 143